HEALTH PSYCHOLOGY

Integrating Mind and Body

GEORGE D. BISHOP

National University of Singapore

ALLYN AND BACON
Boston London Toronto Sydney Tokyo Singapore

Editor-in-Chief, Social Sciences: Susan Badger
Acquisitions Editor: Kevin Stone
Editorial Assistant: Sarah L. Dunbar
Cover Administrator: Linda Dickinson
Composition Buyer: Linda Cox
Manufacturing Buyer: Megan Cochran
Editorial-Production Service: P. M. Gordon Associates
Production Administrator: Deborah Brown

Copyright © 1994 by Allyn and Bacon
A Division of Simon & Schuster, Inc.
160 Gould Street, Needham Heights, MA 02194

Photo Credits: Page 5, © Gale Zucker/Stock, Boston; Page 11, Courtesy David Keough/Boston University Medical Center, Department of Public Relations; Page 19, © North Wind Picture Archives; Page 37, © Mark Antman/Stock, Boston; Page 52, © Ellis Herwig/The Picture Cube; Page 57, © Susan A. Anderson/Lisa Guilmer/The Picture Cube; Page 74, © John Nordell/The Picture Cube; Page 89, © Steve Takatsuno/The Picture Cube; Page 96, © AP/Wide World Photos; Page 109, © Elizabeth Crews/Stock, Boston; Page 114, © AP/Wide World Photos; Page 129, © AP/Wide World Photos; Page 140, Courtesy, Lafayette Instrument Company; Page 158, © Emillo Mercado/The Picture Cube; Page 170, © Steve & Mary Beran Skjold Photographers; Page 174, © Jerry Howard/Stock, Boston; Page 188, © Michael Dwyer/Stock, Boston; Page 193, © Janice Fullman/The Picture Cube; Page 198, © AP/Wide World Photos; Page 215, © Steve & Mary Beran Skjold Photographers; Page 236, © AP/Wide World Photos; Page 244, © AP/Wide World Photos; Page 256, Courtesy Miles Diagnostics Division, Miles, Inc.; Page 262, Courtesy Alzheimer's Association; Page 276, © AP/Wide World Photos; Page 281, © Bohdan Hrynewych/Stock, Boston; Page 289, © Eugene Richards/The Picture Cube; Page 305, © AP/Wide World Photos; Page 308, © Steve & Mary Beran Skjold Photographers; Page 310, © AP/Wide World Photos; Page 333, Courtesy American Cancer Society; Page 334, © Spencer Grant/The Picture Cube; Page 352, Courtesy American Cancer Society; Page 371, Courtesy Boston University Medical Center, Department of Public Relations; Page 376, © Jeff Dunn/The Picture Cube; Page 381, Courtesy Boston University Medical Center, Department of Public Relations; Page 394, George Bishop; Page 408, Courtesy 3M; Page 421, © Jeff Dunn/The Picture Cube; Page 423, © Therese Frare/The Picture Cube.

Library of Congress Cataloging-in-Publication Data

Bishop, George D.
    Health psychology : integrating mind and body / George D. Bishop.
      p.   cm.
    Includes bibliographical references and index.
    ISBN 0–205–13926–4
    1. Clinical health psychology. 2. Mind and body. I. Title.
    R726.7.B54   1994
    616′.0019—dc20
                                 93–17373
                                     CIP

10 9 8 7 6 5 4 3 2   98 97 96 95

To Jane, Sam and Clara
for their love and patience

Contents

PART III   STRESS

PART V   HEALTH PSYCHOLOGY AND SPECIFIC HEALTH PROBLEMS

Preface

Health is a topic that is of vital concern to all of us. A brief stroll through most bookstores, with their substantial selection of health-related books, is testament to the great interest that people have in their health. Recently a revolution has taken place in how we understand health. Whereas in the past health has been thought of primarily in physical terms, there is mounting evidence from a variety of sources that our health is profoundly influenced by our behavior, thoughts, and social relationships. Health psychology, as an area of study, is concerned with exploring these linkages and using the theories and methods of psychology to promote good health, either by preventing disease, promoting healing (when a disease is curable), or aiding adaptation (when a condition is chronic).

With its potential for impact on our health and well-being, health psychology is a tremendously exciting undertaking, full of intellectual challenge and important practical applications. I have written this book as an invitation to the adventure that is health psychology. More specifically, I have several interrelated goals in mind. The first is to provide an accessible and engaging introduction to current research and practice in health psychology. In the last few years there has been a veritable explosion of research in health psychology and related areas. This book is designed as an up-to-date summary of this work, pointing out the progress that has been made as well as what is yet to be learned.

A second goal is to bring to the reader's attention the myriad ways in which the mind and body are closely intertwined. Since the Enlightenment, medical thought in the West has been infused with a mind-body dualism in which the mind and body have been seen as separate and distinct entities. We now know that this distinction is a very artificial one and that the mind and body profoundly influence each other. This book lays out the evidence for this integration of mind and body.

In line with this, a third goal is to point out the ways that psychological methods, both research and clinical, can be used to enhance health. Throughout this book I stress the application of our current knowledge to significant health issues, ranging from disease prevention to the care of persons who are dying.

As an introductory text, this book's goal is to provide students with a base for more advanced study. Given the volume and diversity of current work in health psychology, no textbook can hope to cover all topics in-depth. Rather, this book aims at providing a solid foundation in health psychology research, theory, and application that can provide a springboard for more in-depth study.

Throughout this book I have incorporated a number of features to aid students in their exploration of health psychology. First, the topics in this text are organized around three themes: the interaction of mind and body; coping and adaptation; and the role of interpersonal relationships in health and health care. These themes are introduced in Chapters 1 and 2 and then developed through the rest of the text. In my experience with teaching health psychology I have discovered that students find this theme-approach very useful for understanding the fundamental unity in the diversity of facts and theories. Additionally, in order to help students grasp points that may seem abstract or remote, I make use of numerous case studies and concrete examples as illustrations of more general points. Although anecdotes can never prove a point they can often improve its comprehension. As a further aid to getting a "feel" for health psychology, each chapter contains one or more focus boxes which describe specific research studies, therapeutic techniques, or issues in detail. To assist students in organizing and reviewing material, each chapter begins with a chapter outline and ends with a summary. Finally, to help students in their comprehension, key terms are defined both in the margin next to where they first occur as well as in a glossary at the end of the text: Providing the definition in the margin when a term is first encountered obviates the necessity of flipping to the back of the book for every unfamiliar term and makes the review process easier.

In writing this book I have assumed no other preparation than college-level status and an introductory psychology course. As such, this text is suitable for psychology majors, students going into one of the health professions, as well as interested individuals taking a course in health psychology as an elective.

Completion of this project would not have been possible without assistance from a number of people. My wife, Jane, spent uncounted hours reading through various drafts suggesting many improvements. Many reviewers read and commented on all or part of the manuscript: Larry Gregory, New Mexico State University, Las Cruces; Robert Kaplan, University of California, San Diego; Lynn Durel, University of Miami; Ron Sutterer, Syracuse University; Rock Clapper, Brown University; Dennis Elsenrath, University of Wisconsin, Stevens Point; Robert T. Croyle, University of Utah; Chris Crandall, University of Florida; George Bloch, Brigham Young University; Delia Cioffi, University of Houston; Leonard Doerfler, Assumption College; Suzanne Thompson, Pomona College; David Wittrock, North Dakota State University; John Jung, California State University-Long Beach; Karl Hursey, Texas A&M University; Linda Brannon, McNeese State University; and Andy Baum. Their comments played a significant role in improving the final product. I would also like to express my appreciation to my students, both at the University of Texas at San Antonio and the National University of Singapore, for enduring various drafts of the text and giving me valuable feedback from a student's point of view. Additionally, I would like to thank my colleagues at both institutions for their encouragement and support in this project. Finally, I would like to express my deep appreciation to the editorial staff of Allyn and Bacon for their patience and assistance. Special thanks go to John Paul Lenny, who encouraged me to begin this project, and to Susan Badger, who saw it through to its completion. To these and many others who are too numerous to name, I can only say "Thanks."

HEALTH PSYCHOLOGY

Exploring Health Psychology

"If you have your health you have just about everything." How many times have you heard someone say this? Our health is certainly important to us. For example, in 1991 Americans spent more than $738 billion on health care (Rich, 1992), more than 12% of the American gross national product. In addition, people spend untold amounts of time and effort on remaining healthy.

When we think about health we usually think about the physical aspects of our health: How do we feel physically? Do we have any clinically defined diseases? We are much less likely to think about the psychological and behavioral aspects of our health. Yet there is accumulating evidence demonstrating that the psychological and behavioral aspects of our health are at least as important as the purely physical aspects. Our behavior—in the form of health habits, seeking medical care, and compliance with medical recommendations, to name but a few areas—has a tremendous effect on our health (cf. Matarazzo, Weiss, Herd, Miller, & Weiss, 1984). For example, one habit alone, smoking, has been estimated to account for more than 20% of all deaths in the United States. Table 1.1 illustrates the impact of smoking on specific causes of death. The Centers for Disease Control calculate that in 1988 more than 434,000 deaths were attributable, directly or indirectly, to smoking. Moreover, the CDC estimate, cigarette

TABLE 1.1   *Mortality from Selected Diseases Attributable to Smoking (percentage)*

Disease	Males	Females
Lip and oral cancers	68.8	41.3
Esophageal cancer	58.9	53.6
Lung cancer	79.6	75.0
Cardiac arrest	39.9	34.4
Arteriosclerosis	23.8	31.5
Chronic bronchitis and emphysema	85.0	69.4
Chronic airway obstruction	85.0	69.4
Ulcers	47.9	44.5

Note. Data from "Smoking-attributable mortality and years of potential life list—United States, 1984" (p. 694) by Centers for Disease Control, 1987, *Morbidity and Mortality Weekly Report, 36.*

smoking in the United States collectively resulted in nearly 1.2 million years of potential life lost before the age of 65 (Centers for Disease Control, 1991c).

Psychological states also influence our health. Our feelings and emotions can have either positive or negative effects on our physical well-being. On the positive side, feelings of being loved and supported by others can help us deal with stressful situations (cf. Wallston, Alagna, DeVellis, & DeVellis, 1983). In addition, various psychological interventions can reduce the pain and discomfort experienced from surgery and speed the healing process (cf. Johnson, 1984). The flip side of this is that psychological states can also have negative effects on our physical health. For several decades, psychologists and others have been concerned about the effects of stress on our health. Increasing evidence indicates an association between stress and a variety of negative health effects, ranging from coronary heart disease to cancer and suppression of the immune system (Jemmott & Locke, 1984; Field, McCabe, & Schneiderman, 1985). And although positive social support can reduce the effects of stress, a lack of strong interpersonal relationships can leave one vulnerable to all kinds of physical maladies. The work of James Lynch and others on the consequences of loneliness demonstrates this (see Box 1.1).

WHAT IS HEALTH PSYCHOLOGY?

health psychology
The subfield of psychology concerned with the dynamic interrelationship of behavior and psychological states with physical health.

In general terms, **health psychology** is that specialization within psychology that deals with physical health. We are careful to specify physical health, as opposed to simply health, because the field of psychology has traditionally been associated with issues relating to mental health: the subfield of psychology that focuses on questions of mental health is clinical psychology. Health psychology concentrates on physical health and considers mental health primarily as it relates to a person's physical well-being. As formally defined, *health psychology is the subfield of psychology concerned with the dynamic interrelationship of behavior and psychological states with physical health.*

BOX 1.1 Dying of a Broken Heart

The heart is an organ rich in both medical significance and symbolism. As an organ, the heart is basically a pump providing the necessary push to circulate life-sustaining blood through our arteries and veins. Once the heart ceases to do its job, the person dies; and, indeed, heart disease is a leading cause of death.

The heart also has rich symbolic significance. People speak "from the heart," put their "heart into it," and are at times said to die of a "broken heart." We usually understand this last phrase in a purely symbolic sense. Medically, although people certainly die of heart disease, they do not die of a broken heart, at least not in the way the phrase is usually used. Or do they? James J. Lynch, in his book *The broken heart: The medical consequences of loneliness,* argues that, in fact, people can and do die from the consequences of disappointment and loneliness. The central thesis of his book is that: "The lack of human companionship, the sudden loss of love, and chronic human loneliness are significant contributors to serious disease (including cardiovascular disease) and premature death" (Lynch, 1977, p. 181).

In support of this thesis, Lynch points out that being divorced or widowed presents a considerable health risk, equivalent for some individuals to smoking one or more packs of cigarettes a day. Overall, the death rate for single persons, across race, sex, and age, is 47% higher than for married individuals. For those widowed, the death rate is 46% higher, whereas for divorced persons, the death rate is 84% higher. Lynch notes that the higher death rates for nonmarried individuals hold in different cultures, including the United States, Britain, and Japan, across a wide variety of diseases, and persist

even when known physical risk factors (such as diet, exercise, and smoking for cardiovascular disease) are controlled for.

Particularly striking evidence for the importance of human relationships in health comes from recent studies of patients with coronary heart disease. In one study (Williams et al., 1992), more than 1,300 patients with confirmed heart disease were followed for periods of 9 to 15 years. Analysis of death rates indicated that, even when other medical factors were controlled for, patients who were married or had a close confidant had a significantly lower mortality rate than did those who were either unmarried or did not have a confidant. Whereas 82% of the former lived for five years or more, the comparable figure for the latter was 50%. Overall, unmarried patients without a close confidant had a threefold increase in the risk of death within 5 years compared to those who were either married or had a confidant. Similar results were obtained in another study that examined the effects of living arrangements and marital status on survival after a myocardial infarction (Case, Moss, Case, McDermott, & Eberly, 1992). In this study, individuals living alone showed a 50% greater likelihood of experiencing another heart attack within 6 months compared to those living with other people. Interestingly, having a disrupted marriage (through divorce, separation, or death) did not influence the rate of recurrent heart attacks independently of living arrangements.

Data like these indicate the importance of human relationships for health and survival and demonstrate that people can indeed die of a "broken heart."

The Many Facets of Health Psychology

Although this definition is fairly simple and straightforward, health psychology is exceedingly broad and diverse. Just as psychology covers the broad range of human behavior and psychological states, health psychology includes this same broad range of behavior and psychological states as they influence and are influenced by physical health. In general, the domain of health psychology comprises several broad areas (Matarazzo, 1980). First, health psychology is concerned with the promotion and

Health psychologists are concerned with developing methods for encouraging people to engage in positive habits, such as regular use of seat belts.

maintenance of health. Therefore, considerable attention is paid to the ways in which people's behavior, in the form of habits such as smoking, drinking, seat belt use, exercise, and dietary habits, affects their health. Second, health psychology is concerned with the prevention and treatment of illness. Health psychologists have been active in areas such as stress management and the development of good health habits to help prevent the development of illness. They also work with medical patients to help them cope better with their illnesses and regain their health more rapidly or, in the case of chronic conditions, function as fully as possible in the face of their medical condition.

A third major area encompassed by health psychology is factors associated with the development of illness. There has been discussion for many years (cf. Carmody & Matarazzo, 1991; Kaplan, 1975; McMahon, 1976; McMahon & Hastrup, 1980) about the role of psychological and social factors in the development of illness. Much of this work has centered on the concept of "stress" as a determinant of physical health. Although psychological and social stress has long been suspected in the development of illness, only recently has the complex relationship between stress and illness been teased apart convincingly.

Finally, health psychology is concerned more broadly with the health care system and the formulation of health care policy. Most of us in modern industrialized countries receive our health care from professionals who work independently or as part of a larger clinic or hospital. Thus we are often required to deal with health care institutions that at times seem impersonal or incomprehensible. Further, our interactions with health care professionals involve more than the mechanical dispensing of health care; these interactions are also personal. Health psychologists are interested in how people interact with health care professionals and institutions and the impact of these interactions on their health. For example, the relationship between people and their physicians, or other health care providers, is likely to affect their willingness to follow medical recommendations as well as their rate of recovery from illness or surgery.

Health psychology also draws from the full gamut of specialties within psychology. For example, clinical psychologists contribute to health psychology through the application of clinical diagnostic and treatment techniques to psychological issues and problems that arise in medical treatment. Clinical psychologists work with patients using various psychotherapeutic and behavioral techniques to assist them in coping with illness and disability. In addition, clinical psychologists do research in hospitals and medical clinics on various psychological issues related to illness and health care. Social psychologists have been active in doing research and developing theory on topics such as the interaction process between patient and health care practitioner, stress and social support as they affect health, and the process of coping with illness. Experimental and physiological psychologists have been involved in the development of techniques such as biofeedback to help people regulate autonomic functions. They have played a key role in examining the ways in which physiological responses are influenced by psychological and situational factors. Much of this latter work has involved the use of animals. Developmental psychologists have applied psychological principles to children's health problems, such as those associated with chronic illness or the effects of hospitalization. Finally, cognitive psychologists have contributed to health psychology through work on cognitive processes; in particular, how these are involved in people's understanding of health issues, and how they are influenced by physical disease. Health psychology includes the broad spectrum of human cognition and behavior as it relates to health—hence all areas of psychology play a role.

Why Health Psychology and Why Now?

Health psychology is a new field of endeavor, dating from the late 1970s (Matarazzo, 1980; Stone, 1979b). What accounts for the emergence of health psychology, and why has it emerged so recently? One important reason relates to recent changes in the definition of health and what it means to be healthy. Traditionally, health has been defined as the lack of disease or pathology. More recently, however, the concept of health has been redefined in more positive terms as a state of complete mental, physical, and social well-being (Stone, 1979b). This more "holistic" definition explicitly incorporates the psychological aspects of health.

Paralleling this change in the definition of health has been a questioning of the dominant model in Western medicine. The biomedical model, based on concepts of reductionism and mind-body dualism, has been the foundation of modern medicine

(Engel, 1977). This model, which is discussed in greater detail in Chapter 2, focuses entirely on the physical aspects of health and illness and ignores psychological and social factors. Medical research and practice based on the biomedical model have been tremendously successful in eradicating the killer diseases of the past and developing new medical technologies. However, the biomedical model itself does a poor job of accounting for many phenomena of health and illness. Several theorists have therefore begun to argue for a new model that eliminates the mind-body dualism and reductionism of the biomedical model and explicitly incorporates psychological and social factors in the understanding and treatment of illness (Engel, 1977; Jasnoski & Schwartz, 1985).

A third factor is the shift that has taken place in patterns of illness. Before the tremendous advances of twentieth-century medicine, many of the major killer diseases were acute or infectious illnesses such as pneumonia, influenza, tuberculosis, and diphtheria (U.S. Department of Health, Education, and Welfare, 1979). The advent of modern medicines, such as antibiotics and effective vaccines, as well as vastly improved medical technology, has limited the toll taken by these diseases. However, the reduction in the incidence of these diseases and an increase in longevity have left chronic disease as our main health nemesis. In the latter part of the twentieth century, the primary causes of death are chronic conditions such as cardiovascular disease and the various cancers (National Center for Health Statistics, 1989)—most of which are related to our behavior and are preventable. In his book *Doing better and feeling worse,* John Knowles writes, "Over 99 percent of us are born healthy and made sick as a result of personal misbehavior and environmental conditions" (Knowles, 1977, p. 58). The fact that the major health problems of our time are so closely related to behavior has brought the application of psychological principles to the forefront in the fight against disease.

Economics has also played a major role in focusing attention on psychological and behavioral factors in health. In the past several decades, health care costs have exploded. In the United States, for example, health care now consumes over 12% of the gross national product, a figure that is expected to rise to 14% by the year 2000 (Carmody & Matarazzo, 1991). Figure 1.1 graphically illustrates this increase. Although health care costs are increasing dramatically, Americans are not experiencing a proportional improvement in physical health (Knowles, 1977; Weiss, 1982). Rather, a substantial portion of the cost of health care pays for repairing damage caused by poor health habits and unhealthy life-styles (Knowles, 1977; U.S. Department of Health, Education, and Welfare, 1979). These economic facts, along with the shift in illness patterns to chronic diseases, have focused attention on preventive health measures and, specifically, on changing unhealthy behavior (Agras, 1982; Weiss, 1982).

Finally, the emergence of health psychology at this time can be attributed in part to the coming of age of behavioral technology (Agras, 1982). As noted above, the emphasis in much of earlier psychology was on examining the basic principles of behavior. This emphasis has led to the development of technologies such as behavior modification and biofeedback that can be used to change undesirable behavior and to

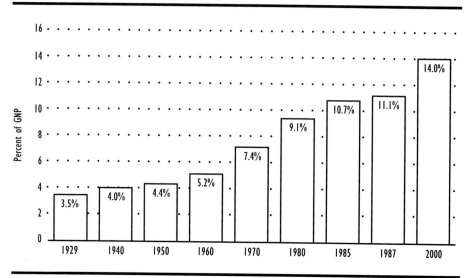

Note. From "Health psychology" (p. 698) by T. P. Carmody and J. D. Matarazzo, 1991, in *The clinical psychology handbook* (2d ed.), ed. M. Hersen, A. E. Kazdin, & A. S. Bellack, New York: Pergamon.

FIGURE 1.1

Health care costs in the United States expressed as a percentage of the gross national product, selected years 1929–1985 with projections through the year 2000.

treat conditions such as asthma, migraine headache, hypertension, and seizure disorders (Andrasik, Coleman, & Epstein, 1982). These efforts, along with basic work in other areas of psychology, have laid the groundwork for developing effective applications of psychological principles to a broad range of health problems.

Health Psychology and Related Areas

Health psychology is certainly not alone in its concern with the role of psychological and behavioral factors in health and health care. Other areas, both inside and outside psychology, address similar questions. Thus it is helpful to examine how some of these fields differ from health psychology as well as overlap with it.

medical psychology
The application of clinical psychological methods to problems of physical illness.

Medical psychology. This term has different meanings depending on where it is used. In Great Britain, **medical psychology** is essentially synonymous with psychiatry. In the United States, it refers to a subspecialty of clinical psychology concerned with the application of clinical methods from psychology to problems of the physically ill. Medical psychologists are therefore involved in psychological assessment of medical patients through techniques such as clinical interviews or standardized psychological tests, and intervention using psychological treatment methods like psychotherapy. As a consequence, medical psychology primarily consists of clinical consultation and service delivery (Adler, Cohen, & Stone, 1979).

Psychosomatic medicine. Psychosomatic medicine, which substantially predates health psychology, initially evolved out of psychoanalysis and the study of psychophysiology (Lipowski, 1977; Schwartz & Weiss, 1977). It traces its roots not

psychosomatic medicine
The specialty within biomedicine that is concerned with psychological factors in the development and course of physical illness.

behavioral medicine
An interdisciplinary field that applies theories and techniques from the behavioral sciences to the treatment and prevention of illness.

behavioral health
An interdisciplinary field that focuses on behaviorally promoting good health habits and preventing disease among those who are currently healthy.

medical sociology
The specialty within sociology that studies the social aspects of health and illness.

to psychology but primarily to the biomedical sciences. Traditionally, practitioners of psychosomatic medicine have focused on psychological factors in the development of physical disease, emphasizing the role of emotional states and stress. Until recently, attention was paid to a few diseases, such as ulcers, bronchial asthma, colitis, and rheumatoid arthritis, that were thought to be caused or substantially influenced by specific emotional and stress factors (Lipowski, 1977). But the focus in this area has now broadened to include psychological factors in the etiology and course of nearly all illnesses (Adler et al., 1979; Lipowski, 1977; Schwartz & Weiss, 1977). Psychosomatic medicine overlaps health psychology, but has a somewhat different history and orientation.

Behavioral medicine. A more recently developed field, **behavioral medicine** is concerned with behavioral approaches to the treatment and prevention of illness (Schwartz & Weiss, 1977). Although many findings and techniques in behavioral medicine have come from psychology, behavioral medicine is a distinct, if overlapping, field. Historically, behavioral medicine grew out of the branch of psychology known as behaviorism, which emphasizes overt behavior and the conditions, most often external or situational, that control it. Thus behavioral medicine tends to focus on theories and techniques derived from behaviorist learning theory, such as behavior modification or biofeedback. For example, a behavioral medicine practitioner might treat migraine headache sufferers using biofeedback techniques or use operant conditioning techniques to help clients lose weight. Many researchers and practitioners in behavioral medicine are psychologists, but a sizable number come from other disciplines, such as biomedicine, public health, sociology, or anthropology (Adler et al., 1979; Schwartz & Weiss, 1977).

Behavioral health. Believing that behavioral medicine tended to place too little emphasis on health maintenance and prevention, Joseph Matarazzo suggested the term **behavioral health** to encompass behavioral approaches to prevention. This specialty focuses on the use of behavioral techniques for maintaining health and preventing illness among individuals who are currently healthy (Matarazzo, 1980; Matarazzo et al., 1984).

Medical sociology. Medical sociology developed as an organized specialty in sociology in the 1940s and 1950s (Olesen, 1975) and involves a wide variety of issues related to social aspects of health and health care. Among the topics covered in medical sociology are social patterns in the distribution of disease and mortality, the effects of social stress on health, social and cultural responses to health and illness, and the institutional organization of health care (Mechanic, 1978). An important distinction in medical sociology is between sociology *in* medicine and the sociology *of* medicine (Straus, 1957). Sociology in medicine refers to the application of sociological perspectives and methods to the study of questions of physical health and patient behavior, such as the seeking of medical care. But the sociology of medicine refers to sociological study of health care organizations and the behavior of health care practitioners. For example, medical sociologists have been actively involved in studying relationships among different kinds of medical professionals in the provision of health services. Although the topics studied by health psychology and medical sociology certainly overlap, the two disciplines have different historical origins and orientation. Medical sociology focuses on social factors in the broader society that influence health, whereas health psychology focuses more on the influence of psychological processes within the individual.

medical anthropology
The specialty within anthropology that studies cultural aspects of health and illness.

Medical anthropology. Another social science discipline interested in matters of health is anthropology. **Medical anthropology** is the study of cultural aspects of health and illness (Foster & Anderson, 1978). In the past, medical anthropologists have tended to focus on health issues in traditional societies. However, there has recently been increased discussion of cultural aspects of health in Western culture (Foster & Anderson, 1978). Although medical anthropologists and health psychologists often have coinciding interests, the two specialties differ in orientation and focus. Medical anthropologists emphasize the cultural aspects of health and how people within a culture understand health matters as a reflection of their overall culture. Medical anthropology strongly emphasizes the cross-cultural comparison of systems of healing and beliefs about health. Health psychologists recognize the importance of culture in how people deal with health matters, but focus more on individual health beliefs and patterns of health-related behavior.

HEALTH PSYCHOLOGY IN ACTION

Now that we have defined health psychology and distinguished it from other related areas, we come to the question of what health psychologists actually do. The activities of health psychologists fall into three broad categories: research, application, and education/training (Weiss, 1982). These three broad categories are found in each of the facets of health psychology described above.

Research in Health Psychology

Of the three categories of activities, research is the broadest. Health psychologists are involved in research on a broad array of issues pertaining to the maintenance of health and the prevention of illness, research that provides the basis for applications in the clinic as well as elsewhere. Much of our discussion in this book is about research. For example, health psychologists are currently engaged in research on sexual practices and their implications for sexually transmitted diseases (STDs) such as genital herpes and AIDS (acquired immunodeficiency syndrome) (cf. Joseph et al., 1987). As we will see in Chapter 12, such research is critical in limiting the spread of AIDS and other STDs. In addition, health psychologists have conducted research on such important topics as the prevention of smoking and obesity, seat belt use and healthy dietary practices. In the area of treatment, health psychologists have been active in developing new ways of dealing with pain (cf. Melzack & Wall, 1982; Turk, Meichenbaum, & Genest, 1983); in developing new behavioral techniques for treating diseases such as hypertension (Shapiro & Goldstein, 1982), asthma (Creer, 1982), and gastrointestinal disorders (Whitehead & Bosmajian, 1982); and in evaluating the effectiveness of different treatment strategies (cf. Prokop & Bradley, 1981). A large body of research in health psychology concerns the factors associated with the development of illness. Health psychologists have intensively studied stress, the way people cope with stress, and, in general, how our health is affected by our interpersonal relationships. An example of these efforts is described in Box 1.1. Finally, health psychologists have been active in researching issues relating to the health care system and health policy. Research on the effects of hospitalization (cf. Raps, Peterson, Jonas, & Seligman, 1982) and the impact of long-term nursing care (cf. Timko & Moos, 1989) has pointed to important psychological factors in how patients react to health care institutions. Considerable discussion has recently focused on how health psychology can be integrated with such areas as public health (DeLeon & Pallak, 1982; Tanabe, 1982) and nursing (DeLeon, Kjervik, Kraut, & VandenBos, 1985).

Applying Health Psychology

Although research is necessary to gain an understanding of basic issues, without application health psychology would be of only academic interest. Health psychologists make major contributions to physical health by applying research findings and behavioral techniques to both the prevention and the treatment of disease. Health psychologists have developed programs for smoking prevention (cf. Hirschman & Leventhal, 1989), helped people with eating disorders (Schlesier-Stropp, 1984), and designed programs for managing stress (Meichenbaum & Jaremko, 1983). Health

Health psychologists are increasingly involved in the treatment of medical patients both as consultants and as service providers.

BOX 1.2 The Psychosocial Crisis of AIDS

Perhaps no disease has been more discussed or feared in modern times than acquired immunodeficiency syndrome (AIDS). Although the first cases of this syndrome were detected only in 1981, as of June 1992, in the United States alone, AIDS had already claimed more than 150,000 lives, and more than 230,000 people had been diagnosed with the syndrome (Centers for Disease Control, 1992). Worldwide, an estimated 10 to 12 million people are infected with the human immunodeficiency virus (HIV), the cause of AIDS, and this number is expected to increase to 40 million by the year 2000 ("HIV infects more than a million people in 8 months," 1992). Although much of the focus has been on the deadly nature of the disease and the speed with which it has spread, AIDS also has a severe psychosocial impact.

The extent of this impact was first outlined by Stephen Morin and Walter Batchelor in their article "Responding to the psychosocial crisis of AIDS" (1984). Morin and Batchelor point out that AIDS has a devastating effect on all involved. Certainly the person with AIDS is the most directly affected. A diagnosis of AIDS is perceived by most as the equivalent of a death sentence and causes immediate distress. They note that at one mental health crisis center, the number of AIDS-related calls had been increasing geometrically over an 18-month period, including an increasing number with threats of suicide or homicide. Among the psychosocial

stressors faced by persons with AIDS are fear of death and dying, the occurrence of repeated infections, and the looming specter of physical deterioration. Added to these are the social stigma of the disease, concern over contagion, fear of possible exposure of a stigmatized life-style, and fear of losing friends, occupation, and financial status. All these stressors point to the need for supportive psychosocial care.

Those with the disease are not the only ones affected. Lovers, family, friends, and health care providers also experience anxieties because of AIDS. Those who have been sexually intimate with the person are now at considerable risk of infection with HIV themselves. Further, Morin and Batchelor point out that for gay men, the largest group of AIDS sufferers in the United States and Europe, lovers "are almost certain to face self-righteousness, discrimination, fear, and legal impediments as they help their lover through the last months or years of his life" (p. 6). Family and friends also experience distress as they work through their feelings about the person's sexual orientation, fears of contagion, and grief about the anticipated death. Health care providers experience stress from working with AIDS patients, who experience heart-rending physical deterioration and often die at a young age. Further, they may be shunned by family, friends, and colleagues because of their work with AIDS patients (Salisbury, 1986). It is clear from all this that AIDS takes a terrible psychosocial toll.

psychologists are involved in the treatment of disease both as consultants to physicians and other health care professionals and as service providers. They offer psychological assessment of medical patients and advise other health care professionals on psychological issues. Health psychologists also employ a wide variety of techniques, including psychotherapeutic methods, behavior modification, and biofeedback to treat conditions ranging from obesity to cardiovascular disease (cf. Prokop & Bradley, 1981). Examples of some issues related to a specific disease, AIDS, are described in Box 1.2.

Education and Training

Finally, health psychologists are engaged in education and training. Many health psychologists are in academic settings, so they are involved in educating students at both the undergraduate and the graduate level about psychological factors in health. In the brief time since health psychology was formulated as a distinct field within psychology, many graduate and postgraduate programs have been developed for training health psychologists (Stone, 1983). In addition, health psychologists teach in medical settings such as medical schools (Thompson & Matarazzo, 1984) and schools of public health (Matthews & Avis, 1982).

THEMES IN HEALTH PSYCHOLOGY

The broad variety of topics encompassed by health psychology can be thought of in terms of three interrelated themes. The overarching theme, which is the basic conceptual framework for this text, is that of the integration of mind and body. All the topics covered are variations and elaborations on the intimate interconnection of our behavior and psychological processes with our physical health.

The second theme, closely related to the first, is coping and adaptation. Human beings are constantly faced with challenges and are forced to make adjustments to meet those challenges. The ways in which we adapt to these challenges affect our physical health significantly. This is most easily seen in work on stress and its relationship to health. The theme of coping and adaptation is also important in how people deal with chronic and life-threatening illness, how people face death, and how they respond to physical symptoms.

The third theme connecting the topics in health psychology is the role of interpersonal relationships in health and health care. Although health is a personal matter for each individual, it is certainly much more than that. Our health is highly influenced by the social fabric of which we are a part. The ways people respond to stress are affected by their relationships to other people. In addition, personal relationships are important in determining how people cope with chronic and life-threatening illnesses and how they respond to death and dying. Finally, our dealings with the health care system involve personal relationships with health care providers.

These few paragraphs only sketch the themes that will be developed in the pages below. Throughout the text, the various topics will be related to these general themes.

ORGANIZATION OF THE TEXT

This text is divided into six sections, each focusing on a particular domain within health psychology. Section I is an introductory section that presents the field of health psychology and lays the theoretical and methodological groundwork for what follows. Already in this chapter we have discussed what health psychology is, illustrated the kinds of issues addressed by health psychologists, and indicated how health psychology relates to other disciplines concerned with health. Chapter 2, "Mind and Body," develops the primary theme for this book: that the subject matter of health psychology can be best understood in terms of the interaction of the psychological and behavioral with the physical. A brief discussion of the biomedical model, currently the dominant model in the Western understanding of health and illness, is followed by some current criticisms of that model and presentation of the biopsychosocial model. This model, which unlike the biomedical model incorporates psychological and social factors, is then illustrated with research on placebos and the role of expectations in healing. Chapter 3 rounds out this introductory section with a discussion of research methods and ethics in health psychology.

Questions of health maintenance and illness prevention are the focus of Section II. As noted above, our behavior has a tremendous impact on our health. Chapter 4, "Human Behavior and Health," discusses the role of behavior in the occurrence of disease by considering such habits as smoking, drinking, and dietary habits, as well as exercise, and their contribution to health and disease. The concept of primary prevention is discussed along with research and theory on the determinants of health behavior.

Chapter 5, "Promoting Good Health," examines the efforts of health psychologists and others to convince people to engage in positive health behaviors such as good eating habits, regular exercise, safe sexual practices, and avoidance of smoking. This chapter addresses the effectiveness of our efforts to prevent illness and disease as well as ways to make those efforts more effective.

Section III examines the fascinating role of stress in the occurrence of disease. Chapter 6, "Stress and Disease," analyzes the term "stress" and its relationship to health. Stress has been defined and measured in a variety of ways. We examine these differing definitions and measures, relating them to theories about how stress operates and how it is related to the development of disease.

Chapter 7, "Dealing with Stress: Who Gets Sick and Who Doesn't," continues this discussion by examining the ways in which people cope with stress. All of us are subject to stress on a fairly regular basis. Certainly in a high-pressure, active society no one escapes the experience of stress. However, stress often has very different effects on different people. The question is why. This chapter considers this question by exploring the roles of personality and social support in the process of coping with stress. We also consider techniques of stress management that have been developed to help people deal with various stresses.

In Section IV, we turn our attention to how people deal with symptoms and disease. One of the most common observations in health psychology is the degree to which people differ in their responses to symptoms and disease. These differences, while fascinating in themselves, have significant implications for people's health-related behavior. Chapter 8, "The Nature of Illness: Perceiving Symptoms and Seeking Help," examines the nature of illness with a specific emphasis on the meaning that people attach to different symptoms and diseases. After a discussion of cultural and social factors in the definition of illness, we analyze the psychological processes involved in perceiving and interpreting symptoms. This is followed by a consideration of the processes involved in conceptualizing illness and seeking help.

Most of us receive our health care from professional health care providers who are often a part of larger health care institutions. Chapter 9, "Interacting with the Health Care System," examines the social and psychological aspects of our relationship to the health care system and to individual health care providers. Although the focus of our interactions with health care practitioners is usually on the symptoms or physical condition for which we are seeking help, these interactions are also very much personal interactions, interactions that often take place under time pressures and the duress of illness. In this chapter, we take up the nature of our relationship with health care providers and the barriers that too often prevent good communication. We also explore the problem of noncooperation with medical recommendations and the contribution that health psychologists can make toward improving the extent to which people follow the advice of health care practitioners. Following this, we examine the psychological aspects of health care institutions, focusing on the experience of hospitalization.

One of the great triumphs of modern medicine has been the development of modern medicines and procedures either to cure or to prevent many conditions that in the past were often fatal. The development of penicillin to cure infections and bacterial diseases such as pneumonia, as well as vaccines for diseases such as smallpox and polio, has added many years to the average person's life expectancy. However, many more people at one time or another will have to deal with some kind of chronic illness or disability. At any one time, approximately 50% of us have one or more chronic conditions that require some type of medical management (Cole, 1974). Chapter 10, "Dealing with Chronic Illness and Disability," examines the psychological aspects of dealing with chronic and disabling conditions. In this chapter, we discuss the psychological and social tasks that face persons with chronic illness and consider the contribution that health psychologists can make to their quality of life.

Chapter 11, "Death and Dying," focuses on the final stage of a person's life. Although few of us like to think about the inevitability of death, it comes to all. Psychologists and others have become increasingly interested in the process of dying and in how people respond to death. In this chapter, we consider the psychological and social aspects of death and dying, from the perspective of both the dying person and those around him or her.

The first four sections of the text are devoted to the basic principles of health psychology. In Section V, we turn our attention to the health psychology of four major health problems. In Chapter 12, "Immunity and AIDS," we examine the nature of immunity and what is known about AIDS. New research in the area of psychoneuroimmunology is uncovering the intricate links between psychosocial factors and the immune system. We discuss the current status of this research and what we currently know about the effects of stress on immunity. We then turn our attention to the nature and causes of AIDS and what can be done to prevent its spread. We conclude our discussion by considering the psychosocial impact of AIDS and ways of helping people cope with this disease and its effects.

One of the leading causes of death in industrialized nations is cancer, the topic of Chapter 13. The term *cancer* actually refers to many different diseases that occur at different sites and often have very different prognoses. In this chapter, we consider the nature of cancer from both physiological and psychological perspectives. After a discussion of the biology and psychoimmunology of cancer, we examine life-style as a major predictor of who will develop cancer. After a discussion of these factors, we examine ways in which health psychologists and other health professionals can help people change their behavior so as to reduce cancer risk. Finally, with the development of more effective treatments for various cancers, people are living longer with these dreaded diseases. At the end of the chapter, we focus on the process of coping with cancer.

Chapter 14, "Coronary Heart Disease," examines current approaches to another leading cause of death. We begin by examining the physiology of heart disease and how cardiovascular functions are influenced by psychological factors. We then probe the ways in which life-style and personality are implicated in the etiology of these disorders and examine behavioral interventions that can be used to prevent heart disease. Our discussion concludes by considering the psychological and social aspects of recovering from a heart attack.

Although it is not a disease as such, pain is a major health problem. Chapter 15 considers the elusive character of pain and its relationship to health. Although pain at first seems like a relatively straightforward phenomenon, even a brief examination of it reveals an unexpected degree of complexity. This chapter examines the social and cultural determinants of the experience of pain along with related physiological and psychological processes. Current theories about pain are then introduced as a framework for understanding these seemingly confusing phenomena. The chapter closes with an examination of different techniques that have been developed to help people cope with acute and chronic pain.

Section VI completes the text by considering the future. In its relatively short history, health psychology has made significant contributions to physical health. But we have really only scratched the surface. In Chapter 16, "Health Psychology: Critical Issues for the Future," we examine likely future directions for health psychology in research and practice, as well as health psychology as a profession. Of course, no one can truly predict the future. The outlines for the health psychology of the future, however, are already becoming apparent. Much has been accomplished, but the adventure has only begun.

SUMMARY

This chapter introduced the field of health psychology, providing a definition of the field as well as examples of applications and a brief history of psychology's involvement in health issues. Health psychology is the application of psychological theory and research methods to problems of physical health and health care. Among the areas addressed by health psychologists are (1) the promotion and maintenance of health, (2) the prevention and treatment of illness, (3) factors associated with the development of illness, and (4) issues concerning the

health care system and the formulation of health policy. Health psychologists contribute to each of these areas through research, application of theories and research findings to medical problems, and education. Health psychology concerns all aspects of health-related cognition and behavior and hence includes contributions from the full spectrum of specialties in psychology.

As a defined specialty, health psychology is very new. Several factors have recently converged to focus attention on psychological and behavioral aspects of health. First, the definition of health has changed from one emphasizing the lack of pathology to one emphasizing complete mental and physical well-being. Second, there has been considerable questioning of the appropriateness of the biomedical model as the foundation for understanding health and illness. Third, a shift has taken place in the patterns of illness, away from acute and infectious diseases as the major killers to chronic diseases as our prime health problems. Fourth, the escalation of health care costs, particularly those related to preventable diseases brought on by poor health habits and unhealthy life-styles, has focused attention on ways of changing these habits and life-styles. Finally, the early emphasis in psychology on the basic principles of behavior has paid off with the coming of age of behavioral technology. In its short history, health psychology has taken great strides in the research and application of psychological and behavioral principles to physical health and shows considerable promise for even greater accomplishments in the future.

KEY TERMS

health psychology (3)
medical psychology (8)
psychosomatic medicine (9)
behavioral medicine (9)

behavioral health (9)
medical sociology (9)
medical anthropology (10)

SUGGESTED READINGS

Carmody, T. P., & Matarazzo, J. D. (1991). Health psychology. In M. Hersen, A. E. Kazdin, & A. S. Bellack (Eds.), *The clinical psychology handbook* (2d ed.). New York: Pergamon. In this chapter Timothy Carmody and Joseph Matarazzo discuss the need for health psychology, review its status, and consider possible future directions.

Stone, G. C. (1979). Psychology and the health system. In G. C. Stone, F. Cohen, & N. E. Adler (Eds.), *Health psychology—A handbook*. San Francisco: Jossey-Bass. In this chapter George Stone gives a history of psychology's involvement with physical health as well as a taxonomy of psychological studies of health.

Taylor, S. E. (1990). Health psychology: The science and the field. *American Psychologist, 45,* 40–50. This article examines the current status of health psychology, the contributions it has made, and factors that can be expected to influence its future development.

CHAPTER **2**

Mind and Body

The relationship between mind and body has been a source of speculation and controversy since ancient times. At some times and in some cultures, mind and body have been viewed as inextricably linked, while at other times and in other cultures, the two have been seen as separate. These notions form a critical basis for a culture's understanding of health as well as the treatment of disease. This chapter examines some of these ideas as they have developed over the centuries, focusing on recent shifts in the understanding of the role of psychological and social factors in health and disease.

MIND-BODY DUALISM AND THE BIOMEDICAL MODEL

Early Ideas

What evidence we have from ancient times suggests that in early societies the mind and body were considered one unit. Diseases of the body were understood in terms of frightening spiritual powers. When a person fell ill, it was believed to happen because demons or other spiritual forces took over and controlled the person. Recovery required that the evil spirits be exorcised from the afflicted body (Kaplan, 1975).

The Greeks were among the first to understand disease in naturalistic terms. According to the Hippocratic theory of humors, disease resulted when there was an imbalance among the different "humors" circulating within the body. Therapy in the Hippocratic system was designed to restore the person to health by restoring the balance between the different humors (Ackerknecht, 1955). Although the emphasis in Greek medicine was on natural causes of illness, the mind and body were still regarded as intimately related, with each affecting the other. Both Aristotle and Plato commented on the ways in which the mind influenced the body and vice versa (Kaplan, 1975).

During the Middle Ages, the practice of medicine was controlled by the Christian church, and healing was performed primarily by priests.

At roughly the same time, the Chinese were also developing a naturalistic conception of health and disease. This conception developed independently of Western concepts but also emphasized disease as a natural phenomenon. Key to this understanding of disease is the concept of balance between forces. Ill health was believed to develop when opposing forces fell out of balance, such as when there was too much heat or too much cold in the body, or when there was an emotional or dietary imbalance. In the Chinese view, the mind and body are closely entwined, and a person's physical health is very much influenced by behavior and emotions. This emphasis on the interrelatedness of mind and body continues to be an important theme in Chinese medicine even today (Pachuta, 1989; Porkert & Ullmann, 1988).

During the Middle Ages (500–1500), the emphasis in understanding disease in the West moved from the naturalistic back to the spiritual. Medicine during this period was practiced under the auspices of the Christian church, and disease was understood in spiritual terms. Violation of divine laws resulted in disease; healing was seen as, at least in part, a function of faith. Healing was believed to take place when the person exchanged sinfulness for mental or physical health. Healing was practiced primarily by priests rather than by physicians (Kaplan, 1975).

Development of the Biomedical Model

Following this religious domination of medicine, the Renaissance saw a return to an emphasis on natural explanations for disease. The period saw a renewed interest in the study of mathematics, chemistry, and physics, paving the way for medical advances. The invention of the microscope provided a powerful tool for gathering medical information necessary for these advances. In addition, Morgagni's work in autopsy, Virchow's in pathology, and Pasteur's in bacteriology laid the foundation for modern medicine (cf. Ackerknecht, 1955).

mind-body dualism
The doctrine that the mind and body are two separate entities with only limited interaction.

Another important foundation for modern medicine was laid at this time in the doctrine of **mind-body dualism.** The doctrine was perhaps best expounded by the seventeenth-century French philosopher René Descartes, who argued that the physical and the spiritual were two separate realms: the body belonged to the physical realm, while the mind was part of the spiritual (Descartes, 1955). According to this view, the body was a machine that could be analyzed in terms of its constituent parts, and understood in essentially mechanical terms. Disease was seen as resulting from the breakdown of the machine; the physician's job was to diagnose the breakdown and repair the machine, a task viewed as similar in principle to that of a mechanic. Thus under the guidance of this conception, health and disease have come to be viewed almost exclusively in biochemical terms, with little consideration of social or psychological factors.

This analytical/mechanistic approach to medicine has undoubtedly produced tremendous benefits. With the development of germ theory in the nineteenth century as well as advances in immunology, public health, pathology, and surgical technique, came dramatic improvements in health. Diseases such as cholera, typhoid, and scarlet fever were brought under control, and mortality rates in the United States and Europe declined appreciably (Ahmed, Kolker, & Coelho, 1979). The advances of biomedicine have been even more dramatic in our own century. The development of "miracle" drugs, such as penicillin and its relatives, and vaccines for a wide variety of previously common diseases, as well as spectacular advances in surgical techniques and medical technology have led to a revolution in health care. With these advances, health care professionals are now able to treat and, if not cure, at least relieve the effects of diseases and physical conditions that in years past were either fatal or simply had to be endured.

CURRENT CRITIQUES OF THE BIOMEDICAL MODEL

biomedical model
The medical model emphasizing the separation of mind and body and the physical causation of disease.

Although the **biomedical model** has undeniably been successful in the fight against disease, this approach to classification and treatment has also engendered growing dissatisfaction. The legacy of the biomedical model has been a medical-care system that is hospital and clinic based and that places its primary emphasis on increasingly sophisticated technology in dealing with disease. Numerous critics have questioned the effectiveness and desirability of this approach. Although biomedicine has made tremendous strides in eradicating infectious diseases, far less progress has been made against the chronic conditions, such as heart disease, cancers, and chronic respiratory ailments, which are currently leading causes of death (Gori & Richter, 1978; Knowles, 1977). Further, as discussed in later chapters, the causes for many of these conditions go well beyond the biomedical and are closely related to behavior.

iatrogenic illness
Illness that is the result of medical intervention.

Critics have also pointed out that our current medical system has definite limitations and dangers. Questions have been raised as to whether hospitals are the best place to treat illness in terms of the effectiveness of the care and the risks of **iatrogenic illness** (Illich, 1976). These and other critiques (cf. Gordon, 1980) have raised significant doubts about the appropriateness of the biomedical model in understanding illness and disease—thus casting doubt on the basic assumptions of the biomedical model as well as its ability to deal with health and illness.

Basic Assumptions

reductionism
The doctrine that the phenomena of health and illness are best understood at the level of physics and chemistry.

One of the most articulate critics of the biomedical model is George Engel. In his critique, Engel (1977) points out that this model rests on two basic assumptions. The first is the doctrine of mind-body dualism, described above, in which a clear demarcation is made between the body as a physical entity and the mind as part of the mental and spiritual domain. The second basic supposition is the principle of **reductionism.** Not only does the biomedical model presume a separation of mind and body, but it assumes that the complex phenomena of disease can be reduced to the language of chemistry and physics. Thus the biomedical model presumes that the important events involved in, for instance, a heart attack are physical in nature—the arterial blockage, tissue damage, pain experienced. Further, these events are best understood in terms of their biochemical characteristics. How the person reacts to these physical events— such as seeking help or the effects on interpersonal relationships—as well as aspects of the person's behavior that might have contributed to the condition—such as diet, stress, or smoking—are generally shunted aside. Likewise, the biomedical approach to treating a heart attack is concerned mostly with managing the physical aspects of the disease, and only secondarily with the patient as a person. The physician concentrates on the person's physiological status, considering the psychological and social ramifications of the disease peripheral (Engel, 1980).

Although this approach to disease has undeniably produced tremendous benefits, Engel argues that it is best understood as dogma. In fact, despite its accomplishments, the biomedical model does not really account adequately for ill health; Engel specifies several ways in which it fails to do so.

Failures

To begin with, in the biomedical model the presence of specific biochemical abnormalities is the criterion for disease diagnosis. This ignores the fact that documented biochemical deviations, at best, define necessary but not sufficient conditions for disease. These biochemical indicators by no means account for all illness.

> Thus while the diagnosis of diabetes is first suggested by certain core clinical manifestations, for example, polyuria, polydipsia, polyphagia, and weight loss, and is then confirmed by laboratory documentation of relative insulin deficiency, how these are experienced and how they are reported by any one individual, and how they affect him, all require consideration of psychological, social, and cultural factors, not to mention other concurrent or complicating biological factors. (Engel, 1977, pp. 131–32)

Second, the diagnosis of physical conditions depends critically on input from the patient. Although physical examination and laboratory tests are certainly important in identifying disease, diagnosis relies a great deal on what the patient is able to communicate to the health professional. Accuracy in diagnosis requires that the health professional have well developed interviewing skills as well as a basic understanding of the psychological, social, and cultural determinants of symptom reports.

Third, the biomedical approach to illness, by concentrating on the physiological, ignores the influence of life situation on the person's health. Engel writes that in order to understand the timing of the onset as well as the course of a disease, it is necessary to consider not only the person's biological susceptibility but also such factors as life changes and the social support the person gets from those around her.

Further, psychological and social factors are critical for determining when, and if, a person comes to view himself as ill when possessing a diagnosable physical abnormality. The same can be said for when other people label the person as being "sick." Since such definitions, whether self or other, are the basis for seeking help, the biomedical model is not capable of explaining why people do or do not seek help and the timing for that decision.

The biomedical model also fails to account for the person's return to health after being ill. We usually think of a person as being cured of a disease when the physiological abnormality has been corrected. However, this may not be the case. Even after the biological abnormality that formed the basis of the original diagnosis is no longer present, the person may still experience illness. A good example of this is the experience of continued pain after the apparently normal healing of a wound (Melzack & Wall, 1982; see Chapter 15).

Finally, Engel indicates that the behavior of the physician as well as the relationship between physician and patient powerfully influence the outcome of therapy. Although the biomedical approach concentrates on applying known medications and technologies to correcting the biological defect, how the physician interacts with the patient can have a significant impact on the effectiveness of such therapies. For one thing, the physician's success in persuading the patient to cooperate in the therapy and implement recommended behavior changes, such as changes in diet or smoking habits, is likely to determine whether the remedy is successful. In addition, the patient's reactions to the doctor's behavior can result in physiological changes that influence the course of the disease. "Thus, insulin requirements of a diabetic may fluctuate significantly depending on how the patient perceives his relationship with his doctor" (Engel, 1977, p. 196).

A NEW UNDERSTANDING OF HEALTH AND ILLNESS

Because of these shortcomings, many theorists have argued that a new model is necessary if we are to make continued progress in understanding and controlling disease (Brody, 1973; Engel, 1977; Jasnoski & Schwartz, 1985). Although the details of this new model are still being worked out and different theorists sometimes take slightly different approaches, there is widespread agreement that this new model must incorporate the positive features of the biomedical model that have been so instrumental in modern medical advances. At the same time, however, the new model must avoid the reductionism and mind-body dualism that have unnecessarily limited the biomedical model.

A Systems Approach

What might this new model look like? The basic theoretical foundation for a new model of health and disease can be found in work on *general systems theory* (von Bertalanffy, 1968). General systems theory is a perspective on natural phenomena that argues that nature is best understood in terms of a hierarchy of systems, in which each system is simultaneously composed of smaller subsystems and part of larger, more encompassing systems. For example, the human body is made up of several interrelated systems, such as the cardiovascular system, the endocrine system, and the nervous system. Each of these is, in turn, composed of various interrelated tissues and cells. Further, the physical body is only one aspect of a person, and each person is a part of larger systems, including family, community, society, and the biosphere. These different systems can be conceptualized in terms of a hierarchy of levels and of a continuum of interacting units. Figures 2.1 and 2.2 give graphic representations of the interrelationship among these different systems. Figure 2.1 shows the hierarchical aspects of a systems approach. Starting from the bottom, with subatomic particles, it is possible to conceptualize each level as comprising the levels beneath it. Although this representation captures one critical feature of the systems theory perspective,

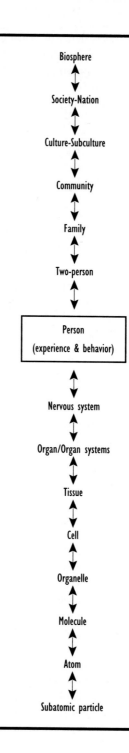

FIGURE 2.1

Hierarchy of natural systems.
Note. From "The clinical application of the bio-psychosocial model" by G. L. Engel, 1980, *American Journal of Psychiatry, 137,* p. 537. Copyright 1980 by the American Psychiatric Association. Reprinted by permission.

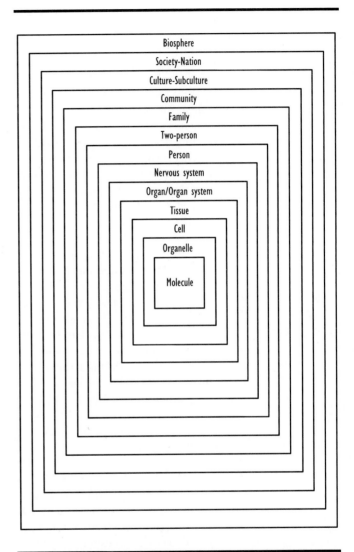

FIGURE 2.2
Continuum of natural systems.

Note. From "The clinical application of the biopsychosocial model" by G. L. Engel, 1980, *American Journal of Psychiatry, 137,* p. 537. Copyright 1980 by the American Psychiatric Association. Reprinted by permission.

Figure 2.2 demonstrates a second important characteristic. Each system is at the same time both a whole and a part. The nervous system, for example, is both a complete system in its own right and a part of the human body. A person is both a separate individual with distinct psychological makeup and functioning and a part of society and of nature in general.

Conceptualizing nature in this way has important implications for our understanding of health and disease. By viewing the different levels of the systems hierarchy as a series of systems with their own internal workings, the general systems approach avoids reductionism. The biomedical model, by assuming that all biological phenomena are reducible basic biochemical processes, both implicitly and explicitly emphasizes finding the most basic level for understanding and treating disease. Since the cellular and molecular levels are lower in the hierarchy than the community or the person, these levels are regarded as more important, and greater emphasis is placed on understanding these levels and developing interventions to be applied there. The systems theory approach makes no such assumptions about the relative importance of different levels, but rather emphasizes the study and understanding of each level in itself. Hence, comprehending the psychological and community aspects of a disease is equal in importance to understanding the disease at the cellular level.

The systems approach also avoids the limitations imposed by mind-body dualism. By emphasizing the interconnectedness of the different natural systems, the systems approach not only bridges the separation between mind and body, but brings the social and cultural levels into the picture. One important feature of the systems approach is the idea that a change or disturbance at one level of the systems hierarchy affects not only that level but levels above and below it. Thus a change at the tissue level, such as the development of a cancerous tumor, has implications at the cellular level as well as the personal level, the family level, and even the community level. But a change at the community level, such as the closing of a major factory, is likely to affect the families of those working at the factory and to produce psychological reactions in those laid off and physiological reactions at the level of the nervous and other bodily systems.

Another essential feature of a systems approach is the concept of *self-regulation* (Carver & Scheier, 1981; Carver & Scheier, 1982; Leventhal, 1983): that systems are goal oriented and strive to achieve a balance in their functioning. A good example of this is homeostasis, first described by Walter Cannon (1929, 1935), wherein organisms attempt to maintain a stability and balance in their internal functioning such that deviations from the norm are met with corrective action. For example, the normal internal body temperature for humans is 98.6°F (37°C). When a person's temperature is above or below this level, corrective action is taken, such as shivering when the person is cold or sweating when the person is hot. This concept applies to other systems as well. For example, when a person experiences symptoms, these deviations lead the person to try to identify the cause of those symptoms so that remedial action can be taken (Leventhal, 1983).

feedback loop
A means of system regulation in which the results of system actions are returned to the system and influence its future behavior.

At the heart of self-regulation are the key concepts of *reference values* and **feedback loops.** Every self-regulating system has a set of reference values that describe the goals of that system. For example, the reference value for human body temperature is 98.6°F (37°C). The reference values for experiencing symptoms are the "normal" bodily sensations that the person experiences on a routine basis. Deviation from these reference values leads to actions aimed at removing the deviation, for example, shivering to increase a low body temperature. The result of the actions is then returned to the system through feedback loops.

These feedback loops can be either positive or negative. In a negative feedback loop, the results of the corrective action reduce the discrepancy from the reference value and eventually lead to a cessation of the action, after which balance in a system is restored. For example, a thirsty person will drink only until the thirst is quenched. However, feedback loops may also be positive: actions taken serve to increase the discrepancy between the current state of the system and the reference value. An amusing example of this can occur with a dual-control electric blanket when the controls are accidentally placed on the wrong side of the bed. If one person under the blanket feels warm he or she is likely to turn down the temperature dial on the control that lowers the temperature on the other side. The other person then feels cold and turns up the other control causing the first person to feel even warmer. This cycle is likely to continue until one or both individuals realize that something is wrong, and the controls are switched back to their correct locations. Similarly, positive feedback occurs when inappropriate treatments for a disease increase rather than decrease symptoms, causing the person's health to deteriorate rather than improve. The increased deviation from the reference value signals the system to change strategies so that attempts to reduce the deviation are more successful. Thus the two people with the electric blanket will probably switch the location of the controls, and the person whose symptoms are getting worse is likely to try a different treatment.

As we will see, the concept of self-regulation plays an important part in understanding health and illness. Feedback loops are found at every level of the hierarchy of systems involved in health, from the molecular and cellular through the community, and describe the means to control the behavior of these systems. For example, at the psychological level, people experience stress when they perceive that their resources are insufficient to deal with challenges at hand. To reduce this stress, people then engage in coping responses that, if successful, help restore a calmer state. Similarly, at the physiological level, responses to stress essentially represent deviations from the person's normal physiological functioning that, if continued for extended periods, can lead to the development of disease. Seeking relief from physical symptoms, such as taking over-the-counter medications or seeing a health professional, is another example of self-regulation through feedback loops (see Chapter 8). When these actions are successful, the person's interpretation of the symptoms is confirmed. However, when the actions are unsuccessful, the person is likely to reinterpret the situation and engage in different actions to restore health.

The Biopsychosocial Model

Viewing health and disease from a systems perspective is more than simply a philosophical shift: it also has important implications for how practitioners approach their patients and for how we go about studying health and disease. Engel (1980) illustrates the clinical application of what he calls the **biopsychosocial model** with the case of Mr. Glover, who becomes ill at work and is taken to the hospital for symptoms of a myocardial infarction after having had one six months earlier. A physician utilizing the reductionistic biomedical model would be primarily concerned with establishing a physical diagnosis for Mr. Glover's condition as quickly as possible and selecting and

biopsychosocial model

A systems approach to illness that emphasizes the interconnectedness of mind and body and the importance of understanding disease at all levels.

applying the appropriate treatment. Although the attending physician requires information from Mr. Glover and the coworker who brought him to the hospital to evaluate the symptoms and establish a diagnosis, primary reliance is placed on various diagnostic tests. Mr. Glover's psychological state, expectations, and other personal characteristics are seen as peripheral. In the situation described by Engel, this lack of attention to the patient as a person became critical when the emergency room staff had difficulty performing an arterial puncture as part of the medical workup, and Mr. Glover went into cardiac arrest. The house staff was able to revive him, but in an interview with the patient a few days later, it became clear that the cardiac arrest had been brought on, at least in part, by the stress associated with the bumbled procedure and his loss of confidence in those attending him. By ignoring signs of Mr. Glover's psychological distress, the house staff hastened the deterioration of his physical condition.

Implications of the Biopsychosocial Model

How might a physician using the biopsychosocial model have approached this case differently? First, from the onset of the episode, a systems-oriented physician would be concerned with factors other than just cardiac status. The initial interview would be conducted in a manner that obtained information about Mr. Glover as a person as well as information to evaluate his cardiac status. In addition to physical symptoms, the interview would ask about the life context of the symptoms, the patient's activities, feelings, and behavior as the symptoms were evolving, and the patient's social and family relationships. Such information would be extremely valuable in anticipating the patient's reactions to various aspects of treatment. Close attention would be paid to the person's psychological state and emotional responses to the ongoing treatment. Finally, the physician would be cognizant of the likely "ripple effects" that can be anticipated from medical intervention. Figures 2.3 and 2.4 illustrate the potential ramifications of two possible outcomes of Mr. Glover's treatment. Both successful and unsuccessful treatment at a physiological level have implications at all the other levels.

A systems approach to treating health and disease has equally important implications for our approach to studying health and disease. In its emphasis on the physiological and the biochemical, the biomedical model focuses attention on the purely physical aspects of disease, and generally considers psychological and social influences at best irrelevant and at worst nuisance variables that cloud the "real" determinants of health status. A systems approach, by contrast, makes it clear that a person's health status is a product of many different influences, ranging from the cellular and the biochemical to the social and cultural. Moreover, changes in the person's health status have wide-ranging effects at the psychological, social, and cultural levels.

The remainder of this book details these interactions. Two particularly fascinating illustrations of the interrelationship of mind and body are placebos and the role of beliefs in health.

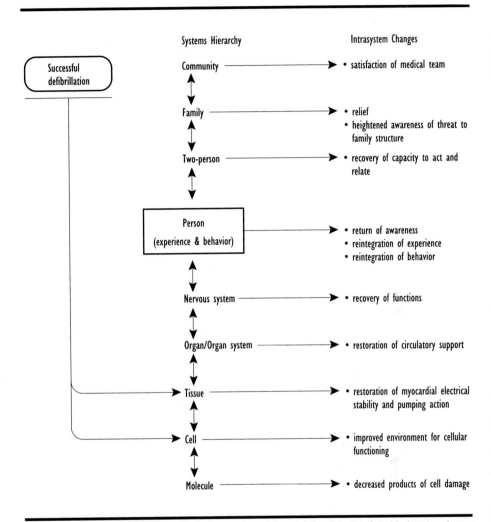

Systems Hierarchy

Successful defibrillation

Community → • satisfaction of medical team

Family → • relief
• heightened awareness of threat to family structure

Two-person → • recovery of capacity to act and relate

Person (experience & behavior) → • return of awareness
• reintegration of experience
• reintegration of behavior

Nervous system → • recovery of functions

Organ/Organ system → • restoration of circulatory support

Tissue → • restoration of myocardial electrical stability and pumping action

Cell → • improved environment for cellular functioning

Molecule → • decreased products of cell damage

Intrasystem Changes

FIGURE 2.3
Effects of successful treatment.

Note. From "The clinical application of the biopsychosocial model" by G. L. Engel, 1980, *American Journal of Psychiatry, 137,* p. 542. Copyright 1980 by the American Psychiatric Association. Reprinted by permission.

PLACEBOS

Mention of the term *placebo* to most people is likely to conjure up images of sugar pills given to hypochondriacs for symptoms that are "all in one's head." The general implication is that when people have been given placebos, and particularly when they find relief with them, the symptoms involved must not have been real, only imagined. Real symptoms, of course, require real medicine.

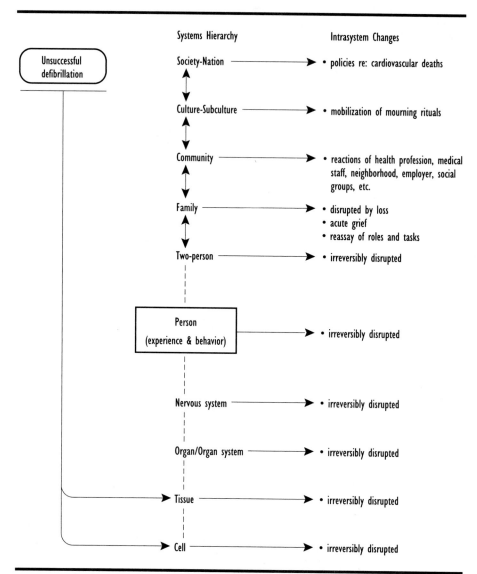

FIGURE 2.4

Effects of unsuccessful treatment.

Note. From "The clinical application of the biopsychosocial model" by G. L. Engel, 1980, *American Journal of Psychiatry, 137,* p. 542. Copyright 1980 by the American Psychiatric Association. Reprinted by permission.

What Are Placebos?

Placebos and their effects have been well known in medicine for some time (cf. White, Tursky, & Schwartz, 1985). The term **placebo** comes from the Latin for "I shall please," and has often been understood to refer to a pharmacologically inert treatment given by a health care provider to mollify the patient. Or, in the case of drug trials, a placebo

placebo
A treatment with no action specific for the condition being treated but that is used for its nonspecific effects.

is used as a baseline against which to evaluate the effects of the drug being tested. Although these are common uses of placebos, the term, in fact, refers to much more than this. Arthur Shapiro (1964; Shapiro & Morris, 1978) defines a placebo as any treatment that has no specific activity for the condition in question, but that is, either knowingly or not, used for its nonspecific, psychological, or psychophysiological effects. Although the proverbial sugar pill falls into this category, so do many other treatments, including those utilizing "real" medications. For example, it has been estimated that between 35% and 45% of all prescriptions are for drugs that have no known effects on the condition for which they are being prescribed; such prescriptions include antibiotics for treating colds or vitamins for treating conditions with no known vitamin deficiency. In these cases, "real" medicines are being prescribed, but for conditions for which they have no known effectiveness (Bok, 1974).

The Effects of Placebos

Even though placebos by definition have no specific activity for the condition being treated, they have very definite effects. Studies of placebos have demonstrated effects on virtually every organ system in the body and for many diseases (Benson & Epstein, 1975). For example, placebos have been shown to have effects on the nervous system, the cardiovascular system, and the digestive system. Among the diseases and symptoms affected by placebos are angina pectoris (chest pain), rheumatoid and degenerative arthritis, hay fever, headaches, coughs, peptic ulcers, hypertension, and pain. In a review of placebo effects involving a total of more than 1,000 patients, Henry Beecher (1955) reported that an average of 35% of patients benefited from placebo treatments. Placebos can even reverse the effects of real drugs, as in the case of a woman who was told that the drug she was receiving would relieve her severe nausea and vomiting. The drug, actually syrup of ipecac, relieved her gastric problems within 20 minutes, even though its usual use is to *induce* vomiting (Ornstein & Sobel, 1987). Further, even though inert, placebos can produce side effects (Park & Covi, 1965).

The placebo effect is so powerful that in clinical drug trials the effectiveness of a test drug is defined as the extent to which it exceeds that of a placebo. For example, if a test drug is effective for 70% of the patients receiving it but the placebo comparison provides relief for 45% the drug effect is assumed to be the difference or 25%. Interestingly, Frederick Evans (1985) has reported that in drug trials involving pain relief placebos are consistently about 55% as effective as the analgesics being tested, regardless of the drug, whether morphine or aspirin.

The placebo effect should also be put in a historical context. Throughout history, patients have been subjected to often bizarre treatments such as potions made from frog sperm, animal dung, or lizard tongues, as well as bleeding, purging, and the royal touch. Although some of these treatments may have had some active ingredients for the condition treated, most of them are now known either to have no specific action on the disease or actually to be harmful. Yet people apparently improved with such treatments, even beyond the number who could be expected to do so because of the self-limiting nature of some illnesses. Such observations have led some to argue that the history of medicine is largely the history of the placebo effect (Shapiro, 1964; Shapiro & Morris, 1978).

Influences on Placebo Effects

Given the power of placebo effects, what determines their action? Although there is still much we do not know about placebos, studies of their effects have shown that many factors influence the occurrence and strength of these effects. For one thing, the specific characteristics of the placebo treatment appear to have a significant effect. For example, it appears that placebos administered through injection may have greater effects that those taken orally. Among those taken orally, capsules are apparently more effective than pills, and larger doses (i.e., more capsules or pills) seem to increase placebo response. The color of the preparation also makes a difference: blue pills or capsules work better as tranquilizers, while red, pink, or yellow ones seem to work better as stimulants (Buckalew & Ross, 1981).

In addition, there is evidence that the brand name on the pill can influence its effectiveness. In one study, a group of British headache sufferers could choose aspirin or a placebo labeled with either a familiar or an unfamiliar brand name. Although 40% of the patients showed improvement with placebos having an unfamiliar brand name, 50% showed relief with placebos bearing a familiar brand. This compared with 56% receiving relief with an unfamiliar aspirin brand and 60% with a familiar brand of aspirin (Branthwaite & Cooper, 1981).

The behaviors and attitudes of the practitioner administering the treatment also contribute to the effectiveness of placebos. When the practitioner is friendly toward the patient, shows an interest in the patient's problems, and is sympathetic, a placebo treatment is more likely to be effective than when the practitioner is cold and distant (Shapiro & Morris, 1978). Indeed, when a doctor is angry, rejecting, or contemptuous of the patient or is preoccupied with personal concerns, negative placebo effects may occur (Shapiro, 1964).

A particularly important role is played by the practitioner's expectations about the treatment. Studies have repeatedly shown that when the practitioner or staff members administering the treatment have high expectations, the treatment is more likely to be effective. Shapiro notes that telling the doctor that a drug is active and not a placebo can dramatically alter its effectiveness. One study reported that placebo effectiveness fell from 70% to 25% when the attitudes toward the treatment changed from positive to negative (Shapiro, 1964).

Although it has often been suggested that certain people are more likely to respond to placebos than are others, attempts at describing the typical person who responds to placebos have generally been unsuccessful. Personality characteristics as such do not appear to be consistently related to placebo responses (Shapiro & Morris, 1978). However, this is not to say that patient characteristics are unimportant. Patient anxiety has been shown to be related to placebo reactions, with more anxious patients showing stronger responses (Shapiro, 1964). In addition, the meaning that the person gives to the symptoms influences the degree of response. Beecher (1960), for example, found that about 35% of patients in a clinic setting found relief of pain with placebos as opposed to only 3% of subjects in a pain experiment. Although there are certainly many differences between pain patients and experimental subjects, one major difference is the meaning they attach to the pain. For clinic patients, pain is likely to be viewed as an indicator of some, perhaps unknown or feared, physical disorder, whereas for experimental subjects pain is an expected result of being in a pain experiment. Interestingly, morphine, which is well known as an effective pain reliever, is also less effective for experimental than clinical pain (Beecher, 1959).

Perhaps the most important patient variable, however, is the faith that the person has in the treatment. In general, the greater the person's confidence in the treatment the more likely that treatment is to be effective (Evans, 1985). Indeed, it has been argued that patient faith is the common pathway by which the different factors described above influence the placebo effect (Plotkin, 1985). Having a treatment that looks, tastes, and feels like "real" medicine, and is administered by an enthusiastic practitioner who has confidence in it, is likely to increase the patient's faith in a positive outcome. This is one of the major reasons why clinical drug trials are conducted through a double-blind procedure in which neither the patient nor the person administering the drug knows who is getting an active drug and who is getting a placebo. If either the patient or the person giving the drug were to know the true nature of the treatment, the results could be significantly altered (Ross & Buckalew, 1985).

Explaining Placebo Effects

How are we to explain placebo effects? How is it that a treatment with no active ingredients for the condition in question can have curative effects? Although many potential explanations have been offered (cf. Shapiro & Morris, 1978; White et al., 1985), three general processes appear most likely. First, placebos may achieve their effects partly through perceptual means. As discussed in Chapter 8, the perception of symptoms and illness is a complex process that depends not only on internal physiological sensations, but also on expectations of what a person should be experiencing. For example, James Pennebaker and Andy Skelton (1981) found that giving subjects a hypothesis about symptoms they should be experiencing significantly affected their symptom perceptions. When a person receiving a placebo expects symptom relief, this expectation in itself may alter symptom perception.

A second possible mechanism is through behavior. When people are given a treatment they fully expect to work, they may change their behavior. For example, if headache sufferers receive medication that they believe will relieve their pain, they may cease to be preoccupied with their problems, begin to relax, and go about regular activities without the restrictions imposed by headache pain (cf. Plotkin, 1985). In addition, the expectation of cure may make people more likely to follow medical recommendations as well as engage in behaviors, such as proper diet and exercise, that themselves lead to an improvement in physical condition.

Particularly intriguing possibilities have to do with physiological effects produced by placebos. Although placebos themselves often have no active ingredients, they have been shown to lead to physiological changes. For example, Richard Sternbach (1964) had six students participate in a three-part experiment in which they swallowed three different pills. These pills, which were actually small magnets used to measure stomach activity, were described as a stimulant that would produce stomach churning and cramps, a relaxant that would lead to a reduction in stomach activity and a bloated feeling, or a placebo that would have no effects at all. Observation of stomach activity showed that the expected reactions were obtained for four of the six subjects. In other words, when given the "stimulant," they experienced stomach churning and cramps, whereas they felt bloated with the "relaxant" and showed no change with the "placebo." Similar results were obtained by Stewart Wolf (1950), who found that when students were given a placebo described as either a stimulant or a depressant, they showed measurable changes in blood pressure and heart rate, as well as in subjective symptoms such as dizziness and abdominal pain. Recent studies have even suggested that placebos may relieve pain through the production of endogenous opioids known as endorphins (see Box 2.1).

All in all, placebos provide an excellent example of the interaction of mind and body by demonstrating the ways in which a person's beliefs about treatment can have remarkable effects on the outcome of that treatment. William Plotkin (1985) goes even further, arguing that placebo effects are in reality a form of self-healing. He contends that an unfortunate side effect of the success of modern medical technology is that it leads people to depend on expensive drugs and a medical elite and to neglect their own self-healing abilities. Placebo effects remind us of those abilities and point to the need to develop self-healing skills and attitudes.

BELIEFS AND HEALTH

The remarkable effects of placebos raise the question of the extent to which beliefs affect one's health. Since faith in an inert treatment has such remarkable outcomes, might it also be the case that other beliefs can have a significant health impact? The answer to this has long been a matter of controversy, but there is increasing evidence that the answer is "yes." Several lines of inquiry are demonstrating that beliefs can profoundly influence one's physical state. We shall be returning to these themes in later chapters. However, for our purposes here, consider some of the evidence relating beliefs to whether a person stays healthy, becomes ill, or even dies, as well as the role of beliefs in the recovery from illness.

The Role of Beliefs in Staying Healthy

All of us at one time or another experience the effects of stress—it is a ubiquitous part of our modern lives. As we will see in Chapters 6 and 7, stress can have profound effects on health, and different stressors have been empirically related to a variety of diseases. The general findings indicate that the greater the amount of stress, the more likely the person is to develop some type of disease (cf. Rahe & Arthur, 1978). Since increased amounts of stress are correlated with poorer health, it is remarkable that some people can endure tremendous amounts of stress without showing ill effects. Particularly remarkable are observations made by Aaron Antonovsky (1979) of Holocaust survivors. In a study concerned with adaptation to menopause, Antonovsky and his coworkers obtained measures of adaptation in a random sample of Israeli women and asked those from Central Europe if they had been in a concentration camp. Not surprisingly, as a group those who reported having spent time in a Nazi concen-

BOX 2.1 ## Do Placebos Relieve Pain Through Endorphins?

The discovery of naturally occurring endogenous opioids (endorphins and enkephalins) as a likely mechanism for pain regulation (see Chapter 15) has raised the possibility that these substances may somehow be involved in placebo relief of pain. Could placebos lead to the production of endorphins that then lead to pain relief?

To test this hypothesis, Jon Levine and his colleagues (1978) administered a placebo or doses of the drug naloxone to dental surgery patients as they recovered from the extraction of an impacted molar. Naloxone is known to counteract the action of endorphins, and Levine et al. (1978) reasoned that if endorphins are involved in placebo-produced pain relief, naloxone should reduce the effectiveness of the placebo. Patients were randomly assigned to one of three groups, all of which received a first injection two hours after surgery, followed by a second injection one hour later. The first group received naloxone, followed by a placebo, whereas the second group received the placebo first, followed by naloxone, and the third group received a placebo both times. As is usually the case, some patients experienced pain relief from the placebo, whereas others did not. Among those who responded to the placebo, however, Levine et al. observed that after the injection of naloxone, they reported greater pain, whereas this was not the case for placebo responders who received a second placebo injection.

Does this demonstrate that placebos operate through the production of endorphins? Possibly. Other studies of naloxone and placebos have produced somewhat conflicting results. For example, Richard Gracely and his coworkers (1983) present evidence that placebo analgesia can occur after administration of naloxone and that naloxone by itself can lead to an increase in pain. As Priscilla Grevert and Avram Goldstein (1985) point out, demonstrating that placebo-induced pain relief is mediated by endorphins can be very tricky. The outcome of studies depends on such factors as the dosage of naloxone used, whether the subjects are aware that drugs are being administered, and the timing of the pain measurements.

In an effort to pin down the role of endorphins in placebo analgesia, Grevert and her colleagues (1983) tested the effects of placebos and naloxone on experimentally induced ischemic arm pain (pain induced by a tourniquet). Subjects participated in three weekly sessions where they were told that they would get a "painkiller" (which was really a saline placebo) through an intravenous drip, but were unaware that they were also receiving a second drug 40 minutes later. Half the subjects received a second placebo, whereas the other half received an injection of naloxone. In addition, all subjects participated in control sessions where they did not receive the "painkiller" but were surreptitiously given a placebo injection, as well as sessions where they were surreptitiously administered naloxone. The control sessions were conducted to monitor the normal course of the pain, whereas the naloxone-only sessions ascertained the effects of naloxone independent of the placebo. The outcome of this study showed that the placebo resulted in a significant reduction of pain and that the group surreptitiously receiving the naloxone experienced less pain reduction. However, the effect of the naloxone was not evident until the second and third sessions, and the naloxone did not completely block the effect of the placebo. Naloxone administered without a placebo did not increase pain.

These results suggest that endorphins may well be an important mechanism in placebo analgesia, but do not rule out the possibility that other mechanisms may be operating as well.

tration camp showed poorer adaptation than did those who did not. What was striking, however, was that within the group of concentration camp survivors, there were several women who were very well adapted regardless of how adaptation was measured. These women had been through one of the most degrading and dehumanizing experiences ever known, yet did not show the physical or psychological scars associated with highly stressful experiences.

On the basis of these observations, as well as other evidence relating stress to disease, Antonovsky argues that the difference between those who show ill effects from stress and those who cope well, and sometimes even thrive on it, is what he calls a sense of coherence. Antonovsky describes the sense of coherence as:

> a global orientation that expresses the extent to which one has a pervasive, endur-ing though dynamic feeling of confidence that (1) the stimuli deriving from one's internal and external environments in the course of living are structured, predict-able, and explicable; (2) the resources are available to one to meet the demands posed by these stimuli; and (3) these demands are challenges, worthy of invest-ment and engagement. (Antonovsky, 1987, p. 19)

In a nutshell, he is describing a belief system in which the person has a strong sense of meaning and faith in one's abilities to meet the challenges of life. According to Antonovsky, this sense of coherence serves as a generalized resource for the person in resisting the effects of everyday stresses.

A closely related concept is what Suzanne Kobasa (1979, 1982b) calls the hardy personality. Kobasa has studied individuals who are under a high level of stress, comparing those who develop illness frequently with those who do not. From these comparisons she has found that individuals who are under stress but have low levels of illness are characterized by a strong sense of commitment to the self, internal control, and meaningfulness, and tend to view life situations as a challenge. Although Kobasa discusses these variations in terms of personality, they clearly reflect different beliefs: hardy individuals believe in themselves and their ability to deal with whatever difficulties may arise.

The flip side of this, however, is that although a person's beliefs can serve as a buffer against the effects of stress, they can also be part of the pathogenesis of ill health. A dramatic example of this is the phenomenon of "voodoo death" that has been described by Walter Cannon (1942). This phenomenon, reported numerous times among so-called primitive peoples, involves a sequence of events wherein an individ-ual either engages in taboo behavior or is condemned by a medicine man or other powerful person and then dies without apparent physical pathology. Although such reports have often been scoffed at, Cannon shows that the kind of condemnation involved, coupled with separation from the social group, can lead to very intense fear and despair, resulting in physiological reactions leading to death. In these cases, belief in the power of the spell and in the consequences of violating taboos profoundly influence the person's physical state. In his discussion of helplessness, Martin Seligman (1975) notes other instances, including prisoners of war and the bereaved, in which death appears to have been brought on by a profound sense of hopelessness and despair.

Beliefs and Recovery from Illness

Another area where there has been considerable interest in the role of beliefs concerns recovery from illness. Here, again, there has been a great deal of speculation and, until recently, not much hard evidence. What are the effects of beliefs on recovery from illness? For one thing, the beliefs that the person has can have a strong impact on how well the person copes with the disease. Shelley Taylor (1983) reports that positive coping with breast cancer is related to certain beliefs that women have about themselves and their disease. In particular, women who cope well are able to find meaning in their experience, utilize various methods to maintain a sense of control over the disease, and are able to perceive themselves as better off than others with the disease, regardless of their objective situation. Taylor refers to these as illusions that serve to help the woman maintain a psychological equilibrium. Taylor does not address the question of whether these beliefs influence the disease process. However, others (cf. Pettingale, 1984) argue that cancer patients' attitudes play a significant role in longevity.

One particularly intriguing way in which a person's beliefs can be harnessed in the healing process is through hypnotic suggestion. While in a hypnotic trance a person is particularly amenable to suggestion from the hypnotist (cf. Hilgard, 1977). Such suggestion can serve to mobilize the person's expectations about positive physical health outcomes, which in turn have been shown to have beneficial effects ranging from relief of pain to the alteration of allergic responses (Ornstein & Sobel, 1987). An example of how hypnosis can be used to alter a person's physical condition is its use in the treatment of warts. Warts are benign tumors of the skin caused by a very common virus. Studies have shown that the use of hypnotic suggestion can be effective in the removal of warts, sometimes even more effective than the usual physical treatments (cf. Ornstein & Sobel, 1987). For example, in one study (Sinclair-Gieben & Chalmers, 1959), fourteen patients with stubborn cases of warts on both sides of their bodies

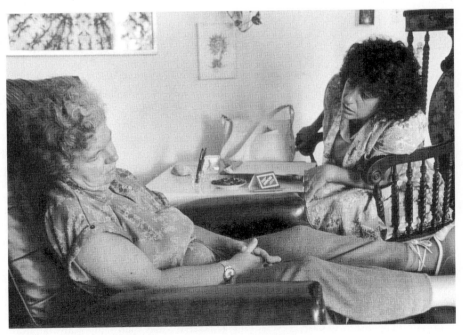

One of the ways a person's beliefs can be used in the healing process is through hypnosis.

were given a suggestion under hypnosis that the warts on one side of the body would disappear, while those on the other side would not. At the end of the study, the warts for nine of the patients had reduced considerably in size on the side where patients expected regression, but not on the other side. Similar results have been found in other studies as well (cf. Ornstein & Sobel, 1987).

Suggestion has also been shown to influence allergic reactions. For example, in one study (Ikemi & Nakagawa, 1962, cited in Ornstein & Sobel, 1987), researchers studied thirteen boys who were highly allergic to a poison ivy type of plant. In the first phase, all the boys were given a suggestion (five under hypnosis, the others not) that they were being touched by the leaves of the plant to which they were allergic. Although in reality they were being touched by a harmless plant, all thirteen showed an allergic reaction. In the second phase, the boys were told that they were being touched by a harmless plant when, in fact, they were being brushed by leaves of the poison ivy type of plant. Eleven boys showed no reaction to leaves that usually resulted in skin eruptions.

Taken as a whole, these results, along with those on the placebo effect, demonstrate the intimate interaction between mind and body. Far from being separate entities with limited mutual influence, the mind and body operate in close coordination with psychological processes and have a profound influence on our physical health (and vice versa). This is a theme that pervades work on health psychology and to which we will be returning continually throughout this book.

SUMMARY

This chapter considers the question of how we are to understand the phenomena of health and disease. A key feature of this puzzle is the intricate connection between psychological and social factors and our physical well-being. The relationship between mind and body has been a matter of debate since ancient times. Although early conceptions of health and disease generally considered the mind and body as one unit, during the Renaissance the doctrine of mind-body dualism was developed, which argued that the mind and body are separate entities that have only limited influence on each other. This doctrine, along with the principle of reductionism, became the bases of the modern biomedical model.

Although research and clinical practice based on the biomedical model have brought many tremendous advances in the understanding of disease and the eradication of many deadly diseases, several criticisms have been leveled at this model. George Engel, in particular,

believes that the biomedical model is a dogma that does not adequately account for the phenomena of illness. He and other theorists have proposed a new understanding of health and disease based on general systems theory. General systems theory argues that nature is best understood in terms of a hierarchy of systems, in which each system is simultaneously composed of smaller subsystems and is a component of larger systems. Each of these system levels is seen as interdependent, with events at one level having "ripple effects" on other levels. Further, events happening at one level are best understood in terms of that level, and no attempt is made to reduce phenomena to a lowest or most basic level. Systems are also conceived as self-regulating, meaning that they are goal oriented and use feedback loops to direct their behavior.

Adopting a systems approach to health and illness has many important implications. For one thing, this approach avoids the problems generated by the doctrines of mind-body dualism and reductionism. A systems-theory approach, sometimes referred to as the biopsychosocial model, explicitly recognizes the interrelationships between the physical body and the psychological and social arenas. With its emphasis on the importance of considering the whole person within a larger social context, this approach also has implications for research and clinical practice. Researchers and medical practitioners using a biopsychosocial model recognize the importance of considering psychological and social factors in illness along with the purely physical.

Two areas that illustrate some of the interactions of mind and body are placebos and the role of beliefs in health. A placebo is a treatment that has no specific action for the condition being treated. By this definition more than 45% of prescription medications, as well as a host of other treatments, may be placebos. Placebos have been shown to affect a wide variety of diseases and to be effective in the relief of a broad spectrum of symptoms. Placebo effects are influenced by such factors as the specific administration of the treatment, brand names, practitioner attitudes toward the patient and the treatment, and the patient's anxiety and confidence in the treatment. Placebos appear to work by (1) changing patient expectations and perceptions, (2) altering behavior, and (3) inducing physiological changes.

In addition to the considerable evidence concerning placebos, a realization has grown that other beliefs that people have influence their health. Recent work on stress and how people cope with it demonstrates that one's beliefs about one's ability to handle life situations and what is termed a sense of coherence play an important role in remaining healthy. In addition, such phenomena as voodoo death show that believing that one is condemned can produce death even without identifiable injury or disease. Beliefs also have a significant influence on the healing process, as illustrated by work showing that the manipulation of beliefs through hypnosis can have a significant influence on such differing conditions as warts and allergies.

KEY TERMS

mind-body dualism (20)
biomedical model (21)
iatrogenic illness (21)
reductionism (21)

feedback loop (26)
biopsychosocial model (28)
placebo (31)

SUGGESTED READINGS

Cousins, N. (1979). *Anatomy of an illness.* New York: W. W. Norton. A personalized account of a life-threatening illness and the nontraditional means used to combat it. A well-written case study of the interaction of mind and body.

Engel, G. L. (1977). The need for a new medical model: A challenge for biomedicine. *Science, 196,* 129–36. Dr. Engel's searching critique of the biomedical model and his call for a new understanding of health and illness.

Ornstein, R., and Sobel, D. (1987). *The healing brain.* New York: Simon and Schuster. A fascinating discussion by a neurobiologist and a physician of the ways in which the brain operates to keep one healthy.

White, L., Tursky, B., and Schwartz, G. E. (Eds.). (1985). *Placebo: Theory, research and mechanisms.* New York: Guilford Press. This edited volume contains a series of chapters exploring in detail what is currently known about placebos and their effects.

Research in Health Psychology

Consider the relationship of beliefs and attitudes to physical disease. For many years it has been popularly believed that a person's beliefs and attitudes influence health. But how do we go about demonstrating this relationship? What is required to go from mere speculation to a scientific certainty that such a relationship exists and then to describe the details of that relationship? To address these questions, this chapter describes the major methods used to investigate issues in health psychology.

The chapter cannot be expected to provide all the tools needed to do effective health psychology research—developing research skills requires far more than the reading of one textbook chapter. Rather, the goal is to offer basic background to help in understanding the research discussed in later chapters.

As shown in earlier chapters, health psychologists are interested in many varied questions, including basic as well as clinical research issues. Given this diversity, health psychologists use a variety of research methods. This chapter examines four basic types of methods: epidemiological, survey, experimental, and clinical. Questions of research ethics are also considered.

RESEARCH BASICS

Each method has its strong points and liabilities. *There is no one best method.* Rather, the choice of which method is best can be made only in relation to the research question being asked. For example, although questions concerning the distribution and etiology of disease are addressed through epidemiological methods, those about the effectiveness of therapeutic interventions are the province of clinical methods. Each type of method requires consideration of which types of questions are most appropriate to that method.

All methods in health psychology share the common goal of providing reliable and valid information about the issues at hand. This is often easier said than done. Regardless of the method used, there are numerous ways in which the results can be invalid. In this respect, the research process can be compared to a game of dodgeball. The goal in this game is to ensure the validity and persuasiveness of research results by avoiding attacks from sources of invalidity.

Sources of invalidity fall into two basic categories. First, research results may be invalid because of errors in research procedure. For example, in a clinical study of the effects of a new behavioral treatment, the results may be invalid because the group receiving the new treatment was less seriously ill at the beginning of the study than was the comparison group receiving a placebo treatment. Under these circumstances, the effects of the treatment are confounded with severity of disease; it is impossible to tell whether the experimental group improved, in comparison to control patients, because of the new treatment or because this group was in relatively better shape at the outset. This is an example of problems that can result from poor **internal validity.** When the research procedures are flawed, drawing valid conclusions about the relationship between variables within a study becomes extremely difficult, if not impossible.

The second general source of invalidity concerns the implications that can be drawn from the study results. Scientists are rarely interested in doing studies for their own sake. Rather, research is usually designed to shed light on some problem of theoretical or practical significance. The results of a research study must not only have internal validity, but should also be generalizable to situations outside the specific research setting, that is, they should have **external validity.** A research study might have poor external validity for many reasons. For example, a survey's interview

internal validity
The degree to which one can validly draw conclusions about the effects of the independent variable.

external validity
The degree to which the results of a study can be applied outside the original research setting.

procedures and questions may be valid, but if the sample is not chosen carefully, the results will apply only to those interviewed. An experiment's setting may be so artificial that the results apply only to that setting. In these cases, the results have few if any implications beyond the study in which they were obtained and are likely to be of very limited use.

EPIDEMIOLOGICAL METHODS

When considering the role of psychological and behavioral factors in health, among the first questions to be asked are who contracts which diseases, and what factors determine whether a person gets a particular disease. Such questions of disease distribution and etiology are addressed through the use of epidemiological methods. Since the first systematic recording of medical statistics in nineteenth-century England, epidemiological methods have provided detailed descriptions of the distribution of different diseases and have contributed to our understanding of the factors that contribute to both mortality and **morbidity** (cf. Hennekens & Buring, 1987; Lilienfeld, 1976). Such data provide a critical starting point for research and practice in health psychology.

morbidity
The occurrence of disease.

Epidemiological Measures

prevalence
The number of people in a given population who have a specific disease at a given time.

incidence
The number of new cases of a disease that occur within a specified population during a given period.

Incidence and prevalence. When addressing the question of the distribution of disease, epidemiologists are concerned with establishing both the **prevalence** and the **incidence** of different diseases. Even though these terms are sometimes used interchangeably, they should be carefully distinguished. The prevalence of a disease refers to the number of people in a given population who have a disease at any particular time. But the incidence of a disease is the number of people in a population who develop the disease over a given period of time. Incidence and prevalence are both expressed in the form of rates (Lilienfeld, 1976).

$$\text{Prevalence rate per } 1,000 = \frac{\text{Number of cases of a disease present in the population at a specified time}}{\text{Number of persons in the population at the specified time}} \times 1,000$$

$$\text{Incidence rate per } 1,000 = \frac{\text{Number of new cases of a disease occurring in a population during specified period of time}}{\text{Number of persons exposed to risk of developing the disease during that period of time}} \times 1,000$$

Thus if we wish to know how many people overall have rheumatoid arthritis, we would examine prevalence rates. If, however, we want to determine the frequency with which AIDS is contracted, we would look at incidence rates. Incidence and prevalence are closely related to each other, as illustrated in Figure 3.1—the prevalence of a disease

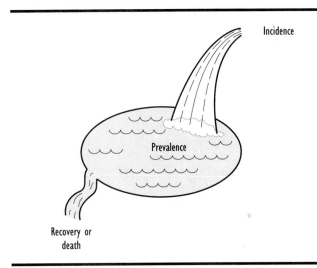

FIGURE 3.1
The relationship between prevalence and incidence.

Note. From *Epidemiology in medical practice* (3d ed.) (p. 50) by D. J. P. Barker and G. Rose, 1984, Edinburgh: Churchill Livingstone. Reprinted by permission.

is a function of the incidence of that disease in conjunction with its duration. Incidence provides the input into the pool of people who have the disease. This pool in turn is depleted when people either die or recover from the disease.

Disease risk. Incidence rates are among the most commonly used morbidity measures and are particularly important for determining risk. "Risk factors" have often been discussed as they pertain to such questions as the likelihood of contracting cancer, having a heart attack or getting some other disease. The identification of such risk factors comes from examination of the incidence rates for given diseases in different populations. In epidemiological usage, *absolute risk,* the overall likelihood of contracting a particular disease, is basically the same as the incidence rate for that disease. **Relative risk,** however, concerns the association between a suspected causal or contributing factor and the occurrence of the disease in question. More formally, relative risk is the ratio of the incidence of the disease among those exposed to the suspected agent in relation to the incidence of the disease among those not exposed, that is:

relative risk
The incidence of a disease among individuals having a particular characteristic divided by the incidence of disease among individuals not having the characteristic.

$$\text{Relative risk} = \frac{\text{Incidence of disease among exposed}}{\text{Incidence of disease among those not exposed}}$$

Table 3.1 gives an example of the calculation of relative risk. In this study lung cancer patients were interviewed about their smoking habits. These data were then compared with the smoking habits of patients without lung cancer. As seen in the table, the relative risk of contracting lung cancer increases dramatically with increased smoking. These data do not prove that smoking causes lung cancer. Rather, the higher

TABLE 3.1   *Calculation of Relative Risk Using Data on Smoking and Lung Cancer*

Daily average cigarettes smoked	Patients		Relative risk of different categories of smokers to nonsmokers
	Lung cancer	Controls	
0	7	61	1.0
1–4	55	129	3.7
5–14	489	570	7.5
15–24	475	431	9.6
25–49	293	154	16.6
50+	38	12	27.6

$$\text{Relative risk (RR)} = \frac{\text{No. of smokers with cancer} \times \text{no. of nonsmokers not having cancer}}{\text{No. of nonsmokers with cancer} \times \text{no. of smokers not having cancer}}$$

Examples:

$$\text{RR (1–4 cigarettes daily)} = \frac{55 \times 61}{7 \times 129} = \frac{3,355}{903} = 3.7$$

$$\text{RR (5–14 cigarettes daily)} = \frac{489 \times 61}{7 \times 570} = \frac{29,829}{3,990} = 7.5$$

Relative risk for nonsmokers is defined as 1.0.

Note. From *Foundations of epidemiology* (2d ed.) by A. M. Lilienfeld, 1980 (p. 210), New York: Oxford University Press. Reprinted by permission.

correlation
Any relationship between two variables, whether causal or not.

relative risk of cancer among smokers simply means that there is a **correlation** between smoking and cancer. Since lung cancer patients and controls are likely to differ from each other on characteristics in addition to their smoking habits, concluding from these data that cigarette smoking causes cancer is not warranted. Although such risk ratios can suggest possible causes for disease, the determination of causal relationships is best established through the use of experimental methods.

Epidemiological Research Strategies

Epidemiologists use a variety of strategies for obtaining data on the distribution and causes of disease. At the most basic level, descriptive methods such as case reports and correlational studies can provide plausible hypotheses about factors that might be related to disease occurrence. Case control and cohort methods can then be used for more systematic testing of these hypotheses.

Case reports. Case reports are detailed descriptions written by one or more clinicians about individual patients who present unique or particularly interesting problems. Although such reports can only be suggestive, given the idiosyncracies of individual patients, they can give clues about potential risk factors. For example, the case of a 40-year-old premenopausal woman who developed a pulmonary embolism after using contraceptives to treat endometriosis (an inflammation of the lining of the uterus) suggested a relationship between contraceptive use and the occurrence of pulmonary embolism (obstruction of a lung artery). Since pulmonary embolisms are much more likely to occur in older, postmenopausal women, this report indicated a possible association between contraceptive use and embolisms, an association that was confirmed in subsequent studies (Hennekens & Buring, 1987).

Correlational studies. Correlational studies compare the occurrence of a specified disease or diseases with the frequency of suspected risk factors across populations or in the same population at different times. The existence of a strong correlation between the suspected risk factor and occurrence of the disease suggests that the risk factor might be related to the disease. For example, Figure 3.2 shows the relationship between per capita meat consumption and colon cancer among women in several different countries. The striking correlation in these data suggests that meat consump-

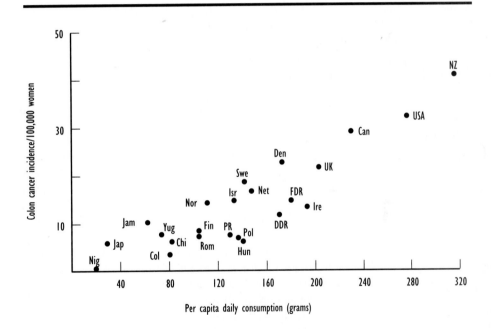

Nig = Nigeria; Can = Canada; Chi = Chile; Col = Columbia; Jam = Jamaica; PR = Puerto Rico;
USA = United States of America; Isr = Israel; Jap = Japan; Den = Denmark; Fin = Finland;
DDR = German Democratic Republic; FDR = Federal German Republic; Hun = Hungary; Ire = Ireland; Net = Netherlands;
Nor = Norway; Pol = Poland; Rom = Romania; Swe = Sweden; UK = United Kingdom; Yug = Yugoslavia; NZ = New Zealand.

FIGURE 3.2

Correlation between per capita meat consumption and colon cancer among women in various countries.

Note. From "Environmental factors and cancer incidence in different countries with special reference to dietary practices" by B. K. Armstrong and R. Doll, 1975, *International Journal of Cancer, 15,* p. 625. Copyright 1975 by John Wiley and Sons, Inc. Reprinted by permission.

tion may be a significant risk factor in colon cancer. Again, however, additional studies are necessary to confirm such a relationship.

case control study
A study matching patients already diagnosed with the target disease to individuals without the disease so as to identify factors associated with its occurrence.

Case control studies. Although correlational studies and case reports can provide valuable leads, much more precise estimates of the relationship between possible risk factors and disease can be obtained from observational studies specifically designed to investigate such relationships. In **case control studies,** the investigators compare a group of patients who have the disease in question with a group of equivalent individuals who do not have the disease. They then check for the presence of possible risk factors that might distinguish the two groups. This type of study, exemplified by the examination of the relationship between smoking and lung cancer discussed above (see Table 3.1), starts with the disease and works back to possible causal factors.

cohort study
A study comparing the rates at which persons with and without a specified risk factor develop given diseases.

Cohort studies. Cohort studies look at this relationship from the other direction, that is, the investigators compare individuals possessing a suspected risk factor with those who do not, to see who develops the disease or diseases of interest. For example, a British study followed a group of women who had contracted rubella during pregnancy for up to two years after the birth of their children. The rate of congenital deformities among children born to these women was found to be substantially higher than it was among those born to women who had not had rubella during pregnancy (Barker & Rose, 1984). This is an example of a prospective (looking forward in time) cohort study: the suspected risk factor was identified at the beginning of the study, well before the congenital deformities were identified.

Cohort studies can also be retrospective (looking backward in time), which means that the investigators ascertain the exposure status of the participants at the initiation of the study and then examine the participants to see how many in each exposure group have the disease or diseases of interest. For example, a study conducted among shipyard workers in Portsmouth, New Hampshire, assessed whether occupational exposure to nuclear radiation led to an increased risk of dying from leukemia or other cancers (Hennekens & Buring, 1987). All white male employees who worked at the shipyards for any length of time between 1952 and 1977 were selected for study. Data on the total amount of radiation exposure during each participant's period of employment were obtained from employee records. This allowed for the classification of participants according to their level of exposure. Information was then recorded on which employees had died and each one's cause of death. In this case, the results did not show the expected increase in leukemia and other cancer deaths for employees exposed to radiation. Figure 3.3 summarizes the case control and cohort study designs.

The various epidemiological methods take different approaches, but they are all concerned with the basic question of what causes particular diseases and are often used in tandem. One example of this is the search for the causes of AIDS (see Box 3.1).

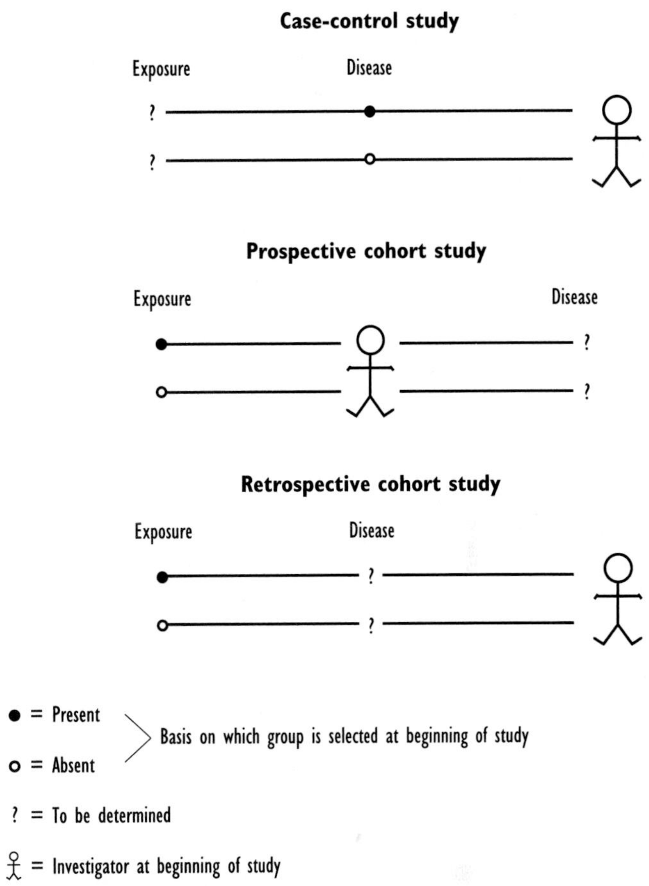

Case-control study

Exposure   Disease

? ——————————•———————————— ⚇

? ——————————○————————————

Prospective cohort study

Exposure   Disease

•——————————⚇—————————— ?

○——————————⚇—————————— ?

Retrospective cohort study

Exposure   Disease

•————————— ? —————————— ⚇

○————————— ? ——————————

• = Present

○ = Absent   ⟩ Basis on which group is selected at beginning of study

? = To be determined

⚇ = Investigator at beginning of study

FIGURE 3.3

Timing of case-control, prospective cohort, and retrospective cohort studies in relation to exposure and outcome.

Note. From *Epidemiology in medicine* (p. 24) by C. H. Hennekens and J. E. Buring, 1987, Boston: Little, Brown and Company. Reprinted by permission.

SURVEY METHODS

Although epidemiological methods provide invaluable information about the distribution and causes of disease, health psychologists are particularly interested in how attitudes and behaviors relate to health. Discussion of these clearly demands going beyond information on mortality and morbidity. We need methods that will provide valid data on people's health-related attitudes and behaviors. Surveys are particularly useful for gathering such information.

BOX 3.1   **The Search for the Causes of AIDS: An Epidemiological Whodunit**

In the never-ending effort to understand and control disease, epidemiologists are sometimes faced with unusual outbreaks of disease that they cannot explain, but which may have important implications. When this happens, epidemiologists swing into action to collect clues as to the origins of the disease and how it is spread. An important recent example is the search for the causes of AIDS.

The first indication that something unusual was happening came from reports of unusual cases of *pneumocystis carinii* pneumonia (PCP). This particular form of pneumonia is extremely rare and is almost always found among individuals whose immune systems have been suppressed in some way. Thus reports by the Centers for Disease Control on the appearance of five cases of this disease among homosexual men in Los Angeles in June 1981 raised perplexing questions. Concern was heightened by another report a month later of additional cases of this disease, along with cases of Kaposi's sarcoma, a rare skin disease, among homosexual men in New York.

Over the next several months, there were additional reports of these two diseases and reports of other opportunistic infections associated with suppression of the immune system. By mid-1982, this mysterious malady, affecting primarily male homosexuals, had afflicted 335 people, killing 136, and had been termed acquired immunodeficiency syndrome.

Since this syndrome had been found primarily among gay men, some observers naturally suspected that the suppression of immunity in AIDS was somehow related to gay life-style or sexual practices. Initial

evidence for the sexual transmission of AIDS came from interviews conducted with PCP and Kaposi's sarcoma patients that showed that the patients were related as friends, roommates, or lovers. These suspicions were confirmed in later case control and cohort studies.

Another troubling development was the appearance of cases of PCP among hemophiliacs. These cases could not be explained through sexual transmission and raised the possibility that AIDS was somehow transmitted through blood transfusions. Given the importance of blood transfusions in surgery and other medical treatments, serious concerns were raised about the safety of available blood for transfusion and about the possibility that AIDS was caused by a blood-borne microbe.

A key piece of the puzzle was identified in May 1983 with the detection of a retrovirus, now known as the human immunodeficiency virus (HIV), in the blood of AIDS patients. The detection of this virus established a cause, prompting work to proceed on developing a vaccine and cure for this deadly disease. Later studies showed that this virus has the ability to develop new strains and that other factors are also involved in AIDS. Such discoveries have indicated the considerable difficulties in developing an effective vaccine.

These few paragraphs give only a brief description of the search for the causes of AIDS, but illustrate the use of epidemiological methods. For a chronology of events related to AIDS, see Malinowsky and Perry (1988). For a detailed discussion of the AIDS epidemic, including both the medical and political aspects, see Shilts (1987).

Even though surveys have become a ubiquitous part of modern life, they are greatly misunderstood and abused. The concepts involved in surveys are quite straightforward, but many surveys, particularly in the popular media, have severe flaws that limit the conclusions that can be drawn from the data. The paragraphs that follow describe the requirements for good surveys and the problems that develop when these requirements are not met.

Survey Samples

How do we go about conducting a valid survey? Most people are likely to agree that a primary ingredient for a good survey is a representative sample of respondents. If the results of the survey are to be applied to a population beyond the original sample, the respondents should be representative of the larger population. But how does one go about obtaining a representative sample? There is a common misperception that the larger the sample, the more representative it is. In reality, the critical question is not the sheer size of the sample but rather how it is selected.

Random samples. Strange as it may seem, the best way to obtain a representative sample is to pay no attention to the characteristics of the respondents, but simply select them at random from the population. More specifically, a **random sample** is one in which every person in the population has an equal chance of being selected for the survey. Based on the laws of probability, such a sample should largely reflect the characteristics of the larger population.

random sample
A sample selected by the rule that every person in the population has an equal likelihood of being selected.

How this works can be easily demonstrated using a jar containing different kinds of beans or marbles. Suppose we have a jar with 55% red marbles and 45% white ones. If we shake the jar to mix the red and white marbles thoroughly and then simply grab handfuls of marbles, we will find upon counting them that approximately 55% of them are red and 45% are white. This is true even though no attention was paid to which marbles were selected from the jar. Further, this will be the case regardless of whether the jar holds 500, a thousand, or a million marbles. In each case, random sampling will approximate the proportion of red and white marbles. The same principles hold in selecting survey respondents.

Given a random sample, how closely the sample approximates the true characteristics of the larger population depends on the size of the sample (but not the size of the population). However, although the accuracy of the estimates increases with sample size, we quickly encounter the law of diminishing returns. For instance, a sample size of roughly 1,100 is needed to be 95% certain that the survey results are accurate within 3 percentage points on either side of the obtained estimate; accuracy within 1% on either side would require a sample of more than 7,000.

The rub comes in making sure that the sample we have selected is, in fact, random. The best way to be sure a sample is random is to have a complete listing of everyone in the population, and then to select randomly from that list. However, for most populations of interest this is highly impractical and, particularly for large populations, extremely expensive and time consuming. Thus survey organizations have developed methods for approximating a random sample.

accidental (convenience) sample
A sample consisting of individuals who happen to be available and willing to participate in the survey.

Nonrandom samples. Given these problems, the use of shortcuts and **accidental** or **convenience samples** is very tempting. Samples of this sort are very easy to obtain because all one has to do is accept whoever is available and willing to participate. For example, one might ask readers of a newspaper or magazine to submit a postcard with their opinions on a particular issue. Or an interviewer might stand in a shopping mall and ask passersby their views on a selected topic. The problem with these procedures is that there is no way of knowing whether the samples obtained are representative of any population beyond the samples themselves. Selecting respondents in a shopping mall, for example, limits the study to people who happen to shop at that mall and leaves out everyone else. Moreover, respondents may volunteer for studies on the basis of their attitudes, with those holding stronger opinions more likely to respond. In mail-in or phone-in surveys, one also has to screen for multiple responses by the same person.

This last point is illustrated by an experience of some friends of mine. Several years ago, a local television station held weekly polls in which a question would be presented on the air, and viewers were asked to phone in their answers, with a small fee charged to the caller's telephone bill. My friends noticed that on nights when a certain babysitter worked for them, several of these charges would appear on their telephone bill. The babysitter apparently was interested in some of the questions and liked to vote early and often.

Thus far we have been concerned with issues relating to **sampling error,** or errors resulting from the selection of survey respondents. Just as important to the validity of a survey are the questions and how they are asked. Inattention to these details can lead to what survey researchers call **non-sampling error.**

sampling error
Errors in survey results attributable to the manner in which the sample of respondents was selected.

non-sampling error
Errors or biases in survey results deriving from factors other than sampling.

Questioning Respondents

Potential biases. For survey answers to be valid, the questions must be fair and unbiased. Asking *leading questions,* which suggest an expected answer, or *loaded questions,* which have emotionally laden connotations, can quickly invalidate a survey regardless of how the sample is chosen. For example, the president of a pro-life lobbying group once proposed to gather opinions on abortion by asking a million Americans "if they favored protecting a defenseless, little child still living in his mother's womb." Even if this survey had been done with a well chosen random sample (it was conducted as a mail-in poll), the results would have still been invalidated by the way in which the question was framed.

Life for survey researchers would indeed be easy (or at least easier) if all they had to watch out for were such obvious biases. However, subtle but still highly important biases can be introduced by the specific wording of a question, as well as by assumptions about the respondents' ability to provide requested information. Just because words are similarly defined does not mean that people respond to them in the same way. For example, questions about public welfare have elicited quite different responses than those concerning provision of public aid to the needy (Marty, 1982). Questions may also be misunderstood. A humorous example of this comes from a study of the economic attitudes of sharecroppers soon after World War II. Responding to a series of questions designed to measure economic liberalism, the sharecroppers were overwhelmingly liberal on all but one question, which concerned government regulation of profits. The respondents gave overwhelmingly conservative answers to this question. It turns out that many of them were illiterate and confused pro*fits* with pro*phets,* believing that the regulation of the latter was best left to God (Selltiz, Wrightsman, & Cook, 1976).

Respondent knowledge. More troubling and potentially more damaging problems may come from assumptions about respondents' ability to provide the requested information. In gathering information about people's health attitudes and behavior, we assume that people are able to provide accurate reports and have reasonably well formed and stable attitudes about the issues in question. Although this is probably true in many cases, research on public opinion has indicated that sometimes, particularly when the issues are relatively abstract or remote from everyday experience, people's attitudes may not in fact be well formed. Rather, the respondents may have what Philip Converse (1964) refers to as *non-attitudes.* In other words, when asked a question about the issue, the person will give an answer that is off the cuff and not based on a true attitude. Ask the person about the issue later on and you may get a different answer.

A similar principle applies when asking people about the reasons for their actions. Richard Nisbett and Timothy Wilson (1977) have shown that when the influences on us are subtle, we often do not really know why we behave the way we do. For example, in a study of pain tolerance, Nisbett and Stanley Schacter (1966) subjected university students to increasingly powerful electrical shocks. Half the subjects received the shocks after being given a placebo that they were told would result in feelings of arousal (heart palpitations, butterflies in the stomach), whereas the other subjects received the shocks without the pill. The results demonstrated that the subjects receiving the pill endured four times as much shock as did the control subjects. However, when asked about factors influencing the amount of shock they were willing to endure, not one of the pill recipients mentioned the pill. These and similar results raise serious questions about surveys that ask about reasons for particular health actions. In such surveys, people might be, in Nisbett and Wilson's words, "telling more than they can know."

An additional area where respondents might be telling more than they can know is the recall of health events. Knowing the frequency with which people engage in various health-related actions such as receiving medical checkups, using specific medications, or engaging in preventive health behaviors, or how often they experience specified health problems is important for studying the psychological and behavioral aspects of health. Thus survey researchers commonly ask about such matters in surveys, assuming that people are able to report accurately when they last visited the doctor or how often they experience headaches. Recent studies in cognitive psychology, however, question these assumptions. Elizabeth Loftus (cf. Loftus, Feinberg, & Tanur, 1985), among others, has noted that the organization of information in memory affects the accuracy of event recall. Respondents remembering events such as visits to the doctor or the frequency of specific symptoms may not be recalling the actual events. Rather, they are probably using various cognitive heuristics (rules of thumb) to

*The validity of survey
results depends on how
the questions are asked.*

estimate dates or frequencies—heuristics that can easily produce biased answers. For surveys to obtain valid information on the recall of health events, such heuristics need to be accounted for and built into the questioning procedures (cf. Lessler, Tourangeau, & Salter, 1989).

Interviewer effects. Finally, a survey's validity depends on the behavior of the interviewer while asking the questions. To obtain a true indication of the respondent's attitudes or an accurate report of behavior, the interviewer must be as neutral as possible in asking the questions and not give clues as to expected answers. For example, in asking about preventive health behaviors such as wearing seat belts or doing monthly breast self-examinations, interviewers should not give their opinions or subtly indicate what they believe to be the correct answer. Rather, the interviewer needs to be a neutral medium through which the questions are asked.

Properly done surveys can provide a great deal of information about people's health-related attitudes and behaviors, so they are invaluable sources of descriptive data and hypotheses for further study. An excellent example of the use of surveys in health research is given in Box 3.2. However, surveys are useful only when the conditions described above are met—otherwise they can be extremely misleading and become a classic GIGO (garbage in, garbage out) system.

Concluding Notes on Correlational Research Methods

The epidemiological and survey research methods described above fall under the general heading of correlational research methods. In using correlational methods, the researcher carefully observes and records data on the phenomena of interest, but makes no effort to intervene or manipulate variables. Such methods provide the basic

| BOX 3.2 | **Measuring the Health of Americans: The National Health Interview Survey** |

One of the most important sources of information about the illnesses, injuries, chronic conditions, health attitudes, and health behaviors of Americans is the National Health Interview Survey (NHIS). The NHIS is a nationwide survey conducted by the National Center for Health Statistics, a component of the Centers for Disease Control of the U.S. government.

The NHIS is conducted as a household survey in which members of randomly selected households are asked questions about personal and demographic characteristics, illnesses, injuries, impairments, chronic conditions, utilization of health resources, and other health topics. Although the content of the core sections of the questionnaire remains fairly constant from year to year, supplemental sections ask about topics of current interest, such as attitudes and beliefs about AIDS or the use of dental services, and vary over time.

The sample for the NHIS, which is drawn from all civilian noninstitutionalized persons residing in the United States, is selected using a multistage probability design. Each year, the sample consists of approximately 49,000 occupied households containing about 127,000 persons. Within each household, generally one respondent, often female, provides the information for all individuals in that dwelling. The response rate over the years has been between 96% and 98%.

Because the data are collected from a large, randomly selected sample, the number of individuals with given ailments and disabilities can be precisely estimated, and the health status as well as health attitudes and behaviors of different demographic groups can be compared. For example, using NHIS data one can note similarities and differences in the occurrence of different illnesses and disabilities among males and females, different ethnic groups, and different age groups. Further, because the survey is a continuing one, trends in these variables can be charted over time.

Data from the NHIS are routinely reported in government publications such as *Vital and Health Statistics* and *Health United States,* and data are available on computer tape for analysis by nongovernmental researchers. For additional information about the NHIS, see Moss and Parsons (1985).

descriptions needed for developing plausible hypotheses about the links between mind and body. Also, since the data are generally collected in natural settings and, when the studies are done well, with representative samples, the results are likely to have a high degree of external validity.

However, valuable as these data are, they cannot be used to definitively test hypotheses about causal relationships. To see why this is true, consider the copious research that has been done on the relationship between life stress and the occurrence of illness (cf. Rabkin & Struening, 1976; Rahe & Arthur, 1978). In general, people who report more stressful life events also report a greater likelihood of getting sick. Such data tempt one to conclude that stressful experiences cause ill health—an unwarranted conclusion on the basis of correlations in this research alone. Although stressful life events may be causally related to illness, illness itself may also cause a person to be more sensitive to life's difficulties and, thus, to report more stressful events. Furthermore, some third factor, such as a disposition toward particular mood states, affects reports of both life events and illness, an argument made by David Watson and James Pennebaker (1989). They point out that measures of both life stress and illness include a significant component of negative affectivity, a general disposition toward negative moods. Their analysis concludes that this "third factor" of negative affectivity significantly inflates the observed correlation between life events and illness.

Thus for every correlation, there are three alternative hypotheses about causality. Variable A may cause variable B. However, variable B might cause variable A, or some third factor might cause both A and B. Correlations simply tell us that two variables are related—the testing of causal relationships requires experimental methods.

EXPERIMENTAL METHODS

To avoid this limitation of correlational studies, researchers can use experimental methods, which have the distinct advantage of being able to test and analyze alternative hypotheses about causality.

The Importance of Control

How is this accomplished? The key to understanding experimental methods is *control*. In a well designed experiment, the experimenters set up an artificial reality in which they are able to exercise specific types of control.

independent variable
The variable manipulated by the researcher in an experimental study.

Independent variable. First, the experimenter exercises control over the **independent variable,** the variable whose effects are the focus of the study. In order to test the effects of the independent variable, the experimenter manipulates it by assigning subjects to different experimental conditions in which they are exposed to different levels of the independent variable. For example, suppose that a researcher wanted to study the effectiveness of different methods of stress management on stress levels and effectiveness of coping. To do this, the experimenter could assign some subjects to a relaxation condition, where they receive training on relaxation techniques. For a contrasting method of stress management, other subjects might be assigned to a psychotherapy condition, where they receive counseling about the causes of their stress. Finally, to control for the possibility that the passage of time or simply being in a study might lead to changes in stress levels and coping, a third group of subjects could be assigned to a control condition in which their stress levels and coping effectiveness are measured at the beginning and end of the study, but they receive no actual treatment. By engaging in this type of manipulation, the experimenter is able to exercise control over the kinds of experiences that the subjects have and test for the effects on the **dependent variable,** or outcome. In this example, there are actually two dependent variables, stress level and coping effectiveness.

dependent variable
The outcome variable for a research study.

Experimental setting. In addition to manipulating the independent variable, the experimenter also exerts control over the experimental setting. In order for the researcher to make meaningful comparisons between experimental conditions, the subjects in the different conditions must have experiences that are the same with the exception of the independent variable. In the example above, no firm conclusions about the effectiveness of different stress management techniques could be made if subjects in one condition were seen in a doctor's office during the winter, whereas those in another condition were seen in a university laboratory during the summer. In this case, the effects of different stress management techniques would be confounded with the influences of experiment location and time of year. We would not be able to tell how much of the difference between groups owed to stress management technique and how much to experiment location and time of year.

Sometimes, ensuring that all subjects are exposed to the same experimental setting is not possible. If this is the case, the experimenter must be careful to *balance* the conditions such that the differences in setting are equally represented in all conditions. For example, the same experimenter might not be able to see all the subjects. In such circumstances, each experimenter should see an equal number of subjects in each condition.

Random assignment. Finally, experimenters exercise control by determining who is in which experimental condition. One major problem with correlational designs is that the participants determine their level of the independent variable for themselves. For example, in the data on smoking and cancer given in Table 3.1, the patients studied determined for themselves whether and how much they smoked—making a determination of causality difficult. The factors that led some participants to smoke might also make them different in other ways. This problem can be circumvented in experimental research through the use of **random assignment.** The principle of random assignment is, simply, that each person has an equal likelihood of being assigned to each of the experimental conditions. Thus in our example concerning stress management, each person in the experiment would be equally likely to be assigned to the relaxation, psychotherapy, or control conditions.

random assignment
The assignment of subjects to experimental conditions such that each subject has an equal likelihood of being in a given experimental condition.

This assignment is decided not by considering the person's characteristics, but rather by using random numbers, flipping a coin, or some other random process. Paradoxically, by ignoring the subjects' characteristics and using random assignment, we can be better assured of having equivalent experimental groups than if we tried to match subjects in the different conditions. With random assignment, the laws of probability make it highly likely that the experimental groups will, on the average, be equivalent regardless of which characteristic we examine. People differ in so many ways that if we were to try matching subjects in the different conditions we could not be sure that they were equivalent in every respect.

When the experimenter has these types of control, the inference of causality becomes fairly straightforward. The experimenter is able to ensure that, with the exception of the independent variable, all subjects are exposed to the same experience and, through random assignment, the groups are equivalent at the beginning of the experiment. Thus one can be confident that any difference in the outcome is because of the independent variable. Box 3.3 describes examples of the use of experimental methods for studying symptom perception.

BOX 3.3 **On Perceiving Physical Symptoms: An Illustration of Experimental Methods**

A key determinant of health and illness behavior is a person's perception of physical symptoms. As discussed in Chapter 8, the perceptions we have of our internal physical state have a significant influence on whether we seek medical attention, practice preventive health measures, and follow medical recommendations. Given the role of symptom perception, we need to understand the processes involved and the factors that influence our symptom reports. But how can we obtain accurate data on such a private experience?

James Pennebaker and his colleagues (cf. Gonder-Frederick, Cox, Bobbitt, & Pennebaker, 1986; Penne-baker, 1982; Pennebaker & Watson, 1988) have used several clever experimental procedures for investigating the processes involved in perceiving symptoms and the accuracy of those perceptions. For example, in a study testing the idea that symptom perception is a function of the balance between internal and external cues, subjects wore headphones while walking on a laboratory treadmill. The sounds heard over the headphones constituted the experimental manipulation that was designed to focus the subject's attention on external or internal cues. One group of subjects heard interesting street sounds; the second group heard their own breathing; and the third group heard nothing. At the completion of their time on the treadmill, subjects filled out a questionnaire about symptoms they were experiencing. The results of this study supported the hypothesis that subjects who focused internally on their own breathing would report more fatigue than those who focused on street sounds (Pennebaker, 1982).

Another study examined the phenomenon of suggestibility in symptom perception by manipulating the subjects' expectations about symptoms they should be experiencing. In this experiment, subjects were told that the study involved the effects of ultrasonic noise

on later task performance. The manipulation of expectations was accomplished by telling one group of subjects that the ultrasonic noise might cause their finger temperature to increase, whereas a second group was told that the noise would cause their finger temperature to decrease. In both cases, the subjects were given elaborate rationales for these increases or decreases. A third group was simply told that finger temperatures would be monitored. Subjects then heard a two-minute tape in which a tone increased in pitch for 15 seconds, followed by 1 minute and 45 seconds of blank tape that subjects were led to believe contained the ultrasonic noise. During the experiment, subjects' finger temperatures were monitored using a thermistor. After listening to the tape, subjects were given a questionnaire asking about perceived finger temperature and the subject's attention to the warmth or coolness of the finger. As predicted, subjects in the temperature increase condition reported a temperature increase, whereas subjects in the decrease and control conditions did not. Further, the perceived increase or decrease was uncorrelated with actual finger temperature, but was significantly correlated with the number of temperature fluctuations. This latter finding argues that subjects paid attention to changes in finger temperature that supported their expectations, but not those that did not. Thus when told to expect an increase, subjects noticed the upward fluctuation, but not the downward one.

In addition to these studies, Pennebaker and his colleagues have also used experimental methods to examine, among other topics, the accuracy of symptom perception among hypertensives and diabetics (cf. Gonder-Frederick et al., 1986; Pennebaker & Watson, 1988). This work is discussed in more detail in Chapter 8.

Types of Experiments

True experiments. What has been described so far is what is called a *true experiment,* that is, ones in which the experimenter has maximal control. Probably the easiest place to conduct true experiments is in a laboratory, where the experimenter

Experiments are the method of choice for addressing questions of causality.

is likely to have the greatest control. However, true experiments may also be conducted in a field setting, in which case they are referred to as *field experiments*. For example, a study of the effectiveness of different methods of preventing preteens from beginning smoking might be done in a school setting. What is critical is not the location of the experiment but rather the experimenter's ability to control the independent variable and setting and to assign subjects to conditions randomly.

Although true experiments provide the strongest data for inferring causality, many topics in health psychology do not lend themselves to such methods. For either ethical or practical reasons, assigning subjects to conditions in a completely random manner or directly manipulating the independent variable may not be possible. Variations of the experimental method can be used in such cases.

quasi-experiment
A research study in which subjects cannot be randomly assigned to conditions but the experimenter still retains control over the independent variable.

Quasi-experiments. One such variation is the **quasi-experiment.** Using this method, the experimenter is able to control the independent variable and most other aspects of the experiment, but is not able to use random assignment. For example, Ellen Langer and Judith Rodin (1976) examined the effects of an induced sense of responsibility among nursing home residents on both psychological and physical well-being. The manipulation in this case was contained in a speech given by the nursing home director. Practical problems prevented the experimenters from randomly assigning individual residents to conditions. Instead they selected two floors in the nursing home, and assigned one to the responsibility-induced condition and one to the control condition.

The possibility cannot be ruled out that some undetected difference between the two groups in quasi-experiments might account for the results. In the Langer and Rodin experiment, for example, the improved well-being of the responsibility-induced group relative to control might have been the result of undetected pre-existing differences, not the experimental manipulation. However, since the experimenter is able to control the manipulation and other aspects of the experiment, experimental logic can be used, even though the conclusions drawn are weakened by the lack of random assignment.

natural experiment
An experiment in which the manipulation of interest occurs without the experimenter's intervention.

Natural experiments. A second variation on the experimental method comes about when the experimenter is able to capitalize on naturally occurring events. In a *natural experiment,* the manipulation of the independent variable is already occurring, and the experimenter "piggybacks" onto these events to study their effects. The experimenter lacks control over both the independent variable and the assignment of subjects, but is able to measure the outcomes for the group experiencing the change as well as for a comparison group that is not exposed to the event. Such designs are particularly useful for studying the effects of experiences that are of such a magnitude as to make it impractical or unethical to produce them for the purposes of research. For example, catastrophic events, such as the nuclear accident at Three Mile Island in New York State, provide a unique opportunity for studying the effects of high levels of stress. Daniel Collins and his colleagues (Collins, Baum, & Singer, 1983) examined the use of coping strategies in dealing with the effects of the Three Mile Island disaster by comparing residents living nearby to people living in the vicinity of an undamaged nuclear power plant more than 100 miles away. Although the conclusions drawn are weakened by the lack of control, natural experiments can provide unique data that could not be obtained by other means.

Limitations of Experiments

Experimental methods clearly have many advantages, particularly for drawing inferences about causality, but they are not without limitations. For one thing, experiments are not always appropriate. Topics such as the effects of severe stress or the impact of hospitalization cannot be studied with true experiments because of ethical and practical considerations. Natural experiments would be more appropriate for topics like these. In addition, experiments are generally not suitable as vehicles for obtaining descriptions of a population's attitudes or behavioral characteristics. Such data are better obtained through the use of surveys.

Moreover, experiments often require considerable care in their interpretation. Recall that in true experiments the experimenter sets up an artificial reality in which to test the effects of the independent variable. Although this artificiality lends itself well to the control needed to eliminate alternative hypotheses, it may also limit the degree to which the results can be generalized to other situations. In brief, experiments tell us what can happen under certain controlled conditions—they do not necessarily tell us what happens in real life.

CLINICAL METHODS

In addition to an interest in basic questions of the causes of disease and the role of attitudes and behavior, health psychologists are also concerned with developing effective treatment interventions. For example, we want not only to document and understand the behavioral risk factors for coronary heart disease, but to help people change their behavior so as to reduce their risk. An essential part of developing intervention methods is the evaluation of their effectiveness.

The basic logic used in clinical trials is essentially the same as that used in experiments. Good clinical trials are well designed experiments, so the principles discussed in the section on experimental methods apply here. However, the nature of the task in clinical trials introduces some unique problems that warrant our consideration (Friedman, Furberg, & DeMets, 1985).

Challenges of Clinical Research

Clinical trials possess unique challenges because the subjects in these experiments are patients who generally have sought help for their distress, and the independent variables are treatments believed to alleviate that distress. Thus clinical trials must take into account the potential complexity of the person's ailments, the treatments he is currently receiving, and his motivation for getting better.

Patient selection. Suppose, for example, that a clinical trial were set up to evaluate the effectiveness of a new behavioral treatment for pain. What considerations are likely to be relevant? One of the first questions to be asked would be the source of the person's pain. Pain can come from a variety of sources and is likely to have quite different histories in different people. Also, various types of pain may respond differently to different interventions. Thus a well designed clinical trial needs to have clearly specified *patient selection criteria*. For example, we may wish to include patients with lower back pain, but not those suffering from joint pain.

The establishment of such selection criteria is almost always a juggling act. On the one hand, selecting a narrow range of patients makes the trial "cleaner" from a statistical standpoint. There is less variability among the patients, and treatment differences are likely to be easier to detect. However, this "cleanliness" comes at a cost. Selection of a narrow range of patients limits the generalizability of the results. Results obtained with one type of pain patient may or may not be applicable to other types. The trick is to use a broad enough range of patients to make the results applicable to a reasonable variety of patients, while avoiding the statistical and interpretive problems involved in having a patient population that is too broad.

Co-morbidity. Other challenges in clinical research come from the occurrence of diseases other than the one under study. Although, from a research point of view, it would indeed be convenient if every patient participating in research had only one disease, in most cases this is highly unrealistic. Patients often have more than one physical problem. For example, patients with diabetes may experience cardiovascular problems and peripheral nerve damage as complications of their diabetes. Even when they do not experience other diseases as complications, patients may have multiple but unrelated conditions. For example, a patient with rheumatoid arthritis might also have a history of coronary heart disease. This co-morbidity tends to add to the variability within groups—making the detection of treatment effects more difficult.

concomitant treatment
Any clinical intervention that is received by patients in addition to the experimental intervention.

Concomitant treatment. Further, patients may be receiving ongoing treatment, either for the disease under study or for coexisting conditions, in addition to the treatment given in the research. This **concomitant treatment** may interact in unexpected ways with the experimental treatment in determining the clinical outcome. Well designed clinical trials will specify the acceptable co-morbidity and concomitant treatments in the patient selection criteria, as well as consider possible biases from other diseases and treatments in the interpretation of the results.

Placebo effects. Thus far we have considered potential difficulties owing to the complexity of the patient's condition and the treatment received. What about the patient's motivation to get better? In the last chapter, we considered the *placebo effect* as an illustration of the dynamic relationship between mind and body. The placebo effect makes it very clear that the patient's belief in a treatment is an important determinant of treatment outcome. But this effect can also considerably complicate the evaluation of treatment effectiveness: If patients get better simply through their faith in the treatment, how can we determine whether the treatment itself is having an effect? Studies of drug effectiveness generally test the effects of an experimental medication against the effects of a placebo medication. In such a study, one group of patients receives the experimental medication, while another group gets a "sugar pill," which is identical in color, shape, taste, and so on. In **single blind studies,** the patients are kept unaware ("blind") of which medication they are receiving. The investigator, however, knows who is getting what. In **double blind studies,** neither the patients nor the investigator knows who is receiving which medication. Instead, patients are given coded medications with the code kept sealed until the termination of the study. By blinding the patient and, preferably, the investigator to the treatment condition, both groups should have the same expectations. Drug effectiveness is then calculated as the extent to which the effectiveness of the "real" medication exceeds that of the placebo. This assumes, of course, that the patient and/or investigator do not guess the treatment condition, in which case the study becomes unblinded and thus invalid.

single blind study
A clinical study procedure in which the researcher knows which treatment condition the patient is in but the patient does not.

double blind study
A clinical study procedure in which neither the patients nor the researchers know which treatment condition a particular patient is in.

The placebo effect can make evaluating psychological and behavioral interventions particularly tricky. Although practicing the same types of controls that are used in drug studies is desirable, devising a believable placebo treatment can present daunting practical difficulties. One strategy has been to use an attention placebo group, in which patients are given information and attention, but no active intervention by the therapist. For example, Florida Bosley and Thomas Allen (1989) evaluated the effectiveness of a program of stress management training for treating hypertension. Changes in the experimental group were compared with those of patients receiving standard clinic care, as well as of patients who received information about the dynamics of stress and the relationship of stress to hypertension, but no training in how to cope. Although a type of placebo control was achieved in this test, the patients, let alone the investigators, could not be kept blinded to the treatment condition.

Thus the placebo effect creates considerable difficulties in interpreting the outcome of clinical trials using psychological and behavioral treatments (cf. Shapiro & Morris, 1978). Often the best available control groups are ones receiving an alternative treatment or people who sign up for treatment but whose treatment is delayed. For example, Sydney Lovibond and his colleagues (Lovibond, Birrell, & Langeluddecke, 1986) compared three programs of behavioral intervention for reducing coronary risk. The three programs included many of the same elements, but differed in their intensity and the feedback given to participants. Studies of this type are very useful for comparing the effectiveness of different treatments and ferreting out active ingredients. However, they do not take account of the extent to which patient expectations affect the outcome.

Patient cooperation. Patient motivation is also relevant to problems of treatment cooperation. As discussed in Chapter 9, patients often do not follow treatment recommendations. Depending on the disorder and type of recommendation, an estimated one-third of patients do not follow recommendations with short-term treatments, and at least half fail to follow recommendations for long-term treatments (cf. Baekeland & Lundwall, 1975; Sackett & Snow, 1979). The implications of noncompliance can be significant and insidious for the evaluation of treatment effectiveness. If patients do not follow the recommendations, an effective treatment might be judged ineffective. Further, since patients are often reluctant to tell practitioners that they are not following the treatment regimen, such noncooperation may go undetected and thus not be accounted for when the results are interpreted. Such considerations indicate the need for clinical trials to include a careful evaluation of the extent of cooperation with the treatment when evaluating treatment effectiveness.

Concluding Comment

The discussion thus far may seem like a putdown of clinical research. Nothing could be further from the truth. The development and implementation of psychological and behavioral treatments for physical disease are an integral part of health psychology. For treatment to be based on solid scientific principles, proposed treatments must be carefully evaluated. Clinical research is absolutely indispensable in that evaluation, but it is difficult to do well, particularly with respect to the challenges discussed above. Box 3.4 describes a clinical trial for the evaluation of a cognitive-behavioral treatment for rheumatoid arthritis.

BOX 3.4 **Treating Rheumatoid Arthritis Using Cognitive-Behavioral Methods: A Clinical Trial**

Rheumatoid arthritis (RA) is a painful and crippling chronic disease in which a person experiences pain and stiffness in the joints, along with fatigue. Although RA is believed to be an autoimmune disease in which the body literally attacks itself, it is also known to be influenced by several psychological factors. There is evidence to suggest that patients who do particularly well in treatment are ones who increase their sense of internal control and self-efficacy.

Based on Albert Bandura's (1986) self-efficacy theory, Ann O'Leary and her colleagues (O'Leary, Shoor, Lorig, & Holman, 1988) developed a cognitive-behavioral treatment designed to enhance patients' feelings of self-efficacy in dealing with their arthritis. The patients in this program received copies of a popular arthritis self-help book, *The Arthritis Helpbook* (Lorig & Fries, 1980), and then met for five weeks in weekly two-hour sessions, during which they were taught a variety of coping techniques, including psychological strategies of pain management and goal setting using self-rewards. In addition, patients were encouraged to develop enjoyable hobbies and activities that would help distract them from their pain. Fifteen RA patients participated in this experimental treatment; another 15 patients who served in a control condition received only the self-help book.

The effectiveness of the treatment was gauged in several ways. First, because one of the primary manifestations of RA is pain, the researchers obtained multiple ratings of pain during the week before treatment began and during the week after treatment ended. In addition, questionnaires recorded their levels of activity, degrees of disability and feelings of self-efficacy, and rheumatologists, blind to the patient's treatment condition, assessed joint impairment.

The results of the study showed that, compared with control patients, those receiving the cognitive-behavioral treatment showed significant improvement in reported pain and joint impairment. Changes in measures of activity and disability were small and did not reach statistical significance. Moreover, patients in the experimental condition reported a greater sense of self-efficacy after treatment. Correlational analyses showed a significant relationship between the amount of clinical improvement and changes in self-efficacy, suggesting that the effects of the treatment were mediated by changes in the patient's perceived self-efficacy.

These results were generally in line with the researchers' hypotheses. However, the conclusions that can be drawn are weakened by the fact that neither patients nor investigators were blind to treatment condition, raising concerns about possible placebo effects.

RESEARCH ETHICS

Research in health psychology is a challenging and exciting venture. Yet as health psychologists and scientists we also have many responsibilities both to our profession and to the people we study and serve.

Research Responsibilities

We have a responsibility to utilize our skills to improve human welfare through the development of new knowledge and new techniques for dealing with health problems. Therefore we must conduct our research competently, report it fairly and accurately, and consider the potential consequences of research results. Although such a responsibility might seem obvious, occasionally there are individuals who disavow this responsibility through *research fraud*. Although scientists rarely engage in such fraudulent practices as the deliberate misrepresentation or outright fabrication of research results, enough instances of this kind of behavior have occurred to evoke considerable discussion in the research community about handling such fraud (cf. Adler, 1989a, 1989b).

We also have important responsibilities to our research participants. Without the cooperation and participation of literally hundreds of thousands of research participants, we could never have developed the empirical knowledge that we have. Beyond gratitude, we have a responsibility to protect them from risks that might be involved in our research.

Research Risks

Research uncertainty. What are the risks for research participants? First, risks can derive from the fundamental nature of science as an uncertain enterprise. If we knew exactly how a research study was going to turn out beforehand, doing the study would be pointless except as a research demonstration. Cutting-edge research aims at learning new things. This adds excitement to our work, but can also produce risks for the participants, for example, reacting badly to our procedures or experiencing adverse effects. An experiment to study the ways in which people cope with mildly stressful experiences, such as seeing an explicit film of an industrial accident, might cause some individuals to become highly upset and to require psychological assistance in dealing with the feelings generated. Or a clinical trial of a behavioral intervention might make some patients worse rather than better, even though in theory patients should improve with the treatment.

Deception. Although there is risk in any study, certain research procedures may increase that risk. One practice that has been the subject of considerable discussion is the use of **deception** (cf. Diener & Crandall, 1978; Kelman, 1972). This practice derives from concern about the possibility that participants' knowledge of the specific purposes and hypotheses of a study might influence the outcome. For example, if participants in a study of the effects of suggestion on symptom perception knew that the experimenters expected them to report certain symptoms under specific circumstances, they might alter their symptom reports to confirm or disconfirm the hypotheses. Another example of the problem of participant expectation is the placebo effect discussed earlier. The mere expectation of improvement may contribute to a positive outcome in clinical trials of potential treatments.

Given these problems, it is easy to see why researchers would consider deceiving research participants. However, deception creates its own difficulties. For one thing, it is simply dishonest. When we use deception, we are, frankly, lying to our research participants. Not only does this breach the trust relationship between researcher and participant, but over time it can be self-defeating. When we gain a reputation for lying to participants, future research participants are likely to be suspicious of what we say

deception
Misleading subjects concerning the purpose(s) or procedure(s) of a research study.

even when we tell them the full truth. In addition, the use of deception prevents participants from making a truly informed decision about whether to participate in the study in the first place.

These considerations argue that deception should be used sparingly, and then only as a last resort. In many cases, the problems that come from participant knowledge about the experiment's purposes and hypotheses can be dealt with by giving participants only a very general description of the experiment. Thus the experimenter omits the specific details with the promise of explaining those details at the end of the study. This maintains the relationship of honesty between researcher and participant and at the same time minimizes the effects of participant knowledge on the outcome. However, such a procedure may not always be effective, so the researcher may resort to active deception to preserve the integrity of the study. If active deception is used, it must be kept to a minimum, and the participants must be told of the deception and its purpose at the conclusion of the study. The goal of such a "debriefing" is to restore the relationship of honesty with participants and remove any harmful effects of the deception before the participants leave the study.

Confidentiality. Another source of risk comes from what we learn about our research participants. Each of us is entitled to privacy about our thoughts, beliefs, medical condition, private behavior, and so on. All these things interest health psychologists, and our research is often directed toward gathering this type of private information. The potential sensitivity of this information makes it critical that we carefully respect participants' right to privacy and invade that privacy only with their permission. Further, after the data are collected, we have a responsibility to maintain the data's **confidentiality** by restricting access to information about individual participants to those directly involved with the research. This can be done by keeping the data in locked files or by encoding the data in such a way that individual identities are concealed. Information about the outcome of the research must be reported in such a way that individuals cannot be identified. To prevent recognition, only group-level data should be reported, and in case studies, the name and other identifying information about the individual should be disguised.

confidentiality
The shielding of individual subjects' data from unauthorized disclosure.

Reducing Research Risk

The risks involved in research must be considered carefully in planning the research and minimized to the extent possible. Further, the possible risks to participants must be weighed against the expected benefits from the research. A *risk/benefit analysis* of this type essentially states that in order for a research study to be considered ethically justifiable, the benefits to be gained from the research must more than outweigh any risk to the participants. Such considerations are particularly critical when doing research with populations that are especially vulnerable, such as children, medical patients, mentally handicapped individuals, or prisoners. In such cases, the participants may be dependent on the researcher or the researcher may have considerable power over them.

informed consent
Agreeing to participate in a research study after receiving an accurate description of the purpose(s) and procedure(s) of the study as well as any risk that might be involved.

Further, our obligations to our participants require that when we ask them to participate in research studies, we describe the research in enough detail that they can freely give their **informed consent** for participation. As noted above, this does not mean that we must tell them all the specific details of the study, only enough so that they can make an informed choice about participating; this should include an accurate description of any known or suspected risks. In addition, under most circumstances participants must have the right to withdraw from the study. The only situation where withdrawal from the study should be restricted is when that withdrawal would jeopardize the participant's health or well-being. Such a circumstance might arise, for example, in clinical trials in which a course of treatment could not be safely terminated before completion.

institutional review
The review of research plans for ethical concerns by an institutional ethics panel before the performance of a study.

Because of concerns about protecting the welfare of research participants, virtually all organizations in the United States involved in research require that research projects be subjected to **institutional review** for ethical considerations before the research is begun. Institutional review boards (IRBs) have been established to consider the potential risks to participants and to rule on whether the risks have been minimized to the extent possible, and are justifiable in light of the benefits from the research. If an IRB is not satisfied with the proposed measures for protecting participants, the research is halted until appropriate measures can be developed. Such review of research plans is essential for protecting research participants and for encouraging a high level of ethical practice in research.

SUMMARY

The validity of our conclusions in health psychology depends on the methods used to gather information about human behavior and health. Without rigorous methods, our statements about phenomena of interest and hypothesized relationships are simply speculations bearing no necessary relationship to empirical reality. The methods described in this chapter are designed to separate fact from myth by providing an empirical grounding for our conclusions.

Epidemiological investigation provides the starting point in health psychology by supplying descriptions of disease prevalence, incidence, and distribution, as well as uncovering factors associated with the occurrence of given diseases. This etiological investigation is important for understanding basic disease phenomena and suggesting possible relationships to psychological and behavioral factors. Case control studies match patients with the specified disease to healthy individuals or patients with other diseases so as to identify factors that are associated with the occurrence of the disease in question. Cohort studies examine the effects of suspected causal agents by comparing the incidence of the disease among those exposed to a suspected causal agent with that among those who have not been exposed. Such studies have been critical in demonstrating the relationships between diseases such as heart disease and behavioral risk factors such as smoking, dietary choices, and lack of exercise.

Although epidemiological methods furnish basic information about the occurrence of disease, survey methods supply valuable data about the attitudinal and behavioral characteristics of large populations. By gathering information from a representative sample, survey researchers are able to make accurate estimates of the prevalence of various health-related attitudes and behaviors in the population as a whole. For surveys to be valid, however, certain conditions must be met. First, the respondents must constitute a random sample of the larger population. Accidental or convenience samples, in which the research simply takes anyone available, are easy to obtain, but are likely to produce nonrepresentative results. Second, the questions in the survey must be carefully selected to weed out those that produce biased answers or that ask for information that the respondent is not able to accurately provide. Third, the interviewer must ask the questions in a neutral manner so as not to influence the respondent's answers.

Although both epidemiological and survey methods provide valuable descriptive data, they are correlational methods, and so cannot be used to test causal relationships. Experimental methods test for causal relationships by manipulating independent variables and examining the effects of these manipulations on the outcome or dependent variables. The key to experimental methods is control: control over the experimental setting, control over the independent variable, and control over who is in which condition. This latter control is exerted through the use of random assignment, in which subjects are randomly assigned to conditions to ensure the equivalency of experimental groups before the beginning of the study.

In addition to the general concerns about validity in experimental studies, clinical studies must take into consideration such potential threats to validity as the placebo effect, differences in patients' medical condition, co-morbidity, concomitant treatment, and patient compliance.

In all our research efforts, the welfare of the subjects must be foremost in our minds. For this reason, ethical standards have been developed to guide researchers. A basic principle in these standards is that every precaution should be taken to reduce risk to study participants. Subjects who participate in a study have the right to be informed about the nature and procedures of the study and to give or withhold freely their consent to participate. Further, except when withdrawal from the study would place the subject at risk, subjects have the right to withdraw from the study if they so desire. Subjects also have the right to privacy and to the confidentiality of their responses. These ethical concerns are particularly important when dealing with vulnerable populations such as children, patients, the mentally handicapped, and prisoners. To ensure subject rights, most educational, medical, and research organizations require that research plans be reviewed by an institutional review board.

KEY TERMS

internal validity (41)
external validity (41)
morbidity (42)
prevalence (42)
incidence (42)
relative risk (43)
correlation (44)
case control study (46)
cohort study (46)
random sample (49)
accidental (convenience) sample (49)
sampling error (50)
non-sampling error (50)

independent variable (54)
dependent variable (54)
random assignment (55)
quasi-experiment (57)
natural experiment (58)
concomitant treatment (60)
single blind study (60)
double blind study (60)
deception (63)
confidentiality (64)
informed consent (65)
institutional review (65)

SUGGESTED READINGS

Diener, E., & Crandall, R. (1978). *Ethics in social and behavioral research*. Chicago: University of Chicago Press. In this book, Edward Diener and Rick Crandall give an in-depth discussion of ethical issues faced by researchers in psychology and other disciplines.

Kazdin, A. E. (1980). *Research design in clinical psychology.* New York: Harper & Row. This textbook discusses research designs used in both experimental and clinical research.

Michael, M., Boyce, W. T., and Wilcox, A. J. (1984). *Biomedical bestiary: An epidemiologic guide to flaws and fallacies in the medical literature.* Boston: Little, Brown. A humorous and engaging discussion of common traps and errors of reasoning in research.

Palinkas, L. A., and Hoiberg, A. (1982). An epidemiology primer: Bridging the gap between epidemiology and psychology. *Health Psychology, 1,* 269–87. An introduction to basic epidemiological methods for those trained in other areas.

CHAPTER **4**

Human Behavior and Health

By emphasizing the interconnectedness of mind and body, the biopsychosocial model indicates the myriad ways in which our physical well being is influenced by our thoughts and behavior. This chapter focuses on one of the major links between mind and body—the impact of everyday behavior on health and disease. Although people often think of disease as being caused by something outside the person's body (such as a virus or bacterium) that attacks it, there is increasing evidence that many of the important determinants of disease are found in behavior and life-style. The discussion that follows considers the evidence for behavioral risk factors in disease, the factors that influence the practice of positive health behavior, and current theories of health behavior.

MIND AND BODY: THE ROLE OF HUMAN BEHAVIOR IN DISEASE

Disease in the 1990s: The Changing Pattern

As noted in Chapter 1, major health indicators have markedly changed during this century. As the Surgeon General of the United States has stated, "The health of the American people has never been better" (U.S. Department of Health, Education and Welfare, 1979). Similar statements can be made about people in other developed or developing countries worldwide. Life expectancy has dramatically increased, primarily because of improvements in public health and medical care. For example, life expectancy at birth for males in the United States has increased from 46.3 years in 1900 to 71.3 years in 1986. For females, the increase has been from 48.3 years to 78.3 years (National Center for Health Statistics, 1989). (See Box 4.1.) This pattern is true throughout the developed world: a baby born in Japan can expect to live an average of 79.1 years, and one born in Sweden can expect to live to 77.1. Life expectancy in the developed world as a whole is currently just under 74 years (Lopez, 1990).

Such changes are encouraging, but other data paint a more sobering picture and indicate the challenges that lie ahead. Much of the increase in longevity can be attributed to reductions in infant mortality and to the dramatic reduction of infectious diseases, such as influenza, rubella, whooping cough, and polio, through immunization programs (Lancaster, 1990; Matarazzo, 1984a). Chronic diseases have replaced these infectious diseases as major causes of death. In 1900, heart disease, cancer, and stroke together accounted for approximately 16 percent of all American deaths. By 1986, these diseases accounted for nearly two-thirds of all deaths, while heart disease, the leading killer, accounted for 36 percent (National Center for Health Statistics, 1988a, 1988d). In addition, even though death rates for many diseases have been declining in the last few decades, mortality for certain diseases has been increasing (see Figures 4.1, p. 71 and 4.2, p. 72).

Particularly noteworthy are increases in lung cancer, suicide, and AIDS. Among males, the death rate for lung cancer in 1986 was 2.7 times the 1950 rate; for females, the increase was 3.3 times. Suicide rates in 1986 were, on average, 30% to 40% higher than in 1950 (Lopez, 1990). The situation with AIDS is even more disturbing. Since the discovery of the first AIDS cases in 1981, the number of AIDS cases has dramatically increased each year. By the middle of 1992, cumulative AIDS cases worldwide were estimated at two million, of which more than 230,000 were in the United States ("HIV infects more than a million people in 8 months," 1992; Centers for Disease Control, 1992). The World Health Organization believes that by the year 2000 up to 40 million people worldwide will be infected with the human immunodeficiency virus (HIV), the identified cause of AIDS.

Life-style and Disease

These abstract statistics demonstrate the challenges we face in the 1990s. The killer diseases of the past were mostly caused by specific micro-organisms that could be

BOX 4.1　Sex Differences in Longevity: The Hazards of Being an American Male

Although the life span for all Americans has steadily increased during this century, the amount of that increase has significantly differed between men and women. In 1900, women enjoyed a two-year longevity advantage over males (48.3 vs. 46.3 years for female and male, respectively). By 1986, this differential had grown to seven years (78.3 vs. 71.3) (National Center for Health Statistics, 1989). Overall increases in longevity can be attributed to better nutrition, public health, and medical care, but the increased differential between men and women presents a more perplexing problem.

Although some have argued that sex differentials in longevity are linked to genetic causes, both medical and behavioral evidence suggest that psychosocial factors, particularly those related to the male role, are the most likely explanation (cf. Harrison, 1978, for a review). According to this view, the requirements of the male role predispose males to behavior patterns that are detrimental to health, such as smoking, drinking, and taking excessive risks.

Medical evidence for this argument comes from examination of sex differentials in death rates for specific diseases. Among the leading causes of death, those with a strong behavioral component show significant differentials between men and women. For example, men die of heart disease nearly twice as often as do women, and they are two and a half times more likely to die of lung cancer, nearly three times as likely to die in auto accidents, nearly four times as likely to commit suicide, and more than twice as likely to die of cirrhosis of the liver. In addition, men, particularly black men, are more likely to die of homicide. White men are nearly three times as likely as white women to die of homicide; black men die of homicide nearly five times as often as black women (National Center for Health Statistics, 1989).

On the behavioral side, James Harrison (1978) has argued that the behaviors that contribute to these diseases are ones encouraged by the American male role. Traditionally, this role has included several themes, including needs for superiority, independence, self-reliance, and power over others, through violence if necessary. These role requirements make it more likely for males to smoke, drink to excess, drive recklessly or too fast, engage in Type A behavior, and become involved in aggressive encounters. All these behaviors are major risk factors for diseases showing higher death rates for males.

conquered through improved medical care and vaccines. In the last decade of the twentieth century, however, the primary killers are diseases associated with human behavior and life-style. This relationship between behavior and major causes of death is illustrated in Table 4.1 (p. 73). The task for the 1990s and beyond is to detail more fully the relationship between behavior and disease and to develop effective methods for encouraging positive health habits and eliminating those habits that cause disease.

behavioral pathogens
Behaviors that increase a person's risk for disease.

Behavioral pathogens. Behaviors that make one more susceptible to disease have been termed **behavioral pathogens** (Matarazzo, 1984a, 1984b). This includes most of the risk factors listed in Table 4.1. Of the factors listed, cigarette smoking, along with alcohol abuse, cause by far the most disease and mortality. The Centers for Disease Control recently estimated that over 20% of all American deaths in 1988 can be attributed to smoking (Centers for Disease Control, 1991c). Cigarette smoking either causes or contributes to the development of a wide range of diseases, including coronary heart disease, chronic bronchitis and emphysema, and cancers of the lung, larynx, pancreas, and urinary bladder, as well as stomach ulcers. In addition, smoking

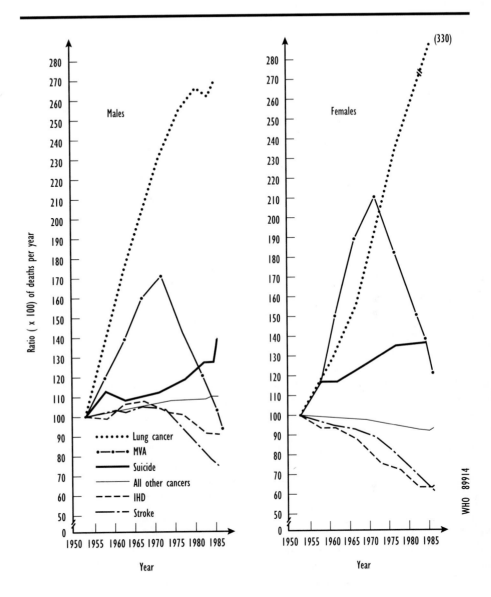

FIGURE 4.1
*Relative change
in mortality
(1950–1954 = 100)
for selected causes of
death in developed
countries from
1950–1954 to 1986.*

MVA = Motor vehicle accidents

IHD = Ischemic heart disease

Note. From "Competing causes of death: A review of recent trends in industrialized countries with special reference to cancer" by A. D. Lopez, 1990, *Annals of the New York Academy of Sciences, 609,* p. 60. Copyright 1990 by New York Academy of Sciences. Reprinted by permission.

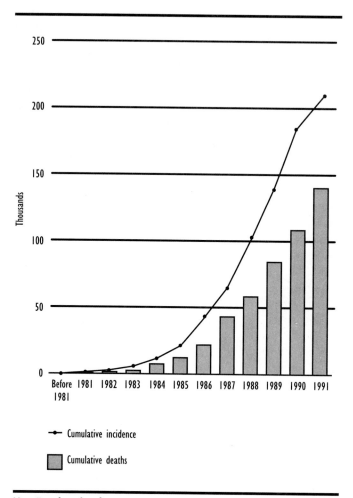

FIGURE 4.2

Cumulative number of AIDS cases and deaths in the United States by year through the end of 1991.

Note. Based on data from *HIV/AIDS Surveillance Report, July, 1992,* Centers for Disease Control, 1992, Atlanta: Centers for Disease Control.

during pregnancy increases the likelihood of birth defects and retardation of fetal growth (U.S. Department of Health, Education and Welfare, 1979). Alcohol abuse is considered a risk factor in more than 10% of deaths in the United States. Cirrhosis of the liver is one of the ten leading causes of death, and alcohol is implicated in approximately 50% of traffic fatalities. Alcohol consumption during pregnancy is a known risk factor for severe birth defects, including mental retardation (U.S. Department of Health, Education and Welfare, 1979).

Behavioral immunogens. But certain behaviors can reduce a person's risk for disease. These behaviors, which Joseph Matarazzo (1984b) terms **behavioral immunogens,** include such positive health habits as eating a healthy diet, sleeping for 7 to

TABLE 4.1 *Major Causes of Death and Associated Risk Factors, United States, 1986*

Cause	Percentage of All Deaths	Risk Factor
Heart disease	36.4	Smoking, hypertension, elevated serum cholesterol, diet, lack of exercise, stress, family history
Malignant neoplasms	22.3	Smoking, worksite carcinogens, environmental carcinogens, alcohol, diet
Stroke	7.1	Hypertension, smoking, elevated serum cholesterol, stress
Influenza and pneumonia	3.3	Smoking, vaccination status
Diabetes	3.3	Obesity
Motor vehicle accidents	2.3	Alcohol, no seat belts, speed, roadway design, vehicle engineering
Accidents other than motor vehicle	2.3	Alcohol, drug abuse, smoking (fires), product design, handgun availability
Suicide	1.5	Stress, alcohol and drug abuse, handgun availability
Cirrhosis of the liver	1.2	Alcohol abuse
Atherosclerosis	1.1	Elevated serum cholesterol

Note. Adapted from "Behavioral health: A 1990 challenge for the health sciences professions" (p. 4) by J. D. Matarazzo, 1984, in J. D. Matarazzo et al. (eds.), *Behavioral health: A handbook of health enhancement and disease prevention,* New York: Wiley; and updated with data from *Health United States 1987,* National Center for Health Statistics, 1988b, DHHS Pub. No. (PHS) 88-1232, Washington, DC: Public Health Service.

behavioral immunogens
Behaviors that reduce a person's risk for disease.

8 hours a night, eating breakfast almost every day, and exercising regularly. The salutary effects of practicing good health habits of this type were shown in a study by Nedra Belloc and Lester Breslow (1972; Belloc, 1973), in which nearly 7,000 adults were surveyed about their health habits. These same individuals were then followed up 5½ and 9½ years later. Results from the 5½ year follow-up are shown in Figure 4.3. Nine and a half years after the initial survey, men who had followed all seven health practices had only 28% of the mortality of those who had followed three or fewer. For women, the comparable figure was 43% (Breslow & Enstrom, 1980).

Environment and Disease

Added to the effects of individual behavior on health are the effects of our collective actions as a society. Health hazards in the environment, such as polluted air and toxic chemicals, have the potential to kill, injure, and sicken individuals, and significantly influence the health of entire communities. An estimated 20% or more of all premature deaths in the United States, as well as a substantial amount of disease and disability, could be eliminated through protection from environmental hazards. Among the primary environmental hazards to health are air pollution, toxic substances such as insecticides, and chemicals used in manufacturing that contaminate air, water, and

Alcohol abuse is a major behavioral pathogen that is associated with such health problems as liver disease, traffic fatalities, and birth defects.

soil, and radiation. Air pollution contributes substantially to respiratory ailments; toxic compounds have been shown to lead to cancer, chronic degenerative diseases, reproductive and developmental impairments, neurological problems, and diseases of the immune system (U.S. Department of Health, Education and Welfare, 1979).

THE CHALLENGE OF PRIMARY PREVENTION

What Is Primary Prevention?

primary prevention
Efforts taken to prevent disease in currently healthy individuals.

secondary prevention
Measures taken to stop the progress of a disease in its early stages.

Fundamental changes in behavior are therefore necessary. **Primary prevention** refers to measures taken to prevent disease in currently healthy persons. Primary prevention can be contrasted with **secondary prevention,** which concerns efforts to stop the progress of a disease in its beginning stages, and **tertiary prevention,** which involves treatment and rehabilitation procedures for diseases that already have clinical symptoms (Fielding, 1978). From the standpoint of minimizing suffering and death, preventing disease from developing in the first place is preferable to repairing the damage after the person becomes ill. For example, elimination of only one habit, smoking, could lead to a 20% reduction in cancer deaths, as well as a substantial reduction in years of life lost to premature death (Stachnik, Stoffelmayr, & Hoppe, 1983). Such estimates do not even begin to address questions of quality of life, or what improvements might be made by changing other habits as well.

Primary prevention involves basically two strategies. The first concentrates on changing people's negative health habits, for instance, smoking, drinking, or dietary

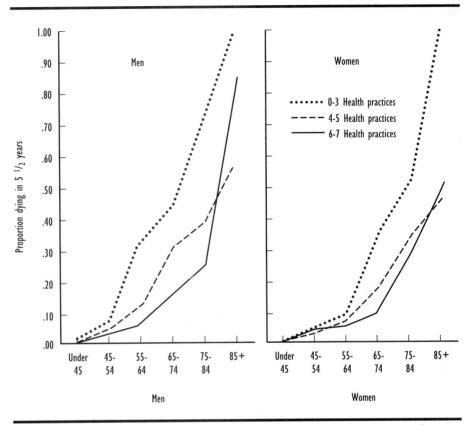

FIGURE 4.3
Age- and sex-specific mortality rates by number of health practices.

Note. From "Relationship of health practices and mortality" by N. B. Belloc, 1973, *Preventive Medicine, 2,* p. 75. Copyright 1973 by Academic Press. Reprinted by permission.

tertiary prevention Procedures for the treatment and rehabilitation of persons with fully developed diseases.

habits. Given the number of people who engage in negative health habits, interventions aimed at changing these behaviors are essential. However, such programs are often only partially successful, and it is not unusual for people to relapse soon after they quit. Cigarette smoking is a prime case in point. Although numerous programs have been developed for changing smoking behavior, these programs typically achieve only short-term success, with a significant proportion of those completing the program eventually resuming their smoking (cf. Leventhal & Cleary, 1980; Lichtenstein & Mermelstein, 1984).

More recently primary prevention efforts have been directed toward preventing bad habits from developing in the first place and encouraging people to adopt positive habits. Examples of such programs include those to help prevent smoking among adolescents (cf. Johnson et al., 1986), prevent the use of drugs (Pentz et al., 1989), and encourage such positive behaviors as regular exercise and healthy diet (cf. Matarazzo et al., 1984). However, programs of this type face several barriers.

Barriers to Primary Prevention

Although many people are more health conscious than ever before, and significant improvements have been made in the number of people practicing primary prevention (cf. Wilson, 1988), many significant impediments block further improvement of health habits. These barriers include cultural attitudes and practices, the nature of health habits, characteristics of the health system, and factors within psychology itself.

Cultural and attitudinal barriers. Most people rank health highly as a value, but as only one value among many (cf. Kristiansen, 1985; Lau, Hartman, & Ware, 1986). Other values, such as success, living a comfortable life, or excitement also serve as powerful motivators. Barriers to primary prevention arise when these other values conflict with the practice of good health habits. Good examples of this are illustrated in Box 4.1. The values embodied in the traditional male role make males particularly susceptible to such diseases as heart attacks, lung cancer, and cirrhosis of the liver, all of which can be prevented through behavioral change.

Thomas Stachnik and his colleagues (Stachnik et al., 1983) believe that prevention efforts are also hampered by specific attitudes. A sense of fatalism about the fact that everyone eventually dies can lead people to conclude that they might just as well die of heart disease, stroke, or cancer. This attitude ignores questions of how long one lives as well as the circumstances of one's death.

A second attitude hampering prevention efforts is one that equates poor health habits with the good life. This attitude questions whether life is worth living if one has to give up such pleasures as eating red meat, living a sedentary life-style, smoking, and consumption of foods like ice cream that are high in cholesterol. The argument is that a life without such pleasures is no life at all. As Stachnik and his associates demonstrate, this ignores the fact that we have learned to enjoy this type of life-style, and thus can learn to find pleasure in a healthier one.

Belief in the powers of technology is another cultural attitude that can impede prevention. Well publicized advances in medical technology and surgical techniques such as organ transplants and artificial body parts have lulled people into complacency about the need for prevention. Such advances, however, are often somewhat overstated and may affect only a small number of people (cf. Thomas, 1977).

Added to these attitudinal barriers are strong economic forces. Several major industries have vested interests in maintaining current life-styles. For example, Americans spend about $30 billion a year on tobacco products (White, 1988), as well as roughly $40 billion for alcoholic beverages (Cavanagh & Clairmonte, 1985). Elimination of tobacco and alcohol consumption would clearly have a major economic impact. Similarly, various segments of the food industry have stakes in promoting the use of their products (see Box 4.2). It is therefore not surprising that both beef and dairy products are touted as being not only pleasurable but necessary to the American diet.

Barriers related to the nature of health habits. Efforts at primary prevention are also often thwarted by the nature of the health habits involved. Many poor health

BOX 4.2 Preventing Cancer: How Important Is the Cereal You Eat for Breakfast?

Many breakfast cereal manufacturers have recently touted the benefits of their products for preventing diseases such as cancer. For example, in one advertisement an earnest young woman cites a recent report by the National Cancer Institute indicating that increased fiber in one's diet can reduce the chance of certain kinds of cancer; she then asks if this will change what she eats for breakfast. "You bet it will," she answers. Advertisements like this and the evidence on which they are based have been the source of considerable controversy (cf. Marshall, 1986; Toufexis, 1985).

At issue in this debate is the strength of evidence relating cancer to specific dietary factors, in this case, dietary fiber. Dietary factors are unquestionably related to cancer. Epidemiological studies and laboratory experiments with animals have demonstrated that although some dietary components, such as fat, are associated with increased cancer, other components, such as vitamin A, are associated with lower risk of cancer (Cohen, 1987; Rogers & Longnecker, 1988). However, there is great controversy over the role of certain dietary substances, such as fiber, and the appropriateness of recommendations for dietary changes. Critics argue that the evidence for the protective effects of diet has been exaggerated and is insufficient to support recommended changes in eating habits. But proponents of dietary changes contend that even if the

evidence is not conclusive, the changes are likely to be beneficial and at worst will do no harm (Marshall, 1986).

Concerning the relationship of breakfast cereal to cancer, advocates of increased fiber argue that people should increase their consumption of dietary fiber to a minimum of 20 to 35 grams per day. According to their estimates, this increase in fiber, combined with a decrease in fat intake, could significantly reduce colon cancer, saving tens of thousands of lives per year (Dranov, 1987).

The evidence for this claim, however, is at best sketchy. Epidemiological studies examining different population groups do show an inverse correlation between the amount of fiber in a group's diet and the number of deaths from colon cancer. However, other studies have shown that only certain types of fiber are related to reduced cancer risk. Animal studies suggest that wheat bran protects against colon tumors, whereas apple, pectin, alfalfa, and oat bran either have no effect or may actually increase tumor growth (Cohen, 1987; Rogers & Longnecker, 1988). Further, as Leonard Cohen writes, "In no case has it been directly demonstrated that implementing dietary changes in a given individual inhibited the onset of cancer or kept an established cancer from spreading" (Cohen, 1987, pg. 48).

gradient of reinforcement
The behavioral principle stating that immediate rewards and punishments are much more effective than are delayed rewards and punishments.

habits—such as the use of alcohol or tobacco, the frequent eating of red meat and other high-cholesterol foods, or unsafe sexual practices—lead to immediate pleasure. Positive health habits—such as exercising regularly, flossing one's teeth, dieting, or receiving regular medical checkups—often require discipline, inconvenience, or the renunciation of pleasure. Since the health effects of such actions are usually apparent only years later, a dilemma for prevention is created. A basic principle of human behavior is that immediate rewards and punishments are much more effective than are delayed ones. This **gradient of reinforcement** (Miller, 1983) helps to explain why highly cost-effective strategies of primary prevention receive much less attention from health care providers and the public than do more expensive treatment procedures. Further, this principle indicates the difficulties that are likely to be encountered in encouraging people to engage in healthy life-styles. Prevention strategies that require delay of gratification or inconvenience in the service of preventing future illness are

Stahler © 1989 Newspaper Enterprise Association. Reprinted by permission.

likely to be far less successful than are those involving immediate reinforcement (Miller, 1983).

Barriers within the health system. The structure of our health care system provides additional barriers to the practice of primary prevention. As was noted in Chapter 2, modern medicine, as based on the biomedical model, is oriented toward treatment and cure. Health care providers are trained to diagnose and treat specific diseases; there are powerful reinforcements, among them money, drama, prestige, and a sense of accomplishment, that are associated with practicing curative medicine (Stanchik et al., 1983). Sadly, fewer reinforcements accompany primary prevention efforts. Although there have been calls for physicians and other health care providers to orient themselves more to primary prevention (cf. Frame, 1989; Wilson, 1988), counseling patients to change their health habits is far less glamorous than producing a dramatic cure. Further, curative procedures are more financially rewarding than are preventive measures. For the most part, health insurance covers treatment for diagnosed conditions. With the exception of some health maintenance organizations (HMOs), health insurance rarely reimburses preventive procedures or counseling on health behavior (Stachnik et al., 1983).

In addition to its emphasis on cure, health care's orientation toward individual treatment tends to block prevention efforts. The basic health care model currently in use emphasizes one-on-one contact between patient and health care provider. This model is perfectly appropriate for dealing with diseases in individual patients, but is far less effective for prevention. Although the personal relationship between patient and health care provider can be a powerful motivator in influencing people to follow medical recommendations (cf. Janis & Rodin, 1979; Stachnik et al., 1983), reliance on this type of one-on-one contact is not very efficient.

Barriers within psychology. Psychologists have been among those calling for increased emphasis on primary prevention, but some factors within psychology itself that have impeded such efforts. For one thing, psychology's focus on mental health has historically overshadowed its interest in other types of health activities. As noted in Chapter 1, only recently have psychologists become involved in significant numbers in efforts aimed at improving physical health.

Second, like medicine, the practice of psychology has emphasized one-on-one interaction between patient and practitioner in an office setting. Among professional psychologists, an attitude prevails that "Only office-based activities are professional" (Stachnik et al., 1983, 458). Such an attitude mitigates against the development of intervention programs in schools, work settings, or the community at large. Stachnik and his associates argue that psychologists and other behavioral scientists need to reorient their efforts to emphasize prevention efforts that reach large groups of people simultaneously. Only when behavioral technology is taken out of the laboratory and office and put to work in more broadly based programs will it be truly effective in promoting health. Examples of such efforts are school-based programs for the prevention of smoking (cf. Flay et al., 1985; McAlister, Perry, & Maccoby, 1979) and large-scale community-based efforts at reducing coronary risk (cf. Farquhar et al., 1977).

HEALTH BEHAVIOR AND ITS DETERMINANTS

The Concept of Health Behavior

health behavior
A behavior that a person engages in while healthy so as to prevent disease.

The challenge in primary prevention is to persuade people to change their behavior so as to reduce the risk of disease. **Health behaviors** are behaviors that a person engages in, while still healthy, for the purpose of preventing disease (Kasl & Cobb, 1966). These include a wide range of behaviors from stopping smoking and losing weight to exercising regularly and eating right. Thus, the concept of health behavior comprises both efforts at reducing behavioral pathogens and the practice of behaviors that act as behavioral immunogens.

Although healthy or unhealthy life-styles are commonly discussed as if a person either does or does not practice good health behavior, research on health behaviors has shown that the practice of one health behavior is often only weakly related to the practice of others (Kirscht, 1983; Mechanic, 1979). Why is this? The major reasons seem to be that health behaviors differ on a number of dimensions and may be influenced by different factors. For one thing, some health behaviors require that a person actively engage in positive activities, whereas others require the avoidance of harmful ones. Thus, although a person may initiate good habits such as exercising and eating right, that same person may have difficulty in avoiding the temptations involved in cigarette smoking and excessive use of alcohol. In addition, some health behaviors, such as brushing one's teeth, eating right, and exercising, can be performed by the individual without professional assistance, whereas others, such as receiving regular check-ups or immunizations, require medical supervision. Health behaviors also differ considerably in their complexity. Some, like immunizations or check-ups, are relatively simple and are performed only occasionally. Many health behaviors, however, are repeated and are embedded in important habit patterns. For example, obtaining health benefits from exercise requires that the person exercise on a regular basis. Positive habits, like brushing one's teeth, and negative habits, such as smoking and overeating, are closely related to the person's daily routines and general habit patterns. Beyond this, complex, long-term habits may become integrated together as a part of the person's overall life-style (Kirscht, 1983). Finally, different health behaviors may well be determined by different factors.

Determinants of Health Behavior

Social and demographic determinants. Health researchers have long noted that health behaviors differ significantly between social groups. Such relationships are best documented for medically based preventive actions. Individuals with higher income or education, for example, are more likely to be immunized than are those of lower socioeconomic status. Gender is also a determinant—women are more likely to obtain dental care, immunizations, and regular checkups than are men. In addition, individuals in small families are more likely to engage in preventive actions as are those who participate more in social activities and who have high levels of social support. One particularly important social factor is a person's access to a regular source of medical care. Not surprisingly, having regular access to medical care makes it more likely that a person will engage in preventive behavior (Kirscht, 1983).

Situational determinants. In addition to these broad social factors, health behaviors are also considerably influenced by social situations. Family members and peers can exert considerable influence on the health habits a person develops. For example, Howard Leventhal and his coworkers have noted that a young person's first cigarette is typically smoked in the presence of peers and is often obtained from a parent or older sibling. Further, having a parent or sibling who smokes seems to make smoking more acceptable (Leventhal, Prohaska, & Hirschman, 1985). Along these same lines, many studies have found peer pressure and the influence of older "more mature" models to be critical determinants of smoking initiation (cf. McAlister, Perry, & Maccoby, 1979; Evans, 1984).

Symptom perception. A person's health behaviors are also often influenced by perceived symptoms. A man who considers himself healthy, but finds that he is winded after climbing only one or two flights of stairs, may decide that he really needs to begin an exercise program. Or a smoker may vow to quit smoking after she begins to have a persistent cough. In such cases, the person regards current symptoms as an indicator of potential physical problems. Changes in behavior are made as a way of reducing perceived risk. However, although such symptoms can be very useful in motivating a person to adopt positive health habits, their influence is likely to be transitory (cf.

Leventhal et al., 1985). A smoker may quit when alarmed by a persistent cough, only to begin smoking again after the cough has ceased.

Psychological determinants. Finally, a person's health behaviors are likely to be influenced by psychological factors, both emotional and cognitive. Emotional needs and states can have a potent effect on health practices. Young people who become regular smokers soon after smoking their first cigarette may do so in response to perceived stress. The act of smoking itself is often related to emotional factors such as anxiety or boredom (Leventhal et al., 1985). Studies of other health habits have shown a similar pattern. For example, a study of health habits among young people found that those who reported higher levels of emotional distress were less likely to engage in positive health behaviors, such as eating breakfast, exercising, and not smoking, than were those with lower levels of distress (Leventhal et al., 1985). Negative emotional states apparently interfere with good health habits, but emotional distress can also lead one to seek medical care (cf. Mechanic, 1978).

Beyond these emotional factors, the practice of health behaviors is a function of a person's thoughts and beliefs. In an extensive program of research, Leventhal and his colleagues (Leventhal, Meyer, & Nerenz, 1980; Leventhal, Nerenz, & Steele, 1984) have documented the ways in which "common sense" illness representations influence people's health actions. In particular, they note that in responding to potential illness threats people make use of cognitive models that they have for different illnesses, models that may or may not correspond to the medical understanding of the illness. These models are discussed in greater detail in Chapter 8. For our purposes here, however, the important point is that preventive health actions are guided by these models. Thus a woman who believes that AIDS affects only homosexual males and intravenous drug users will most likely not be particularly concerned about using "safe sex" practices. However, someone who is convinced that nutrition is the key to avoiding cancer is likely to be careful about eating habits.

One set of cognitions that seems to be particularly important in motivating people to practice good health habits are those relating to perceived vulnerability (see the discussion of the Health Belief Model below). In general, people who perceive themselves to be vulnerable to a given disease are more likely to engage in measures to prevent that disease. In this regard, Neil Weinstein (1982, 1984, 1988) has pointed out that people tend to be unrealistically optimistic about their future health. When asked what they perceive to be the likelihood that they will experience given health problems in the future, on average people tend to see themselves as being less likely than others to get those diseases. This demonstrates an important psychological barrier in convincing people to change their health habits.

THEORETICAL APPROACHES TO HEALTH BEHAVIOR

With these factors as background, we are now ready to examine some of the theories that have been developed to explain people's health behavior and recommend possible methods for helping people adopt more positive health habits.

The Health Belief Model

Developed by psychologists working for the Public Health Service, the Health Belief Model (HBM) has been extensively researched and applied to preventive health actions ranging from immunizations (Rosenstock, Derryberry, & Carriger, 1959) to breast self-exams (Calnan & Moss, 1984). The HBM has also been applied to questions concerning sick role behavior, use of medical services, and compliance with medical regimens (cf. Wallston & Wallston, 1984, for a review).

Basic assumptions and concepts. The HBM is quite straightforward in its assumptions and concepts. Fundamental to this model is the assumption that health behaviors are more or less rationally determined by the person's perceived vulnerability to a health threat. In the terminology of the HBM, readiness to take a health action is primarily a function of two factors: the person's perceptions of *susceptibility* to disease and the perceived *severity* of the consequences of getting the disease. Thus the model predicts that Joe will be most ready to take action (for example, stop smoking or change sexual practices to avoid getting AIDS) when he believes that he is in danger of contracting the disease in question and when he believes that the disease has important consequences. Conversely, he is least likely to take action when the likelihood of contracting the disease is perceived to be low or the disease is believed to have only minor consequences.

Given that Joe feels vulnerable, whether he actually takes action will depend on his evaluation of potential health behaviors. Specifically, potential behaviors will be evaluated in terms of their perceived benefits and any barriers or costs that might be present. In addition, his behavior is likely to be influenced by cues that can trigger action. For example, if Joe feels susceptible to developing lung cancer from smoking and believes that he can successfully reduce his risk by stopping smoking, he is likely to take steps to do so. This is particularly true if he knows a smoker who has just been diagnosed with cancer, or there is some other cue for him to stop smoking, such as a persistent cough or a recommendation from his doctor. But he is unlikely to stop smoking if he doubts his ability to quit, believes that it will do him no good, or comes to the conclusion that the costs of quitting are too great.

Although these factors form the heart of the model, research based on these hypotheses has indicated that other factors are involved as well. These other factors, labeled "modifying factors," include a variety of demographic variables (e.g., sex, age, race, ethnicity) and social psychological factors (e.g., personality, social class, peer group pressure). These variables are assumed to have their effects indirectly by influencing perceived threat and benefit (Becker & Maiman, 1975). Figure 4.4 summarizes this expanded Health Belief Model.

Putting the Health Belief Model to the test. As noted above, the HBM has generated a substantial amount of research. These studies have generally been supportive of the model, finding that specific health behaviors are related to measures of perceived vulnerability as well as the perceived benefits of taking action. In one study, Marshall Becker and his colleagues (Becker, Maiman, Kirscht, Haefner, & Drachman, 1977)

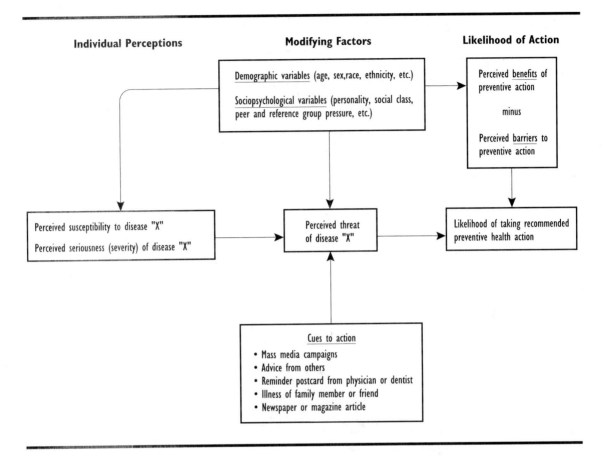

FIGURE 4.4

The Health Belief Model.

Note. From "Sociobehavioral determinants of compliance with health and medical care recommendations" by M. H. Becker and L. A. Maiman, 1975, *Medical Care, 13,* p. 12. Copyright 1975 by J. B. Lippincott Co. Reprinted by permission.

used the Health Belief Model to predict whether mothers kept clinic appointments and adhered to a prescribed diet for their obese children. To make these predictions, the researchers queried the mothers about their perceptions of their children's susceptibility to illness and continued obesity, as well as their beliefs about the seriousness of these illnesses and obesity. The mothers were also questioned about their perceptions of the benefits and potential drawbacks of their children's dietary regimen and about their overall health motivation. The HBM was then tested by correlating these measures of perceived vulnerability, benefits/barriers, and motivation, with appointment keeping and dietary compliance. Overall, the results indicated that the HBM did a credible job of predicting whether the mothers would keep appointments and would keep their children on the prescribed diet. Other studies have found the components of the HBM to be significant predictors of who practices breast self-examination (Calnan & Moss, 1984; Champion, 1990), participates in screening for cervical cancer (Hennig & Knowles, 1990), seeks information about hypertension and herpes (Wallston & Wallston, 1984), and engages in preventive behavior against HIV infection (Wilson, Lavelle, Greenspan, & Wilson, 1991).

Although the results of these studies have been generally favorable, significant questions have been raised about the HBM. Not all the studies done using this model have produced confirming results. One study found that individuals with higher susceptibility to dental problems were not more likely than those with lower susceptibility to seek preventive care (Tash, O'Shea, & Cohen, 1969). Another study, using fear appeals to motivate college students to become immunized against tetanus, found no relationship between perceived vulnerability and getting tetanus shots (Radelfinger, 1965). In addition, even in those studies that report confirming results, the relationships obtained are often not particularly strong. In the study of dietary compliance described above, the correlations tended to be modest, with an average correlation of .34 (Becker et al., 1977; Wallston & Wallston, 1984). Similarly, in a study of HIV prevention, HBM variables predicted only 12%–15% of the differences between individuals in their HIV-preventive behavior (Wilson et al., 1991). Finally, there are questions about whether the HBM is applicable cross-culturally. In a study of preventive health behavior in three ethnic groups in Singapore, Stella Quah (1985) found that the usefulness of the HBM in predicting behavior varied considerably between different groups. Further, cultural variables, such as gender roles and modernization, were often among the strongest predictors of behavior.

On close examination, the HBM appears highly plausible but suffers from several problems. First, some theorists (cf. Wallston & Wallston, 1984) argue that the Health Belief Model is more a catalogue of variables than a real model because it lists variables that ought to be related to health behavior, but is imprecise in specifying the exact relationships involved. In addition, research on the model has tended to operationalize the various components in different ways, thus there is little consistency in how the variables are actually measured (Wallston & Wallston, 1984). This makes it very difficult to assess adequately the usefulness of the model. Finally, by emphasizing abstract, conceptual beliefs about vulnerability and the benefits of health actions, the HBM overlooks the sensory aspects of symptom experience and the cognitive models that people develop for understanding specific diseases (cf. Leventhal & Diefenbach, 1991; Leventhal et al., 1984; Safer, Tharps, Jackson, & Leventhal, 1979).

The Theory of Reasoned Action

Like the Health Belief Model, the Theory of Reasoned Action (TRA) seeks the reasons for people's behavior in their thoughts and beliefs. The models differ, however, in the specific beliefs involved and in the hypothesized relationships of these beliefs to behavior.

Basic assumptions and concepts. According to the TRA, developed by Martin Fishbein and Icek Ajzen (Ajzen & Fishbein, 1980; Fishbein, 1980; Fishbein & Ajzen, 1975), the key determinant of a person's behavior is behavioral intentions. These intentions, in turn, are determined by the person's attitudes toward the action and beliefs about how others will respond to that action. For example, whether Susan goes on a diet is primarily a function of her intention to do so. Whether Susan intends to diet reflects her attitudes toward dieting and her beliefs about how others will respond to her as a result of her diet. Thus if Susan believes that her diet will bring her weight down to a desired level, and will not result in too much discomfort, then she is likely to have a positive attitude toward dieting, which will contribute to her intention to do so. In addition, if she believes that her family supports her dieting and that her boyfriend will be delighted with her new slimmer figure, this makes it even more likely that she will resolve to diet. However, if she doubts the effectiveness of the diet, believes that it will cause a great deal of discomfort or inconvenience, or thinks that she will encounter resistance to her plans, she is less likely to want to go on it. In determining her resolve to diet, each of these factors is assumed to be weighted by the relative importance that Susan places on them. Figure 4.5 shows the hypothesized relationships between each of the factors in the theory.

Putting the Theory of Reasoned Action to the test. How useful is the TRA as a model of health behavior? To date, fewer studies have tested the TRA than the HBM. However, the results of these studies have been encouraging. For example, Robert Brubaker and David Wickersham (1990) used the TRA to predict the practice of testicular self-examination (TSE) for detecting testicular cancer in young men. In this

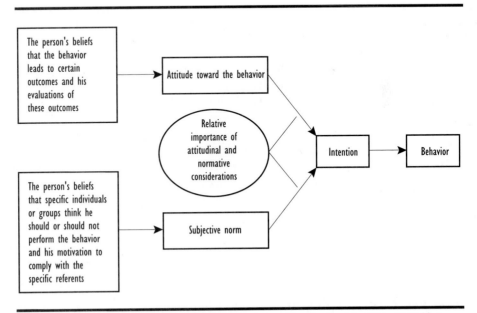

FIGURE 4.5

The Theory of Reasoned Action. Arrows indicate the direction of influence.

Note. From "A theory of reasoned action: Some applications and implications" (p. 69) by M. Fishbein, 1980, in M. M. Page (Ed.), *1979 Nebraska Symposium on Motivation,* Lincoln: University of Nebraska Press. Copyright 1980 by the University of Nebraska Press. Reprinted by permission.

study, more than 200 male college students were given instruction in TSE and completed a questionnaire operationalizing the components of the TRA. Included in the questionnaire were items concerning their attitudes toward TSE, beliefs about subjective norms (i.e., whether others wanted them to practice TSE), beliefs about the outcome of TSE, self-efficacy, and intention to perform TSE during the next month. A follow-up questionnaire six weeks later asked whether subjects had in fact performed the TSE, as well as whether they had seen posters placed around campus promoting TSE. In support of the TRA, the results showed that both attitudes toward TSE and beliefs about subjective norms significantly predicted intentions to perform TSE. Taken together, differences on these two variables accounted for 39% of the differences in behavioral intentions. These intentions, in turn, were significantly correlated with reported TSE performance, particularly for subjects exposed to posters promoting TSE. Other studies have applied this model to weight loss (Saltzer, 1978; Schifter & Ajzen, 1985), smoking (Fishbein, 1980; Norman & Tedeschi, 1989), breast cancer detection (Montano & Taplin, 1991), and alcohol and drug use (Bentler & Speckart, 1979).

Although it has been applied to health behavior in a relative few studies, the TRA holds considerable promise. It is a parsimonious theory that is more tightly reasoned, and often better operationalized, than is the HBM (cf. Wallston & Wallston, 1984). Despite these strong points, the model is not without its drawbacks. In order to make clear predictions about behavior, beliefs and attitudes specific to that behavior must be measured. Thus new measures must be developed for each behavior, measures that are often specific to the sample. This can be a very time-consuming process. Also, there is some question about how well the model works with relatively uneducated, low-income samples, and there is little consideration of factors other than beliefs and attitudes that may affect the person's behavior (Wallston & Wallston, 1984).

A closing comment on using cognitions to predict health behaviors. Both the HBM and the TRA assume that the primary determinants of health behavior reside in people's beliefs and attitudes. Therefore they assume that a person's health behavior is the outcome of conscious intention. Is this really true? William Hunt and his associates (Hunt, Matarazzo, Weiss, & Gentry, 1979) argue that many health behaviors can be best understood as habits that have become largely automatic for the person, and thus are likely to be controlled by cues of which the person is no longer aware. For example, the behavior of smoking a cigarette may become somewhat automatic for a smoker in certain social situations or when under stress. In these situations, the person reaches for a cigarette without really thinking about it. This argues that models like the HBM and the TRA are likely to be most useful for explaining health behavior that requires conscious intent, such as deciding to go on a diet or getting check-ups or immunizations. Once a behavior has become a habit, these models are likely to be considerably less useful in predicting the person's behavior.

Learning Theory Approaches to Health Behavior

Whereas the Health Belief Model and the Theory of Reasoned Action both emphasize the cognitive determinants of health behavior, learning theory approaches emphasize the role of situations and reward. In this approach, health behaviors are viewed as learned responses controlled by rewards and punishments. Thus the key to understanding why a person does or does not engage in particular health protective actions lies in the rewards and punishments that maintain that behavior.

Types of learning and their relationship to health behavior. Learning theorists have shown that behavior is influenced by a variety of basic learning processes. As early as 1898, Edward Thorndike indicated that behavior can be strengthened or weakened by its consequences. This observation laid the groundwork for the development of the principles surrounding operant conditioning. **Operant conditioning** emphasizes that behaviors followed by reinforcement (rewards) are likely to be repeated, whereas those that are punished—or at least are not followed by reinforcement—will decrease in frequency. Research on operant conditioning has established the conditions under which reinforcement and punishment are most effective, and has demonstrated the wide variety of reinforcements that control human behavior (cf. Chesney, 1984; Miller, 1984).

One operant conditioning principle that has profound implications for health behavior is the *gradient of reinforcement*. As noted earlier, this principle refers to the fact that immediate rewards and punishments are much more effective than are delayed ones. In many cases, the effects of good health habits become evident only over a period of years, whereas immediate pleasures are associated with behaviors that are deleterious in the long run, such as smoking, drinking, or eating junk foods. Other operant conditioning principles with implications for health behavior are **shaping**, the principle that reinforced behaviors gradually evolve through changes in reinforcement, and **intermittent reinforcement,** the finding that behavior that is rewarded only part of the time is more resistant to extinction through nonreward than is behavior reinforced all the time (Miller, 1984).

A second type of learning with important implications for health behavior is **respondent learning**, also known as *classical conditioning.* Based on the work of Ivan Pavlov and others, respondent learning emphasizes the learning of associations between stimuli. In his work with dogs, Pavlov demonstrated how previously neutral stimuli can come to elicit responses when paired with stimuli that already elicit those responses. The classic example of this, of course, is Pavlov's conditioning of dogs to salivate on hearing a bell. In addition, work on respondent learning has shown that once an organism has been conditioned to respond to a stimulus, similar stimuli will also come to elicit the response. Thus if a person has become conditioned to reaching for a cigarette when under stress at work, that response is likely to generalize to other stressful situations (cf. Miller, 1984).

In applying these principles to health behavior, health psychologists often utilize the strategy of **applied behavior analysis.** In this strategy, the behavior to be changed (e.g., smoking or overeating) is clearly specified, and careful observations are made of the conditions that seem to promote the behavior and the consequences of the behavior (Chesney, 1984). Thus in applying this approach to Susan's habit of overeating, careful records would be made of when Susan eats, how much she eats, the situational cues that precede her eating, and the immediate consequences of her behavior. These

operant conditioning
Learning in which behavioral responses are increased through reward.

shaping
Teaching a response by reinforcing successive approximations to the desired behavior.

intermittent reinforcement
Reinforcement that is given for only some occurrences of a response.

respondent learning
Learning in which a previously neutral stimulus comes to evoke the same response as another stimulus with which it is paired.

applied behavior analysis
A strategy for modifying behavior involving the careful specification and observation of the behavior to be changed followed by attempts to alter the conditions that control the behavior.

observational learning
Learning that takes place through watching another's behavior.

vicarious reinforcement
Reinforcement of a behavior through seeing another person being rewarded.

self-efficacy
A person's beliefs about his or her ability to attain particular goals in a particular situation.

discriminative stimulus
A stimulus that acts as a cue, releasing a given behavior.

records would then be analyzed to uncover cues, such as loneliness or situational stress, that appear to set off eating binges as well as reinforcements, such as reduction of tension, that work to maintain the overeating.

Both operant and respondent conditioning involve learning by direct experience. There is also ample evidence that a considerable amount of learning takes place indirectly through observation of others' behavior. Work by Albert Bandura (1969, 1977b) and others has demonstrated the importance of **observational learning** and developed the principles behind it. In particular, Bandura notes that people are most likely to be influenced by prestigious models, and are likely to imitate behavior when they see the model being rewarded, but not when that person is punished. Thus **vicarious reinforcements** that a person obtains by watching another get rewarded for, say, stopping smoking can be an important determinant of behavior.

A particularly important aspect of Bandura's work concerns the process of *self-regulation* and the role of **self-efficacy** in guiding behavior. In line with the concept of self-regulation that was discussed in Chapter 2, Bandura (1977a, 1977b) emphasizes that people actively set goals for themselves and direct their own behavior. In Bandura's view, the key to understanding behavior is that people actively monitor their actions, comparing their outcomes to their goals, and regulate their behavior so as to achieve those goals. Central in this is the person's beliefs in his or her ability to attain the selected goals, what Bandura refers to as the sense of self-efficacy (Bandura, 1977a). For example, in this view, the key to understanding Bob's efforts to stay with an exercise program is his belief in his ability to follow through with his intentions to work out on a regular basis.

Putting learning theory approaches to the test. These basic principles form the foundation for techniques for eliminating bad health habits and encouraging good ones. Chapter 5 discusses several of these techniques in detail. For now, two studies will be described that illustrate the application of learning theory approaches to health behavior.

In a classic study of behavioral approaches to the problem of obesity, Sydnor Penick and his colleagues (Penick, Filion, Fox, & Stunkard, 1971) used applied behavior analysis to alter the eating habits of a group of obese patients. The program involved four basic elements. First, in order to obtain a description of baseline eating behavior, patients were asked to keep daily records of how much they ate, when they ate, and under what circumstances. These records showed that the patients tended to eat under a wide variety of circumstances. In addition, certain situations, such as watching television, had apparently become cues for eating. The second element of the program aimed at controlling the cues or **discriminative stimuli** that had become associated with eating. During this part of the program, patients were encouraged to confine their eating to one place, usually the dining room, and to avoid other activities, such as reading or watching television, when eating. In addition, to further limit the cues associated with eating, patients used a distinctive table setting, including an unusually colored place mat and napkin. Once eating had become paired with a single place and the distinctive table setting, patients were taught techniques for controlling their food intake: counting each mouthful of food, and placing their utensils on the plate after every third mouthful until they had completely chewed and swallowed that mouthful. Finally, patients were rewarded for changed eating behavior through a reinforcement schedule in which they were given points for using the suggested control procedures when eating. These points could then be converted into cash. When the patients were weighed at the end of the research, the results indicated that the program had been highly successful. Compared with a group of patients receiving psychotherapy for their weight problems, the patients participating in the behavioral program were substantially more likely to lose weight and to keep it off. Similar results have been found in other programs using similar approaches. The principles involved have also been successfully used in many large-scale programs (cf. Stunkard, 1979).

In addition to helping people change health behaviors, health psychologists are also concerned with maintaining these changes over time. Unfortunately, long-term studies of health behavior indicate that a high percentage of those who change their health behaviors eventually revert to their old habits (Krantz, Grunberg, & Baum, 1985). Research by Mark Condiotte and Edward Lichtenstein (1981) argues that self-efficacy plays a central role in maintaining new health habits. In their research, Condiotte and Lichtenstein followed smokers in two different smoking cessation programs for 3 months. At the beginning and several times after the completion of the programs, participants were questioned about their smoking behavior and their perceived self-efficacy in resisting the temptation to smoke. The findings indicated that both smoking programs significantly increased the participants' sense of self-efficacy for staying tobacco free. Changes in self-efficacy, in turn, predicted whether participants were successful in resisting relapse. Further, for those participants who did go back to smoking, the situations in which they began smoking were ones in which they had a low sense of self-efficacy.

The results of these studies give a sample of the contributions that learning theory can make to understanding and modifying health behaviors. By focusing on the process by which health habits are acquired, as well as the situational and cognitive determinants of behavior, learning theory provides the health psychologist with extremely powerful tools for promoting healthier life-styles. These tools are not

Behavioral methods have been used to successfully alter eating behavior in obese individuals.

without their shortcomings, however. For example, techniques that rely on direct reward of desired health behaviors may produce increases in the target behavior that are maintained only while the reward is being given, and which evaporate after the behavior is no longer reinforced. For example, Adrian Lund and Stephen Kegeles (1984) found that although direct rewards were effective in encouraging young adolescents to use a fluoride mouthwash, use of the mouthwash declined substantially after the rewards were no longer given. Similar results have been obtained when using rewards to encourage the use of seat belts (Roberts & Fanurik, 1986). Results such as these emphasize that long-term change in health behaviors requires that those changes be internalized.

In conclusion, these three approaches to health behavior emphasize a variety of different determinants. The Health Belief Model and the Theory of Reasoned Action both emphasize conscious beliefs and attitudes, and assume that health behaviors are more or less rationally determined. By contrast, learning theory approaches stress the various ways in which health behaviors are either directly or indirectly learned. As we will see in Chapter 5, these different approaches suggest very different methods for promoting healthier behavior.

SUMMARY

The evidence linking behavior and disease is very strong. Although there have been tremendous improvements in health and longevity during this century, a great deal of preventable disease and mortality remains. Chronic conditions, such as heart disease and the cancers, are the current major causes of death. These diseases have direct links to behavior and life-style. A major challenge for the 1990s and beyond is to detail further the relationships between behavior and disease, and to develop effective methods for encouraging healthier life-styles. In particular, methods are needed to combat behavioral pathogens, such as smoking, alcohol abuse, and unhealthy diet, as well as to encourage behavioral immunogens such as exercising regularly, eating right, and getting enough sleep. Epidemiological evidence demonstrates that the rate of mortality is lower among people who practice good health habits than among those who do not.

Such evidence strongly suggests the need for primary prevention, that is, measures to keep healthy people from developing disease. However, there are many barriers to primary prevention efforts. Cultural attitudes, such as fatalism about the inevitability of death and the equation of poor health habits with the good life,

are often obstacles, and so are certain economic forces. The fact that good health habits may require discipline, inconvenience, or the renunciation of pleasure can also discourage the adoption of such habits. Beyond this, the medical system's orientation toward the treatment and cure of individual patients and psychology's traditional emphasis on mental health impede primary prevention efforts.

Health behaviors are behaviors a person engages in for the purpose of remaining healthy. Whether a person practices good health behaviors is determined by many factors, for instance, social and demographic factors (sex, income, education, and access to medical care). Some health behaviors are controlled by perceived symptoms, whereas others are heavily influenced by family and peer influence. Finally, psychological factors including both emotional and cognitive factors are important determinants of whether a person practices particular health behaviors.

Theories of health behavior have focused on both the cognitive and situational determinants of health practices. The Health Belief Model (HBM) focuses on the person's perceived susceptibility to disease, perceptions of the severity of the disease, and beliefs about the perceived benefits and barriers to action. This model is intuitively appealing, but research evidence for it is mixed. Although some studies have been supportive, others have not. Fishbein and Ajzen's Theory of Reasoned Action (TRA) also emphasizes cognitive determinants of health behavior but focuses on the person's behavioral intentions. According to this model, whether a person engages in a behavior is a direct function of behavioral intentions, which, in turn, are determined by the person's attitudes toward the action and beliefs about how others will respond. This model has been applied to health behaviors in only a few studies, but has shown considerable promise. Both the HBM and TRA work best for behavior that requires conscious intent and are likely to be less effective in predicting behavior that has become habitual.

Learning theory approaches to health behavior emphasize how behavior is acquired and maintained. Therefore, these approaches tend to focus on the situational determinants of health actions, particularly the rewards and punishments associated with different behaviors. In addition, Albert Bandura has argued that a person's sense of self-efficacy is a key factor in behavior. Research on learning theory approaches to health behavior have demonstrated that these concepts provide health psychologists with important tools for understanding health actions and for bringing about desired changes.

KEY TERMS

behavioral pathogens (70)
behavioral immunogens (73)
primary prevention (74)
secondary prevention (74)
tertiary prevention (75)
gradient of reinforcement (77)
health behavior (79)
operant conditioning (87)

shaping (87)
intermittent reinforcement (87)
respondent learning (87)
applied behavior analysis (88)
observational learning (88)
vicarious reinforcement (88)
self-efficacy (88)
discriminative stimulus (88)

SUGGESTED READINGS

Kirscht, J. P. (1983). Preventive health behavior: A review of research and issues. *Health Psychology, 2,* 277–301. This article reviews what is currently known about preventive health behavior.

Matarazzo, J. D., et al. (1984). *Behavioral health: A handbook of health enhancement and disease prevention.* New York: Wiley. The chapters in this volume provide a comprehensive overview of current work by health psychologists and others on health promotion.

U.S. Department of Health, Education and Welfare. (1979). *Healthy people: A report of the Surgeon General on health promotion and disease prevention.* (Report No. 9-55071.) Washington, DC: U.S. Government Printing Office. This landmark report describes in detail the challenges and possibilities for improving America's health through behavior change.

Wallston, B. S., & Wallston, K. A. (1984). Social psychological models of health behavior: An examination and integration. In A. Baum, S. E. Taylor, & J. E. Singer (eds.), *Handbook of psychology and health,* Vol 4. Hillsdale, NJ: Erlbaum. In this chapter, Barbara and Kenneth Wallston review current theories of health behavior, noting the strengths and weaknesses of each.

CHAPTER **5**

Promoting Good Health

As we saw in Chapter 4, the relationship between behavior and disease is very strong. A person's behavior can either increase susceptibility to disease or protect against it. Finding ways to encourage people to practice good health behaviors and avoid poor ones presents a major challenge for health psychologists and others concerned with promoting good health. This chapter examines some of the techniques that have been developed for changing health behaviors and then considers how these can be applied to specific health behavior problems. In the course of this discussion, the effectiveness of these efforts will be critically evaluated.

MIND AND BODY: PROMOTING HEALTH

Behavioral Health

Joseph Matarazzo (1980) has coined the term *behavioral health* to refer to efforts by psychologists and other health professionals to encourage positive health behaviors. In Matarazzo's words:

> *Behavioral health* is an interdisciplinary field dedicated to promoting a philosophy of health that stresses *individual responsibility* in the application of behavioral and biomedical science knowledge and techniques to the *maintenance* of health and the *prevention* of illness and dysfunction by a variety of self-initiated individual or shared activities. (p. 813; italics in original)

Behavioral health is an action-oriented *application* of our knowledge to the promotion of health. Therefore, it concerns the development of specific techniques for encouraging behavior change. Given the variety of behaviors and diseases involved, any one technique is not likely to be sufficient in itself to produce the changes necessary. Rather, behavioral health draws on a wide variety of techniques applied in diverse settings to promote healthy living.

Challenges Presented by Modern Life-styles

What specific features of current life-styles are most in need of change in order to promote better health? We can begin answering these questions by recalling the major behavioral pathogens and immunogens identified in Chapter 4. As we saw, the current major causes of death are associated with such factors as smoking, alcohol use, diet and sedentary life-style.

In this respect there is both good news and bad news. On the positive side, there is evidence of a move on the part of at least some toward a healthier life-style. For example, the percentage of Americans who regularly smoke has declined from 52% among men and 34% among women in 1965 to 31% and 27%, respectively, in 1987. Correspondingly, the percentage of individuals who have quit smoking has risen from 20% to 31% among men and 8% to 18% among women in the same time period (National Center for Health Statistics, 1989). Progress has also been made in reducing cholesterol levels and encouraging physical exercise. The percentage of Americans with high levels of serum cholesterol has fallen from approximately 27% in 1960–62 to just under 22% in 1976–80 (National Center for Health Statistics, 1989). Further, the number of adults between the ages of 18 and 64 who engage in regular vigorous physical exercise has risen from an estimated 35% in 1978 to 42% in 1985 (National Center for Health Statistics, 1987). Similar positive trends have been reported in other countries as well. For instance, in Finland a recent analysis of trends in coronary risk showed positive changes for serum cholesterol, smoking, and blood pressure (Vartiainen et al., 1991).

Although these data are encouraging, they also point out areas of concern. Despite positive trends, approximately 30% of American adults regularly smoke as do nearly 40% of Japanese (Shimao, 1988). Worldwide, tobacco use causes an estimated two and a half million deaths annually (Masironi & Rothwell, 1988). Similarly, the drinking of alcoholic beverages continues to be prevalent throughout the world. On an annual basis, the average American consumes alcoholic drinks containing the equivalent of approximately 8 liters of pure alcohol compared to 13.5 liters for the French, 8.5 for Canadians, and 5.7 for the Japanese (Sournia, 1990). Further, even though progress has been made in reducing high cholesterol levels and encouraging exercise, many people still have elevated cholesterol or lead sedentary lives. These statistics provide only a partial picture of the current state of behavioral health, but they indicate important challenges ahead.

CHANGING ATTITUDES AND BELIEFS TO PROMOTE GOOD HEALTH

How can we encourage healthy living? One means is through changing people's attitudes and beliefs. As noted in Chapter 4, two of the major theoretical approaches to health behavior, the Health Belief Model and the Theory of Reasoned Action, emphasize beliefs and attitudes as determinants of people's health practices. Both theories also argue for changes in attitudes and beliefs as a prerequisite for changes in health behaviors. Thus, according to the HBM, promoting positive health behaviors requires that we persuade people that they are susceptible to given diseases, such as AIDS, cancer, or heart disease, and that there are effective means of preventing these illnesses. Alternatively, the TRA argues that attempts to change health behaviors need to produce change in people's attitudes toward behaviors such as smoking cessation and exercise, as well as convince people that such behavior changes will be viewed positively by others.

Using Attitude Change to Promote Positive Health Behavior

How can we go about promoting these attitude changes? This question has been the focus of a great deal of research among social psychologists and others. Beginning in the 1950s many studies have examined in detail how people respond to persuasion attempts and the processes involved. From this research has come principles that can be used to promote attitudes and beliefs conducive to good health behavior.

Informational appeals. Promoting good health behavior requires that people be aware of the connections between behavior and health and know what is involved in healthy behavior. For example, motivating people to engage in more physical exercise and eat a healthier diet demands that they be made aware of the role of diet and exercise in health and realize their importance. So, a necessary step in changing health behavior is providing people with information to guide their actions.

This is a simple enough proposition, but there is more to an informational appeal than simply providing the information. Bringing about changes in behavior through informational appeals involves at least five different processes (McGuire, 1969). First, we need to get the audience's *attention*. This is no mean feat, considering the amount of information that people are constantly bombarded with. Once a message is received, the next step is *comprehension*. For a message to be effective, it must be presented in terms that are understandable to the audience and that fit their conceptions of health and illness (see Chapter 8). Assuming that the message is understood by the audience, the third step in persuasion is *yielding*, that is, accepting the position advocated by the message. For information to have a long-term effect, there must also be message *retention* and, finally, *action* in which the person's behavior changes to become healthier.

How can we facilitate these processes and increase the likelihood that health information will be effective in changing behavior? Studies of persuasion have indicated several key factors in persuasion. First, the effectiveness of a message often depends on who presents it: it is clearly advantageous for the message to be delivered by a communicator who is perceived as expert and trustworthy (Hovland & Weiss, 1951). For health messages, physicians and other health professionals—such as the Surgeon General—are ideal communicators, particularly when they are well known or prestigious. Messages are also more likely to be accepted when they are presented by communicators who are attractive (Chaiken, 1979), confident in their delivery (Erickson, Lind, Johnson, & Barr, 1978), and perceived as similar to the audience. For example, Theodore Dembroski and his colleagues (Dembroski, Lasater, & Ramirez, 1978) found that black junior high school students were more persuaded by a message on dental hygiene from a black dentist than from a white one.

How we construct the message is also critical (cf. Petty & Cacioppo, 1981). Messages must be clear, concise, and not overly complex. Complex and technical messages are best reserved for audiences that are well educated. The exact arguments to be used also depend on the audience. For audiences that are well informed or who tend to be skeptical of the position advocated, a communicator should anticipate objections and use a two-sided argument, one that refutes opposing arguments while presenting the communicator's position. But if the target audience already leans toward the advocated position, a simple presentation of the arguments supporting that position will suffice. Finally, in order to make sure that the point of the message gets across, the communicator should draw explicit conclusions from the information presented and not leave those conclusions up to the audience. Thus, for example, a message about the benefits of exercise should explicitly point out the specific benefits of physical exercise and make recommendations as to amounts and type of exercise.

Fear appeals. One of the more common approaches to attitude change is to try to motivate change through the use of fear. The idea is that people will be more likely to accept a message and change their attitudes and behavior if their fears and apprehensions are appealed to. Such an approach is particularly relevant to health behavior since the object of changing health habits is to avoid future disease and disability. Thus the message often has a built-in component of fear. For example, recent

Health campaigns often use fear appeals in an attempt to motivate behavior change.

efforts aimed at encouraging "safe sex" are designed to convince people to change their sexual behavior so as to avoid the threat of AIDS. Given the fear of AIDS, such messages are implicitly, if not explicitly, designed to motivate behavior change through arousing fear. Similarly, efforts to persuade people to stop smoking are often based on appealing to their fear of cancer and heart disease.

How effective are fear appeals? The answer to this question often depends on whom you ask. On the one hand, there is evidence that greater levels of fear do lead to greater attitude change. In his review of the effects of fear communications, Howard Leventhal (1970) discusses several studies in which higher levels of fear have been associated with greater acceptance of such recommendations as stopping smoking, getting chest x-rays, and obtaining tetanus shots. On the other hand, Irving Janis (1967) argues that moderate levels of fear produce the greatest attitude change and that high levels of fear can actually interfere with acceptance of health recommendations. In a classic study, Janis and Seymour Feshbach (1953) found that junior high school students exposed to a moderately fear-provoking message on dental hygiene showed greater acceptance of new hygiene practices than did those receiving a high fear message.

The resolution to this controversy seems to be in the specific content of fear appeals and the cognitive responses that they evoke. Current evidence indicates several necessary conditions for fear appeals to be effective (Rogers 1975, 1983). First, a fear appeal must make plain to people the extent to which negative health practices produce undesirable health consequences. In addition, the message must convince them that those consequences are real and are likely to happen to them. Once this message is conveyed, ways of avoiding those consequences must be explicitly described. Finally, the message should persuade people that they have the ability to follow through on the recommended changes (Maddux & Rogers, 1983). Thus in using fear to motivate people to stop smoking, for example, one must convincingly describe the effects of smoking on health, make the listeners realize that they are personally at risk, and provide them with effective ways of quitting. Unfortunately, fear appeals often fail to produce these changes when these conditions are not met.

Does Changing Attitudes Change Health Behaviors?

Studies of persuasion demonstrate convincingly that people's attitudes can be changed through informational and fear appeals. Although this is encouraging and provides us with an important first step, it is only a first step. For attitude change to promote good health, the changes must be not only in attitudes but in behavior. Our interest in attitude change is predicated on the assumption that changes in attitudes will be reflected in people's behavior.

Is this assumption warranted? Like studies of the effects of fear, research on the relationship of attitudes to behavior has produced mixed results. Many studies have shown fairly strong relationships between attitudes and behaviors, but others have shown little or no connection (cf. Fishbein & Ajzen, 1975; Wicker, 1969). The effects of health promotion attempts based on attitude change have similarly been mixed. In a study of weight change in obese children, John Kirscht and his coworkers (Kirscht, Becker, Haefner, & Maiman, 1978) found that weight change was greatest when mothers were given high-threat messages. Although these results suggest that belief changes can have positive effects on health behavior, other studies have found little or no effect for attitude change attempts. Howard Leventhal and Paul Cleary (1980), for instance, point out that although attempts to stimulate feelings of vulnerability in smokers are successful, they often fail to change actual smoking behavior.

The tenuousness of the relationship between attitude and behavior change serves as a warning against relying too heavily on attitude change techniques for promoting healthy behavior. Health behaviors *can* be influenced by stimulating attitude change. However, this is much more likely under some conditions than others. Studies of the relationship between attitudes and behavior indicate that attitudes are most likely to have a strong influence on behavior when they are based on direct experience, are easily accessible, and are made salient to the person (cf. Fazio, 1989; Petty & Cacioppo, 1981). Further, attitudes have their greatest effect when they are consistent with, or at least not contradictory to, prevailing norms (Fishbein & Ajzen, 1975).

USING BEHAVIORAL TECHNOLOGY TO PROMOTE GOOD HEALTH

Attitude change is certainly not the only, nor even most effective, route to influencing people's health behaviors. A more direct means is through the application of the principles of learning theory. Chapter 4 discussed the different types of learning, and how learning principles can be used to explain people's health actions. How might these principles be used to promote better health?

Cognitive-Behavioral Approaches to Health Promotion

Cognitive-behavioral approaches to health promotion encompass a diverse group of strategies. Although diverse in their application of behavioral principles, these strategies share some guiding principles (Kendall & Turk, 1984), beginning with the assumption that behavior and cognition must be considered together in bringing about change. The reason for this is that people do not respond directly to environmental events, but rather to their cognitive representations of those events. Much human learning is controlled by people's cognitions. Their thoughts, feelings, and behaviors are often causally related. Thus, in trying to understand why a person engages in seemingly self-destructive behavior, such as smoking, or neglects to practice good health habits such as exercise or proper nutrition, one must look at the person's cognitions as well as at the behavior itself. In applying cognitive-behavioral techniques, the goal is to identify the undesirable behaviors and their cognitive supports, and then design and implement learning experiences that will be effective in bringing about change. No one technique is likely to be effective for all individuals and all problematic health behaviors. Rather, the objective is to fit the technique to the person and the behavior. Further, two or more techniques will often be used simultaneously. This point is elaborated in the section on multimodal approaches.

Specific Techniques

Numerous techniques have been developed for behavior change. Those described here are ones that are particularly applicable to problematic health behaviors. Later chapters consider additional cognitive-behavioral techniques as they apply to other health issues such as stress reduction and pain control.

Respondent conditioning. As noted in Chapter 4, respondent learning is based on the principle that when two stimuli occur together on a repeated basis they come to elicit the same response. For example, if every time a child goes to the doctor he gets a shot, the child will eventually show the same aversion to simply going to the doctor that he does to getting the actual shot.

aversion therapy
The use of respondent conditioning to pair an undesirable health behavior with a noxious stimulus.

How might the principles of respondent conditioning be applied to changing health behavior? One application is the use of **aversion therapy,** that is, associating an undesirable health habit with a negative experience. For example, the drug Antabuse (disulfiram) causes unpleasant reactions such as nausea and vomiting when taken in conjunction with alcohol. Thus when a patient on Antabuse drinks alcohol it produces a highly aversive experience. Other aversion treatments for alcohol abuse include the pairing of electric shock with the sight, taste, and smell of alcoholic beverages and the use of other chemicals, such as emetine, to produce nausea, which is then paired with alcohol (Fuller et al., 1986; Nathan & Goldman, 1979).

How effective are such treatments? Antabuse is likely to keep the person from drinking while taking the drug. However, patient compliance is a major problem. Antabuse not only makes drinking highly unpleasant, but it also has its own side effects. Not surprisingly, patients often stop taking it at the first opportunity. Overall, treatment with Antabuse is only moderately effective in producing long-term behavior change (Fuller et al., 1986). Other aversion therapies also lose their effectiveness over time. Arthur Wiens and Carol Menustik (1983) found that although 63% of the alcoholics at one hospital who were treated with emetine stayed sober for one year, after three years the percentage had dropped to 31%.

Operant conditioning. Whereas respondent conditioning is concerned with the formation of associations between stimuli, operant conditioning focuses on the consequences of behavior, that is, the kinds of rewards and punishments that follow behavior. Behavior that is followed by rewards will increase in frequency, whereas behavior that results in no reward or is punished will decline. Beyond this, when behavior is rewarded in one situation but not another, the person will learn to discriminate between those situations, increasing the behavior in the situation where it is rewarded.

The principles of operant conditioning have been applied to health behavior in several ways. Probably the most straightforward application is the use of direct rewards to encourage positive health behaviors. For example, Adrian Lund and Stephen Kegeles (1982, 1984) used prizes (ranging in value from 10 cents to $5.00) to encourage schoolchildren to use a fluoride mouth rinse. Their studies have shown that although the rewards were quite effective in getting the children to use the mouth rinse, participation in the program dropped off considerably after the rewards were no longer given. Similar results were obtained by Michael Roberts and Debra Fanurik (1986) in their efforts to use rewards to encourage the use of seat belts. Seat belt usage was high when the rewards were given, but dropped off precipitously after the rewards were withdrawn.

contingency contracting
A treatment procedure in which the person contracts with the therapist or other person specifying the behavior change desired and the consequences for failure to adhere to those changes.

Another application of operant conditioning principles is the technique of **contingency contracting.** In contingency contracting, the person negotiates a contract with another person, often the therapist, specifying the desired behavior change along with the consequences for not reaching the goal. For example, Joanne, a smoker, might deposit a sum of money with her therapist with the instructions that if she remained smoke free for 6 months, she would get the money back. However, if she goes back to smoking during that period, the money would be donated to a specified charity. In effect, Joanne is making a bet with her therapist that she will be able to stop smoking, a bet with monetary consequences.

Does it work? Tim Wysocki and his colleagues (1979) used this technique to encourage physical exercise among college students. The participants deposited items of personal value with the experimenters and contracted to engage in a specified amount of aerobic exercise in the presence of another participant. Failure to fulfill the contract resulted in forfeiture of the items. Students entering into this contract significantly increased their exercise during the program and continued to show an increased level of exercise a year later. A note of caution is in order, however: a third of those in the program dropped out.

So far we have been concerned with the simple reward and punishment of behavior. **Stimulus control** focuses on the cues that become associated with particular behaviors. Smoking, for example, is often associated with specific situations, such as after-dinner conversation or the sight of cigarettes or an ashtray.

stimulus control
Arranging the environment so as to minimize or eliminate the stimuli that tend to trigger problem health behaviors.

Stimulus control aims at changing the person's environment so as to remove the cues that trigger the undesirable behavior. The person is encouraged to gradually reduce the range of stimuli that trigger the behavior until the behavior is eliminated. A stimulus control program for smokers, for instance, would encourage them to gradually reduce the situations in which they smoke, until all smoking takes place in a few well defined situations. After the number of smoking situations is reduced in this way, efforts would be made to eliminate the cues, such as ashtrays or packages of cigarettes, that remind the person of smoking.

Programs using stimulus control have been used to help people change such negative health habits as smoking (Bernstein & Glasgow, 1979; Leventhal & Cleary, 1980) and overeating (Leon, 1979); however, the results of these efforts have been mixed. Stimulus control does seem to help people to lose weight (cf. Leon, 1979; Stunkard, 1979), but its effectiveness with smoking appears limited. Although stimulus control procedures help smokers to cut down on their cigarette consumption, they tend to stabilize at about 10 to 12 cigarettes per day (Bernstein & Glasgow, 1979), but not really quit.

Modeling. Health habits, like other behaviors, are strongly influenced by the example of other people. For example, a recent study of automobile safety belt use found that passengers were two and a half times more likely to use seat belts when the driver used them than when the driver did not (Howell, Owen, & Nocks, 1990). Other studies have shown that exposure to heavy drinking models substantially increases alcohol consumption (Marlatt, 1979), and that the presence of parents, siblings, or peers who smoke makes it much more likely for a young person to begin smoking (Leventhal & Cleary, 1980; Ary & Biglan, 1988).

Since models can influence people in developing unhealthy habits, it stands to reason that they can also be useful in fostering positive health behaviors. The key would appear to be making sure that attractive models are available to model the desired behavior. An example of the use of models for this purpose is the Counseling Leadership Against Smoking Pressure (CLASP) program developed at Stanford University (McAlister, Perry, & Maccoby, 1979). In this program, attractive high school students served as nonsmoking models for junior high students. These models encouraged the junior high students to stay smoke free through their own example as well as by training them to resist peer pressures to use tobacco. What were the results of this program? At the end of two years, the schools with the CLASP program had only half as many smokers as did a control school without the program (McAlister, Perry, Killen, Slinkard, & Maccoby, 1980).

Modeling techniques are also used in the clinic. Such techniques can be particularly useful in helping people deal with fears and anxiety. As noted in Chapter 4, emotional factors, such as anxiety, can interfere with the practice of positive health habits and make it more likely that people will engage in negative health habits such as smoking and overeating. Reducing the person's anxiety, then, should make it more likely that the person will resist negative health behaviors and engage in positive ones. In the technique of **vicarious counterconditioning,** the patient observes the model repeatedly do something that the patient fears. Seeing the model do this without fear or negative consequences serves as reassurance to the patient that he too can do what he fears without harm. **Vicarious systematic desensitization,** also known as *contact desensitization,* is a related technique, in which the model successfully works through a hierarchy of anxiety-producing situations similar to situations that the patient fears. Watching the model do this then helps the patient deal with those situations (Bandura, 1969).

Modeling often plays a significant role in self-help approaches to problem health behaviors. For example, in Alcoholics Anonymous (AA) established members who have successfully dealt with their alcohol problems serve as models to new members who are just beginning their efforts.

Self-control. The methods described so far all require the intervention of an outside person, most often a therapist. This can be a significant disadvantage. For behavioral techniques to be successful in the long run requires that the behavior changes be internalized. It is all well and good for behavior to change in response to operant or respondent conditioning, but if the behavior change is limited to the treatment period, very little has been accomplished. Self-control techniques involve teaching people to monitor their own behavior and administer rewards and punishments on a self-determined schedule.

A critical first step in self-control is the process of **self-monitoring.** Before change procedures can be initiated, the person must be aware of the problem behavior and have some idea of the kinds of cues that trigger it. Indeed, it has been argued that a lack of conscious awareness of the specific acts in behaviors such as drinking may contribute to a person's difficulty in controlling the behavior (cf. Wegner, Vallacher, & Dizadji, 1989).

In self-monitoring, the person is taught to discriminate the actions in question and then to keep an ongoing record of when they occur and under what circumstances. For example, in his work with alcoholism, Alan Marlatt (1979) has developed a Daily Drinking Diary that requires the person to record any alcohol consumed during the day, along with the time and social and situational context in which it occurred. Similar techniques have been used with other problem health behaviors, such as overeating (Leon, 1979).

Although self-monitoring is primarily used as an initial step in a broader program of behavior change, the simple act of observing one's own behavior can have effects of its own. For example, studies using self-monitoring in programs for the control of smoking have found that having smokers record their tobacco usage results in a

vicarious counterconditioning
A treatment method for helping people deal with fear in which the patient repeatedly observes a model engaging in a feared behavior.

vicarious systematic desensitization
A treatment technique in which the patient observes a model successfully dealing with a hierarchy of anxiety-arousing situations.

self-monitoring
A self-control technique in which the person keeps detailed records of the behavior in question and the circumstances in which it occurs.

reduction in smoking. These changes tend to be small and transitory, but they do occur (Bernstein & Glasgow, 1979).

After the behavior has been charted and its relationship to triggering cues established, a second step is the specification of goals for change. These goals must be laid out carefully: they should focus on specific behaviors (as opposed to vague outcomes), be incremental, and be publicly stated (Mahoney & Arnkoff, 1979). For example, to lose weight one should select goals relating to specific behaviors such as eliminating between meal snacks, avoiding certain foods, and limiting calorie intake, rather than aiming to lose a certain number of pounds. Also one should set out a series of intermediate goals that can be achieved in reasonably short periods of time instead of focusing on the end result. A task with intermediate goals does not look so onerous, and the person can be rewarded by the successful achievement of each goal. In addition, announcing weight loss intentions to family or friends may elicit support in this effort.

self-reinforcement
A treatment tech-
nique in which the
person is trained to
give self-rewards for
desired behavior.

After appropriate goals are set, the person can use stimulus control and **self-re-inforcement** strategies to bring about the desired changes. For example, a person trying to lose weight should limit eating to particular places and times and be careful to remove cues, such as tempting desserts and other high-calorie foods, from the house. In addition, self-rewards can provide additional encouragement for attaining goals. Of course, one should be careful about the nature of the self-rewards. A hot fudge sundae would not be an appropriate self-reward for someone trying to lose weight. Finally, to maintain the behavior change, the person should rehearse the new behaviors and practice them consistently.

Self-control techniques would certainly seem to have many advantages, but do they work? The evidence suggests that they do. For example, Michael Mahoney and his colleagues (Mahoney, Moura, & Wade, 1973) used different self-control techniques to help overweight patients lose weight. As can be seen in Figure 5.1, patients who engaged only in self-monitoring showed more weight loss that did those in a control group, but somewhat less than those who used different forms of self-reinforcement. More important, the losses at the end of the program were not only maintained but enhanced at a 7-week follow-up.

Skills training. Among the barriers that people sometimes encounter in developing good health habits is a lack of social skills. People who lack skills in interacting with others and dealing with upsetting situations may well respond maladaptively by engaging in behavior that is deleterious to their health. For example, a person who has trouble dealing with interpersonal conflict may deal with the anxiety aroused by such conflicts through drinking alcohol. Another might deal with situations of loneliness by eating large amounts of food. In such situations, programs to encourage healthy behavior are likely to be stymied by the person's lack of social skills.

The objective of **skills training** is to foster positive health behaviors by teaching the person to identify personal and social needs and then develop the skills for meeting those needs (Tapp, 1985). The specific skills involved will, of course, depend on the person and the targeted behavior. A person who has difficulty dealing with an

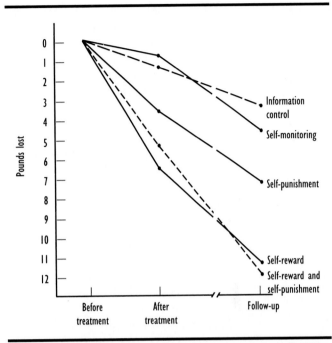

FIGURE 5.1
Weight loss using different self-management techniques.

Note. From "Self-management" by M. J. Mahoney and D. B. Arnkoff, 1979, in O. F. Pomerleau and J. P. Brady (Eds.), *Behavioral medicine: Theory and practice* (p. 90), Baltimore: Williams and Wilkins. Based on data from "The relative efficacy of self-reward, self-punishment, and self-monitoring techniques for weight loss" by M. J. Mahoney, N. G. M. Moura, and T. C. Wade, 1973, *Journal of Consulting and Clinical Psychology, 40,* 404–7. Reprinted by permission.

skills training
A treatment procedure in which the person is given training in dealing with interpersonal situations that tend to result in poor health behaviors and training for dealing with situations involving temptation.

overbearing boss would benefit by assertiveness training. Someone having difficulty in organizing daily activities needs training in time management (Everly, 1984).

How might this be applied to a specific problem health behavior? One example comes from work with alcoholics. In one study, male alcoholics assigned to a skills training treatment met biweekly in eight 90-minute sessions. During these sessions, they worked with therapists to develop skills in dealing with situations that tended to trigger drinking, such as those involving anger or social pressure to drink. In each session, patients were taught a general problem-solving orientation to deal with a particular situation and were then encouraged to generate their own coping strategies. Evaluation of this program showed that in comparison to patients in two control conditions, patients receiving the skills training were significantly better able to control their drinking (Marlatt, 1979).

Multimodal approaches. One strong advantage to having a variety of different methods is the ability to pick and choose among the available techniques to select ones that fit the particular person and target behavior. As noted earlier, individual techniques are usually not used in isolation, but are combined in a multifaceted treatment.

multimodal approach
A treatment approach that combines the use of several different techniques.

For example, to deal with her weight problem Silvia might first engage in self-monitoring to gain an understanding of her eating habits and the cues that trigger overeating. Next, she might go through a program of skills training to help her work through distressing interpersonal relationships that contribute to her overeating. After she has developed the needed social skills, she might enter into a contingency contract in which she deposits money with a therapist or other person that will be returned as she meets specific goals for eating habits and weight loss. The final phase might involve training in self-control techniques that she can use following the termination of her therapy. This ability to mix and match techniques depending on the patient and the behavior vastly increases the likelihood of success in changing the behavior and maintaining that change over time.

The Problem of Relapse

Throughout our discussion, we have been concerned not only with changing health behaviors but also with maintaining that change over time. How big a problem is backsliding or relapse? The evidence suggests that it may well be one of the major obstacles to successful risk reduction. Tabulation of the proportion of people who return to destructive health habits after treatment show that more than 75% of those who successfully stop behaviors such as smoking, drinking, or drug usage during a given treatment will start up again within a year (Hunt, Barnett, & Ranch, 1971). The size of the relapse problem is shown graphically in Figure 5.2.

Alan Marlatt (1985) has developed a program of relapse prevention based on principles of self-control, which aims at increasing the person's awareness of choice among behaviors and helping the person develop the coping skills needed to deal with possible relapse situations. Therefore, it is a multimodal program that emphasizes helping clients to identify possible relapse situations and then develop the skills necessary to get through those situations without slipping. For example, to help Harry stay sober, a therapist following Marlatt's relapse prevention program would have Harry engage in self-monitoring to identify situations in which he is most likely to be tempted to return to drinking. Once these are identified, the therapist would work with Harry to develop the skills that he needs to cope with those situations and stay sober. The techniques that might be used run the gamut of those available in the cognitive-behavioral approach. Although it has been somewhat neglected in efforts to foster good health behaviors, the prevention of relapse is clearly a critical ingredient in bringing about long-term changes in health behaviors.

PUTTING ATTITUDE AND BEHAVIOR CHANGE PRINCIPLES TO WORK

With these principles as background, the next question is how best to put them to work in changing health attitudes and behaviors. Might physician recommendations to patients be effective in bringing about change? What about using the mass media for altering health attitudes and behaviors? Might schools or work places be good sites

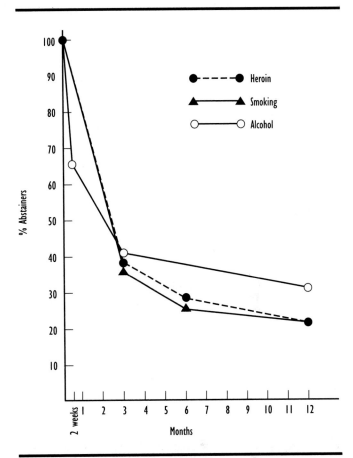

FIGURE 5.2
Relapse rates in the treatment of addictive behaviors.

Note. From "Relapse rates in addiction programs" by W. A. Hunt, L. W. Barnett, and L. G. Ranch, 1971, *Journal of Clinical Psychology, 27* (p. 456). Copyright 1971 by Clinical Psychology Co., Inc. Reprinted by permission.

for influencing people? Attempts have been made to use all these channels to promote good health. As we shall see, each has its particular strengths and liabilities.

Appeals by Physicians

The prestige of doctors and their expertise in health matters would seem to make the doctor's office an ideal place for promoting healthy behavior. And, indeed, there is evidence that a simple appeal to patients from their physicians can have a significant impact on behavior. For example, a group of researchers in London found that having British doctors give brief but firm advice to their smoking patients to stop smoking resulted in a significant increase in the number of smokers who gave up cigarettes (Russell, Wilson, Taylor, & Baker, 1979). Although such results are hopeful, they must be kept in perspective. Among those given advice to stop smoking only 3% to 5%

remained smoke free after a year. Although this is higher than the number who stopped smoking without advice from the doctor (0.3% to 1.6%), it is still a rather low percentage. Also, studies of patient cooperation with medical recommendations in general show that patients often do not understand or remember instructions given to them by their physicians or may simply disregard them (DiMatteo & DiNicola, 1982). Some of the reasons for this and possible remedies are discussed in Chapter 9. However, we must not discount the potential effects of physician appeals. Even though only 3% to 5% of those advised to stop smoking by their doctors actually did, the authors point out, if every physician were able to persuade even this percentage of patients to stop, the cumulative effect would be greater than would vastly increasing the number of specialized smoking clinics (Russell et al., 1979).

Health Promotion in the Clinic

If simple recommendations from a physician lead to relatively small changes in health behaviors, might better results be obtained through the application in clinics of some of the psychological and behavioral techniques described above? In some ways, such an approach would seem to have advantages. It certainly makes sense to take techniques that show promise in research studies and apply them on a wider clinical scale. By working with individual patients, the clinician is able to tailor the intervention to the specific person and problem health behavior. In addition, the bond developed in the one-on-one interaction between therapist and patient may increase the likelihood of success.

clinical health promotion
The application of health promotion principles in a clinical setting.

Clinical health promotion involves a variety of techniques including biofeedback, operant conditioning techniques, cognitive methods, stress management, and social skills training (cf. Tapp, 1985). There is no doubt that these methods can work. For example, operant conditioning approaches to obesity have generally been quite successful in helping people to lose weight (cf. Stunkard, 1979). Behavioral treatments to help people stop smoking have reported success rates as high as 90% (cf. Leventhal & Cleary, 1980).

Although such results are certainly encouraging, clinical interventions also have their drawbacks. For one thing, success rates likely to be touted are those for the short-term. Long-term success rates are often much lower. For example, the percentage of smokers who remain smoke free one year after treatment is often in the range of 10% to 25% (Leventhal & Cleary, 1980). Drop-out rates, often reaching 50%, are also a problem. Finally, although the one-on-one relationship between therapist and patient may help bring about behavior change, using it as a means for bringing about behavior changes would be inefficient on a larger scale. These considerations, along with those discussed in Box 5.1, suggest that although clinical health promotion can be effective, it can also easily be oversold.

Mass Media Appeals

Another means of influencing people's attitudes and health behaviors that would seem promising is through the mass media. In modern technological societies, there are few people who are not touched in one way or another by television, radio, newspapers, and other mass media. Surveys have found, for example, that in a typical American

BOX 5.1   Clinical Health Promotion: Some Notes of Caution

Clinical health promotion assumes that the application of psychological and behavioral principles to change health behaviors will result in improved health and well-being for the clients. Evidence certainly shows that this can be the case, but there is also a danger in promising more than we can deliver. For example, Robert Kaplan (1984) describes a telephone conversation between a psychologist and an endocrinologist in which the psychologist declared that diabetes could be "cured" through stress inoculation training. Another psychologist claimed in a newspaper advertisement that genital herpes could be controlled through psychotherapy. Such claims clearly go well beyond the effects demonstrated by controlled research and could discredit the efforts of health psychologists as a group.

Kaplan strongly urges that health psychologists applying the principles of health psychology to clinical health promotion recall that our ultimate aim is to improve health (as opposed to simply reducing presumed risk factors) and that we confine our claims to

those that can be clearly supported through research. In this regard, we must carefully examine the assumptions behind the interventions and critically evaluate their likely effects on health. For example, considerable effort has been devoted to changing dietary habits in the hope of reducing the number of deaths from coronary heart disease. The primary focus of such interventions is the reduction of serum cholesterol levels. Although serum cholesterol has been shown to be related to heart disease, the mechanisms are far from simple, and there is considerable question as to whether dietary changes will, in fact, reduce coronary risk. Beyond this, there is the question of cost effectiveness. Psychologists often assume that behavioral interventions are cost effective even though, to date, evidence is inconclusive.

Kaplan is certainly not trying to discourage clinical health promotion efforts. Rather, he is urging us to be wary of undue enthusiasm and carefully evaluate our interventions before we offer them.

home the television is on for an average of six hours a day and that on any given day 65% of Americans will watch television. Children are particularly likely to be television viewers; by high school graduation, the average child has be estimated to have spent nearly twice as many hours watching television as in school itself (cf. Lau, Kane, Berry, Ware, & Roy, 1980). Such statistics demonstrate a vast potential for using television and other mass media to influence health habits.

Given this potential, it is disappointing to find that research on the effects of mass media campaigns show relatively weak effects. Review of the effects of televised health campaigns (Lau et al., 1980) shows that television campaigns usually have little or no measurable effect on people's health attitudes and behaviors. For example, attempts to use public service announcements (PSAs) to influence seat belt use (Robertson et al., 1974), family planning behavior (Kline, Miller, & Morrison, 1974), and alcohol and drug abuse (Morrison, Kline, & Miller, 1976) have failed.

Some campaigns, however, have been successful—generally, those that provided extensive information over an extended period of time. A good example of this is the Stanford Three Community Study, an ambitious project aimed at reducing coronary risk (Farquhar et al., 1977; Maccoby, Farquhar, Wood, & Alexander, 1977). This three-year project selected three small California cities for study and involved systematic evaluation of coronary risk factors at the beginning of the study, as well as at the end of each of the following three years. Tracy was selected as a control city; it received no health information other than that routinely presented through the media. The researchers mounted a two-year multimedia campaign in Gilroy that included more than 50 spot announcements, several hours of radio programs in addition to over 100 radio spots, and weekly newspaper columns, as well as mailings to inform people about coronary risk and how it could be reduced. This media campaign was repeated in Watsonville, where it was supplemented with intensive face-to-face instruction. Over the three years of the study, coronary risk for those at high risk for heart disease declined in all three cities with a significantly greater decline in the two experimental cities (see Figure 5.3). The greatest reduction was obtained in Watsonville, which received the media campaign plus intensive instruction. Interestingly, different risk factors showed different effects from the interventions. The largest effects were found for consumption of high-cholesterol foods and smoking, whereas weight loss was unaffected.

Why are mass media appeals so variable in their results? Many reasons could be cited. Although the mass media are ubiquitous, the number and variety of programs

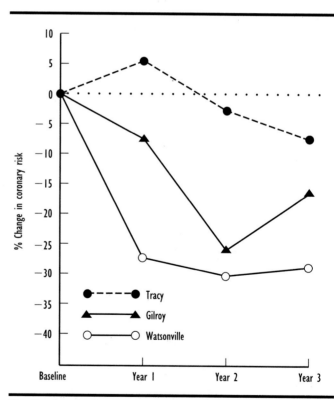

FIGURE 5.3

Changes in coronary risk for high-risk individuals in three California cities.

Note. Based on data from "Promoting positive health behaviors in adults" by N. Maccoby, 1980, in L. A. Bond and J. C. Rosen (Eds.), *Competence and coping during adulthood* (p. 213), Hanover, NH: University Press of New England.

Televised health messages are not likely to have large effects individually but can have a considerable cumulative effect.

and messages available mean that any particular message is likely to reach only a very small percentage of the population. Thus only campaigns that are extensive and intensive are likely to reach large numbers of people. Just because a message arrives in people's homes does not mean that it is actually received. People are very adept at "tuning out" messages that they are uninterested in or that present unwelcome information. As was noted in our discussion of the persuasion process, reception of a message does not guarantee understanding, acceptance, or action. Beyond this, health messages in the media compete with an often greater number of advertisements promoting unhealthy behaviors such as smoking and drinking.

Overall, the primary value in mass media appeals apparently lies in their cumulative effects. Although individual media messages and campaigns may have relatively weak effects, the summation of multiple messages over time can be quite impressive. A good example of this is the effect of antismoking messages. In a study of per capita cigarette consumption from 1947 to 1975, Kenneth Warner (1977) found that antismoking messages such as reports of smoking health scares in the 1950s, the Surgeon General's report on smoking and antismoking commercials in the late 1960s were each associated with an immediate, though transitory, 4% to 5% decrease in cigarette consumption. According to Warner's analysis, without these events annual cigarette consumption would have been 20% to 30% higher by 1975 than it actually was. Although each message produced a relatively small change in smoking, the cumulative effects were substantial.

Promoting Health in the Schools

By their nature, schools provide an ideal setting for promoting positive health behavior. Childhood is the time when many lifelong behavior patterns are being formed, and the amount of time children spend in the classroom makes school settings attractive as an intervention site. Thus many have called for comprehensive health education in the schools (cf. Kolbe & Iverson, 1984). Such programs would help children to understand personal and societal health issues, and increase their competency to make informed decisions about behaviors that affect health.

How effective are school-based health promotion programs? The evidence is promising, but questions still remain. For example, Richard Evans and his colleagues (Evans, 1984) have developed school-based smoking prevention programs targeted at junior high school students. Based on attitude change principles, Evans and his coworkers developed a series of films to present students with the facts about smoking and to help them deal with social pressures to smoke. An important feature of these films is that they were specifically geared to a young adolescent audience, using attractive adolescent narrators and language geared to the audience's level of comprehension. The results of this effort have been encouraging. Over a three-year period, students participating in this program were significantly less likely to begin smoking than were nonparticipants. Another good example of school-based health promotion programs is the CLASP program described earlier. In spite of the impressive results of such programs, questions have been raised about their long-term success. For example, follow-up of the participants in four smoking prevention strategies found that the programs had little residual effect after five to six years (Murray, Pirie, Luepker, & Pallonen, 1989).

Health Promotion in the Work Place

Whereas schools provide a seemingly ideal location for promoting health in children, the work place has considerable potential for encouraging good health habits in adults. Working adults spend a great deal of time at their places of work. Thus the work place has a large captive audience that can potentially be influenced to adopt positive health habits. From an employer's point of view, there are some strong economic, not to mention humanitarian, reasons for promoting healthy living. The annual costs of preventable disease run into the hundreds of billions of dollars, including the direct costs of disease treatment and indirect costs from lost productivity, absenteeism, and employee turnover. Employers end up paying the lion's share of these costs (Fielding, 1984), so they stand to benefit from reducing them.

Recent years have witnessed a veritable explosion of health promotion programs in the work place. Programs range in size from a few lectures on a health topic such as nutrition or exercise to extensive programs involving large, well-staffed exercise and health facilities. In a survey of California employers, the most frequent health promotion activities were accident prevention, cardiovascularpulmonary resuscitation (CPR), and choke saver. Alcohol and drug abuse programs as well as hypertension screening, smoking cessation, fitness, and stress management programs were also offered (Fielding & Breslow, 1983).

How successful are these programs? Good data are hard to find, but those available suggest that such programs can be very successful. For example, preliminary data from Johnson & Johnson's "Live for Life" program indicate a 43% increase in employee physical fitness, along with a 15% reduction in the number of smokers, a 32% reduction in the number of employees with high blood pressure, and a 9% reduction in sick days (Wilbur, 1982, cited in Fielding, 1984).

But work place health promotion programs are not without their caveats. First, simply setting up a program does not ensure success. Jonathan Fielding (1984) contends that success in such programs requires long-term commitment, top management support, employee involvement, professional leadership, and strong and continuing promotional efforts. Second, as Richard Sloan (1987) has argued, current work place health promotion programs have inherent limitations. By focusing on changes in individual health behaviors, such programs overlook organizational factors, such as work stress, exposure to toxic substances, and the use of hazardous equipment and procedures, that can significantly affect employee health.

Self-help Groups

The discussion above considers programs that generally rely on professionals to assist in bringing about behavior change. What about programs in which people with problem health behaviors help themselves and others with similar problems? Interest in self-help groups for a variety of problems, including chronic illness, grief, alcoholism, and weight problems, has dramatically increased in recent years (cf. Borman, Borck, Hess, & Pasquale, 1982; Gartner & Riessman, 1984). All these groups are based on the idea that no one is better able to help another with a problem than someone who has experienced that problem firsthand. Further, by helping others the helper is also helped. This is what Alan Gartner and Frank Riessman (1984) call the "helper-therapy" principle. The group plays a critical role in providing its members with support, reinforcement, sanctions, and feedback. Thus it enhances the power of the individual members to deal with the problem.

The most prominent self-help groups in health promotion are those concerned with appetitive or addictive behaviors such as eating problems and drug and alcohol abuse. Examples are Alcoholics Anonymous (AA), Take Off Pounds Sensibly (TOPS), Overeaters Anonymous, and Smokenders. How effective are these groups? Given the nature of the groups (many are, after all, "anonymous"), there are few hard figures. The available data are mixed. For example, although one study of AA reported a 75% success rate (Tiebout, 1944, cited in Robinson, 1979), another more carefully controlled study found a 68% dropout rate (Brandsma, Maultsby, & Welch, 1980). Thus self-help groups may be effective in helping people alter negative health behaviors, but current empirical evidence is inconclusive.

Targeting Whole Communities

Several of the approaches already described have been aimed at specific segments of the population such as schoolchildren, adult employees, or participants in self-help groups. What about health promotion programs that target entire communities? Might there be advantages to developing programs that can be applied across the board to everyone living in a particular area? The answer is clearly yes. Stephen Weiss (1984) points out several advantages for community-based prevention programs. For one thing, such programs use prevention methods that apply to the environments in which people live. One problem with programs limited to the clinic, work place, or school is that the person's behavior might be effectively changed in that setting, but the change may not generalize to other environments. Because members of the target population all live in the same community, community-based programs enhance opportunities for information exchange and social support among program participants. Further, because of their scale, community-based programs can minimize the per capita cost.

By their nature, community-based interventions are complex undertakings. To be comprehensive and effective, such programs typically involve multiple channels such as mass media campaigns, work place programs, health education programs in the schools, physician appeals, and face-to-face counseling (cf. Kittel, 1984; Lasater et al., 1984; Puska, 1984). An example of a comprehensive community-based prevention program is described in Box 5.2.

Are such programs effective? Given their complexity and the difficulty of establishing appropriate comparison groups, accurate evaluation of these programs is difficult. However, there is accumulating evidence that well designed programs are quite effective. A good example is the North Karelia Project in Finland (Puska, 1984). Begun in 1972, this program was a multidimensional health education effort aimed at reducing coronary risk in the Finnish county of North Karelia. This effort included the development of educational materials on coronary risk, as well as training in the skills needed to bring about healthy behavior changes and the mobilization of social support to maintain those changes. In addition, environmental changes were introduced, such as smoking restrictions and reductions in the fat content of foods available in the local stores. These efforts appear to have paid off. In the first five years of the project, significant reductions were obtained in smoking, cholesterol levels, and blood pressure. Overall, coronary risk for males was reduced by 17%, whereas risk for women declined 11%. More important, death rates from coronary heart disease showed a significant decline.

ADDRESSING SPECIFIC HEALTH BEHAVIOR PROBLEMS

So far we have considered the processes that determine people's health behavior and some of the basic techniques available for influencing those behaviors. We are now ready to take up the application of these principles to specific health behavior problems. The sections that follow consider alcohol abuse, weight control, and exercise—only a small sampling of problem health behaviors. Discussions of specific health problems in later chapters will consider other problem health behaviors such as diet, smoking, and risky sexual behavior.

Alcohol Abuse

Data on the consumption of alcoholic beverages indicate that the use and abuse of alcohol is widespread throughout the world. Alcohol consumption differs significantly between countries, but all countries have at least some individuals who drink to excess

BOX 5.2 **Community Health Promotion: The Pennsylvania County Health Improvement Program**

Intensive large-scale efforts are required to meet the challenges of effective health promotion. At the same time, limited resources demand that such interventions be cost effective. With these considerations in mind, the Pennsylvania County Health Improvement Program (CHIP) was initiated as a multiple risk factor, multiple channel intervention aimed at reducing coronary risk in Lycoming County, Pennsylvania.

Based on the extensive literature about coronary risk factors, CHIP planners selected five risk factors for intervention: elevated cholesterol levels, hypertension, smoking, physical inactivity, and excess body weight. To reduce these risk factors, interventions were then selected that targeted the detection and control of hypertension, smoking cessation, exercise, weight loss, and dietary changes.

A key aspect of CHIP is the active participation of the community in the planning and execution of the program. Early in the planning process, a Steering Committee was established consisting of key community leaders and leading local medical practitioners. The involvement of these community opinion leaders helped to pave the way for acceptance of the program and its interventions.

In order to have maximum impact, CHIP uses five channels to convey its message. First, the mass media in Lycoming County have played a vital role in introducing CHIP to the community and helping to establish its credibility; the mass media also disseminate information about heart disease risk reduction, mostly through articles and columns in the newspapers as well as radio programs on health.

The second major channel has been the work site. Employers in Lycoming County have been encouraged to support CHIP by developing their own health promotion programs for employees. During the first three years of CHIP, 58 different health promotion programs were begun through work sites employing 3,800 individuals. Key features of these programs include the sense of program ownership developed among employees involved and the amount of creativity displayed by employees implementing the programs. For example, weight loss competitions were organized both within and between companies.

Health care providers are the third channel. Because of their prestige in the community and credibility in health matters, physicians and other health care providers play a central role in encouraging good health behaviors. Local physicians have been critical in both hypertension control and smoking cessation in CHIP.

Schools and voluntary organizations are the final two channels used by CHIP. An antismoking curriculum based on the successful CLASP program by McAlister et al. (1979) was implemented in the junior high schools to prevent young people from beginning smoking, and educational programs concerning hypertension and nutrition were planned. Planner hope that these interventions will influence not only the health behaviors of the children but will also have an influence on the parents' behavior through the children. Finally, voluntary organizations, such as social, fraternal, and religious organizations, were contacted and mobilized in the program. These groups were encouraged to motivate behavior change through special events and to provide social support for maintaining healthy behaviors.

The long-range goal of CHIP is to reduce coronary risk factors to the point that coronary morbidity and mortality show a measurable decrease. Although the final results are not yet in, preliminary data indicate that CHIP has been successful in nearly doubling the number of health promotion programs in Lycoming County. Additional details about CHIP can be found in Stunkard, Felix, and Cohen (1985).

(Sournia, 1990). Surveys in the United States indicate that nearly two thirds of adult Americans drink alcoholic beverages, with 8% indicating that they are heavy drinkers and 22% labeling themselves as moderate drinkers (National Center for Health Statistics, 1989). Along with tobacco, alcohol consumption is a major source of disease

*Alcohol use is closely
related to homicides
and suicides as well as
to traffic deaths.*

and death. Although some evidence indicates that the consumption of moderate amounts of alcohol may, in fact, be beneficial to one's health (cf. Klatsky, Friedman, & Siegelaub, 1981), the extended heavy drinking of alcohol and the consumption of alcohol under certain circumstances can produce serious health effects, including cirrhosis of the liver, gastrointestinal problems, cardiovascular problems, lung disease, and neurological problems. Among the latter is the Wernicke-Korsakoff Syndrome, a psychotic condition characterized by severe memory deficits and confusion, as well as visual and movement difficulties. One of the most heart wrenching effects of alcohol use is the Fetal Alcohol Syndrome (FAS), in which the consumption of alcohol by a woman during pregnancy can lead to serious health problems for the child, including growth deficiencies, central nervous system difficulties, facial abnormalities, and mental retardation (Benzer, 1987).

In addition to these direct medical complications of alcohol use, the consumption of alcohol also has many indirect effects. For example, 50% of all traffic deaths in the United States are estimated to be alcohol related, as are 30% of suicides and 50% of homicides. The abuse of alcohol cost the American economy nearly $117 billion dollars in 1983, in direct costs of treatment and indirect costs including lost time, crime, and motor vehicle accidents (National Institute on Alcohol Abuse and Alcoholism, 1987).

alcoholism
Compulsive, addictive, or habitual consumption of alcohol that poses a serious threat to the person's well-being.

What causes alcoholism? Alcoholism generally refers to alcohol consumption that is compulsive, addictive, or habitual, and results in serious threat to a person's health and well-being. Of the roughly two-thirds of the American population that consumes alcoholic beverages, between 5 million and 15 million individuals are estimated to be alcoholics (cf. Marlatt, 1979). What is it that leads to alcoholism? Why are so many people able to consume alcohol in small or moderate quantities, while others become alcoholic?

The causes of alcoholism have been hotly debated for a long time. Probably the most popular theory is that alcoholism is a disease (Gitlow, 1973; Jellinek, 1960). According to this model, the alcoholic somehow differs from others who consume alcohol. Although most people can control their drinking, the alcoholic cannot. After a drink or two, the alcoholic experiences a physiological addictive response triggered by the alcohol consumed, which leads to an irresistible craving for more alcohol. The person is then unable to stop drinking until intoxication occurs or the person runs out of alcohol to drink. Alcoholics Anonymous (AA) is one of the best known and chief proponents of this view. According to the AA philosophy, the alcoholic is completely powerless over alcohol, and alcoholism can never be cured but only controlled. In this view, the only way an alcoholic can stay in control is never to have another drink (Robinson, 1979).

Despite its popularity, the disease model of alcoholism has been seriously criticized by several alcoholism researchers (cf. Marlatt, 1979; Peele, 1984). Among the criticisms are that the disease model does not address the question of why people drink or adequately describe the process by which a person becomes an alcoholic. Further, it does not explain how it is that many problem drinkers cease their problem drinking without treatment (more than 50% in some studies) or account for alcoholics who learn to drink in a controlled manner (Marlatt, 1983; Peele, 1984).

Whereas the disease model seeks the causes of alcoholism in the biological makeup of the person, the social learning model looks to the social environment. According to this model, alcoholism is a learned addictive behavior that can be understood through the principles of social learning and cognitive psychology. Thus the emphasis is on the determinants of drinking and the consequences that alcohol consumption has for the person. Several studies have provided evidence that drinking patterns are related to the person's social environment. For example, parental drinking and drinking by peers are significantly related to whether an adolescent begins drinking (Hansen et al., 1987; Monti, Abrams, Kadden, & Cooney, 1989). In addition, as we saw earlier, the amount that a person drinks in a particular situation can be significantly influenced by the drinking behavior of a model (Marlatt, 1979). Beyond this, there is also evidence that the likelihood of becoming an alcoholic is increased if the person has a history of deviant behavior and lacks the social skills for dealing with distressing situations (Monti et al., 1989; Zucker & Gomberg, 1986).

Treating alcohol abuse. Many techniques have been developed for dealing with alcohol abuse, each of which has its proponents. Among the techniques are medical intervention, self-help groups, aversion therapy, psychotherapy, self-control techniques, and skills training. The most common approach combines several of these into a multimodal program that attempts to fit the therapy to the specific patient.

Depending on the length and severity of alcohol abuse, detoxification may be necessary. Alcoholics who have been drinking heavily for some time are likely to experience withdrawal symptoms that may range from relatively mild to severe. These

symptoms include such reactions as irritability, restlessness, hyperventilation, para-
noid reactions, severe confusion, and outright hallucinations (delirium tremens or
DTs). Although the more serious reactions occur in a minority of alcoholics, they
require medical observation and intervention (Schuckit, 1989).

Self-help groups are among the oldest and most widely used methods for treating
alcoholism. Alcoholics Anonymous, founded in 1935, is the best known of the
self-help groups and has thousands of chapters throughout the world. As noted before,
AA is a strong proponent of the disease model of alcoholism. AA members believe that
the only way to deal with alcoholism is through complete abstinence. Central to this
program are the "twelve steps," in which members admit their powerlessness over
alcohol, acknowledge their dependence on God, ask for help in overcoming their
personal defects, and commit themselves to righting past wrongs and living a new life.
AA members also subscribe to a philosophy that the person who is best able to help
an alcoholic is another alcoholic. During AA meetings, members relate their drinking
problems, how they are dealing with them, and provide support for others who are
attempting to stay sober (cf. Robinson, 1979).

Aversion therapy is also used in treating alcoholics. Based on the principles of
classical conditioning, this therapy pairs the consumption of alcohol with an aversive
experience such as nausea and gagging. Drugs such as emetine are commonly used;
electric shock has also been employed, even though it has generally proved ineffective.
Aversion therapy drugs have been shown to be moderately effective in treating alcohol
abuse, but "booster" sessions are often required to maintain the association between
alcohol consumption and nausea and vomiting. In most treatments, aversion therapy
is not used alone, but rather as part of a comprehensive treatment plan (cf. National
Institute on Alcohol Abuse and Alcoholism, 1987).

Since alcoholics often have personal problems in addition to their abuse of alcohol,
psychotherapy is often included in the treatment program. The type of psychotherapy
used depends on the orientation of the therapist. Virtually every kind of psychotherapy
has been used, including individual and group methods (National Institute on Alcohol
Abuse and Alcoholism, 1987). The basic goal of psychotherapeutic treatment is to help
the person come to grips with personal conflicts and deal more effectively with
problems that are associated with alcohol abuse. The effectiveness of psychotherapeutic methods has been a matter of some debate. Some studies report success rates in the
range of 65% to 80% after one year (Brownell, 1982), but questions have been raised
about the methods often used to assess outcome. Chad Emrick and Joel Hansen (1983)
point out that such factors as patient selection and attrition, other therapies received
by the patients outside of the study, the timing of the evaluation, and criteria for success
significantly affect outcome figures. When these factors are carefully accounted for,
success figures are often somewhat lower than they first appear.

In addition to these techniques, self-control and social skills training play a
significant role in treating alcoholism. One of the first steps in treatment is often
self-monitoring, in which the person is required to keep a running record of drinking
behavior and its relationship to social and situational cues. This provides the therapist
and the patient with information about the amount and type of drinking taking place
and the events that seem to trigger it. Contingency contracting is also sometimes used,

in which specific consequences are agreed upon for continued drinking. However, such procedures do not seem to be particularly effective (Nathan & Goldman, 1979). Skills training does appear to be effective: the person is taught to deal with situations that cause distress and are likely to lead to a relapse in drinking. Among the skills commonly taught are those relating to communication, giving and receiving criticism, drink refusal, and problem solving (Monti et al., 1989).

Obesity and Weight Control

Obesity is another extremely common health risk. More than one fourth of all Americans are estimated to be overweight. Problems with weight generally increase with age, particularly for women, and are worse for minorities. Nearly half of all black women are considered overweight (National Center for Health Statistics, 1989). In addition, the "battle of the bulge" is being lost. There is evidence, for example, that from the 1960s to the 1970s the average weight for American women (controlling for height) went up 13 pounds, while the average weight for men increased nearly 10 pounds (Thompson, Jarvie, Lahey, & Cureton, 1982). Of all of the New Year's resolutions that people make, probably the most common is to lose some weight.

There is good reason to be concerned about the number of people who are overweight. Epidemiological evidence has long demonstrated that obesity is associated with an increased likelihood of death and is a risk factor for many diseases (cf. Bray, 1984). For example, men who are 5% to 15% overweight are 25% more likely to die of diabetes than are men at or near their ideal weight. Death rates are five times as high for men more than 25% overweight. Similar patterns are obtained for heart disease, coronary artery disease, and digestive diseases. The risks are particularly great for individuals who are grossly overweight. In one group of young obese men with an average weight of over 300 pounds, death rates were up to 12 times that of the general population (Bray, 1984). In addition to an increased likelihood of death, obesity is also a risk factor for hypertension, heart disease, gallbladder disease, diabetes, and kidney problems.

Obesity also has social and psychological costs. Obese individuals tend to be rated as less likeable, are at a disadvantage in dating relationships, get lower grades, earn less, and are generally the subject of negative social attitudes (Bray, 1984; Crandall & Biernat, 1990). Not surprisingly, individuals who are obese often have problems with self-esteem and depression, and become preoccupied with their weight (Wilson, 1984; Wolman, 1982).

What leads to obesity? Although it is tempting to take the view that obesity is simply a result of overeating, current evidence shows that this view is far oversimplified (Rodin, 1981). In fact, people who are overweight often do *not* eat more than their thin counterparts. Rather than being a simple result of overeating, obesity is a complex phenomenon involving both biological and behavioral factors (Rodin, 1982; Shah & Jeffery, 1991).

To begin with, twin studies contain evidence of a genetic basis for obesity. Obesity tends to run in families, and obese parents often have obese children. Thus from the beginning, some people apparently have more potential to become fat than do others.

This potential for obesity may then be built upon by maternal as well as childhood eating habits. Although the evidence is still sketchy, Ruth Striegel-Moore and Judith Rodin speculate that "maternal nutrition and hormonal changes during pregnancy influence fetal taste responsiveness by altering the composition of amniotic fluid" (1985, p. 79). In addition, both the number and the size of a person's fat cells are influenced by childhood eating habits. When a child is obese, fat cells increase in both size and number, making it more likely that he or she will become an obese adult. Overeating during adulthood increases the size but not the number of fat cells. These considerations indicate the importance of preventing obesity in childhood (Epstein & Wing, 1987).

Once a person becomes obese, the body begins to play some dirty tricks. Evidence has shown that the fatter a person is, the fatter he or she is likely to become. First, as a person grows fatter, the size of the fat cells increases, as does their ability to make and store fat. Second, with increased weight, a person's basal insulin level tends to go up. As the person's basal insulin level rises, so does the ability to store fat. Increased insulin also tends to increase feelings of hunger and thus to promote overeating. To compound matters, when a person is obese, fewer calories are necessary to maintain body weight. In one study, subjects who were forcefed from normal weight to 10% above their ideal weight required up to twice as many calories to maintain that weight as did subjects who entered the study obese (Lukert, 1982). In addition, obese individuals tend to be less active, so they use up fewer of their calories in energy expenditures, thus leaving them to accumulate in fat cells. Finally, the emotional stress of being fat in a thin-oriented society can lead obese individuals to be even more likely to overeat (Rodin, 1982).

The obvious way to stop this cycle would seem to be to recommend going on a diet, but it turns out that diets themselves may exacerbate the problem. One of the effects of decreased food intake is that the body adjusts itself to require fewer calories, an effect that seems to be increased with additional diets. Some researchers have argued that the human body has a *set point* for weight. Deviations above this level, which is specific to each person, will trigger responses to bring the person's weight down to the set point. A loss of body fat, however, will trigger responses such as hunger and metabolic slowdown to increase body weight (Bennett & Gurin, 1982; Stallone & Stunkard, 1991).

Treating obesity. Obesity is thus a very difficult condition to treat. In many respects, the problem is not so much taking weight off as it is keeping it off. Anyone who has ever dieted to lose weight knows this. The measure of weight reduction plan's effectiveness is not the amount that the participants lose initially, but rather the amount that stays off over a period of months or years.

There are basically two ways to fight "the battle of the bulge." One can reduce the number of calories consumed or increase the number of calories expended. Many methods have been attempted for reducing caloric intake, some of them rather extreme. In some cases of morbid obesity (obesity that is a clear danger to the person's health), surgical techniques have been used, such as stomach stapling or removal of a portion of the small intestine. In stomach stapling, for example, portions of the stomach are literally stapled together surgically to reduce the stomach's overall capacity and thus the amount that the person can eat. Another technique is to wire the patient's jaws closed so as to curtail food intake. Such methods are effective in producing weight loss; however, their extremity and potentially serious side effects limit their use to cases of severe obesity (Garrow, 1988).

More commonly, people attempt to lose weight through some form of diet, which aims at altering food intake so as to reduce the number of calories. A walk through any bookstore will give an idea of the variety of potential diet plans available. Authors of these plans recommend everything from low-carbohydrate to single-food diets, with a variety of other strategems in between. Although some of these plans may prove helpful for some individuals, the amount of weight lost is usually disappointing, and all too often it comes right back (Bennett & Gurin, 1982). The main beneficiaries of these programs are generally their authors.

Greater success has been obtained with cognitive-behavioral methods for changing people's eating habits. As noted in the discussion of cognitive-behavioral methods above, several techniques can be applied to the problem of weight control. Cognitive-behavioral weight loss programs typically use many different procedures to help the person change dietary habits so as to lose weight. Rather than attempting to produce quick and dramatic losses, these programs emphasize gradual weight loss (1 to 2 pounds per week), in the assumption that this will reduce the likelihood of increased hunger and make it more likely that behavioral changes will be successfully integrated in the person's life-style (Wilson, 1984).

A typical cognitive-behavioral program for weight reduction includes a combination of operant conditioning, self-control, and cognitive restructuring, in which the person learns to control self-defeating thoughts about dieting and weight control (Abramson, 1982). A first step is likely to involve self-monitoring to obtain a clear picture of the person's eating patterns, along with the circumstances associated with eating. This might then be followed by the use of either reinforcement or self-control techniques for altering eating behavior. For example, contingency contracting might be used, in which the person puts up a sum of money to be earned back as goals are attained in changing eating behavior or losing weight. Another possibility is using stimulus control procedures to limit the number of stimuli that trigger eating. Along with these changes, the person may also be counseled about beliefs and expectations. Many overweight individuals begin treatment with unrealistic expectations and self-defeating thoughts; they believe that they should be able to lose weight quickly and effortlessly, or think of themselves in vague, negative ways (e.g., as "fat slobs"). Cognitive restructuring aims to change these beliefs to remove these barriers to successful treatment (Abramson, 1982). An example of a successful program containing several of these elements is the program developed by Sydnor Penick and his colleagues (Penick et al., 1971) at the University of Pennsylvania. This program is described in detail in Chapter 4.

The other side of the equation is the expenditure of calories through activities, a particularly important element since overweight individuals tend to be somewhat less active than those of normal weight. This argues for the inclusion of regular exercise in programs for weight reduction. Unfortunately, the use of exercise for this purpose has been relatively neglected (Abramson, 1982; Thompson et al., 1982). Programs utilizing exercise have found that obese individuals who exercise do lose significant amounts of weight, with the heaviest individuals losing the most weight. However, exercise must be frequent if it is to be effective. Exercising four or five times a week produces greater weight loss than does exercising less often (Thompson et al., 1982). Exercise also has beneficial effects other than weight loss. For that reason, we next consider exercise in health promotion.

Exercise

Proper exercise has been long part of a routine prescription for maintaining good health because of its many beneficial effects on the body. Even though both health professionals and laypeople widely accept this view, many people do not get sufficient exercise. Surveys have shown that less than 10% of the American adult population met the 1990 national goals for physical activity and fitness (Koplan, Caspersen, & Powell, 1989). Further, 50% of those individuals who begin a formal exercise program drop out within the first six months (Dishman, 1982). What are the health effects of exercise, and what can be done to encourage people to begin and maintain an appropriate exercise regimen?

Many studies have demonstrated the benefits of exercise. Among the largest of these is a recent study by Steven Blair and his colleagues (Blair et al., 1989), which followed more than 10,000 men and 3,000 women for an average 8 years, examining the role of physical fitness in mortality rates. The subjects, all of whom had received complete physical exams at a Dallas clinic, were in good health at the beginning of the study. The results of a treadmill exercise test, included in the exam, provided a basis for placing subjects into one of five physical fitness categories. Category one included the least fit individuals, whereas category five contained the most fit. The results were quite dramatic. For both men and women, the overall risk of death was 3 to 5 times higher for individuals in the least fit category as compared to the risk for those who were most fit. These benefits were found across age groups and remained when allowances were made for other risk factors, such as smoking, blood pressure, serum cholesterol, weight, and family history of heart disease. In fact, exercise appeared to be particularly important for those who also had other known risk factors. For example, for a woman who both smoked and got little exercise, the risk of dying was 12.6 times that of a woman who was physically fit and did not smoke. For a man with high cholesterol who was out of shape, the risk of death was nearly 7 times that of a man who had low cholesterol and was in good shape. Figure 5.4 shows these relationships graphically. Most of the differences in mortality owed to a lower likelihood of dying from cardiovascular disease or cancer. However, exercise seemed to reduce the risk of death from other causes as well.

In addition to the physical benefits of exercise, exercise has psychological benefits. In a review of studies examining the psychological effects of exercise, Wesley Sime found that "exercise produces a greatly improved state of mind" (1984, p. 503). Among the benefits are reduced anxiety, lowered tension, less depression, and a greater sense of well-being. The results to date, however, must be taken as suggestive rather than conclusive because of limitations in the studies done. Single- or double-blind studies

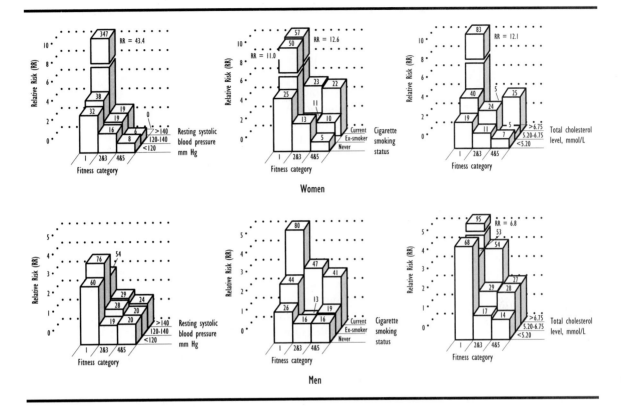

FIGURE 5.4

Relative risks for all causes of death among 10,224 men and 3,120 women, by fitness category and blood pressure, smoking habits, and cholesterol level. Each bar represents the relative risk based on age-adjusted, all-cause mortality rates per 10,000 person-years of follow-up, with the relative risk of the front-right cell set at 1.0. Numbers on top of the bars are the all-cause death rates per 10,000 years of follow-up for each cell.

Note. From "Physical fitness and all-cause mortality: A prospective study of healthy men and women" by S. N. Blair, H. W. Kohl, R. S. Paffenbarger, D. G. Clark, K. H. Cooper, and L. W. Gibbons, 1989, *Journal of the American Medical Association, 262,* 2395–2401. Copyright 1989 by the American Medical Association. Reprinted by permission.

of exercise are virtually impossible, and, given the popular belief in the benefits of exercise, placebo effects are highly likely.

What steps can be taken to persuade people to exercise more? Several behavioral techniques have been used (cf. Martin & Dubbert, 1982), including offering people various types of reinforcement. For example, one study (Martin & Dubbert, 1982) incorporated the use of reinforcement, in this case praise and individual feedback, into a community-based exercise program. Three months after the program began, 54% of those encouraged through these procedures were still jogging as compared to 17% who did not receive this reinforcement. A variant of this, of course, is contingency contracting. As noted earlier, Tim Wysocki and his coworkers (1979) successfully used contingency contracting to motivate students to stay with an exercise program.

Stimulus control has also been employed to increase exercise participation. For example, Kelley Brownell and his colleagues (Brownell, Stunkard, & Albaum, 1980) were able to significantly increase stair climbing by posting a cartoon near an elevator and stairway. The cartoon depicted a heart coaxing people to use the stairway rather than the elevator. Telephone prompts to health club dropouts have also been shown to boost participation (Martin & Dubbert, 1982). Apparently, one key to getting people to exercise is simply to remind them and make exercise salient.

In addition to these strategies, self-control techniques can be used to encourage exercise. One study, for example, used a combination of self-monitoring, self-reward, and self-punishment (essentially self-contracting) to encourage young women to participate in a fitness-improvement program (Turner, Polly, & Sherman, 1976). In another study, self–goal-setting in which participants were able to set their own exercise goals led to better attendance and better three-month maintenance of an exercise program than was the case when goals were set for the participants by an instructor (Martin & Dubbert, 1982). Finally, cognitive strategies may also be helpful for distraction while exercising. For example, one study found that training participants to think pleasant thoughts, set small mental goals, and "go slowly and smell the flowers" resulted in better attendance and exercise adherence than did having participants focus on bodily sensations (Martin & Dubbert, 1982).

SUMMARY

This chapter has examined the role of health psychology in promoting good health. These efforts, which come under the rubric of *behavioral health,* are concerned with altering behavior so as to maintain health and prevent illness. Two major strategies have been developed for changing health behaviors. One, based on theories such as the Health Belief Model and Theory of Reasoned Action, attempts to bring about the alteration of health behaviors by changing people's attitudes and beliefs. There is good evidence that such appeals can indeed change attitudes. However, such attitude change is only a first step and may or may not be related to actual change in behaviors.

The second major strategy attempts to bring about direct changes in health behaviors through the application of cognitive-behavioral methods. This approach derives from learning theory and involves techniques based on respondent and operant conditioning, as well as modeling and self-control principles. Among the techniques employed are aversion therapy, contingency contracting, stimulus control, modeling, and skills training. Most treatment plans do not use these techniques separately, but rather combine them into a multimodal approach. Such programs are designed not only to change the health behavior, but also to prevent a relapse to the person's previous habits.

Both attitude change and cognitive-behavioral strategies have been put to work in a variety of ways. Physician appeals rely on "doctor's orders" to convince people to improve their health habits. Although such appeals are often not heeded, physicians can have an important impact on their patients' health behaviors. Health behavior change techniques have also been applied in clinics. Clinical health promotion can be effective in changing the health behaviors of individuals, but is rather inefficient and is sometimes oversold. In order to reach large numbers of people, the mass media can be employed to spread the word. The evidence suggests that mass media appeals are valuable primarily for their cumulative effects, but are often ineffectual in the short run. School and work place health promotion programs are becoming more common and have proved reasonably effective in bringing about health behavior changes. Recent attempts have been made to bring these different venues for health promotion together into programs that target whole communities. These programs involve a multichannel approach, including advice by health professionals, media appeals, worksite programs, and school health programs.

The actual application of these techniques depends on the target health behavior in question. Alcohol abuse is commonly treated through medical interventions, self-help groups, aversion therapy, psychotherapy, self-control techniques, and skills training. Obesity, however, is treated through interventions designed to reduce caloric intake or increase energy expenditure through exercise. Among the most successful interventions for obesity are cognitive-behavioral programs for changing people's eating habits. These typically involve a combination of operant conditioning, self-control, and cognitive restructuring. Successful programs for encouraging exercise have utilized principles of reinforcement, stimulus control, self-control, and cognitive strategies for distraction while exercising.

KEY TERMS

aversion therapy (98)
contingency contracting (99)
stimulus control (100)
vicarious counterconditioning (101)
vicarious systematic desensitization (101)
self-monitoring (101)

self-reinforcement (102)
skills training (103)
multimodal approach (104)
clinical health promotion (106)
alcoholism (114)

SUGGESTED READINGS

Dishman, R. K. (1982). Compliance/adherence in health-related exercise. *Health Psychology, 1,* 237–67. In this article, Rod Dishman reviews current methods for encouraging people to engage in regular physical exercise.

National Institute on Alcohol Abuse and Alcoholism (1987). *Alcohol and health: Sixth special report to the U.S. Congress.* DHHS Pub. No. (ADM) 87-1519. Washington, DC: Public Health Service. This special report to Congress details the effects of alcohol on health and the treatments currently in use for dealing with alcohol abuse.

Shah, M., & Jeffery, R. W. (1991). Is obesity due to overeating and inactivity, or to a defective metabolic rate? A review. *Annals of Behavioral Medicine, 13,* 73–81. In this article, Meena Shah and Robert Jeffery review what is known about behavioral factors involved in the etiology of obesity.

CHAPTER **6**

Stress and Disease

You are on your way to an important appointment with little time to spare when you encounter a major traffic backup on the expressway. Or you're having one of those days when you have several important exams back to back. Whether it comes from traffic on crowded expressways, having heavy duties at work or school, or strains in interpersonal relationships, all of us at various times have felt "under stress." But what is stress, and how does it affect our health? These questions at the heart of health psychology have been the focus of research for several decades. This chapter examines the concept of stress, how it is measured, what makes something stressful, and the current evidence linking stress to physical illness. Chapter 7 continues the discussion by examining the coping process and the factors that moderate the effects of stress.

124

MIND AND BODY: EXPLORING THE STRESS LINK

Of all the topics in health psychology perhaps none exemplifies the integration of mind and body more than does stress. Strong suspicion has long existed that various aversive experiences can take their toll on a person's health, but the exact nature of the link between stress and disease has been a matter of speculation and controversy. Although many believed that stressful experiences could result in disease, solid data proving the relationship were difficult to find. Evidence demonstrating a link between life stress and disease has continued to mount, and advances in the psychophysiology of stress have begun to uncover the intricacies of the linkages between mind and body. As we will see, stress has many important effects on several systems of the body—most prominently the nervous, endocrine, and immune systems—effects that can lead to the development of disease. These linkages are at the heart of the mind-body nexus.

Defining Stress

Although the experience of stress is extremely common, stress is a rather elusive term to define. The term stress has been used in conjunction with a wide variety of phenomena including such disparate events as natural disasters, being unemployed, feeling aroused or anxious, having a disagreement with a close friend, having financial troubles, and getting married. Given the diversity of experiences included under this one rubric, it is not surprising that the term itself is difficult to pin down.

In general, stress has been defined in three basic ways (Coyne & Holroyd, 1982). First, stress is commonly defined in terms of particular events in the environment. According to this *stimulus* view of stress, certain events are particularly likely to produce feelings of tension or upset. Thus stress is seen as being a characteristic of environmental stimuli. This is the definition that people are using when they talk about how stressful their jobs are or how much stress they are under at school.

Researchers using this definition of stress have focused their attention on how people respond to different events believed to be stressful; this view assumes that different people respond similarly to given events and thus the amount of stress that people are experiencing can be determined by assessing the events that have occurred in their lives. For example, the Social Readjustment Rating Scale (Holmes & Rahe, 1967; Rahe & Arthur, 1978), one of the more common self-report measures of stress, asks people to indicate which events from a list they have experienced in the last year. Each event is assigned a scale value, and the amount of stress that the person has experienced is taken to be the sum of the scale values for the events marked. An alternative method is to examine the effects of specific events such as unemployment (Gore, 1978), war (see Box 6.1), or natural or manmade disasters (Melick, Logue, & Frederick, 1982).

Stress has also been defined in terms of the reactions that people have in stressful situations. This *response* definition of stress focuses on the physiological and psychological effects of particular events. For example, Hans Selye (1976, 1982) has argued that any time an organism is challenged or threatened, it will exhibit a predictable pattern of physiological responses, including the release of various hormones and

BOX 6.1 When Stress Lingers: Posttraumatic Stress Disorder

Although stress is a common experience, most of the stressors that people encounter are relatively minor, and their effects are transitory. Some stressors, however, are so traumatic for the person that the effects of the experience linger and can produce extreme, and sometimes bizarre, symptoms for months and even years after the event. These continuing reactions to highly traumatic events have been termed *posttraumatic stress disorder* (PTSD) (cf. Boulanger, 1985; Brett, Spitzer, & Williams, 1988).

PTSD can occur in response to many extremely stressful experiences including combat, civilian catastrophes, kidnapping, rape, torture, and witnessing mutilation and violent death. Symptoms for PTSD have been a matter of debate, but generally include three categories of symptoms that can be linked to a recognized stressor. Perhaps the most dramatic symptom involves reexperiencing the traumatic event. Individuals with PTSD may experience recurrent waking recollections or nightmares of the event, or may suddenly act or feel as if the event were recurring.

> Lou, a 37-year-old former Marine infantryman with two tours in Vietnam, was troubled by nightmares. His wife's fear was exacerbated when he awakened and shot at a nightstand across the room, mistaking it for an oncoming North Vietnamese soldier. A few weeks later, he

woke to find that the North Vietnamese soldier that he was throttling was his nine-year-old son (Smith, 1985, p. 130)

Other symptoms of PTSD include a numbing of responsiveness to the things going on around the person and a heightened level of arousal. Individuals with PTSD often show a reduced interest in people and events around them and feel a sense of detachment or estrangement from others. In addition, they have sleep disturbances as well as problems with concentration and memory.

How common are the symptoms of PTSD? Accurate estimates of the actual incidence of PTSD are hard to find, in part because the disorder has received so much publicity and the symptoms involved can appear in other disorders. A survey of American veterans who had served in Vietnam, however, indicates widespread prevalence of PTSD symptoms among those who had a medium or high exposure to combat. Among those with medium combat exposure, half reported nightmares, 61% had troubled memories, and 86% indicated problems with depression. Among veterans with a high level of combat exposure, 75% had nightmares, 91% had troubled memories, and 92% reported depression. These levels were substantially higher than those for nonveterans or veterans who had not seen combat duty (True, Goldberg, & Eisen, 1988).

changes in heart rate, blood pressure, respiration, and gastrointestinal activity. These responses are essentially the same regardless of the stimulus that evoked them; hence the important features of stress are to be found in how the person reacts, as opposed to the events to which the person has been exposed.

A third approach to stress argues that neither a stimulus- nor a response-based definition is adequate. Rather, stress is best understood as a *process* that incorporates both the events experienced and psychological and physiological responses to those events (cf. Coyne & Holroyd, 1982; Lazarus & Folkman, 1984). In this view, the critical determinant of stress is how the person perceives and responds to different events. What is important is not the event itself, but how it is interpreted. This approach to stress introduces a psychological dimension that is missing in the other definitions. In particular, stress is understood as a *transaction* between the person and the environment, in which the person appraises situations along with available

stress
A transaction between a person and the environment that includes the person's appraisal of the challenges posed by the situation and available coping resources, along with the psychological and physiological responses to those perceived challenges.

resources for coping with those situations. A person is said to be under stress when the situation is perceived to demand more by way of coping resources than the person believes are available (Lazarus & Folkman, 1984). This perception of a discrepancy sets in motion the psychological and physiological stress responses.

The remainder of this discussion uses the third approach, the process definition of stress. Thus, **stress** is *a transaction between the person and the environment that includes the person's appraisal of the challenges posed by the situation as well as available coping resources, along with the psychological and physiological responses to those perceived challenges.*

This definition brings together important themes in research on stress and helps to put the various findings on stress into perspective. We now consider how this definition developed.

Cannon's Fight-or-Flight Response

fight-or-flight response
Arousal of the body either to fight off or flee from a perceived threat.

epinephrine (adrenaline)
A catecholamine produced by the adrenal medulla that has effects similar to arousal of the sympathetic nervous system.

norepinephrine (noradrenaline)
A catecholamine produced by the adrenal medulla as well as the neurons of the sympathetic nervous system that has effects generally similar to those of epinephrine.

Modern stress research dates from the early twentieth century and the work of physiologist Walter Cannon (1929, 1935). In his studies of the physiological processes involved in the body's maintenance of homeostasis, Cannon observed what he came to term the **"fight-or-flight" response.** He noted that when an organism perceives itself to be threatened, it takes measures to either fight off the threat or flee from it. Physiologically, this involves a series of events beginning with the stimulation of the sympathetic nervous system and endocrine system. As a result of this stimulation, there is a precipitous rise in **epinephrine (adrenaline)** and **norepinephrine (noradrenaline)** in the blood, along with increases in heart rate, blood pressure, blood sugar, and respiration, and a movement of blood away from the skin and toward the muscles.

Evidence for the processes postulated by Cannon comes from studies of both animals and humans. In his earliest studies, Cannon (1929) found that when cats were frightened by a barking dog, measurable amounts of epinephrine were detected in their blood. This was not the case when the cats were not frightened. Further, removal of the adrenal glands eliminated this effect. Recent studies have shown that when humans are exposed to situations usually considered stressful, they show a rise in the level of epinephrine and norepinephrine in both the blood and the urine (cf. Frankenhaeuser, 1975; Mason, 1968). For example, one study (Bloom, Euler, & Frankenhaeuser, 1963) found that paratroop trainees showed a significantly higher level of adrenaline secretion when they were engaged in parachute jumps compared to periods of ground activity. These results are illustrated in Figure 6.1. Similar results have been obtained for subjects engaged in athletic competition, gravitational stress, viewing gruesome films, and taking examinations (Mason, 1968).

In some instances, the fight-or-flight response can be very adaptive in that the organism is prepared to make a rapid response to physical threats. Suppose you are confronted by someone in a dark alley. Being aroused in this way gets you ready to either fight off the mugger or run from him. This rapid mobilization comes at a cost, however, in that it disrupts normal functioning and, when sustained for long periods of time, can lead to a depletion of the organism's energy reserves and potentially result in health problems. Cannon (1935) described *critical stress levels* as involving threats of such a magnitude as to disrupt normal homeostasis and create a situation of

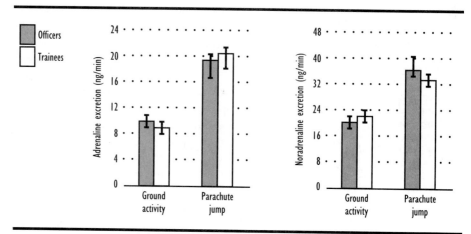

FIGURE 6.1

Comparison of adrenaline secretion by paratroop trainees during ground training and when doing parachute jumps.

Note. From "Sympathetic-adrenomedullary activity, behavior and the psychosocial environment" by M. Frankenhaeuser, 1975, in P. H. Venables and M. J. Christie (Eds.), *Research in psychophysiology* (p. 77), New York: Wiley. Reprinted by permission.

imbalance. Under these circumstances the fight-or-flight response can result in considerable wear and tear on the body.

Selye's General Adaptation Syndrome

Although the studies of Cannon and others provided the initial data, it was Hans Selye who developed and popularized the idea of a stress response (Mason, 1975a, 1975b; Selye, 1976). While seeking to uncover a new sex hormone, Selye noticed that injecting rats with extracts of cattle ovary tissue resulted in unexplained changes in several body organs. Specifically, he noted that the cortex (outer layer) of the adrenal glands became enlarged and hyperactive, while glands such as the thymus and spleen, as well as several structures in the lymphatic system, shrank, and bleeding ulcers appeared in the stomach and intestines. To his surprise, the injection of other substances and exposure to cold, heat, and trauma produced the same reaction.

General Adaptation Syndrome (GAS)
The body's generalized response to threat that includes the phases of alarm, resistance, and exhaustion.

These observations led to Selye's formulation of the **General Adaptation Syndrome (GAS).** In Selye's view, the GAS is the generalized way in which an organism mobilizes to protect itself from harm. In particular, he argued that any threat to an organism will result in a fixed set of responses that fall into three phases. In the first phase of this response, termed *alarm,* the organism mobilizes to fight off the threat. During alarm, the sympathetic branch of the central nervous system is activated, and adrenal activity increases. Heart rate and blood pressure increase, and the body is mobilized for action. This part of the GAS is essentially the same as Cannon's fight-or-flight response and is what Selye initially observed when he injected rats with ovarian extracts.

Assuming that the organism survives the initial threat, continued threat leads to the second stage, the stage of *resistance.* During this stage, the organism continues to fight off the threat, using available coping mechanisms. The organism focuses on

When a person is faced with a stressor such as being robbed at gunpoint, the fight-or-flight response prepares the body for action.

fighting off the threatening stimuli, but in the process other physical and psychological functions are likely to be neglected. In essence, the organism's resources are being diverted from their usual functions in order to bring about a suitable adaptation to the threat. Although there may be the outward appearance of normality as the threat is resisted, over time resistance takes its toll in the rapid usage of the body's resources.

Should the threat occur repeatedly or continue for a long time, the organism enters stage three, *exhaustion.* When the organism reaches this stage, the resources for resistance to threats are depleted, and the organism becomes susceptible to physiological damage and disease. Selye identified several diseases, termed *diseases of adaptation,* that he believed were at least partially the result of the depletion of resources used to deal with stressful threats. Among these are kidney disease, cardiovascular disease, and allergic conditions. This three-phase response to stress is illustrated in Figure 6.2.

A key feature of the GAS is that Selye believed it to be *nonspecific,* meaning that the body shows the same response to a threat regardless of its origin. Thus the physiological changes observed during the alarm reaction are the same regardless of whether the organism is being assaulted by heat, cold, x-rays, injections, or muscular exercise (Mason, 1975b; Selye, 1976). Selye defined this nonspecific reaction as *stress,* while he used the term *stressors* to refer to the stimuli that produced this reaction. In addition, Selye distinguished between harmful stress, which he called *distress,* and positive stress, termed *eustress.* Although the physical reactions were believed to be largely the same, he considered eustress much less damaging to health.

Selye has provided a conceptually appealing model of how the body responds to threat and has laid out some of the details on how external threats may be related to

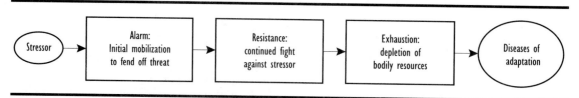

FIGURE 6.2 *The General Adaptation Syndrome.*

physical diseases. In essence, he describes the sequence of events that take place as the body utilizes its resources to defend against harm. However, the body's resources are limited, and, while it is able to fend off most noxious agents, a prolonged struggle depletes the body's defenses and can result in disease.

Selye's ideas are intuitively appealing, but have also generated a great deal of controversy (cf. Mason, 1975b), mostly because of his definition of this syndrome as nonspecific. Critics have argued that, in fact, responses to threat are not nonspecific but vary with the type of threat. John Mason (1975b) has suggested that one of the reasons that Selye and others have found similar responses to different threats in the laboratory is that, although the specific stimuli that have been used may be different, they all evoke an emotional response in the animals tested. He argues that it is this emotional response that produced the effects obtained by Selye and others, and that threats that do not evoke emotional reactions will show a different physiological pattern.

A number of studies support Mason's view. For example, fasting monkeys that were isolated from non-fasting monkeys and given a non-nutritive pellet to mask the fact that they were being deprived of food did not show the same increase in secretion of 17-hydroxycorticosteroid (17-OHCS; a stress hormone) as did monkeys that were deprived of their food in the presence of other monkeys who were eating (Mason, 1971). In addition, a comparison of hormonal responses to different types of stressors suggests at least two patterns: one associated with unpredictable or ambiguous stressors, and another associated with what he terms "signaled" stressors (Mason, 1975b).

On the basis of his studies of stress responses, Mason suggests an analogy between stress and pathogens such as bacteria or viruses. Being exposed to bacteria or viruses puts one at risk for developing the disease associated with the pathogen, but not everyone who is exposed develops the disease. In fact, many pathogens are commonly harbored within an individual without the person experiencing any ill effects. Whether the person becomes ill depends on conditions including the nature of the pathogen and the body's ability to resist infection (Mason, 1975b). Similarly, exposure to stressors does not automatically produce the effects described in the GAS. Rather, stressors have the *capability* of evoking these responses. Whether they do or not depends on intervening host factors.

A second major problem with Selye's theory is that stress is conceptualized as a strictly biological response, therefore, there is little or no attempt to address nonbiological aspects of stress. In many ways, this is not particularly surprising since the theory was developed from experiments on animals. However, because all threats are felt to produce the same response, there is little room in this theory for consideration of different sources of stress or of how these threats are evaluated and dealt with on a psychological level.

Stress and Psychological Appraisal

Whereas the work of Cannon, Selye, Mason and others has provided important insights into the physiological aspects of stress, Richard Lazarus and his colleagues (Coyne & Holroyd, 1982; Lazarus & Folkman, 1984) have developed a very influential model of the psychological processes involved in stress. According to this view, stress is best understood in terms of the person's cognitive interpretation of potentially stressful events. In fact, how events are perceived is more important than the objective events themselves. Thus stress is neither an environmental stimulus nor a physiological response, but rather "a relationship between demands and the power to deal with them without unreasonable or destructive costs" (Coyne & Holroyd, 1982, p. 108). In brief, stress is seen as a *transaction* between person and environment. Key to this transaction are the two fundamental processes of appraisal and coping.

Appraisal. Appraisal refers to people's constant assessment of situations and the resources available for dealing with them—a process regarded as key to the amount of stress experienced and the person's emotional responses to it. Thus a person faced with a potentially stressful situation, such as a visit to the dentist or an important exam, will appraise the amount of potential danger as well as the resources that are available for dealing with that danger. The person will experience stress to the extent that perceived threat exceeds resources perceived to be available for coping with it. The assessment of potential danger is termed **primary appraisal,** whereas the evaluation of available resources is called **secondary appraisal.**

When engaging in primary appraisal, the person is asking the question "Am I in danger?" The answer to this question involves judgments of the extent to which the situation involves harm or loss, threat, or challenge. All of these involve the potential for negative outcomes, but the assessment of the situation as one of challenge is clearly the most positive and is likely to be seen as having the most potential for a positive outcome. Depending on the person, the same objective situation can be appraised in any of these ways. For example, suppose that Ken has just been told that he is being transferred by his company. Ken may see the transfer as a loss, in that he will have to leave his current colleagues and community to relocate. Or he may perceive the transfer as a threat to his status in the company. Or he may see his new position as a challenge that, handled properly, can lead to advancement. The transfer is likely to be viewed as least stressful when Ken regards it as a challenge.

Whereas primary appraisal concerns potential danger in the situation, secondary appraisal considers the question of "What can I do about it?" To answer this question, the person takes stock of the resources available and evaluates coping strategies with respect to their cost and likelihood of success. Among the determinants of this appraisal are previous experiences that the person has had with similar situations,

primary appraisal
The initial appraisal of a threat in which the person assesses the amount of danger involved.

secondary appraisal
Appraisal of a threat in terms of what the person believes that he or she can do about it.

beliefs about the self and personal capabilities, perceived social support, and the availability of material resources. Continuing with our example of Ken, after engaging in primary appraisal, he is likely to consider experiences with previous transfers, thinking about coping strategies that worked or did not work before. In addition, he may think about how well he deals with such changes, reflect on how his family will react to the move, and estimate available financial resources.

The distinction between primary and secondary appraisal is largely designed to demonstrate the basic cognitive processes involved. In everyday situations, these two types of appraisal are often closely intertwined and are likely to occur iteratively. For example, Ken's assessment of the threat posed by his job transfer may be heightened by his knowledge that his family is very happy in its current location and not anxious to move. Support for the move from family and colleagues, however, may encourage him to look on the transfer as a challenge rather than a threat. In addition, reevaluation of how well such moves have gone in the past may help him change his mind about how much of a threat this new situation poses. In this case, Ken has engaged in *reappraisal*.

The importance of this type of appraisal has been demonstrated in an extensive series of studies by Lazarus and his colleagues (cf. Lazarus & Folkman, 1984; Lazarus, Averill, & Opton, 1970, for reviews). In a classic study, Joseph Speisman and his coworkers (Speisman, Lazarus, Mordkoff, & Davison, 1964) examined the role of appraisal in subjects' responses to a film of a primitive genital mutilation ceremony. This film shows a graphic depiction of crude genital surgery and generally evokes severe discomfort in viewers. Appraisal was manipulated experimentally through a narration provided for the film. In one condition, the subjects heard a "trauma track" that emphasized the pain and mutilation experienced by the initiates; subjects in a second condition were presented with a "denial track" downplaying the pain and mutilation involved and pointing out positive emotions experienced in the ceremony. A third group was exposed to an "intellectualization track" that presented the events from a detached anthropological perspective. Subjects hearing either the denial or intellectualization tracks reported feeling less upset and showed less physiological response to the film than did subjects hearing the trauma track. In a related study, Lazarus and Elizabeth Alfert (1964) found that reactions to the film were reduced even more when subjects were provided with a denial orientation to the film before it was shown.

coping
Efforts taken to deal with stressful situations.

Coping. The second major process involved in the stress experience is **coping.** Coping refers to a person's efforts, both cognitive and behavioral, to deal with a stressful situation. These efforts can range from finding a new way to look at the situation to direct attacks on the problem. Which coping strategy is selected will be largely determined by the specific appraisal of the situation. In addition, the results of these coping efforts can lead to a reappraisal of the nature of the situation and what can be done about it. The coping process is considered in greater detail in Chapter 7.

To summarize, Lazarus and his colleagues view stress as a dynamic process involving both the person and the objective situation. The objective situation provides the initial stimulus, but the key determinants of stress are how the person perceives

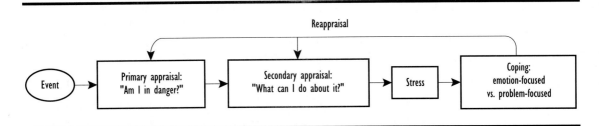

FIGURE 6.3 *Stress and the appraisal process.*

the situation and the coping resources that can be brought to bear. The person's perceptions and coping responses are interrelated and dynamic. Coping depends on appraisal, but, conversely, the results of coping are likely to alter the person's appraisal. Figure 6.3 shows these processes and their interrelationships.

This approach is clearly an advance over earlier models of stress that focused entirely on physiological responses. Physiological responses are certainly a central part of the stress process, but Lazarus's approach brings in the psychological and social factors that determine the type of response, both psychological and physiological, that a person will show in a given situation.

HOW IS STRESS MEASURED?

Given the different definitions that have been used for stress, numerous measures of stress are used. How stress is defined affects the measurements that are believed to be most useful. A stimulus-based definition implies the use of measures designed to quantify characteristics of stressful events, whereas a response-based definition suggests measures focused on psychological or physiological changes.

In general, stress is measured in four different but complementary ways (Baum, Grunberg, & Singer, 1982). Researchers using a stimulus definition of stress have tended to emphasize self-reports, whereas researchers defining stress in terms of response have generally used performance, psychophysiological, and/or biochemical measures. From a process point of view, none of these measures is sufficient in itself. Rather, each is useful for examining a particular aspect of stress, and a complete analysis requires a combination of measures. The ultimate test of a measure is the extent to which it is reliable and useful in predicting a given outcome, for our purposes, illness.

Self-report Measures

Among measures of stress, self-report measures are by far the most commonly used. Self-report measures are attractive to investigators because they are often relatively straightforward in format and easy to administer and score. Their ease of administration and scoring, however, has also made them subject to considerable abuse. Self-report stress measures are frequently reprinted in popular magazines and newspapers, along with instructions for scoring and cut-off points for determining the likelihood of becoming ill in the near future. Such presentations almost invariably ignore important conceptual and measurement issues that complicate the interpretation of self-report measures.

Measures of major life events. One type of self-report measure assesses stress by obtaining reports of major life events. Of these measures, the first, and most popular, is the Social Readjustment Rating Scale (SRRS) developed by Thomas Holmes and Richard Rahe (1967). On the basis of data from more than 5,000 patients, Holmes and Rahe identified 43 life events that appeared to precede illness onset. These events (listed in Table 6.1) include a wide variety of occurrences, both positive and negative, that Holmes and Rahe felt would involve significant change in the person's life. To obtain a quantitative estimate of the amount of stress produced by these events, Holmes and Rahe asked 394 adults to rate each one in terms of the degree of "necessary readjustment" required. In making these ratings, subjects were asked to compare the amount of change required by the event with the change required by marriage, which was assigned an arbitrary value of 500. Ratings from individual subjects were then averaged to obtain a single scale score for each event, which was divided by 10 to obtain the values listed in Table 6.1.

Assessment of stress using this instrument is straightforward. Subjects are given the list of events and asked to check the ones they have experienced during a specified period, most often the previous 6 or 12 months. The subject's stress score is determined by adding up the values of all the events checked. In line with their emphasis on stress as the result of the amount of change experienced, scores on the SRRS are stated in terms of life change units or LCUs.

How well does the SRRS predict illness? Initial work with this instrument was quite encouraging. In early retrospective studies, Rahe and his colleagues (Rahe, 1972) obtained data on life events (using the SRRS) and illness episodes from more than 2,000 navy personnel and other respondents. Examination of the data indicated that reports of illness were significantly related to scores on the SRRS. In general, higher LCU scores were associated with a greater likelihood of illness. Results were similar in a later prospective study, in which the life events reported by nearly 2,500 navy personnel for a six-month period before going to sea were found to be significantly related to the number of illnesses during the subsequent six-month cruise.

Although these results stimulated much interest and have been replicated by other investigators (cf. Rabkin & Struening, 1976, for a review), they have also been the subject of a great deal of criticism. For one thing, critics pointed out that although the relationship between the SRRS and measures of illness was generally significant from a statistical point of view, it also tended to be relatively weak (Rabkin & Struening, 1976). This raises questions as to exactly how important stress is as a precursor of illness and suggests that other factors need to be taken into account.

Criticisms have also been leveled at the SRRS as a measurement tool. Critics have argued that the 43 items included are not a valid sampling of all life events. Life events scales constructed more recently have sometimes included 100 or more events (cf.

TABLE 6.1   *The Social Readjustment Rating Scale*

Rank	Life Event	Mean Value
1	Death of spouse	100
2	Divorce	73
3	Marital separation	65
4	Jail term	63
5	Death of close family member	63
6	Personal injury or illness	53
7	Marriage	50
8	Fired at work	47
9	Marital reconciliation	45
10	Retirement	45
11	Change in health of family member	44
12	Pregnancy	40
13	Sex difficulties	39
14	Gain of new family member	39
15	Business readjustment	39
16	Change in financial state	38
17	Death of close friend	37
18	Change to different line of work	36
19	Change in number of arguments with spouse	35
20	Mortgage over $10,000	31
21	Foreclosure of mortgage or loan	30
22	Change in responsibilities at work	29
23	Son or daughter leaving home	29
24	Trouble with in-laws	29
25	Outstanding personal achievement	28
26	Wife begin or stop work	26
27	Begin or end school	26
28	Change in living conditions	25
29	Revision of personal habits	24
30	Trouble with boss	23
31	Change in work hours or conditions	20
32	Change in residence	20
33	Change in schools	20
34	Change in recreation	19
35	Change in church activities	19
36	Change in social activities	18
37	Mortgage or loan less than $10,000	17
38	Change in sleeping habits	16
39	Change in number of family get-togethers	15
40	Change in eating habits	15
41	Vacation	13
42	Christmas	12
43	Minor violations of the law	11

Note. From "The social readjustment rating scale" by T. H. Holmes and R. H. Rahe, 1967, *Journal of Psychosomatic Research, 11,* p. 216. Reprinted by permission.

Dohrenwend, Krasnoff, Askenasy, & Dohrenwend, 1978; Hurst, Jenkins, & Rose, 1978; Zimmerman, 1983). Concern has also been expressed about the lack of specificity of some of the items (e.g., "change in financial state") and the fact that some items such as "personal injury or illness" or "change in eating habits" may actually reflect rather than predict physical and psychological illness. Although one critic has argued that 29 of the 43 items can be seen as being possible reflections of illness (Hudgens, 1974), studies that have compared the predictive power of events scales such as the SRRS both with and without the illness-related items have produced mixed results. Some studies have found that elimination of potential illness related items substantially reduces the relationship between life events stress and illness (Schroeder & Costa, 1984), but other studies have found little effect (Zimmerman, O'Hara, & Corenthal, 1984).

In addition, some of the basic assumptions of the SRRS have been questioned. A primary premise of much of the work on life events stress is that the critical feature of life events relating them to illness is that they require some sort of readjustment. As can be seen in Table 6.1, the events in the SRRS include both positive and negative events, and the events vary substantially in their controllability. Recent studies suggest that different types of events may be differentially related to illness. For example, Gary Stern and his colleagues (Stern, McCants, & Pettine, 1982) found that illness was related to the occurrence of greater numbers of uncontrollable events, but not controllable ones. Similarly, other studies have found that the occurrence of negative events is related to illness, yet this is not the case for positive events (cf. Anderson & Arnoult, 1989; Ross & Mirowsky, 1979). Moreover, by using a single set of event weights for all individuals, Holmes and Rahe assumed that events require the same amount of readjustment by different people. Thus, for example, they assumed that the amount of readjustment required by divorce is the same regardless of the person or the circumstances involved. This assumption makes the scoring of the SRRS simpler, but it also conflicts with common experience.

These concerns have led researchers to develop additional measures of life events, which attempt to improve the measurement of stress by providing a more comprehensive listing of life events (Horowitz, Schaefer, Hiroto, Wilner, & Levin, 1977; Lewinsohn, Mermelstein, Alexander, & MacPhillamy, 1985), specifying the events more clearly (Cochrane & Robertson, 1973), or having respondents provide their own weightings for the aversiveness of the events that they have experienced (Sarason, Johnson, & Siegel, 1978).

Daily hassles and uplifts. Thus far we have considered only major events, such as marriage, getting fired from work, and death of a close friend. What about the day-to-day events that people find irritating or annoying but are not of the same magnitude as the major events? Do these events create stress that can have an adverse impact on health? Richard Lazarus and his coworkers (Kanner, Coyne, Schaefer, & Lazarus, 1981; Lazarus, 1980; Lazarus & Cohen, 1977) argue that such events, termed *hassles*, are a major source of stress, and may be even more important than the major life events. In their view, "it is these day-to-day events that ultimately should have proximal significance for health outcomes and whose cumulative impact, therefore, should be assessed" (Kanner et al., 1981, p. 3).

But our lives also include events that bring us joy, relief, or pleasure. Lazarus and his colleagues (Kanner et al., 1981; Lazarus, Cohen, Folkman, Kanner, & Schaefer, 1980) contend that positive events such as relaxing, spending time with family, getting a good night's sleep, and using skills well at work may serve as a buffer against the effects of more negative events. Such *uplifts* may serve as a respite from stressful encounters, help sustain us in our coping efforts, or help us to recover when we feel down.

To test these ideas, Lazarus and his colleagues have developed two scales: the Hassles Scale and the Uplifts Scale. The Hassles Scale consists of 117 different events that are generally considered annoying or irritating—such as an argument with a friend, difficulty with traffic, or not having enough money to do what we want—that characterize our everyday experience. When filling out the Hassles Scale, respondents are asked to indicate which of these hassles they have experienced recently and to score how severe each was. The Uplifts Scale is similar, except that it contains 135 positive experiences. Table 6.2 shows the ten most frequent hassles and uplifts as reported by a sample of middle-aged adults.

What is the relationship between hassles, uplifts, and illness? Although these are relatively new scales, accumulating evidence shows that everyday events are indeed related to both our physical and psychological well-being. For example, one study (Kanner et al., 1981) found moderately high correlations (between .41 and .66) between hassles and psychological symptoms reported on a symptom checklist; another (DeLongis, Coyne, Dakof, Folkman, & Lazarus, 1982) obtained correlations ranging from .27 to .35 between hassles and physical symptoms. In both cases, hassles showed a greater correlation with symptoms than did a measure of major life events. Similar results have been obtained by several other investigators (Burks & Martin, 1985; Holahan, Holahan, & Belk, 1984; Monroe, 1983; Wolf, Elston, & Kissling, 1989; Zarski, 1984). In general, measures of uplifts have shown little or no relationship to health outcomes, suggesting that uplifts may not play a role in buffering the effects of stress.

Although the results from the Hassles Scale have been promising, the scale has not escaped criticism. Barbara Dohrenwend and her colleagues (Dohrenwend, Dohrenwend, Dodson, & Shrout, 1984) argue that, like the SRRS and some of the other measures of major life events, the Hassles Scale contains items that are similar to the health events that the scale purports to predict. This confounding artificially raises the correlation between scores on the Hassles Scale and reported symptoms. In defense of the Hassles Scale, Lazarus and his colleagues present data showing that the correlation between Hassles scores and psychological symptoms remains strong even when potentially confounding items are removed from the scale (Lazarus, DeLongis, Folkman, & Gruen, 1985).

In summary, self-report measures of stress, whether of major life events or everyday hassles, provide researchers with an essential tool for measuring stress from the respondent's point of view. As indicated, however, there are continuing controversies about the exact meaning of these measures, and the scores obtained can be

TABLE 6.2   *Ten Most Frequent Hassles and Uplifts*

Item	Percentage of Times Checked
Hassles	
1. Concerns about weight	52.4
2. Health of a family member	48.1
3. Rising prices of common goods	43.7
4. Home maintenance	42.8
5. Too many things to do	38.6
6. Misplacing or losing things	38.1
7. Yard work or outside home maintenance	38.1
8. Property, investment, or taxes	37.6
9. Crime	37.1
10. Physical appearance	35.9
Uplifts	
1. Relating well with your spouse or lover	76.3
2. Relating well with friends	74.4
3. Completing a task	73.3
4. Feeling healthy	72.7
5. Getting enough sleep	69.7
6. Eating out	68.4
7. Meeting your responsibilities	68.1
8. Visiting, phoning, or writing someone	67.7
9. Spending time with family	66.7
10. Home (inside) pleasing to you	65.5

Note. From "Comparison of two modes of stress management: Daily hassles and uplifts versus major life events" by A. D. Kanner, J. C. Coyne, C. Schaefer, and R. S. Lazarus, 1981, *Journal of Behavioral Medicine, 4,* p. 14. Reprinted by permission.

overinterpreted. Moreover, self-report measures reflect the person's conscious experience and are likely to miss physiological and behavioral changes of which the person is unaware (Baum et al., 1982).

Performance Measures

In addition to self-reports of stress, one can also measure the effects of stress on performance. One of the commonly noted effects of stress is that people often find it difficult to perform well when they are in stressful situations. For example, people often have difficulty in their work or in doing fairly simple tasks when they have experienced a distressing event such as a financial reversal or the death of a friend. Such events can have a significant effect on concentration and motivation, which in turn adversely affect the person's performance. Therefore, several researchers have proposed using task performance as a measure of stress (Baum et al., 1982). Andrew Baum and his colleagues (Baum, Gatchel, Fleming, & Lake, 1981) used a proofreading task and an embedded figures task as measures of the stress engendered by living near the Three Mile Island nuclear plant after the accident there. Their results showed that these measures mirrored the amount of subjective stress reported by the respondents. Similar results have been obtained by other researchers using other stressors as well as a variety of perceptual and performance tasks (cf. Cohen, 1980, for a review). Such results suggest that these measures can be a useful behavioral alternative to self-reports. Since performance measures do not rely on the respondents' memory for and interpretation of events, they may provide a more objective measure of the stress response. However, they only measure one aspect of stress. In addition, interpretation of the scores can be complicated by such nonstress-related factors as individual differences in specific abilities related to the task being used.

Physiological Measures

sympathetic nervous system The branch of the autonomic nervous system responsible for arousing the body to action.

Since a key aspect of stress is the arousal of the **sympathetic nervous system** (SNS), another method for measuring stress is through the use of physiological indicators such as increases in heart rate, blood pressure, and respiration, or changes in the skin's resistance to electrical current (glavanic skin response or GSR) (Baum et al., 1982). For example, Lazarus and his colleagues (Lazarus, Speisman, Mordkoff, & Davidson, 1962) used GSR and heart rate to measure stress reactions to gruesome films; Sheldon Cohen and his colleagues (Cohen, Evans, Krantz, & Stokols, 1980) used blood pressure as a measure of stress resulting from aircraft noise.

Although physiological measures are useful for charting aspects of the physical response to stress, they also have their drawbacks. For one thing, the instrumentation required to obtain these measures can present problems when investigators venture beyond the confines of the laboratory. The measurement of arousal requires delicate instruments that must be carefully calibrated and often become decalibrated when moved. Also, accurate measurements may require that the subject remain still and endure intrusive electrodes. Recent technological advances in instrumentation have made physiological measurements more accurate and easier to obtain, but such difficulties persist (Baum et al., 1982; Dimsdale, 1987). A second difficulty concerns the interpretation of the results. Studies have found substantial individual differences in these physiological measures, and the measures obtained may be confounded with such nonstress factors as the novelty of being tested or the invasiveness of the procedures (Dimsdale, 1987).

Biochemical Measures

corticosteroids A group of hormones produced by the adrenal cortex that are involved in the regulation of bodily functions.

In addition to its effects on heart rate, respiration, and other physiological measures, stress also has an important impact on the endocrine system. As noted earlier, the work of Selye (1976) and Mason (1968) has demonstrated some of the typical endocrine changes that take place when an organism is exposed to known stressors. Of particular interest have been increases in the secretion of **corticosteroids** by the **adrenal cortex** and **catecholamines** by the **adrenal medulla**. Elevation of these hormones can be detected through assays of either blood or urine and provides researchers with a means of monitoring an important link in the stress process. For example, increases in corticosteroids have been related to stressors

A person's physiological responses are a measure of the effect of a stressor on autonomic arousal.

adrenal cortex
The outer layer of the adrenal gland.

catecholamines
A group of chemicals produced by the body that act as neurotransmitters.

adrenal medulla
The inner portion of the adrenal gland.

associated with athletic competition, emergency duty in hospitals, stress among flight crews, and situations involving loss of control. In addition, excretion of catecholamines has been shown to increase when subjects are exposed to stressors such as cold, pain, parachute jumps, and failure (Baum et al., 1982; Frankenhaeuser, 1975).

Although biochemical measures can provide a very useful window for monitoring stress, interpretation of these measures can be tricky. Individuals differ in their adrenal responses to stress, and their responses can be influenced by factors other than stress. For example, a study of helicopter ambulance medics in Vietnam found that some medics showed an increase in corticosteroid excretion in response to the stress of combat, but others actually showed a decrease. These variations apparently reflected the medics' differing coping styles (Bourne, Rose, & Mason, 1967). Catecholamine levels can also be affected by diet, exercise, and even the act of drawing blood for analysis (Dimsdale, 1987).

As can be seem from this discussion, the measurement of stress is complex and has many pitfalls. Each of the measures described has been used successfully in various studies, but has drawbacks and taps only a specific aspect of the stress process. A comprehensive view of stress requires the use of multiple measures. Self-report measures can be used to examine stress from the respondent's point of view, whereas physiological and biochemical markers help shed light on what is happening inside the body, and performance measures tap the behavioral aspects of stress.

HOW IS STRESS RELATED TO DISEASE?

As we are all very much aware, stress can be an unpleasant experience. But how is it related to disease? What are the mechanisms by which these unpleasant experiences are translated into negative effects on our health?

There are basically two generic ways in which stress influences health. First, stress can have a direct impact on health through various physiological mechanisms. In addition, stress can have an indirect effect through behavior. Chapters 4 and 5 showed that behavior has a strong effect on health. If stress alters a person's health behavior, these changes can be expected to have a health impact. The sections that follow examine the impact of stress on health by considering how stress affects health indirectly through behavior as well as more directly through physiological mechanisms.

Stress and Behavior

How might stress influence health through behavior? To the extent that stress causes a person to behave in unhealthy ways, it can have a negative effect on health. Such an effect might come about either because stress leads to the practice of less favorable health behavior or because it causes the person to be more sensitive to symptoms and engage in more illness-related behavior.

Health behavior. Chapters 4 and 5 discussed behaviors, such as eating, smoking, alcohol consumption, and exercise, that influence health. Such behaviors are known not only to be related to health but also to be influenced by stress. People under stress will often change their eating, drinking, and smoking habits (Conway, Vickers, Ward, & Rahe, 1981; Grunberg, Sibolboro, & Talmadge, 1988; Newcomb & Harlow, 1986). For example, one study (Conway et al., 1981) found that increases in perceived occupational stress were related to increased cigarette and coffee consumption among men in high stress jobs. Also, several studies have shown that increased stress is associated with increases in alcohol and drug usage (cf. Newcomb & Harlow, 1986). These changes in health behaviors can then lead to poorer health outcomes (Leiker & Hailey, 1988; Wiebe & McCallum, 1986).

Illness behavior. Stress also has an effect on illness when it leads to changes in how people respond to potential signs of illness. Chapter 8 includes a detailed discussion of the processes involved in perceiving and seeking help for symptoms. At this point it is sufficient simply to mention that whether people become aware of symptoms and what they do about them involves several factors including stress levels. When people are under stress, they tend to perceive their health in more negative terms (Tessler & Mechanic, 1978) and may be more likely to seek help for symptoms they might otherwise ignore. For example, Steven Gortmaker, John Eckenrode, and Susan Gore (1982) found that both the major life events and daily stress were associated with increased use of health care facilities, independent of reported symptoms. These findings suggest that stress is an important factor in determining whether the person is defined, by self or others, as being sick.

Conversely, when a person is under pressure the mental effort involved in dealing with the situation may lead the person to ignore important signs of illness. This may be particularly true for individuals who are hard-driving or task-oriented. Several studies have found that individuals with a Type A personality (characterized by time urgency, hostility, impatience, and strong achievement striving) report fewer symptoms than do individuals without Type A characteristics (cf. Carver, Coleman, & Glass, 1976; Matthews & Carra, 1982; Weidner & Matthews, 1978). In their time urgency and drive for achievement, Type A individuals apparently fail to pay attention to physical symptoms. Although these findings have provoked controversy (cf. Offutt & Lacroix, 1988), such a tendency to suppress symptoms could lead the person to overlook important signs of illness, which in turn might result in the development of more serious disease than if it had been treated in a more timely fashion.

The Psychophysiology of Stress

Stress is also a psychophysiological phenomenon. A full understanding of the relationship between stress and disease requires a consideration of the physiological mechanisms involved. Although these mechanisms are complex and not completely understood, an idea of how stress gets translated into disease can be conveyed by considering the way in which stress affects key systems of the body. For present purposes, this discussion focuses on the autonomic nervous system, the endocrine system, and the immune system.

The discussion that follows will be concerned with the general physiological mechanisms linking stress to disease. But there are significant individual differences in physiological stress responses; people have different genetic constitutions and may have very different vulnerabilities. For example, people characterized as having a Type A behavior pattern appear to have significantly stronger cardiovascular responses to stress than do others, and may be more vulnerable to heart disease (Rhodewalt & Smith, 1991; see Chapter 14). Yet individuals who are more passive in the face of stress and tend to suppress negative emotions, a pattern known as the Type C personality, may be more likely to develop cancer (Temoshok, 1987). This interplay of both psychological and physical factors in disease causation is reflected in the *diathesis-stress model*. In brief, this model states that disease outcomes are the result of both the person's physical and psychological vulnerabilities in combination with stressors experienced.

The autonomic nervous system. Think about the last time you had a heated argument with someone or had a close call on the expressway. Afterward you may have noticed that your heart was pounding, your hands were clammy, and you felt generally keyed up. These sensations come from the activation of the **autonomic nervous system.** This network of nerve fibers provides the pathways by which messages are carried back and forth between the central nervous system and the internal organs of the body, and makes the initial and most rapid response to stress.

autonomic nervous system
The branch of the nervous system that relays messages from the central nervous system to the internal organs of the body.

The human nervous system is a marvelously complex network that makes it possible for us to think, feel, and behave. Although the nervous system is complex, its basic organization is quite straightforward. As can be seen in Figure 6.4, the nervous system is divided into central and peripheral systems. The central nervous system (CNS) includes the brain and spinal cord and is the central processing unit and command center of the body; the peripheral nervous system connects the CNS to the rest of the body. The autonomic nervous system (ANS), along with the somatic nervous system, make up the peripheral nervous system. Whereas the ANS provides the connections between the CNS and internal body organs, the somatic nervous system is the channel by which sensory input comes into the CNS and messages from the CNS are carried to skeletal muscles to control voluntary movement (Asterita, 1985).

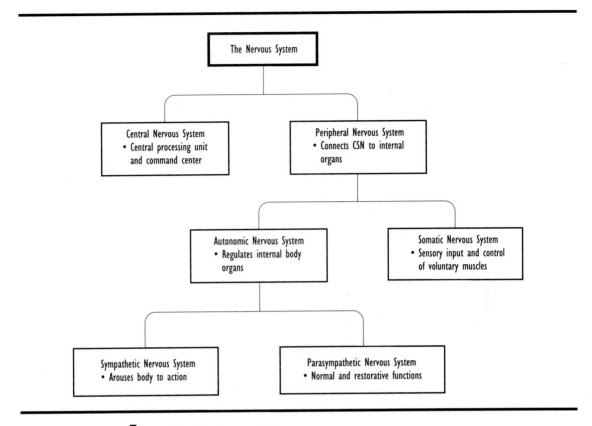

FIGURE 6.4 *The divisions of the nervous system.*

The ANS serves as the channel for information between the CNS and the internal body organs, and therefore regulates bodily functions, such as heart rate, breathing, and digestion, that are essential for survival. Although we can become aware of the functioning of the ANS, most of its operation takes place outside our awareness. The ANS itself is organized into two major divisions that connect to the same organs but affect them in different and often opposite ways. These two divisions, the parasympathetic and sympathetic nervous systems, along with some of their major effects, are shown in Figure 6.5.

parasympathetic nervous system The section of the autonomic nervous system concerned with normal and restorative functions.

Normal and restorative functions are the province of the **parasympathetic nervous system.** This system is referred to as an *anabolic* system because it restores and builds up the body's energy stores. As noted in Figure 6.5, activation of the parasympathetic system slows the heart, stimulates digestion, and has a generally calming effect. After the body is aroused by a perceived threat, the parasympathetic nervous system brings the affected body functions back to normal (Asterita, 1985).

Operating in opposition to the parasympathetic system, the sympathetic nervous system (SNS) arouses the body to action. This is the portion of the nervous system that

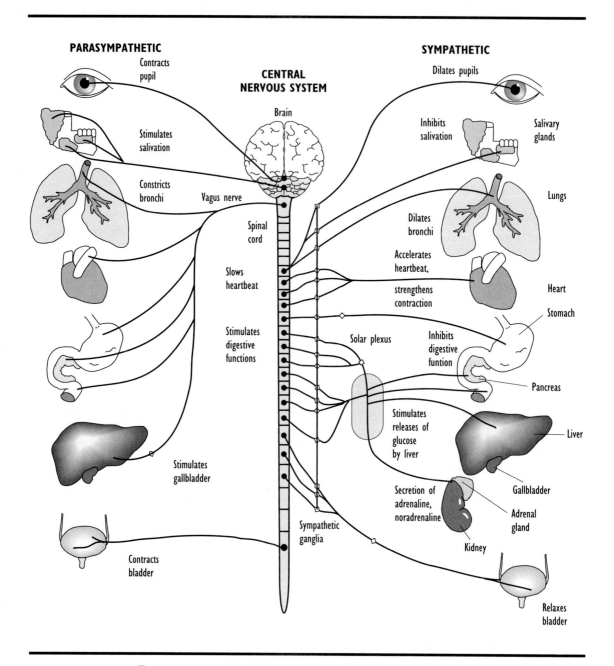

FIGURE 6.5 *The autonomic nervous system.*

is activated when the person perceives a potential threat and prepares to act. As can be seen in Figure 6.5, arousal of the SNS results in an increase in heart rate, dilation of the pupils, secretion of epinephrine and norepinephrine, and an inhibition of digestion. In addition, more stored energy converts to useable energy, and blood flow to the skin is restricted, while blood flow to the muscles is increased. In short, the body mobilizes for meeting the threat. Because of its role in releasing energy for dealing with potential threats, the SNS is described as a *catabolic* system. Cannon's observations of the fight-or-flight response were observations of the arousal of the SNS.

The endocrine system. The physiological effects of stress do not stop with activation of the SNS. The second major body system involved with stress is the endocrine system. This system works very closely with the ANS in regulating body functions, but acts through a different means. Whereas the nervous system sends messages to the various muscles and body organs through nerve impulses, the endocrine system achieves its effects chemically through hormones released into the blood. This method of communication with body organs is slower than can be achieved through nerve impulses but the effect is much longer lasting (Asterita, 1985).

A key role in the stress response is played by the adrenal glands, located on the top of the kidneys. When stimulated by the SNS, the adrenal medulla (the inner part of the adrenal gland) responds by releasing large quantities of the catecholamines, epinephrine, and norepinephrine into the blood stream. Epinephrine is a product solely of the adrenal medulla, whereas norepinephrine is also produced by the neurons of the SNS and serves as a neurotransmitter in that system. Together, these hormones have much the same effect as does SNS stimulation. Thus their presence in the blood stream stimulates increases in cardiovascular activity, respiration, perspiration, muscle strength, and mental activity. These effects are much longer lasting than those generated by the SNS on its own; thus adrenal medullary responses reinforce and extend the effects of SNS activation. The synergistic activity of the SNS and adrenal medulla is termed the *sympathoadreno-medullary (SAM) system* (Asterita, 1985; McCabe & Schneiderman, 1985).

Endocrine responses to stress are not limited to the SAM system. The second major way in which the endocrine system is involved in stress is via the hypothalamus, pituitary gland, and adrenal cortex, or what has been termed the *hypothalamic-pituitary-adrenocortical (HPAC) system*. This system is activated by messages from the CNS to the hypothalamus, a small structure at the base of the brain, which in turn secretes *corticotropin-releasing factor* (CRF). CRF acts on the pituitary gland to stimulate the production of *adrenocorticotrophic hormone* (ACTH), which then activates the cortex (outer layer) of the adrenal glands to produce corticosteroids. Like other hormones, corticosteroids are involved in the regulation of body functions. There are two types of corticosteroids: mineralocorticoids, which function to regulate the electrolytes in the blood as well as control the utilization of minerals in the body, and glucocorticoids, which regulate the amount of glucose (sugar) in the blood. Their function in the stress response is apparently to step up the release of energy in support of heightened arousal and to suppress inflammation that might result from injury or infection. In addition, glucocorticoids inhibit the immune response (McCabe & Schneiderman, 1985). A summary of the role of the endocrine system in stress is shown in Figure 6.6.

The immune system. Whereas the ANS and the endocrine system are concerned primarily with regulating internal bodily functions, the immune system has the task of defending the body from outside invaders such as bacteria and viruses. The processes involved in immunity are extraordinarily intricate and have only recently begun to be understood. The functioning of the immune system is treated in greater detail in Chapter 12 ("Immunity and AIDS"). For our purposes here, it is sufficient to note two types of immunity, humoral and cell-mediated, both of which can be influenced by stress (cf. Campbell & Cohen, 1985; McCabe & Schneiderman, 1985). **Humoral immunity** fights invaders through antibodies, which circulate in the blood and attach themselves to "foreign" substances such as bacteria, fungi, and viruses while they are still in the blood and before they enter body cells. This type of immunity is based on the functioning of B cells, which mature in the bone marrow and, when

humoral immunity
Immunity based on antibodies that circulate in the blood and attack foreign substances before they enter body cells.

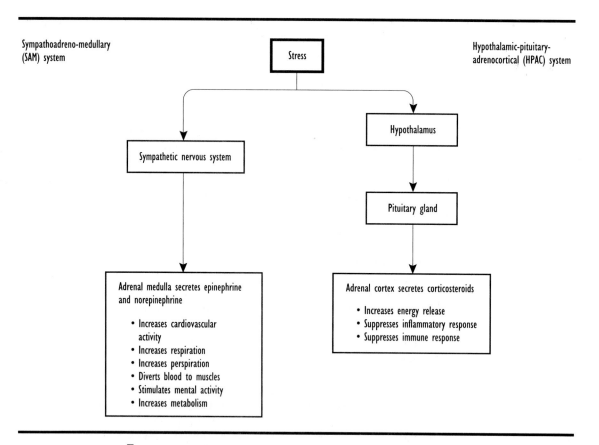

FIGURE 6.6 *Stress and the endocrine system.*

cell-mediated immunity
Immunity based on sensitized lymphocytes known as T cells, which directly attack invading foreign substances in the body.

activated by *antigens* (foreign bodies), secrete antibodies (also known as immunoglobulins), which attack the invader. **Cell-mediated immunity,** however, is based on cells known as *sensitized lymphocytes,* which directly attack invaders without the use of antibodies. Cell-mediated immunity is a function of T cells, which mature in the thymus gland, and is much longer lasting than humoral immunity.

Although there is still a great deal to be learned about the effects of stress on the immune system, the evidence to date suggests that stress has the general effect of suppressing immune function. On the one hand, severe stress is known to lead to reduction in the size of the thymus gland, which as just mentioned is the source of the T cells involved in cell-mediated immunity. On the other hand, there is evidence that stress can inhibit the secretion of antibodies. For example, John Jemmott and his coworkers (Jemmott et al., 1983) found that when students were under high levels of academic stress, they secreted lower levels of immunoglobulin A (IgA) than when they were under less pressure. IgA is involved in defending the body against infections, particularly those of the upper respiratory tract.

As we have seen, stress has complex effects on physiological functioning. Just how are these effects related to increased disease? Many of the mechanisms involved are still being uncovered. However, some generalizations can be made. In addition to wear and tear on the body, the changes brought about by stress can increase the likelihood of disease through specific effects on body organs as well as through a general reduction in the body's defenses. For example, the SNS activation associated with stress has been implicated in the development of hypertension, atherosclerosis, and cardiac arrhythmias (McCabe & Schneiderman, 1985). In addition, there is accumulating evidence that reduced immunocompetence occasioned by stress can lead to an increase in infectious disease (Jemmott & Locke, 1984) and more rapid growth of certain types of cancer (Justice, 1985). As emphasized above, the development of disease is a function of the person's physical and psychological vulnerabilities in addition to stress experienced.

STRESS AND SPECIFIC HEALTH PROBLEMS

The previous section examined some major mechanisms by which stress is related to disease. Now we turn our attention to the role of stress in specific diseases. Traditionally, diseases believed to be related to psychological factors such as stress have been referred to as *psychosomatic diseases* (also sometimes referred to as *psychophysiological diseases*). In reality, this term is misleading. As we will see throughout the rest of this text, stress has an influence on many, if not most, diseases, including those with known physical causes. For example, even though cancer is not classified as being a psychosomatic disorder, increasing evidence demonstrates that psychological factors play an important role in several aspects of these diseases. The importance of psychological factors in a wide variety of diseases is reflected in the fact that the current *Diagnostic and Statistical Manual of Mental Disorders of the American Psychiatric Association* (DSM-III-R) no longer has a category for psychosomatic conditions. This has been replaced by the designation "psychological factors affecting physical condition" (Reid

& Wise, 1989). We now turn our attention to the role of stress in peptic ulcers, asthma, and the occurrence of sports injuries.

Peptic Ulcers

peptic ulcer
A lesion (wound) in the wall of the stomach or upper part of the small intestine (duodenum).

Peptic ulcers are lesions in the walls of the stomach or upper part of the small intestine that lies just below the stomach. Those that occur in the stomach are termed *gastric ulcers,* whereas those in the upper part of the small intestine, or duodenum, are referred to as *duodenal ulcers.* Although both types of ulcers are termed peptic, they differ in important ways, and many physicians considered them different diseases. For example, although patients with duodenal ulcers tend to secrete abnormally high levels of hydrochloric acid and pepsin, those with gastric ulcers often show normal or reduced gastric secretion. Also, gastric ulcer patients tend to be older than those with duodenal ulcers. Of the two, duodenal ulcers are by far the most common (Brooks, 1985; Kaplan, 1983).

What causes ulcers? Studies of ulcer patients suggest several possibilities (Brooks, 1985). Genetics appear to play an important role in gastric ulcers. Children of gastric ulcer patients show an increased likelihood of developing gastric (but not duodenal) ulcers themselves. In addition, heavy use of aspirin appears to be associated with the development of gastric ulcers, as does smoking. Smoking is also associated with duodenal ulcers. However, for these ulcers a key factor appears to be excessive excretion of highly acidic gastric juices, principally hydrochloric acid and pepsin, that are produced during digestion. Although the stomach and small intestines normally have effective defenses against the corrosive effects of these juices, excessive amounts combined with reduced defenses can lead to erosion of the wall of the stomach or small intestine and eventually an ulcer.

Both professionals and lay people have long regarded stress as an important factor in ulcers. Early thinking was heavily influenced by psychoanalysis and tended to focus on the psychological needs and defenses of ulcer patients (Bachrach, 1982). Attention has more recently focused on the role that specific stressors play in the development of ulcers. Observations of human gastric functioning have shown that the secretion of gastric juices is heavily influenced by emotional states (Engel, Reichsman, & Segal, 1956; Wolf & Wolff, 1947). Studies with animals have shown that stressors such as electric shock, immobilization, prolonged food deprivation, and conflict can lead to the development of ulcers. The effects of these stressors are particularly evident in situations where the stressors are applied without warning and/or the animal has no control (Weiss, 1984). This suggests that being placed in a situation where one anticipates negative outcomes but is unable to do anything about them may be particularly likely to lead to the development of ulcers.

Asthma

Bronchial asthma is a common respiratory disorder that afflicts 4% to 7% of the population and results in several thousand deaths every year (Wolman, 1988). In this disorder, the bronchial airways in the lungs become blocked, and the person experiences paroxysms of wheezing, coughing, and shortness of breath. This blockage may have several causes, including excess mucus in the airways, a swelling of the walls of

bronchial asthma
A respiratory disorder in which the bronchial airways become blocked and the person experiences wheezing, coughing, and shortness of breath.

allergic (extrinsic) asthma
Asthma that results from failure of immunological defenses or from allergies.

idiosyncratic (intrinsic) asthma
Asthma that is not related to allergies and may be related to psychological factors.

the bronchi, or a contraction of the muscles surrounding them. Whatever the cause, the result is a drastic reduction in the person's ability to breathe. Asthma attacks often come on suddenly and can last anywhere from a few minutes to several hours or even days. In between attacks, the person is symptom free and able to breathe normally (Weinstein, 1987).

Two types of asthma have been identified. **Allergic (or extrinsic) asthma** is related to allergies and to failure of immunological defenses. Attacks of allergic asthma tend to be seasonal and occur frequently in all age groups. When allergic asthma is not seasonal, it may be related to allergies to substances such as feathers or molds. **Idiosyncratic (or intrinsic) asthma** is not related to allergies, but may develop out of a common cold or be related to psychological factors (Wolman, 1988).

Although asthma is commonly classified as a psychophysiological disorder, it is not, properly speaking, caused by stress or other psychological factors. Rather, once a person has asthma, psychological factors may be important in triggering asthmatic attacks. Studies of asthmatics have found evidence of abnormalities in the responses of the autonomic nervous system and a tendency to overreact to stress (Werry, 1979). Evidence also shows that, at least for children, asthmatics' relationships with their families may play a role. Some children have been observed to suffer substantially fewer asthma attacks when they are away from home; this effect has been demonstrated even when other factors such as the presence of house dust (to which the children might be allergic) have been controlled (Long et al., 1958).

This is not to say that psychological variables are a primary or even contributing factor to most asthma attacks. An assessment of the factors precipitating attacks in a consecutive sample of 487 asthma patients found that although psychological factors were present for 69% of the patients, most of the asthma attacks were the result of a combination of factors including allergies, infections, and psychological variables (Williams, Lewis-Faning, Rees, Jacobs, & Thomas, 1958).

Sports Injury

Every year between 3 million and 5 million people in the United States are injured while engaging in sports and recreation. Sports injuries account for the majority of accidental injuries experienced by adolescents and young adults and therefore constitute a major health problem. Although many factors are involved and no one has suggested that such injuries are psychophysiological in origin, increasing evidence indicates that psychological factors, and stress in particular, play an important role in vulnerability to sports injuries. For example, Steven Bramwell and his coworkers (Bramwell, Masuda, Wagner, & Holmes, 1975) found that life change (as measured by a modification of the SRRS) was significantly related to athletic injuries. Among football players reporting a low level of life change, 30% experienced injuries, as compared with 50% and 73% of those who reported medium or high levels of life change. Similar results have been obtained for participants in noncontact sports (Hardy & Riehl, 1988).

Why should stress influence injuries? No one really knows for sure, but two general hypotheses have been put forward (Smith, Smoll, & Ptacek, 1990). On the one hand, stress may interfere with the concentration needed to perform a sport well and avoid danger. It is well known that stress has negative cognitive effects; athletes experiencing a great deal of stress may become less vigilant and thus less likely to notice danger cues and to take self-protective action. On the other hand, the physiological arousal involved in stress may be a key factor. The arousal associated with stress tends to increase muscle tension as well as reduce a person's motor coordination. Since athletes rely on their coordination and fluidity of movement in their sports, a reduction in these may make the person more likely to experience injury. But social support and coping skills can help to counteract the effects of stress and therefore to reduce injuries. Ronald Smith, Frank Smoll, and John Ptacek (1990) found that high stress predicted increased sports injuries only among athletes who had low levels of social support and coping skills.

These are only a few of the health problems that have been related to stress; however, they illustrate some possible relationships between stress and specific diseases. Stress can play a direct role in causing a health problem or may be a factor that exacerbates an already existing condition. The relationship of stress to disease is explored further in our discussions of AIDS (Chapter 12), cancer (Chapter 13), and coronary heart disease (Chapter 14).

SUMMARY

Experiencing stress is extremely common in modern life, and stress as a topic presents a prime example of the interplay between mind and body. Although virtually everyone has experienced stress, definition of the term itself is elusive. Stress has been defined in three basic ways: as a stimulus, as a response, or as a transaction. This discussion views stress as a transaction between the person and the environment.

Early research on stress focused primarily on the physiological processes involved. Among the earliest contributions were those of Cannon and Selye. In the fight-or-flight response, observed by Cannon, the sympathetic and endocrine systems are activated to help the organism either fight off or flee from harm. Selye's description of the General Adaptation Syndrome (GAS) extended these observations by delineating three phases of the stress response: alarm, resistance, and exhaustion. Selye argued that the GAS was nonspecific, meaning that the body has the same response to any kind of threat. This claim has been widely criticized, and there is now evidence that different stressors may produce different physiological responses.

In order to better represent the psychological processes involved in stress, Lazarus and his colleagues have developed a transactional model. According to this model, the key factors in stress are appraisal and coping. In primary appraisal, the person assesses the challenge posed by a situation, whereas in secondary appraisal, an assessment is made of the resources available for dealing with the challenge. Coping refers to a person's actual efforts, both cognitive and behavioral, to handle the situation.

Several methods have been developed to measure stress. Self-report definitions generally take a stimulus approach to stress and measure stress by obtaining reports of potentially stressful experiences. Other stress measures focus on people's responses to stress. Performance measures take advantage of the fact that stress tends to degrade task performance and quantifies stress by measuring that degradation. Physiological measures examine the stress response by measuring the effects of stress on indicators of sympathetic nervous system activation; biochemical measures focus on the impact of stress on the endocrine system.

The link between stress and disease can be either indirect or direct. Stress influences the development of disease indirectly through the person's health or illness behavior. Thus stress may either lead to the practice of poorer health habits or influence whether the person becomes aware of and seeks help for symptoms.

Stress may also lead to disease directly through changes in physiological functioning. Central to the linkage between stress and disease are the impact of stress on the autonomic nervous system, the endocrine system, and the immune system. The initial responses to stress are made by the sympathetic branch of the autonomic nervous system. Activation of the sympathetic nervous system results in an increase in heart rate, secretion of epinephrine and norepinephrine, blood flow to the muscles, and conversion of stored energy to usable energy. These responses are followed and reinforced by action of the endocrine system, particularly the adrenal gland. The adrenal medulla releases large quantities of epinephrine and norepinephrine into the blood stream, and the adrenal cortex releases corticosteroids. Stress also affects the immune system, generally suppressing immune functioning and rendering the body more susceptible to bacteria and viruses.

Although diseases believed to be related to psychological factors are have been traditionally termed psychosomatic or psychophysiological, current evidence indicates that psychological factors are involved in many, if not most, diseases. Among the diseases that have long been suspected of having a psychological component are peptic ulcers and asthma. Research on these health problems has supported the widely accepted notion that stress is implicated in either the etiology or exacerbation of these ailments. In addition, recent evidence points to the role of stress in sports injuries.

KEY TERMS

stress (127)
fight-or-flight response (127)
epinephrine (adrenaline) (127)
norepinephrine (noradrenaline) (127)
General Adaptation Syndrome (GAS) (128)
primary appraisal (131)
secondary appraisal (131)
coping (132)
sympathetic nervous system (139)
corticosteroids (139)
adrenal cortex (140)

catecholamines (140)
adrenal medulla (140)
autonomic nervous system (142)
parasympathetic nervous system (143)
humoral immunity (146)
cell-mediated immunity (147)
peptic ulcer (148)
bronchial asthma (149)
allergic (extrinsic) asthma (149)
idiosyncratic (intrinsic) asthma (149)

SUGGESTED READINGS

Asterita, M. F. (1985). *The physiology of stress.* New York: Human Sciences Press. This is a detailed discussion of the physiological aspects of stress and the relationship of stress to disease.

Fleming, R., Baum, A., & Singer, J. E. (1984). Toward an integrative approach to the study of stress. *Journal of Personality and Social Psychology, 46,* 939–49. In this article, the authors discuss the different approaches to the study of stress and argue for an integrated approach that includes the role of environmental events, psychosocial processes, and physiological responses.

Lazarus, R. S., & Folkman, S. (1984). *Stress, appraisal, and coping.* New York: Springer. Richard Lazarus and Susan Folkman discuss their psychosocial approach to stress with a specific emphasis on psychological appraisal and coping.

Selye, H. (1976). *The stress of life* (rev. ed.). New York: McGraw-Hill. In this book, Hans Selye gives the chronology of his efforts to understand stress and describes his seminal findings in nontechnical terms.

CHAPTER **7**

Dealing with Stress: Who Gets Sick and Who Doesn't

As we have just seen, stress involves a complex set of phenomena that can have very important, and often deleterious, effects on physical health. Overall, people who are under high levels of stress experience higher than average rates of disease. However, the data show that this relationship can vary considerably. Although some people experience increased disease and illness in the face of stress, many others do not. This chapter explores some of the factors that mediate between stress and the development of disease and that help to account for why stress sometimes leads to disease but often does not. The question of psychological resistance factors that help to moderate the effects of stress are also addressed. As John Mason (1975b) has pointed out, stress can be considered similar to physical pathogens in that it has the *potential* to produce disease. Whether it actually does depends on how much resistance a person can muster.

What determines this resistance? We begin our exploration of this question by first considering the nature of coping and how coping fits into the mind-body relationship. Next we examine three major categories of resources—perceived control, personality, and social relationships—and how these help to moderate the stress experience. Finally, we explore some techniques that have been developed to help people manage stress.

MIND AND BODY: COPING WITH STRESS

The issues relating to how people deal with stress go to the heart of the three themes of this book. As was pointed out in Chapter 6, stress involves a transaction between person and environment that has important psychological and physiological effects. The coping resources that people mobilize in response to stress play a key role in determining the nature and extent of the stressor's impact. Thus, in its role as a mediator of the effects of stress, coping is an important component in the mind-body relationship. Further, the process of dealing with the challenges presented by stress is clearly central to our second theme of coping and adaptation. In their efforts to deal with stress, people use strategies and resources that help determine their adaptation to environmental demands. Coping well with stressors greatly facilitates successful adaptation, whereas failure to cope puts one at risk for poor adaptation. Finally, the process of coping involves more than just the person alone. Our relationships with other people provide a major set of resources for dealing with stress. Social support, in particular, is a prime example of our third theme, the role of interpersonal relations in health.

The Coping Process

Stress, as defined in the previous chapter, involves a dynamic interplay between environmental events, a person's appraisal of those events, and his or her coping responses. The first of these may set the process in motion, but the key to understanding stress lies in the latter two. The coping process includes all of a person's efforts to deal with perceived threats—whether overt or covert, positive or negative, adaptive or maladaptive.

What are the characteristics of this process? First, coping is closely related to a person's appraisals. How a situation is appraised will determine what the person does about it, which in turn may well change the initial appraisal. To illustrate this, consider the case of Bill, who has just been told that the company he works for is closing down. Initially, he views the impending loss of his job as a serious threat, portending possible economic catastrophe. Bill thus evaluates possible ways of dealing with this threat and decides to seek specialized training in another, better paying, field. After receiving the training and gaining employment in his new field, Bill may well look back on the closing of the company as one of the best things that has happened to him. Of course, events do not always turn out this well; unsuccessful coping might result in reappraising the threat as more menacing.

The coping process is also dynamic. Coping is not just a one-time response. Rather, it involves constantly changing efforts to deal with stressful situations. Situations themselves are constantly changing, as are our perceptions of them. People's efforts at coping often shift with these changes. Take your last visit to the dentist, an event commonly associated with anxiety. The way you coped with this anxiety probably changed considerably, depending on whether you were waiting for your appointment in the reception room, having a tooth filled, or preparing to leave. In a study of dental patients, May Wong and Danny Kaloupek (1986) found that the specific strategy used in dealing with anxiety associated with dental treatment differed substantially before, during, and after the procedure. For example, patients tended to use avoidant strategies (e.g., not thinking about bad feelings) more before and after the procedure than they did during it. Behavioral strategies (e.g., preparation for or cooperation with the treatment), however, increased steadily in frequency throughout the three phases, reaching their highest point in the period after the procedure.

Third, coping is goal directed. Specifically, it is directed toward managing perceived threats. How is this accomplished? People cope in many different ways, which can generally be divided into those that are concerned with the person's reaction to the situation and those that deal with the problem itself (Lazarus & Folkman, 1984). We now turn to a consideration of these two types of coping, and the specific strategies associated with them.

Coping Goals and Strategies

problem-focused coping
Coping concerned with changing the objective situation.

Coping may be aimed at altering the situation itself. **Problem-focused coping** attempts to change the objective situation by changing either something in the environment or how the person interacts with the environment. For example, if Sally is faced with several exams on the same day, she might try to reschedule one of the exams or change her study habits so as to improve the efficiency of her studying. In either case, she would be using problem-focused coping in that she would be attacking the problem itself.

emotion-focused coping
Coping that focuses on controlling the emotional effects of stress.

Emotion-focused coping, by contrast, consists of a person's efforts to control the emotional distress associated with a situation. This type of coping is most likely to occur when the person believes that there is little or nothing concrete that can be done to alter the actual events. Under these circumstances, the person focuses attention on learning to adapt to the negative events. A good example of this is found in Shelley Taylor's (1983) work on cognitive adjustment to breast cancer. Taylor shows that women who cope well with breast cancer develop and maintain beliefs about the meaning and cause of their cancer, their ability to master the cancer and its effects, and how well they are doing relative to other women with the disease. These beliefs help them to manage the emotional stresses associated with breast cancer, even though they do not change the objective situation. Most of the time, emotion-focused coping aims at reducing emotional arousal. Emotion-focused coping can also be directed toward *increasing* emotionality, such as when athletes "psych" themselves up just before a competition.

These coping goals can be accomplished through different strategies (cf. Carver, Scheier, & Weintraub, 1989; Cohen & Lazarus, 1979; Pearlin & Schooler, 1978). One strategy is to take *direct action* in dealing with the stressor. For example, a person faced with a serious illness might seek out immediate medical treatment in order to limit the effects of the disease. Alternatively, a person might *seek information.* Parents of a child with a congenital heart defect might consult different physicians as well as other sources of information to learn about the condition and what can be done about it. Another strategy is to seek *social support,* either for practical help with the problem or for emotional support. As we will see shortly, social support can provide a powerful buffer against stress. A fourth strategy a person might use is to *focus on emotions* so as to vent them. For example, while grieving for a loved one, a person might focus on feelings of sadness to work through the loss. These are only a few of the possibilities. Table 7.1 gives a taxonomy of coping strategies developed by Charles Carver and his colleagues (Carver et al., 1989). This taxonomy illustrates common strategies used in dealing with stress and how they relate to problem-focused and emotion-focused coping.

How effective are these different strategies? The answer to this question clearly depends a great deal on the situation. Although a strategy of taking direct action is likely to be effective when there is reason to believe that the situation can be changed, such strategies can easily lead to frustration when the person is faced with circumstances that cannot be altered. In such a case, emotion-focused coping is likely to be the most effective. This was apparently the case for residents near the Three Mile Island nuclear plant. Examination of the psychological, biochemical, and behavioral effects of the stress of living near the plant indicated that residents coped best when they used an emotion-focused strategy in which they attempted to seek out the good that might result from the accident (Collins, Baum, & Singer, 1983).

The effectiveness of a strategy also depends on the time-frame involved. Strategies that are immediately effective in reducing stress may not be effective in helping the person to cope over the long haul and vice versa. In a meta-analysis of studies on coping, Jerry Suls and Barbara Fletcher (1985) analyzed the effectiveness of avoidant and nonavoidant strategies for coping with stress in both the near and long terms. Avoidant tactics are ones in which the person tries to direct attention away from the source of the stress or one's reaction to it, whereas nonavoidant strategies are ones in which the person focuses attention on the stressor and its effects. In general, Suls and

TABLE 7.1   *A Taxonomy of Coping Strategies*

Strategy	Description
Problem-Focused Strategies	
Active coping	Taking active steps to try to remove or circumvent the stressor or ameliorate its effects
Planning	Thinking about how to cope with a stressor
Suppression of competing activities	Putting other activities aside so as to deal with the stressor
Restraint coping	Waiting for an appropriate opportunity to act
Seeking social support for instrumental reasons	Seeking advice, assistance, or information
Emotion-Focused Strategies	
Seeking social support for emotional reasons	Getting moral support, sympathy, or understanding
Positive reinterpretation	Reinterpreting the situation in a positive manner
Acceptance	Accepting the reality of the situation
Denial	Denying the reality of the situation
Turning to religion	Praying, seeking God's help, or looking for comfort in religion
Focusing on and venting emotions	Focusing on whatever is distressing and ventilating those feelings
Behavioral disengagement	Reducing one's efforts to deal with the stressor or giving up
Mental disengagement	Turning to other activities so as to distract one's attention from the situation

Note. Based on "Assessing coping strategies: A theoretically based approach" by C. S. Carver, M. F. Scheier, and J. K. Weintraub, 1989, *Journal of Personality and Social Psychology, 56,* 267–83.

Fletcher found that avoidant strategies seemed to be most effective in the short term, particularly if the emphasis was on dealing with emotions, but nonavoidant strategies produced better outcomes in the long run. Thus avoidant strategies can be useful for getting though the initial shock of a situation, but long-term resolution of the problem depends on dealing with it directly.

In reality, people use more than one strategy in dealing with any given stressor. For example, data for one study (Folkman & Lazarus, 1980) were gathered from 100 middle-aged adults on how they coped with stressful events during the course of a year. Each subject reported an average of fourteen stressful episodes, along with the thoughts and behaviors that they used for coping. The results showed that in almost every case multiple methods were used for dealing with the episodes and that subjects almost always used both emotion-focused and problem-focused coping strategies.

Coping and Health

Given the different ways that people cope with stressful situations, how do these coping strategies affect health? As is the case with stress, coping can influence health either indirectly, through health and illness behavior, or directly, through physiological mechanisms.

Indirect effects. To the extent that a person's coping strategies influence health and illness behavior, we can expect that they will have an impact, which could be either positive or negative, on health outcomes. Taking direct action to deal with a serious illness can have a positive effect on health. By seeking appropriate medical care in a timely fashion, the person might prevent more serious health problems. Also, as Irving Zola (1964) has shown, people often seek medical care when symptoms of potential illness create interpersonal difficulties (such as when obesity or impotence leads to a marital quarrel) or interfere with social activities. In such cases, the person copes with the social stressor by seeking diagnosis and treatment.

Not all coping responses are adaptive, however. Particularly when attempting to deal with emotional responses to a stressful situation, a person may cope by denying the reality of the situation or by using substances such as alcohol, drugs, or tobacco. For example, studies of delay in seeking help for symptoms of cancer have demonstrated that one reason why people put off diagnosis and treatment is that they fear the diagnosis itself (cf. Antonovsky & Hartman, 1974). Further, coping with stress through the use of drugs, alcohol, or tobacco may reduce the person's emotional arousal but, as we saw in Chapter 5, can have very adverse effects on health.

Direct effects. How people cope with stress can also have direct health effects through physiological changes. There is accumulating evidence that people's coping strategies have significant effects on their physiological responses to stressful situations. A good example of this is a study of the effects of coping on blood pressure (Harburg, Blakelock, & Roeper, 1979). In this study, subjects were interviewed about how they dealt with work-related anger when interacting with an angry boss. Blood pressure readings were taken several times during the interview and then related to subjects' coping style. The findings indicated that using a reflective style, in which the person analyzed the boss's attack and dealt with it either through reason or delayed response, was linked to lower blood pressure. But responding to the attack immediately through denial or protest was related to higher blood pressure. Other studies have shown that how people deal with events, such as the impending death of a child or a near disaster at a nuclear power plant, can also affect levels of corticosteroids and catecholamines. For instance, parents who responded with denial to their child's impending death from leukemia showed decreased levels of corticosteroid excretion compared with parents not using this defense (Friedman, Mason, & Hamburg, 1963). Also, among individuals living near the Three Mile Island nuclear plant, those who coped by looking for possible positive outcomes excreted significantly lower levels of norepinephrine than did those not using this coping strategy (Collins et al., 1983).

How we cope with stressors like difficulties with a boss can have significant physiological effects.

Ultimately, of course, we are interested in how coping affects health status. Several studies have illustrated that how people cope with stressors can influence overall health and even mortality. Studies of health among the elderly, for example, contain evidence that how elderly individuals cope with the stress of being dislocated and institutionalized influences their well-being and longevity. Elderly who respond with passivity or denial tend to show the poorest health, whereas those who respond with anger and a "fighting spirit" have better health and are likely to live longer. Similar effects have been found for cancer patients (Lazarus & Folkman, 1984; Pettingale, 1984). These studies show that how people cope affects health outcomes, but a person's health status may also affect coping: A person who is in poor health may well cope less well at the beginning of a study than one who is in better health, making it difficult to determine the actual impact of coping on health.

Now that we have considered the coping process and its relationship to health, we are ready to discuss some of the major factors that moderate the stress experience. These factors consist of the resources that the person has to draw on and the constraints faced in dealing with stressors. We begin by examining internal moderators of stress, namely psychological control and personality characteristics, and then move on to the role of social relationships.

PSYCHOLOGICAL CONTROL AS A MODERATOR OF STRESS

Most people like to feel in control of things. In fact, recent research has indicated that the need to feel in control is so strong that people will indulge in an *illusion of control.* Such an illusion allows people to feel as if they are in control when, objectively, they clearly are not (Langer, 1983). How might control be related to stress? For one thing, a lack of control may well be a significant factor contributing to the stress experience itself. Research with both humans and animals has shown that when events are uncontrollable, a sense of helplessness can develop, which in turn can lead to feelings of depression and hopelessness, as well as reduced motivation to cope (Seligman, 1975). Thus we can expect that experiences that are associated with a low sense of control will be experienced as being particularly stressful. In fact, this has been repeatedly shown to be the case. When people are exposed to such experiences as unpredictable shock, uncontrollable noise, insoluble problems, or loss of personal freedom, they report greater feelings of distress and increased physiological arousal (cf. Abbott, Schoen, & Badia, 1984; Glass, 1977; Thompson, 1981).

The flip side of this is that a sense of control can reduce stress and contribute to effective coping. Although people inevitably experience stress, research studies have shown that control-enhancing procedures can substantially reduce the amount of distress experienced as well as the aftereffects of such experiences (Thompson, 1981).

Gaining a Sense of Control

How can people gain a sense of control? Although the concept of control at first seems fairly straightforward, in fact, a sense of control can be stimulated in various ways. Researchers studying the effects of control have used such diverse procedures as giving people information about upcoming events, providing a means of stopping aversive stimuli, giving people choices, or encouraging them to see the positive side of the situation. Out of this diversity emerge two general types of control, which have their effects by either providing the person with a concrete course of action, or helping the person to think about the experience in a different way (Averill, 1973; Fiske & Taylor, 1991; Thompson, 1981).

Believing that one has the ability to affect the aversiveness of a stressful situation provides a sense of **behavioral control.** This might involve terminating the event, making it less likely, less intense, or altering its timing or duration. Although behavioral control bears an obvious similarity to problem-focused coping, the person does not necessarily have to *do* anything to benefit from behavioral control. Simply the *belief* that one has control seems to be sufficient.

behavioral control
The belief that a person has the ability to influence the aversiveness of a situation.

How does behavioral control affect stress? Substantial evidence indicates that behavioral control has significant effects on the stress experience and its aftereffects. Sometimes the worst part of a stressful experience is waiting for it to happen. Giving people a sense of behavioral control can help reduce the strain of anticipation. For example, telling people that an unpleasant experience can be avoided, even if the person never actually tries to do so, helps reduce the anxiety and arousal involved in waiting (Thompson, 1981).

Behavioral control can also affect the impact of the stressful situation itself. Studies on the impact of stressful events have shown that having behavioral control can alleviate the negative effects of stress on cognitive performance, as well as influence social behavior and even longevity. For example, in a study of elderly nursing home residents, Ellen Langer and Judith Rodin (1976) induced a sense of behavioral control through a speech by the nursing home director emphasizing all the choices available to the residents (responsibility condition). To bolster their sense of control, residents were given their choice of a movie night, were asked to give their opinions about how complaints should be handled, and were allowed to select a plant that they would care for themselves. A comparison group from the same home heard a speech from the director emphasizing the staff's responsibility in caring for the residents, were assigned a movie night, were told how complaints would be handled, and were given a plant that would be taken care of by someone else. Questionnaires filled out three weeks after the speech showed that, compared with residents in the comparison condition, residents in the responsibility condition reported themselves as happier and more active. In addition, they were rated by nurses as showing more general improvement and as spending more time in social activities and less time talking to and watching staff. A comparison of health status eighteen months later found that, whereas 30% of the residents in the comparison group were now deceased, only 15% of those in the responsibility group had died. This difference was obtained even though, according their health records, the overall health of the two groups was equivalent at the beginning of the study (Rodin & Langer, 1977).

cognitive control
Having a cognitive strategy for reducing the effects of a stressful situation.

If believing that one can do something can make a situation less stressful, what about exercising control over how you think about it? **Cognitive control** refers to having a cognitive strategy for mitigating the effects of a stressful situation. This can take the form of focusing on the positive aspects of an otherwise stressful event, engaging in distraction, gathering new information, or reappraising the threat value of the situation (Averill, 1973; Thompson, 1981). For instance, a patient undergoing surgery might be instructed to focus on the benefits of the surgery instead of the pain; a person having blood drawn might direct her attention to what is occurring in the room.

What are the effects of having cognitive control? In general, cognitive control seems to be effective in reducing stress. Studies have shown that the use of cognitive control techniques can reduce the amount of subjective distress both before and during a stressful event, as well as reduce at least some aspects of physiological arousal. For example, in a study by David Holmes and Kent Houston (1974), subjects who were instructed either to detach themselves emotionally from expected electrical shocks or to redefine them as "an interesting new type of physiological sensation" experienced less anticipatory anxiety and less physiological arousal than did subjects who expected the shocks but did not engage in cognitive control.

The effects of cognitive control also appear to continue after the event is over. Studies have found, for instance, that using cognitive control techniques can reduce anxiety and pain after surgery or other stressful events. One study found that surgery patients who engaged in cognitive reappraisal, calming self-talk, and selective attention reported less pain and required fewer pain relievers and tranquilizers than did other patients (Langer, Janis, & Wolfer, 1975). Jean Johnson and her colleagues (Barsevick & Johnson, 1990; Johnson, 1984; Johnson, Lauver, & Nail, 1989) have found that preparing patients with information about what they can expect to experience during and after medical and surgical procedures can improve their later adjustment. In one study (Johnson et al., 1989), men undergoing radiation therapy for prostate cancer showed better emotional adaptation both during and after the procedure if they had first been given concrete and objective information about what they could expect to experience than if they had not been given this information.

Although inducing a sense of cognitive control can clearly be beneficial in helping people cope with stressful situations, some caveats should be considered. For one thing, the long-run effectiveness of cognitive control is likely to depend on the specific strategy used. As noted earlier, there are significant differences between avoidant and nonavoidant coping strategies. Both types of coping strategies are essentially cognitive in nature, but, as previously discussed, avoidant strategies seem to work better in the short run, whereas nonavoidant strategies result in better coping over time (Suls & Fletcher, 1985). Moreover, although providing information seems to help people to cope, the information by itself may not be sufficient to reduce the stressfulness of an experience. Some studies have suggested that information is most likely to aid in coping with aversive events when it prompts the person to use appropriate coping strategies (Thompson, 1981).

Individual Differences in Perceived Control

Thus far we have been concerned with specific types of control that can be exercised in a situation. Although these different types of control are available to anyone, people differ in their beliefs about how much control they have. Some people believe that they can exert a great deal of control; others see themselves as largely at the mercy of outside forces. These individual differences in perceived control have been examined using the related concepts of locus of control and self-efficacy.

locus of control
Beliefs that people have about what determines their outcomes.

Locus of control. "It's all a matter of luck." "If it's meant to be, it will happen." Sentiments like these express a belief that what happens to a person owe to outside forces over which the person has little control. Such beliefs represent what has been termed external **locus of control.** The construct of locus of control refers to generalized beliefs that a person has about what determines outcomes (Rotter, 1966; 1975). Individuals with an internal locus of control (termed *internals*) generally believe that what happens to people is the result of their own efforts; those with an external locus of control (termed *externals*) see outcomes as the result of external forces such as luck or the efforts of other people. According to Rotter (1966), such beliefs are relatively stable personality dispositions that develop through experience. This general concept has been applied both to beliefs about outcomes in general and to outcomes specifically related to health (Wallston & Wallston, 1981; Wallston, Wallston, & DeVellis, 1978).

How are differences in locus of control related to coping and health? From the nature of the construct, internals would appear more likely to take a direct approach to dealing with stress than would externals. A study of information seeking among tuberculosis patients, for example, found that internals sought out more information and knew more about their disease and its treatment than did externals (Seeman & Evans, 1962). In addition, health locus of control beliefs appear to influence health protective behavior as well as adaptation in the face of illness. For instance, one recent study of sexual behavior among gay men found that those with an internal health locus of control were more likely engage in safe sex practices than were those with a more external orientation (Kelly et al., 1990). In addition, a recent study of hope in the face of potential or actual HIV infection found that, regardless of their HIV status, gay men with an internal health locus of control expressed more hope for the future and also had fewer symptoms of depression (Rabkin, Williams, Neugebauer, Remien, & Goetz, 1990).

Although results like these demonstrate that locus of control beliefs can be an important influence in coping and health, here, too, caveats should be noted. First, not all studies have found significant effects for locus of control, and even among those that have, the effects are sometimes quite modest. For example, a study of psychological factors in genital herpes found no relationship between health locus of control beliefs and either the recurrence of genital herpes lesions or distress in the face of this condition (McLarnon & Kaloupek, 1988). Also, data from two community surveys of health behavior in England found that health locus of control beliefs were at best only modestly related to such behaviors as exercise, smoking, and alcohol use (Calnan, 1989).

One possible reason for these contradictory results is that many studies have attempted to demonstrate the influence of locus of control beliefs without taking other important beliefs and values into account. These studies seem to have assumed that locus of control should have a direct effect on outcome variables. In fact, the effects of locus of control are probably influenced by other variables, such as the relative values placed on the outcomes or behaviors in question. For example, effects of locus of control on the practice of positive health behaviors is likely affected by the values that the person places on healthy living as compared with other values, such as career success or the pleasure obtained from unhealthy behaviors.

In addition, the effects of locus of control might depend on context. For example, Katherine Parkes (1984) has shown that differences in coping strategies between internals and externals depend on the type of situation. In a study of coping among nursing students, she found that when the students felt that something could be done about a situation, internals were much more likely than externals to engage in direct coping and much less likely to use suppression techniques such as inhibiting action or suppressing distressing thoughts. Yet differences in coping strategy were much smaller when the situation was one that the students felt they must simply accept. Overall, though, internals appeared to show a more adaptive pattern of coping than did externals.

self-efficacy
A stimulus that acts as a cue, releasing a given behavior.

Self-efficacy. Whereas locus of control concerns generalized expectations about control, self-efficacy refers to a person's beliefs about being able to achieve desired goals in particular situations. For example, a person who is confident about her ability to overcome the effects of a back injury has a high sense of self-efficacy with regard to coping ability in that situation. But a person with little confidence in being able to deal with rheumatoid arthritis has a low sense of self-efficacy in that area. Although self-efficacy is determined by many different elements, in general people develop a greater sense of self-efficacy for activities and situations in which they experience success. Conversely, failure tends to lead to a low sense of self-efficacy. In his work on self-efficacy, Albert Bandura (1977a, 1986) argues that self-efficacy is a key determinant of several aspects of human behavior, including how people deal with stress. In particular, he suggests that a person's sense of self-efficacy determines whether and what kind of coping behavior an individual will engage in, how long coping efforts will continue, and the amount of effort the person will put into coping.

The role of self-efficacy in coping has been explored in several recent studies. Bandura and his colleagues (Bandura, O'Leary, Taylor, Gauthier, & Gossard, 1987) examined the role of self-efficacy in coping with pain. In this study, university students who had difficulty enduring pain were taught cognitive strategies for pain control, given a placebo that they believed was an analgesic, or received no intervention. Included in the cognitive strategies were diversion of attention from the pain sensations, imagery techniques, and self-encouragement. Following this, all participants were given a pain tolerance test known as the cold pressor procedure, which consists of submerging one's hand in circulating ice water. Compared to pre-test pain tolerance scores, after training the scores of participants who were taught the cognitive strategies indicated an ability to endure substantially more pain. Little change in pain tolerance was found for the placebo or no intervention groups. Other findings indicate that changes in pain tolerance were mediated by changes in participants' perceived self-efficacy in withstanding pain. Perceived self-efficacy was found to be strongly correlated with pain tolerance, and increases in pain tolerance were directly mirrored by increases in perceived self-efficacy. Parallel results have been found for patients suffering from chronic pain. For example, Ann O'Leary and her colleagues (1988; described in Box 3.4) found that a cognitive-behavioral intervention to help rheumatoid arthritis patients better cope with their disease resulted in heightened feelings of self-efficacy, which in turn predicted improvements in pain and joint impairment.

These studies strongly argue for the importance of self-efficacy in coping and point to the possibility of improving how people deal with stress through improving their sense of self-efficacy (see also Smith, 1989). The sense of self-efficacy is also implicated in a person's overall health, as is illustrated by studies that have found self-efficacy to be a moderator between life stress and illness. In these studies, the relationship between life stress and illness is significantly reduced for individuals with a high sense of self-efficacy (cf. Holahan, Holahan, & Belk, 1984).

A Closing Caveat

This section discussed studies that have demonstrated a positive relationship between control and coping. These studies illustrate that having a sense of control can help people to cope with stress and can have positive effects on both psychological and physical well-being. At the same time, however, feeling a sense of control is not always beneficial. In her review of the relationship between control and coping, Susan Folkman (1984) indicates that having control can actually increase feelings of threat when it negatively influences other areas of the person's life or is contrary to the person's usual means of coping. For example, telling cancer patients that they can control the cancer through the use of chemotherapy gives them a sense of control.

However, the side effects of the chemotherapy may produce as much distress as the cancer itself. Under such circumstances people may find the means of control highly aversive. Similarly, a person who ordinarily copes with stressors through avoidance may find it aversive to be asked to make choices or engage in behavioral control.

PERSONALITY AND COPING

Given that stress is defined as a transaction between the person and the environment, the role of personality has been repeatedly raised as a determinant in coping. Current evidence indicates that people tend to be relatively consistent over time in how they deal with situations (Stone & Neale, 1984). Do certain personality traits mediate the stress experience? Do some traits help the person cope, whereas others make coping more difficult? Are certain types of individuals relatively immune to the effects of stress? These questions have generated a considerable amount of research and are the basis for our next area of discussion.

Personality Traits and Stress

How do personality traits affect the stress experience? The most common conception is that certain personality traits reflect personal resources on which the person can draw in coping, whereas other traits are liabilities that the person needs to overcome. The traits involved and how they have their effects have inspired considerable discussion. Among the traits proposed as possible moderators of stress are optimism (Scheier & Carver, 1987), self-concept (Linville, 1987; Hobfoll & Leiberman, 1987), and hostility (Hardy & Smith, 1988). In addition, Box 7.1 discusses the role of laughter and a sense of humor in dealing with stress.

Optimism. We all know people who always seem to look on the bright side of things, as well as others who are more pessimistic and are routinely able to find a cloud beneath every silver lining. Recent evidence suggests that such differences in outlook on life may have important effects on a person's well-being. For example, Michael Scheier and Charles Carver (1987) have found that people who are optimistic report fewer physical symptoms and may recover more rapidly from cardiac surgery. In one study, patients undergoing coronary artery bypass surgery who scored high in optimism showed fewer complications during surgery and were rated by health professionals as recovering more rapidly than did more pessimistic patients.

The long-term effects of a pessimistic outlook have recently been documented in a longitudinal study of Harvard graduates (Peterson, Seligman, & Vaillant, 1988). The study assessed the tendency to explain negative events in a pessimistic way at age 25 and then related the results to physical health over the next 35 years. Even when initial physical and emotional health were statistically controlled, men who expressed a pessimistic view evinced poorer health than did those who were more optimistic. This suggests that being a pessimist may well be hazardous to one's health.

BOX 7.1   **Humor and Stress: Laughing Your Way to Good Health**

Everyone likes a good laugh. Humor often helps to ease one through difficult situations and can make adversity seem less serious. Although these aspects of humor have long been recognized, possible health benefits of laughter have recently come to the forefront of discussion. In his account of his experience with a serious, debilitating disease, Norman Cousins (1979) describes how he used laughter to regain his health. In his unorthodox treatment program, Cousins found that ten minutes of belly laughter seemed to have an anesthetic effect and to help him get pain-free sleep. He credits this laughter, along with massive doses of vitamin C, with helping him regain his health.

Cousins's account, engrossing though it may be, provides only anecdotal evidence for the health benefits of humor. What is the scientific evidence? How effective is laughter as a moderator of stress?

To date, only a few studies have addressed this issue systematically. Studies of the psychological benefits of laughter have proved promising. For example, Rod Martin and Herbert Lefcourt (1983) found that both the ability to appreciate humor and the ability to produce it acted as moderators of stress. In their study, individuals who scored high on measures of humor showed fewer negative effects from life stress. Similar results were obtained by Arthur Nezu and his colleagues (Nezu, Nezu, & Blissett, 1988). Interestingly, humor appeared effective in fending off symptoms of depression, but not anxiety.

The evidence for the physical benefits of humor is much sketchier. Many health professionals certainly believe that humor helps in healing (cf. Pasquali, 1990; Simon, 1988; Trent, 1990). Studies of the physiological effects of laughter have suggested that laughter increases heart rate, respiration, oxygen exchange, and the production of catecholamines (cf. Fry, 1979). In addition, recent studies have suggested that the ability to laugh can assist people in coping with serious illness or disability. To date, however, there is no definitive evidence that humor actually speeds healing or affects the course of illness.

The best conclusion at this time is that humor should be enjoyed for its own sake. A good laugh can certainly help people feel better and can act as a buffer against some of the psychological effects of stress. Whether it can foster physical healing remains to be seen.

---

self-complexity
The extent to which people make and maintain cognitive distinctions between different aspects of their lives.

Self-concept. How one thinks about oneself also seems to have an impact on dealing with stress. This can be seen in recent work by Patricia Linville (1987) concerning the effects of **self-complexity** as a buffer against stress. Self-complexity refers to the extent to which people are able to make and maintain cognitive distinctions between different aspects of their lives. For example, a man who views himself primarily in terms of being a husband and a lawyer would have a low self-complexity, while someone who has distinct ideas about herself as a wife, businesswoman, tennis player, and charity volunteer would have a somewhat higher level of complexity. Linville argues that greater self-complexity helps to buffer against the effects of stress by limiting the extent to which the effects of stressful events "spill over" from one area of a person's life to another. Consider, for example, a man having marital difficulties. If his self-concept focuses primarily on his roles as husband and businessman and these are seen as closely linked, as might be the case if his wife also worked in the business, the stress of marital difficulties would likely affect most aspects of his life. However, if his self-concept includes a variety of roles, such as husband, businessman, sports enthusiast, and community leader, he would likely experience less spillover. To test these ideas, Linville examined the relationships between stressful life events, self-complexity, and physical illness and depression in a sample of college students. Overall, self-complexity buffered the effects of stress for depression and for different physical illnesses. Subjects who were high in self-complexity became ill less often in the face of stress than did those low in this characteristic.

People's conceptions of themselves vary in not only complexity but feeling. **Self-esteem** refers to a person's sense of self-worth. Individuals who have a high sense of self-esteem have a positive sense of self-worth and tend to describe themselves in positive terms such as confident, successful, outgoing, and energetic. By contrast, people with low self-esteem usually describe themselves in negative terms and have a low sense of self-worth. Having a high sense of self-esteem seems to buffer the effects of stress by helping the person to see stressful events as less threatening or making it less likely that the person will feel a sense of failure when experiencing negative outcomes.

Many studies provide the evidence on the effectiveness of self-esteem as a buffer. For example, Stevan Hobfoll and Joseph Leiberman (1987) investigated the roles of self-esteem and spousal support in dealing with the stresses associated with pregnancy and childbirth. Included in the study were women who had had an uncomplicated birth as well as women who delivered by Caesarean section, had a premature birth, or experienced a spontaneous abortion. The results showed that women with high self-esteem experienced fewer feelings of depression both immediately after the birth and three months later. In another study, Charles Holahan and Rudolf Moos (1985), using data from a community survey, found that men whom they described as stress-resistant (i.e., experienced few physical and psychological symptoms in the face of high stress) tended to be more easy-going, self-confident, and less inclined to use avoidance coping strategies than those who were less stress-resistant.

Hostility. A person's characteristic level of hostility is another personality variable that influences stress responses. In particular, people who are more cynical and hostile in the face of adversity show stronger reactions to stressful situations and have poorer health outcomes. For example, one study found that college men who scored high on a questionnaire measure of hostility tended to be less friendly, show greater anger, and have higher diastolic blood pressure during role-played interactions involving inter-personal conflict than did low-hostility subjects (Hardy & Smith, 1988). Further, differences in hostility are associated with disease outcomes. One study found that high levels of hostility were prospectively associated with increased mortality over a 20-year period. Compared with those whose hostility scores at the beginning of the study were in the bottom 20% of the distribution, people with scores in the highest 20% had 42% greater overall mortality (Shekelle, Gale, Ostfeld, & Paul, 1983). Another study found that over a 25-year period, individuals with high hostility scores were five times as likely to experience angina pectoris and myocardial infarction as were those with lower scores (Barefoot, Dahlstrom, & Williams, 1983). Finally, a recent meta-analysis of studies relating personality to disease has found that across

self-esteem
A person's sense of self-worth.

many studies anger/hostility is significantly related to such diseases as heart disease, asthma, and arthritis (Friedman & Booth-Kewley, 1987). As we will see in Chapter 14, hostility appears to be a key component in the Type A or so-called coronary-prone behavior pattern.

Is There a Disease-Prone Personality?

Results linking personality characteristics to stress and disease raise the possibility that a certain type of personality might be particularly prone to the effects of stress and the development of disease. Might there indeed be a "disease-prone" personality? To explore this possibility, Howard Friedman and Stephanie Booth-Kewley (1987) did a meta-analysis of 101 studies relating personality traits to five different diseases, including coronary heart disease (CHD), asthma, ulcer, arthritis, and headache. The results showed small but highly reliable associations between the personality variables of anxiety, depression, anger/hostility, and extraversion with the different diseases. In general, anxiety and depression showed the most consistent associations. People who scored higher on measures of anxiety and depression were at significantly higher risk for developing any of the five diseases. The associations for extraversion were more variable, but were also significant for all diseases. Anger/hostility was significantly related to CHD, asthma, and arthritis, but was not associated with ulcers or headache.

On the whole, these results suggest the possibility of a generic disease-prone personality, in which people who are prone to experience negative emotions are more susceptible to disease. Although these results are intriguing, the associations obtained are by definition correlations (since randomly assigning people to personality is not possible), and may or may not reflect a causal relationship. For example, as yet unspecified genetic factors might lead to particular personality dispositions and predispose one to certain diseases. Along these same lines, the mechanisms by which these traits are related to disease is currently unclear. As we will see in Chapter 14, the relationship between hostility and CHD might be the result of excess cardiovascular reactivity on the part of people high in hostility. However, the mechanisms by which anger/hostility affects other diseases or the means by which anxiety and depression have their effects is still undetermined.

Is There a Hardy Personality?

The other side of the notion of a disease-prone personality is the possibility that a certain personality type may be particularly resistant to stress, that is, that there exists a particular combination of personality characteristics that reliably describes individuals who stay healthy in the face of adversity. Is there such a personality, and, if so, what are its basic characteristics?

To date, the most extensive efforts to address these questions have been the studies by Suzanne Kobasa and her colleagues (Kobasa, 1979, 1982b; Kobasa, Maddi, & Kahn, 1982; Kobasa, Maddi, & Zola, 1983; Kobasa & Puccetti, 1983) of what they call the hardy personality. According to Kobasa, the person most likely to stay healthy in the face of stress is a person who possesses three key traits, what we can call the three Cs. The first of these is *commitment*. Hardy individuals believe in themselves and what they are doing. Second, people with hardy personalities possess a sense of *control* over what happens to them. This prediction is in line with the work we discussed earlier on the stress-buffering effects of an internal locus of control. The final characteristic is *challenge*. Kobasa believes that hardy individuals expect change and see stressful events as challenges that offer the opportunity for growth.

To test these ideas, Kobasa and her colleagues conducted a series of studies examining the role of these traits in health outcomes. In an early retrospective study, Kobasa (1979) gathered data from a group of executives on their levels of life stress and illness over the previous 3½ years. On this basis, she was able to identify those individuals who were under high stress and experienced either high or low levels of illness. These executives were then sent a second set of questionnaires designed to measure personality traits relevant to the hardiness concept. Analysis of the responses to these questionnaires indicated that executives who reported high levels of stress but low levels of illness were those who scored low on measures of alienation (the opposite of commitment), nihilism, external control, and vegetativeness (the opposite of challenge). Conversely, those with high stress and high illness were ones who scored high on these measures.

Although these results support the idea of a hardy personality, the observed relationships might have been inflated by collecting the data retrospectively or might have been unique to the population studied. Therefore, Kobasa replicated the study using a prospective design and different populations. For example, another study (Kobasa et al., 1982) collected personality data from 670 middle- and upper-level managers at the beginning of the study and related these to stress and illness over the next two years. This time rather than comparing the personality differences between high and low illness subjects, Kobasa and her colleagues used the personality measures to identify individuals who were high and low in hardiness and examined the differences in illness rates. These differences are shown in Figure 7.1. As expected, executives experiencing high levels of stress reported more illness, but the levels were substantially lower for those high in hardiness. Also, as expected, hardiness had no effect on illness rates when stress levels were low. Since hardiness is conceptualized as a buffer against the effects of stress, it is not expected to reduce illness rates when stress is low. The generality of these results has been demonstrated in studies examining the role of hardiness among lawyers, army officers, and women being screened for cervical cancer (Kobasa, 1982a; Gentry & Kobasa, 1984).

Additional studies have explored the relationship between hardiness and other coping resources such as social assets, perceived social support, and exercise (Kobasa, Maddi, & Puccetti, 1982; Kobasa & Puccetti, 1983). In general, the results have suggested that hardiness has effects that are independent of and add to these other resources. Thus, perceived social support and exercise both help to buffer stress on their own, but individuals with hardy personalities benefit even more.

Although the data collected by Kobasa and her colleagues would seem to present a strong case for the existence of a hardy personality, several researchers have voiced criticisms (cf. Carver, 1989; Funk & Houston, 1987; Hull, Van Treuren, & Virnelli, 1987). For one thing, questions have been raised about the measurement of hardiness.

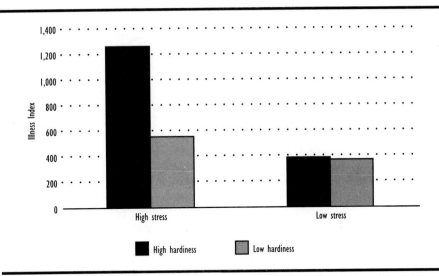

FIGURE 7.1

Illness as a function of life stress and hardiness.

Note. Based on data from "Hardiness and Health: A Prospective Study" by S. C. Kobasa, S. R. Maddi, and S. Kahn, 1982, *Journal of Personality and Social Psychology, 42,* 168–77.

As noted earlier, Kobasa has measured hardiness negatively by looking for people low on alienation, external control, and vegetativeness. So what was measured might have been the presence or absence of maladjustment, rather than a positive trait of hardiness (Funk & Houston, 1987). There is also a question as to whether the three hypothesized components of hardiness form a unified personality type or whether they are best considered independently. Evidence from some studies suggests the latter and further argues that hardiness effects result primarily from commitment and control. The dimension of challenge actually appears to have relatively little effect (Hull et al., 1987). Finally, questions have been raised about the role of hardiness in mediating stress. Although Kobasa's data have suggested that hardiness serves as a buffer against stress, other studies have not found this to be the case (cf. Funk & Houston, 1987; Hull et al., 1987; Wiebe & McCallum, 1986). These questions need to be answered definitively before we can conclude that there is indeed a hardy personality.

COPING WITH STRESS THROUGH SOCIAL SUPPORT

Thus far our discussion has centered on internal resources for dealing with stress. As we have seen, a person's beliefs about control as well as certain personality characteristics seem to play a role in mediating responses to stress. Clearly, however, such internal resources are not the entire story. As the poet John Donne has so eloquently written, "No man is an Island, entire of itself" (1624/1972, p. 98). We are profoundly influenced by our relationships with others, in both positive and negative ways. We now turn to the role of these relationships in coping with stress.

What Is Social Support?

social support
The aid and support that people receive from their interactions with others.

Most of the research on social relationships as they relate to stress has focused on the concept of **social support,** which refers to the kind of aid and backing that people receive from their interactions with others (Cohen & Wills, 1985; Wallston et al., 1983). This includes events such as a husband advising his wife on problems with her job, a teenager helping an elderly person across the street, a parent providing financial assistance to a college student, or a minister comforting someone who has just lost a loved one.

The diversity of these events lends itself to identifying different types of support. Sheldon Cohen and Thomas Wills (1985) suggest that social support performs four basic functions. First, social support helps people feel better about themselves and their relationships with others. *Esteem support* performs this function by letting people know that they are loved and accepted despite their faults and shortcomings. Thus the encouragement and acceptance that we receive from friends, family, or colleagues would be classified as esteem support. In contrast, *information support* refers to the help that people receive in understanding or defining situations. When events are ambiguous or not easily understood, others can provide us with important information about how to understand or cope with what is happening (Goethals, 1986; Suls & Miller, 1977). Hence, the advice that we receive on how to do something or what to

Studying with a friend can provide both informational support and social companionship.

expect are examples of information support. *Instrumental support* consists of concrete assistance in the form of financial aid, needed services, or material resources. For example, if you borrow a lawn mower or a ladder from your neighbor, you have received instrumental support. Finally, others can help simply by being there, in other words, through *social companionship*. This type of support, which includes spending time with others in recreational or leisure activities, can help people deal with difficult situations by either distracting them from their troubles or facilitating positive moods.

Social Support and Health

Certainly the support of others can help us to feel better, but how, specifically, is it related to our health? Although strong speculation has long arisen about the positive effects of social support on health, proving this relationship has been tricky. Part of the problem derives from the wide diversity of social support measures available (cf. Bruhn & Philips, 1984; Heitzmann & Kaplan, 1988; Sarason, Shearin, Pierce, & Sarason, 1987). These measures often tap different aspects of social support and may show different relationships to health measures. In general, however, they fall into two types (Cohen & Wills, 1985). Measures of *social network structure* assess the number, density, or proximity of relationships that a person has available to provide support. These measures indicate whether the person has others available to provide support, but give only an indirect indication of the availability of various support functions. Measures of *support function*, however, attempt to assess directly whether the person's need for various types of support is being met. Asking people if they are married is a measure of structure, as is counting the number of friends a person has. But asking about the availability of someone to talk to in time of difficulty or the number of times the person has received monetary assistance are measures of support function. Both types of measures can be further subdivided by the extent to which they are global or specific in their assessment. Global measures attempt to obtain an overall measure of either structure or function; specific measures examine designated aspects of the person's support. The distinction between measures of structure and function is important because, as we will see, the nature of the relationship between social support and health often depends on how support is measured.

In general, social support is thought to have its effects on health in one or both of two ways (cf. Cohen & Wills, 1985; Wallston et al., 1983). The most common view is that social support acts as a buffer against the effects of stress. According to this view, when a person is experiencing stress, the support of other people provides needed resources for dealing with the situation and hence "buffers" the person against possible ill effects. If social support operates as a buffer, the effects of such support should be evident only in the presence of stress. Thus when stress is low, health outcomes will differ little as a result of social support. However, when stress levels are high, individuals with high levels of social support will have better health outcomes than will those with low levels of support.

A second approach argues that social support has effects independent of stress. Being a member of a large social network can provide a person with positive experiences and a set of ongoing socially rewarding roles in the community. This being the case, social support could enhance well-being by promoting positive affect as well as giving the person a sense of belonging and self-esteem. Such effects would certainly be helpful in dealing with stress, but may also be important even when the person is not faced with stressful experiences. Thus social support may have a main effect on illness regardless of stress levels. If this is so, the effects of social support will be evident in both high and low stress situations. A graphic illustration of the difference between social support as a buffer and social support as a main effect is given in Figure 7.2.

Which of these models best describes the effects of social support on health? The answer to this question depends a great deal on how one measures social support. When social support is measured by the number of different persons that an individual can rely on for support (i.e., through global social network structure measures), the typical result is a main effect for social support. For example, Nan Lin and his colleagues (Lin, Simeone, Ensel, & Kuo, 1979) examined the relationship of life stress and social support to psychiatric symptoms among Chinese-Americans in Washington, DC. In this study, social support was measured by assessing respondents' interactions and involvement with friends, neighbors, and the local community. Overall, they found that greater levels of social involvement were associated with lower levels of psychiatric symptoms, regardless of stress levels. There was no indication that social support buffered the effects of stress. Further, social support was more strongly related to symptoms than was life stress. These data are consistent with the main effects model, but since they are correlational, no causal conclusions can be drawn. In other words, it is just as possible that psychiatric symptoms reduced social support as it is that social support reduced symptoms.

However, when social support is measured in functional terms the evidence favors buffering effects. For example, Anita DeLongis and her coworkers (DeLongis, Folkman, & Lazarus, 1988) examined the effects of daily hassles as well as social support and self-esteem on both psychological and physical symptoms in 75 married couples. In this prospective study, the couples were interviewed monthly for a period of six months concerning recently experienced stress, social support, self-esteem, and health outcomes. Overall, the effects of stress on symptoms depended on the respondents'

FIGURE 7.2

Possible relationships between stress, social support, and illness. A—Social support as a main effect. B and C—Two illustrations of social support as a buffer.

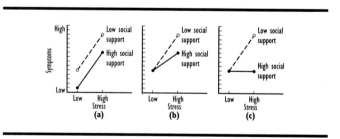

Note. From "Stress, social support, and the buffering hypothesis" by S. Cohen and T. A. Wills 1985, *Psychological Bulletin, 98*, p. 313. Reprinted by permission.

social support and self-esteem. Respondents who had unsupportive relationships and had low self-esteem showed more illness in response to stress than did those with supportive relationships and high self-esteem. Other studies have shown buffering effects for social support on psychological health as well as for such physical outcomes as genital herpes flare-ups and the occurrence of sports injuries (Evans, Palsane, Lepore, & Martin, 1989; Norbeck & Tilden, 1983; Smith, Smoll, & Ptacek, 1990; Vanderplate, Aral, & Magder, 1988). Although these results support the buffering hypothesis, not all studies have found these effects. Some evidence indicates that whether social support buffers stress depends on the specific social support function that is measured. Further, more evidence is available for the buffering effects of social support on psychological than physical illness (Cohen & Wills, 1985).

Finally, our social relationships may not always be positive. Having others around for companionship or to provide information or other support can help people get through stressful experiences. However, our relationships with others can also themselves be a source of stress. Arguments with a friend or one's spouse can be highly distressing. Further, help that is offered sometimes turns out to exacerbate problems rather than ameliorate them. The way in which social support networks can sometimes make things worse is illustrated in a recent study of social support for family members caring for Alzheimer's patients (Pagel, Erdly, & Becker, 1987). In this study, 68 spouses of patients with Alzheimer's disease were interviewed about their perceptions of the disease, stresses in their lives, and the positive and negative aspects of their social networks. In addition, respondents were given several scales designed to measure psychiatric symptoms. The results showed that caregivers who reported more upset with their social networks had greater depression than those reporting less upset. This relationship was shown to persist over time as well as when initial depression was controlled, indicating that upset with one's social network served to predict changes in depression. Thus while our social relationships can certainly be a benefit in staying healthy, they can also make us more vulnerable to disorder when they are perceived as upsetting or frustrating.

STRESS MANAGEMENT

As we have seen, a person's internal and external resources can play significant roles in mediating the stress experience. Because of the effects that stress can have on physical and psychological well-being, there has been a great deal of interest in developing techniques for alleviating stress. What kinds of techniques can be used to help people deal with stress, and how effective are these? As with other moderators of the stress experience, stress management techniques can be directed toward helping people manage their psychological and physical reactions to stressful events or toward aiding them in reappraising situations as being less stressful. Let us consider some techniques that have been developed, along with the evidence for their effectiveness in reducing stress.

Relaxation

progressive relaxation
A relaxation technique in which the person is taught to relax by successively tensing and relaxing different muscle groups.

systematic desensitization
A relaxation technique in which the person is taught to relax while imagining encounters with feared objects or situations.

Stress results in physiological arousal and feelings of tension. Almost by definition, a person who is under stress experiences tension of one sort or another. Relaxation can be used as a stress management technique to reverse this process and help the person to feel more at ease when dealing with stressful situations.

Different procedures have been developed to induce relaxation (cf. Lavey & Taylor, 1985). In **progressive relaxation** (Jacobson, 1938), the person is taught to relax by tensing and relaxing different muscle groups with the eyes closed in a quiet environment. The person is trained to become aware of tension within the body and learn how to eliminate that tension by relaxing the muscles completely. Relaxation of mental activities is assumed to follow from the physical relaxation. A variant of this is the technique of **systematic desensitization** developed by Joseph Wolpe (1958). In systematic desensitization, individuals suffering from anxieties or phobias are taught to relax while imagining encounters with situations or objects that generally cause them to be fearful. Other variations of relaxation therapy include the use of relaxing images or the use of repeated words (such as "one" or "relax") to help the person avoid distracting thoughts.

An analysis of the different relaxation techniques indicates that, although they differ in some of their specifics, they tend to share many central features (Lavey &

Although studies of meditation have suggested that it can be an effective technique for dealing with stress, these outcomes primarily result from its effect in relaxing the person.

Taylor, 1985). Relaxation techniques generally require that the person be in a tranquil setting, seated or lying down with eyes closed, and have reduced muscle activity. In addition, the person is generally encouraged to engage in deep, regular breathing, to focus attention inwardly away from outside activities, and to enter a passive frame of mind by excluding distracting thoughts. Entering this state produces mental calmness and reduces the arousability of the central nervous system.

How effective is relaxation for dealing with stress? Relaxation techniques certainly help a person feel more comfortable and relaxed, and therefore affect the subjective experience of stress. In addition, relaxation training has been shown to have a significant effect on health problems associated with stress, such as high blood pressure, muscle tension headaches, and insomnia, and may help to improve the functioning of the immune system (Crowther, 1983; Ewart et al., 1987; Kiecolt-Glaser et al., 1985; Lavey & Taylor, 1985). For example, in a study of the role of relaxation in lowering blood pressure, Craig Ewart and his colleagues (Ewart et al., 1987) found that, compared to an assessment only condition, a program of progressive relaxation helped to lower the blood pressure of high school students. Students selected for this study consistently had blood pressure readings above the 85th percentile. In another study, geriatric patients given relaxation training showed a significant increase in natural killer cell activity as well as changes in other measures of cellular immuno-competence (Kiecolt-Glaser et al., 1985).

Studies such as these suggest that relaxation not only helps people feel better, but can have some potentially significant effects on important health functions. However, studies of the effectiveness of relaxation and other stress reduction techniques are difficult to evaluate because of the potential for placebo effects (see Chapter 2). It is quite obvious when a person is receiving relaxation treatment as compared with being in a control group, and the differential expectations generated by these differing conditions may well influence the outcome. Thus relaxation treatments appear to be effective, but question remains about the exact mechanisms involved.

Meditation

meditation
Techniques in which the person focuses inwardly in a non-analytical way and attempts to become aware of the process of thoughts coming and going.

Interest in the use of **meditation** as a technique for controlling stress has recently grown. Spurred by reports from India and other Asian countries about extraordinary feats of bodily control and altered states of consciousness by meditation masters, Western scientists have begun to examine the meditation process and its effects (cf. Benson, 1984; Shapiro, 1985). Meditation comes in many forms, but the term generally refers to "techniques that have in common a conscious attempt to focus attention in a nonanalytical way and also an attempt not to dwell on discursive, ruminating thought" (Shapiro, 1985, p. 310). The person attempts to focus away from thoughts of everyday life and instead become aware of the *process* of thoughts coming and going. Meditation may be either formal—in which case the person may meditate using a specific posture (such as the lotus position) at particular times of the day—or informal. Informal meditation is generally practiced throughout the day without a specified place or position and involves an attempt to be conscious of everything that one does. Although many forms of meditation are based in religious belief systems, meditation does not imply any particular religion and, in fact, can be practiced without reference to religion.

Scientific interest in meditation has focused on its potential as a self-regulation strategy for controlling stress. Hence, the question has been whether meditation has measurable effects on feelings of stress and physiological arousal. The evidence demonstrates that meditation does indeed help people to deal with stress. Studies of meditation have found that the use of these techniques can help people to cope better with a variety of phobias and anxiety. In addition, meditation has measurable physiological effects, including reduced heart rate, decreased oxygen consumption, decreased blood pressure, increased skin resistance (GSR), and changes in alpha activity in the brain (Benson, 1984; Shapiro, 1985). Meditation can also be useful in dealing with such stress-related conditions as insomnia, asthma, and hypertension (Shapiro, 1985).

Although these results are promising, comparisons of meditation with other self-regulation strategies such as progressive relaxation or self-hypnosis have found that meditation is neither better nor worse than these other treatments. This suggests that there is nothing particularly unique about meditation as a stress management tool. In fact, meditation apparently has the same effects as does relaxation and most likely has its effects primarily by relaxing the person (Shapiro, 1985).

Biofeedback

biofeedback
A technique in which a person learns to exert control over a specific physiological function by responding to feedback from that function.

Relaxation therapy and meditation are mostly applied in a global manner, in other words, without trying to influence specific physiological functions. In contrast, **biofeedback** is a technique that aims at changing specific physiological indicators. Biofeedback training generally tries to teach a person to consciously control physiological functions that are considered automatic and thus outside conscious control. For example, a person might be trained to control skin temperature, heart rate, or brain waves. This is accomplished by attaching the person to sensors that monitor the selected physiological function and provide the person with a visual or audible signal as to the current level of that function—such as temperature electrodes, in the case of skin temperature. The output from these sensors would then be amplified and presented to the person in the form of, perhaps, a series of soft tones. As skin temperature dropped, the tones would speed up, whereas they would slow as skin temperature rose. In training a person to raise skin temperature, the individual would be instructed to attempt to slow the tones down as much as possible.

Studies of biofeedback as a technique have shown that people can be trained to control reliably such functions as heart rate, skin temperature, and muscle tension (Andrasik, Blanchard, & Edlund, 1985). Such results have encouraged researchers and clinicians about the possibilities of using biofeedback to help people control stress as well as to treat stress-related health problems. In line with this, some studies have examined the effects of biofeedback on such disorders as hypertension, mandibular joint pain, and migraine and muscle tension headaches (Andrasik, Blanchard, & Edlund, 1985; Dahlstrom, Carlsson, Gale, & Jansson, 1985; DeGood & Redgate, 1982; Jessup, 1982; McGrady, Woerner, Bernal, & Higgins, 1987). The results from these studies have largely been promising. For instance, Lars Dahlstrom and his colleagues (Dahlstrom et al., 1985) found that the use of biofeedback helped to reduce the signs and symptoms of mandibular dysfunction; Angele McGrady and her coworkers (McGrady et al., 1987) reported statistically and clinically significant decreases in blood pressure using biofeedback with hypertensives.

Despite these encouraging results, considerable debate continues over the nature of biofeedback and its role in producing these improvements. Although biofeedback has been conceptualized in terms of voluntary control of specific physiological functions, there is little evidence that such control produces the results attributed to it. During biofeedback training, patients are instructed to relax in a seated position while they learn to control the target physiological function. Biofeedback produces no better outcomes overall than does relaxation alone, and the outcomes attributed to biofeedback might be primarily the result of this relaxation (Jessup, 1982).

Physical Activity

The beneficial effects of exercise for overall fitness and health are well documented, and we know that exercise has beneficial physiological effects (see Chapters 4 and 5). What about the use of exercise as a technique for managing stress? What are the psychological effects of exercise? People often rave about how good they feel mentally as well as physically after they exercise. What is the empirical evidence?

A growing number of studies support the contention that exercise can have beneficial psychological effects (cf. Sime, 1984, for a review). Studies of exercise have suggested that engaging in an appropriate amount of exercise (as defined by the person's age and physical condition) can result in a significant reduction of anxiety for between 30 minutes and several hours. In addition, physical exercise is now being prescribed by some clinicians as an adjunct therapy for patients who are depressed.

The potential role of exercise as a general buffer against stress is illustrated in a recent study by Jonathan Brown and Judith Siegel (1988). In this prospective correlational study, high school girls first filled out a series of questionnaires measuring life stress, physical exercise, and illness, and then repeated these questionnaires nine months later. As expected, the results of the study showed that life stress at the beginning of the study significantly predicted later illness. However, this relationship was much stronger for girls who reported low levels of exercise. For girls with high levels of exercise, high levels of stress did not seem to have a deleterious effect.

Why does exercise have these effects? Unlike what we saw with meditation and biofeedback, relaxation does not seem to be the primary active ingredient. In fact, exercise and relaxation seem to have a synergistic relationship. Each has effects of its own, and when combined they have an even more powerful impact (cf. Sime, 1984). Although the exact mechanisms have not been definitively identified, several possibilities have been suggested. First, exercise may help to reduce anxiety by reducing muscle tension. In addition, evidence indicates that increased cortical blood flow and increases in norepinephrine after exercise may play a role. One particularly exciting possibility has to do with the role of beta-endorphins, substances known to be related to the perception of pain. Recent studies have suggested that exercise leads to an increased level of beta-endorphins in the blood, which may result in improved mood (Sime, 1984).

Advocating exercise as a means of dealing with stress does not come without caveats. First, the exercise program needs to be appropriate to the person's age and physical condition. Not everyone can or should engage in an intensive exercise program. From the standpoint of dealing with stress, the most effective exercise programs seem to be those that (a) elicit sustained heavy breathing without resulting in exhaustion, (b) last between 20 minutes and 2 hours, and (c) are engaged in 3 or more times per week (Berger, 1984). The importance of moderate- as opposed to high-intensity exercise is underscored by Andrew Steptoe and Sara Cox (1988), who found that, although having subjects engage in moderate exercise resulted in improved mood, high-intensity exercise resulted in increased tension and anxiety. These results are for short-term mood changes, but they show that one can have too much of a good thing.

Stress Inoculation Training

stress inoculation training
An approach to stress management designed to help people build their coping skills and enhance their resistance to stress.

Thus far we have discussed specific techniques for helping people to manage their psychological and physical reactions to stressful situations. Although these techniques can be very useful in managing stress, they only address limited aspects of the problem. **Stress inoculation training** (SIT; Meichenbaum, 1985) is an eclectic approach to stress management that provides a framework for dealing with different aspects of the stress experience. Based on a transactional approach to stress, SIT is designed to help people build their coping skills and enhance their resistance to stress. Specific goals of SIT are given in Table 7.2.

In practice, SIT consists of three phases. In the initial, or *conceptualization*, phase, the basic objectives are to establish a collaborative relationship with the client and begin the process of helping the client to deal with stressors that are of concern. As a part of this, the therapist collects information on the client's stress-related problems, assesses expectations for the training, and educates the client about the transactional nature of stress. This phase of the training provides the client with a framework to understand stress reactions and sets the stage for developing specific interventions.

The second phase of SIT is the *skills acquisition and rehearsal* phase. The goal of this phase is to ensure that the client develops the capacity to cope effectively with the identified stressors. Thus, once an assessment has been made of the client's needs, the therapist can design a program to help the client develop needed skills. Obviously, the specifics of this part of the training depend on the stressors involved and the client's existing skills. However, the therapist has a range of possibilities to choose from, including relaxation training, cognitive strategies designed to help the client think about the situation differently, problem-solving training, and self-instructional training. In the latter, the client is taught various self-statements that can be used when confronting a stressor. For example, a person might reassure herself that she can handle the situation or instruct herself to "relax and slow things down." During this phase, the client is taught the appropriate skills and then rehearses them with the therapist (and possibly others) so as to have them available when the need arises.

TABLE 7.2   *Major Goals of Stress Inoculation Training*

1. Teach clients the transactional nature of stress and coping.

2. Train clients to self-monitor maladaptive thoughts, images, feelings, and behaviors in order to facilitate adaptive appraisals.

3. Train clients in problem solving, that is, problem definition, consequence, anticipation, decision-making, and feedback evaluation.

4. Model and rehearse direct-action, emotion-regulation, and self-control coping skills.

5. Teach clients how to use maladaptive responses as cues to implement their coping repertoires.

6. Offer practice in in vitro imaginal and in behavior rehearsal and in vivo graded assignments that become increasingly demanding, to nurture clients' confidence in and utilization of their coping repertoires.

7. Help clients acquire sufficient knowledge, self-understanding, and coping skills to facilitate better ways of handling (un)expected stressful situations.

Note. From *Stress inoculation training* (p. 22) by D. Meichenbaum, 1985, New York: Pergamon. Reprinted with permission.

In the *application and follow-through* phase, the client is encouraged to implement the skills learned during the training phase in everyday situations. Thus the therapist works with the client to reinforce the skills learned and maximize the likelihood that they will generalize to "real world" situations. As a part of this, the therapist might use *imagery rehearsal*, in which the client is asked to rehearse coping efforts while imagining being in a stressful setting. For example, a person who finds social situations stressful might rehearse coping strategies while imagining being in different social settings. In addition, rehearsal might be accomplished through role playing stressful situations or through the use of behavioral assignments in which the person seeks out stressful but not overwhelming situations in which to practice coping. The client's goal is to gain sufficient practice in using coping skills so that, by the end of the training, the person feels a positive sense of self-efficacy for dealing with challenging situations.

Given the complexity of this program, its effectiveness is difficult to evaluate in toto. However, the techniques advocated by Meichenbaum have been applied in many different settings with apparent success. For example, stress inoculation training has been used with nurses to help them deal with the demands of their profession (West, Horan, & Games, 1984), as well as with police trainees (Sarason, Johnson, Berberich, & Seigel, 1979), teachers (Forman, 1982), and athletes (Kirschenbaum, Wittrock, Smith, & Monson, 1984). Although these programs are different in their specifics, they have all followed the basic outlines of SIT and have apparently been successful in helping the clients deal with stress.

SUMMARY

Although stress can certainly have negative effects on health, evidence is growing that the effects of stress depend a great deal on how people cope with it. Coping refers to all of a person's efforts to deal with perceived threats. These efforts can take many forms and involve numerous strategies, but, in general, can be divided into efforts aimed at controlling the emotional distress associated with the situation (emotion-focused coping) and those that focus on changing the situation or how one deals with it (problem-focused coping).

Coping affects health in two basic ways. First, coping may have indirect effects on health through changes in health and illness behavior. Coping efforts that lead the person to seek medical attention in a timely fashion can have a positive effect on health, whereas the use of alcohol, drugs, or tobacco to deal with problems can lead to negative effects. Coping can also have direct effects on health through physiological mechanisms. Research evidence indicates that the coping strategies can have significant effects on physiological responses, which, in turn, influence health.

People have many resources, both internal and external, to draw on in coping with stress. Psychological control is an internal resource that can help people deal with stress by avoiding the sense of helplessness that can sometimes accompany stressful situations. Feelings of control can achieve their effects by either providing the person with something concrete that can be done about the situation (behavioral control) or helping the person to think about the situation differently (cognitive control). In addition, people differ in their beliefs about the amount of control they have over situations. In general, people with an internal sense of control or a positive sense of self-efficacy are better able to cope than are those with an external sense of control or a poor sense of self-efficacy.

Personality is a second internal resource on which a person can draw in coping with stress. Several personality characteristics have been identified as moderating the effects of stress. Among these are optimism, self-concept, and hostility. Recent evidence suggests the possibility of a "disease-prone" personality, in which individuals with a disposition to experience negative emotions are also at greater risk for disease. In addition, individuals with a strong sense of commitment, control, and challenge are thought to be better able to deal with stress than are persons lacking these traits.

How well people deal with stress is also influenced by their relationships with others. Social support refers to the kind of assistance we get from our interactions with others. Research studies have provided evidence that social support can either buffer the effects of stress or have a direct effect on health outcomes independent of stress. However, our social relationships can also be themselves a source of stress. Relationships that are restrictive or unsupportive can lead to negative health outcomes.

Given the importance of coping in mediating the effects of stress, considerable interest has arisen in identifying techniques for stress reduction. Such techniques could have an effect by helping the person either to manage their psychological and physiological reactions to adverse events or to reappraise events as less stressful. Among the techniques that have been developed are relaxation, meditation, biofeedback, and the use of physical exercise. In general, all of these seem to be effective in helping people cope with stress. Research has suggested, however, that meditation and biofeedback accomplish their results primarily through relaxing the person. Stress inoculation training is a multimodal approach to stress management designed to help people build their coping skills and enhance their resistance to stress.

KEY TERMS

problem-focused coping (154)
emotion-focused coping (154)
behavioral control (159)
cognitive control (160)

locus of control (161)
self-efficacy (162)
self-complexity (165)
self-esteem (166)

SUGGESTED READINGS

Benson, H. (1984). *Beyond the relaxation response.* New York: Times Books. This book describes Herbert Benson's work on relaxation in nontechnical terms, linking it to the effects of beliefs on health.

Cohen, S., & Edwards, J. R. (1989). Personality characteristics as moderators of the relationship between stress and disorder. In R. W. J. Neufeld (ed.), *Advances in the investigation of psychological stress.* New York: Wiley. In this chapter, the authors critically evaluate what is currently known about the role of personality traits in coping with stress.

Meichenbaum, D. (1985). *Stress inoculation training.* New York: Pergamon. In this book, Donald Meichenbaum describes his stress inoculation program and how it can be applied to a variety of different stressors.

Wallston, B. S., Alagna, S. W., DeVellis, B. M., & DeVellis, R. F. (1983). Social support and physical health. *Health Psychology, 2,* 367–91. This review article examines the literature on the buffering effects of social support, pointing out weaknesses in the data as well as future directions for research.

CHAPTER 8

The Nature of Illness: Perceiving Symptoms and Seeking Help

All of us have had the experience of getting sick. It may have been something as mild and transitory as a cold, or as serious and long-lasting as a chronic, life-threatening disease such as cancer. Illness is certainly a universal human experience. But what is illness? When we think of the physical infirmities that we have had, we most often think in terms of what is wrong with our bodies biologically; for instance, a virus producing a disease such as chicken pox or the flu, or a failure of the body to produce needed substances such as insulin in diabetes, or an abnormal growth as in cancer. In other words, we usually think in terms of some type of disease. When we look more closely, however, the phenomena of ill health are much more varied than that.

MIND AND BODY: THE NATURE OF ILLNESS

Although the biological state of our bodies is certainly a critical aspect, the phenomena of ill health include far more than just the biological. People often perceive symptoms and report them to a health care provider, only to have them dismissed as trivial or "all in the mind." Yet the person still feels ill. More than 50% of the patients who present symptoms to family practitioners are estimated not to have a clinically identifiable disease but to be seeing the practitioner for emotional or personal reasons (Jennings, 1986).

Alternatively, a person may have a disease and not feel ill. Hypertension is called the silent killer because it can exist for a long time without being detected (Galton, 1973). Many cancers can exist and develop for weeks, months, or even years without being detected. This is particularly troublesome because early detection of cancers is one of the keys to their control (cf. Renneker, 1988).

In order to understand why these disparities exist and why a person's biological state often does not coincide with experience, we must examine another dimension of the integration of mind and body. When we speak of disease, we are referring to a primarily biological concept. **Disease** refers to pathological conditions within the body, conditions that may be clinically diagnosed by a health professional. **Illness,** by contrast, refers to the experience of discomfort and suffering (Barondess, 1979; Jennings, 1986). As a subjective experience, illness is influenced by not only the person's biological state but also cultural and social factors, situational variables, stress, personality, and concepts held by the person about the nature of disease. Thus, illness represents a true interaction between the physical and the psychological.

This distinction between disease and illness becomes particularly important when we consider the actions that people take concerning their health. Although we usually think of people as seeking medical attention because they are sick and have a disease, the reality is that help-seeking for health problems is a function of illness and not disease. In other words, people respond to their perceptions of their physical state and not to the objective state itself (cf. Kasl & Cobb, 1964; Mechanic, 1972; Robinson, 1971). **Illness behavior** refers to the actions that people take in response to perceived illness. The study of illness behavior includes examination of all the factors that influence a person's response to symptoms and discomfort (Mechanic, 1962, 1978).

With this as background, let us now take a closer look at this experience called illness and what people do about it. We begin by examining sociocultural influences on people's responses to suffering and discomfort. Following this, we explore the processes involved in experiencing and interpreting symptoms and illness. Finally, we conclude our discussion by examining behavioral responses to illness, paying particular attention to when and why people seek, or fail to seek, appropriate medical attention.

disease
The occurrence of objective pathological abnormalities in the body—which may or may not be clinically apparent.

illness
The experience of suffering and discomfort, which may or may not be related to objective physical pathology.

illness behavior
The reaction component of illness, specifically the behavior that a person exhibits in response to experienced suffering and discomfort.

THE SOCIOCULTURAL CONTEXT OF ILLNESS

Cultural Factors in Illness

Understanding the nature of illness and how different people respond to physical distress requires a consideration of the cultural context in which illness takes place. Although the biological processes involved in disease are the same across cultural boundaries, how people understand and experience discomfort is often radically different. For example, many of us would blanch at the very thought of having steel hooks embedded in the skin and muscles of the back and then being suspended from a pole by those hooks. Yet the hook-hanging ritual is practiced in parts of India as a ceremony for blessing the children and crops. Remarkably, the participant in this ritual shows no signs of pain, but rather seems to be in a state of exultation (Melzack & Wall, 1982).

Anthropological studies of differences in illness across cultures have shown repeatedly that illness conceptions do not occur in isolation, but are part of the larger cultural belief system. Western technological societies tend to think of illness in terms of specific dysfunction within the body and look for the causes in such things as germs, stress, or other attacks on the body. Other cultures view illness differently. In his study of illness beliefs and medical care among the Spanish-speaking peoples of the state of Chiapas in southeastern Mexico, Horatio Fabrega (1974) describes two contrasting approaches to illness that differ from the Western model. Indians of Mayan descent regard illness as either a sign of sin or an indication that one's enemies have plotted with devils and witches to cause harm. A return to health requires that the sick person and his family make certain social, moral, or religious reparations. These beliefs are part of the Mayans' overall cosmology, which emphasizes the person's connectedness with the social system and regards illness "as a direct or indirect extension of the workings of the social system" (p. 231). Individuals of direct Spanish descent, however, have a more individualistic view of illness, seeing the occurrence of illness as evidence that the person's strength has been overcome and depleted. For these individuals, illness can be caused by biological, social, and psychological factors, with the principal causes found in the person's emotions and social relationships. These beliefs, in turn, reflect the more differentiated world view that conceives of the individual as a separate person but with strong ties to the social group.

Even within Western technological society, cultural groups differ in their responses to suffering and discomfort. For example, a classic study of cultural differences in responses to physical symptoms (Zola, 1966) found considerable differences between Irish-American and Italian-American clinic patients in their presentation of symptoms for treatment. Whereas patients of Irish descent tended to describe a relatively small number of localized symptoms and downplay any pain, patients of Italian descent reported more symptoms relating to more areas of the body and were vocal about their pain. Along similar lines, another study (Zborowski, 1952) compared reactions to pain among Italians, East European Jews, Irish, and "Old Americans" treated at a New York hospital. Italian and Jewish patients tended to be emotional about their pain, often exaggerating their pain experience. Irish tended to deny the pain, and "Old Americans," a white, predominantly Protestant group whose grandparents had been born in the United States, tended to be more stoical and "objective" about their discomfort. Further, even though both Jews and Italians tended to be more expressive about their pain than were the others, they apparently did so for different reasons. Italians were primarily concerned with the pain sensations and were satisfied simply to find relief. Jews, however, were more concerned with the meaning of the pain and with its potential consequences. In both studies, the different responses to discomfort reflect overall cultural differences between the groups. Another good example is found in Box 8.1, which describes beliefs about illness and healing among Mexican-Americans in the Southwest. In all these cases, culture influences the illness experience by providing the person with basic illness orientations and categories for interpreting somatic experience (Lewis, 1981).

The Social and Situational Context of Illness

Culture provides the overall context in which illness takes place. The experience of ill health, however, is further shaped by various social and situational factors.

Demographic differences in illness. Numerous studies have shown that the perception of ill health differs substantially depending on the person's place in the social structure. James Pennebaker (1982), citing surveys of symptom experience and various illness-related behaviors—such as medication use, activity reduction because of illness, and physician visits—notes that the prevalence of illness appears to depend on such variables as age, sex, marital status, living arrangements, and socioeconomic status (SES).

With regard to age, the data suggest that frequency of illness increases as one gets older, with older people reporting more activity restriction, aspirin use, and physician visits. Although these findings are influenced by physical decline in the later years, older people appear to interpret symptoms differently than do their younger counterparts. For example, as people age, they tend to attribute relatively mild symptoms to aging rather than illness (Leventhal & Prohaska, 1986; Prohaska, Keller, Leventhal, & Leventhal, 1987).

Most studies have also shown that women report more illness and illness behavior than do men. Interestingly, studies asking about past illness experience almost universally find this difference, whereas studies asking for current reports of symptoms have found few differences (Bishop, 1984; Pennebaker & Skelton, 1978), suggesting that some differences found in other studies may be the result of differential recall. Although there is some question as to whether women actually experience more symptoms, one study has found evidence that women have a more "diffuse" view of illness, often reporting symptoms that "radiate" throughout the body. In addition, men often appear unaware of serious health problems when reporting symptoms to a doctor (Verbrugge, 1980).

Marital and living arrangements also seem to have a significant effect on illness. Studies have consistently shown that, compared with those who are married, unmar-

BOX 8.1   Curanderismo: Folk Medicine Among Mexican-Americans

One of the fastest growing ethnic groups in the United States is Mexican-Americans, many of whom live in the Southwest. A significant part of the Mexican-American cultural heritage is a system of folk medicine known as *curanderismo* (from the Spanish verb *curar,* to heal) (Trotter & Chavira, 1981). The beliefs of curanderismo have roots in Judeo-Christian religious beliefs, Native American herbal lore, witchcraft, spiritualism, and scientific medicine. Although curanderismo recognizes many of the same diseases as scientific medicine, it sees illness as deriving from both natural and supernatural causes. Thus, certain illnesses, including those recognized by scientific medicine, are seen as the result of natural forces, and are amenable to treatment by physicians or through herbal remedies. Other illnesses, however, are regarded as supernatural in origin. These illnesses cannot be treated by physicians and require the ministrations of a *curandero* (traditional healer). A curandero is a member of the community who is recognized as having a gift of healing (*el don*) and who practices traditional methods of diagnosis and healing. The work of a curandero is not limited to physical ministrations but also deals with the person's social, psychological, and spiritual concerns.

Included in curanderismo are illnesses that are believed unknown to scientific medicine and are thus treated by curanderos. Among the best known are *mal de ojo, susto, caída de mollera,* and *empacho.*

Mal de ojo is an illness of children and infants that can occur when someone, especially a woman, looks admiringly at someone else's child. When this happens, the child may begin to show symptoms such as fitful sleep, excessive crying, diarrhea, vomiting, and fever. Treatment of this condition involves having the child lie down and making the sign of the cross over him or her with an egg while the healer recites the Apostle's Creed three times. The egg is then cracked and dropped into a

glass of water. The jar is placed on the child's head while the Apostle's Creed is again recited. Finally, the glass is placed under the child's bed. The child is expected to be cured by morning.

Other diseases are believed to be caused by the person's emotional state. For example, *susto* results from strong feelings of fright. Weakness is the primary symptom of *susto,* but if the illness lasts for a long time it can lead to the more serious *susto pasado,* which can include symptoms of stomach trouble, diarrhea, lack of appetite, lethargy, irritability, and loss of weight. *Susto* can be cured in several ways, including rituals involving branches from a sweet pepper tree.

Caída de mollera ("fallen fontanel") is a disease that may be caused by pulling the bottle from a baby's mouth while the child is sucking, by a fall from a crib or bed, or by throwing the baby into the air. In this condition, the area directly under the anterior fontanel (the soft space between the front bones of an infant's skull) is believed to drop. When this happens, the child experiences severe diarrhea and vomiting. Treatment for *caída de mollera* involves various techniques designed to move the mollera back into its rightful place. For example, the infant might be suspended upside down for one to two minutes so that the mollera can fall back into place. Or a curandero might apply pressure to the child's hard palate with his fingertips.

Empacho is a condition caused by overeating certain foods and is characterized by the presence of a large ball in the stomach. Children under two years of age are believed to be particularly at risk for *empacho.* When a child gets *empacho,* he will continue trying to eat but will vomit the food as rapidly as he eats it. Other symptoms include excessive crying, diarrhea, and fever. Treatment for *empacho* can involve the use of certain herbal medicines and purgatives.

ried individuals report more symptoms, take more aspirin, and think themselves in poorer health. Further, the number of residents in the person's household also influences the experience of symptoms. Overall, individuals living with one to three others report the fewest symptoms and claim to be in the best health. Perceived symptoms appear to be most numerous for those living alone or with four or more others (Pennebaker, 1982).

Finally, social class or socioeconomic status (SES) plays an important role. In general, the higher a person's SES, the fewer symptoms are reported, the less aspirin is used, and the more positive is the person's perception of current health (Pennebaker, 1982). Beyond this, compared with their white-collar counterparts, blue-collar workers are less informed about illness, more skeptical of medical care, more dependent when ill, and also have more difficulty in adopting the sick role (Rosenblatt & Suchman, 1964). We can certainly expect from this that the illness experience itself would differ significantly between these two groups. A concrete example of this difference comes from a study of class differences in the experience of pregnancy (Rosengren, 1964). Compared with middle-class women, lower-class women were more likely to see themselves as "sick" when pregnant, a view that often conflicted with that of their physicians. Further, lower-class women were more likely to have superstitious beliefs about pregnancy and childbirth (such as "if a husband and wife quarrel, the baby will be ugly").

In addition to these demographic differences, the experience of ill health is significantly influenced by our interactions with others, as well as the situational context in which it occurs.

Interactions with others. As we will see shortly, the processes by which we perceive and interpret symptoms are complex and often involve considerable uncertainty. For example, people may be unsure about whether particular sensations constitute symptoms, and, if so, whether they are serious, what they indicate, or what is the most appropriate treatment. This uncertainty often leads people to discuss their symptoms with others and seek their advice about what they should do. For example, a study of illness episodes in a community sample (Suchman, 1965) found that approximately three fourths of the respondents who reported having had a relatively serious illness discussed their symptoms with another person, usually a family member, before seeking medical attention. In more than 90% of the cases, this discussion took place as soon as the initial symptoms appeared. This kind of **lay referral** is likely to occur any time people have symptoms for which they have no ready interpretation and may result in either a referral to a professional or a substitute for professional care (Sanders, 1982).

lay referral
Informal discussion of symptoms and physical concerns with friends, family, or other nonprofessional individuals.

These discussions with others often have an important impact on how people interpret their symptoms and their subsequent actions. In the study of illness episodes just described (Suchman, 1965), most of the conversations initiated by the respondents concerned obtaining validation of the symptoms experienced. Thus people wanted to make sure that their symptoms were indeed worth being concerned about. In roughly two thirds of the cases, those consulted interpreted the symptoms as indicative of illness, and in more than half the cases recommended that the person seek medical attention. When given, this advice was heeded in the vast majority of cases. Data like these show that the advice that people receive from others often plays a significant role in shaping their illness experience (Sanders, 1982).

When people are deeply involved in what they are doing, they are less likely to notice symptoms of injury or illness.

Situational context. Although often overlooked, the situation in which those symptoms occur heavily influences the perception of symptoms. Usually we think of injury or disease as having an urgency that transcends the situation, but this is often not the case. For one thing, our perception of symptoms and what we do about them often depend on our activities at the time and our ability to "contain" the symptoms within the ongoing situation. Bodily sensations occur all the time. However, whether people notice aberrant sensations, interpret them as symptoms, and do something about them depend on how involved the people are in what they are doing, and whether they can continue their activities in the face of the symptoms. An example of this comes from an interview with a man who had recently experienced a heart attack while bowling. Even though he was experiencing chest pain, shortness of breath, and perspiration, he continued his game because he "could not 'let down' his fellow teammates" (Alonzo, 1979, p. 398).

Another situational factor that plays an important role is the amount of stress the person is experiencing. As we saw in Chapters 6 and 7, stress has been shown to be significantly related to the development of disease. In addition, stress can make a person more sensitive to symptoms and more likely to do something about them. Studies of the relationship between stress and illness behavior have consistently found that psychological distress is significantly correlated with the perception of poorer health and greater likelihood of seeking medical attention (Gortmaker, Eckenrode, & Gore, 1982; Mechanic, 1976; Mechanic & Volkart, 1961; Tessler & Mechanic, 1978).

Particularly for individuals with a high propensity to use health services, seeking medical care can be a means of coping with stressful life situations.

PERCEIVING SYMPTOMS

Social and cultural factors provide the context for the experience of ill health, but what are the processes involved? How do we come to notice symptoms and perceive ourselves to be ill? An obvious beginning is the perception of symptoms. When we perceive ourselves as ill, this assessment is often based on the perception of certain symptoms. For example, a person feeling the onset of a cold might note the occurrence of nasal congestion, a cough, fever, and a general malaise. In perceiving such symptoms, we generally assume that these are the result of aberrant physiological states within our bodies, that is, that the nasal congestion perceived corresponds to actual physiological changes taking place in the nasal passages and that the fever represents an actual rise in body temperature. Such assumptions may be accurate in many cases, but symptom perception may represent far more than this.

Physiological Changes and Symptoms

symptom
Subjective experience
of a physiological
state.

Just how do we perceive **symptoms**? Symptom perception is more than merely a direct perception of physiological states, but such states are important and provide a first step in the process. Awareness of these physiological states begins with sensory receptors throughout the body that transmit nerve impulses to the brain, where they are interpreted as various sensations. Andy Skelton and James Pennebaker (1990) note three types of somatic senses that are relevant to the perception of symptoms. *Mechanoreceptive senses* detect the displacement of tissue and are sensitive to touch, pressure, vibration, and kinesthetic changes. *Thermoreceptive senses* distinguish heat and cold, and *pain senses* are usually related to tissue damage. Stimulation of the receptors related to these senses give rise to the bodily sensations that we call symptoms.

But how much of our symptom experience is the result of these sensations? The answer is still being debated, but current evidence suggests that at best only a part of our symptom experience derives from physiological receptors. In fact, Skelton and Pennebaker (1990) argue that symptom reports "should be regarded as representing subjects' *understanding* of their bodily states, but not necessarily the actuality of those states" (p. 29; italics in original). Data supporting this statement come from recent studies that have investigated the factors influencing symptom reports.

Psychological Factors in Symptom Perception

Focus of attention. One of the more subtle, but pervasive, influences on our perception of symptoms is our focus of attention. Several studies (Fillingim & Fine, 1986; Pennebaker, 1980, 1982; Pennebaker & Lightner, 1980) have demonstrated that symptom perception often depends on what the person happens to be attending to. For example, one study (Pennebaker & Lightner, 1980) found that perceptions of fatigue among joggers are, in part, a function of terrain over which they are jogging.

When doing laps on an oval track, joggers tended to run more slowly than they did while jogging cross country through a wooded area, even though they reported equal levels of fatigue. Since joggers may well set their pace by their perceptions of fatigue, this suggests that joggers on the cross-country course paid less attention to fatigue. Apparently, the varied scenery encountered in the cross-country course distracted the joggers from internal sensations associated with fatigue. Along these same lines, Roger Fillingim and Mark Fine (1986) found that having runners focus on a target word repeated over headphones would result in fewer reports of symptoms than those same runners who listened to their own breathing and heart rate while running or were given no special instructions. Similarly, people are more likely to notice itching or tickling in their throats, and hence cough, during the boring parts of a movie than they are during more exciting parts (Pennebaker, 1980).

These findings accord with the common observations by parents concerning injury perception in their children. Children, particularly younger ones, often come home with various cuts and scratches, sometimes even bleeding, but think nothing of it until the injuries are pointed out—at which point they become extremely concerned, perhaps even bursting into tears. These observations and research findings can be explained by noting that symptom perception is, in part, the result of a competition among cues for our attention. We are continually bombarded by cues from many sources, both from the external environment and from our bodies. Given limitations on our information-processing capabilities, we can attend to only a small portion of these. Thus, the more we are engrossed in ongoing activities, the stronger the visceral cues need to be in order to break into awareness. Children deeply engrossed in playing with friends are less likely to notice relatively minor cuts and scratches than they would be when playing alone or when less engrossed.

However, under some circumstances, paying close attention to physical sensations can result in reduced feelings of distress. For example, several studies have found that instructing people to pay attention to the discrete sensory aspects of sensations can reduce the distress associated with both experimental and clinical pain. In one study (Leventhal, Brown, Shacham, & Engquist, 1979), male college students reported experiencing less pain in a pain experiment (involving submerging one's hand in ice water) when they were given detailed information about the specific sensations they would be experiencing. When subjects were told about likely feelings of apprehension, given only procedural information and/or warned about strong pain sensations, they reported feeling higher levels of pain. Other studies have found that giving this type of sensory information can reduce distress from cancer chemotherapy (Love, Nerenz, & Leventhal, 1983) as well as childbirth pain (Leventhal, Leventhal, Shacham, & Easterling, 1989). This sensory monitoring, as it is called, apparently reduces distress by focusing the person's attention on relatively objective aspects of the sensations involved and away from more negative and emotional interpretations. In so doing, the person is able to take a more neutral, detached approach to otherwise distressing sensations (Cioffi, 1991).

Cognitive set. Closely related to focus of attention is one's cognitive set. Making certain symptoms salient by having people think about them or even simply making

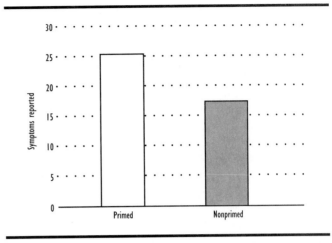

FIGURE 8.1
The effect of cognitive set on the perception of symptoms.

Note. Primed subjects had health-related thinking activated, whereas non-primed subjects did not. Based on data from "Priming symptom reports with health-related cognitive activity" by J. A. Skelton and D. B. Strohmetz, 1990, *Personality and Social Psychology Bulletin, 16,* p. 452.

thoughts about health in general more prominent can increase symptom reporting. For example, one study examining the effects of cognitive set on symptom reporting (Skelton & Strohmetz, 1990) had subjects engage in a semantic decision-making task designed to activate health-related thinking. To test for the effects on symptom reporting of making health-related thoughts prominent, half the subjects filled out a symptom checklist before the task, and half filled it out afterward. The effects of cognitive set were demonstrated in the fact that subjects filling out the checklist after the task reported significantly more symptoms than did those filling out the checklist before the task. These effects are shown in Figure 8.1. A related experiment (Skelton, Oppler, Taylor, & Thomas, 1988) had subjects imagine different physical symptoms (such as "cold hands," "upset stomach," and "itchy ankle"). Compared to other subjects asked to think about non-health-related images (such as a friend's face), subjects thinking about symptoms reported experiencing more of the symptoms they were thinking of.

Expectations. Suggestibility is particularly strong when people have a specific idea as to what they should be experiencing. In fact, James Pennebaker (1982; Pennebaker & Skelton, 1981) contends that the process of experiencing symptoms can be thought of in terms of a hypothesis-guided search. Bodily sensations occur continually, and are often rather vague and ambiguous. Given this ambiguity, how we experience these sensations is likely to be influenced strongly by our hypotheses as to what we should be experiencing.

In an experiment testing this idea (Pennebaker & Skelton, 1981), subjects were told that they would be exposed to two minutes of ultrasonic noise. Further, subjects

TABLE 8.1   *The Effects of Hypothesis on Perceived Finger Temperature*

Measure	Hypothesis		
	Increase	*Decrease*	*None*
Self-reported finger temperature	69.6	48.1	57.8
Attention to warmth	66.5	33.5	29.9
Attention to coolness	21.3	42.5	24.8
Correlation between self-reported temperature and temperature fluctuations	+.48	−.49	+.11

Note. Self-reported finger temperature ranged from 1 = finger became cooler to 50 = no change to 100 = finger became warmer. The two attention items required subjects to rate the degree to which they attended to warmth (coolness): 1 = not at all and 100 = a great deal. From "Selective monitoring of bodily sensations" by J. W. Pennebaker and J. A. Skelton, 1981, *Journal of Personality and Social Psychology, 41,* 216.

in three conditions were told that this noise would result in either an increase or a decrease in finger temperature or, in a control condition, were told nothing about a change in finger temperature. After exposure to a tape with the "ultrasonic noise" (in actuality all but 15 seconds of the tape was blank), subjects were asked to rate their finger temperature and indicate the extent to which they paid attention to the warmth and coolness of their fingers. Actual finger temperature was monitored during the session using a thermistor. During the experiment, there was, in fact, no overall change in finger temperature for subjects in any of the conditions. However, as can be seen in Table 8.1, those led to believe that they would experience an increase in finger temperature showed a rise in perceived finger temperature; this was not the case for those expecting a decrease or who were given no hypothesis at all.

Particularly revealing was the finding that the amount of increase or decrease in perceived skin temperature was correlated with the *number* of fluctuations in recorded skin temperature during the session. This suggests that subjects were paying attention to the random fluctuations in skin temperature during the session and inferring from these the amount of increase or decrease. When expecting an increase in temperature, subjects inferred that more fluctuations indicated a greater increase in temperature, whereas subjects expecting a decrease concluded that more fluctuations meant more of a decrease in temperature.

Emotions. So far we have been concerned with various cognitive influences on symptom perception. What about our emotions? Do they also influence the symptoms that we perceive? Experience seems to suggest that they do. We have all had days when we were in such a good mood that we did not notice various aches and pains that we would ordinarily pay attention to. Yet we have also had days when we have been in a bad mood and seemed to notice every discomfort, no matter how minor. Research evidence backs up these experiential observations. For example, one study (Croyle &

We learn a great deal about which symptoms are important—and hence to be noticed— by the way in which others respond to those symptoms.

Uretsky, 1987) found that inducing a temporary bad mood in subjects led them to judge their health more negatively and to report more symptoms than was the case for subjects put into a positive mood. Along these same lines, another study, in which respondents kept a diary of symptoms and moods, found that bad moods were a consistent trigger for the reporting of symptoms (Verbrugge, 1985b).

More general mood dispositions seem to have a similar effect. In particular, recent research indicates that people who are prone to negative affectivity (NA)—a general disposition to experience negative emotions such as anger, disgust, guilt, and depression—are more sensitive to physical discomforts than are people less prone to these negative states (Watson & Pennebaker, 1989, 1991). Overall, there is evidence of a fairly strong relationship between negative mood states and self-report measures of physical health, but there is, at best, only a weak correlation between negative mood states and physiological health measures. This suggests that people who are high in NA probably experience no more actual physical pathology than do others, but they tend to be more sensitive to physical discomforts and hence report more symptoms.

Learning. In considering the symptoms that people experience, we also need to include the role of learning. In a very real sense, we learn how to experience symptoms. From the time children are very small, they are taught both directly and by example which symptoms are important and which are trivial. A mother's concern over a rash and seeming unconcern about a superficial cut provide a child with powerful cues about which symptoms to attend to and which to ignore. In addition, symptom reports can be used as a means of communication. When we want attention, medical help, emotional support, or even to avoid unpleasant obligations, we can use statements about symptoms in order to achieve those ends (Skelton & Pennebaker, 1990).

An example of the role of learning in symptom experience is found in research on menstrual symptoms. One survey of adult nursing students and their mothers (Whitehead, Busch, Heller, & Costa, 1986) found that how her mother reacted to menstrual symptoms when the student was an adolescent was significantly associated with the student's experience of menstruation as an adult. Students whose mothers exhibited menstrual distress or who were encouraged to take on a sick role when menstruating reported significantly more menstrual symptoms and were more likely to take time off or seek help for those symptoms than were students whose mothers did not respond to menses with distress. A similar pattern of findings was obtained for other symptoms as well. A more detailed analysis of menstrual symptoms is described in Box 8.2.

Accuracy in Symptom Perception

Given that the experience of symptoms is influenced by a range of psychological and physical factors, what can be said about the accuracy of our perception of bodily states? Are we capable of accurately detecting what is going on internally? We detect general or fairly pervasive bodily states, such as hunger or fatigue, accurately enough to know when to eat or when to rest. However, on closer examination, the evidence suggests that people's symptom perceptions are often highly inaccurate. For example, one study (Pennebaker, Gonder-Frederick, Stewart, Elfman, & Skelton, 1982) had subjects participate in 20 laboratory tasks that were separated by two-minute baseline periods. After each task and baseline period, physiological measures were taken, and subjects were asked to report symptoms they were experiencing. Correlations between the physiological measures and self-reported symptoms for individual subjects showed little evidence of accuracy of symptom perceptions. Although some correlations were high, up to .82, on the average, correlations between perceived symptoms and physiological measurements were quite low, ranging from .05 to .20. Similar results have been obtained when subjects have been asked to track their heart rate. Here the average correlations between actual and perceived heart rate were in the range of .065 to .12 (Pennebaker, 1981).

This lack of accuracy would appear to pose particular problems for individuals with diseases such as hypertension and diabetes, where regulation of internal body states is essential and patients often believe that they can monitor these states using specific symptoms (cf. Baumann & Leventhal, 1985; Gonder-Frederick & Cox, 1991; Gonder-Frederick, Cox, Bobbitt, & Pennebaker, 1986; Leventhal, Meyer, & Nerenz, 1980). For example, studies of hypertension patients have shown that beliefs about perceived relationships between high blood pressure and specific symptoms are generally inaccurate, but still influence treatment behavior (cf. Baumann & Leventhal, 1985; Leventhal et al., 1980; Pennebaker & Watson, 1988). In these cases, whether a person continues to take blood pressure medication, or even continues in treatment at all, may be based on monitoring symptoms that, in fact, have little to do with actual physiological state.

BOX 8.2 Menstruation and Cognition

Discussion of the relationship between menstruation and a woman's mood and behavior has recently grown. Long a topic of taboo and euphemisms, Americans are now more willing to discuss menstruation and its effects. Survey evidence shows that Americans have strong beliefs about menstruation; many believe that women cannot function normally at work during menstruation and that menstruation affects a woman's ability to think, among other effects (Delaney, Lupton, & Toth, 1988).

Diane Ruble and Jeanne Brooks-Gunn (1979) note that both popular and scientific discussions of the relationship of menstruation to behavior and psychological functioning rest on three basic assumptions: (1) women's fluctuations in symptoms, moods, and behavioral characteristics across the menstrual cycle are a well documented fact, (2) these changes are hormonally based, and (3) the changes are believed to be severe and possibly debilitating.

Hormonal changes undeniably occur during the menstrual cycle. But how valid are the above assumptions? Ruble and Brooks-Gunn argue that many of the changes that are presumed universal have little basis in fact. Although some women do experience debilitating symptoms during menstruation, the evidence for pervasive and severe symptoms among all or most women is very weak. Some studies show statistically significant relationships between a woman's menstrual cycle phase and physical and emotional symptoms. However, these changes are small and, with the exception of pain, water retention, and breast swelling, not consistently found. Further, virtually no evidence supports changes in performance related to the menstrual cycle, and no convincing physiological reasons exist for such changes. The strongest results obtained with regard to the relationship of the menstrual cycle to behavior and psychological functioning appear to be in the beliefs that people, both men and women, have about the effects of menstruation. Although there is relatively weak evidence for the actual effects, there are strong beliefs about those effects.

If, in fact, the psychological and behavioral effects of menstruation are relatively small in relationship to the beliefs that people have about those effects, how can we account for the beliefs? Ruble and Brooks-Gunn argue

that the answer to this question can be found in recent work in social cognition that investigates the cognitive processes involved in the formation of social beliefs. These cognitive processes may result in the development of beliefs about the effects of menstruation in the absence of evidence and, once developed, in the strengthening of those beliefs.

With regard to the development of beliefs, research in social cognition has indicated several factors that can lead to beliefs in the absence of evidence. Beliefs about menstrual symptoms may well develop from connotations that people associate with menstruation. Ruble and Brooks-Gunn write that bleeding has negative connotations of injury or illness and that "menstruation is almost universally perceived in negative terms and to be in need of control by means of various rituals and taboos" (p. 183). These connotations set the stage for the development of beliefs about menstrual symptoms. In addition, when an event is salient to a person, as menstruation is to a woman, people are more likely to make attributions to that event and to perceive relationships between that event and others. Thus bad moods or off days occurring premenstrually may be attributed to the menstrual cycle because of its salience, when, in fact, such moods or off days occur at other times as well but are attributed to other factors. Third, research in social cognition has shown that people are much more likely to remember when salient events occur together than they are to notice times when such co-occurrence does not take place. This selectivity in information processing may lead women to remember a few occasions when symptoms occurred premenstrually or menstrually, but not pay attention to the other times when those symptoms were not present. These factors can easily lead to the development of beliefs about the occurrence of symptoms during the menstrual cycle in the relative absence of evidence.

Once these beliefs become established, other cognitive processes maintain and strengthen them. When people have a belief about something, they may distort evidence so that it is consistent with that belief. Moreover, after a belief has become established, it becomes resistant to disconfirmation and tends to bias the recollection of events. With regard to beliefs about menstruation, people will ignore evidence that would disconfirm the expected association between menstrual phase and symptoms and selectively recall information that fits with the beliefs.

Does all this argue that menstrual symptoms are "all in her head"? Not at all. What it illustrates is that the symptoms experienced during different phases of the menstrual cycle, like other symptoms experienced by both men and women, are a function of both the physiological changes involved and beliefs about which symptoms should be occurring.

UNDERSTANDING ILLNESS

Although the perception of symptoms is an important part of experiencing illness, it is by no means the whole story. People do not just experience individual symptoms; they organize these symptoms into more global entities. In other words, people develop mental representations of different physical diseases. For example, when experiencing such symptoms as a fever, chills, headache, nasal congestion, and generalized achiness, a person will most likely think of these symptoms in terms of a specific illness, for example, the flu. As we will see, people's representations of different diseases have important implications for how they experience and respond to illness.

The Nature of Illness Representations

How can we best describe these illness representations? Research in cognitive psychology is clear in indicating that when people process information about objects or events they do not do so in terms of discrete pieces of information, but rather in terms of organized "bundles" of information, or **schemata** (Fiske & Taylor, 1991). With respect to physical illness, these schemata represent a person's overall understanding of particular illnesses. Therefore, illness representations include information about the identity of the illness in question, its symptoms, possible causes, likely time course, and potential consequences (Bishop, 1991b; Leventhal & Diefenbach, 1991; Leventhal, Nerenz, & Steele, 1984).

schema (pl., schemata)
An organized "bundle" of information about a specific object, idea, or event.

These illness representations provide the basis for the person's active attempts to understand and appropriately respond to potential health threats (Bishop, 1991b; Leventhal & Diefenbach, 1991). For the person experiencing symptoms of fever, chills, headache, nasal congestion, and generalized achiness, these symptoms provide signals that something may be wrong, but of themselves have no necessary meaning or implications. They merely indicate perceived bodily sensations. Illness representations provide a means of interpreting symptoms and giving them meaning. Thus relating the symptoms to a cognitive schema for the flu helps the person to make sense of the symptoms and have an idea of what to do about them. Illness representations also provide the basis for interpreting and responding to other health-related information, such as health warnings or medical diagnoses. Having a cognitive schema for lung cancer provides people with a basis for interpreting and responding to warnings about cigarette smoking. Similarly, a person gives meaning to a diagnosis of hypertension by applying a cognitive schema for that disease.

Where do these illness representations come from? At least three sources can be identified (Leventhal et al., 1980). One is the semantic associations people have with disease names. When disease names have strong semantic associations, they are likely to influence how people think about the disease. For example, hypertension is often considered related to emotional tension. Second, we construct illness representations from our experience with different illnesses, both our own and those of others around us. Having had a particular disease or being around someone with it gives a person information about the symptoms involved, how long it lasts, and so on. In this regard, serendipitous factors appear to play an important role. For example, when a person is diagnosed with hypertension after having engaged in heavy physical activity or had a recent interpersonal conflict, these events may be seen as causally related to the hypertension (Leventhal et al., 1980). In addition, our illness schemata are heavily influenced by information that we receive from others and from our culture in general. Folk illness concepts, media discussions, information from parents, friends, and health providers, and articles in newspapers and magazines all provide us with information about different diseases.

Illness Representations in Action

Once developed, the schemata that people have for different illnesses can have profound effects on how they deal with illness-related situations. The next few paragraphs explore two major ways in which illness representations influence how people experience and deal with illness.

Illness experience. As already noted, people's illness schemata serve as a basis for interpreting symptoms that they experience. How does this work? One likely possibility is that a person's schemata for different diseases provide templates that the person can match against symptoms experienced to provide an interpretation of the illness (Bishop, 1991b; Bishop & Converse, 1986). Illness representations can be thought of as **prototypes,** or idealized representations of the symptoms and other attributes associated with particular diseases. When a person experiences symptoms, a cognitive search is initiated, in which the person attempts to make sense of those symptoms by matching them against available prototypes. Assuming success in finding a prototype that provides a reasonable match, the person identifies the symptoms as representing that disease. This allows the person to access other information about the disease contained in the prototype, such as likely cause, duration, other symptoms, and potential curative actions. When the person is unsuccessful at matching the symptoms to a prototype, he may experience confusion about the cause and implications of the symptoms that, at least in the case of relatively serious symptoms, can be quite anxiety provoking (Bishop, Briede, Cavazos, Grotzinger, & McMahon, 1987; Bishop, Sikes, Schroeder, McGregor, & Holub, 1985).

prototype
An idealized or typical instance of a category. Disease prototypes are idealized conceptions of specific diseases.

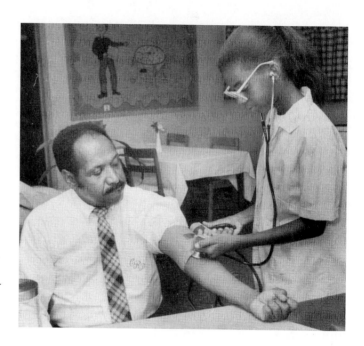

The beliefs that hypertensives have about their disease has a considerable impact on whether they stay in treatment.

One implication of this is that the specific disease prototypes that the person has available will channel the illness experience. Having a particular prototype can produce illness experiences that the person would not have in the absence of the prototype. A vivid example of this phenomenon is what is known as medical students' disease (Mechanic, 1978; Woods, Natterson, & Silverman, 1966). Medical educators have long observed the tendency among medical students to believe that they are experiencing the illnesses that they are studying. This affliction, which affects approximately 70% of medical students, is likely to occur when the student is under stress (which is almost ubiquitous in medical school) and notices bodily symptoms, usually benign, that bear at least a vague resemblance to symptoms of the condition being studied. Having recently acquired new, but as yet incomplete, information about the disease in question, the student jumps to the conclusion that the symptoms, in fact, signal that disease. The cure for medical students' disease consists of time, reassurance from a trusted instructor or physician, and additional information about the disease. In this case, a little knowledge can indeed be a dangerous thing.

Treatment behavior. Illness schemata also have a considerable impact on how people cope with chronic or life-threatening diseases and the treatment for those conditions. Howard Leventhal and his colleagues (Baumann & Leventhal, 1985; Leventhal et al., 1980, 1984; Leventhal, Nerenz, & Straus, 1982) have pointed out that the cognitive representations that patients develop of diseases such as hypertension and cancer play a central role in guiding their behavior in treatment, as well as in coping with the disease and side effects of treatment.

Good examples of this are the disease representations held by hypertensive patients (Leventhal & Diefenbach, 1991; Leventhal et al., 1982, 1984). Although hypertension is a condition that is described by most medical authorities as having no overt symptoms (other than elevated blood pressure), most patients studied by the Leventhal group believed that they could monitor certain symptoms to determine when their blood pressure was elevated. The symptoms identified varied from person to person, and often seemed to have been identified on the basis of a semantic association in which "hyper-tension" was seen as indicating high levels of tension. Although other research (Pennebaker et al., 1982) has shown that these perceived associations are generally erroneous, patients were convinced of their validity and seemed to use them as a basis for treatment decisions (Meyer, Leventhal, & Gutmann, 1985).

In addition, patients seemed to be using three different "models" of hypertension as a disease. One group saw hypertension as an acute disease, meaning that it is like an infection that can be cured through treatment. A second group viewed hypertension as a cyclic disease in which the elevated blood pressure would come and go. The third group had a model of hypertension closer to the medical understanding of the disease and viewed it as being a chronic condition that requires life-long control. These models were in turn related to the person's treatment behavior. Among newly treated patients, those holding an acute model of hypertension were more likely to drop out of treatment within six months (58%) than were patients holding a chronic model (17%) (Leventhal et al., 1984).

RESPONDING TO ILLNESS

So far in our discussion of illness we have examined the cultural, social, and cognitive aspects of illness. We turn now to the behavioral side of illness, and consider what people do when they perceive themselves to be ill.

Types of Illness Response

Traditionally, the question of what people do about illness has focused on the seeking of medical attention (cf. Mechanic, 1978). Although seeking medical help for illness is an important aspect of illness behavior, it is only a minor aspect of people's behavioral responses to illness. For example, a recent study of symptom perception and illness behavior using daily health diaries found that a group of relatively healthy young respondents reported one or more symptoms on about 20% of the days surveyed, took remedial action for just over half those symptoms, reduced activity for roughly 30% of them, but sought medical attention for fewer than 8% (Bishop, 1984). In another health diary study, respondents reported symptoms on 38% of the diary days, with lay consultation for 48% of those symptoms, curative actions for 58%, but medical care for only 5% (Verbrugge, 1985b).

The range of behaviors in response to illness is exceedingly broad, encompassing such diverse behaviors as curtailing activities, discussing it with a friend or family member, taking an over-the-counter medication, making an appointment with a health care provider, and making a hurried trip to the emergency room. A glimpse of the various different illness behaviors can be found in a recent study by Michael Diefenbach, Howard Leventhal, and Linda Patrick-Miller (1990). In this study, undergraduate students were asked to describe their thoughts and likely actions in response to two different illness scenarios, one involving flu, the other, appendicitis. Classification of subjects' responses required 25 categories for thoughts and 15 categories for actions. Thoughts elicited by the two illnesses included those related to its cause, realization of being ill, thoughts about action, and positive and negative emotions. When asked about actions, subjects listed such behaviors as continuing with normal activities, reducing activities, relaxing, seeking professional help, looking to others, gathering information, taking medication, and engaging in health-promoting behaviors.

sick role
The role taken by a person who is defined as sick.

Responses to illness may also be organized into a special role, known as the **sick role,** in which people are relieved of their usual social responsibilities, such as going to school or work. For example, if a student wakes up on the day of a class presentation with clear symptoms of the flu or other illness, he or she is generally given a reprieve and allowed to do the presentation at a later time. Similarly, we do not expect a person who has just had surgery to report immediately for work. Rather, in both cases we define the individuals as ill and exempt them from their usual responsibilities. This exemption, however, is accompanied by the expectation that those involved will do whatever they can to return to health (Twaddle, 1972).

Illness Behavior as Coping

As we shall see below, illness behavior is determined by many factors. However, the underlying theme concerns how people cope with discomfort. At its most basic, illness behavior reflects a coping process. Thus the study of illness and illness behavior fits very well into the second general theme of this text, coping and adaptation. People use illness behavior to cope with physical discomforts and perceived symptoms. Actions taken in response to symptoms and perceived illness often involve direct attempts to find relief. But illness behavior as a coping response goes well beyond this. People also use illness behavior to deal with emotional, psychological, and social difficulties. David Mechanic (1978) shows that people often use physical complaints as a way of dealing with psychological distress. In particular, people who have difficulty expressing emotional distress directly may complain of physical symptoms and visit the doctor in order to ask for help with feelings of loneliness or other distress. Relatedly, the person may use illness to attract attention or sympathy from others.

In addition, illness can be used to deal with difficult social situations. For example, a student who conveniently becomes ill the morning of a big exam may, consciously or not, be using illness to avoid a potentially unpleasant situation. Because a person who is defined as ill and placed in the sick role is generally relieved of his or her usual obligations, being sick can sometimes be an attractive alternative. In such cases, as well as when the person uses illness to gain sympathy or deal with personal problems, illness behavior is reinforced by the **secondary gains** the person receives (Mechanic, 1978).

Deciding to See a Doctor

secondary gain
Gain or advantage that a person obtains by being ill.

As we have seen, people respond to illness in many ways. Most of the time, people deal with illness on their own or with the help of family or friends. However, for an important minority of their illnesses, people seek professional help. Although individuals seek medical attention for only a small proportion of their illness episodes (Bishop, 1984; Verbrugge, 1985b), this results in a very large number of medical visits overall. For example, Americans seek advice from medical practitioners more than a billion times per year, with the average person making more than five visits to physicians (National Center for Health Statistics, 1988b). What determines whether a person seeks medical attention for a particular illness? The person's medical condition clearly plays a role. However, that is only the beginning. Studies of medical care utilization demonstrate that some people are more likely than others to seek medical attention. In addition, people are more likely seek help at certain times than at others.

Who seeks help? How likely a person is to seek medical care depends in part on who that person is. Sociological studies of health care utilization have illustrated several demographic and sociocultural characteristics that seem to predispose people to seek health care (McKinlay, 1972; National Center for Health Statistics, 1987). These factors closely parallel those that shape the illness experience. First, age plays an important role. In particular, the very young and the old are more likely to seek medical attention than are those in between, partly because of the particular health needs of these age groups. Very young children generally receive periodic vaccinations and well-baby checks, and are prone to developing the various infectious diseases of childhood. As adults age, they are likely to develop chronic conditions and diseases associated with aging.

Gender is another important factor. Overall, females use health care services more than do males. With the exception of early childhood, when males and females see the doctor equally often, this finding holds across age groups and persists even when gender-specific conditions, such as pregnancy and gynecological problems, are excluded (Nathanson, 1977; National Center for Health Statistics, 1987; Verbrugge, 1979, 1982). These differences are particularly striking when we take into account the fact that women live longer than do men (Nathanson, 1977; National Center for Health Statistics, 1988b; also see Box 4.1). This greater longevity for women seems at odds with the greater illness seemingly implied by their more frequent use of health services.

The reasons for these differences are not entirely clear, although it appears that sex roles may play a critical role (Harrison, 1978; Nathanson, 1977; Verbrugge, 1982, 1985a). As noted in Chapter 4, male sex roles tend to emphasize aggression and risk taking, as well as "macho" behaviors such as smoking and drinking. These factors then increase males' risk of death from accidents and chronic diseases such as heart disease and lung cancer. Moreover, seeking medical care may be more in keeping with the female role: females tend to be more involved in health and health care than are males. For example, it is usually the mother in a family who attends to the health care needs of family members. In addition, it is often more socially acceptable for girls and women to express bodily discomforts than is the case for boys and men (Verbrugge, 1982, 1985a).

Use of health services is also influenced by socioeconomic status. Data from surveys of health care utilization indicate overall that poor people use health services more than do those at higher income levels. Generally, low-income people visit the doctor more and are more likely to be hospitalized than are the affluent (National Center for Health Statistics, 1987). In addition, where people at different SES levels obtain their care and the type of care that they seek differ. Those with higher incomes are likely to receive their care at private doctors' offices and to schedule visits for preventive care as well as to seek medical attention when they feel ill. The poor are more likely to use hospital emergency rooms and outpatient clinics, and tend to seek care only when they are experiencing symptoms of illness (Cockerham, Lueschen, Kunz, & Spaeth, 1986).

What accounts for these differences in health care utilization? The greater use of health services by the poor, at least in part, reflects social class differences in over-all health. For many reasons, poor people have more health problems and are in poorer health than those who are more affluent. On the average, low-income individuals are hospitalized more often, have longer hospitalizations, and are more likely to perceive their health as "fair" or "poor" (Health Resources and Services Administration, 1986). Differences in where people receive their care are to some extent a function of costs. Private health care is expensive, and the cost can be prohibitive for low-income persons, leading them to rely more on hospital emergency rooms and public clinics.

Health orientation and integration into the health care system also play a role. Recent surveys of health attitudes among low-income individuals argue that poor people often see themselves as less susceptible to illness (Rundall & Wheeler, 1979) and take less personal responsibility for their health (Cockerham et al., 1986). As a result, they are less likely to seek preventive health care, which, in turn, leads to higher illness rates. In addition, poor individuals are less likely to have a regular physician from whom they seek care. This lack of integration into the health care system contributes to their lack of preventive care and means that when they do fall ill, they are likely to seek help in a clinic or hospital emergency room (Rundall & Wheeler, 1979).

As we have seen, some groups in society are more likely than others to use health care services. These findings, however, should be kept in perspective. The differences that have been described reveal *average* differences based on age, sex, and income. However, each of these groups varies widely. For example, although on the average males use health services less than females do, some men go to the doctor frequently, and some women rarely go. The same points can be made with respect to age and socioeconomic status. In addition, these findings tell us nothing about *when* people seek medical attention.

When do people seek medical care? The seeking of medical care is more than just a matter of going to the doctor when a person has the most objective need. Studies of illness behavior indicate that *when* a person seeks help is a function of the specific nature of the symptoms experienced, the situation, personal needs, the person's illness schemata, and other factors.

Perhaps the most obvious determinant of when a person seeks help is the type of symptoms experienced. In particular, symptoms that are unexpected, visible, or defined as serious or disruptive are particularly likely to lead the person to seek medical attention (Mechanic, 1978). Additional insight into how symptoms affect illness behavior comes from a recent study of the basic cognitive dimensions used by middle-class white Americans in thinking about physical symptoms and their relationship to different actions (Bishop, 1987). The results of this study suggest four different dimensions used in thinking about symptoms. Specifically, people in this study seemed to be organizing symptoms on the basis of whether those symptoms are caused by a virus, have a physical or psychological cause, are disruptive to activities, and where they are located in the body. These dimensions were, in turn, related to three types of action. Perception of a symptom as caused by a virus was associated with self-care, for example, taking a non-prescription medicine or using a home remedy, whereas attributing a symptom to physical causes and location in the lower part of the body were related to seeking professional help. Disruptiveness of the symptoms was related to curtailing activities.

Whether a person seeks medical attention is also a function of the situation. As we saw earlier, a person's involvement in activities and the amount of stress in a situation are important determinants of illness experience. Situational factors are also of considerable importance in determining action after symptoms are perceived. For example, Irving Zola (1964) has identified five "triggers" that determine when a person will seek medical care. Three of these relate to the situation. First, seeking medical attention may be the result of an *interpersonal crisis*. In this case, an interpersonal situation causes the individual to notice symptoms and to dwell on them. An example of this is when a person uses illness or medical care as a means of manipulating others. Seeking medical care can also be triggered by *social interference*. This occurs when the person's symptoms disrupt valued social activities, such as when flu symptoms prevent a person from attending a party. A third trigger is *sanctioning*, in which the person is told by others to seek medical attention for a problem. This is likely to happen when the person's illness becomes too obvious for others to continue to ignore, or when the person's condition becomes disruptive for others, for example, when a person's progressive hearing loss begins to make normal conversation difficult for others in the family.

Beyond the symptoms and the situation, the individual's personal needs also play a role. We often think of good health as one of our paramount values. After all, "if you have your health, you have just about everything." However, health is often not the primary motivator of our health actions (Lau, Hartman, & Ware, 1986). Some needs may lead a person to ignore symptoms or put off seeking medical care. For example, fear of being diagnosed with cancer may lead a person to delay seeking help for suspected cancer symptoms (cf. Antonovsky & Hartman, 1974). Practical considerations, such as the need to go to work to earn a living or lack of money for doctor bills or medications, may also prevent a person from seeking help (Mechanic, 1978).

But people's needs may lead them to engage in illness behavior even in the absence of physical pathology. This may be conscious, as in the case of malingering, in which a person continues to occupy the sick role after the disease or injury is no longer present. For example, individuals seeking compensation for injuries may continue to exhibit illness behavior after the injuries have healed. Unconscious needs may also be the motivation, as in neurotic conversion reactions, in which the person uses physical symptoms as a way of dealing with unconscious neurotic conflicts. The term *abnormal illness behavior* has been coined to refer to these kinds of persistent, maladaptive illness behavior that reflect the person's personal needs rather than state of health (Pilowsky, 1978). Such illness behavior can be either "illness affirming," in which case the person engages in illness behavior in the absence of actual pathology, or "illness denying," where the person refuses to acknowledge or respond to known pathology.

Whether people seek help is also determined by their cognitive representations, or schemata, for different illnesses. As noted earlier, people understand symptoms in terms of their schemata for specific illnesses. These schemata include ideas about the kinds of actions required to cure a condition or at least ameliorate its symptoms. When a schema for a particular condition is accessed, the person is provided with ideas for actions to take. Whether a person seeks medical attention or engages in self-care or other illness behavior is likely to depend on the illness schema that the person uses for interpreting the symptoms. For example, consider the case of Bill, who experiences congested sinuses, moderate fever, lack of energy, chest congestion, and gastrointestinal upset. These symptoms fit most people's schema for the flu, thus he will probably conclude that that is what he has. On the basis of this interpretation, he is likely to consider that the appropriate response is simply to take it easy for a while and use over-the-counter medications to ameliorate the symptoms. Further, he is likely to expect that the symptoms will last for no more than a few days. However, if symptoms continue to get worse and the medications prove ineffective in providing relief, Bill is likely to question his interpretation. Perhaps, rather than the flu, these symptoms actually indicate something more serious, such as pneumonia. For most people, the schema of pneumonia includes the action component of seeking medical attention. Accessing this schema, Bill is then likely to decide to see his doctor.

Delaying Medical Care

For certain illnesses, the person must seek medical attention quickly in order to even survive. For example, 70% of deaths from myocardial infarction (MI) occur within four hours of the onset of symptoms (Gillum, Feinleib, Margolis, Fabsitz, & Brasch, 1976). In such cases, getting immediate medical attention can literally make the difference between life and death. Similarly, seeking timely medical care for cancer symptoms can make the difference between catching the disease in its early stages, when it is still localized, and dealing with cancers that have metastasized to other areas

appraisal delay
The amount of time that it takes a person after experiencing symptoms to decide that he or she is ill.

illness delay
The time required for a person to decide that professional help is required after deciding that he or she is ill.

utilization delay
The time it takes a person to decide to seek professional help after deciding that such help is

of the body and thus are much more difficult to treat (Renneker, 1988). Despite the obvious need for timely treatment, many patients postpone going to the doctor. MI patients often wait several hours or more before seeking treatment; cancer patients sometimes delay for months. Why? What causes people to delay seeking medical attention for serious conditions?

Addressing this question is assisted by conceptualizing the process of seeking medical help in terms of stages. In their analysis of the determinants of delay behavior, Martin Safer and his coworkers (Safer, Tharps, Jackson, & Leventhal, 1979) outline three basic stages in the decision to seek medical care, each of which can result in delay. First, the person must decide if he or she is ill. The time involved in this decision is termed **appraisal delay.** After illness has been recognized, the person must decide whether professional help is needed. This can result in **illness delay.** Finally, the person must decide to actually seek help. The time required to make this decision is referred to as **utilization delay.** Together, these three stages represent the amount of time between first noticing the symptoms and the seeking of care (see Figure 8.2).

What determines the amount of delay at each of these stages? Interviews with patients seeking care at hospital clinics revealed that appraisal delay was related to the sensory aspects of the person's symptoms, as well as whether the person had read about the symptoms. Patients showed less delay when they were in pain or bleeding, but showed more delay when they took time to read about their symptoms. In fact, those

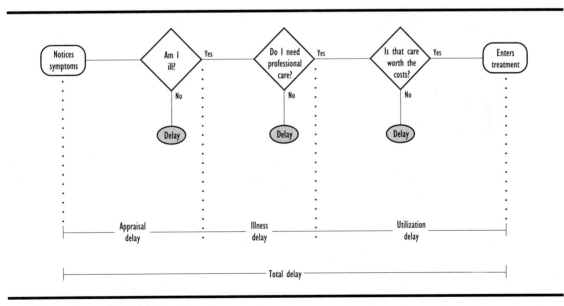

FIGURE 8.2   *Three stages of delay in seeking medical help for symptoms.*

Note. From "Determinants of three stages of delay in seeking care at a medical clinic" by M. A. Safer, Q. Tharps, T. Jackson, and H. Leventhal, 1979, *Medical Care, 17,* p. 12. Reprinted by permission.

who read a great deal about their symptoms delayed more than five times as long as those who did not read about their symptoms. Those who read about their symptoms were probably less certain about whether the symptoms indicated illness and were looking for additional information to help them make up their minds (Safer et al., 1979). A similar pattern of results was obtained in a study of patients who had experienced a heart attack. Initial pain led to short delay, whereas talking with others about symptoms was associated with longer delay (Matthews, Seigel, Kuller, Thompson, & Varat, 1983).

Illness delay showed a somewhat different pattern. The sensory aspects of the symptoms were still important, but other factors also came into play. At this stage, longer delay was associated with having symptoms that the person had had before. Apparently, because of their previous experience with the symptoms, patients experiencing old symptoms did not feel the same urgency to seek care as did those experiencing particular symptoms for the first time. Images and thoughts evoked by the symptoms also affected delay. Patients who imagined negative consequences of being sick—such as being on the operating table—or who spent time thinking about the symptoms and their consequences tended to delay longer than those who did not. In addition, males delayed longer than did females.

Whereas appraisal and illness delay largely depended on sensory aspects of the symptoms and how the person thought about them, utilization delay was most closely related to practical concerns. The strongest predictor of utilization delay was concern over the cost of the treatment. Not surprisingly, those very concerned about cost delayed longer than others who were less concerned. In addition, patients with painful symptoms and who felt that their symptoms could be cured showed less delay. Here, patients seemed to be evaluating the urgency of their need for care as well as its likely utility.

The studies discussed so far have focused on adults seeking care for themselves. Do the same factors hold when parents seek care for their children? The evidence suggests that they do. For example, one study found that mothers' delay in seeking pediatric care for their children was determined by the nature of the symptoms, age of the child, family history, and the level of the mother's worry about the symptoms. Mothers sought care more quickly when their children had fever or respiratory problems, or when there was a history of chronic illness in the family. But mothers with younger children or who worried about their child's symptoms tended to take longer to seek care. In the latter case a primary reason for seeking care appeared to be concern about symptoms that had persisted for a week or more combined with continuing complaint from the child (Turk, Litt, Salovey, & Walker, 1985).

Overusing Medical Care

The opposite of delay is the seeking of medical care without good reason. As was noted at the beginning of this chapter, many patients seeking care from family practitioners have no diagnosable disease. Such overuse of medical services exacts a cost in both monetary and physical terms. The "worried well," those who are not sick but believe that they might be, are estimated to be responsible for 50% of the cost of adult ambulatory health care (Barsky & Klerman, 1983). In addition, patients who seek medical care needlessly may be subjected to unnecessary medical tests, given unneeded medications, and put through needless surgery. An example of this, as described by internist Timothy Quill (1985), is a 74-year-old woman, who over the course of a single year had been evaluated by a cardiologist for chest pain, a gastroenterologist for abdominal pain, a pulmonologist for shortness of breath, and was currently being referred for severe headache and weakness. Beginning when she was 24, she had had over 30 operations for vague problems and was currently taking six different prescription medications. Yet physical examination showed her to be in remarkably good health.

hypochondriasis
A false belief, also known as hypochondria, in having a disease or an exaggerated fear of contracting disease.

What leads to this overuse of medical services? Such overuse can be attributed largely to patients who seek medical attention for emotional reasons. Some of these patients suffer from psychiatric disorder, whereas others use symptoms and help seeking as a way of getting attention or manipulating others. **Hypochondriasis,** or hypochondria, is a false belief in having a disease or an exaggerated fear of contracting one. These beliefs persist despite medical reassurance that nothing is, in fact, wrong (Kellner, 1987). Patients with hypochondriasis often experience vague symptoms that they interpret as being signs of disease. These symptoms, often related to the head, neck, abdomen, and chest, are ones that healthy people experience from time to time but generally think little of. Because they are preoccupied with their bodies, hypochondriacs see such symptoms as cause for alarm and resist the suggestion that the symptoms are normal. This conviction that they are ill, despite reassurance from health care givers, often leads hypochondriacs to "doctor shop," seeking advice from physicians until they find one who finds some kind of physical cause for the symptoms.

neuroticism
A broad personality trait including self-consciousness, inability to inhibit cravings, vulnerability to stress, and a tendency to experience negative emotions.

One major underlying component of hypochondriasis appears to be the personality dimension of **neuroticism.** Neuroticism is a broad trait that includes self-consciousness, inability to inhibit cravings, vulnerability to stress, and a tendency to experience negative emotions such as anxiety, hostility, and depression. According to Paul Costa and Robert McCrae (1980, 1985), the tendency to overreport and seek help for physical complaints is closely related to neuroticism, even for individuals who do not suffer from psychiatric disorder. In support of this contention, Costa and McCrae show that there is a strong correlation between neuroticism and physical complaints, both for people who would qualify as emotionally disturbed and for those whose neuroticism scores are within the normal range. Thus even people with mildly elevated neuroticism scores tend to overuse health care, though not to the extreme extent found among some hypochondriacs.

Overuse of health services may also be a learned social response, in which a person attempts to attract attention and manipulate others (Barsky & Klerman, 1983). Thus the person complains of symptoms so as to obtain sympathy or encouragement, and uses the sick role to avoid responsibilities or challenges. Visiting the doctor is a way to gain sympathy and to have one's entry into the sick role validated.

Beyond this, physical complaints seem to serve as a means by which people can protect their self-esteem. Along these lines, hypochondriacal individuals may use physical symptoms as a self-handicapping strategy. Self-handicapping provides people with ready excuses for failure by placing impediments in their own paths. Thus, should they perform poorly, they can save face and preserve their own self-esteem by attributing their failure to the impediment, rather than to their own lack of ability. A study supporting this notion (Smith, Snyder, & Perkins, 1983) found that hypochondriacal subjects reported the largest number of symptoms when they performed a task described as a test of "social intelligence," and were allowed to believe that physical symptoms might be an excuse for poor performance. Fewer symptoms were reported when they were told that performance was unrelated to physical health, or when the task was described as simply a pilot test of some materials for a future study.

In summary, people respond to illness in various ways. Underlying the different responses to illness are the ways in which people cope with both physical and psychological discomfort. Most symptoms result in either self-care or simply business as usual. Although in most cases this may be appropriate, many people delay seeking help for symptoms of serious disease or seek help when none is needed. This underscores the fact that whether, as well as when, a person seeks medical attention results as much from psychological and social factors as from the kinds of symptoms experienced.

SUMMARY

This chapter examines how lay people understand and interpret physical symptoms and illness. Although the terms "disease" and "illness" are often used interchangeably, they are, in fact, quite different. Disease refers to biological events occurring in the body, events that can be confirmed objectively through examination and medical tests. But illness refers to the person's subjective experiences of suffering and discomfort.

The experience of illness and the person's response to it are a function of many influences. Culture provides people with a set of basic illness orientations and conceptual categories for understanding suffering and discomfort. This can be seen clearly in cross-cultural comparisons of illness conceptions and in differences in the reporting and response to symptoms among cultural groups within a single society. The experience of illness is also a function of the person's social situation. People are more likely to experience and do something about symptoms when they are under stress. Further, they are less likely to experience and respond to symptoms when they are deeply engrossed in activities. Age, sex, social class, and living arrangements also affect the experience of illness.

The starting point for many illnesses is the experience of symptoms. The process by which we experience symptoms is a complex one that is certainly influenced by the person's physiological state, but is also a function of numerous other influences. In fact, studies of the accuracy of symptom perception have demonstrated that people are often highly inaccurate in their perception of internal states. Symptom perception has been shown to be strongly influenced by situational cues, cognitive set, the person's expectations, emotional states, and learning. The question of symptom perception takes on particular relevance in the case of chronic conditions such as diabetes and hypertension, where patients often believe that they can detect changes in blood glucose and blood pressure by monitoring certain symptoms. Studies have proved that these beliefs are often inaccurate and can lead the person to erroneous conclusions about the need to continue on medication or to seek medical attention.

A person's cognitive representations of different illnesses are also important in the perception of physical health. People do not just experience symptoms—they actively construct cognitive models of physical illnesses that include the identity of the illness, its symptoms, cause, expected time course, consequences, and cure. These cognitive models, which develop out of the person's illness experiences, as well as through socialization and receiving information from others, play a critical role in directing the person's coping with suffering and discomfort and their response to perceived health threats.

Our goal as health psychologists is ultimately to understand people's behavioral responses to illness or illness behavior. These responses can take forms ranging from a minimal reduction in activities to seeking immediate medical attention, and can best be understood in terms of how people cope with discomfort. The specific form of a person's illness behavior, and in particular whether and when he or she seeks medical care, depends on who the person is, the symptoms perceived, the cognitive models used to interpret them, and personal needs and situational factors. These factors also help to explain why some people delay seeking care for symptoms of serious illness, while others overuse medical services.

KEY TERMS

disease (183)
illness (183)
illness behavior (183)
lay referral (187)
symptom (189)
schema (196)
prototype (197)

sick role (200)
secondary gain (201)
appraisal delay (205)
illness delay (205)
utilization delay (205)
hypochondriasis (207)
neuroticism (207)

SUGGESTED READINGS

Burbach, D. J., & Peterson, L. (1986). Children's concepts of physical illness: A review and critique of the cognitive-developmental literature. *Health Psychology, 5*, 307–25. Daniel Burbach and Lizette Peterson discuss how children develop their ideas about physical illness and how these ideas are often quite different from those of adults.

Leventhal, H., Nerenz, D., & Straus, A. (1982). Self-regulation and the mechanisms of symptom appraisal. In D. Mechanic (ed.), *Symptoms, illness behavior, and help-seeking*. New York: Prodist. In this chapter, Howard Leventhal, David Nerenz, and Andrea Strauss describe their self-regulation model for understanding how people deal with illness and treatment.

Pennebaker, J. W. (1984). Accuracy of symptom perception. In A. Baum, S. E. Taylor, & J. Singer (eds.), *Handbook of psychology and health*. Vol. 4. Hillsdale, NJ: Erlbaum. In this chapter, James Pennebaker empirically evaluates the extent to which people are able to report accurately on physiological changes occurring in their bodies.

Skelton, J. A., & Croyle, R. T. (eds.) (1991). *Mental representation in health and illness*. New York: Springer-Verlag. The chapters in this book summarize recent research on the cognitive representation of illness and its implications for understanding health-related behavior.

CHAPTER 9

Interacting with the Health Care System

L inda, now in her thirties, had been having earaches off and on since childhood, so it was really no surprise when she developed yet another one. This one, though, seemed different. It did not go away with the usual combination of prescribed ear drops and time. After several visits to her primary care physician, Linda was referred to an ear, nose, and throat specialist who diagnosed the problem as a possible cholesteatoma, a cyst in the middle ear that can be the result of repeated ear infections. To prevent possible serious damage to the middle ear, Linda would need surgery to remove the cholesteatoma. Although having surgery meant taking time away from her job and family and was certainly not a pleasant prospect, it was going to be necessary to preserve her hearing.

A date was set for the surgery, and, on the appointed day, Linda checked into the hospital. Efforts were clearly being made to make the hospital as pleasant as possible.

However, it still had a rather drab institutional air about it. Linda's room, on a seemingly endless corridor, was pleasant enough, but thoroughly impersonal. The nurses were constantly on the go, and, even though they tried to be friendly, never seemed to have much time for individual patients as they struggled to keep up with their various duties. Most of Linda's first day was spent with various lab tests and examinations in preparation for the surgery. After having blood drawn numerous times and being poked and prodded in seemingly every possible way, she began feeling less like a person and more like simply a body to be operated on. Her first response was to try to take it in stride. But then she began to rebel in various minor ways, like refusing to get out of her street clothes and into a hospital gown until absolutely ordered to. Finally, in a weakened state after the surgery, she gave up and tried to do what she was told.

MIND AND BODY: PSYCHOLOGY AND HEALTH CARE

Sooner or later, all of us come into contact with the health care system. The encounter may be brief, as with a visit to a clinic for an immunization or a doctor's appointment for troubling symptoms, or it may involve more extended contact such as being hospitalized or recuperating in a nursing home. What is the nature of these interactions with the health care system? What psychological factors are involved? What is the impact of these psychological factors on health? This chapter explores these questions by considering the relationship between patients and the individuals, as well as the institutions, that make up the health care system.

When we are ill and seek medical attention, we are primarily concerned with the direct effects that medical attention may have on our health. Therefore, we are likely to focus on the physical and technical aspects of the health care system. Has the doctor made the correct diagnosis? Will the treatment be effective? Does the hospital have modern facilities and the latest medical equipment? These aspects of health care are obviously important. However, few people realize the extent to which psychological factors influence health care. As we will see, evidence is mounting that the psychological aspects of health care have both direct and indirect effects on treatment outcome. For one thing, how we feel about individual health care providers has an impact not only on our satisfaction with care but also on how well we respond to treatment. Relatedly, the quality of our communication with doctors and other health professionals has an indirect effect on health by influencing whether we follow treatment recommendations. These are but two examples of the mind-body connection and the importance of interpersonal relations in health and health care. Other important examples will be found in analyzing the psychological aspects of hospitalization.

PATIENT-PRACTITIONER RELATIONSHIPS

At the heart of our interactions with the health care system are relationships with individual practitioners. These relationships may be brief and impersonal, such as when a person goes to the emergency room and is seen by whichever doctor is on duty, or they may be longer lasting and more personal, as when a person has a regular primary physician or routinely consults with a particular specialist. Regardless of whether it is brief or longer lasting, this relationship can have important implications for how the person evaluates the care received and for health outcomes. To better understand this, let us examine the nature of patient-practitioner interactions and their effects on both psychosocial and health outcomes.

The Psychology of Patient-Practitioner Interaction

Think about the last time you visited a doctor. What was the interaction like? How did the doctor behave toward you? How did you behave toward the doctor? What about your interaction with nurses? These questions lead one to realize that interactions between patients and practitioners have several characteristic features. First, they often involve emotional intensity, which derives from the fact that health care providers are often given access to the patient's body and intimate details of the patient's life; the intensity also results from the emotional dependency that can develop when people are ill (DiMatteo, 1979). Second, the interaction involves significant status differences. As professionals, physicians are generally perceived as high in social status. In health care settings, physicians are the highest-ranking professionals, followed by nurses and other health care staff. Patients, however, come from all walks of life and vary considerably in social status. In health care settings, they rank below health care staff, and are expected to defer to them. Finally, interactions between patients and health care providers frequently involve various types of social influence. Healing is, in part, a persuasive art that often depends on the practitioner's ability to influence the patient's health-related attitudes and behavior (Rodin & Janis, 1979).

Interactions between patients and health care providers can be viewed as mini-dramas in which the behavior of each is governed by socially prescribed roles. The behavior of health care providers is guided by people's expectations about how doctors and other health professionals should act. These professionals are viewed as having a special responsibility for promoting and restoring the health of their patients. As a part of this, they are expected to possess a high degree of technical competence and have a commitment to serving people. In addition, they are expected to maintain emotional neutrality when interacting with patients, while expressing compassion for their suffering. In return for their performance of this role, health care providers, especially doctors, are accorded a high degree of status and power (Menke, 1975; Parsons, 1975).

Patients also have a specific role. When people are ill, they are normally relieved of usual social duties and take on the *sick role* (see Chapter 8). As a part of this role, patients are usually viewed as the victims of forces beyond their control and, therefore, are not held responsible for their condition. In addition, they are expected to profess a desire to get better, seek appropriate medical attention, and, in general, to do whatever is necessary to return to health (Arluke, Kennedy, & Kessler, 1979; Parsons, 1975).

How these roles are played out in practice depends on how practitioners and patients approach their respective roles. Differences in practitioner orientations are illustrated in a study by Michael Calnan (1988). Doctors with a *social orientation* viewed their role in broad terms that included concern with both the physical and the social aspects of health. These doctors indicated a greater interest in the psychosocial aspects of medicine and reported more involvement in such activities as health education, consultation on health behaviors, and screening activities. In addition, they were less concerned with the financial incentives in medicine and were more likely to work in smaller towns. Doctors with a *medical orientation,* by contrast, focused more on the organic disease and were less concerned with the patient's personal or social concerns; they were also less concerned with health education, health behaviors, and screening activities. As a group, they placed more emphasis on financial rewards and were more likely to work in larger towns and cities.

Not surprisingly, doctors' orientations toward patients have significant implications for patients' evaluations of their competence. In particular, patients express the greatest confidence in a doctor when they feel that the doctor spends sufficient time with them, is interested in them as individuals, and demonstrates devotion to helping them deal with their illnesses (Ben-Sira, 1980).

Patients also differ considerably in how they approach the patient role. One difference concerns expectations about who should make the final decisions about their health. Some patients prefer a passive role in which the doctor decides what is best for them, whereas other patients prefer to take a more active role and make health decisions for themselves. For example, some patients prefer simply to be told what they should do about their illness. Other patients prefer to have the doctor discuss with them the various treatment options and then make the decision jointly. These different orientations have clear implications for the interaction that takes place between the patient and the practitioner. In addition, a recent study (Brody, Miller, Lerman, Smith, & Caputo, 1989) suggests that these differing orientations may have an impact on patients' recovery, at least in the short-term. In this study, patients attending a general internal medicine clinic were questioned about their involvement in health decisions just before their interaction with the doctor. In addition, they were interviewed about their current level of symptoms and discomfort both before the visit and one week later. Patients who preferred to take an active role during their visit to the doctor generally showed more improvement in their symptoms than did patients taking a more passive role. The time frame for this study was short, and most of the illnesses were relatively minor, but the results are suggestive and bear follow-up.

Communication Between Patient and Practitioner

Communication is crucial to any interaction between patient and practitioner. Patients come to practitioners with various types of health problems and requests. Practitioners need to obtain information from patients (or a parent or companion, if the patient is a child or unable to respond) about the health needs involved if they are to respond appropriately. Once this is done, the practitioner needs to communicate back to the patient a diagnosis and a treatment plan. Although this may sound simple enough, communication between patient and practitioner is often far from simple. This communication takes place on both verbal and nonverbal levels, and is often fraught with barriers.

The verbal level. The most obvious communication between patient and practitioner occurs on the verbal level. Patients come with requests, and practitioners attempt to respond to them. What kind of requests are involved? The first things that come to mind are concerns about symptoms and illness. However, research on patient requests indicates that much more is involved. For example, in one study of question-asking in a medical clinic, direct medical questions made up less than 3% of the interaction between doctor and patient (Roter, 1984). In an examination of the kinds of requests that patients make in primary care settings, Mary-Jo Good and her colleagues (Good, Good, & Nassi, 1983) identified five categories of requests. Among the most prominent were requests for the treatment of psychosocial problems, including requests for help with emotional problems or requests for comforting. A second category was requests for medical explanations, such as an explanation of symptoms or advice about medical treatment. The remaining three categories included requests related to obtaining support in dealing with an illness or problem, getting test results explained, and requests to ventilate emotions and obtain legitimization.

How well do practitioners respond to these requests? The data here are mixed. Some studies have found that patients seem largely satisfied with the information that they obtain from practitioners (Kincey, Bradshaw, & Ley, 1975; Kindelan & Kent, 1987). But other evidence indicates that many patients are anything but satisfied (Cousins, 1985). How can this discrepancy be explained? One possibility is that patients differ considerably in the kind of information they seek from their doctors. For example, one study (Kindelan & Kent, 1986) asked patients in a general practice clinic to rank their preferences for five different types of information. On average, patients ranked information about diagnosis and prognosis the highest. However, although diagnosis was ranked first by 38% of the patients, it was ranked last by 26%. To confound matters, there seems to be little correspondence between patient preferences and doctors' perceptions of patient preferences. In another study (Kindelan & Kent, 1987), patients showed the greatest preference for information on prognosis, followed by diagnosis and etiology. Physicians, however, believed that patients were most interested in information about treatment.

The nonverbal level. Although verbal communication may be the most obvious in medical settings, communication at the nonverbal level may, in many respects, be the most important. Since the earliest days of medicine, physicians and other healers have relied on observations of patient behavior for diagnosis and have cultivated their bedside manner. Similarly, patients rely on far more than just a practitioner's words to judge how seriously the practitioner views the illness, and what the prospects are for recovery. Cues such as the tone of voice used, a look in the practitioner's eye, or a reassuring touch often communicate as much as do the words themselves (Friedman, 1979). Indeed, nonverbal communication between patient and practitioner has been

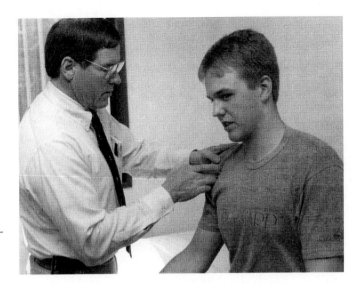

Often the most important communication between doctor and patient takes place on the nonverbal level.

shown to be related to patient satisfaction as well as whether the person returns for follow-up appointments (DiMatteo, Hays, & Prince, 1986; Hall, Roter, & Rand, 1981).

Which nonverbal cues are most important in interactions between patients and practitioners? One of the most important elements of nonverbal communication in medical settings is touch (Blondis & Jackson, 1977; Friedman, 1979). During a medical examination, practitioners learn a great deal about a person's physical condition by feeling and palpating various areas of the body. The importance of touch as nonverbal communication, however, goes far beyond this practical use. Touch also has enormous symbolic value. Touch symbolizes concern and reassurance; patients generally feel better about their interaction with the practitioner if they have been touched during the examination, rather than simply questioned. In fact, touch is of such strong symbolic value that for centuries Europeans sought relief of symptoms through the "royal touch," and even today faith healers use the technique of "laying on hands" (Friedman, 1979).

How the practitioner looks at the patient also conveys important information. Reassuring glances from a practitioner may encourage a patient to open up on a sensitive topic or help a patient who is having a difficult time. But a practitioner is likely to upset the person if he or she avoids looking at a patient or seems to stare. Avoidance may be interpreted by the patient as indicating that the practitioner is trying to hide something, or that there is something awry in the interaction. Staring may also leave the impression that there is something bad or freakish about the patient, particularly when the person has a physical deformity or for some other reason feels especially self-conscious (Friedman, 1979).

More generally, a great deal of information is conveyed between patient and practitioner through facial expression. The patient's facial expression can provide the practitioner with invaluable information about how the patient is feeling both physically and emotionally. Facial expressions can communicate the intensity of a patient's pain as well as such feelings as fear, anger, and frustration. Practitioners too convey feelings and expectations to patients through facial expressions. A doctor's frown at learning that a patient has not followed treatment recommendations or a nurse's wince at seeing a patient's deformity can convey powerful messages to the patient. Similarly, facial expressions can convey sympathy, understanding, or optimism that can encourage patients who are having difficulty (Friedman, 1979).

Another important channel for emotional expression is the person's tone of voice. Indeed, how something is said may be as important as what is said. Listening to a person's tone of voice often allows one to detect when the person is happy, sad, angry, or in pain. Thus by paying close attention to voice tone, practitioners can gain valuable clues as to what the patient is feeling. For example, even if the patient does not mention any personal difficulties, the fact that the words are spoken in a dull monotone may suggest an underlying depression, which can then be further explored. Similarly, practitioner's feelings are conveyed to patients through voice tone. Feelings communicated in this way can have important effects on patient satisfaction (Hall et al., 1981) as well as treatment outcome (Friedman, 1979). For example, one study found the judged expressiveness of physicians to be significantly correlated with patient satisfaction (Friedman, DiMatteo, & Taranta, 1980); another found that the perceived amount of anger in a doctor's voice was inversely related to the doctor's success in dealing with alcoholic patients (Milmoe, Rosenthal, Blane, Chafetz, & Wolf, 1967).

Barriers to good communication. As we have seen, patient-practitioner communication is complex and takes place on multiple levels. When all goes well, the patient and practitioner are able to establish good rapport, which facilitates mutual understanding. Unfortunately, several barriers often interfere with good communication (DiMatteo & DiNicola, 1982; Quill, 1989). For example, communication may be blocked by the practitioner's use of *medical jargon.* Terms such as *protein, umbilicus,* or *malignant* may have little meaning for patients, particularly those who are relatively unsophisticated (McKinlay, 1975; Samora, Saunders, & Larson, 1961). Telling a patient that a test result is negative (which is usually a positive thing) or that alcohol use during pregnancy is "contraindicated" may leave the person confused about what is actually meant. Why do practitioners use medical jargon? One reason is simple habit. During their training, practitioners become accustomed to using medical terms with other professionals and continue that habit with patients. Jargon may also be used to establish the physician's authority, impress patients, or simply to keep patients quiet (DiMatteo & DiNicola, 1982; Hinkley, Craig, & Anderson, 1990).

Communication may also be hindered by *sociocultural differences between patient and practitioner.* Differences in age, social class, ethnicity, or gender may prove important barriers. As noted in Chapter 8, ethnic groups often differ in how they understand and respond to illness (Zborowski, 1952; Zola, 1966). Many of these folk concepts of illness differ considerably from those held by medical practitioners, and this can lead to misunderstandings. Patients may also be more willing to open up to some practitioners than they are to others. For example, one study (Young, 1979) found that patients were more willing to disclose symptoms to a physician of the same sex than they were one of the opposite sex. In addition, patients showed a greater willingness to discuss symptoms with a more physically attractive physician.

Patients also contribute their share to poor communication. Illness often stirs up *emotions* that can impair the patient's ability to communicate and understand what the practitioner is saying (Quill, 1989). When patients are anxious, angry, or feeling shame or helplessness, they may find it difficult to make themselves understood. In addition, anxiety is known to hinder a person's ability to learn and retain information (Mandler, 1975). In such cases, the practitioner should be sensitive to the emotions that the patient is experiencing and take the time to explore these and provide emotional support (Quill, 1989).

Communication is also complicated by *patient cognitive limitations.* Numerous studies have shown that patients often misinterpret or forget much of what they are told during medical consultations. For example, one study found that, when they were questioned shortly after a visit to the doctor, patients had already forgotten roughly a third of what they had been told (Ley & Spelman, 1965). Particularly disturbing was the fact that patients failed to recall 56% of the instructions they had been given and 48% of the treatment information. Other studies have found that the more patients are told, the more they forget, and that instructions and advice are more likely to be forgotten than other information. Interestingly, the intelligence and age of the patient seem to make little difference in how much is remembered (DiMatteo & DiNicola, 1982). Even information that is remembered may well be misinterpreted. One study discovered that, even when instructions were typed by the doctor, patients misinterpreted as much as 64% of the medication instructions they had been given (Mazullo, Lasagna, & Griner, 1974).

What can be done to overcome these barriers? The difficult circumstances under which patients and practitioners interact make a complete solution to all these barriers unlikely. However, innovative programs are attempting to lower the barriers to communication by emphasizing the human side of medicine early in medical training. Programs like those at the medical schools of University of Missouri at Kansas City and Harvard University focus on the patient-practitioner relationship from the beginning of medical training through course work as well as early hands-on experience. Students in these programs take courses in the social sciences and humanities, along with the usual courses in biomedical science. In addition, small groups of students work closely with a physician and begin seeing patients on hospital wards from the beginning of their training; in other programs, they generally do not interact with patients until later. These programs aim to teach students to focus on the patient who has the disease, rather than on the disease itself (Gibbs, 1989).

Results of Patient-Practitioner Relationships

As we have just seen, relationships between patients and practitioners are complex, and many barriers hinder the development of rapport. Although the quality of patient-practitioner interactions is important in itself, its true importance becomes clear when we consider some of the outcomes of these relationships.

Patient satisfaction. That frustration with medical care seems to be increasing just when medical science is making unprecedented strides in conquering disease is indeed ironic (Cousins, 1985; Gibbs, 1989). Many factors account for this, yet one that stands out is the patient-practitioner relationship. Although the curative powers of medicine have never been greater, many patients complain that their doctors do not listen to them, are not sympathetic to their needs, or that they do not understand what their doctors tell them (Cousins, 1985). Recent studies indicate that patient satisfaction with medical care is a function primarily of the quality of the patient-practitioner relationship (Buller & Buller, 1987; DiMatteo et al., 1986; Feletti, Firman, & Sanson-Fisher, 1986; Ross, Mirowsky, & Duff, 1982). In particular, the quality of the interaction between patient and practitioner determines reported satisfaction with the practitioner, whether the patient wants to return to that practitioner, and whether the patient keeps future appointments (DiMatteo et al., 1986; Ross & Duff, 1982). Patients show a strong overall preference for practitioners who have a warm and expressive emotional style as compared with those who remain emotionally neutral (Buller & Buller, 1987; DiMatteo, 1979; DiMatteo, Linn, Chang, & Cope, 1985).

A particularly important consequence of this is that patients often judge the competence of a practitioner by their emotional satisfaction with care (Ben-Sira, 1976; Bloom, 1963). In reality, most lay people are unable to assess technical competence directly, so they rely instead on their feelings about the practitioner. The result is that when patients are dissatisfied with the emotional aspects of their care, they are more likely to "doctor shop," going from one doctor to another until they find one that suits them. In addition, emotional dissatisfaction with care appears to be a major reason why terminally ill patients sometimes reject their doctors and turn to quacks, faith healers, and other nonmedical healers (DiMatteo, 1979). Box 9.1 provides a somewhat different perspective on the problem of dissatisfaction.

Malpractice litigation. Rapport between patient and practitioner also relates to who is sued for malpractice. Statistics show that three in five obstetricians and gynecologists in the United States have been sued at least once, one in ten dentists will be sued in any given year, and one fourth of all physicians will be sued at least once during their careers (Fish, Ehrhardt, & Fish, 1985). Patients sue medical practitioners for many reasons, not the least of which is clear medical incompetence. However, all medical procedures have risks, and even the best practitioners sometimes make mistakes. Well-known malpractice attorney Melvin Belli writes that even routine medical procedures can lead to litigation when the practitioner shows insensitivity by poking fun at patients, ignoring them, talking tough, or being careless in reporting test results (Belli & Carlova, 1986). Overall, practitioners who are most prone to being sued by patients are those who feel insecure with their patients, are unable to admit their own limits, and, when confronted with dissatisfied patients, tend to dismiss their

BOX 9.1 Patients Aren't the Only Ones Who Are Frustrated

Most discussions of the shortcomings of the patient-practitioner relationship tend to focus on patient frustrations. But practitioners are also frustrated. One recent survey of American physicians showed that nearly two thirds are pessimistic about their professional futures and a similar number would not want their children to go into medicine. In addition, between the 1986–87 and 1988–89 academic years, applications to medical school in the United States dropped 15%, a reflection of concern about medicine as a career (Gibbs, 1989).

What are the sources of this frustration? Doctors name several (Gibbs, 1989), including, ironically, recent advances in medicine. As medical "miracles" have become more common, patients have increased their expectations about doctors' ability to deal with any and all medical problems. These expectations often reach unrealistic heights and place considerable pressure on doctors to cure whatever conditions are presented to them, or face being denigrated as a quack or sued for malpractice.

Recent advances in medical technology have also increased the emotional distance between patient and practitioner. Physicians now spend much of their time on medical tests, rather than getting to know their patients. In addition, technology can have a dehumanizing effect, reducing the patient to just a body to be worked on.

Changes in medicine as a social institution are also a source of frustration. In an effort to contain medical costs and provide greater efficiency in medical care, more than half of all physicians in the United States now work in some kind of a group practice, often a health maintenance organization (HMO) in which patients pay a flat annual fee for medical services. Although such arrangements have economic benefits, they force doctors to consider not only their patients' interests but also corporate demands, demands that may conflict with patient needs. In addition, government and private health insurers have adopted strict guidelines for how much treatment for given conditions should cost. These guidelines often seriously restrict the doctor's independence in determining the kind of treatment a patient can receive.

Ever lurking in the background, of course, is the threat of malpractice litigation. In the face of heightened patient expectations, physicians are painfully aware that anything less than a perfect outcome may land them in court. The extent of the litigation threat is illustrated by the experience of a Manhattan cardiologist treating an elderly woman who had arrived in the emergency room for treatment of a heart attack and pneumonia. Hovering near her and keeping tabs on the entire proceedings was the family attorney (Gibbs, 1989). The threat of malpractice litigation as well as the cost of malpractice insurance has led some physicians to hire risk managers to advise them of potential legal risks and has driven others out of practice entirely.

Although such frustrations cast a pall over the practice of medicine for many physicians, fortunately many still see medicine as a career of challenge and compassion. Also, in light of increased pressures placed on physicians, some medical schools are responding by altering their curricula to emphasize the humane side of medicine and assist new doctors in dealing with the increased pressures.

complaints as trivial (DiMatteo, 1979; Vaccarino, 1977). When practitioners behave this way, patients tend to retaliate by hitting them in the wallet.

Response to treatment. The relationship that patients have with practitioners has also been shown to affect the outcome of treatment. First, providing patients with the kind and level of information that they desire can significantly reduce their anxiety before surgery, particularly when that information is presented in a warm and personal fashion (Auerbach, Martelli, & Mercuri, 1983). This reduction in anxiety may, in turn, speed recovery. For example, Lawrence Egbert and his colleagues (Egbert, Battit, Welch, & Bartlett, 1964) provided one group of abdominal surgery patients with information about the kind of pain they could expect to experience after their surgery, along with advice on how to minimize that pain. A control group was given routine treatment without specific information on pain. Patients in the information group, on the whole, reported less pain, requested fewer pain relievers, and spent 2.7 fewer days in the hospital than did patients in the control group. These results as well as those of other studies (see Johnson, 1984) emphasize the importance of providing patients with appropriate information.

Subtle features of the patient-practitioner interaction can also have important effects on specific body systems. For example, one study (Orth, Stiles, Scherwitz, Hennrikus, & Vallbona, 1987) found that the blood pressure in hypertensive patients was significantly related to the verbal interaction that took place during a clinic visit. The more time patients spent describing perceived symptoms, the more their blood pressure dropped in the following two weeks. In addition, the more time practitioners spent during the clinic visit explaining the patient's illness and treatment, the lower the patient's blood pressure was two weeks later. These findings may reflect a greater tendency for patients who were allowed more time to describe their symptoms and who got more detailed explanations to stick more closely to their treatment regimen. In addition, greater interaction between patient and practitioner may have helped to reduce the patient's anxiety level.

NON-COOPERATION WITH MEDICAL RECOMMENDATIONS

When people seek assistance from health care practitioners, they are generally motivated by a desire either to avoid ill health or to obtain relief from a health problem. Since seeking help from a health care practitioner often requires a substantial investment of time, effort, and money, one would expect that once they have gotten the practitioner's advice, they would follow it. Going to the trouble of seeking medical advice, only to disregard it, would certainly be a waste. Yet this is precisely what many people do.

Traditionally, failure to follow medical recommendations has been referred to as non-compliance. To some, however, this terminology suggests a somewhat authoritarian approach and the assumption that the practitioner, as expert, gives orders that the patient is obligated to follow. This infers a somewhat one-sided relationship in which the patient has little, if any, say (DiMatteo & DiNicola, 1982; Trostle, 1988). To emphasize the bidirectional nature of patient-practitioner interactions, we will use the term *non-cooperation*. Since cooperation requires the willing participation of both parties involved, use of this term indicates the extent to which the actions of patients and practitioners jointly determine health outcomes.

How Prevalent Is Non-cooperation?

The answer to this question depends on how you ask it and whom you ask. At its most basic, non-cooperation refers to any deviation from the treatment plan. Thus it encompasses such diverse behaviors as missing appointments, neglecting to take prescribed medication, taking too much medication, taking it at the wrong time, cheating on a recommended diet, and continuing to smoke in the face of recommendations to stop (DiNicola & DiMatteo, 1984).

Given this diversity of behaviors, it is not surprising that estimates of non-cooperation vary widely, ranging from 15% to 94%, with an average of about 30%. Cooperation with short-term curative regimens, such as taking antibiotics for an infection, is high, often around 70% to 80% (i.e., 20% to 30% non-cooperation). For longer term regimens, however, cooperation drops off substantially and is often low (50% or less) for recommendations involving long-term changes in life-style (DiNicola & DiMatteo, 1984; Feinberg, 1988; Sackett & Snow, 1979; Stone, 1979a). For example, a recent study of medical cooperation among hemophiliacs found that nearly three fourths of the patients studied experienced problems in adhering to their medical regimens (Weiss et al., 1991).

A critical consideration in assessing the amount of non-cooperation is the method by which it is measured (DiNicola & DiMatteo, 1984; Gordis, 1979; Roth, 1987). One simple method is to ask practitioners whether their patients are following recommendations. Although such data are easy to obtain, they also tend to be highly inaccurate. In general, practitioners overestimate the extent to which their patients cooperate with treatment and have a great deal of difficulty identifying which of their patients are non-cooperative (Gordis, 1979).

As an alternative, some studies have assessed cooperation by means of self-reports from patients (Berenson, Groshen, Miller, & Decosse, 1989; Gordis, 1979). Although questioning the patient gets closer to the source of the behavior, these self-reports are likely to be biased by errors in memory, as well as the person's desire to look good in the eyes of others. Again, estimates of cooperation are likely to be inflated (DiMatteo & DiNicola, 1982; Gordis, 1979). One study examining cooperation with a preventive course of antibiotics found that 73% of the patients reported good cooperation with the regimen. However, when cooperation was assessed by the more objective measure of counting pills, only 55% of the patients qualified as showing good cooperation (Feinstein et al., 1959).

Because of problems with physician and self-report measures of cooperation, researchers and practitioners have devised more direct means of assessment. When the medical recommendation involves taking medication, cooperation can be assessed by measuring the amount of medication that the patient has taken. For example, medication use might be judged by counting the number of pills remaining from a prescription or by checking on prescription refills at the patient's pharmacy (Gordis, 1979). Although such measures are more objective than simply asking the patient or practitioner, they are relatively crude in that they do not indicate when the medication was taken or even whether it actually was. Before an appointment, a patient who has not been taking the medication regularly might take a larger than prescribed amount at one time so as to seem cooperative or might simply dispose of the medicine. Although clever ways can be devised to guard against such abuses (cf. Masur, 1981), these measures may seem more accurate than they really are.

Even more directly, medication use might be monitored through chemical analysis of the patient's blood or urine. This can done by testing for the presence of the drug itself or by testing for a **tracer**, a compound added to the medication that is then detectable when the medication is ingested (Dubbert et al., 1985; Gordis, 1979). For example, the vitamin riboflavin, which is cheap, nontoxic, and easily detected in urine, has been used as tracer for measuring cooperation in taking a variety of drugs (Dubbert et al., 1985). Chemical analysis can provide the most accurate measures of treatment cooperation. Despite this potential accuracy, these measures have serious drawbacks. First, they are invasive and require blood or urine samples from patients. They may also be expensive and time consuming. More important, individuals often differ as to the rate at which they absorb and excrete drugs, and the drugs themselves remain in the body for different lengths of time. Such technical difficulties can seriously limit the usefulness of these measures (Babiker, Cooke, & Gillett, 1989; Gordis, 1979).

What does all this say about the prevalence of non-cooperation? Simply, that there is no completely foolproof way of determining whether patients are following medical recommendations. Each of these methods encounters significant problems of both reliability and validity (see Chapter 2). Researchers and practitioners interested in an accurate assessment should use several different measures and then view the results with skepticism. Since most measures overestimate the number of people who follow the treatment, the estimates given for non-cooperation, discouraging as they are, are probably low.

tracer
A substance added to a medication that can be used as a marker of whether and how much of it has been ingested.

The Impact of Non-cooperation

The importance of non-cooperation as a problem comes into focus when we consider the possible impact of patients' failure to follow treatment recommendations. To be sure, patients may at times be well advised *not* to follow the recommendations of their health care providers. Medical practitioners, like everyone else, are human and make mistakes. However, such cases are generally the exception rather than the rule.

One possible effect of non-cooperation is that the patient forfeits whatever benefit is to be derived from the treatment. When patients neglect to take prescribed medicine, or fail to make recommended changes in life-style or behavior, or to follow other recommendations, they may substantially reduce the possibility of recovery (Epstein, 1984). This, in turn, may result in repeat outpatient visits, unneeded hospitalization, and unnecessary expense. The end result is an inefficient use of the health care system (Masur, 1981). Consider as an illustration the increased medical expenses involved with non-cooperation as it relates to hypertension. Figure 9.1 shows the estimated increase in the cost of extending the life of a hypertensive patient by one year when the person either follows or fails to follow treatment. Some observers have gone so far as to argue that allocating funds to increase treatment cooperation would be more

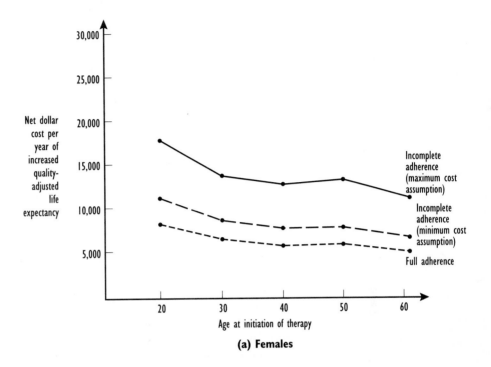

(a) Females

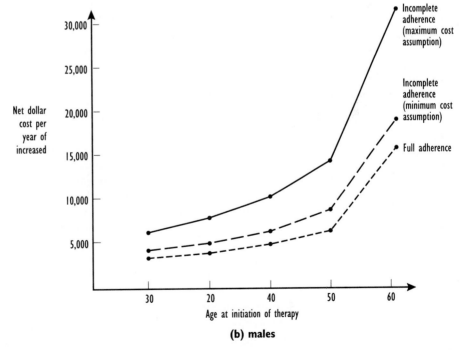

FIGURE 9.1

Effects of lack of treatment cooperation on the cost-effectiveness of hypertension treatment.

Note. From "Hypertension: A policy perspective" by M. C. Weinstein and W. B. Stason, 1976 (p. 128), Cambridge: Harvard University Press. Reprinted by permission of the publishers and by the President and Fellows of Harvard College.

(b) males

effective in reducing disability and death from diseases like hypertension than using the same amount of money to identify and treat new cases (Weinstein & Stason, 1976).

Another result of non-cooperation is that it can lead to errors in diagnosis and treatment. When patients fail to respond to treatment, practitioners may change the medication dosage, try a new medication, or order diagnostic tests to determine why the treatment is not working. These efforts are likely to be futile when the actual reason for treatment failure is that the patient simply was not following the treatment plan. Relatedly, when non-cooperation occurs in the context of clinical research, research results may be misleading (Masur, 1981).

Causes of Non-cooperation

Given the prevalence of non-cooperation and its potential impact, the question naturally arises as to why people would go to the trouble of seeking medical attention, only to disregard the treatment advice. Such behavior would certainly seem irrational. Investigations of non-cooperation have turned up several important determinants, including features of the treatment regimen, characteristics of the patient, and the nature of the patient-practitioner relationship.

Nature of the treatment. The type of treatment involved is important in determining cooperation. Patients are most likely to cooperate with treatment when it is of short duration, relatively simple, and requires few changes in the person's usual routine. In addition, cooperation is highest when the treatment is effective in relieving troublesome symptoms, has few side effects, and is relatively low in cost (DiNicola & DiMatteo, 1984; Haynes, 1979a; Hunt, Jordan, Irwin, & Browner, 1989; Kirscht & Rosenstock, 1979).

Such findings certainly make intuitive sense. People prefer treatments that are effective but impose relatively little cost, either in time or money. However, such findings also indicate major problem areas. Cooperation is likely to be lowest for those health problems that have the most serious long-term consequences. For example, hypertension is a major risk factor for health problems including heart disease, stroke, kidney disease, and blindness (Herd & Weiss, 1984). Yet hypertension is also asymptomatic, so many people who have high blood pressure are unaware of it, and even those who are aware often leave it untreated. Approximately 15% of those with hypertension in the United States are thought to be ignorant of their condition (Roccella & Horan, 1988). In addition, after hypertension is detected, a substantial percentage of patients drop out of treatment within a year. To compound matters, treatment of hypertension is a lifelong process that often involves medications that can produce distressing side effects. The result is that, even among patients remaining in treatment, only about two thirds actually follow their treatment regimens (Dunbar-Jacob, Dwyer, & Dunning, 1991).

Patient characteristics. Health care practitioners are tempted to view non-cooperation as the result of simple contrariness by the patient. Some patients, according to this view, simply have an uncooperative personality (Davis, 1966).

Although little empirical evidence supports the existence of such a personality (Kirscht & Rosenstock, 1979), patient characteristics have been shown to play an important role in cooperation.

One important determinant of cooperation is the patient's comprehension of the treatment instructions. As we saw earlier, instructions to patients are often misinterpreted or forgotten (Ley & Spelman, 1965; Mazullo et al., 1974). Obviously, patients are unlikely to be able to follow a treatment plan if they do not understand what is expected of them. This strongly suggests that before patients leave the examining room, practitioners should make sure that patients understand the treatment instructions. One way of doing this is to provide patients with written instructions, by either writing out instructions for an individual patient or providing the patient with preprinted information about the health problem and its treatment. Studies evaluating the effectiveness of preprinted information have found that providing this type of information can be effective in increasing cooperation, at least for relatively short-term treatments (Morris & Halperin, 1979). This assumes, of course, that the information is presented at a level appropriate for the patient.

Closely related are patients' beliefs about illness and the efficacy of treatment. Chapter 8 discussed lay illness representations and their role in various kinds of health-related behavior. These "common sense" ideas about illness help people to make sense of their experience and provide a guide for behavior (Bishop, 1991b; Leventhal et al., 1984). In his work on treatment cooperation, Howard Leventhal and his colleagues (Leventhal et al., 1984) found that whether hypertensives stay in treatment depends a great deal on their "common sense" notions about the nature of the disease. Those patients who believe that hypertension is a chronic disease requiring lifelong efforts at control are much more likely to stay in treatment than are those who see hypertension as an acute condition that, once treated, is cured. Similarly, other studies have found that treatment cooperation is higher when patients believe that a disease is serious, that they are susceptible to it, and that the prescribed treatments are effective in either treating or preventing it (Kirscht & Rosenstock, 1979).

Patients' social circumstances are also important in determining cooperation. Cooperation or non-cooperation with medical treatment does not take place in a social vacuum, but, rather, is influenced by relationships to others (Kirscht & Rosenstock, 1979). First, the roles that people play can significantly influence whether they follow a practitioner's advice. For example, advice to a salesman to limit his working hours and avoid stress is likely to be disregarded if it interferes with his ability to earn a living and meet his financial obligations. Similarly, a mother with small children is likely to find it difficult to follow a practitioner's advice to avoid lifting, unless she has someone to help take care of the children. Various kinds of stress can interfere with treatment cooperation. Several studies have found that when people are experiencing high levels of stress, they are less likely to follow medication recommendations and are more likely to miss follow-up appointments (Kirscht & Rosenstock, 1979). Finally, social support from family and friends can be an important determinant of cooperation. Particularly when the treatment recommendations involve changes in life-style or habit, having the support of others can give the person the necessary boost to keep going (Kirscht & Rosenstock, 1979; Morse et al., 1991).

Patient-practitioner relationship. One of the most important factors in treatment cooperation is the quality of the patient-practitioner relationship. As we saw earlier, patient-practitioner relationships are complex and subject to potential difficulties. Two aspects of this relationship are of particular importance for treatment cooperation. The first is the communication of information between the practitioner and the patient, including both the patient's communication of symptom information and the practitioner's communication of information about the treatment. One study, for example, found that cooperation with treatment was significantly higher when the communication between patient and practitioner was bidirectional, meaning that patients not only answered the practitioner's questions but also independently volunteered information (Rost, Carter, & Inui, 1989). In addition, as noted earlier, the failure of practitioners to communicate treatment information to patients effectively is a major barrier to treatment cooperation.

Equally important is the communication of concern and caring for the patient. This affective dimension of the patient-practitioner relationship has been found to be closely related to patients' efforts to follow treatment recommendations. For example, one series of studies (Francis, Korsch, & Morris, 1969; Korsch, Gozzi, & Francis, 1968; Korsch & Negrete, 1972) discovered that whether mothers followed the treatment recommendations of pediatricians largely depended on how satisfactory they regarded their relationship to the pediatrician. Mothers who felt that their pediatrician lacked warmth or who were dissatisfied with the care that their children received were much less likely to follow the doctor's recommendations. Similarly, a recent study of pediatric seizure patients found that cooperation with medical regimens was significantly higher when both the patients and their parents expressed satisfaction with the care received (Hazzard, Hutchinson, & Krawiecki, 1990).

Improving Cooperation

At this point, the question naturally arises as to what can be done to improve treatment cooperation. This is a thorny problem, and as yet no comprehensive solution has emerged. However, many promising techniques have been developed to deal with at least parts of the problem (DiNicola & DiMatteo, 1984; Kirscht & Rosenstock, 1979; Masur, 1981).

One prerequisite for cooperation is the patient's *intention* to follow the treatment recommendation (DiNicola & DiMatteo, 1984). Even complete understanding of the treatment regimen will not lead to cooperation unless the patient makes a decision to adhere to it. This suggests that, after explaining the treatment, practitioners should obtain from patients a verbal commitment to cooperate. The effects of this type of commitment have been experimentally explored by James Kulik and Patricia Carlino (1987). This study randomly assigned parents of children suffering from ear infections to one of two groups. Parents in the experimental group made an oral promise to the physician that they would give their children all the antibiotic medication. In the control condition, the same treatment regimen was prescribed, but parents were not asked to make a commitment. Cooperation was significantly higher when parents made the oral commitment. Although these results are promising, the commitment will be effective only if it is freely made (i.e., not coerced) and internalized (DiNicola & DiMatteo, 1984).

Commitment is only the first step. Everyone has made commitments (e.g., a New Year's resolution) that were later abandoned. As noted in Chapters 4 and 5, health behaviors are strongly influenced by habit; treatment cooperation is no exception. Thus several theorists have argued that treatment cooperation is best approached as a problem in long-term behavioral self-control (DiNicola & DiMatteo, 1984; Epstein & Cluss, 1982; Kirscht & Rosenstock, 1979; Masur, 1981). In this regard, behavioral modification techniques can be used to good effect. Cuing techniques, for instance, can be used to remind patients of appointments or of their medication schedule. Telephone or postcard reminders have been shown to increase significantly the likelihood that patients will return for follow-up appointments or come in for vaccinations (Jones, Jones, & Katz, 1988; Masur, 1981). Self-monitoring techniques can be used to draw the patient's attention to the behavior that needs to be changed. For example, in one study, hypertensive patients were taught to measure and chart their own blood pressure, and were required to keep track of when they took their medication. Compared to a control group, the self-monitoring group showed a 21% improvement in treatment cooperation (Haynes, 1979b).

Beyond this, techniques such as operant conditioning, contingency contracting, and self-reinforcement can be used to shape and maintain positive treatment behavior. **Token economies** have been successfully used to increase cooperation with dietary regimens for children undergoing renal dialysis (Magrab & Papadopoulou, 1977). In addition, contingency contracting techniques have been used to improve treatment cooperation among cardiac patients, diabetics, and hypertensives (Masur, 1981).

Behavioral techniques like these generally work best when they are buttressed by appropriate cognitions and social support from others. Dante DiNicola and Robin DiMatteo (1984) demonstrate that whether desired behaviors are maintained over time often depends on whether the behavior is attributed to the person's own volition or to the influence of an outside agent, such as a practitioner. Thus the person must develop a strong sense of internal control and self-efficacy concerning treatment cooperation. This argues that practitioners should be sensitive to patients' concerns about their ability to follow the prescribed treatment and that every opportunity should be taken to reinforce patients' sense of commitment and self-confidence. In addition, as we saw earlier, people are most likely to cooperate with treatment when they have the support of family and friends. Therefore, practitioners should explore possible sources of social support for the patient and, where possible, enlist the aid of significant others in helping the patient follow the prescribed treatment (DiNicola & DiMatteo, 1984).

token economy
A behavioral modification technique in which patients are given points for exhibiting desired behavior, which can later be exchanged for various rewards.

THE EXPERIENCE OF HOSPITALIZATION

People receive most of their medical care as outpatients or in a clinic. Occasionally, however, a person needs to be hospitalized, either for treatment or to receive tests that, for one reason or another, cannot be performed on an outpatient basis. Although the points made earlier about patient-practitioner relationships still apply, the experience of hospitalization goes well beyond simply the interactions that people have with practitioners. Being hospitalized means dealing with a large-scale institution that is strange to most people and can be overwhelming. Hospitals have their own rules and procedures, often developed primarily for staff convenience and efficiency, that many times seem to be at cross purposes with patient needs. For this reason, hospitals are generally considered aversive places, and hospitalization is seen as a very negative experience.

Hospitals as Institutions

Understanding the experience of being hospitalized requires an examination of hospitals as institutions. The modern hospital as we know it is a relatively recent invention. When hospitals were first developed during the Middle Ages, they were places that catered to the ill poor. The wealthy were generally cared for at home. In their role as charitable institutions, hospitals also took in travelers, orphans, and the poor who had nowhere else to go (Anderson & Gevitz, 1983; Wilson, 1965). Since little effective medical care was available, hospitals gained the well-deserved reputation as places of last resort, where people went to die. Anyone who could afford it steered clear of hospitals. Even into the 1920s, many hospitals were still thought of as charitable institutions for those who had no other alternative. Only in the last few decades have hospitals been used routinely by people from all levels of society (Wilson, 1965).

Modern hospitals are generally large complex institutions charged with performing a wide variety of health-related activities, including preventing illness, curing disease, repairing injury, providing health education, conducting research, and training medical personnel. Accomplishing these tasks requires a diverse and highly trained staff as well as a complex social hierarchy. At the top of this hierarchy is the board of trustees, which is generally concerned with overall policy-making and fundraising. Directly below the board of trustees are the administrators and medical staff. The hospital administration deals with the practical everyday matters of running the hospital, such as ordering supplies, maintaining the physical plant, keeping patient accounts, and purchasing equipment. The dramatic growth in health care costs in the recent years and increased competition for patients have put hospital administrators under increasing pressure to keep costs down, while providing facilities for state-of-the-art medical care (Kiesler & Morton, 1988).

The medical staff, which has a completely separate line of authority, is responsible for medical treatment. Curiously, physicians are often not employees of the hospital. Rather, they are usually private practitioners or members of group practices or health plans who are granted the right to treat their patients at that hospital. Therefore, their services are billed separately from those of the hospital, and physicians generally act independently of the hospital administration. Below physicians is the nursing staff. Unlike physicians, nurses are paid hospital employees who are charged with the management of hospital wards and the day-to-day care of patients. This arrangement often puts nurses in difficult situations, since they are expected to follow the directives of both the administration that employs them and the physicians who outrank them on the medical staff (Aiken, 1983; Kastenbaum, 1982; Wilson, 1965).

In addition to physicians and nurses, the hospital staff includes allied health professionals such as social workers, dieticians, and physical therapists. These professionals provide important services in the hospital setting, but are often defined by physicians as ancillary to what they consider the hospital's primarily medical purpose (Ginzberg, 1983). Lowest in rank are the orderlies and technicians who perform less skilled patient care duties, but are nonetheless critical to the hospital's functioning.

The Role of the Hospital Patient

total institution
An institution that takes control of virtually every aspect of a person's life.

Where does the patient fit into all this? Ostensibly, patients are the entire reason for the existence of hospitals. However, patients are guests in the hospital environment and generally powerless ones at that. They come unbidden into an environment that most find entirely alien and generally confusing (Wilson, 1965). Upon entering the hospital, they find it to be what Erving Goffman (1961) describes as a **total institution.** In other words, the hospital takes control of virtually every aspect of patients' lives. They are expected to follow the hospital's schedule, eat and sleep at designated times, receive visitors only during specified hours, conform to hospital procedures, and make their bodies available for examination when requested.

In addition, hospital patients are often treated in a depersonalized manner. For a variety of reasons, whether the practitioner's simple habit, to minimize emotional involvement, or to keep a patient quiet, patients are often treated more like objects than persons. For example, during examinations, the focus may be so much on the medical problem at hand that it is almost as if the patient weren't there. One psychologist reports how, during an examination when he was fully conscious and able to respond for himself, the doctor began speaking about him in the third person and asking questions of his companion rather than directing them to him (Zimbardo, 1969). Although the practitioner may find minimizing the personal aspects of the interaction more convenient, this depersonalization often makes patients feel confused and angry (Taylor, 1979).

Patients differ considerably in how they deal with the patient role. Judith Lorber (1979) has identified three basic types of patient response, as seen by hospital staff. Most patients are either "good patients" or "average patients," in that they passively conform to the requirements of the patient role and are generally cooperative. The difference between "good" and "average" patients is that whereas "good" patients are uncomplaining and stoical, "average" patients have minor complaints that can be easily handled. Both "good" and "average" patients tend to be well liked by hospital staff because they make few demands on staff time and generally do not interrupt staff routine. But a minority of patients are seen by staff as "problem patients," because they

complain a great deal, become emotional about their problems, demand extra attention, or refuse to cooperate with treatment. When problem patients are seriously ill,
and the staff can attribute their disruptiveness to the seriousness of the illness, they
are generally forgiven. However, problem patients who are not viewed by the staff as
seriously ill are likely to be roundly condemned. In this case, they are likely to be seen
as being troublemakers and may be tranquilized, referred for psychiatric evaluation,
or even discharged early.

What leads to these different responses to the patient role? One major determinant
appears to be how people respond to the loss of control that is experienced when
entering a hospital. Turning over control of one's life to the hospital is certainly stressful
enough. In addition, patients are placed at the mercy of an institution that they
generally do not understand and are kept in a state of low information. The result is
likely to be a considerable amount of confusion and anxiety (Skipper, Tagliacozzo, &
Mauksch, 1964; Taylor, 1979). Most patients deal with this confusion and loss of
control by acquiescing in the demands of the patient role. Other patients, particularly
those who are younger, better educated, or accustomed to being able to control their
environment, respond with **reactance** (Brehm, 1966). For these patients, loss of
control is perceived as an unacceptable challenge to the person's freedom, which may
arouse anger and must be resisted. Thus the so-called problem patient's complaints
and demands for additional attention may be angry attempts by the person to
reestablish at least a small measure of personal freedom (Taylor, 1979).

Patient reactions may also change over time. Even though some patients may enter
the hospital with the expectation of maintaining control, frustrating experiences with
hospital routine and lack of information may convince them that their efforts at control
are futile. When this happens, the person is likely to enter a state of learned
helplessness (Seligman, 1975). In this state, people show characteristic cognitive
deficits and fail to exercise even the control that they have. In support of this, one
study (Raps, Peterson, Jonas, & Seligman, 1982) found that the longer patients were
in the hospital, the more likely they were to perform poorly on cognitive tasks and
show symptoms of depression (see Figure 9.2). These findings were obtained even
though physically the patients were improving.

The psychological processes of reactance and learned helplessness may also have
important implications for how well patients recover from their illnesses. In her
discussion of hospital patient behavior, Shelley Taylor (1979) shows that neither good
patient nor problem patient behavior is likely to be adaptive for the patient. Although
good patients may be well liked by hospital staff, they may be suffering from learned
helplessness, which is associated with possible norepinephrine depletion, general
erosion of health, and the possibility of sudden death. Patients who respond with
reactance, by contrast, are likely to experience anger, heightened secretion of stress
hormones, and the possible aggravation of cardiovascular problems. A summary of
these consequences is shown in Table 9.1. This argues for changing the hospital patient
role so as to provide patients with more information and give them as much control
in hospital settings as possible (Taylor, 1979).

reactance
A patient's psycho-
logical motive to
preserve a sense of
freedom that is being
threatened.

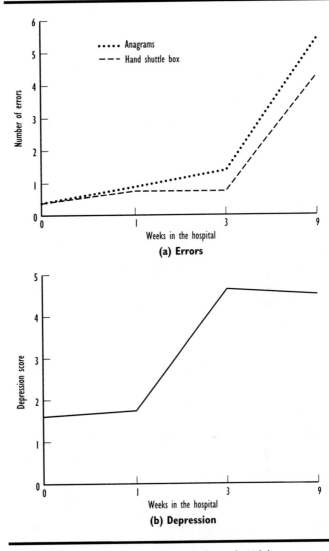

FIGURE 9.2

Cognitive effects of hospitalization: Errors on cognitive tasks and level of depression by length of time in the hospital.

Note. Based on data from "Patient behavior in hospitals: Helplessness, reactance, or both?" by C. S. Raps, C. Peterson, M. Jonas, and M. E. P. Seligman, 1982, *Journal of Personality and Social Psychology, 42,* 1036–41.

Preparation for Surgery

One aspect of hospitalization where these considerations seem particularly relevant is patient preparation for surgery. Studies of surgical patients have found that most express moderate to high degrees of fear and anxiety before the surgery. Among the

TABLE 9.1   *The Possible Consequences of Loss of Control, Good Patient Behavior, and Problem Patient Behavior in Hospital Patients*

State	Behaviors	Cognitions	Affect	Physical State	Response from Staff
Loss of control (Depersonalization)	Non-discriminant information seeking and use; complaints to staff	Inadequate expectations; confusion	Anxiety	Heightened physical reactions to symptoms and noxious medical procedures; possible increased need for medication, lengthened hospital stay	Non-person treatment
Good patient behavior (Helplessness)	Compliance Passivity Learned helplessness Inability to take in information Failure to provide condition-relevant information	Feelings of helplessness, powerlessness, possible denial or fatalism	Anxiety and depression	Possible norepinephrine depletion; helplessness also related to sudden death and gradual erosion of health	Responsiveness to emergencies but routine failure to solicit information from patient
Bad patient behavior (Reactance)	Complaints to staff Demands for attention, mutinous behavior Possible self-sabotage	Commitment to a right to know; suspicion (or paranoia) regarding condition, treatment and staff behavior	Anger	Heightened catecholamine secretion and hydrocortisone production; possible aggravation of blood pressure, hypertension, tachycardia, angina; eventual adrenalin depletion	Condescension; ignoring patients' complaints; "medicate to placate"; psychiatric referrals; possible premature discharge

Note. From "Hospital patient behavior: Reactance, helplessness, or control?" by S. E. Taylor, 1979, *Journal of Social Issues, 35,* p. 175.

most common fears are understandable worries about pain and discomfort, side effects from the surgery, possible reactions to anesthesia, disruption of life plans, and the possibility of death. Concern about the effects of this anxiety has stimulated a considerable amount of research on the best ways to prepare patients for their surgery (Anderson & Masur, 1983; Johnson, 1984; Ray, 1982).

The most effective methods for preparing surgical patients appear to be those that provide the patient with a sense of control, be it cognitive or behavioral. For example, earlier we discussed a study by Lawrence Egbert and his colleagues (Egbert et al., 1964) in which surgical patients given information about postsurgical pain were able to leave the hospital between two and three days sooner than patients not given this information. In addition, other studies have suggested that some types of information may be particularly effective. In a study comparing different types of information (Johnson, Rice, Fuller, & Endress, 1978), one group of patients received procedural information about what would be done to and for them during and after the operation; a second group got this procedural information, along with descriptions of the sensations that patients usually experienced from the surgery. A third group received neither type of information. Within each group, half the patients were given instruction in behavioral methods, such as deep breathing and leg exercises, that might make them more comfortable. The results of the study showed that for anxious patients both types of information and the behavioral instructions were effective in reducing postsurgical anxiety. In addition, patients who received the sensory information were released from the hospital sooner and became active more rapidly after returning home.

Another study (Langer, Janis, & Wolfer, 1975) examined the effectiveness of an attentional strategy for helping patients cope with surgery. In this study, one group of patients was taught to exercise cognitive control by directing their attention away from their current discomfort to the positive outcomes that they expected from their surgery. A second group of patients did not receive this training. In addition, half the patients in each group were given preparatory information about what they could expect from their surgery, while the other half were not. Patients who were taught to direct their attention were rated by nurses as having less anxiety and as dealing better with their surgery than patients not given the training. In addition, patients given the training required fewer pain relievers and sedatives.

These are only three of the dozens of studies that have investigated various methods of psychologically preparing patients for surgery. The results of these studies have shown that when patients receive orienting information before surgery, particularly information about which physical sensations to expect, they are less emotional after surgery, show less physiological arousal, require fewer pain relievers, and may be released sooner. Similar effects are obtained when patients are instructed in cognitive and behavioral control (Anderson & Masur, 1983; Johnson, 1984; Ray, 1982).

Although these results are impressive, people are likely to differ in how they respond to these interventions. For example, some people (known as "monitors") welcome information and seek it out, whereas others (called "blunters") avoid it. An example of how these individual differences may affect responses to information about medical procedures is provided in a study by Suzanne Miller and Charles Mangan (1983). In this study, women about to undergo a diagnostic procedure for cervical cancer were divided into monitors and blunters according to their expressed preference for information. Following this, half the patients in each group were given a large amount of preparatory information about the procedure, whereas the others were given a minimal amount. The patients who showed the least physiological stress in response to the exam were those who were given the amount of information that fit their preferences. In other words, monitors given a large amount of information

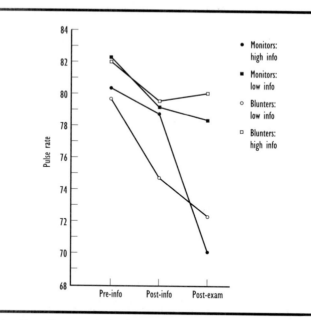

Note. From "Interacting effects of information and coping style in adapting to gynecologic stress: Should the doctor tell all?" by S. M. Miller, and C. E. Mangan, 1983, *Journal of Personality and Social Psychology, 45*, p. 230.

FIGURE 9.3
The effects of information on physiological stress: Mean pulse ratings before information, after information, and after the examination.

showed low physiological stress as did blunters given little information. However, monitors who were given little information and blunters given a large amount showed much greater stress. These results are shown in Figure 9.3. Although the patients in this study were undergoing only a diagnostic procedure, not actual surgery, the results suggest that information will be most effective in reducing surgical stress when it fits the patient's personality.

Providing patients with a sense of control is only one psychological factor that influences response to surgery. Surgical outcomes may also be affected by patient-practitioner relationships, as well as aspects of the patient's surroundings. Box 9.2 describes some unexpected effects of operating room conversation on surgical outcome.

When Children Go to the Hospital

Hospitalization is a stressful experience for almost anyone. However, it can be particularly stressful for children. Between 10% and 35% of hospitalized children are estimated to show significant behavioral disturbances (Schaffer & Challender, 1959), and more than 92% show at least some psychological upset (Cassell, 1965).

Such responses to hospitalization among children are certainly understandable. As we noted earlier, hospitals are alien and confusing environments for almost anyone. When the patient is a child, however, developmental factors intensify emotional responses to hospitalization. Particularly for young children, hospitalization stress

BOX 9.2 | Do Surgical Patients Still Hear Despite Anesthesia?

During most surgical procedures, patients are put to sleep or anesthetized to block awareness of pain and other stimuli during the operation. Since the patients are asleep, most surgical staff assume that they are unable to hear what is going on in the operating room and thus feel free to comment, joke, or even make disparaging remarks.

But are anesthetized patients actually oblivious to what is going on around them? Recent studies suggest not. In fact, although they do not remember the operation itself, evidence suggests that patients may well register what goes on. For example, in one study, Henry Bennett and his colleagues (Bennett, Davis, & Giannini, 1985) randomly assigned 33 surgical patients to either a suggestion or a control condition. In both conditions, after the induction of anesthesia, headphones were placed over the patients' ears. Patients in the suggestion condition heard a tape that included suggestions for rapid healing, along with music and songs. Also included near the end of the tape was a suggestion to the patient that during a postsurgical interview "you pull on your ear so that I know you have heard this." Patients in the control condition heard sounds from the operating room. Although none of the patients consciously remembered hearing the suggestion, patients in the suggestion condition tugged on their ears six times more

often during the postsurgical interview than did those in the control condition. Similar results have been reported by other investigators (Goldman, Shah, & Hebden, 1987; Miller & Watkinson, 1983).

What is the practical significance of such findings for patient recovery? To answer this question, another study (Evans & Richardson, 1988) compared the post-operative recovery of hysterectomy patients in suggestion and control conditions. During surgery, patients in the suggestion condition heard a tape containing suggestions such as "How quickly you recover from your operation depends on you—the more you relax, the more comfortable you will be," or "You will not feel sick, you will not have any pain." Patients in the control condition heard a blank tape. Again, none of the patients was consciously able to recall the suggestions made during surgery. However, patients in the suggestion condition spent 1.3 fewer days in the hospital after surgery and had significantly fewer complications.

These data, combined with others suggesting that negative comments during surgery can have a deleterious effect on recovery (Levinson, 1965), argue that what goes on around the patient during surgery can have significant psychological and physical effects. The data also indicate the need for the surgical staff to take care in what they say around anesthetized patients.

separation anxiety
Anxiety felt by a child when separated from parents or primary caretakers.

may be intensified by **separation anxiety** (Ainsworth, 1979; Bowlby, 1973). When young children are separated from their parents and placed in a strange situation, such as a hospital, they typically become distressed and exhibit emotional behaviors such as crying.

In addition, children often have a great deal of difficulty understanding what is going on in the hospital and why they are there. For example, hospitalized children may have no idea why their parents have brought them to the hospital, what is wrong with them, or what is going to happen while they are there (Gofman, Buckman, & Schade, 1957). Although some of this may come from the fact that they simply have not been told, studies of children's understanding of physical illness indicate that children understand illness differently than do adults and may misunderstand what they are told (Bibace & Walsh, 1979; Burbach & Peterson, 1986). Children may blame themselves for their illness or see treatment as punishment (Eiser, 1985).

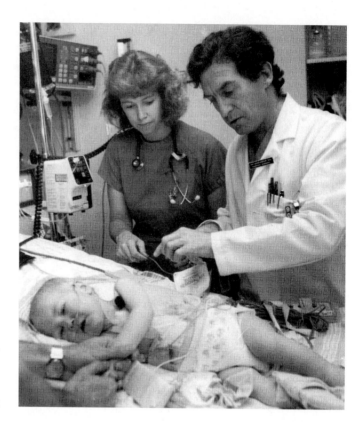

The stress of hospitalization for children may be intensified by such factors as separation anxiety, difficulty in understanding what is happening to them, and enforced inactivity.

Beyond this, separation from friends and schoolmates, the enforced inactivity of hospitalization, fears about the outcome of the illness and its treatment, and the embarrassment of being physically examined by strangers all contribute to the young patient's distress. The result is likely to be a great deal of anxiety as well as possible bed-wetting, temper tantrums, behavioral regression, and general acting out (Eiser, 1985).

For these reasons, most experts now recommend that children be psychologically prepared for hospitalization. Many negative effects of hospitalization can be reduced if the child understands better what the illness is, why hospitalization is necessary, and what will happen while in the hospital.

There are different ways to accomplish this (Saile, Burgmeier, & Schmidt, 1988). One of the most common is to expose the child to a model who is coping well with hospitalization. For example, in a classic study, Barbara Melamed and Lawrence Siegel (1975) prepared a group of young surgical patients by showing them a film entitled "Ethan has an operation." This film showed a 7-year-old boy being hospitalized for a hernia operation. Various scenes showed Ethan as he was admitted to the hospital, had a blood test, was separated from his mother, and went through surgery. In the film,

Ethan candidly described his fears, but was able to overcome them. A control group of patients saw a film about a nature trip in the country. Overall, as compared to the control group, the children who saw the hospitalization film exhibited less anxiety both before and after the operation. In addition, their parents reported fewer behavioral problems after the children returned home.

In addition to simply providing information, other preparation techniques focus on teaching parents how to help their children cope. One study (Zastowny, Kirschenbaum, & Meng, 1986) randomly assigned surgery patients and their parents to one of three preparation conditions. A week before admission, all patients and their parents were shown a film designed to provide reassuring information about the child's upcoming hospitalization. In addition, parents in an anxiety reduction group were given instruction on the nature of stress and how to reduce their own anxiety as well as that of their child. Parents in a coping skills groups were instructed in the use of various skills for coping with stress and how these could be used to reduce hospitalization stress. Parents in a control condition were simply instructed to spend extra time with their children. Compared to the control group, both patients and their parents in the anxiety reduction and coping skills groups showed less distress both before and after hospitalization. In addition, patients in the coping skills group showed less behavioral disturbance during their hospitalization.

These are only two of the techniques that have been used. Others include cognitive-behavioral methods such as self-control techniques and desensitization, emotional support, and simply providing information. Despite the variation, all the techniques appear at least somewhat effective. Overall, programs that include the emotional support of significant others (such as parents) in addition to other techniques are somewhat more effective than those that do not (Pinto & Hollandsworth, 1989; Saile et al., 1988).

In sum, although hospitalization is a stressful experience for both children and adults, its effects can be significantly ameliorated through appropriate preparation. Key to this preparation is providing patients with information about what to expect and a sense of psychological control.

SUMMARY

All of us interact with the health care system at one time or another. At the heart of these interactions are our relationships with individual health care practitioners. These interactions are governed by socially prescribed roles that specify appropriate behavior for both patients and practitioners. How these roles are played out in practice depends on the specific orientations of the practitioners and patients involved.

Central to patient-practitioner relations is communication. This communication takes place on both the verbal and nonverbal levels and is subject to many barriers. At the verbal level, patients present their requests to physicians, who then respond to them. Among the most common requests are those relating to psychosocial problems and medical explanations. Much important information in patient-practitioner interactions is conveyed nonverbally through touch, eye contact, facial expression, and tone of voice. Unfortunately, effective communication is often blocked by the practitioner's use of medical jargon, sociocultural differences between patients and practitioners, depersonalization, patients' emotions and cognitive limitations, and individual differences in the way patients experience and report symptoms. Problems in patient-practitioner relationships can have serious implications for patient satisfaction, malpractice litigation, and the outcome of treatment.

One particularly important problem in the patient-practitioner relationship is non-cooperation with medical treatment. On the average, patients fail to follow an estimated 30% of treatment recommendations. Non-cooperation is even higher for long-term treatments and those involving life-style changes. When patients fail to follow practitioner recommendations, they forfeit the full benefit of their treatment. In addition, patient non-cooperation can lead to errors in diagnosis and treatment. Among the determinants of non-cooperation are the nature of the treatment, patient comprehension of treatment instructions, beliefs about the nature of the illness, and patients' social circumstances. Some of the most important determinants of non-cooperation, however, are found in difficulties with the patient-practitioner relationship, particularly communication problems and difficulties in patient-practitioner rapport. Methods for reducing non-cooperation include obtaining verbal commitment from patients to follow the treatment and behavioral techniques such as cuing,

self-monitoring, contingency contracting, and self-reinforcement.

When patients are hospitalized, they enter complex institutions that are often alien and confusing. As total institutions, hospitals take control of virtually every aspect of a patient's life while they are there. The resulting loss of control and lack of information often leave patients confused and anxious. Although some patients seem to adapt well to the patient role, others respond with reactance or learned helplessness, both of which can have negative consequences for recovery. One aspect of hospitalization that has received wide attention is the psychological preparation of patients for surgery. Numerous studies have found that providing patients with a sense of control can aid them in coping with surgery and its aftermath. Among the types of control most commonly used are informational, cognitive, and behavioral control.

Issues of preparation are particularly critical for hospitalized children. Hospitalization is often a stressful experience for a child. Hospitalization stress among children is likely to be intensified by such factors as separation anxiety, difficulty in understanding the illness and treatment, separation from friends, enforced inactivity, and embarrassment about physical examination. Several programs have been developed to prepare children for hospitalization. Methods such as exposing the child to filmed models as well as teaching parents how to help their children cope have been shown to be effective in reducing anxiety and behavioral problems both before and after surgery.

KEY TERMS

tracer (222)
token economy (227)
total institution (229)

reactance (230)
separation anxiety (235)

SUGGESTED READINGS

Anderson, K. O., & Masur, F. T. (1983). Psychological preparation for invasive medical and dental procedures. *Journal of Behavioral Medicine, 6,* 1–40. In this paper, Karen Anderson and Frank Masur provide a comprehensive review of the effectiveness of

psychological methods for preparing people for medical procedures.
DiMatteo, M. R. (1979). A social-psychological analysis of physician-patient rapport: Toward a science of the art of medicine. *Journal of Social Issues,*

35, 12–33. Robin DiMatteo provides a cogent social psychological analysis of the components of doctor-patient rapport and their implications.

Eiser, C. (1985). *The psychology of childhood illness.* New York: Springer-Verlag. Chapter 3: "Children in the hospital" gives a detailed discussion of the effects of hospitalization on children and how these effects can be ameliorated.

Taylor, S. E. (1979). Hospital patient behavior: Reactance, helplessness, or control? *Journal of Social Issues, 35,* 156–84. This paper analyzes the psychological aspects of the hospital patient role and points out the consequences of that role.

Dealing with Chronic Illness and Disability

Previous chapters have discussed the way in which life stress can lead to disease. This chapter reverses the discussion by considering the ways in which disease produces stress, emphasizing the influence of the body on the mind. To begin our discussion, consider the following vignette:

The Martez family—Carlos, Anita, Maria, and Ana—left their Cuban homeland in the early 1960s and settled in Queens, New York, to start a new life together. Carlos, a skilled cabinetmaker, was unable to find steady employment to support Anita (his wife), Maria (Anita's sister), and Ana (his daughter). After Carlos' untimely death in the mid-1970s,

Ana graduated from college and started working in the public library system. Anita and Maria spent their days keeping house and praying for Ana's success.

Anita gradually began to experience short-term memory losses; she would walk into the kitchen and forget why she was there or pick up the phone to call Ana and forget the phone number. She developed other symptoms—dizziness, headaches, and confusion—and was worried sick about her health. After several trips to the doctors, Ana was encouraged to take Anita to a city medical center for more extensive tests. Their worst fears were confirmed; Anita was diagnosed as having Alzheimer's disease.

For several years, Maria and Ana were able to care for Anita. As her disease progressed, she lost bladder and bowel control, became unable to walk, and was disoriented most of the time. Maria was losing her strength to provide daily care and Ana had to work to support the family. Everything they believed about family bonds told them a nursing home was out of the question, but caring for Anita at home seemed equally impossible. They desperately needed to figure out what to do (Goldfarb, Brotherson, Summers, & Turnbull, 1986, pp. 4–5).

This vignette illustrates the tremendous impact that chronic and debilitating illness can have on patients and their families. Such illnesses disrupt lives and families, and pose important challenges. In this chapter we examine the sequence of events after a person is diagnosed with a chronic illness and consider how people adapt to the challenges presented. The term *adapt* is used advisedly since chronic illnesses, by definition, are long term and often have no effective cure. In the absence of a definitive cure, individuals with chronic diseases are faced with the necessity of learning to live with their condition. The discussion begins by examining people's initial responses to the diagnosis of a serious chronic illness. Next the chapter covers the psychosocial issues involved in adapting to chronic illness; finally it focuses on these issues as they relate to three major chronic diseases.

MIND AND BODY: THE CRISIS OF CHRONIC ILLNESS

A diagnosis of chronic illness brings with it a host of changes and challenges. An immediate response may well be one of shock and disbelief. "It can't be true!" "Why me?" As the reality of the situation sinks in, the person is faced with coping with the symptoms, dealing with sometimes painful and almost always unfamiliar medical procedures, and dealing with the reactions of family and friends. How can we best describe this process?

Obviously, the diagnosis of chronic illness produces stress for the person. But the challenges involved go well beyond those involved with ordinary stressors. Rudolf Moos (Moos, 1982; Moos & Tsu, 1977) has argued that responses to chronic illness are best understood in terms of **crisis.** People faced with stressful situations ordinarily call upon their various coping mechanisms and resources to deal with the situation and restore a sense of normalcy. A crisis occurs when a person is faced with a situation so novel or so major that the usual methods of coping are simply insufficient. Under such circumstances, the person is at a loss as to how to respond and experiences a

crisis
A situation so novel or so major that a person's usual methods of coping are insufficient.

disequilibrium
A state of physical,
psychological, or
social imbalance.

state of psychological, social, and physical imbalance, or **disequilibrium.** While in this state, usual responses to situations are disorganized, and the person is likely to experience extreme fear, guilt, or other unpleasant emotions.

This situation cannot last indefinitely because of the intensity of disequilibrium stress. Rather, some kind of resolution must be achieved, even if only temporarily. Thus, a crisis can be thought of as a *transition period* with important implications for the person's long-term adaptation. The person must develop new ways of coping with drastically altered circumstances. The critical question is whether these new coping methods will be adaptive or maladaptive in the long run. If the person responds to the crisis by developing coping methods that deal effectively with the challenges posed, the new equilibrium will probably be a healthy one. The person may well come through the experience stronger than before. But failure to deal effectively with the challenges will produce a new equilibrium that is unhealthy and likely to signal psychological deterioration and decline (Moos, 1982).

Studies of patients dealing with chronic illness demonstrate that throughout this process the person is faced with important tasks (Moos, 1982). Some of these relate to the illness itself, whereas others are more general in nature. Table 10.1 summarizes these tasks.

Perhaps most obvious is the task of dealing with the symptoms and incapacitation of the illness itself. Chronic illnesses often involve highly distressing symptoms such as pain, weakness, dizziness, incontinence, disfigurement, or paralysis. In addition, patients often need to be on the alert for symptoms of impending health crises. For example, a person with diabetes must monitor blood sugar so as to maintain proper levels and avoid both sugar shortage and insulin shock (Hendrick, 1985).

TABLE 10.1   *Major Adaptive Tasks with Chronic Illness*

Illness-Related Tasks

1. Dealing with pain, incapacitation, and other symptoms

2. Dealing with the hospital environment and special treatment procedures

3. Developing and maintaining adequate relationships with health care staff

General Tasks

4. Preserving a reasonable emotional balance

5. Preserving a satisfactory self-image and maintaining a sense of competence and mastery

6. Preserving relationships with family and friends

7. Preparing for an uncertain future

Note. From "Coping with acute health crises" by R. H. Moos, 1982, in T. Millon, C. Green, and R. Meagher (eds.), *Handbook of clinical health psychology* (p. 135), New York: Plenum.

Beyond the effects of the disease itself, patients also have to cope with the treatment process and maintain at least adequate relationships with health care staff. Many chronic illnesses require the use of special procedures and equipment to keep the disease in check. Patients with end-stage renal disease (kidney failure), for instance, are required either to receive a kidney transplant or to undergo hemodialysis, in which the person's blood is circulated through an artificial kidney for several hours, several times a week. Such life-saving measures, while essential to maintain life, can also be very stressful for the person (cf. Binik, Devins, & Orme, 1989). In addition, the person must deal with the treatment environment. As we saw in the last chapter, hospitals and clinics are often confusing and depersonalizing environments—which can add to an already stressful situation (cf. Taylor, 1979).

Developing and maintaining good relationships with health care providers present special problems in their own right. Frustrations associated with disease and treatment may produce anger against health care staff that can interfere with communication. Moreover, patients may be hesitant to ask for information or tell the doctor about concerns, even when valid. All this may be compounded by frequent turnover in personnel, requiring the patient to develop new relationships with health care staff repeatedly (Moos, 1982).

Other adaptive tasks, which are more general in nature, are relevant to many types of life crises. A major task for patients is maintaining emotional balance in the face of illness. As noted earlier, a diagnosis of serious or chronic illness is likely to engender negative emotions including fear, failure, guilt, helplessness, and apprehension. A key to healthy coping is maintaining at least some hope and optimism in the face of sometimes seemingly insurmountable circumstances (Moos, 1982; Taylor, 1983).

Closely related is the need to preserve a satisfactory self-image along with a sense of mastery and accomplishment. The physical changes that often accompany disease can be damaging to self-image and esteem. For example, the loss of a breast through mastectomy can be a serious blow to a woman's sense of femininity (Taylor, 1983; Wood, Taylor, & Lichtman, 1985). A person who must rely on a pacemaker or other device may experience feelings of being "half human–half machine" (Moos, 1982). Further, living with a chronic disease often requires people to redefine their capabilities and accept help with things they once did for themselves.

Relationships with family and friends also present important challenges. Studies of patients with chronic diseases have shown that the diagnosis of serious illness can act as a barrier to communication and interaction at the very time when the support of others is needed most (cf. Wortman & Dunkel-Schetter, 1979; Dunkel-Schetter & Wortman, 1982). In addition, simply being labeled as a "patient" or "seriously ill" can disrupt relationships. This is particularly likely to be the case when the disease itself is stigmatized, such as with AIDS (cf. Morin & Batchelor, 1984; Triplet & Sugarman, 1987).

Finally, individuals with chronic and life-threatening illnesses must prepare for an uncertain future. Many diseases, including cancer and AIDS, involve cycles of disease activity followed by remission. In addition, new medical procedures are constantly being developed that can treat or cure previously incurable conditions.

Ironically, this may actually make coping more difficult in that the person must prepare for the likelihood that the condition is irreversible, while being aware of the hope that future medical advances may change all that. Added to this are the serious financial pressures that can be brought by medical costs and reduced earning capacity (Strauss et al., 1984).

Dealing effectively with these tasks requires that patients and their families develop various coping skills (Moos, 1982). Like other stressors (see Chapter 7), these coping skills may focus on the emotions stirred up by the illness or on the practical aspects of the illness. Among the ways that people deal with the emotions involved are to deny or minimize the seriousness of the situation, prepare oneself mentally by going over possible alternative outcomes, or look for some sort of meaning in what has happened (Moos, 1982; Taylor, 1983). Skills for coping with the illness itself include seeking information about the disease and its possible outcomes, mastering specific illness-related procedures, and goal setting. Social skills are also important in dealing with illness. Chronic illnesses may reduce people's ability to perform chores for themselves, and thus they need to be able to ask for assistance. In addition, patients need emotional support and reassurance from friends and family, without getting trapped into passive-dependent roles (Moos, 1982).

Success at developing these skills and coping with chronic illness depends on the illness, who contracts it, and the resources available. Different illnesses present different challenges and produce different psychosocial impacts. Some conditions, such as AIDS, genital herpes, or epilepsy, are stigmatizing. Because of the strong public attitudes and fears about these conditions, a person with one of these diseases may be shunned by others or experience discrimination (Herek & Glunt, 1988; Scambler & Hopkins, 1990; Triplet & Sugarman, 1987; VanderPlate & Aral, 1987). Other diseases,

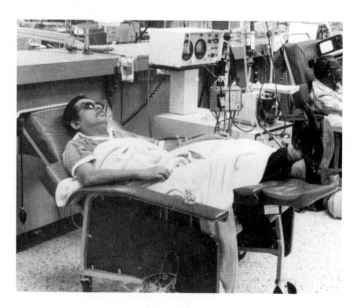

One of the major challenges of chronic illness is coping with treatment procedures. Some patients with end-stage kidney disease, for example, are required to undergo frequent sessions of dialysis.

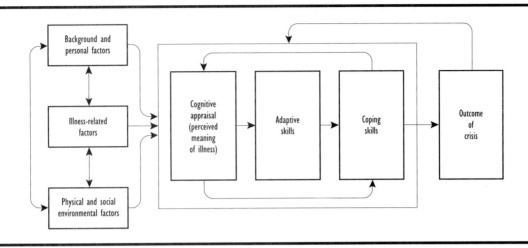

FIGURE 10.1 *A model of the crisis of physical illness.*

Note. From "Coping with acute health crises" by R. H. Moos, 1982 (p. 132), in T. Millon, C. Green, and R. Meagher (eds.), *Handbook of clinical health psychology,* New York: Plenum.

such as rheumatoid arthritis or Alzheimer's disease, are highly debilitating. Here important challenges relate to maintaining one's abilities and dignity as the disease progresses (Altman, 1987; Genest, 1989). Some chronic conditions are also life threatening. Diseases like AIDS and cancer evoke strong concerns about mortality, which can further complicate the coping process (Mages & Mendelsohn, 1979; Weitz, 1989). Finally, whether life-threatening or not, many chronic conditions require long-term medical management or significant life-style changes. For example, persons with insulin-dependent diabetes are required to take regular injections of insulin to control their blood sugar levels and are required to follow strict diets (Davidson, 1986).

Beyond the disease itself, factors such as age, gender, socioeconomic status, intelligence, emotional maturity, and ego-strength are likely to influence how the illness situation is appraised as well as the psychological and intellectual resources available for coping (Moos, 1982). Finally, the physical and social environment can significantly affect the coping process. The aesthetic quality of surroundings, the problems that they pose for mobility, and the degree of support that a person receives from friends and family are likely to have a major impact on adaptation (Moos, 1982).

The factors involved in the coping process are closely interrelated. As can be seen in Figure 10.1, background, illness, and environmental factors set the stage for the overall coping process. Within the coping process itself, the appraisal of the illness influences both the adaptive tasks required and the coping skills brought to bear. These, in turn, strongly influence the outcome of the crisis. Just as in other coping situations, the coping skills available and the outcome of the crisis are likely to strongly influence the perceived meaning of the illness.

PSYCHOSOCIAL DIMENSIONS OF CHRONIC ILLNESS AND DISABILITY

After the crisis of chronic illness has passed, the person begins the transition to a new social and psychological equilibrium. By their very nature, chronic illness and disability substantially alter the person's life. Just because the crisis has passed, however, does not mean that the struggle is over. Rather, it has only begun. Patients and those around them are still faced with significant challenges both psychologically and socially.

Psychological Aspects

Emotional adjustment. As we have already seen, the diagnosis of a chronic illness elicits emotional reactions. Initially, the person's response is likely to be one of denial, fear, shock, and apprehension (cf. Dimond & Jones, 1983; Eisenberg, Sutkin, & Janssen, 1984; Shontz, 1975). The sheer intensity of these emotions may lessen with time, but emotional adjustment remains critical.

One major concern in the long-range adaptation to chronic illness is depression. Many studies (cf. Binik et al., 1989; Devins & Seland, 1987; Thompson, Sobowlew-Shubin, Graham, & Janigan, 1989; Turner & Noh, 1988) have found that people with chronic illness and disability are more likely than others to show symptoms of depression. Although the percentages vary from study to study and disease to disease, a recent community survey found that about 35% of individuals with disabilities from all sources showed clinically significant depression, as compared with 12% of a non-disabled comparison sample (Turner & Noh, 1988). A major reason for this appears to be that illness and disability, by their nature, lead to significant loss of control in important areas ranging from control over one's body to control over everyday activities. This loss of control can, in turn, produce feelings of helplessness and depression (Devins & Seland, 1987; Peterson, 1982; Seligman, 1975).

Of course, not everyone with a chronic illness or disability becomes depressed. In the Turner and Noh (1988) study, 65% of those with disabilities were not depressed. What accounts for the difference? One important determinant seems to be age. Among those with chronic illnesses or disability, depression and other psychological problems were more common among younger people (Cassileth, Lusk, Strouse, Miller, Brown, Cross, & Tenaglia, 1984), as illustrated in Figure 10.2. Although this finding has yet to be adequately explained, one possibility is that people expect greater illness and disability with advancing age; thus the development of chronic illness in an older person comes as less of a shock. Another possibility is that older people have had more experience in developing effective coping skills. Consistent with this is the fact that people who have had an illness or disability longer seem to cope better with it (Casilleth et al., 1984; Thompson et al., 1989).

The nature of the disease itself also has a strong influence on emotional adaptation. Physical conditions that involve highly visible disfiguration—such as severe burns of the face—or that are stigmatizing—such as AIDS or epilepsy—can make adaptation difficult (cf. Scambler & Hopkins, 1990; Weitz, 1989; Wisely, Masur, & Morgan, 1983). The psychological difficulties involved in dealing with burns are described in Box 10.1. Also, in general, the more severe the disease, the more difficult the emotional

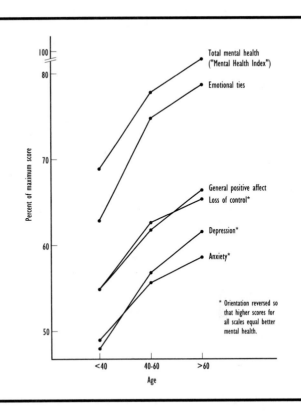

FIGURE 10.2

The relationship between age and mental health among patients with chronic illness.

Note. From "Psychosocial status in chronic illness: A comparative analysis of six diagnostic groups" by B. R. Cassileth, E. J. Lusk, T. B. Strouse, D. S. Miller, L. L. Brown, P. A. Cross, and A. N. Tenaglia, 1984, *New England Journal of Medicine, 311,* 506–11. Reprinted by permission.

adaptation to it. For example, in a study of Parkinson's disease, a degenerative, disabling neurological condition, Gayle Dakof and Gerald Mendelsohn (1989) identified four clusters of patients on the basis of emotional adaptation. One cluster of patients was reasonably well adapted, whereas a second cluster was depressed and apprehensive, a third felt depressed, ashamed, and misunderstood, and a fourth cluster was passive and resigned. Overall, patients who were reasonably well adapted were also the ones with the least severe disease.

Cognitive adjustment. Closely related to emotional adjustment is how the person thinks about the disease. The process of adaptation is not only an emotional process but a cognitive one. One aspect of this concerns the beliefs that people have about the illness. As seen in Chapter 8, people develop various beliefs about the nature of illness and its causes. These beliefs, which may or may not correspond to a medical understanding of the disease, serve as a guide for directing treatment efforts (cf. Leventhal et al., 1984) and play an important role in adjustment. For example, Shelley Taylor (1983) found that nearly all the women interviewed in a study of breast cancer developed beliefs about what caused their illness. Regardless of whether these beliefs made medical sense, they seemed to help the women to cope. Interest-

BOX 10.1 The Psychological Impact of Burns

Every year hundreds of thousands of people experience burns. Although most burns are relatively minor, a significant number are severe enough to require hospitalization. Burns this severe exact not only a physical but a psychological toll. Beginning with the trauma of the burn itself, burn patients face psychological issues that can have a profound effect long after they are released from the hospital (Wisely et al., 1983).

The immediate effect of severe burns is likely to be physiological and psychological shock. Skin loss and the presence of burned tissue expose the person to infection as well as threats from fluid loss, respiratory complications, edema, and electrolyte imbalance. In addition, removal of dead tissue (debridement) and even amputation may be required. These procedures are very painful and likely to be psychologically traumatic. For the more than 33% of burn patients who are children, the trauma can be particularly difficult. Children are thrust into an alien environment full of the smell of burned flesh and painful procedures they do not understand. Not surprisingly, they often experience anxiety and sometimes disorientation, hallucinations, and delusions (Wisely et al., 1983).

After the person's condition is stabilized, he or she must still deal with both physical and psychological pain. Burns themselves are often extremely painful, and

the frequent dressing changes required to avoid infection only add to this pain. This pain may be accompanied by anxiety and depression, as well as phobic reactions to treatment procedures (Kiecolt-Glaser & Williams, 1987; Wisley et al., 1983). These and other reactions are likely to be more intense among patients who blame themselves for the incident that caused the burns (Kiecolt-Glaser & Williams, 1987).

Even after release from the hospital, burn patients continue to face psychological challenges. Many of these challenges relate to functional impairment and disfigurement brought by the injuries. Despite repeated plastic surgery, the person's appearance may never be what it was before. Particularly when the burns affect visible body areas such as the face, this change in appearance can have profound psychological and social effects. Body image may be distorted, and others may react with curiosity or disgust. A major danger is that the patient will react to this by withdrawing into a social shell.

The psychological effects of burns demonstrate the need for the involvement of psychologists in the care of burn patients. Psychologists can serve as resources for helping burn patients and their families deal with the difficulties encountered in adapting to severe burns and their aftermath.

ingly, most of the causes identified were either controllable (such as diet) or were in the past. Apparently, the women were selecting explanations for their illness that allowed them to believe that the disease would not come back because "things are different now."

Other illness beliefs relate to the person's sense of mastery and control over the disease. As we saw in Chapter 7, feelings of control can act as a buffer against the effects of stress. The same applies when coping with chronic illness. As with attributions about the cause of the illness, whether the beliefs about control are logical to an outside observer seems to make no difference. All that seems to be required is that people *believe* that they can control the disease. Cancer patients, for example, apparently develop beliefs about how they can control the disease, ranging from a positive attitude to strictly following doctors' orders to giving direct commands to the body. Although some of these beliefs may seem strange or irrational to outsiders, holding them seems to help people cope (Taylor, 1983).

Cognitive adjustment is also reflected in people's outlook on life. An important feature of this is the meaning that people give to events. Although chronic illness and disability are objectively undesirable events, people are quite adept at finding positive meaning in the midst of catastrophe. In her study of breast cancer patients, Taylor (1983) discovered that many of the women interviewed found that they had gained new self-insights and that their lives had taken on new meaning in the face of their illness. For example, one woman stated: "You take a long look at your life and realize that many things that you thought were important before are totally insignificant. That's probably been the major change in my life. What you do is put things into perspective" (Taylor, 1983, p. 1163). Although not everyone was able to find a positive meaning, being able to do so was related to better psychological adjustment. Similar findings have been obtained with stroke patients. Patients who reported having a sense of meaning in life were less likely to be depressed after a stroke (Thompson et al., 1989).

Finally, cognitive adaptation depends on how people with chronic or disabling diseases come to view themselves. The physical changes brought about by such conditions are often threatening to the person's sense of self. To deal with these threats, people need to find ways of feeling good about themselves. One way of doing this is by comparing oneself with others with the disease who are faring less well. Breast cancer patients, for example, seem to use this process, known as downward comparison, to help them maintain positive feelings about themselves and their future (Taylor, 1983; Wood et al., 1985).

Most people adapt remarkably well to the challenges of chronic illness, even though some certainly continue to have significant difficulties; these were the conclusions of studies of the long-term psychological adaptation of patients with chronic diseases and disability. In a study of patients with several different types of chronic disorders, Barrie Cassileth and his colleagues (1984) found that, on the whole, mental health differed little among patients with arthritis, diabetes, cancer, renal disease, and skin disorders. More significant, the overall mental health of these patient groups was essentially equivalent to that of a physically healthy comparison group.

Social Aspects

Chronic illness and disability also present important social challenges. Healthy adaptation requires that the person deal successfully with the effects of the illness on interactions with family and friends.

Interaction with others. One of the most distressing aspects of chronic illness for many patients is the effect that it can have on their relationships with other people. The challenges associated with chronic illnesses, not surprisingly, can disrupt interpersonal relationships. First, the patient may voluntarily withdraw from social interaction (Strauss et al., 1984). This may be caused by the physical effects of the disease itself, such as when a loss of energy makes engaging in interaction difficult; social isolation may also be sought because of the person's concern about stigma or physical appearance. For example:

A retired professional man in his sixties was treated for squamous cell carcinoma of the nostril and lip with radiation and surgery. After the surgical repair, he reported, "I awoke and saw a monster in the mirror." He avoided people and retired from his work. Four years later, he still remained mostly indoors, isolated, brooding about his deformity, and fearing a recurrence. To the interviewer he clearly had a moderate degree of facial scarring, but nothing like the gross deformity he experienced in himself (Mages & Mendelsohn, 1979, p. 263).

The other side of this is that friends and acquaintances may withdraw from the person with the disease. Serious diseases may well conjure up fears and anxieties in them that lead them to avoid the person. For example, cancer patients may be avoided because friends and acquaintances cannot bear to face the physical changes that have taken place in the person, or may subconsciously fear that they can contract the disease from the person (Wortman & Dunkel-Schetter, 1979; Strauss et al., 1984). Such avoidance is particularly likely when the disease is highly feared and has a stigma attached to it. People with AIDS, for example, have been shunned, barred from schools, fired from their jobs, and run out of their communities by people panicked about being near someone with the disease (Foster, Somerville, & Duckett, 1990; Mather, 1985; Shilts, 1987).

Particularly disturbing is that this disruption of interpersonal relationships occurs at a time when the person is likely to need social support the most. When patients are attempting to cope with their own fears and anxieties, having others around for support is likely to be particularly critical (Wortman & Dunkel-Schetter, 1979; Singer & Lord, 1984; Strauss et al., 1984). Many studies have demonstrated that having supportive social relationships can play an important role in helping people cope more effectively with illness (Manne, Sandler, & Zautra, 1986; Singer & Lord, 1984; Walsh & Walsh, 1989). For example, a recent study of individuals with multiple sclerosis found that having emotional support from others helped maintain a sense of self-esteem (Walsh & Walsh, 1989).

Chronic illness and the family. Chronic illness also has important effects on the patients' families. When a family member is diagnosed with a serious illness, the concerns and disruptions experienced by the patient are likely to be experienced by other members of the family as well. The ill family member is likely to become more dependent on help from others in the family. For example, individuals who have had strokes or have a mobility-impairing condition such as arthritis may need to rely on other family members to help them with even simple tasks like getting dressed or moving around. In addition, aspects of the person's treatment may well place a burden on other family members. Chronically ill individuals are often seen by several different medical specialists. Getting to and from appointments can require a considerable amount of time and effort. Added to this is the impact that illness is likely to have on family finances. Chronic illness is often very expensive and can eat heavily into available funds, sometimes even leading to financial ruin (Strauss et al., 1984).

Beyond these practical problems, chronic illness can also affect the overall functioning of the family. The strains associated with illness can lead to marital difficulties (Binik et al., 1989; Garrison & McQuiston, 1989; Lewis, Woods, Hough, & Bensley, 1989) and various difficulties for children in the family. When the ill family member is a child, parents may focus their concerns and attentions on the child's illness, leading to resentment by siblings. Studies of the siblings of chronically ill children have found higher levels of emotional and behavioral disturbance among these children than among siblings of healthy children (Garrison & McQuiston, 1989; King & Hanson, 1986).

Yet families are an essential source of support for individuals with chronic illnesses and disabilities. Family members can provide the person with emotional and practical support, and often play a key role in the person's adaptation. For example, social support from family members has been shown to play an important role in helping diabetic children to control their disease (Garrison & McQuiston, 1989) and in helping kidney disease and cancer patients to cope (Christiansen, Turner, Slaughter, & Holman, 1989; Mages & Mendelsohn, 1979; Taylor, 1983).

Helping People Cope

Given the challenges presented by chronic illness and disability, what can be done to help people cope? The answer to this question depends, of course, on the nature of the disease, the particular vulnerabilities of a given patient, the person's coping resources, available social support, and other factors. Thus interventions need to be tailored to the specific person and situation.

In many cases, a critical intervention, particularly in the initial period after diagnosis, is *patient education* about the nature of the disease, its treatment, and consequences. Patients and their families may be unfamiliar with the disease before diagnosis, and may find the symptoms experienced and treatment procedures somewhat bewildering. They may also be confused as to where to turn for help and information. Patient education can assist patients and their families to cope by helping them understand the disease and its treatment. For example, arthritis self-help courses help arthritis patients to understand the nature of arthritis, provide training in pain management and goal setting, and give the participants hints on how to accomplish everyday tasks with the least strain on their joints. Evaluation of one such course suggests that this type of education can allow patients to increase their sense of self-efficacy and improve psychosocial functioning (O'Leary, Shoor, Lorig, & Holman, 1988).

Certainly not all the problems encountered with chronic illness can be dealt with fully through education. When the emotional strains on the individual or other family members become too great, *psychotherapy* may be necessary. Through psychotherapy, the person and family members can work through emotional difficulties and learn to adapt to the illness. Therapy may be done with the patient individually or involve the entire family. Group psychotherapy brings together patients with chronic illness so that they can help each other cope. Psychotherapy with medical patients differs in important ways from standard psychotherapy in that it is concerned not with psychopathology but rather with specific problems of illness-related adaptation (Garrison & McQuiston, 1989; VanderPlate, 1984); moreover, the therapy tends to be episodic rather than long term. Thus therapy sessions are generally scheduled primarily in response to medical crises or when particular issues arise (Wellisch, 1981).

Behavioral interventions can also play an important role in helping people cope with illness. Conditions known to be caused or aggravated by stress, even many where a stress link is not evident, can benefit from relaxation and other behavioral interventions. In addition, behavioral methods can be used to improve cooperation with medical recommendations. A good example of how behavioral methods can be used to improve patient coping is the case of diabetes. Behavioral interventions used with diabetes include relaxation training and the use of behavioral treatments, such as self-monitoring, skills training, contingency contracting, and shaping, to improve cooperation with medical regimens (Surwit, Feinglos, & Scovern, 1983).

Finally, *self-help groups* can help patients cope by providing them with information about their diseases and offering them an opportunity to compare their experiences with others who have the disease. These groups generally meet on a regular basis and share personal experiences and coping solutions, and provide each other with social support (Hinrichsen, Revenson, & Shinn, 1985). Although some have questioned their effectiveness, self-help groups have been shown to have beneficial effects on helping people cope with diseases including cancer, diabetes, genital herpes, scoliosis, and genetic diseases (Hinrichsen et al., 1985; Manne et al., 1986; Swavely, Silverman, & Falek, 1987).

Thus far we have focused on general aspects of coping with chronic illness and disability. Although this provides an overview of the issues involved, the overview is incomplete. The processes discussed take place in the context of specific diseases. People cope with different diseases in similar ways, but some diseases require unique coping methods: to illustrate, we now turn our attention to how people live with diabetes, arthritis, and Alzheimer's disease.

LIVING WITH DIABETES

diabetes mellitus
A metabolic disorder in which the body is unable to properly convert glucose into usable energy.

Diabetes mellitus is a common chronic disease and a major health problem worldwide (Alberti & Krall, 1990). According to current estimates, in the United States alone nearly 6 million people have been diagnosed with diabetes, and an additional 4 million to 5 million have diabetes, but have not yet been diagnosed (National Center for Health Statistics, 1988c; National Diabetes Data Group, 1985). When the complications of diabetes are taken into account, diabetes is directly or indirectly responsible for more than 300,000 American deaths annually, making it the third leading cause of death in the United States (Davidson, 1986).

What Is Diabetes?

Diabetes is a metabolic disorder in which the body is unable to properly convert glucose (sugar) into usable energy. In normal metabolism, the body produces the hormone **insulin,** which plays a key role in the process. After a person eats, the level of glucose in the blood rises, which normally stimulates the production of insulin. Insulin then makes cell membranes more permeable to glucose and stimulates the

insulin
A hormone produced by the pancreas that regulates the body's use of sugar.

hyperglycemia
A condition of having too much sugar in the blood.

liver to make and store glycogen, an animal starch derived from sugar. Thus glucose is converted to usable energy and glycogen (stored energy), and glucose levels in the blood drop. In addition, insulin stimulates the incorporation of amino acids into muscle protein for tissue growth and fosters lipogenesis (fat formation) for long-term energy storage (Hendrick, 1985).

A diabetic has defective insulin production or use such that the body either produces insufficient amounts of insulin or the insulin does not have its intended effects. Therefore the glucose cannot be readily used by body cells, so it accumulates in the blood, producing a condition known as **hyperglycemia.** Because the cells are unable to metabolize glucose, they instead metabolize glycogen, fat, and protein, effectively depleting the body's supply of stored energy. In addition, the body attempts to flush the excess glucose from the system through the kidneys and urine. This leads to the classic diabetic symptoms of high levels of thirst and excessive urination. If this process continues for a long time, the person experiences fatigue, weight loss, and dehydration, and may lapse into a coma and die. Appropriate treatment can restore insulin and blood glucose to proper levels and prevent the effects of hyperglycemia (Davidson, 1986; Hendrick, 1985; Surwit et al., 1983).

Although the direct effects of hyperglycemia are certainly serious, much of the concern over diabetes has to do with its serious medical complications. Over time, even mildly elevated levels of blood glucose can produce serious health problems. Compared to the general population, diabetics are twice as likely to have heart disease and stroke, 17 times more likely to suffer from kidney problems, 20 times more likely to have gangrene, and 25 times more likely to go blind (Davidson, 1986). These potential problems shorten the life expectancy of diabetics.

Diabetes takes two major forms. The most serious, and fortunately less common, type is insulin-dependent or Type I diabetes. This type of diabetes is most commonly diagnosed in childhood or adolescence and is often referred to as juvenile diabetes. In insulin-dependent diabetes (IDDM), the body produces little or no insulin; thus, the person relies on exogenous (external) insulin to achieve proper metabolism of glucose. Approximately 5–10% of diabetics are insulin dependent (Davidson, 1986).

More common and less serious is adult-onset or noninsulin-dependent diabetes (NIDDM). Although NIDDM can be diagnosed at any age, it is most commonly discovered in individuals over the age of 40. In normal weight individuals, insulin is produced but at subnormal levels. In individuals who are overweight, the situation is different; they may produce normal or even above-normal amounts of insulin. However, because the fat cells are enlarged and more resistant to insulin's actions, the same amount of insulin does not have the same effects as it does in normal weight persons. NIDDM accounts for about 90–95% of all diabetes (Davidson, 1986).

Treatment of diabetes involves both medical and behavioral interventions. Individuals with IDDM generally require intravenous injections of insulin, which are often self-administered and are designed to help the person maintain appropriate blood glucose levels. Diet and exercise are two additional components of effective diabetic control. Insulin-dependent diabetics are encouraged to eat frequent, small meals so as to maintain a relatively constant level of blood glucose and watch what they eat so as to keep their weight down and get a proper balance of protein, carbohydrates, and fats. Exercise is also important: it helps people to stay fit and keep their weight down, and reduces their need for insulin (Davidson, 1986; Hendrick, 1985; Tsalikian, 1990).

Treatment of NIDDM is less complicated. Although some NIDDM patients require intravenous insulin, many can maintain appropriate blood glucose levels through the use of oral medications or even through diet and exercise alone. Since obesity is often a factor with NIDDM, weight control is likely to be a major part of the treatment (Davidson, 1986; Zimmerman, 1990).

Behavior and Diabetes

Diabetes is closely related to behavior. Living with diabetes requires that the person engage in complex behaviors to control the disease and its effects. A person with IDDM needs to monitor blood glucose levels carefully and then administer the appropriate amount of insulin so as to maintain normal blood glucose levels. In addition, the person must carefully control diet and exercise, as well as reduce stress, which can disrupt metabolic control. The treatment regimen for NIDDM is generally not as rigorous, but the person still needs to maintain careful control of diet and exercise and take medications when prescribed (Wing, Epstein, Nowalk, & Lamparski, 1986).

How successfully have diabetics followed these regimens? Research evidence paints a somewhat pessimistic picture. Insulin-dependent diabetics often either do not monitor their blood glucose with appropriate frequency or make significant errors in estimating glucose levels. For example, one study found that among children attending a diabetes clinic, only 26% were monitoring their blood sugar three times daily, and 25% were monitoring it less than once per day. Further, only 36% of the children estimated their blood sugar within ±10% (Wing et al., 1985). Dietary cooperation is also a problem. Studies examining cooperation with diets have routinely found that a significant number of diabetics fail to follow recommendations about meal scheduling and foods (Wing et al., 1986). The picture is similar for NIDDM. Although noninsulin-dependent diabetics are generally prescribed less rigorous regimens, they still often fail to monitor glucose levels, do so inaccurately, or stray from their recommended diets (Wing et al., 1986).

As seen in the previous chapter, several interventions have been developed to increase cooperation with medical recommendations. Behavioral strategies appear to be particularly useful for diabetics. For example, Rena Wing and her colleagues (Wing et al., 1986) conceptualize diabetes control in terms of a behavioral self-regulation model involving the steps of self-observation, self-evaluation, and self-regulation. In order to improve glucose control, the person must be taught to monitor and evaluate glucose levels accurately and then take the necessary steps to correct imbalances. Behavioral programs to do this typically include strategies such as specific assignments to define unambiguously what needs to be done, skills training to develop new behaviors, cuing behaviors with salient stimuli, behavioral contracts, self-monitoring, and programs of reinforcement (Surwit et al., 1983). For example, researchers in one program (Epstein et al., 1981) used a "traffic light diet," in which foods were divided into Red (Stop) foods that were to be avoided, Yellow (Caution) foods that could be eaten in moderation, and Green (Go) foods that could be consumed without restriction. Children in this program self-monitored their intake of Red foods and received points for staying below their Red food goal. The results indicated that this program was successful in improving dietary cooperation.

In addition to the role of behavior in treating the disease, behavior is also implicated in a diabetic's insulin requirements. In particular, psychological stress has been shown to increase insulin needs (Hanson & Pichert, 1986). Activation of the sympathetic nervous system leads to the secretion of hormones such as epinephrine, norepinephrine, and cortisol, which are known to counteract the effects of insulin (Citrin, Kleinman, & Skyler, 1986). This suggests that behavioral relaxation techniques can be useful in the treatment of diabetes. In support of this, several studies have found that various types of relaxation and anxiety management training can help to improve glucose tolerance and reduce insulin requirements (Rose, Firestone, Heick, & Faught, 1983; Surwit et al., 1983).

Psychosocial Dimensions of Diabetes

Diabetes also has psychosocial implications. As with other chronic illnesses, a diagnosis of diabetes is likely to be upsetting for the person. Newly diagnosed diabetics often respond with disbelief or denial, followed by anger and, eventually, passive resignation. Anxiety and depression have been found in many diabetics and their families, perhaps because they feel overwhelmed by the requirements for controlling the disease, angry, or afraid of long-term complications (Hendrick, 1985).

Added to these feelings are common problems with sexual dysfunction. Impotence has been reported for more than half the men who have had diabetes for more than six years. In addition, women may experience sexual difficulties because of painful intercourse or decreased genital sensitivity or orgasmic capacity (Newman & Bertelson, 1986). Some of these problems derive from neurological or vascular changes caused by the disease itself. In addition, psychosocial problems, such as depression, anxiety, anger, and alcohol use, often increase sexual difficulties. Studies of the effects of diabetes on marriage have found that, although diabetes can increase marital stress, it often serves as a "medium" for acting out existing marital conflicts (Hendrick, 1985).

Diabetes in Children and Adolescents

Psychosocial difficulties can be particularly intense for children and adolescents diagnosed with diabetes. Although a diagnosis of diabetes is likely to be a blow for an adult, it can be particularly upsetting for a child. Children often understand illness differently than do adults and may well construct their own explanation for the disease (Bibace & Walsh, 1979; Burbach & Peterson, 1986). Thus children with diabetes may see the disease as punishment for negative behavior or as reflecting their parents' failure to protect them from harm (Hendrick, 1985). In addition, the emotional impact of diagnosis with diabetes is likely to be compounded by emotional changes that take place during adolescence. Adolescence is a time when most young people test limits and when anger and rebellion are common. Diabetics may do so in the form of eating forbidden food or altering insulin dosage (Hendrick, 1985; LaGreca, 1987).

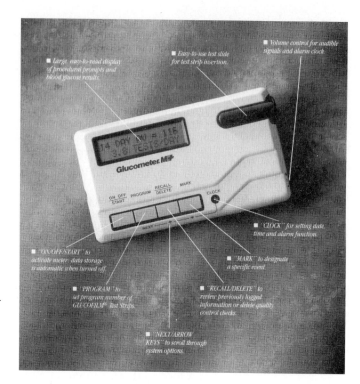

Treatment, non-coop-eration, and medica-tion errors are major problems among chil-dren and adolescents with diabetes, but tech-nology has made it much easier to meas-ure and keep track of blood glucose levels and insulin dosage.

A particular concern has to do with medical cooperation among children and adolescents. Children or adolescents who are diagnosed with diabetes almost always have the more serious IDDM, which requires the more rigorous treatment regimen. When the patient is a young child, the parents assume responsibility for making sure that the treatment regimen is followed. Under these circumstances, the degree of adherence is essentially a function of the knowledge, motivation, and skills of the parent. For older children, more of the treatment responsibility falls to the child. Thus the degree of adherence is a function of the child's knowledge and skills (LaGreca, 1987). Significantly, the fact that the child willingly assumes responsibility and adheres to the treatment regimen does not necessarily mean a better outcome. In one study, Annette LaGreca (1982) found that children who assumed more responsibility for their care actually had poorer metabolic control. This was the case even when the children had good knowledge of the disease and made efforts at following the regimen. Knowledge and motivation, by themselves, do not mean that the person is able to be *effective* in monitoring glucose or measuring insulin for injection. The children apparently had the knowledge and motivation but had not yet adequately acquired the necessary skills. Overall, studies of adherence to medical regimens among chil-dren and adolescents show an alarmingly high rate of error and noncooperation (LaGreca, 1987).

With young diabetics, the family plays a key role in disease control. Studies of the dynamics of the families of diabetics have found that poor family coping is common. Parents and other family members may become obsessively concerned with diabetic control, or may engage in denial and be uninvolved. Either approach can be maladaptive (Hendrick, 1985). In general, support from parents and high family cohesion are associated with good diabetic control, whereas the opposite is associated with poor control (Johnson, 1980; Hanson et al., 1989). This argues for some kind of therapeutic intervention when families show maladaptive responses to diabetes. Although few controlled studies have been done, family therapy does appear beneficial in such cases (Johnson, 1980).

LIVING WITH ARTHRITIS

Most of us take for granted our ability to move and go about our everyday activities with a minimum of pain. For the millions of people who suffer from arthritis, however, such ease of movement cannot be taken for granted. Rather, even simple movements like walking across the room, buttoning clothes, or opening a jar can produce excruciating pain. Although arthritis has plagued humankind since the beginning of time (Benedek, 1988), the psychosocial dimensions of this affliction have only recently been explored in depth.

The Nature of Arthritis

rheumatoid arthritis
A chronic, systemic, inflammatory condition causing pain and swelling of the joints.

osteoarthritis
A degenerative joint disease characterized by the progressive loss of cartilage and other changes in the joints.

Several conditions have been collectively described as arthritis. The term *arthritis* itself means "an inflammation of the joints." The two most common forms of arthritis are **rheumatoid arthritis** (RA) and **osteoarthritis** (OA). Although RA and OA are both arthritis and involve joint pain, they are actually very different diseases. RA is a chronic, systemic, inflammatory condition affecting various joints in the body. Typically, joint inflammation is symmetrical, that is, the same joints are affected on both sides of the body. Although a person with RA may experience periodic remission of the disease, over time the disease produces destruction of the joints, deformity, and, ultimately, varying degrees of disability (Zvaifler, 1988). In addition, patients with RA experience other health problems such as skin nodules, heart problems, lung disease, neurological complaints, and eye problems (Bennett, 1988; Genest, 1989). The causes of RA are as yet unknown, though it is believed to be an autoimmune disease: a disease in which the immune system literally attacks the body's own tissues. Since no cure exists for RA, treatment focuses on relieving symptoms, primarily pain and stiffness, and helping the person to maintain use of the joints (Hess, 1988).

OA, by contrast, is a degenerative joint condition that commonly afflicts people as they get older. This form of arthritis is characterized by progressive loss of cartilage and other changes in the joints. People with OA experience joint pain that worsens slowly over time, as well as stiffness and enlargement of the affected joints. Unlike RA, OA is not a systemic disease but rather affects joints individually. The joints affected are likely to be the ones that receive heavy usage. Thus people who are overweight are at greater risk for OA in the knees. In addition, the joints affected vary with the person's occupation. For example, coal miners develop OA of the spine, whereas bus drivers get OA of the shoulders. No cure currently exists for OA either; thus treatment is primarily symptomatic, with a view toward minimizing additional joint damage (Moskowitz & Goldberg, 1988).

Psychosocial Dimensions of Arthritis

Arthritis is rarely fatal, so the primary concerns about it relate to psychosocial effects and the ability of arthritics to carry out their day-to-day functions. Studies of arthritics, done mostly with RA patients, have shown that the psychosocial impact of arthritis can be profound (see Anderson, Bradley, Young, McDaniel, & Wise, 1985; Genest, 1989, for reviews).

In most cases, the outstanding symptom of arthritis is pain. This pain comes primarily from inflammation of the affected joints, but can also come from complications of the disease or side effects of medication. Studies of the overall health of arthritics and their medication usage have found that self-reported pain is by far the strongest predictor of how much medication they take, as well as both physician and patient assessments of general health. In addition, the amount of pain experienced by the person is an important predictor of psychological well-being and overall prognosis of the disease (Anderson et al., 1985; Genest, 1989).

Functional impairment in dealing with activities of daily living is another major concern with arthritis. Arthritics often report considerable difficulty with even simple movements; these limitations are generally viewed as one of the most frustrating aspects of the illness (Genest, 1989). Table 10.2, which lists responses to items on a measure of functional impairment, gives a glimpse of some of the difficulties experienced by arthritics. As can be seen, the limitations experienced by arthritics tend to be general and thus likely to affect adversely a broad spectrum of the person's activities. Therefore, a major emphasis in patient education is on helping arthritics develop ways of accomplishing their everyday activities with a minimum of pain and strain on the joints (Lorig & Fries, 1986; Porter, 1984).

TABLE 10.2 *Functional Impairment in RA*

Item	Percent Checking
Walk more slowly	73
Walk shorter distances or frequent rests	63
Walk with difficulty (limp, wobble)	56
Move hand or fingers with limitation or difficulty	62
Stand for only short periods	43

Note. Items are paraphrased from the Sickness Impact Profile in "Physical and psychosocial function in rheumatoid arthritis" by R. A. Deyo, T. S. Inui, J. Leininger, and S. Overman, 1982, *Archives of Internal Medicine, 142,* p. 880.

The activity limitations and pain often lead arthritics to experience emotional problems as well as difficulties with social relationships, sexual activity, and employment. Studies of RA patients have found that they express lower self-esteem, less work satisfaction, and a greater sense of meaninglessness than do healthy controls (Earle et al., 1979). In addition, several studies have found evidence of increased depression among arthritics (Genest, 1989; Smith, Peck, & Ward, 1990). But not all arthritics experience emotional difficulties to the same degree. Those who have significant social support from family or friends have fewer emotional difficulties than those with less support (Brown, Wallston, & Nicassio, 1989; Fitzpatrick, Newman, Lamb, & Shipley, 1988; Goodenow, Reisine, & Grady, 1990). In addition, those who are able to maintain a sense of control or self-efficacy in the face of their disease show better emotional health (Affleck, Tennen, Pfeiffer, & Fifield, 1987; Genest, 1989; Smith et al., 1990).

Arthritis can also have negative effects on the person's relationships with others. Roughly half the arthritics surveyed in one study reported that they had trouble with communication or interaction with others (Deyo, Inui, Leininger, & Overman, 1982). In addition, several studies have noted negative changes in family functioning (Anderson et al., 1985). One area that is particularly relevant for marriage relationships is sexual functioning. Although the data are sketchy, sexual desire and capacity appear diminished, at least among RA patients (Genest, 1989). The extent to which arthritis places strains on marriages is somewhat unclear. Early studies suggested that arthritics had higher rates of divorce, but later studies have produced more mixed results (Anderson et al., 1985). The psychosocial effects of arthritis in children are explored in Box 10.2.

Finally, arthritis can have significant financial ramifications. Surveys of patients with RA have found that financial concerns are one of the most serious sources of stress among arthritics (Genest, 1989). Medical treatment costs can be substantial, especially for older patients on fixed incomes. In addition, the pain and disability associated with arthritis can have a serious impact on the person's ability to work. One study of patients with RA found that, on the average, their yearly earnings were 50% of what they would have been had they not contracted the disease. Of those patients who were working at the time they were diagnosed, 59% were no longer working at the time of the study (an average of 9 years later) (Meenan, Yelin, Nevitt, & Epstein, 1981).

Helping People Live with Arthritis

What can be done to help people cope with their arthritis? As indicated earlier, no cures exist for either OA or RA. The most that medical treatments can do is relieve some of the symptoms and try to prevent further damage to the joints. Thus various drugs are used to relieve pain and inflammation, and patients are advised to rest often and carefully pace their activities (Anderson et al., 1985; Hess, 1988).

The psychosocial effects of arthritis can be addressed in several ways. Traditional psychotherapy techniques can be used to help arthritics deal with the emotional impact of the disease. Psychotherapy under these circumstances tends to be brief and focused on the effects of the disease. In addition, the empirical relationship between

BOX 10.2 Arthritis in Children

Although arthritis is usually thought of as a disease of older adults, more than 250,000 children in the United States alone suffer from juvenile rheumatoid arthritis (JRA) (Gewanter, Roghmann, & Baum, 1983). These children have a disease that is similar to adult rheumatoid arthritis but occurs at a much earlier age. Unless properly managed, this disease can result in permanent joint damage and disability.

JRA presents important psychosocial challenges for patients and their families. Perhaps because arthritis is thought of as something that affects old people, children with JRA have problems with self-concept, thinking of themselves as "different," "inferior," and "less worthy" (King & Hanson, 1986). In addition, children with JRA have been found to exhibit behavioral disturbances and to be at risk for psychological maladjustment (Billings, Moos, Miller, & Gottlieb, 1987; Varni, Wilcox, & Hanson, 1988). These problems tend to be more serious for children with more severe disease, although some evidence indicates that children with less severe disease sometimes experience more problems (King & Hanson, 1986).

In addition to psychological problems, JRA can also have negative effects on social interaction and school participation. Children with JRA often experience fatigue and may be required to restrict their physical activities. These restrictions are likely to mean that they are unable to participate in normal school and social activities, or may be forced to do so at a reduced level. Thus children with severe JRA are likely to miss school more often and tend to participate in relatively few social activities (Billings et al., 1987).

As with most other chronic diseases, the family also feels the effects of the child's illness. Studies of the effects of JRA on the family have found that parents of children with JRA experience a considerable amount of anxiety and express fears about the possibility for long-term handicap and the potential effects of the disease on the child's height or appearance. Moreover, the cost of medical care can impose a serious financial burden on many families (King & Hanson, 1986).

Fortunately, the long-term prospects for JRA patients appear positive. Studies of long-term adaptation generally show that children with JRA adapt well. Although some JRA patients still have disabilities as adults, they appear to attain the same level of education and income as similar individuals without JRA and, overall, to function well as adults (King & Hanson, 1986).

social support and the impact of arthritis suggests that interventions to increase social support should help arthritics deal with the disease. To date, few controlled evaluations have been done on the effects of social support interventions. Some evidence has suggested that these interventions can be effective, but the data are mixed (Anderson et al., 1985). More promising are strategies that focus on self-regulation, such as those using relaxation or biofeedback to help patients reduce their pain, or that teach arthritics specific techniques for accomplishing daily activities with a minimum of pain. These self-regulation strategies appear effective in reducing pain and minimizing disability (Anderson et al., 1985; O'Leary et al., 1988).

LIVING WITH ALZHEIMER'S DISEASE

One of the triumphs of modern medicine has been a significant increase in life expectancy. As we saw in Chapter 4, life expectancy has increased substantially throughout the developed world (Lopez, 1990; National Center for Health Statistics,

1989). With the increase in life expectancy has come an increase in diseases associated with old age. Now that people die less often from acute and infectious diseases, they are more likely to live long enough to develop diseases that generally only afflict people in their later years. One of the most significant of these is Alzheimer's disease, which is estimated to affect 10% of American adults over age 65 and 47% of those who live to be at least 85 (Evans et al., 1989).

What Is Alzheimer's?

People have long thought that the memory loss and cognitive deficits characteristic of dementia are a natural part of old age, that senility is inevitable. We now know that it is not (Birren & Schaie, 1990). Many elderly people maintain their cognitive faculties and remain mentally alert until they die. This is not true, however, for victims of Alzheimer's disease.

Alzheimer's disease
A degenerative brain disease producing progressive and irreversible loss of cognitive function.

Alzheimer's disease is a brain disorder that is characterized by a progressive and, currently, irreversible loss of memory and intellectual function. The onset of the disease is insidious, and patients often show only mild deficits in the early stages. Over time, however, the symptoms of dementia worsen, and the person's condition progressively deteriorates. One of the major difficulties in diagnosing Alzheimer's is that many other conditions can produce similar symptoms. For example, serious depression, excessive alcohol use, or reactions to some medications can mimic the effects of Alzheimer's. Thus a diagnosis of Alzheimer's is generally made by eliminating other possible causes of the person's symptoms. At present, a definitive diagnosis can only be made through autopsy or by taking a brain biopsy (Heckler, 1985; Zarit, Orr, & Zarit, 1985). This uncertainty in diagnosis creates the likelihood that individuals with reversible dementia may be misdiagnosed as having Alzheimer's.

Although the course of Alzheimer's varies considerably from person to person, the progressive deterioration goes through several phases. In the early stages of the disease, loss of memory may be the only discernible sign. Later, the person may show subtle personality changes, for example, becoming less spontaneous or showing signs of apathy or withdrawal. As the disease progresses into the middle stages, the changes in the person become more pronounced. The intellectual impairment becomes more severe, and the person's appearance may begin to deteriorate. Behavioral problems, such as wandering, become more apparent. In the later stages, the individual begins to show more profound cognitive changes, including serious disorientation, and the person can deteriorate to the point of being mute, incontinent, and totally dependent on others (Heckler, 1985; Zarit et al., 1985).

As yet we do not know what causes Alzheimer's, nor are there effective treatments for it. We do know that the disease involves a progressive deterioration of the neurons and other changes in the brain. This may be the result of genetic factors, neurochemical imbalances or deficits, an autoimmune process, or the accumulation of environmental toxins (Altman, 1987; Miner, Richter, Blass, Valentine, & Winters-Miner, 1989). Although experimental drugs are being tested, no reliable means have been discovered as yet to arrest or reverse the disease and its effects (Giacobini & Becker, 1989).

The Impact of Alzheimer's on the Family

The cognitive and behavioral changes caused by Alzheimer's can have a devastating effect on family members. In the early stages of the disease, Alzheimer's patients retain their physical vigor and may not, to outside observers, seem changed. However, to family members who interact with the person on a daily basis, the person's transformation into a confused and helpless stranger is all too evident. The deterioration brought on by Alzheimer's can be particularly hard to deal with because the person involved is often a parent or spouse on whom family members have depended over the years (Heckler, 1985; Zarit et al., 1985).

One of the most difficult aspects of the disease for family members is the loss of identity experienced by Alzheimer's patients (Orona, 1990). Relationships with significant others and memories of past shared experiences are important aspects of a person's identity. As memory and cognitive faculties deteriorate, Alzheimer's patients are typically unable to recall significant family experiences and, over time, arrive at a point where they no longer recognize those closest to them. In the later stages of the disease, patients may not even recognize themselves (Biringer, Anderson, & Strubel,

Caring for Alzheimer's patients often puts a serious strain on families.

1988). This loss of identity and relationship can be devastating for family members. As one woman said of her mother:

> I knew I was losing her. . . . When she did not recognize me, that's what bothered me the most. I'm under the illusion—well, she birthed me. I know she knows me. I've been here, and I *know* she knows me! But she didn't know me. And that was very traumatic for me (Orona, 1990, p. 1254).

As the disease progresses, the person's need for care and attention increases substantially. The memory losses and other cognitive deficits mean that the person becomes increasingly dependent on others for tasks that once could be handled with ease. Behavioral problems, such as wandering, mean that Alzheimer's patients may have to be watched carefully for their own safety. The person may eventually become bedridden and totally dependent on others for all aspects of care. Since most Alzheimer's patients are cared for at home, this often presents a tremendous burden for family members. Family members, most often the spouse, eldest daughter, or a daughter-in-law, become responsible for observing the patient, providing needed custodial care, initiating medical treatment, and filling medical prescriptions (Maletta & Hepburn, 1986). In addition, the financial burden can be considerable, particularly in the later stages of the disease, when caring for the person may require professional assistance or placement in a nursing home.

Helping Families Cope

Not surprisingly, the emotional, physical, and financial burden of caring for Alzheimer's patients often takes a significant toll on family members, particularly those who act as caregivers (Maletta & Hepburn, 1986; Zarit et al., 1985). What can be done to ease this burden? The primary key seems to be providing caregivers with as much support as possible. This support can come from different sources. One obvious source is other family members and friends. Having the support and assistance of family and friends is likely to make the caregiver's task much easier. Unfortunately, support from family and friends is not always helpful and can sometimes be upsetting. These upsetting aspects of social networks make the primary caregiver more vulnerable to such problems as depression (Pagel, Erdly, & Becker, 1987).

Physicians and other health professionals also play an important role. Gabe Maletta and Kenneth Hepburn (1986) indicate that physicians can help families cope by educating caregivers about Alzheimer's and its effects, as well as by teaching them practical care techniques. In addition, they can assist by supporting caregivers both emotionally and practically. Thus they can make suggestions on how to deal with difficult behavior problems and help caregivers understand and deal with their own feelings.

Finally, community resources can be utilized to help caregivers cope. Many communities now have adult day-care facilities available that accept Alzheimer's patients (cf. Graham, 1989). These facilities can be extremely helpful by providing a respite for caregivers and can make it possible for family members to care for aging family members at home while still keeping their jobs. In addition, self-help groups such as local chapters of the Alzheimer's Disease and Related Disorders Association can assist by providing education, counseling, and support groups for families of patients (Smith, 1988).

SUMMARY

Chronic illness is often a significant source of stress for patients and those around them. This stress can be understood in terms of crisis, a situation that is so novel or so major that the person's usual methods of coping are simply insufficient. Crises produce a state of imbalance or disequilibrium, in which usual responses are disorganized, and the person is likely to experience intense emotions. A crisis can also be thought of as a transition period with important implications for later adaptation.

Throughout this crisis, the person is faced with adaptive tasks. These tasks include dealing with the symptoms and incapacitation of the disease itself, coping with the treatment process, maintaining adequate relations with health care staff, keeping an emotional balance, preserving a satisfactory self-image, maintaining relationships with family and friends, and preparing for an uncertain future. Dealing with these tasks requires both emotion-focused and problem-focused coping skills. How well people cope with chronic illness depends on the disease, personal resources, and the physical and social environment.

Long-term adaptation to chronic illness and disability involves several psychosocial aspects. One major concern is emotional adjustment, particularly depression. Depression is a common problem among those with chronic illness and disability. Adaptation is also a cognitive process. Studies of chronic illness have found that the beliefs that people have about their diseases, what caused it, how much control they feel that they have, the meanings they can find in events, and how they view themselves are important dimensions in cognitive adaptation. Finally, chronic illness has important implications for social relationships with family and others. Social relationships with others may be disrupted just at the time the person needs social support

the most, and chronic illness can seriously affect family functioning.

Several interventions have been developed to help patients and their families deal with the challenges of chronic illness and disability. Patient education provides people with information about the disease and its treatment; psychotherapy can help people deal with the emotions involved. Behavioral interventions can aid the coping process by relieving stress or increasing treatment cooperation. Finally, self-help groups can provide patients and their families with information about diseases and treatment and give them an opportunity to compare their experiences with others in similar circumstances.

Diabetes mellitus is a metabolic disorder in which the body is unable to properly convert glucose to energy. Living with this disorder presents many challenges. Insulin-dependent diabetics need to monitor their blood glucose level and administer insulin; both insulin-dependent and noninsulin-dependent diabetics must carefully follow dietary and exercise regimens. Noncooperation and treatment errors are important problems that need to be addressed to help people maintain good diabetic control. In addition, diabetes can have psychosocial effects including anxiety and depression, sexual dysfunction, and negative effects on families. Psychosocial and medical cooperation problems can be particularly difficult when the patient is a child or adolescent.

For people who suffer from arthritis, even simple movements can bring pain. Rheumatoid arthritis is a chronic, systemic, inflammatory condition affecting various joints in the body. Osteoarthritis is a degenerative joint condition that affects people as they age. The primary manifestations of arthritis are pain and functional impairment, which, in turn, can have important emotional effects and adversely affect the person's social relationships. Techniques that can be used to help arthritics include psychotherapy, social support intervention, and self-control strategies.

Alzheimer's disease is a brain disorder characterized by a progressive and irreversible loss of memory and intellectual function. This disease affects an estimated 10% of Americans 65 and over and 47% of those 85 and older. Alzheimer's is an insidious disease that develops slowly, but over time robs the person of cognitive func-

tion and identity. The emotional impact of Alzheimer's on the family is often devastating, as family members deal with their loved one's progressive deterioration. Moreover, the physical and financial burden of care can be overwhelming. The key to helping families cope is to provide them with as much support as possible. This support can come from family members and friends as well as health care professionals and community support organizations.

KEY TERMS

crisis (241)
disequilibrium (242)
diabetes mellitus (252)
insulin (253)

hyperglycemia (253)
rheumatoid arthritis (257)
osteoarthritis (257)
Alzheimer's disease (261)

SUGGESTED READINGS

Frank, J. (1985). *Alzheimer's disease: The silent epidemic.* Minneapolis: Lerner. This book provides a nontechnical introduction to Alzheimer's disease and its impact on patients and their families.

Genest, M. (1989). The relevance of stress to rheumatoid arthritis. In R. W. J. Neufeld (ed.), *Advances in the investigation of psychological stress.* New York: Wiley. This chapter discusses stress as both a factor in causing rheumatoid arthritis and an effect of having this disease.

Moos, R. H. (1982). Coping with acute health crises. In T. Millon, C. Green, and R. Meagher (eds.), *Handbook of clinical health psychology.* New York: Plenum. In this chapter, Rudolf Moos discusses his crisis theory of people's initial responses to serious illness.

Surwit, R. S., Feinglos, M. N., & Scovern, A. W. (1983). Diabetes and behavior: A paradigm for health psychology. *American Psychologist, 38,* 255–62. Richard Surwit and his colleagues give an overview of diabetes mellitus and the role of behavior in its treatment and control.

CHAPTER 1

Death and Dying

We all labour against our own cure, for death is the cure of all diseases.
Robert Browne (1605–1682)
Religio Medici, pt. ii, 9

There is no Death! What seems so is transition;
This life of mortal breath

Is but a suburb of the life elysian,
    Whose portal we call Death.

Henry Wadsworth Longfellow (1807–1882)
Resignation

Cowards die many times before their deaths;
The valiant never taste of death but once.
Of all the wonders that I yet have heard,
It seems to me most strange that men should fear;
Seeing that death, a necessary end,
Will come when it will come.

William Shakespeare (1564–1616)
Julius Caesar, II, ii, 32

Few of us like to contemplate death. The topic seems so gloomy and uninviting. Yet all of us will die sooner or later. The recent improvements in health and longevity have allowed death to come ever later, but it still comes. What is death, and what are the related psychological issues? These are topics that are taken up in this chapter, beginning with current understandings of death and how healthy people face the prospect of their own demise. We then move on to the psychological issues involved with terminal illness. How do people react when they learn that they will die in the foreseeable future? Are there stages to these reactions? Terminal illness also raises questions of patient management. How can health professionals and others best help dying patients to deal with their impending deaths? Where is the "best" place to die? In a hospital? In a hospice? At home? After discussion of death from the patient's point of view, we turn to the survivors. The death of a loved one generally involves intense emotions including, among others, grief, anger, self-pity, and resentment. We will explore these emotions and how they fit into the process of bereavement, and what can be done to help survivors cope. Finally, we will examine death as it relates to children. We usually think of death in terms of older adults. But children die as well; moreover, they are certainly affected when someone close to them dies. How do children understand death? How can parents and others help children to deal with death in the midst of childhood?

MIND AND BODY: DEATH AS THE LAST STAGE OF LIFE

Birth, growth, decline, and death form a universal cycle in nature. Despite its universality, we know relatively little about the last stage in this cycle.

What Is Death?

The answer to this question may at first seem obvious; death is the cessation of life. However, when we dig deeper, we find that death is far from a simple concept. Robert

Kastenbaum (1991; Kastenbaum & Aisenberg, 1976) writes that death is a relative and changing concept. How a person understands death is relative to developmental level, situation, and culture, and is likely to change as these factors change. As discussed below, children understand death differently than do adults. In addition, cultures differ in how they view death. In Western technological culture, death is generally viewed in biological terms. Other cultures, however, often have very different views, regarding death in metaphysical or magical terms (see Box 11.1).

Even in modern technological culture, concepts of death change over time. Advances in technology have significantly altered the medical definition of death. Before the mid-twentieth century, death was determined by a lack of respiration, lack of pulse, and failure to respond to such stimuli as light, movement, and pain (Kastenbaum, 1991). Modern technology, however, has made such indices inadequate. Through the use of respirators, intravenous feeding, and other technological devices, vital signs can now be maintained artificially for long periods. Is such a person dead or alive? Some argue that the person is alive and that life supports should be maintained so long as there is even the most remote possibility that the person will improve. Others argue that from a social and humane point of view, the person is already dead and that the body should be allowed to expire in dignity (Sugarman, 1986; Veatch, 1989).

BOX 11.1   A Cross-Cultural Perspective: Death in New Guinea

Death is a universal human experience. Members of all societies die, and survivors must deal with those deaths. Although death is universal, explanations for death are not and vary substantially between cultures. In Western technological society, death is understood in biological terms; the body ceases to function biologically and the person is declared dead. Some people believe in an afterlife; most, however, consider beliefs in spirits that come back to haunt the living to be the stuff of superstition and fantasy.

This view of death contrasts sharply with that found in other cultures. For example, according to anthropologist Peter Huber (1980), the Anggor people of New Guinea understand death in terms of sorcery. Although illness, accident, or violence may be proximate causes of death, all deaths are seen as ultimately the result of the work of a sorcerer: the Anggor believe that a person's death, though perhaps the result of violence, was possible only because the person had already been attacked by sorcery. Further, the Anggor generally assume that the sorcerer is someone from outside the village—a reflection of their underlying hostility toward outsiders.

For the Anggor, death represents the final separation of two basic aspects of the person: the *ifiaf* ("vital spirit") and the *hohoanum* ("consciousness" or "personality"). During life, the *ifiaf* is subordinated to the *hohoanum* and controlled by it. At death, the *hohoanum* ceases to exist, and the *ifiaf* is liberated from its control. The Anggor believe that the *ifiaf* has considerable powers and thus poses potential danger to the village. Thus Anggor mortuary practices are intended to isolate and banish the spirits of the deceased. Further, they believe that the *ifiaf* will repeatedly visit the home of the sorcerer responsible for the death. For several days after a death, the men of the village maintain a nightly vigil to watch for signs of the *ifiaf's* return to the sorcerer. Their motive is not revenge, but simply to identify the source of sorcery.

In his discussion of the Anggor understanding of death, Huber stresses that how a society understands death is a reflection of the structural relationships within the culture. For the Anggor, ideas about death are best understood in relationship to the undercurrent of intervillage hostility that is characteristic of that culture.

brain death
The definition of biological death based on the lack of brain wave activity and circulation in and to the brain.

To deal with such issues, physicians have developed the concept of **brain death,** meaning that a person is truly dead when the brain is no longer functioning. Along these lines, a group of Harvard Medical School faculty members developed what have become known as the *Harvard Criteria* for death. These guidelines define death as a state in which the person (1) is unreceptive and unresponsive to stimuli, (2) has no movement or breathing, (3) has no reflexes, (4) has a flat EEG (electroencephalogram), and (5) has no circulation to or within the brain (Ad Hoc Committee, 1968). In practice, the first three criteria are sufficient for most cases, but the final two criteria can be used when there is any doubt.

This definition, however, really addresses only one aspect of death. Although biological death is certainly important, we can also talk about other kinds of death. *Psychological death* is said to occur when the person's mind ceases to function; *social death* takes place when other people act toward the person as if he or she were dead. *Legal death* occurs when the person is adjudged dead by a legal authority. Such judgments are generally made after a person has been missing in action or cannot be found for a specified period of time (Aiken, 1985).

Even these definitions do not tap the full meaning of death. Death also has philosophical and religious meaning. Some of these meanings are illustrated in the quotations at the beginning of this chapter. For some, death means simply the final end of life. For others, death is a transition to a new and better existence, whereas for still others, death is the cure for all human infirmities. Such meanings are a matter of personal preference but can exert a tremendous impact on how people deal with the thought of death.

Facing the Thought of Death

Early in life, during childhood and young adulthood, people generally do not spend much time thinking about the end of life. Rather, at these ages, people are most likely to be focusing their thoughts on what the future holds. Somewhere around the middle of life—the exact age varies substantially between individuals—people begin to realize that life is finite and that they have a limited number of years remaining in which to accomplish their goals. As the years unfold, people are likely to become ever more aware that their lives are measured more in terms of the years they have already lived than those that they have left (Aiken, 1985).

How do people deal with the thought of death? Although many different ways can be identified, research on death attitudes has focused on three basic responses to death: denial, anxiety, and acceptance (Kastenbaum, 1991). Some people respond predominantly with denial. Thoughts of death are simply pushed out of conscious awareness. The person may simply refuse to think about death or may engage in death defying behavior such as dangerous sports or reckless driving (Doka, Schwarz, & Schwarz, 1990; Thorson & Powell, 1990).

When people do think of death, a common response is anxiety. Studies of people's attitudes about death have shown that, on the average, people report feeling moderately anxious about death (Kastenbaum, 1991; Pollak, 1979). This average, however, masks important differences between people. For example, death anxiety shows significant variation by sex, age, sense of well-being, and religious beliefs.

Perhaps because they feel more comfortable in expressing such feelings, women express more death anxiety than do men (Da Silva & Schork, 1984; Pollak, 1979). Gender differences, however, go well beyond just differing levels of anxiety. Anthony Da Silva and Anthony Schork (1984) found that women typically thought more about death than did men, tended to feel that religion played a significant role in their feelings about death, and believed in life after death. Men, by contrast, reported having fewer thoughts about their own deaths, felt that religion had not played a role in their feelings about death, doubted the existence of an afterlife, and, when thinking of their own mortality, felt motivated to achieve more. This suggests that men and women may have different orientations toward death.

Although one might think that fear of death would increase as its likely time draws near, research on age differences does not support this. Instead, death anxiety shows an early peak during late adolescence and early adulthood, after which it declines somewhat, only to rise again during middle age and then decline as people enter later adulthood (Kastenbaum, 1991). In fact, one study found that of three age groups studied (young, middle-aged, and elderly) the elderly group showed the least fear and most acceptance of death (Gesser, Wong, & Reker, 1987). Apparently, as death becomes more of a reality, people are able to make their peace with it.

Fears of death are also a function of the person's sense of well-being and religious beliefs. Overall, death anxiety is lower for people who have a positive sense of well-being and a sense of meaning in life (Pollak, 1979). In addition, evidence indicates that religious beliefs influence death anxiety. For example, one study (Florian & Kravetz, 1983) found that highly religious Jews expressed less concern about death as personal annihilation but more fear of punishment in the hereafter than did those who were less religious.

thanatology
The study of death and dying. Professionals who study death and dying are known as thanatologists.

Since death is inevitable, the ideal orientation toward death is acceptance. However, the anxieties that people have about death often preclude a ready acceptance. For this and other reasons, **thanatologists** have argued the need for death education. Death education courses introduce people to what is known about death-related topics and urge them to bring their death-related thoughts, fantasies, and fears out into the open, where they can be discussed and faced realistically. Does it work? Research evidence indicates that inducing people to think about death realistically can help them to reduce their fear of death and develop a keener sense of the meaning of life (Kastenbaum, 1991; Kuiken & Madison, 1987).

THE PSYCHOLOGY OF DYING

From a biological point of view, the moment of death can be pinpointed. But what of the events leading up to death? Whereas death is an event, dying is a process, one that has a well-defined end and definite effects, but only an ill-defined beginning.

Exactly when a person changes from someone who is living to one who is dying depends on the frame of reference used (Kastenbaum, 1991). For health care professionals, the determining factors are most likely to be biomedical. Patients are defined as dying either when diagnosed with a terminal condition or when nothing more can be done to preserve the patient's life. Under these circumstances, medical efforts are likely to change from a focus on curing the illness and returning the person to health to one of custodial care aimed at making the person as comfortable as possible.

For patients and their families, however, the primary criteria of dying are likely to be psychosocial. Although the medical diagnosis still plays a key role, patient and family members are likely to see dying as a function of when the facts are communicated and when they are realized and accepted. Doctors and nurses often already know that a patient's condition is terminal but delay telling the patient and family members. In fact, until relatively recently the prevalent thinking was that patients should not be told that they were dying. Many health care professionals feared that informing patients of their terminal status would only upset them. In addition, many doctors and nurses find it emotionally difficult to discuss death with patients. The result has been a *conspiracy of silence* in which medical personnel, as well as family and friends, pretend that everything is fine and that the patient will soon recover. Although this conspiracy of silence is meant to protect the patient's feelings, it often has the opposite effect. Many patients either know or suspect that they are dying. The lack of acknowledgment by others only deepens their sense of isolation and leaves patients to face death feeling psychologically abandoned (Aiken, 1985; Kastenbaum, 1991).

Regardless of the perspective, the definition of a person as dying has profound effects on how people relate to the person. First, the person is viewed differently by health care professionals. As already noted, the emphasis of care is likely to change from curing to simply making the person comfortable. In addition, the interactions between the patient and the health care staff are likely to become briefer and more cursory. In the context of the dominant biomedical model, death represents an uncomfortable defeat on which few health professionals wish to dwell. One study found, for example, that nurses took significantly longer to answer calls from dying patients than they did patients who were expected to recover. Even when the researcher noted the discrepancy and the nurses attempted to respond more rapidly, the old pattern reestablished itself after a few weeks (Bowers, Jackson, Knight, & LaShan, 1964). In extreme cases, defining a patient as dying, and thus hopeless, can lead to outright neglect (Kastenbaum, 1991).

Being labeled as dying also has strong effects on relationships with family and friends. The impending death of a loved one evokes strong emotions, which are often difficult to deal with and can create barriers between the patient and others. One college-aged leukemia patient described it this way:

> I had to develop almost a whole new set of friends. My good old buddies just felt awfully uncomfortable around me. They couldn't be themselves anymore. I realized they'd be relieved if I would just sort of drift away from them. (Kastenbaum, 1991, p. 78)

Tragically, this kind of disengagement from the dying person comes just when the person is likely to need the support of family and friends the most.

Dying Trajectories

Dying, as a process, takes time. Although in some cases a person is fully alive one moment and dead the next, the transition more often takes at least hours, if not days, months, or years. Bernard Glaser and Anselm Strauss, in their pioneering work *Time for dying* (1968), describe the process of dying in terms of "trajectories" that involve characteristic amounts of time and typical events. More important, these trajectories have profound effects on how the person is treated and how people respond to the person's death.

One of the more common trajectories, particularly in an age when death results increasingly from chronic ailments, is the *lingering trajectory*. The person has generally been ill for a long time, and death comes after a period of gradually declining health. Under these circumstances, medical staff may make efforts to reverse the person's decline, but dramatic rescue attempts are rare. The staff's general attitude seems to be that everything possible has been done and that death is only a matter of time. Thus care is likely to focus on making the person comfortable. The medical staff "allow" many patients to die quietly. Perhaps because those involved have been socially dead for some time, deaths after a lingering trajectory are often more acceptable than those coming after other trajectories. Although family and staff are likely to feel grief, it is comparatively muted, and the death may even be seen as a "blessing." As Glaser and Strauss point out:

> In effect, then, these patients drift out of the world, sometimes almost like imperceptibly melting snowflakes. The organization of work emphasizes comfort care and custodial routine, and is complemented by a sentimental order emphasizing patience and inevitability. (1968, p. 64)

In sharp contrast, patients who are on an *expected quick trajectory* receive often heroic attention from medical personnel. In this trajectory, the person's life is in imminent danger, and the difference between life and death may be literally a matter of seconds or minutes. This could be the case, for example, when a person has had an accident or has experienced a sudden heart attack. Glaser and Strauss note several ways in which this trajectory can be played out. In what they term the *pointed trajectory,* the person is exposed to risky medical procedures that might either preserve life or result in death. Patients in a *danger-period trajectory,* such as those in intensive care or recovering from major surgery, however, are in considerable danger of dying but can be expected to survive if they make it through the current critical period. Closely related is the *crisis trajectory,* in which the patient is not in imminent danger of dying, but a crisis, such as renal failure, could result in death if not immediately tended to. In all these cases, medical staff watch the patient's condition closely and are prepared to take whatever measures are necessary to preserve life. The most salient features of these trajectories are time urgency, intense treatment efforts, and rapidly shifting expectations about the patient's chances.

Deaths from quick trajectories are not always expected. A patient experiencing an *unexpected quick trajectory* is not believed to be in imminent danger of dying. Although the person may be ill and may even be perceived as dying, death is not expected in the foreseeable future. However, without warning, the patient's condition takes a turn for the worse and suddenly death is near. This state of affairs is likely to cause a crisis for the medical staff as they mobilize to deal with this new turn of events. Because they are unexpected, deaths after this trajectory are likely to be particularly disturbing for medical personnel, as well as for loved ones.

Are There Stages in People's Reactions to Dying?

These trajectories describe some of the different ways in which people die, but what of the actual experience of dying? What does dying look and feel like from the perspective of the dying person? Probably the best-known answers to these questions come from the work of Elizabeth Kübler-Ross (1969) and her theory of the stages of dying.

Kübler-Ross's five stages. Based on interviews with more than 200 dying patients, Kübler-Ross concluded that the process of dying involves a series of five stages that differ in content and emotional intensity. In her view, these stages, which begin at the time of a terminal diagnosis, are normal and predictable ways of dealing with the prospect of death. Although people differ in how they go through them, the stages are seen as a universal description of how people approach death.

The initial response to the news of impending death is *denial*. In response to the shock of receiving the news, the person simply refuses to acknowledge the facts. "No, it can't be true. The diagnosis is wrong." Even though observers may view this denial as irrational, it often serves a self-protective purpose and gives the person time to grapple with the situation psychologically. In fact, people often respond with denial to any kind of bad news. So long as this response is only temporary, it can be healthy. However, a person who persists in denial or who steadfastly refuses to accept the facts may require psychological intervention.

After the news sinks in and is acknowledged, the person's response is likely to change to *anger*. "Why me? What have I done?" In response to the felt unfairness of the situation, the person is likely to express anger and resentment in a multitude of directions: against God, the medical staff, family members, friends, or anyone who is healthy. This kind of response can be distressing to those around the person, particularly when they are targets, unless they realize that the anger is not really directed at them but rather at the perceived unfairness of death.

Anger usually does not last indefinitely and, in the normal course of events, fades into *bargaining*. During this stage, the person attempts to alter the situation by striking a bargain with God, fate, the medical staff, or anyone or anything that can offer the hope of reprieve. The patient hopes that being on his or her best behavior will lead justice to prevail, and life will be allowed to continue. Thus the patient may promise to attend church regularly, take medicine without complaint, or give generously to charity, if only allowed to live.

When bargaining fails to alter the basic situation, the person enters the stage of *depression*. Despite all of the person's efforts, the situation is unchanged, and the person becomes dejected at all that has been suffered and all that will be lost in death. Kübler-Ross describes this stage as one of **anticipatory grief** and as being a necessary step toward final acceptance. Thus she advises medical personnel and loved ones to accept the person's depression, share in the sadness, and, when appropriate, offer support and reassurance.

anticipatory grief
Grieving that takes place before a death actually occurs.

The final stage is *acceptance*. After the emotional turbulence of the first four stages, the person finally comes to a full acknowledgment that death is inevitable. The person accepts this inevitability and is able to face death calmly. According to Kübler-Ross, this is also a time when the person begins to disengage from all but a few close friends and family members.

Criticisms. How useful is Kübler-Ross's description? Her work has undoubtedly had a tremendous impact on how people view the dying. Before her work, the experiences and feelings of dying patients were essentially ignored. Her detailed descriptions have alerted both health professionals and lay people to complex emotions experienced by people who are dying. Despite the importance of this contribution, however, her theory has been seriously criticized by several thanatologists.

One of the primary criticisms is that, although the descriptions are compelling, Kübler-Ross has never really demonstrated the existence of stages. The concept of stages implies a progression from one stage to the next. In her research, Kübler-Ross did not follow patients as they died, but, rather, interviewed different patients who were at various points in the process of dying. Therefore, her descriptions are better understood as simply detailing different emotional reactions that people have to dying. There is no real evidence that people actually progress from denial to anger, bargaining, depression, and acceptance. Instead, these are responses that most dying patients have at one time or another, and a patient will just as likely go from denial to depression to bargaining as experience these reactions in the order given by Kübler-Ross (Kastenbaum, 1991; Schulz & Schlarb, 1988).

A second major criticism is that Kübler-Ross's descriptive stages are often confused with a prescription of how people should react to dying (Aiken, 1985; Kastenbaum, 1991). Even though Kübler-Ross herself has argued against viewing the stages prescriptively, many are tempted to interpret her stages as providing a pattern for "normal" dying. Thus caregivers or family members may draw the inference that the person should be progressing through a specified sequence of reactions and become disturbed when the person does not proceed through the stages "on schedule." Expectations about how the person "should" be responding only add additional pressure to an already stressful situation.

Finally, Kübler-Ross's work describes only one aspect of the person's response to dying and leaves out the totality of the person's life. Her theory focuses on supposedly universal aspects of dying, but in the process ignores the unique aspects of the person's experience. Dying people vary by gender, age, ethnicity, socioeconomic status, and other variables, all of which may profoundly influence the dying experience.

Alternative conceptions. Although Kübler-Ross's theory is the best known, it is by no means the only description of the emotional aspects of dying. Edwin Shneidman (1980), for example, uses the term "death work" to describe how a person prepares for death. This death work includes preparing oneself for death and preparing loved ones to be survivors, and is complicated by the strong emotions involved. Rather than a series of stages, Shneidman describes the process of dying as:

a hive of affect, in which there is a constant coming and going. The emotional stages seem to include a constant interplay between disbelief and hope and, against these as a background, a waxing and waning of anguish, terror, acquiescence and surrender, rage and envy, disinterest and ennui, pretense, taunting and daring and even yearning for death—all of these in the context of bewilderment and pain. (Shneidman, 1980, p. 447)

Another formulation, proposed by Mansell Pattison (1977), argues that the process of dying can be best described as a three-phase process. In the first phase, known as the *acute phase,* the person experiences intense emotions over the prospect of dying. During this phase, which corresponds roughly to Kübler-Ross's denial, anger, and bargaining stages, fear and anxiety are high and are dealt with through denial and other psychological defense mechanisms. Next, the person enters the *chronic living-dying phase,* in which anxiety is reduced and the person begins to grapple with the realities of impending death. During this phase, the person begins to accept death gracefully. Finally, the person enters the *terminal phase.* Although the person still wants to live, death is now accepted as inevitable. The person operates at a relatively low energy level and begins the final withdrawal from loved ones.

Social Relationships and the Dying

As we have seen, the process of dying is often stressful and filled with intense emotions. It is also a process that includes family and friends as well as the patient. Indeed, dying is very much a social process. Ideally, when a person is dying, family and friends are readily available to provide emotional support for the person in this last battle. Sadly, this is often not the case. In fact, the very fact that the person is dying may lead to a reduction in social interaction and support just at the time the person needs it the most (Caughill, 1976).

The reasons for this are not hard to find. The stress of learning that one is dying may lead the person to withdraw from social contact. This may be a response to concern about how others will deal with the person's impending death, or simply a desire for psychological space in which to deal with the emotions involved. One common fear is that the person's status as dying will depress family and friends. In an effort to keep from becoming an emotional burden, the person may simply avoid interaction. Moreover, when obvious mental or physical changes have been brought about by disease, the person may be concerned that these changes will upset unprepared visitors (Carey, 1975). These concerns, added to the normal tendency for dying persons to begin taking leave of loved ones, can lead to a considerable reduction in the person's social contacts.

Moreover, family members and friends may find interaction difficult. They, too, are likely to be feeling grief and other emotions about the fact that the person is dying. Unless dealt with openly and realistically, these emotions can easily lead to avoidance of the dying person. In addition, visitors often find it difficult to know what to talk about when someone is dying. For many, death is still something of a taboo topic and thus is something to be avoided in polite conversation (Kastenbaum, 1991). Further, people often have assumptions about what others want to hear or want to talk about. In particular, visitors, as well as the dying person, may be concerned that bringing up

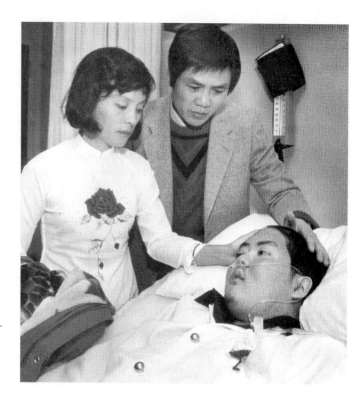

Social support is essential for dying patients, but communication is often impaired by the emotions involved.

topics relating to the person's death or plans for after the person is gone will only be upsetting to all involved. Further, those involved may not really want answers to their questions. The end result is likely to be a forced cheerfulness in which only trivial topics are discussed and no one ever really communicates what they are thinking.

These communication problems can be overcome. The key is to face fears and emotions directly and communicate as openly and sensitively as possible. Kastenbaum (1991) offers several suggestions for how to facilitate communication with the dying. First, he advises that people be alert to indirect and symbolic forms of communication. Given the emotions involved, people who are dying may not directly state what they are feeling, but only hint at it. For example, they might express their feelings in dreams or through symbols. Thus, attention should be paid to these. Second, he urges people to help make competent and effective behavior possible for the dying. By paying attention to the person's physical and emotional state, visitors can provide the level and kind of support that the person needs to maintain a sense of dignity without feeling like others are completely taking over. Relatedly, people should allow the dying person to set the pace in activities and discussions. Finally, communication is facilitated when people refrain from projecting their own needs and fears on the dying. Rather, they should allow the dying to be themselves and deal with death in their own ways.

MANAGEMENT OF THE DYING PATIENT

Given their choice, most people would prefer to die at home rather than in an institution (Garrett, 1978). The reality, however, is that many people die in hospitals and other medical care institutions (Raether and Slater, 1977). What are the implications for the patient of dying in an institution as compared with dying in familiar surroundings at home? What can be done to help ease the transition between life and death?

Dying in an Institution

The reasons so many people die in institutions are readily apparent. Hospitals and other health care facilities have the life-saving equipment and medical know-how to deal with patients' medical problems and, where possible, extend life. However, despite the medical advantages of hospitals and nursing homes, they are not ideal places in which to die. The basic orientation of most medical institutions is toward cure. Therefore, the efforts of the staff are generally focused on maintaining life and preventing death. In this context, death represents failure and is thus to be avoided if at all possible.

Not surprisingly, the medical care that patients receive often declines considerably after the staff determines that they are dying (Brown & Thompson, 1979). Formally, this attitude toward the dying may be reflected in **coding,** a medical decision that is made about the efforts that will be taken to revive a patient if the heart and lungs should cease functioning. *Code blue* indicates that all-out efforts will be made to resuscitate the person, even including extraordinary or heroic efforts. A *slow code* directs nurses to initiate cardiopulmonary resuscitation (CPR) but nothing else; a *no code* indicates that neither CPR nor heroic efforts are warranted. In the last case, the patient is simply allowed to die (Aiken, 1985). Informally, staff attitudes toward the dying are likely to be reflected in slower responses to calls from dying patients (Bowers et al., 1964) and in derogatory comments about patients.

coding
A medical decision about the amount of effort to be expended in reviving the patient in the event of cardiopulmonary failure.

Perhaps the most distressing aspect of dying in an institution, however, is that little emphasis is placed on the psychosocial needs of the patients. As was noted in Chapter 9, being hospitalized is a stressful and depersonalizing experience for anyone. The emotional needs of the dying person make it even more so. At a time when the person is most in need of the comfort of familiar surroundings, hospitals and nursing homes provide only a sterile and impersonal institutional setting. In addition, busy doctors and nurses are unlikely to have time to deal with psychosocial needs, and they do not find dealing with death easy either (see Box 11.2). However, the overall result is that the needs of the dying patient are unlikely to be met in institutional settings.

The Hospice Alternative

Because of concerns that hospitals and nursing homes are really rather poor places to die, many health professionals have argued that an alternative is needed. Out of this concern has developed what has become known as the **hospice** movement (Aiken & Marx, 1982; Butterfield-Picard & Magno, 1982; Kastenbaum, 1979; Vandenbos, DeLeon, & Pallak, 1982). Originated by British physician Cicely Saunders in the

BOX 11.2 The Psychological Costs of Dealing with Death: Burnout in the Health Professions

Most people find watching another person die an emotionally wrenching experience. Emotions such as grief over the person's death, anger at the pain the person has endured, and feelings of helplessness at not being able to do anything are likely to be intense as survivors cope with the death. Although we expect that health care professionals will be prepared through their training to deal with death, they clearly pay a high psychological cost as a result of dealing with death on a regular basis.

The term *burnout* refers to the physical and mental exhaustion experienced by individuals who work intensively with other people, and who often give more than they receive from their clients, colleagues, or supervisors. Professionals experiencing burnout exhibit symptoms including physical and emotional exhaustion, the development of negative and callous attitudes about the people they are working with, and reduced personal accomplishments. Even though they may put up a good front for others, burned-out professionals are experiencing weariness and despair that may manifest itself through drug and alcohol abuse, increased smoking, or career changes (Maslach & Jackson, 1982; Pines & Aronson, 1981).

In their discussion of burnout, Ayala Pines and Elliot Aronson (1981) note that the most striking cases of burnout they encountered in their work involved hospital nurses working with terminally ill cancer patients. Even though these nurses initially cared deeply about their patients and volunteered for the assignment in order to help them, over time they began to distance themselves from the patients emotionally and even came to resent them. For example, nurses might come to view the patient as just another "case" or engage in gallows humor, in which they would put down or mock patients. As nurses became aware of their resentment, they also developed considerable feelings of guilt and shame. A common statement was "I, of all people, am

not supposed to be feeling this way" (Pines & Aronson, 1981, p. 5).

Ironically, as the nurses were hurting on the inside, to others they often appeared crisp, efficient, and even ebullient as they went about their duties. These intense efforts at hiding their feelings led many nurses to feel alone in their psychological turmoil. Since others seemed to be handling the stress of the situation with aplomb, they believed that their own feelings of distress must be abnormal and a sign of professional inadequacy. This conclusion, of course, served only to heighten their distress.

Tragically, burnout robs patients of truly compassionate care when they need it the most and may lead to poorer medical care. Nurses experiencing burnout not only have a greater tendency to be emotionally distant and callous, but are also more likely to make serious on-the-job mistakes (such as erroneous medication dosage) and to be more neglectful of their duties. Not surprisingly, they are disciplined more often by supervisors (Bram & Katz, 1989).

What can be done about burnout? Pines and Aronson (1981) argue that dealing with burnout requires a systematic approach involving several steps. The first essential step is awareness of the problem. Before constructive actions can be taken, the person needs to understand the nature of burnout and the fact that it is a function of the situation, rather than a result of personal inadequacy. Once awareness of the problem is established, the next step is taking responsibility for changing the situation. For such efforts to be effective, however, those involved must clearly distinguish between those aspects of the situation that can be changed and those that cannot. Once this is done, tools for coping can be developed. Among the techniques that can be used are workshops focusing on burnout, the development of peer support groups, and the teaching of stress management skills.

1950s, the hospice concept focuses on providing a maximally supportive environment for the dying and their loved ones. In her work in London hospitals, Saunders was disturbed at her colleagues' inability to respond adequately to the needs of the dying

hospice
An approach to care for the dying that emphasizes patient comfort and death with dignity.

and was determined to do something about it. The result was the founding in 1967 of St. Christopher's Hospice in London. Since that time, hospices have been established throughout the world; more than 100,000 people in the United States alone, most of them terminal cancer patients, are estimated to receive hospice care at any given time (Schulz & Schlarb, 1988).

How does care in a hospice differ from other forms of care? The term *hospice* itself, which comes from medieval Europe, denotes a place where travelers on pilgrimage were welcomed and provided with food and shelter. Therefore, a sense of journey is central to the hospice concept. Dying is seen as a journey and the hospice as a way station for providing comfort and care on that journey (Kastenbaum, 1979). The primary emphasis of the hospice concept is on "comfort-care." Medical attention is provided not so much to extend life as to make the person's remaining life more useful and desirable. Thus, medical staff rarely engage in heroic efforts to save the person's life but rather focus their attention on making the person more comfortable (Butterfield-Picard & Magno, 1982).

Hospice care revolves around several basic principles (Saunders, 1984; Kastenbaum, 1979, 1991). A key principle concerns control of patient pain and discomfort. Pain is often the major physical symptom experienced by the dying, so hospice treatment pays a great deal of attention to pain control (Levy, 1988). After a person is admitted to a hospice program, painful, invasive treatments are typically discontinued, and the person is provided with medication to control pain. Care is taken to avoid sedating the patient to the point that communication is hindered, since that would disrupt the person's social relationships. Instead, a special pain preparation known as the *Brompton mix,* consisting of cocaine, morphine, ethyl alcohol, and a sweetener, is used to relieve pain with a minimum of sedation. Other pain relievers may also be used. In the course of treatment, patients learn to regulate their own medication intake so as to maintain their desired level of comfort (Aiken, 1985).

A second major component of hospice is an emphasis on personal caring and open discussions of death and dying. Patients may be cared for either in their own homes or in inpatient facilities. Regardless of the location of care, patients are encouraged to personalize their surroundings. Patients are addressed by their first names, and visitors are subject to few, if any, restrictions. The goal is to make the surroundings as comfortable as possible for the person. Staff are trained to be sensitive to patients' needs and to care for them in a loving and personal manner. For patients who remain in their homes, trained volunteers visit regularly to help with various practical chores as well as to read to the patient, stay with the patient while family members are out, and, generally, provide support (Patchner & Finn, 1987). Open communication is a priority. Family members are encouraged to take an active part in the patient's final days and months, to spend as much time as possible with the patient, and to deal openly and honestly with their feelings.

The watchword in all of this is death with dignity. Hospice treatment emphasizes the importance of living one's last days to the fullest and making the most of each moment. Whereas the highly technological care obtained in institutions can serve to dehumanize and isolate the person, hospice care is designed to help the person maintain feelings of self-worth and connectedness to others.

How successful is hospice as an alternative? To answer this question, the National Hospice Demonstration Study (NHDS) examined various aspects of care received by dying patient in 31 hospices and 8 hospitals throughout the United States (Mor, Greer, & Kastenbaum, 1988). In terms of cost, hospice care was generally less expensive than hospital care. This can be attributed in part to the fact that hospice patients spent more time at home and were less likely to receive intensive medical treatments—an appropriate approach for many patients. For the most severely debilitated patients, however, hospital care may be preferable. There were some indications that hospice patients obtained greater pain relief than did hospital patients. Particularly important, the social quality of life remained quite high for hospice patients, and they seemed able to spend their final days in the manner they preferred. Overall, these data suggest that, at least for the organizations studied, hospice care is successful in fulfilling its objectives.

Dying at Home

Many people wish to die at home surrounded by family. This is certainly understandable since the person will probably be more comfortable psychologically. With proper support, dying at home can be practical, but it also has its drawbacks.

One concern is the quality of medical care (Turnbull, 1986). Hospitals and nursing homes can clearly provide superior medical facilities. However, if family members and other caretakers are properly trained and remain in close communication with medical personnel, medical care at home can be adequate to the patient's needs. This assumes, of course, that the person's health problems are appropriate for home care.

Another potential difficulty is stress on the family. Although the patient may find dying at home psychologically easier, other family members can suffer considerable stress. Terminally ill patients often require continuous care, which generally requires that one or more members of the family take responsibility for overseeing that care. Even if the family is financially able to hire full-time nursing help, family members often experience considerable strain as they attempt to adjust their schedules to meet the needs of the patient. In addition, care of a dying person can be emotionally draining as family members grapple with their emotions (Hinton, 1967). The benefit, of course, derives from the emotional satisfaction of having shared time and feelings with the patient, knowing that the patient's last moments of life are being spent with family in familiar surroundings.

Thus the emotional rewards may well outweigh the practical problems involved in having someone die at home. This is particularly true when the family has outside support. As noted in the discussion of hospices, many hospice patients die at home. When a hospice patient is at home, hospice volunteers work with the patient and family to help relieve some of the burden and make the process of caring for the patient a bit easier.

Counseling with the Terminally Ill

As we have seen, dying can be an emotionally difficult process. Because of the strong emotions involved, the dying may need the assistance of a qualified counselor. Such a counselor, who might be a psychologist, psychiatrist, social worker, or pastoral

Therapy with dying patients can help them deal effectively with their anxieties and fears.

clinical thanatology
Counseling techniques used with dying patients.

counselor, can be of invaluable assistance in helping the person to face and sort through many fears and anxieties. This type of counseling has come to be known as **clinical thanatology.**

The therapeutic techniques used with the dying range from traditional psychotherapy to behavioral and cognitive-behavioral methods (Sobel, 1981). Each of these aims to help the person concentrate on making the most of the time remaining. Even though it uses the same methods, therapy with the dying differs considerably from therapy in other settings (Shneidman, 1984). First, the time-frame is limited. Of necessity, therapy with the dying is limited to the time that the person has left. This means that the goals are fundamentally different and more finite than is the case in other therapy. The overriding goal is to enhance the person's comfort and assist the person in tying off loose ends and attaining a sense of psychological peace.

The rules of psychotherapy are also different. Whereas most therapy requires a degree of professional distance between the therapist and patient, therapy with the dying allows for a much closer and deeper relationship, with the therapist openly responding to the patient's feelings. As Shneidman notes, "intensive work with the dying generally permits a depth of transference and countertransference that should not be done or countenanced in perhaps any other professional relationship" (1984, p. 279). The therapist is not simply a neutral observer who stands back and only observes and interprets the patient's feelings, but may also act as the patient's friend and advocate.

Success in the therapeutic relationship is also gauged differently. Dying patients probably cannot be expected to work through all their concerns. Patients often die before they have had a chance to deal with all their fears and anxieties. Thus therapists need to realize that the therapy may have a lack of closure and a sense of incompleteness. In the therapeutic relationship, the dying person sets the pace and nothing absolutely has to be accomplished. Rather, the therapy should deal, or not deal, with whatever the dying person wishes. The therapist is likely to identify important issues that the patient simply does not wish to discuss. In other settings, the therapist would probe and confront such denial. With the dying, however, the therapist needs to respect the patient's wishes.

Finally, the context of the therapeutic relationship is different with the dying. Rather than meeting with the patient in a private office at regularly scheduled times, therapy sessions are likely to be conducted in the patient's room and at times that are appropriate for the patient's needs and physical condition. Moreover, the therapist must coordinate closely with the medical staff to stay abreast of the patient's condition and to inform them of significant issues that are of concern to the patient.

GRIEF AND BEREAVEMENT

bereavement
The experience of losing a loved one to death.

grief
Emotional responses to bereavement.

mourning
Socially prescribed ways of expressing grief.

Regardless of how well prepared they are, the death of a loved one can be emotionally devastating for survivors. Now that the loved one has died, those remaining behind must deal with both the practical and emotional aftermaths. The term **bereavement** refers to the objective fact that someone close has died. A person is bereaved any time a loved one dies. **Grief,** by contrast, refers to the response to bereavement. People differ substantially in how they respond to death; thus an understanding of grief requires that we carefully consider how different people understand and deal with death. Much is determined by culture. The culturally prescribed patterns for the public expression of grief are known as **mourning.** Every society expects bereaved individuals to express their grief in culturally prescribed ways such as funerals, public crying, or wailing, or the performance of certain rituals.

The Bereavement Process

Bereavement begins as soon as the loved one dies and often follows a characteristic pattern depending on the society. In Western societies after a death, those close to the deceased are expected to experience grief and go into mourning. Friends and family members generally express their concern and support for the bereaved by providing both practical assistance and emotional comfort. Often this includes help with household chores, preparation of meals, and assistance with child care, as well as a sympathetic ear. After a few days, or at most a few weeks, this support decreases, and the bereaved are expected to deal with these matters on their own. Friends and family members go their separate ways, and the person may be left alone for large amounts of time (Glick, Weiss, & Parkes, 1974). This can be a particularly lonely time since the person is still grieving, but no longer has others' support in dealing with the grief.

People who are bereaved are expected to experience grief, but the intensity of that grief varies a great deal among people. Although some people grieve intensely, others do not seem to grieve at all. Overall, men tend to show less overt grief than do women (Glick et al., 1974). In addition, grief is generally less intense when the deceased is elderly, perhaps because death among the elderly is more expected (Aiken, 1985; Ball, 1977). But grief may be particularly intense when the death was unexpected, as in the case of accident victims (Shanfield, Swain, & Benjamin, 1987), or when the death was the result of suicide (Range & Calhoun, 1990).

Grief is likely to affect many aspects of the person's life. In particular, grief is accompanied by distressing physical and psychological symptoms. The grieving person is likely to experience sensations such as tightness in the throat, choking and shortness of breath, a need for sighing, a feeling of emptiness in the abdomen, and a sense of physical weakness. These are likely to be joined by psychological symptoms such as insomnia, absentmindedness, problems with concentration and memory, and a tendency to do things over and over (Parkes, 1988). The symptoms of grief are so intense and striking in some people that some observers have suggested that grief can be thought of as a disease (Engel, 1961). Given the symptoms of grief, people who are bereaved are often subject to increased levels of illness (Parkes, 1988). In addition, bereaved individuals have higher death rates than others their age (Bowling, 1988; Helsing, Szklo, & Comstock, 1981; Parkes, Benjamin, & Fitzgerald, 1969).

Grief is never a pleasant experience, but for most people it subsides with time. In *pathological grief,* however, the symptoms either continue in an intense form for long periods or are notable for their absence (Aiken, 1985). When a person experiences *chronic grief,* the feelings of intense sadness and sorrow last for years after the death. Even though the loved one died two, five, or ten years earlier, the person still experiences physical and mental symptoms of grief and may even have hallucinations about the deceased. In other cases of pathological grief, the person's feelings of grief are delayed for five or ten years or more after the death. In some cases, the person may never express grief. However, even though the person shows no emotions about the death, his repressed grief will likely show up in the form of neurotic or even psychotic behavior (Aiken, 1985; Pincus, 1976).

When a Spouse Dies

Some of the best available descriptions of bereavement come from the classic research of Ira Glick, Robert Weiss, and Murray Parkes on the experiences of men and women who lost their spouses (Glick et al., 1974; Parkes & Weiss, 1983). In this research, 49 widows and 19 widowers, all of whom were 45 years old or younger and living in the vicinity of Boston, Massachusetts, were contacted by the researchers soon after the death of the spouse and interviewed about their experiences. These individuals were then followed for up to four years after they were first bereaved.

The initial responses to bereavement were almost universally feelings of pain and desolation. Reports of feeling overwhelmed were common, and some of the newly bereaved felt so numb that they wondered whether they would ever move, act, or think again. These feelings were present regardless of whether the death was expected, though they tended to be most intense when the death was sudden. Women who knew that their husbands were dying were likely to report that they had been grieving even before the death took place. However, this anticipatory grieving did not eliminate the shock of the death when it occurred.

In general, men and women responded in many similar ways. However, there were significant differences in how widows and widowers interpreted their feelings and in how they dealt with the death. For women, the most common response was of feeling abandoned, whereas for men, the predominant feeling was one of being dismembered. These differences are most likely traceable to gender differences in the meaning of marriage. For women, marriage was understood in terms of social relationships, which were disrupted by the death of the husband. But for men, marriage had sustained the man's capacity to work. After bereavement, men tended to become disorganized in their work, whereas women often found that going to work helped them in dealing with their interpersonal needs.

Gender differences were also evident in emotional reactions and attempts to maintain emotional control. Physical symptoms of the type described earlier were common, with reports of aches and pains, poor appetite, insomnia, headaches, dizziness, and other symptoms. Widowers were more likely to report feeling choked up, whereas widows were more likely to express their grief in tears. Widows reported that they tried hard to maintain emotional control and often longed for someone to take over and help them organize their lives. Widowers generally felt more uncomfortable with direct expression of grief and attempted to maintain control because they felt that expressing too much emotion was unmanly. In addition, women tended to feel anger at being widowed, whereas men felt guilt. The men often felt that they should have been more sensitive or made life easier for their wives. Feelings of guilt were particularly strong when the wife had died in childbirth: the husband tended to blame himself for his wife's death.

Among the most important events early in bereavement is the *leave-taking ceremony,* which often takes the form of a funeral. The bereaved bid their final farewell to the deceased at this ceremony. For the respondents in this study, the funeral seemed more important for women than for men. Widows were generally seen as the central figure at the funeral and were viewed as the final authority for all arrangements. Hearing that they had done well tended to bolster their confidence; the funeral served as the event that marked their acceptance as the new head of the family. Men tended to give less attention to the funeral and to be more concerned with the practical details, often feeling that the cost had been too high. For men, the funeral did not signal a new status as family head and was often viewed simply as something to get through.

After the funeral, the bereaved spouse was generally left alone as family and friends went back to their normal routines. This period was particularly difficult for both widows and widowers because they were left to handle their grief on their own. For widows, this was often a period of social withdrawal through which they signified their mourning status and continued to work through their feelings. An important feature of this was the process of **obsessional review,** in which the widow would continuously review the events surrounding her husband's death. This review seemed to be a way in which she could come to grips with her husband's death and integrate the event with her daily life. In addition, widows would idealize the dead husband by emphasizing his positive traits and forgetting his faults.

obsessional review
The continuous review of the events surrounding the death of a loved one.

Men seemed to accept the reality of their wife's death more readily. Although widowers engaged in obsessional review, this review was briefer and quickly gave way to more practical concerns. From outward appearances, men seemed to recover more quickly than did women. However, a closer examination showed that, although men showed fewer outward signs of grief, they showed deficits in energy, competence, and satisfaction. Widowers apparently made a more rapid social recovery than did widows, but their emotional recovery actually took longer.

What about the long-term recovery from grief? In a follow-up study, Murray Parkes and Robert Weiss (1983) conducted interviews with the study participants two to four years after the death. Their results indicated that the pattern of recovery two to four years later generally reflected what had occurred during the first year of bereavement. Those who had handled their grief well during the first year were also those who made the best long-term recovery. They had developed a clear understanding of what had happened and had used this understanding to help them get on with their lives. In addition, they had been successful in developing a new identity for themselves. By contrast, those who were still having difficulty had not been able to conceptualize adequately what had happened and were unable to develop a new self-concept. Many of these individuals showed signs of the types of pathological grief discussed earlier.

Helping Survivors Cope

Survivors having difficulty dealing with their grief may require professional help. Counseling can be helpful in assisting people with the process of letting go of their loved ones. Sometimes, just having someone to mourn with can make the difference (Kastenbaum, 1991), whereas other cases require special therapeutic techniques.

One technique that has been developed for helping people work through their grief is **guided imagery** (Melges, 1982). Guided imagery leads grieving individuals through a series of exercises in which they relive aspects of their relationship with the deceased. In the first session, they are instructed to recall their affection for deceased before the person died. This procedure is distressing, but is deemed necessary for the person to reestablish a sense of self-identity and self-worth. In later sessions, with eyes closed, the person is instructed to relive receiving the news of death as well as the experience of the funeral and viewing the body. The person is encouraged to engage in dialogues with the deceased in which secrets and feelings are shared and the person re-

guided imagery
A counseling technique in which bereaved individuals are taken through exercises in which they relive aspects of their relationship with the deceased.

ceives permission from the deceased to seek out new relationships. Finally, the bereaved is urged to exchange final words and say goodbye to the deceased loved one.

Another important source of help for survivors is the support of other people. Having warm and supportive family members and friends often makes a tremendous difference in how well the person copes (Parkes, 1988). In addition, grief support groups can help people who have lost loved ones (Merkner, 1990). These groups are generally made up of others who have experienced similar losses and help survivors by providing them with support and understanding. Among these groups are Compassionate Friends, for parents who have lost a child, Hope for Youth, which provides support for young people whose parents have died, and Survivors of Loved Ones' Suicides for the families and friends of suicide victims. Although these groups can be helpful for survivors, they also have their dangers. For example, some groups adhere to rigid beliefs about the nature of grief, such as a belief in an invariant set of stages that have no real basis in fact. Such beliefs may hinder rather than help recovery (Kastenbaum, 1991). Thus prospective members should investigate a group thoroughly and exercise caution when joining.

CHILDREN AND DEATH

When we think of childhood, death is often the last thing we think about. Childhood is supposed to be a happy time when the child has few cares. The topic of death seems out of place when talking about children. However, like everyone else, children are affected by death. In the past, when people lived shorter lives, death was a more familiar experience for children than it is today. Still, even today children die and are affected when family members or friends die.

Children's Concepts of Death

Adults are sometimes wont to believe that children who think about death are abnormal in some way. However, casual observation and research studies show that even very young children think about and respond to death. For example:

> A boy, aged 16 months, was taken to a public garden by his father, an eminent biomedical scientist. This was a regular visit, one of their favorite expeditions together. The boy's attention was captured by a fuzzy caterpillar creeping along the sidewalk. Suddenly, large adult feet came into view, and the caterpillar was crushed (unwittingly) by another visitor to the garden. Immediately, the boy showed an alarmed expression. He then bent over the remains, studying them intently. After a long moment, he stood up and informed his father, in a sad and resigned voice, "No more!" (Kastenbaum, 1991, p. 151)

Other examples of children's thoughts about death can be found in such games as ring-around-the-rosy, which dates from the time of the Black Plague, or peek-a-boo, which comes from an old English word meaning dead or alive (Stillion & Wass, 1984).

How do children understand death? Studies of children's concepts of death show that these concepts, like others, pass through a predictable set of developmental stages. A classic description of these stages comes from the work of Maria Nagy (1948). From her interviews with 378 Hungarian children aged three to ten, Nagy identified three basic stages. Very young children (ages three to five) generally think of death in terms of separation. Some of the youngest children in this group expressed the idea that death was just a continuation of life, but in a diminished form. Death was viewed as temporary and something that might be reversed, a bit like sleeping. A major advance in the understanding of death seemed to occur at about age five or six. During the second stage, which generally lasts until about age nine, the child comes to understand death as final. The dead are not just sleeping, but are gone permanently. Although death is seen as final, the child believes that death can be eluded if one is clever or lucky. Thus death is not seen as personal or universal—it happens only to some people. With stage three, beginning at about age ten, the child develops a concept of death that resembles that of adults. Death is now seen as not only final but also as personal, universal, and inevitable. The child now understands that everyone, even the child, will eventually die.

With a few exceptions, Nagy's findings have been confirmed by more recent studies. In general, ideas about death follow the stages of cognitive development as outlined by Jean Piaget (1960). In a study among American children, Gerald Koocher (1973) found a steady progression toward understanding death in abstract and universal terms as children moved from the preoperational to the concrete-operational to the formal-operational stage. For example, when asked "what makes things die?" children at the preoperational stage generally cited specific or concrete causes of death, such as guns or poison, whereas children at the stage of formal operations mentioned more general causes, such as old age or illness. Also, in line with Piaget's observations of egocentrism in children's thought, Koocher found that children had difficulty taking the viewpoint of others and imagining how other people would respond if they were to die. Only as children progress to the stage of formal operations are they able to see death from another's perspective (Koocher, 1973).

When a Child Is Terminally Ill

Most children regard death as something that happens to other people. Their own death, if they think about it at all, is seen as far away. However, for children with terminal illness, death is not an abstraction but a grim reality.

How do terminally ill children deal with their impending deaths? Many parents and physicians would prefer that children not be told when they are dying (Stillion & Wass, 1984). They seem to believe that children are best off not knowing. However, studies of terminally ill children have shown that, even when not told, they are often well aware of their condition and demonstrate their anxiety in both their words and actions (Katz, Kellerman, & Siegel, 1980). This awareness of impending death seems to develop gradually as the child attempts to grapple with the situation.

Some of the most detailed and systematic information about dying children's thoughts and feelings comes from the work of Myra Bluebond-Langner (1977). On the basis of extensive observation of hospitalized children, Bluebond-Langner describes five stages that children pass through as they attempt to understand their illness. Initially, children are aware that they have a serious illness but have little understanding beyond that. They are concerned about the seriousness of the illness and feeling sick. In the second stage, which often occurs after the first remission of the disease, they become more sophisticated about the illness, often learning the names of the medicines used and their side effects. During this stage, they are optimistic about recovery and their self-concept changes to one of "seriously ill but will get better." As time passes and they experience a relapse of the disease, their understanding of the illness changes further. During the third stage, children continue to learn more about the treatment procedures and their purposes and come to realize that the illness is long term. At this point, their self-concept becomes "always ill but will get better." As the illness continues, even this optimism fades. During stage four, children think in terms of always being ill and never getting better. Finally, declining health and observation of other dying patients make the children realize that death is likely to follow. Now their self-concept changes to "dying."

As difficult as terminal illness is for dying children, it is at least as difficult for those around them. Parents of dying children are likely to experience powerful emotions of grief, anger, guilt, and anxiety as they watch their child die (Klass & Marwit, 1988; Stillion & Wass, 1984). These emotions are likely to be particularly strong when the death is unexpected, as when the death occurs through accident or suicide, or when the child was initially healthy (Aiken, 1985; Littlefield & Rushton, 1986). Unless dealt with effectively, these emotions can literally tear a family apart. Communication can break down as parents cope with the death and, in some cases, divorce may occur (Feeley & Gottlieb, 1988; Klass, 1986).

Siblings are also profoundly affected. They also experience strong emotions as they watch a brother or sister die. On top of this, they must cope with a changed family situation. Parents are likely to focus their attention on the sick child, leaving other children feeling neglected. Not surprisingly, siblings of dying children often experience problems in behavioral adjustment at the time and later in life (Birenbaum, Robinson, Phillips, Stewart, & McCown, 1989; Stillion & Wass, 1984). Such effects indicate the need for interventions to help family members deal with the death of a child.

When a Parent Dies

In the normal course of events, parents are expected not only to precede their children in death but to die after the child has reached adulthood. Some children, however, experience parental death while they are still in childhood, a loss that can be a real tragedy for the child. After a parent dies, the child not only must deal with the strong emotions of losing a loved one, but is also deprived of the comfort and guidance of the parent.

Studies of parental bereavement show that children have many of the same feelings and go through many of the same reactions to death that adults do (Aiken, 1985; Kastenbaum, 1991), but with some important differences (Furman, 1974). Whereas adults can deal with the death through such cognitive means as replaying memories, young children are likely to express their loss through actions. For example, a toddler who has lost a parent may repeat play activities that he or she had engaged in with the parent. In addition, children are likely to remember parents in terms of a few salient images, in contrast to the many memories that a bereaved spouse can draw on. Beyond this, the loss of a parent may also lead to adjustment difficulties for the child. Studies of bereaved children have uncovered psychological and behavioral difficulties that are common after parental death. Bereaved children tend to be more submissive, dependent, and introverted than children who have not lost a parent. In addition, they show a higher frequency of emotional disturbance and maladjustment and may be more likely to exhibit delinquent and criminal behavior (Kastenbaum, 1991).

The effects of parental loss extend well beyond childhood. Studies have shown that adults who lost parents as children are more likely to have problems with loneliness (Murphy, 1986). In addition, they are more likely to have psychiatric problems such as depression and suicidal behavior, as well as to have physical disorders such as cardiovascular disease (Aiken, 1985).

Helping Children Deal with Death

How can parents and others help children to better understand and deal with death? Adults often prefer simply to ignore the topic of death when talking with children (Stillion & Wass, 1984), under the assumption that death will frighten or upset children and thus is best left undiscussed. However, as we have seen, even young children think about and are affected by death. Therefore, they often have questions to which they seek answers.

The death of a parent is a devastating event for a child and underscores the importance of helping children understand and deal with death.

To help adults handle children's concerns better, Robert Kastenbaum (1991) offers some suggested guidelines. First, parents should be good observers and be sensitive to their children's concerns. Parents can best respond to children's concerns when they are relaxed and attentive enough to learn what those concerns really are. Thus parents should not plan for "one big tell-all," but rather deal with questions as they come up and maintain a continuing dialogue. Parents should not expect that the child's responses to death will be obvious or immediate. Rather, these responses are likely to come out over time and to express themselves in various ways. Parents should be prepared to deal with these responses as they occur. Just the fact that parents are available to talk at these times can be reassuring to children.

When explaining death, parents should be prepared to provide children with accurate information expressed in simple and direct language and to avoid fanciful or sentimental explanations. Simply stating that Grandpa is dead is better than talking about how Grandpa is "with the angels" or has "gone away." Adults should also resist the impulse to remove children from the scene when a death occurs or when the topic of death is discussed. Although this may sometimes be appropriate, children should be exposed to the experience and helped to learn from it. Finally, parents should be prepared for the fact that what a child thinks or feels about death may disturb or anger adults. Parents should accept the child's thoughts and feelings for what they are and provide support as the child works through them.

SUMMARY

In its simplest terms, death is the cessation of life. However, the meaning of death goes far beyond this simple definition. How a person understands death is relative to developmental level, situation, and culture, and changes as these evolve. In modern technological culture, the concept of death is primarily biomedical, but we can also speak of psychological, social, and legal death—any of which may or may not parallel biological death.

When people think about death, they often respond with denial or anxiety. Less commonly, they may exhibit acceptance. Studies of death anxiety have shown that most people report feeling moderately anxious about death. In addition, death anxiety varies significantly by sex, age, sense of well-being, and religious beliefs. Although ultimately acceptance is the healthiest response toward death, such acceptance is often precluded by feelings of anxiety. Thanatologists have developed death education courses to help people overcome such feelings and encourage them to deal realistically with their misconceptions and fears of death.

Whereas death is an event, dying is a process that takes place over time. The beginning of this process is defined differently depending on the person's point of view. Medical professionals tend to define dying in terms of biomedical criteria, whereas the patient and family members are more likely to use psychosocial criteria. Regardless of the perspective, defining a person as dying has profound effects on how others relate to the person, including changes in the focus of medical care and difficulties in interacting with family and friends.

Kübler-Ross has argued that the emotional reactions of dying patients can be understood in terms of identifiable stages including denial, anger, bargaining, depression, and acceptance. These stages have been useful in directing attention to the thoughts and feelings of the dying, but have been heavily criticized by thanatologists. Alternative conceptions of the dying process emphasize the complex interplay of emotions associated with dying or propose different phases of dying.

Dying patients' difficulty with social relationships is an important aspect of the dying process. Just when they are most in need of social support, many patients feel the most isolated and alone. Such problems can be overcome if family and friends of the dying person are sensitive to the person's needs and are willing to face their own feelings and fears.

Given their choice, most people would prefer to die at home. However, in developed countries most people die in institutions such as hospitals and nursing homes. Although such institutions are generally well equipped to handle medical problems, they are not ideal places to die. The hospice movement attempts to change this by providing patients with a maximally supportive environment that focuses on the psychosocial needs of dying patients and their families.

Terminally ill patients often seek psychological counseling to help them handle the the stresses involved in dying. This counseling is similar to other psychotherapy, but differs in terms of the time-frame and goals involved. Counseling the dying is designed primarily to help patients deal with their concerns and face death with acceptance and a sense of peace.

Death also is a stressful experience for survivors. Bereavement refers to the objective fact of losing a loved one, whereas grief refers to the person's response to that loss, and mourning is the public expression of grief. People who are bereaved experience many psychological and physical symptoms that usually pass with time. However, a person with pathological grief either continues to display symptoms in an intense form for a long time or shows a notable absence of symptoms.

Studies of children's concepts of death indicate that children think about death and come to understand it through a series of stages that parallel those found in cognitive development. Children initially see death as something that is sad but reversible; later, they come to realize that death is permanent and universal. Similar stages in understanding are found as terminally ill children attempt to deal with their illness.

The illness and death of a child often has profound effects on parents and siblings. The intense emotions involved can literally tear a family apart unless they are dealt with effectively. Siblings typically show adverse affects at the time as well as later. Similarly, the death of a parent is likely to be a genuine tragedy for a child, which can have lasting psychological and physical effects. Parents can help children deal with death by being available and sensitive observers of children's concerns and by providing children with accurate and developmentally appropriate information.

KEY TERMS

brain death (269)
thanatology (270)
anticipatory grief (273)
coding (277)
hospice (279)
clinical thanatology (281)

bereavement (281)
grief (282)
mourning (282)
obsessional review (285)
guided imagery (285)

SUGGESTED READINGS

Kastenbaum, R. J. (1979). "Healthy dying": A paradoxical quest continues. *Journal of Social Issues, 35,* 185–206. In this article, thanatology pioneer Robert Kastenbaum analyses the American death system and questions its goal of "healthy dying."

Kastenbaum, R. J. (1991). *Death, society, and human experience* (4th ed.). New York: Merrill. Kastenbaum discusses a wide variety of topics related to death.

Shneidman, E. S. (ed.) (1984). *Death: Current perspectives* (3d ed.). Palo Alto, CA: Mayfield. This book of readings contains provocative articles from several leading researchers on important aspects of death.

CHAPTER 12

Immunity and AIDS

Probably no disease has stirred more controversy or caused more anxiety in modern times than has acquired immunodeficiency syndrome (AIDS). Although the first cases were identified only in 1981, by the middle of 1992 more than two million people worldwide had been diagnosed with AIDS ("HIV infects more than a million people in 8 months," 1992). Of even greater concern is the rapid spread of human immunodeficiency virus, the identified cause of AIDS. As of the beginning of 1992, the World Health Organization estimated that between 10 million and 12 million individuals were infected with HIV worldwide, a number expected to increase to 40 million by the year 2000 ("HIV infects more than a million people in 8 months," 1992). According to some estimates, more than one in five people in some African countries may be infected with HIV (Simpson, 1989).

The phenomenon of AIDS forcefully directs our attention to the question of how the body defends itself from disease. In reality, no one dies from AIDS itself. Rather, AIDS renders the body incapable of fighting off viruses and other disease-causing

292

organisms that would ordinarily be harmless to the person. "Opportunistic infections," as they are called, then ravage the body, eventually causing death. This chapter examines first the nature of the body's defenses against disease and how these defenses are influenced by psychological and behavioral factors, and then focuses on the AIDS epidemic. What is AIDS, and how is it transmitted? What can be done to prevent AIDS? How do people cope with this disease? As we shall see, many concepts discussed in previous chapters find direct application in dealing with AIDS.

MIND AND BODY: DEFENDING AGAINST DISEASE

When we fall victim to a virus or "bug," we often ask ourselves why we got sick, perhaps looking to some environmental or emotional factor. In many ways, a much more appropriate question would be "How is it that we stay well most of the time?" Our bodies are continually under assault from various disease-causing conditions and organisms. We are exposed to viruses and bacteria in the air. We come in contact with toxic substances, and we continually harbor disease-causing organisms in our bodies. Yet most of us remain remarkably healthy much of the time—thanks to the immune system.

Unraveling the Mystery of Immunity

Although humans have long marveled at the capacity of the body to fend off disease and heal itself, only recently have scientists begun to understand the intricate mechanisms by which this is accomplished. Central to an understanding of these mechanisms is the immune system, a widely dispersed collection of organs, ducts, and specialized cells that can detect foreign matter when it enters the body and destroy it before it causes illness. In addition, the immune system is able to detect and destroy internal threats such as cancer cells. Through its vigilance against both internal and external threats, the immune system provides the body with an extraordinary degree of resistance to disease (Langman, 1989).

immunity
The body's ability to protect itself from a disease, particularly one that is infectious.

What is immunity? Immunity refers to the body's ability to defend itself from disease-producing organisms and conditions. This immunity comes in several forms. Some immunity is inborn in the form of a nonspecific *natural immunity*. From birth, our bodies are able to detect and respond to hostile foreign matter. A second type of immunity is *acquired immunity*. Through experience with disease-producing organisms, the body builds up immunity to specific diseases. After experiencing certain diseases such as measles or chicken pox, the body develops the ability to fight off those diseases in the future. In addition, the use of vaccines, such as those for polio or tetanus, provides the person with *artificial immunity*. Even though the person has never had the disease, once vaccinated, the body develops the capacity to resist the microorganisms that cause it (Cooper, 1982; Langman, 1989).

Regardless of its source, immunity is based on the body's capacity to detect the difference between cells that are "self" and cells and other matter that are either abnormal or "not self." This is accomplished through the use of subtle markers that

antigen
Any substance from inside or outside the body that is recognized as foreign and induces a response from the immune system.

nonspecific immunity
Immune responses to any antigen without concern for its identity.

allow the immune system to distinguish the cells of the "self" from those that are foreign. After detecting a foreign invader, termed an **antigen,** the immune system mounts a multifaceted attack against it. This attack includes both a general, nonspecific immune response that targets anything foreign and a response that is specific to the particular antigen (Cooper, 1982; Langman, 1989; see Table 12.1).

Nonspecific immunity. The most general type of immunity, termed **nonspecific immunity,** involves a broad spectrum defense against a wide variety of invaders. When the immune system is activated by the presence of an antigen, specialized white blood cells, known as **phagocytes** ("cell eaters"), swing into action. These phagocytes seek out the invaders, engulf, and ingest them. Phagocytes (including **macrophages,** or "big eaters," which attach themselves to tissues, and **monocytes,** which circulate in the blood) are not very choosey and will consume anything suspicious that they happen to encounter. Hence the term "nonspecific." In their role as general scavengers,

TABLE 12.1   *Key Cells in Immune Responses*

Cell	Function
Nonspecific Immunity	
Phagocytes (monocytes and macrophages)	Act as general scavengers, consuming a wide variety of antigens before they can infect body cells. Present pieces of antigens to B and T cells.
Natural killer (NK) cells	Attack and destroy body cells that are cancerous or have been infected by viruses. Do not need to be sensitized to specific antigens.
Specific Immunity	
Humoral immunity	
B cells	Produce plasma cells that then secrete antibodies against specific antigens.
Memory B cells	Specialized B cells that record information about previously encountered antigens.
Cell-mediated immunity	
Killer T cells	Destroy body cells that are cancerous or virus-infected. Require prior sensitization.
Memory T cells	Specialized T cells that record information about previously encountered antigens.
Helper T cells	Gather information about antigens and signal other immune system cells to respond.
Suppressor T cells	Slow down and terminate immune responses when no longer needed.

phagocyte
A cell, such as a macrophage, with the ability to ingest micro-organisms and cell debris.

macrophage
A large cell, part of nonspecific immunity, that surrounds an antigen and digests it.

monocyte
The largest of the white blood cells. Monocytes participate in the nonspecific immune response.

natural killer (NK) cells
Leukocytes that play a role in nonspecific immunity by destroying cancer cells and cells infected with viruses.

specific immunity
An immune response to a specific antigen.

humoral immunity
Immunity based on antibodies that circulate in the blood and attack foreign substances before they enter body cells.

antibodies
Protein molecules produced by activated B cells that act to protect the body against specific antigens.

phagocytes provide a front-line defense against invading antigens be they viruses, bacteria, fungi, or other foreign matter (Eisen, 1990; Langman, 1989).

In addition, a second group of cells, known as **natural killer (NK) cells,** attack and destroy body cells that are cancerous or infected with viruses. Phagocytes attack invaders before they enter body cells; once a virus or other invader enters a cell, however, phagocytes become ineffective. At this point, NK cells take over and continue the battle against the invader. In this way, NK cells play an important role in protecting the body against cancer and certain viral diseases. Like phagocytes, NK cells are nondiscriminating and respond to any cell that they perceive as cancerous or virus-infected (Eisen, 1990).

Specific immunity. In addition to this generalized immune response, the immune system responds in a focused way to specific invaders. Through **specific immunity,** the immune system can detect the presence of a specific antigen, such as the virus for chicken pox or the bacterium that cause diphtheria, and mount an attack that is directed only at that antigen. This type of immunity, acquired through experience with the antigens in question, involves a fascinating form of communication between the phagocytes and second group of white blood cells known as lymphocytes. After ingesting an antigen, the phagocytes break down the antigen and display pieces of it on their surface. These pieces are then presented to the lymphocytes. If the antigen has been encountered before, those lymphocytes that are specialized for that antigen are activated. If the antigen is unknown, the immune system responds by making a record of the new antigen and "commissioning" new lymphocytes to respond to it. These lymphocytes, in turn, operate by either attacking invaders while they are in the blood and other body fluids (humoral immunity) or destroying infected cells (cell-mediated immunity).

Humoral immunity (also known as antibody-mediated immunity) allows antigens to be intercepted while they are still in various body fluids and attacked through the use of **antibodies.** Antibodies are proteins derived from plasma cells produced by a specific class of lymphocytes known as **B cells.** When secreted by the plasma cells, some antibodies attach to the surface of the antigen, slowing it down so that it can be consumed by phagocytes. Other antibodies attack antigens, causing them to explode, while still others neutralize the toxins produced by the antigens.

Antibodies (also known as *immunoglobulins*), come in five known varieties, each of which has specialized functions. For example, immunoglobulin A (abbreviated as IgA) defends the surfaces of the body against invading antigens, whereas IgE is concentrated in the lungs, skin, and mucous membranes, and defends against environmental antigens, such as pollens or molds in the air. People who suffer from hay fever or other allergies can blame their IgE. When present in abnormally high levels, as it is with allergy sufferers, IgE is responsible for allergic reactions (Desowitz, 1987).

In addition, some B cells are specialized to "remember" antigens that have been encountered previously. After they first encounter a particular antigen, these

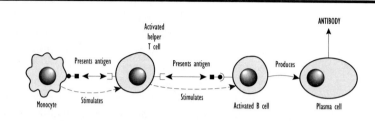

FIGURE 12.1 *Simplified view of the processes in humoral immunity. Monocytes stimulate the helper T cells and present them with pieces of the antigen. The helper T cells, in turn, stimulate and present pieces of the antigen to B cells, which produce plasma cells, which, in turn, manufacture antibody.*

B cells
Circulating white blood cells also known as B lymphocytes that, when activated by an antigen, produce antibodies.

cell-mediated immunity
Immunity based on sensitized lymphocytes known as T cells, which attack invading foreign substances in the body.

T cells
White blood cells that originate in the bone marrow but mature in the thymus gland.

thymus gland
An organ located above the heart and behind the breastbone, where T cells mature and differentiate into several different varieties.

memory B cells are primed to respond quickly when that antigen is encountered again. This provides the immune system with the capacity to mobilize its response to specific invaders rapidly. The sequence of events in humoral immunity is depicted in Figure 12.1.

Cell-mediated immunity. Although humoral immunity is effective in fighting off invaders in the blood and body fluids, some antigens do get through and go on to infect body cells. When this happens, **cell-mediated immunity** comes into play. Cell-mediated immunity detects cells that are cancerous or that have been infected and taken over by micro-organisms such as viruses. This is accomplished by another set of lymphocytes known as **T cells** (so-called because they mature in the **thymus gland**). T cells possess the ability to identify and destroy body cells that have become abnormal and thus pose a threat.

How does this work? The functions of cell-mediated immunity are carried out by several different varieties of T cells. As is the case with B cells, some T cells serve as an immunological memory. These *memory T cells* carry inside of them information about previously encountered antigens so that, when one of those antigens is encountered again, the response can be rapid, saving valuable time. *Killer T cells*, by contrast, are specialized to attack and kill their targets directly. After detecting a cancerous cell or one infected with a virus or other invading micro-organism, a killer T cell closes in on its target, makes contact with it, and then lyses (dissolves) it, apparently by releasing chemicals that destroy the target cell's outer membrane. Killer T cells also attack foreign tissue and are responsible for the body's rejection of transplanted skin and organs (Desowitz, 1987; Roitt, 1984).

While killer T cells do the work, two additional strains of T cells are charged with stimulating and inhibiting immune responses. *Helper T cells* account for 55% to 70% of all of the T cells and incite other immune system cells to multiply rapidly when faced with a threat. These cells gather information about invasions taking place and secrete chemicals to stimulate other leukocytes (including both B and T cells) to reproduce and attack. Thus helper T cells are important in "turning on" the immune response. After the invasion is quelled and the invading antigens destroyed, *suppressor T cells* come into play. These cells slow down and eventually stop the proliferation of the other immune cells and their associated chemicals. In effect, suppressor T cells "turn off" the immune response when it is no longer needed. The action of the helper and suppressor T cells allows the immune system to mount the right size attack at the right time. An overview of the processes involved in cell-mediated immunity is given in Figure 12.2.

Defending against infection. Whatever our environment, we are constantly surrounded by antigens. Most of these antigens, however, are stopped by the skin and mucous membranes lining the nose, mouth, lungs, intestines, and other body orifices before they ever enter the body's interior. Skin provides a physical barrier for repelling

FIGURE 12.2

The cell-mediated immune response. Monocytes stimulate and present pieces of the antigen to both helper T cells and pre-killer T cells. Helper T cells produce T cell growth factor and other chemical messengers that lead to proliferation and maturation of killer T cells. Killer T cells then attack and destroy virus-infected target cells.

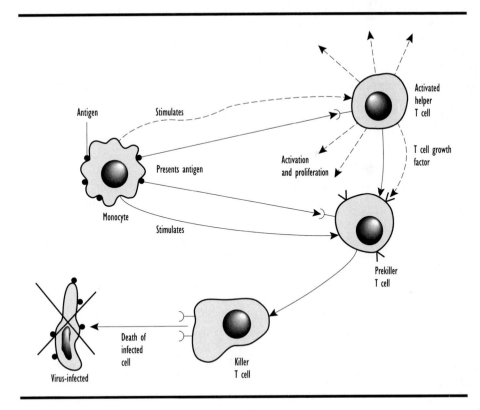

antigens, whereas the mucous membranes contain fluids saturated with antibodies, principally IgA and IgE, that attack the antigens as they try to penetrate these barriers. Despite these defenses, some antigens manage to get through either because of breaks in the skin or because the external defenses are overwhelmed.

Once inside the body, antigens provoke both specific and nonspecific immune responses. The phagocytes of nonspecific immunity seek out and consume antigens, presenting pieces of those antigens to the B and helper T cells. Helper T cells then activate the specific immune response, and the battle is joined in the bloodstream to repel the invaders. B cells, stimulated by the helper T cells, multiply and produce plasma cells, which, in turn, produce antibodies for destroying the antigen.

Antigens that make it through the defenses in the bloodstream are met by yet another line of defense before they can do their real damage. When the phagocytes present pieces of the antigen to the helper T cells, the helper T cells also chemically signal the killer T cells about the presence of the antigen. After the antigen invades body cells, the killer T cells multiply and attack the invaded cells, destroying both them and the antigen.

These defenses continue so long as the body is under assault by the antigen. As the attack subsides, suppressor T cells slow the immune response, halting the increased production of B and T cells, and reducing the counterattack. Eventually, the battle ends, and the immune system returns to its baseline state. A memory of this attack is retained, however, by the memory B and memory T cells so that, should the antigen be encountered again, the response will be even more swift.

Psychoneuroimmunology

As researchers learn more about the immune system and how it keeps us healthy, they find increasing evidence that immunity is more than just a physiological process. It is also a psychophysiological process involving the person's attitudes and feelings. Emotional states, the kinds of stress a person is under, and a person's social relationships all influence the activity of the immune system. These influences are the focus of **psychoneuroimmunology,** a new specialty that examines the ways in which psychosocial processes are intertwined with both the nervous and immune systems.

psychoneuro-immunology
The study of the interrelationships between psychosocial factors and the immune, nervous, and endocrine systems.

Conditioning immunity. When we think about the process of conditioning, we generally think of the conditioning of behavior. A serendipitous discovery by Robert Ader, however, has led to the realization that the immune system, long thought to function autonomously of psychosocial stimuli, can also be conditioned. In an experiment on taste aversion in rats, Ader attempted to produce aversion to a saccharine solution by injecting the rats with the drug cyclophosphamide just after they had drunk some of the solution. Since cyclophosphamide rapidly causes nausea, this produced a strong negative reaction to the normally attractive taste of the saccharine. After this taste aversion had been established, Ader stopped the administration of cyclophosphamide to see how long the aversion would last in the absence of reinforcement. As expected, the rats gradually returned to drinking the saccharine solution. Unexpectedly, however, they also began to die from infections and cancer (Ader & Cohen, 1975, 1981). In the search to discover the reasons for these deaths, Ader and Nicholas Cohen (1975) found that rats conditioned this way suffered from seriously impaired immunity. Cyclophosphamide is a known immunosuppressant, and, even though one dose would not by itself result in the level of immune impairment found in this study, pairing this drug with the saccharine solution apparently resulted in a conditioned suppression of the immune system. This effect was confirmed by subsequent experiments, which showed that pairing immunosuppressants with other stimuli can indeed lead to conditioned immune suppression (Rogers, Reich, Strom, & Carpenter, 1976).

Several other effects of conditioning on immune responses have also been noted. For example, conditioning has been used to reduce the immune system's natural tendency to reject skin grafts. In addition, NK cell activity has been altered through conditioning, as has the release of histamines during allergic reactions (Lloyd, 1987). Particularly exciting are findings that conditioning can be used to enhance the immune response. For example, a study by Vithal Ghanta and his colleagues (Ghanta, Hiramoto, Solvason, & Spector, 1985) found that the temporal pairing of an odor (camphor) with the injection of an immunity-enhancing drug resulted in a conditioned increase in NK cell activity such that, after conditioning, exposure to the camphor alone increased NK cell activity.

Findings like these have potential clinical applications. For example, conditioning procedures might be used to behaviorally suppress an overactive immune system in individuals with autoimmune diseases such as systemic lupus erythematosus (SLE, also known as lupus), a condition that includes severe inflammation of the blood vessels, kidney disorders, and tumors of the skin and nervous system. In conditions like SLE, the immune system becomes hyperactive and attacks the body's own cells. Currently, such conditions are treated with powerful immunosuppressant drugs that can reduce the impact of the disease but also have toxic side effects. Experiments in rats with an SLE-like disease have shown that behavioral conditioning can substantially reduce the amount of these drugs needed to keep the disease under control (Ader & Cohen, 1982).

Stress and immunity. The kind of stresses a person is experiencing also has important effects on immune functioning. As was discussed in Chapter 6, evidence now indicates that stress can suppress the immune system, but exactly how does this work? Preliminary answers to this question are being provided by research examining the effects of stress on **immunocompetence,** that is, the immune system's effectiveness in identifying and destroying antigens.

The impact of stress on immunocompetence emerges in several different ways. First, stress has been shown to alter the number and type of immune system cells circulating in blood and other body fluids. For example, William McKinnon and his colleagues (McKinnon, Weisse, Reynolds, Bowles, & Baum, 1989) examined the number of T, B, and NK cells in blood samples taken from individuals living near the

immunocompetence
The extent to which the immune system is able to fight off disease.

Three Mile Island nuclear plant after the near disaster there, and compared these with samples taken from individuals living more than 80 miles away. Overall, people living near TMI exhibited fewer B, killer T, and NK cells than did people living further away. Since these cells are key players in immunity, a decrease in their numbers is taken as an indication of reduced ability to fight off invaders.

Stress also appears to affect the responsiveness of leukocytes. Several studies examining the ability of phagocytes to digest antigens or the capability of killer T and NK cells to kill invading or abnormal cells have found that leukocytes are less responsive when the organism is under stress. For example, one study using mice (Kandil & Borysenko, 1987) found a marked reduction in the ability of NK cells to bind to and kill tumor cells after the mice had been subjected to stress by being rotated on a turntable. Similarly, Michael Irwin and his colleagues (Irwin, Daniels, Smith, Bloom, & Weiner, 1987) found that NK cell activity was significantly lower among recent widows than it was among women with healthy husbands.

Although these studies and others (Antoni, 1987; Kiecolt-Glaser et al., 1986; Locke et al., 1984) have produced promising results, controversy lingers concerning these effects. For example, Ronald Moss and his colleagues (Moss, Moss, & Peterson, 1989) found no relationship between everyday life stresses in humans and level of NK cell activity, suggesting that the relationship is more complicated than a simple one-to-one correspondence between stress and immune functioning.

Finally, some evidence demonstrates that stress can increase the rate of tumor development. For example, Joanne Weinberg and Joanne Emerman (1989) surgically injected cancer tumor cells into mice and then stressed some of them through daily exposure to novel environments. Examination of the tumors at the end of the experiment showed significantly greater tumor growth among the stressed mice as compared to the unstressed ones. Interestingly, this was the case only for mice separated from their siblings and kept in separate cages. Mice kept with their siblings showed much less tumor growth. These results were interpreted as indicating that stress has a suppressive effect on the immune system that can be substantially ameliorated by the presence of familiar others. Again, however, the results are not entirely consistent. Although other studies have obtained this effect, still others have not (cf. Antoni, 1987; Justice, 1985). Benjamin Newberry and his colleagues (Newberry, Gildow, Wogan, & Reese, 1976), for example, found no increase in tumor growth when they stressed rats by the application of electrical shock.

The presence of contradictory results tells us that the relationship between stress and immune functioning is far from simple. The various components of the immune system can be influenced by a variety of non-stress factors such as time of day, food intake, alcohol, and smoking (Kiecolt-Glaser & Glaser, 1988). Even minor variations in these factors can produce unexpected results. However, as noted in Chapters 6 and 7, the stress-disease relationship is moderated by variables relating to the nature of the stressful experience and how the person experiences and copes with it. Along these same lines, evidence is accumulating that the effects of stress on immune functioning are influenced by such variables as the person's coping style and the duration of the stressful events. For example, it appears that stress that is dealt with passively (through avoidance or withdrawal from the situation and taking a passive, pessimistic outlook) tends to lead to suppression of the immune system, whereas stress that is met with direct action does not (Antoni, 1987).

Enhancing immunity. The effects of stress on immune functioning raise the question of how one might ameliorate those effects. Might it be possible, for example, to use social support or stress management techniques to enhance immunocompetence? The answer seems to be a qualified yes.

Several studies of the role of social support in immune functioning have suggested that people who enjoy high levels of social support tend to exhibit higher levels of immunocompetence than is the case for people with less social support. For example, a recent study of immune functioning among the spouses of cancer patients (Baron, Cutrona, Hicklin, Russell, & Lubaroff, 1990) found that spouses who reported high levels of social support showed greater NK cell activity as well as a stronger immune response to chemical challenge than did those with less social support. Along these same lines, a recent study by John Jemmott and Kim Magloire (1988) found that students with higher levels of perceived social support exhibited higher levels of salivary IgA (indicating greater immunocompetence) during exam periods than did students who perceived less social support. Although these studies are suggestive, these data are correlational and thus must be interpreted cautiously. As seen in Chapter 2, correlations provide evidence of a relationship between two variables, but do not prove that the relationship is causal. Before we can conclude that social support results in increased immunocompetence, supporting data are needed from studies in which social support is experimentally manipulated.

Another possible means of enhancing immune functioning is through the method of catharsis, in which the person actively confronts traumatic experiences from the past. Everyone experiences traumatic experiences at one time or another. Although putting these out of one's mind is tempting, the results of an experiment by James Pennebaker and his colleagues (Pennebaker, Kiecolt-Glaser, & Glaser, 1988) suggest that actively disclosing those events to others can have beneficial effects on immune functioning. In this experiment, college students were assigned to write about either trivial or traumatic experiences on four consecutive days. Before and after the experiment and six weeks afterward, blood samples were drawn which were analyzed for lymphocyte responsiveness. The results showed that students who wrote about traumatic events showed higher levels of lymphocyte responsiveness than did those who wrote about trivial experiences. This suggests that perhaps the "talking cures" of psychotherapy may have physical as well as psychological effects.

Finally, some of the stress management techniques described in Chapter 7 may be useful in minimizing stress-related immunosuppression. For example, in a study of the effects of examinations on immunocompetence in medical students, Janice Kiecolt-Glaser and her colleagues (Kiecolt-Glaser et al., 1986) randomly assigned half the subjects to a hypnotic/relaxation condition in which they were provided an overview of hypnosis and other relaxation methods, were hypnotized, and then encouraged to practice relaxation techniques during and outside scheduled group sessions. Although overall the subjects exhibited reduced immunocompetence during exams, this immunocompromise was significantly ameliorated for subjects who frequently practiced relaxation techniques. Similarly, another study found that use of relaxation techniques resulted in increases in immunocompetence among a group of elderly residents in an independent living facility (Kiecolt-Glaser et al., 1985). Although these findings are promising, they should be interpreted cautiously because other studies have failed to obtain these effects. For example, Bengt Arnetz and his colleagues (Arnetz et al., 1987) found no immunological effects for a psychosocial program designed to help unemployed women.

Overall, the evidence suggests the possibility of enhancing immunity through various psychosocial interventions. The conflicting results, however, suggest that the relationship between psychosocial factors and immunocompetence is mediated by other factors that have yet to be uncovered. Thus considerably more research is required before drawing the definite conclusion that social support, catharsis, relaxation, or other interventions can indeed reliably improve immunocompetence.

THE AIDS EPIDEMIC

Under normal circumstances, the immune system is able to fight off most infections and to protect the body from a wide variety of diseases. However, when the immune system is seriously compromised, the body becomes subject to diseases to which it is normally relatively immune. Until recently, severe immune deficiency was rare, confined primarily to cases of organ or tissue transplant, in which the immune system was artificially suppressed, as well as the exceptional case of natural immune deficiency. The advent of AIDS, however, has changed all this.

What Is AIDS?

acquired immunodeficiency syndrome (AIDS)
A disease caused by the human immunodeficiency virus (HIV), which causes severe impairment of immune functioning.

As we have seen, the acronym AIDS stands for **acquired immunodeficiency syndrome,** a condition in which the body loses its ability to fight off infection. When this happens, the person becomes subject to infections and cancers, which eventually result in death.

In fact, it was the unexplained occurrence of certain rare diseases that led to the identification of AIDS as a disease. In June 1981, the Centers for Disease Control (CDC) reported five cases of an extremely rare form of pneumonia, *pneumocystis carinii pneumonia* (PCP), among homosexual men in the Los Angeles area. PCP is so uncommon that the drugs used to treat it were considered experimental and dispensed only by the CDC. At about the same time, the CDC received several reports of a rare form of cancer known as Kaposi's sarcoma, a disease generally found only among elderly men or patients receiving immunosuppressive therapy. The occurrence of these diseases among individuals whose immune systems had no apparent reason to be compromised set off a search for the cause of these unusual occurrences (see Box 3.1).

What causes AIDS? Although the causes of these illnesses were initially a mystery, evidence developed quickly that the disease was sexually transmitted. For example, a case control study among gay men in 1981 found that the variable most clearly distinguishing AIDS patients from non-patients was the number and frequency of sexual contacts. Further, data on the sexual partners of 13 of the first 19 AIDS cases found that during the previous five years nine of them had had sexual contact with a person who later developed AIDS. In 1982, however, it became evident that AIDS was not solely transmitted through sexual contact. The appearance of AIDS among individuals who had received blood transfusions or who had shared hypodermic needles during intravenous (IV) drug use strongly suggested that the disease was caused by some sort of transmissible agent in the blood (Heyward & Curran, 1988).

A major breakthrough in the search for a cause came with the discovery of the **human immunodeficiency virus (HIV).** HIV is a particular type of virus known as a **retrovirus.** First discovered in humans in the late 1970s, retroviruses replicate by injecting themselves into host cells and literally taking over the genetic workings of those cells. After this happens, these cells become virtual virus factories, producing viral particles that then move out of their host cells to infect new cells. Among human retroviruses, HIV is the most prolific in its replication and the most deadly in its effects (Redfield & Burke, 1988; Streicher & Heller, 1989).

The effects of AIDS on the body. The opportunistic infections that first called attention to AIDS are, in reality, a late manifestation of a long chain of events. This chain begins with the entry of HIV into the body through the bloodstream. After HIV enters the bloodstream, it seeks out and attaches itself to a particular molecule on the surface of target cells known as CD4. CD4 molecules are found on many cells but are particularly prevalent on the T cells of the immune system—which helps explain why HIV has such a devastating effect on immunity. After binding to the CD4 molecule, HIV injects itself into the cell, incorporates its genetic material into the cell's DNA, and destroys the cell's ability to function. The infection produced continues for the life of the cell and is also carried in any daughter cells produced by the cell's division (Weber & Weiss, 1988).

Current evidence suggests that when HIV first enters the body, the immune system responds to it like any other antigen and is able to contain the infection. Recent studies of patients newly infected with HIV have found that, within a few weeks after infection, the body mounts a massive counteraction that effectively suppresses the amount of HIV in the body (Clark et al., 1991; Daar, Moudgil, Meyer, & Ho, 1991). During this time, at least a third of newly infected individuals may experience a fever or severe sore throat, but these clear up on their own. However, although the immune system is apparently able to handle the initial infection, HIV remains in the body in a latent state. At varying lengths of time after infection, HIV begins to destroy the helper T cell population (Bowen, Lane, & Fauci, 1985; Volberding, 1989). Since the helper T cells bear a primary responsibility for triggering the immune system's response to foreign invaders, this has a serious effect on the ability of other immune system cells to do their jobs. Some of these effects are shown in Figure 12.3.

human immunodeficiency virus (HIV)
A retrovirus that causes AIDS and ARC by invading and taking over helper T cells.

retrovirus
A type of virus that carries its genetic information in the form of ribonucleic acid (RNA).

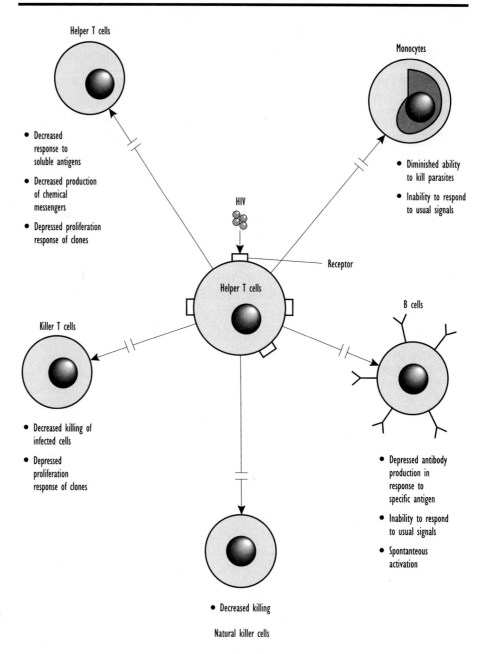

FIGURE 12.3

Some of the many functional defects caused by infection of helper T cells with HIV. Cells affected include other T cells, B cells, natural killer (NK) cells, and monocytes.

Note. Adapted from "Immunopathogenesis of the acquired immunodeficiency syndrome" by D. L. Bowen, M. D. Lane, and A. S. Fauci, 1985, *Annals of Internal Medicine, 103,* 704–9.

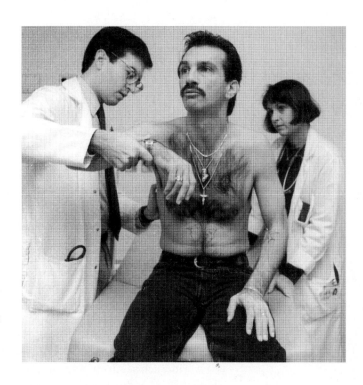

The suppression of immune functioning caused by AIDS leaves a person vulnerable to opportunistic infections.

AIDS-related complex (ARC)
A medical syndrome that is similar to AIDS but does not involve the same degree of impairment in immune functioning or as severe symptoms as AIDS.

Clinically, the immunocompromise resulting from HIV infection manifests itself in a sequence of increasingly serious conditions. One of the first signs of HIV infection is chronic swelling of the lymph glands. During this stage, which typically lasts from three to five years, the person generally feels well, but the swollen lymph glands are testament to the body's attempts to fight off the virus. Although the person feels well, the immune system's ability to fight off infection is steadily declining. As this decline progresses, the person begins to develop symptoms known as **AIDS-related complex (ARC).** Among these symptoms are diarrhea, spiking fevers, fatigue, night sweats, and chronically swollen lymph glands. With further decline in immune functioning, the person develops full-blown AIDS. Now the immune system is unable to fight off viruses and other invaders that would normally cause no problem, and the person becomes subject to opportunistic infections and diseases. The most common of these are PCP and Kaposi's sarcoma, but AIDS patients also suffer from herpes, yeast and fungal infections, cytomegalovirus, and other conditions.

In addition to its effects on immunity, HIV produces serious effects on the central nervous system. Although these effects were initially overlooked because of the dramatic impact of AIDS on the immune system, observations of AIDS patients showed that they suffered from neurological problems ranging from mild memory loss, lethargy, and social withdrawal to severe dementia, ataxia, and seizures. Thus in addition to infecting the cells of the immune system, HIV also appears to infect cells of the central nervous system directly (Janssen, 1989).

The Transmission and Prevention of AIDS

Ever since the initial identification of AIDS, professionals and lay people have been greatly concerned about the disease's transmission. Despite widespread fears that HIV can be contracted through casual contact with an infected person, available evidence clearly shows that the virus is only passed through contact that involves the exchange of blood, semen, or other bodily fluids. Specifically, HIV is passed through sexual contact or contact with the blood of an infected person such as occurs when two people share hypodermic needles during intravenous drug use or when a person receives a transfusion of HIV-infected blood. Fortunately, tests for HIV infection in blood and blood products have drastically reduced the risk of transfusion-related AIDS. In addition, HIV can be passed from an infected mother to her unborn child.

Sexual transmission. The vast majority of HIV infections to date have been through sexual transmission. In the Americas and Europe, this transmission has most often been through homosexual encounters. For example, 58% of the AIDS cases in the United States reported through June 1992 involved gay or bisexual men who contracted HIV through sex with other men, most frequently receptive anal sex without the use of a condom (Centers for Disease Control, 1992). In other parts of the world, such as Africa, Asia, and the Caribbean, AIDS apparently spreads primarily through heterosexual contacts. Most AIDS cases in Africa have occurred among heterosexuals, affecting roughly even numbers of males and females (Mann, Chin, Piot, & Quinn, 1988; N'Galy & Ryder, 1988). The World Health Organization estimates that more than 90% of new HIV infections in adults worldwide occur through heterosexual intercourse ("HIV infects more than a million people in 8 months," 1992).

Behind these statistics are sexual practices associated with the spread of HIV. Although HIV can be transmitted in any sexual encounter in which semen or other bodily fluids pass from one person to the other, several factors increase the risk of infection. One of the most important is the number of sexual partners. The more sexual partners a person has, the more likely it is that at least one of those partners will be infected with HIV, particularly if one or more of those partners is from a high-risk group such as homosexual men, prostitutes, or IV drug users. Relatedly, anonymous sex, such as in bathhouses or with prostitutes, also increases the risk of contracting HIV. Studies of early AIDS cases in gay males found that a large percentage of them had had sexual relations in bathhouses and barely knew their partners, if indeed they knew them at all (Shilts, 1987). In addition, sexual practices such as anal intercourse and oral-anal contact appear to substantially increase the likelihood of HIV infection (Gerberding & Sande, 1989). Conversely, the risk of HIV infection decreases substantially when a person is sexually abstinent or is involved in a long-term monogamous relationship. Using condoms during intercourse can prevent the exchange of semen and thus reduce the risk of infection (see Box 12.1).

BOX 12.1 How Safe Is "Safe Sex"?

The clear evidence for sexual transmission of HIV has led to urgent calls for people to engage in "safe sex." But what is safe sex, and how safe is it?

In reality, the only truly safe sex is no sex at all or activities that do not involve direct sexual contact such as sharing sexual fantasies, talking sexy, caressing each other, or masturbation without physical contact. Kissing, even "French kissing," also appears to be safe. Although HIV has been isolated in saliva, the amount of the virus in saliva is apparently too small to produce infection (Frumkin & Leonard, 1987). Finally, sex within a mutually monogamous relationship of long standing (ten years or more) is considered safe. All other forms of sexual activity involve some risk. Although it is not possible to attach hard numbers to the level of risk involved, various activities can be classified according to their relative level of risk.

Low-risk sex. These activities involve sexual contact but not the mingling of body fluids. For example, mutual masturbation is a low-risk activity so long as there are no cuts or sores on the partners' skin through which HIV could enter. When cuts or sores are present, one should wear rubber gloves to reduce the risk. Intercourse of any type using a condom with a partner whom you know well and have every reason to believe is uninfected generally carries a low risk.

Medium-risk sex. Risk increases with the likelihood that your partner is from a high-risk group (e.g., gay or bisexual men, prostitutes, IV drug users) or when you know little about your partner. Thus intercourse using a condom with a partner who might be from a high-risk group or about whom you know little is considered to entail a medium level of risk. Even though condoms have been shown to reduce the risk of HIV exposure, they do not eliminate it entirely.

High-risk sex. Activities that involve the exchange of bodily fluids (semen, vaginal secretions) with someone who may be infected fall under the category of high-risk sex. Thus intercourse without a condom or oral-anal contact without a latex barrier carries a high risk of infection. Unprotected anal intercourse seems to carry a particularly high risk of infection for the receiving partner because of the likelihood of tears in the lining of the rectum. Any contact with a partner's blood or the sharing of sexual toys with an infected partner should be considered high risk.

These risk levels are only relative. To protect yourself against HIV infection, the most important factors are *who* your partner is and *what* you do together. The only way to be completely safe is either through celibacy, long-standing mutually monogamous relationships, or activities that involve no direct sexual contact. For more information, see Kaplan (1987) or Health Care Information Network (1989).

Although the facts of sexual transmission have clear implications for AIDS prevention, development of effective prevention programs has faced formidable obstacles. The association of AIDS with sexuality and, in particular, homosexuality, has created political and moral barriers to prevention. In the United States, for example, efforts to promote the use of condoms to prevent the spread of HIV have often met with opposition from religious and community leaders who view such efforts as implicitly condoning homosexual or promiscuous behavior (Moskop, 1989). Further, the strong association of AIDS with homosexuality has led many non-homosexuals to believe that AIDS is solely a gay problem that does not pertain to them. These factors, along with conflicting governmental responses and public uncertainty about the magnitude of the actual risk of contracting AIDS, have hampered prevention efforts (Fineberg, 1988).

Sexually active adolescents represent a particular source of concern about the spread of AIDS because they often believe themselves at low risk yet engage in high-risk sexual behaviors.

Despite these barriers, "safe sex" campaigns and behavioral interventions have successfully led to altered sexual behavior. For example, Jeffrey Kelly and his coworkers (Kelly, St. Lawrence, Hood, & Brasfield, 1989) used a behavioral intervention, consisting of AIDS risk reduction information, training in self-control, sexual assertiveness, and the development of self-affirming social supports to reduce high-risk sexual behaviors among gay men. Compared to a waiting-list control group, men randomly assigned to the intervention group greatly reduced the frequency with which they engaged in high-risk sexual behaviors, a change that was maintained at a follow-up eight months later. Other studies have obtained significant reductions in high-risk behaviors through informational interventions. One study among black inner city adolescent males found a significant reduction in high-risk sexual behaviors in response to a five-hour informational intervention comprising focused games, videotapes, and role-playing exercises (Jemmott, Jemmott, & Fong, 1990). Studies among gay and bisexual men have consistently reported decreases over time in the number of sexual partners and frequency of unprotected anal intercourse, along with increases in the number of men in monogamous relationships (Becker & Joseph, 1988; Doll et al., 1990; Joseph et al., 1987; Stall, Coates, & Hoff, 1988).

Although these studies are encouraging, caution is in order. Other studies have found a high degree of recidivism over time with many men relapsing at least temporarily into unsafe sexual practices (Kelly, St. Lawrence, & Brasfield, 1991; Stall, Ekstrand, Pollack, McKusick, & Coates, 1990). Relapse appears to be most common among men who are younger and those who had previously engaged in more frequent risky sexual behavior (Kelly et al., 1991). The fact that HIV can be transmitted through a single encounter makes this recidivism particularly worrisome.

Studies of sexual attitudes and behaviors among heterosexuals are also a source of concern. Although evidence clearly proves that HIV can be readily transmitted through heterosexual activities, many heterosexuals still think of AIDS as a disease of white gay males and downplay their own risk. For example, Vickie Mays and Susan Cochran (1988) report that, although black and Hispanic women are at higher risk than white women for contracting HIV from their sexual partners, they see themselves as less likely than white women to get AIDS and often take few, if any, precautions. Similarly, studies of sexually active adolescents have found that many adolescents think themselves unlikely to contract AIDS (Strunin, 1991) and engage in high-risk sexual behaviors (Biglan et al., 1990).

AIDS and IV drug use. The second major route for HIV transmission is through intravenous drug usage. An estimated one fourth of the AIDS cases in the United States and Europe involve IV drug use as a risk factor (Des Jarlais & Friedman, 1988). Transmission through IV drug use occurs when drug users share needles in the process of injecting drugs. Unless the needles are carefully cleaned between uses, small amounts of blood remain on the needles, which can then infect the next user. The likelihood that a person will contract HIV through IV drug use increases substantially with the frequency of such use and with the injection of drugs in "shooting galleries" or other places where injection equipment is borrowed or rented. After HIV becomes established among IV drug users in an area, it can spread to non–drug-using hetero-sexuals via sexual transmission as well as to children through perinatal transmission. In New York City, for example, an estimated 90% of the cases of heterosexual transmission of HIV occurs between IV drug users and their non–IV-drug-using sexual partners, while more than 80% of the perinatal transmission involves children of IV-drug-using mothers (Des Jarlais, Casriel, & Friedman, 1989; Des Jarlais & Fried-man, 1988).

Although the ideal way to stop the spread of HIV through needle-sharing is to convince IV drug users to stop using drugs, research has shown that the rate of IV drug use has not declined substantially in response to the AIDS threat (Des Jarlais, Friedman, Casriel, & Kott, 1987). Evidence, however, does indicate that IV drug users are well informed about the risks of AIDS and are engaging in risk-reducing behavior. In one study of patients in a methadone maintenance program in New York, 93% knew that AIDS was transmitted through needle-sharing and more than half reported that they engaged in such risk-reducing behaviors as only using sterile needles or cleaning their needles frequently (Friedman et al., 1987, cited in Des Jarlais & Friedman, 1988). Moreover, programs in which addicts are encouraged to exchange their old needles for new sterile ones or in which they have been taught to clean their needles with bleach have resulted in significant risk reduction. Such programs, however, have often met with considerable resistance from community groups and government officials, who see them as implicitly condoning drug usage. Changes in IV drug use behavior have generally been toward risk reduction, not risk elimination (Des Jarlais & Friedman, 1988).

Perinatal transmission. Most HIV transmission takes place through either sex-ual contact or the sharing of needles during IV drug use. However, a growing number

An HIV-infected mother has an estimated 30% chance of passing the infection on to her child. Infants born infected with HIV make up the vast majority of HIV-infected children.

of children have acquired HIV from their infected mothers. In the United States, for example, more than 3,000 children of HIV-infected mothers developed AIDS between 1981 and mid-1992 (Centers for Disease Control, 1992). The World Health Organization estimates that by the year 2000 between five million and ten million babies worldwide will have been born with HIV infection ("HIV infects more than a million people in 8 months," 1992). These children were infected through contact either with the mother's blood while *in utero* or with infected blood and other fluids during birth (Goedert, Duliege, Amos, Felton, & Biggar, 1991). The increasing number of HIV-infected babies emphasizes the need for preventing HIV infection in women of childbearing age and for programs aimed at preventing pregnancy among HIV-infected women (Grossman, 1989).

HIV and health care workers. Because health care workers come in close contact with patients, contact that may involve invasive medical procedures, considerable discussion has arisen of the possibility of HIV transmission between patient and health care workers. Health care workers are worried that they may contract HIV from infected patients. For example, observations of surgical procedures in one hospital found that surgical personnel had direct contact with patient blood in more than 30% of the operations observed. Although most of these were skin contacts, a small number (7%) included needle sticks, which have the potential for transmitting HIV (Panlilio et al., 1991). Observations like these have led to the institution of protective measures, such as the use of face guards or rubber aprons during surgery. Fortunately, the risk of contracting HIV from patients appears to be low and can be reduced even further through safeguards. Current estimates indicate that the likelihood of HIV transmission from a single needle stick during surgery on an infected person is less than 0.4%, whereas the risk of transmission through skin contact with infected blood is nearly zero (Gerberding & Schecter, 1991).

But patients are also worried—about the possibility of contracting HIV from an infected health care worker. Such concerns have been heightened by reports of patients who apparently contracted HIV from an infected dentist who failed to use appropriate precautions (Centers for Disease Control, 1991a). Although these cases underline the need for adherence to infection control procedures, the current evidence shows that public fears are exaggerated: the likelihood of HIV transmission from practitioner to patient is even lower than that from patient to practitioner. An examination of more than 2,000 patients of an HIV-infected surgeon showed no evidence of transmission of the virus (Mishu, Schaffner, Horan, Wood, Hutcheson, & McNabb, 1990).

Women and AIDS

Because of the preponderance of gay and bisexual men among persons with AIDS in the United States, many of the efforts at prevention have been aimed at this group. This emphasis, however, glosses over important aspects of AIDS among women, who now make up a growing proportion of new AIDS cases. Among these are the principal routes of infection, gender roles, and issues related to pregnancy.

Although homosexual behavior has played a prominent role in the spread of HIV among males, the predominant routes of infection for women are through intercourse with infected men and IV drug use. Just over half (51%) the women with AIDS in the United States were infected through drug use, and another 30% were infected through intercourse with infected men. Of particular concern is the fact that the proportion of women contracting HIV through infected partners has been increasing annually since the inception of the AIDS epidemic (Ellerbrock, Bush, Chamberland, & Oxtoby, 1991). The vast majority of women worldwide contract HIV through heterosexual contact ("Gloomy figures from WHO," 1991; Mann et al., 1988). Data such as these argue that prevention efforts aimed at women must emphasize the ways in which women can protect themselves from infection in heterosexual encounters and alter IV drug use behavior.

Efforts to prevent the sexual transmission of HIV to women are complicated by gender roles and power inequities in heterosexual relationships (Kaplan, 1987; Leonardo & Chrisler, in press). Women have been traditionally socialized to take a submissive role in intimate relationships and to defer to their male sexual partners.

Such socialization mitigates against women taking a more assertive role in sexual encounters by questioning a partner about past sexual encounters, insisting that he use a condom, or resisting his advances if he refuses. In some cases, women who have insisted on the use of a condom have been subjected to verbal and physical abuse by their physically stronger male partners (Cochran & Mays, 1989).

An area of particular concern relates to pregnancy and the possibility of infecting an unborn child. Most women with AIDS are of reproductive age, and more than 80% of all AIDS cases in children derived from perinatal transmission. An HIV-infected mother is estimated to have a 30% chance of passing the virus on to the fetus (Gwinn et al., 1991). The majority of infants born infected with HIV live less than three years and die of opportunistic infections (Grossman, 1989). The facts of perinatal transmission raise troubling ethical questions concerning reproductive freedom and responsibility. Does a woman who is HIV positive have the right to choose to become pregnant? If she does become pregnant, should the pregnancy be terminated or allowed to continue to term, despite the odds that the child will be infected? As yet, there are no agreed upon answers to these questions, nor are there likely to be in the foreseeable future (Murphy, 1989). However, they highlight some of the unique issues related to women and AIDS.

COPING WITH AIDS

In addition to their concern with prevention, health psychologists are concerned with the tremendous psychosocial impact of AIDS. Perhaps no other disease has raised so many urgent questions about coping with life-threatening illness or the ways in which people respond to individuals with disease. The next sections explore some of the critical issues involved in how persons with AIDS cope with their condition, as well as society's response to AIDS.

Living with AIDS

As noted earlier, AIDS is a disease with a long incubation period. In addition, the destruction of the immune system and resulting opportunistic infections associated with AIDS are progressive in nature, occurring over a period of months and often years. Therefore, individuals with AIDS or at risk for developing AIDS must deal with this disease intensively over a period ranging from a few months to several years.

Being HIV positive. Often the first indication that a person will eventually develop AIDS is a positive test for HIV. Analysis of blood samples for the antibodies produced in response to HIV allows a fairly accurate determination of whether a person has been exposed to HIV (see Box 12.2). HIV testing does not detect the actual virus in the blood, but the presence of HIV antibodies is considered a reliable indicator that HIV is present (Institute of Medicine, 1986). What proportion of HIV-positive individuals will eventually develop AIDS is still not known but is almost certain to be high.

BOX 12.2 HIV Testing: Its Uses and Abuses

One of the major breakthroughs in the fight against AIDS has been the development of tests for HIV infection. Because years generally pass between initial infection and the development of AIDS symptoms, early detection of HIV infection is important for preventing its spread, medically monitoring infected individuals, and providing available treatment. The development of tests for HIV infection, however, has also spawned considerable public debate, leading some to support mandatory testing; others argue against testing for fear of stigma and discrimination against those who test positive (Coates et al., 1988; Field, 1990; Institute of Medicine, 1986).

What are the key issues here? HIV testing has been critical in helping to slow the number of new infections. Among the first indications that HIV is a blood-borne virus was the development of AIDS among transfusion patients, raising fears about the possible rapid spread of HIV through the blood supply. The development of tests for HIV antibodies in 1984 made possible the comprehensive screening of blood and blood products used in transfusions—which has virtually eliminated the risk of infection (Institute of Medicine, 1986). HIV testing has also been instrumental in reducing the rate of infection via sexual transmission and IV drug use. Studies of the effects of knowledge of HIV status have found greater reductions of high-risk behavior, such as unprotected anal intercourse and needle-sharing, among individuals who learn that they are seropositive than among those who find out they are seronegative or who elect not to learn the results of the testing (Coates et al., 1988).

Yet HIV testing raises troubling questions. Tests for HIV are considered reliable, but they are not 100% accurate. Ensuring that HIV antibodies will be detected in infected samples requires that the tests be as sensitive as possible. However, the more sensitive a test, the greater the likelihood of false positives. Because of this

problem, the most common procedure is first to test blood using the ELISA method, which is inexpensive and highly sensitive, but also produces false positives, and then to confirm positive test results using the more accurate, but expensive, Western blot test. Even with these safeguards, however, the possibility of falsely labeling someone as HIV positive still exists.

HIV tests can also produce a false sense of security. A negative result of an HIV test is not necessarily a clean bill of health. Antibodies for HIV do not appear immediately after infection, but may take several months to develop to a detectable level. In general, most infected persons will have developed antibodies within six months of infection, but tests done earlier may be negative. In the meantime, the person is capable of spreading the virus to others through sexual or blood contact.

Confidentiality is another major issue. Because of the psychosocial consequences of a positive HIV result and because HIV is most often spread through stigmatized and sometimes illegal behavior, considerable concern has arisen over who should have access to the results and the potential consequences for those who test positive. AIDS activists and others have strongly argued that results should be kept completely confidential, with only the person involved having access. One concern is that a potential lack of confidentiality or even the suspicion of it will discourage those who may be infected from being tested. Others argue that reporting of HIV infections to medical authorities is essential for tracking the epidemic and for identifying others who may have been infected by the person, so that they can be tested and receive treatment when appropriate.

Considerations like these demonstrate that HIV testing can easily be abused and have led some experts to argue against mandatory and in favor of voluntary testing that includes strong guarantees of confidentiality (Institute of Medicine, 1986).

The deadly nature of AIDS, along with the uncertainty associated with being HIV positive, produce considerable psychological strain. Recent studies have found that, after learning of their status, HIV-positive individuals show significant increases in anxiety, depression, and mood disturbance, which may persist for several weeks

(Chuan, Devins, Hunsley, & Gill, 1989; McKusick, 1988; O'Hearn et al., 1990). Interestingly, this distress may be greatest for those who have no symptoms of AIDS. One study, for example, found that men who were asymptomatic but HIV positive reported greater death anxiety, less optimism, and greater overall psychological distress than did HIV-positive men who had AIDS symptoms (Kurdek & Siesky, 1990). The reason for this appears to be the greater strain produced by the uncertainty of being HIV positive but not having symptoms and not knowing when or if those symptoms will appear.

The amount of distress experienced on notification of HIV status also depends on the person's coping style and perceived social support. Overall, more negative psychological functioning for both symptomatic and asymptomatic individuals is associated with frequent use of coping strategies based on avoidance and dissatisfaction with perceived social support (Kurdek & Siesky, 1990). Being notified of HIV-positive status may also lead to a decline in perceived social support (Friedman, Antoni, Ironson, Laperrier, & Schneiderman, 1991). Data such as these underline the need for effective counseling programs for individuals who are tested for HIV, particularly those who test positive.

Dealing with ARC and AIDS. After symptoms begin, the person is faced with new challenges. Now the likelihood of developing full-blown AIDS is much higher, and the person is faced with the problems attendant in dealing with the disease itself. As mentioned in Chapter 10, individuals with chronic or life-threatening illnesses are faced with adaptive tasks including those related to the illness itself and to psychosocial aspects of the illness. These tasks are well illustrated in the case of persons with ARC and AIDS.

As we have seen, the impact of AIDS on the body is devastating. Over time the person must deal with increasingly serious symptoms and opportunistic infections that often go through unpredictable cycles of flare-up and remission. As one person with AIDS stated:

> Probably the hardest thing is not knowing when you're well what's going to happen tomorrow because when you're well all you're thinking about is, "What am I going to get? What's the next infection I'm going to have to put up with?" Of course, when you're sick it's like, "Well, I hope they can make me well. I wonder if they can or not" (quoted in Weitz, 1989, p. 275).

In addition, AIDS has serious effects on the nervous system, producing symptoms ranging from mild memory loss to severe dementia (Janssen, 1989). Individuals who would normally be in the prime of life are likely to find these physical and mental symptoms particularly difficult to handle.

Not surprisingly, AIDS is often accompanied by considerable psychological distress and, for some, psychopathology. Studies have found that a high percentage of persons with AIDS show significant mood disturbances, including depression, and suffer from feelings of guilt and thoughts about suicide (Catalan, 1988). Examination of suicide rates in New York City found that men with AIDS were 36 times more likely to commit suicide than were other men of the same age (Marzuk et al., 1988). The extent of psychological distress among persons with AIDS appears to be related in part to feelings of self-blame for contracting the disease. In a recent study, Jeffrey Moulton and his colleagues (Moulton, Sweet, Temoshok, & Mandel, 1987) found that attributing the cause of the disease to oneself was associated with greater psychological distress among persons with AIDS than was attributing it to factors outside the self.

These difficulties are compounded by the social stigma attached to AIDS and to the behaviors by which it is transmitted. Despite more open attitudes toward sexuality in many countries, homosexuality is still stigmatized and widely considered deviant (Herek, 1989). Further, IV drug use is illegal in most places. For some, a diagnosis of AIDS results in the exposure of a life-style that previously had been hidden from family members and acquaintances (Morin & Batchelor, 1984). Under these circumstances, the person may be faced with embarrassing questions or recriminations about life-style while simultaneously attempting to cope with debilitating illness. Moreover, because of the strong association of AIDS with homosexuality and IV drug use, individuals who were infected through blood transfusions or heterosexual contact may be the subject of suspicion and innuendo concerning sexual orientation or drug usage. Beyond these attitudes, persons with AIDS have also been subjected to outright discrimination. Numerous cases have been reported in which persons with AIDS have been dismissed from their jobs, put out of their homes, or banned from school because of their disease (Bayer & Gostin, 1990; Kirp, 1988).

As discussed in Chapter 10, a person's relationships with others, particularly relationships that provide support during the illness, can be a key factor in coping with any serious illness. In the case of AIDS, the stigma associated with the disease and people's concern about contracting it may erect significant barriers to effective support. Not only are persons with AIDS subjected to discrimination, but recent studies of health care workers' attitudes toward patients with HIV have documented considerable fear of HIV, with some providers simply refusing to treat patients who are HIV positive (Gerbert, Maguire, Badner, Altman & Stone, 1988). Family members may reject the person because of attitudes toward homosexuality and the stigma associated with AIDS (McDonell, Abell, & Miller, 1991). Thus persons with AIDS who need support the most may be the least likely to get it (Newton, Temoshok, Haviland, & O'Leary, 1991). One response to problems such as these has been the development of organizations such as the San Francisco AIDS Foundation and Gay Men's Health Crisis to provide services and support for persons with AIDS (Shilts, 1987).

AIDS and bereavement. Because of its extremely high mortality, bereavement is a major part of dealing with AIDS. As noted in Chapter 11, bereavement commonly exacts a heavy emotional toll; when dealing with AIDS that toll is likely to be compounded by several factors unique to this disease (Lennon, Martin, & Dean, 1990). For one thing, most of those who have contracted AIDS have been in what is usually considered to be the prime of life, a time when death is not expected and is likely to be considered tragic. As one 39-year-old person with AIDS stated:

> I've had the shedding of contemporaries that I would not have expected to experi-
> ence until I was 65 or 70. . . . It would have been difficult to imagine anything as
> far-fetched as what has happened. Where totally healthy, beautiful 30-year-old peo-
> ple are reduced to the shivering weightlessness of 90-year-old men in 7 months
> (quoted in Lennon et al., 1990, p. 478).

Because AIDS has been concentrated among certain groups, members of these groups are likely to experience multiple bereavements from AIDS. In turn, the experience of multiple bereavements has been found to increase symptoms of psychological distress significantly (Martin, 1988). This psychological distress is likely to be exacerbated further by the stigma associated with the disease and the fact that in many cases the bereaved are themselves at risk for AIDS and may, in fact, have already developed symptoms (Lennon et al., 1990).

Research on AIDS-related bereavement indicates that grief reactions follow similar patterns to other bereavement, including symptoms such as yearning to have the person back, crying, preoccupation with the deceased, and, in some cases, denial that the death has occurred. These reactions appear to be particularly strong when the bereaved has been involved in caring for the deceased. Here as well, social support appears to be critical. In a sample of bereaved gay men, Mary Clare Lennon and her colleagues (Lennon et al., 1990) found that, although the sheer availability of support did not appear to make a difference, those who perceived that they had adequate instrumental and emotional support experienced less intense grief reactions than did those who perceived their support to be inadequate. Data such as these reinforce the critical need to provide appropriate social support for those affected by the AIDS epidemic.

Psychosocial interventions. AIDS clearly raises many challenges for coping. What interventions can be used to help people deal with these? Several approaches have been used to address the challenges at different stages in the person's encounter with AIDS (Grant & Anns, 1988). For those first receiving the results of HIV antibody testing, crisis intervention may be necessary to help them deal with the emotional impact of a positive test result. As a part of this intervention, counselors help the person deal with the anxiety and fear associated with what is often viewed as tantamount to a death sentence. In addition, counselors help the person work through issues relating to sexuality and intimacy and the stigma associated with the disease (McKusick, 1988). Organized support groups can also be used. Such groups allow persons with AIDS the opportunity to discuss their concerns with others in similar circumstances and to hear from other HIV-positive individuals who have worked through their own issues. Through this sharing, persons with AIDS find that they are not alone in their experiences and concerns, which can help in relieving feelings of anxiety and hope-lessness (DiPasquale, 1990). Finally, long-term counseling may be necessary to help

Doonesbury

BY GARRY TRUDEAU

Despite strong evidence to the contrary, many people still act as though HIV can be spread through casual contact.

Note. Doonesbury © 1989 G. B. Trudeau. Reprinted with permission of Universal Press Syndicate. All rights reserved.

the person cope with the various crises that accompany AIDS and to deal with issues raised by impending death.

AIDS Phobia

One of the most troubling aspects of the AIDS epidemic has been the accompanying epidemic of fear. As has been noted throughout our discussion, persons with AIDS and even those who are HIV positive but not symptomatic have been subjected to considerable hostility and discrimination. What accounts for these attitudes?

One key factor is the nature of AIDS as a disease. AIDS is a deadly disease that is also transmissible. As a deadly disease, AIDS confronts people with the reality of death and, therefore, raises deep-seated anxieties (Herek & Glunt, 1988). The fact that AIDS is transmissible significantly compounds this anxiety. Transmissibility raises in people's minds the possibility of "catching" the disease from an infected person. Although strong evidence proves that HIV is not transmitted through casual contact, recent research evidence shows that people categorize AIDS as contagious and associate contagion primarily with casual contact (Bishop, 1991b; Bishop, Alva, Cantu, & Rittiman, 1991). As noted in Box 12.3, considerable difficulties are involved in convincing people that AIDS is not transmitted through casual contact.

Fears about AIDS have probably been exacerbated by the extensive media coverage of the epidemic. The continuing barrage of news stories about AIDS as well as the often voiced skepticism about the reliability of reassurance from health experts have most likely had the cumulative effect of increasing people's concerns. Research in social cognition has indicated that people often make judgments of the frequency of events by the ease with which they come to mind. For example, studies of perceptions of the

BOX 12.3 **Why Is It So Difficult to Convince People That AIDS Is Not Transmitted Through Casual Contact?**

One of the striking aspects of the efforts to educate people about how HIV is and is not spread is the difficulty of convincing people that HIV is not spread through casual contact. Although the available evidence argues strongly against the transmission of HIV through casual contact, many people seem to act as if HIV could be transmitted through the air or by simply being near someone with HIV. Such concerns are attested to by the many well-publicized instances in which persons with AIDS have been shunned or children infected with HIV have been barred from school (Conrad, 1986). In addition, data from the National Health Interview Survey revealed that a substantial percentage of respondents harbored suspicions that HIV could be passed through casual contact. For example, 24% of the respondents believed that it was somewhat or very possible for a person to catch AIDS from eating in a restaurant where the cook had HIV, and 20% believed that it was possible to get AIDS by using public toilets. But only 18% said it was definitely not possible to get AIDS by sharing plates, forks, or glasses with someone with AIDS, and only 17% believed it was not possible to get AIDS by being coughed or sneezed on by someone with AIDS (Dawson, 1990). These findings seem remarkable in light of the intense education efforts mounted to inform people about AIDS and HIV.

Although such results, to some extent, may reflect some people's lack of authoritative information on AIDS and HIV, research on cognition and lay illness representations suggests reasons why people may find accepting the actual facts about HIV transmission difficult.

First, convincing people that something does not exist or cannot happen is not easy. No evidence to date indicates that anyone has contracted HIV through casual

contact. However, the fact that it has not happened yet does not logically rule out the possibility that it could happen. Thus no one can say with absolute certainty that cases of transmission through casual contact will not occur in the future. Experts are careful to couch their conclusions in such terms as "highly unlikely" or "virtual impossibility." However, such hedging does not rule out the possibility and may serve to exacerbate people's fears.

Another important factor is how people think about diseases, particularly contagious diseases. As seen in Chapter 8, people interpret symptoms and other illness information through the use of cognitive prototypes that embody their understanding of different diseases (Bishop, 1991b). In addition, people cognitively organize disease information into categories according to features such as whether the disease is contagious or life threatening, and appear to view certain diseases as prototypical of a particular category. For example, in one study (Bishop, 1991a) subjects defined contagious disease as a disease that is passed from one person to another, most often by casual contact, and saw diseases like a cold, the flu, or chicken pox as prototypical contagious diseases. Thus people might apply (or misapply) a generic concept of contagious disease to any disease that falls into that category. Since 77% of the subjects named AIDS a contagious disease and rated it as a fairly typical contagious disease, it may well be the case that people are (mis)applying their generic concept of a contagious disease to AIDS. This suggests that convincing people that HIV is not transmitted through casual contact requires overcoming their tendency to identify contagious diseases with casual contact and to view AIDS as a typical contagious disease.

frequency of diseases and other events as causes of death have found strong correlations between how much a person has heard about a disease as well as the number of news stories about it and the number of people believed to die from it. These results have been found even when controlling for the actual number of deaths caused by the disease (Bishop, Madey, Salinas, Massey, & Tudyk, 1992; Slovic, Fischoff, & Lichtenstein, 1982). Thus, although news coverage of the epidemic has been essential for keeping people informed, it has probably also had the undesirable side effect of heightening anxiety. In addition, the probabilistic statements used by health officials to reassure people about risks from AIDS have often been greeted with skepticism, resulting at times in more, rather than less, anxiety (Herek & Glunt, 1988).

Another critical factor is the history of the epidemic itself. AIDS was first diagnosed among male homosexuals, and in the United States and Europe, gay men and IV drug users make up the majority of persons with AIDS. Both of these groups have long been stigmatized, and the association of AIDS with homosexuality and drug usage has led to stigmatizing those afflicted with the disease (Herek & Glunt, 1988). Studies of attitudes toward persons with AIDS have found a strong association between these attitudes and negative feelings about persons with AIDS (Pryor, Reeder, Vinacco, & Kott, 1989).

What can be done to change these attitudes? Dealing with these complex attitudes is likely to require concerted efforts that include both changing individual attitudes and the implementation of enlightened public policy (Herek & Glunt, 1988). With respect to individual attitudes, efforts directed toward reducing irrational fears and stigma surrounding AIDS should address concerns about contracting AIDS and confronting individual prejudices. In addition, public policies that guarantee anonymity of HIV test results and prohibit discrimination against persons with AIDS can help to encourage more rational attitudes toward AIDS and those who live with it.

SUMMARY

Immunity plays an important role in health by defending the body against disease-producing organisms and conditions. Based on the body's ability to detect the difference between the body's normal cells and foreign antigens, as well as body cells that have become abnormal, immunity may be accomplished either through nonspecific or specific mechanisms. In nonspecific immunity, phagocytes seek out and ingest antigens circulating in the blood and other body fluids, whereas natural killer cells attack and destroy cells that are infected or cancerous. In specific immunity, specialized leukocytes, known as B and T cells, seek out and attack specifically targeted antigens either in the blood and other body fluids (humoral immunity, involving B cells) or after they have infected body cells (cell-mediated immunity, involving T cells).

Recent research in psychoneuroimmunology has shown that immunity is significantly influenced by psychosocial factors such as conditioning and stress. Recent studies have demonstrated that immune functioning can be both suppressed and enhanced through conditioning, findings that have potentially significant clinical applications. Further, immunocompetence appears to be influenced significantly by stress. Some studies have shown that stress can lead to a reduction in the number and type of immune system cells available for fighting infection and a reduction in leukocyte responsiveness. In addition, tumors may develop more rapidly under conditions of stress, indicating a reduction in the effectiveness of the immune system in seeking out and destroying cancerous body cells. Conversely, new evidence suggests that immune functioning can be enhanced through social support and stress reduction techniques.

Acquired immunodeficiency syndrome (AIDS) is a condition in which the body loses its ability to fight off infection. This condition is caused by a retrovirus, human immunodeficiency virus (HIV), which attacks the cells of the immune system, in particular, the helper T cells. Since helper T cells are a key link in the immune system's response to antigens, the destruction of these cells significantly reduces the body's ability to fight infection. HIV infection progresses through a series of stages marked by increasingly serious symptoms, including both opportunistic infections and neurological deficits. AIDS-related complex (ARC) is a condition in which the person experiences symptoms such as diarrhea, spiking fevers, fatigue, and night sweats, but has not yet developed the opportunistic infections characteristic of AIDS.

HIV is blood-borne and transmitted through sexual and blood contact. In the Americas and Europe, the most common means of transmission are through homosexual contact and the sharing of needles during IV drug use. In Africa, Asia, and the Caribbean, HIV appears to be spread primarily through heterosexual contact. In all parts of the world, a growing number of children are contracting HIV from their infected mothers through perinatal transmission. Because of the association of AIDS with certain high-risk behaviors such as having multiple sexual partners, anonymous sex, engaging in receptive anal intercourse without the use of a condom, and sharing needles during IV drug use, programs have been developed to encourage safer sexual practices as well as to reduce the risks of HIV transmission through needle-sharing. However, these programs have often met with resistance from religious and community leaders who believe that they implicitly condone homosexual or promiscuous behavior or IV drug use. Overall, prevention programs have produced mixed results.

In addition to its impact on physical health, AIDS also has important psychosocial effects. Many people consider receiving a positive HIV test tantamount to a death sentence and experience considerable psychological strain, including symptoms of anxiety, depression, and mood disturbance. This psychological distress continues with the development of ARC and AIDS, and is compounded by the social stigma associated with AIDS and the behaviors by which it is transmitted. Persons with AIDS are frequently rejected by family and acquaintances and often face outright discrimination. Because of the extremely high mortality rate among AIDS patients, bereavement is a major aspect of dealing with AIDS.

One very troubling aspect of the AIDS epidemic has been people's fearful reactions to AIDS and persons living with it. These attitudes have played a key role in the hostility and discrimination faced by persons with AIDS. Among the factors accounting for these attitudes are the transmissible and deadly nature of HIV, the extensive media coverage of the epidemic, and the association of AIDS with homosexuality and IV drug use. Changing attitudes toward persons with AIDS requires both a concerted effort at changing individual prejudices and enlightened public policy.

KEY TERMS

immunity (293)
antigen (294)
nonspecific immunity (294)
phagocyte (295)
macrophage (295)
monocyte (295)
natural killer (NK) cells (295)
specific immunity (295)
humoral immunity (295)
antibodies (295)

B cells (295)
cell-mediated immunity (296)
T cells (296)
thymus gland (296)
psychoneuroimmunology (298)
immunocompetence (299)
acquired immunodeficiency syndrome (AIDS) (302)
human immunodeficiency virus (HIV) (303)
retrovirus (303)
AIDS-related complex (ARC) (305)

SUGGESTED READINGS

Backer, T. E., Batchelor, W. F., Jones, J. M., & Mays, V. M. (eds.) (1988). Special issue: Psychology and AIDS. *American Psychologist, 43,* 835–987. In this special issue of the *American Psychologist,* several leading researchers discuss psychological issues related to HIV and AIDS.

Davis, J. (1989). *Defending the body: Unraveling the mysteries of immunology.* New York: Atheneum. In this book, science writer Joel Davis discusses recent advances in our understanding of the immune system. Provides a good introduction to immunology for the nonspecialist.

Nichols, E. K. (1989). *Mobilizing against AIDS.* Cambridge: Harvard University Press. In this book, Eve Nichols discusses important aspects of AIDS and its physical, psychological, and social effects.

Shilts, R. (1987). *And the band played on: Politics, people and the AIDS epidemic.* New York: St. Martin's Press. Randy Shilts describes the political, medical, and human side of the AIDS epidemic.

Cancer

With the possible exception of AIDS, no disease has been more feared than cancer. Part of the reason for this is the number of people who develop cancer and die from it. Currently the second leading cause of death in the United States and most industrial countries, cancer claims more than half a million lives each year in the United States and four million worldwide (Davis, Hoel, Fox, & Lopez, 1990; Renneker, 1988). Further, current statistics indicate that in industrialized countries roughly a third of the population will develop cancer during their lifetime (Renneker, 1988). Even more important as a source of fear, however, is the common perception of cancer as an insidious degeneration of the body, leading to a slow painful death (Berman & Wandersman, 1990; Sontag, 1978). Despite the recent strides that have been made in treating and curing cancer, many people still react to a diagnosis of cancer as if it were a death sentence. This chapter reviews what is known about cancer and how it reflects the mind-body relationship, and examines health psychology's contribution to preventing cancer and helping people to cope with it.

MIND AND BODY: THE BIOLOGY AND PSYCHOLOGY OF CANCER

Although cancer afflicts all living organisms and almost certainly has been around since the time of the dinosaurs (Renneker, 1988), a scientific understanding of cancer really developed only in the last few decades. The priority given to cancer research since the early 1970s has led to tremendous strides in understanding the biological mechanisms by which cancer begins and progresses, as well as the ways in which the biology of cancer is intertwined with psychosocial factors.

Biological Aspects of Cancer

What is cancer? Although the term *cancer* is commonly used in the singular, in reality speaking of cancers in the plural would be more appropriate. What is commonly referred to as cancer actually encompasses several hundred different diseases. These diseases differ in terms of how rapidly they progress, where they are located, and their prognosis, but share certain common biological characteristics (Garrett, 1988).

Chief among these characteristics is that cancers (also called neoplasms) involve the uncontrolled growth and abnormal spread of cells. Under normal conditions, body cells reproduce in an orderly fashion and have a specified life span. Further, when they reach a particular point in their life cycle, they stop reproducing. Thus when a person reaches maturity, the number of new cells being reproduced roughly equals the number of cells dying off. Cancer, however, changes all this. Cancerous cells lose the ability to stop reproducing, and continue to multiply beyond what is necessary for the replacement of dying cells. The result is the development of tumors that, if undetected or their growth not halted, can kill the person. Death may follow because of organ failure, as in the case of cancer of the liver or kidney, or the obstruction of vital organs, as can occur with intestinal cancer. In addition, cancer may lead to hemorrhaging or strokes, or can cause profound alteration to bodily functions, rendering the person susceptible to other health problems (Renneker, 1988).

tumor
An abnormal growth of tissue, which may be either benign or malignant.

benign tumor
An abnormal growth that is not cancerous and generally not considered to be threatening to health.

malignant tumor
An abnormal growth that is cancerous and has the capacity to spread to other parts of the body.

metastasis
The process by which malignant tumors spread to distant parts of the body.

Tumors certainly can wreak havoc. However, not all tumors are cancerous. **Benign tumors** are made up of cells that are relatively typical of the tissues from which they originate. Such tumors are usually confined to the area in which they begin to grow and generally develop relatively slowly. Although removing benign tumors is often necessary, such growths are considerably less dangerous than cancerous ones. By contrast, tumors made up of cancer cells are described as **malignant.** Cells in malignant tumors are often different from surrounding cells and tend to reproduce relatively rapidly. Even more important, malignant tumors often grow beyond their original location and invade other body organs, or **metastasize,** spreading cancerous cells through the bloodstream and implanting new cancers throughout the body (Garrett, 1988).

What causes cancer? Certain substances are considered **carcinogenic,** or cancer-causing. In fact, at times almost everything appears carcinogenic even though this is assuredly not the case. But how do carcinogenic substances lead to the development

DUNAGIN'S PEOPLE

The high number of substances known to cause cancer sometimes leads people to believe that everything is carcinogenic.

"AS OF THE SIX O'CLOCK NEWS LAST NIGHT, THAT IS STILL GOOD FOR YOU."

Note. Reprinted with special permission of North American Syndicate.

carcinogen
Any substance capable of converting normal cells into cancerous ones.

DNA (deoxyribonucleic acid)
A large molecule, found primarily in cell nuclei, which carries the cell's genetic information and controls cell functioning.

of cancer? The answer to this is still not completely understood, but available evidence indicates that carcinogens cause mutations or genetic "mistakes" that alter cell functioning and are then passed on when cells reproduce.

In particular, the key to understanding the development of cancer appears to reside in the role of **DNA (deoxyribonucleic acid)** in cell reproduction and growth (I. Weinstein, 1988). DNA, often called the master molecule of life, contains the genetic codes that direct cell development and growth. Through this control, DNA determines the characteristics of tissues and organs as well as the organism as a whole. Should the DNA in a cell be altered in some way, the way the cell functions may dramatically change. Further, alterations in a cell's DNA, if left uncorrected, are passed on to daughter cells when the cell divides.

Carcinogens lead to cancer when they produce alterations in cell's DNA. These alterations may include the insertion or deletion of material into the DNA, or transposition of the amino acids that make up the DNA molecule. For example, ultraviolet light can cause a chemical reaction in cells that alters both the components and the shape of the DNA molecule (Garrett, 1988). In most cases, alterations such as these are detected by the cell and repaired before they can do any damage, or are lethal to the cell and kill it before it has a chance to reproduce. However, some alterations go undetected and provide the basis for the development of cancer.

oncogenes
Genes that control cell growth and reproduction and may play a pivotal role in the development of cancer.

One type of alteration that seems to be particularly important are those that affect areas of the DNA known as **oncogenes.** Oncogenes code for growth factors and help promote or retard the growth of cells as well as individuals. Thus oncogenes control when cells reproduce and when a person goes into a growth spurt, such as during infancy or adolescence. One leading theory of cancer development is that carcinogens and some viruses instigate an alteration of key oncogenes, causing uncontrolled cell reproduction and growth and eventually cancer (I. Weinstein, 1988).

The alteration of DNA is just the beginning of cancer. After this alteration has occurred, the cells involved may or may not develop into a cancerous tumor. A key role in this is played by *tumor promoters,* which are substances that are not carcinogens themselves, but which hasten the development of cancer after the DNA damage caused by carcinogens. Exposure of altered cells to tumor promoters transforms benign, slow-developing tumors into malignant ones (I. Weinstein, 1988). Figure 13.1 illustrates the progression through which normal cells become malignant tumors.

One might think that after cancer gets started, the body is defenseless against it. In fact, nothing could be further from the truth. As seen in Chapter 12, the immune system actively defends the body against disease by searching out cells that are foreign or infected and destroying them. Cancer cells characteristically have chemical markers on their surface identifying them as being foreign or "not self." As part of what is referred to as its *immunosurveillance* function, the immune system fights against the development of cancer by destroying cancerous cells before they have a chance to develop into malignant tumors. The natural killer (NK) cells appear to play a key role in this (Bovbjerg, 1991; Clark, 1988).

Psychological Factors in Cancer

So far we have focused exclusively on the biological aspects of cancer. How do psychological factors fit in? Although psychological factors have long been suspected of being important in the development of cancer, only recently has empirical evidence been found for such a link. Much of the evidence is still somewhat indirect. However, recent studies have provided evidence for several ways in which psychological factors may influence the development and prognosis of cancer.

Personality. The idea that cancer is related to personality goes back at least to the Greek physician Galen, who taught that melancholy women were much more likely to develop breast cancer than were sanguine women (Renneker, 1988). Similar ideas have been put forward more recently by researchers such as Lawrence LeShan (1977), who argued that cancer was associated with feelings of rejection, suppression of negative emotions, and feelings of helplessness in the face of stressful life events. However, despite arguments by researchers and theorists supporting the role of personality in cancer (cf. Fox, 1988), solid evidence has been hard to compile, in part because of the methodological difficulties of demonstrating such a link. A key problem

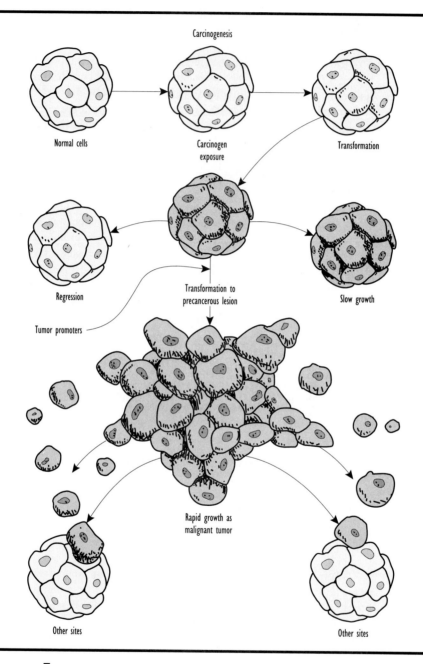

FIGURE 13.1 *The process of carcinogenesis.*

Note. Adapted from "The biology of cancer" by L. Garrett, 1988 (p. 44), in *Understanding cancer* (3d ed.) by M. Renneker, Palo Alto, CA: Bull Publishing Co.

here is that cancer develops over many years and often decades. Determining whether the personality traits measured preceded the cancer or came about because of it is not possible unless studies are done longitudinally over a long period. Further, as seen in Chapter 2, a correlation between personality and cancer indicates only that there is a statistical relationship and does not prove causality.

Recent longitudinal studies, however, have circumvented at least some of these difficulties by relating the incidence of cancer to personality variables measured well before disease onset. For example, John Shaffer and his colleagues (Shaffer, Duszynski, & Thomas, 1982; Shaffer, Graves, Swank, & Pearson, 1987) related the incidence of cancer among male physicians to personality measures taken while they were in medical school some 30 years earlier. Their findings provide evidence that cancer incidence is related both to family relationships and to personality variables. In particular, men who later developed cancer tended to have poorer relationships with their families, especially their fathers (Shaffer et al., 1982). In addition, men who were "loners" while young as well as those who suppressed their emotions behind a bland exterior tended to have high rates of cancer later in life. Yet men who were high in emotional expressiveness had relatively low rates (Shaffer et al., 1987). Another study (Dattore, Shontz, & Coyne, 1980) using scores on the Minnesota Multiphasic Personality Inventory (MMPI) to predict the occurrence of cancer found that increased incidence of cancer was related to emotional suppression and low levels of depression. The relationship of depression to cancer, however, is somewhat questionable, since other studies have found cancer to be related to higher levels of depression, while still others have found no relationship at all (Fox, 1988).

To summarize the relationship between personality and cancer, Lydia Temoshok and her coworkers (Temoshok, 1987; Temoshok et al., 1985) have proposed the concept of the Type C or cancer-prone personality, which is conceptualized as the polar opposite of the Type A personality (see Chapter 14). According to this formulation, the person most likely to get cancer is passive, cooperative, suppresses negative emotions, and has a high potential for learned helplessness. Evidence relating personality to the prognosis of cancer is discussed in Box 13.1.

Stress. Researchers have also been interested in the possibility that cancer development and growth may be related to stress from life events. Since the early part of this century, many research studies have attempted to establish such a link in both humans and animals. However, most of these studies have used retrospective designs. Studies comparing cancer patients with non-cancer controls have found that cancer patients report significantly more negative life events such as loss of loved ones, marital problems, and parental separation than do controls (Sklar & Anisman, 1981). In addition, patients who experienced a recurrence of cancer after surgery reported having had more difficulties in adjusting to the disease and its treatment than those not having a relapse (Rogentine et al., 1979).

Although the results of retrospective studies can be considered only suggestive, they have generally been confirmed by studies using a prospective design. For example, one study found that patients who developed lung cancer were more likely to have experienced job instability and the loss of a significant relationship in the

BOX 13.1 **Cancer and a Fighting Spirit**

As we have seen, evidence is growing that the development of cancer is related to personality factors, in particular the so-called Type C personality. But what about the prognosis of cancer after it has been diagnosed? Do the chances of recovery differ according to personality? A recent longitudinal study of cancer patients indicates that the answer may be yes.

In a ten-year investigation of the role of personality in cancer prognosis, K. W. Pettingale and his coworkers (Greer, Morris, & Pettingale, 1979; Pettingale, 1984; Pettingale, Philalithis, Tee, & Greer, 1981) interviewed breast cancer patients three months after surgery for removal of the cancer and classified them according to their response to their cancer diagnosis. Ten of the 57 patients exhibited denial in that they downplayed the seriousness of their condition and showed little or no emotional response to the cancer. Another 32 patients showed what the researchers termed stoic acceptance. These patients acknowledged the seriousness of the cancer and indicated that it was something they would just have to live with. Five of the patients expressed strong feelings of helplessness and hopelessness in the face of the cancer. Finally, ten patients expressed a highly optimistic attitude about their cancer, tended to ask for information and vowed to do everything in their power to "conquer" their disease, an attitude the authors termed a "fighting spirit."

Follow-up of the patients at both five and ten years showed that their initial response to their cancer was strongly related to the course of the disease. Among those who showed a stoic acceptance 10 (31%) had died at the five-year follow-up and 24 (75%) had died by ten years. Similarly, by five years four of the five patients exhibiting helplessness were dead. By comparison, for those with a fighting spirit only one (10%) had died at five years and three (30%) by ten years. Patients who responded with denial had intermediate death rates; one (10%) had died by five years and five (50%) by ten.

Although these results are promising, they should be interpreted cautiously. First, the number of patients is small. Before accepting the proposition that a fighting spirit does indeed improve prognosis, the study should be replicated with a larger number of patients. Second, the observed relationship is correlational and may be due to some third factor. Third, the patients were classified through clinical interviews that may not be reliable. Finally, not all studies have found an association between psychosocial factors and cancer prognosis (cf. Cassileth, Lusk, Miller, Brown, & Miller, 1985). Despite these shortcomings, the results are suggestive and point to important avenues for further investigation.

previous five years than was the case for patients with benign lung tumors (Horne & Picard, 1979). More recently, a series of studies in Yugoslavia and Germany followed nearly 4,000 individuals for ten years, examining personality, stress, and potential life-style factors in the development of cancer and heart disease. Overall, death from both diseases was significantly related to the amount of stress reported at the beginning of the study. Further, the effects of stress depended on personality type. Individuals fitting the description of the Type C personality and experiencing high stress levels showed high deaths from cancer. But those more resembling the Type A personality were most likely to die of cardiovascular disease. Statistical analysis indicated that those reporting high levels of stress had a 40% higher death rate from these diseases than did those who were less stressed (Eysenck, 1988).

Even though these data appear to present a strong case for the role of stress in cancer, even prospective studies cannot be considered conclusive evidence. As noted earlier, cancer is a disease that generally develops over several years; thus even when stress measures are taken years before the appearance of clinical symptoms, the cancer may have actually predated the stress. Further, the physiological changes associated with cancer can affect mental and behavioral processes before the detection of the cancer, which may result in increased stress (Sklar & Anisman, 1981).

One way around some of these difficulties is through the use of animal models. For example, the impact of stress on tumor development can be experimentally determined by implanting cancer cells in rats or other animals, and then exposing some animals to stress while others are not stressed. Studies using this type of paradigm have generally confirmed the role of stress in cancer growth and development, but have also noted potential caveats. For one thing, not all stressors have the same effects. In line with human studies showing that uncontrollable events are generally more stressful than controllable ones, one study found that rats exposed to inescapable electrical shock were more likely to develop cancer tumors than were those either exposed to escapable shock or no shock at all (Visintainer, Volpicelli, & Seligman, 1982).

The effects of stress may also differ depending on the type of tumor involved. One puzzling finding is that whereas stress often enhances tumor development, in some cases it leads to reduced tumor growth (Sklar & Anisman, 1981; Justice, 1985). Some of these differences may derive from methodological differences between studies. However, they are also likely related to the types of tumors involved. In general, tumors can be classified into those that are caused by viruses and those that are caused by other carcinogenic processes. Alan Justice (1985) notes that viral and nonviral tumors seem to respond differently to stress. In particular, he argues that the growth of viral tumors is enhanced during the application of stress, but then slows after the stress is removed. In nonviral tumors, which make up the bulk of those affecting humans, tumor growth tends to be slowed during the actual application of stress but then to increase after the stress is removed. These relationships are shown in Figure 13.2. This argues that the effects of stress on cancer depend on both the timing of the stressor and the type of tumor involved. This raises the intriguing possibility that whereas stress may have the negative effect of enhancing tumor growth in some cases, in other cases it may actually be beneficial in protecting against cancer. However, this conclusion is tentative, still open to debate, and based on animal studies, which may or may not generalize to humans.

Psychoimmunity. The burning question in all the studies linking psychosocial factors to cancer growth and development relates to the mechanism by which this occurs. One strong possibility concerns the impact of personality and stress on the immune system. As noted earlier, the immune system is actively involved in seeking out and destroying cancer cells before they can develop into tumors. Also, as seen in the discussion of psychoneuroimmunology in Chapter 12, the functioning of the immune system is significantly influenced by psychological stressors and how people deal with them. Thus psychological stress probably influences the development of

FIGURE 13.2
The hypothesized effects of stress on different types of tumors.

Note. Arrows indicate increase or decrease in tumor growth. Rebound refers to the period after the stressor is terminated. From "Review of the effects of stress on cancer in laboratory animals: Importance of time of stress application and type of tumor" by A. Justice, 1985, *Psychological Bulletin, 98,* p. 110.

cancer by suppressing the immune system's ability to guard against cancer cells (Bovbjerg, 1991; O'Leary, 1990).

Recent evidence suggests that two psychoimmune processes are particularly important. One key process relates to what is known as DNA repair. As we noted earlier, DNA damage is critical in the initiation of cancer. However, in most cases, DNA damage is found and corrected before it leads to cancer. Recent studies indicate that this process of DNA repair may be significantly influenced by psychosocial factors. For example, in one study, Ronald Glaser and his coworkers (Glaser, Thorn, Tarr, Kiecolt-Glaser, & D'Ambrosio, 1985) exposed rats to a carcinogen and then subjected half of them to stress through rotation on a turntable. At the conclusion of the experiment, they found that, compared to unstressed rats, stressed rats had lower levels of methyltransferase, a DNA repair enzyme that is produced in response to carcinogen damage. Lower levels of this enzyme can be expected to lead to reduced DNA repair. Similar results have been obtained in humans. In another study (Kiecolt-Glaser, Stephens, Lipetz, Speicher, & Glaser, 1985), blood samples from highly distressed psychiatric patients showed less DNA repair in response to irradiation damage than did samples taken from less distressed patients or non-patient blood donors.

Psychological stress also appears to play a significant role in altering the effectiveness of natural killer (NK) cells. NK cells seek out and destroy cancer cells before they can develop into tumors; a reduction in their effectiveness makes a person more susceptible to tumor development. In a series of studies, Sandra Levy and her coworkers (Levy, Herberman, Lippman, & d'Angelo, 1987; Levy, Herberman, Maluish, Schlien, & Lippman, 1985; Levy, Lee, Bagley, & Lippman, 1988) found that psychosocial variables such as feelings of distress, perceived social support, fatigue, and feelings of joy were related to NK cell activity, which in turn was related to cancer development. A study by Steven Locke and his colleagues (Locke et al., 1984) found significantly reduced in vitro NK cell responsiveness in blood samples taken from subjects who reported both high levels of stress and numerous psychiatric symptoms. The presence of psychiatric symptoms suggests that the subjects not only experienced high stress but also had difficulty dealing with it. NK cell activity was highest for subjects who reported high stress but few psychiatric symptoms, suggesting that stress only suppresses NK cell activity when the person does not deal with it effectively.

Since these studies are all correlational, experimental confirmation is needed before firm conclusions can be drawn. Such studies would be clearly unethical with humans, but animal experiments have provided supportive evidence. For example, experiments with rats have shown that experimental stresses such as rotation lead to a substantial reduction in blood leukocytes (of which NK cells are one variety) and a significant increase in certain types of tumor growth (Riley, 1981).

LIFE-STYLE AND CANCER

Cancer has often been called, and rightly so, a life-style disease. Current evidence indicates that 75% to 80% of all cancers are caused by modifiable life-style factors and are thus preventable (Doll & Peto, 1981). As specialists in health-related behavior, health psychologists are in a unique position to contribute to the control of cancer. The next sections consider some of the major life-style factors that are associated with cancer, as well as interventions for their modification.

Tobacco Use

The use of tobacco is one of the key life-style factors in cancer. According to current estimates, tobacco use is directly or indirectly implicated in more than 390,000 deaths in the United States alone (Centers for Disease Control, 1989b). The annual death toll from tobacco is estimated to be 2.5 million worldwide (Masironi & Rothwell, 1988). Tobacco use is responsible for 30% of all cancer deaths (including 75% to 80% of those from lung cancer), 30% of all deaths from heart disease, as well as thousands of deaths from chronic bronchitis, emphysema, asthma, and chronic obstructive pulmonary disease. Little wonder that it was described by the U.S. Surgeon General as "the largest single preventable cause of illness and premature death in the United States" (U.S. Department of Health, Education and Welfare, 1979).

Smoking and cancer. The smoke that smokers inhale contains several chemicals known to be carcinogenic and otherwise detrimental to health. Chief among these are nicotine, which is largely responsible for the addictive nature of smoking, tar, and carbon monoxide. Tar, in particular, is known to be a powerful carcinogen and has a strong effect on the initiation and promotion of cancer. The major site for this cancer is the lungs. Every year more than 135,000 Americans die of lung cancer, which accounts for 25% of all American cancer deaths.

Epidemiological studies show that the likelihood of developing lung cancer increases dramatically with smoking. A person who smokes one pack of cigarettes a day is ten times more likely to die of lung cancer than is a nonsmoker. For individuals who smoke two or more packs per day, the risk is 25 times as great (American Cancer Society, 1989).

Although it is most prominently associated with lung cancer, in fact, smoking is related to many different cancers. Individuals who smoke are seven times as likely to develop cancer of the mouth, more than twice as likely to develop cancer of the bladder or pancreas, and significantly more likely to develop other cancers, such as leukemias and lymphomas (Doll & Peto, 1981). In addition, studies have shown that nonsmokers who live with smokers are significantly more likely to develop cancers of all types than are those not exposed to "passive smoking" (Garfinkel, Auerbach, & Joubert, 1985; Sandler, Everson, Wilcox, & Browder, 1985). Even the use of smokeless tobacco has been found to increase the risk of cancer, as Box 13.2 explains.

Beginning smoking. Most smokers acquire their habit at a young age. Surveys among middle school and high school students indicate that the modal age for beginning smoking is 12 to 13 years (McAlister, Perry, & Maccoby, 1979). An estimated 80% to 90% of American young people admit to having experimented with smoking, and more than 15% of adolescents 12 to 18 years old smoke regularly (Centers for Disease Control, 1989a; Leventhal & Cleary, 1980). This early smoking is, in turn, related to smoking later in life. One study found that among those who smoked regularly in adolescence, more than 70% went on to become regular adult smokers. Even those who only experimented with smoking were twice as likely to become adult smokers as those who did not (Chassin, Presson, Sherman, & Edwards, 1990).

What leads to the development of a smoking habit? Current evidence suggests that becoming a smoker is a gradual process, involving several stages (Leventhal & Cleary, 1980). Before trying their first cigarette, future smokers go through a stage of *preparation,* in which the attitudinal foundation is laid for smoking. Much of this preparation includes smoking models. Young people who start smoking are likely to have at least one parent who smokes, as well as friends who smoke. In addition, young people who begin smoking are likely to have a positive attitude toward smoking and a positive image of smokers, be less academically oriented, have a relatively low sense of self-esteem, and have an external locus of control (Ary & Biglan, 1988; Burton, Sussman, Hansen, Johnson, & Flay, 1989; Chassin, Presson, Sherman, Corty, & Olshavsky, 1981; Clarke, MacPherson, & Holmes, 1982; Leventhal & Cleary, 1980).

In trying the first cigarette, the person enters the *initiation* stage. Experimentation with smoking is greatly influenced by social factors, in particular, peer pressure. Studies of adolescent smoking have found that the majority of smoking occurs in the presence of others, most often peers. Interestingly, many of these cigarettes are smoked at home, suggesting that parents at least implicitly condone the young person's smoking (Biglan, McConnell, Severson, Bavry, & Ary, 1984). The first few cigarettes appear to be particularly crucial in developing the smoking habit in that young people who smoke as few as four cigarettes are much more likely to become adult smokers than those who experimented with three or fewer (Leventhal & Cleary, 1980).

After trying the first few cigarettes, the person enters the stage of *becoming* a smoker. This stage, which typically lasts from one to two years, is characterized by a gradual increase in cigarette consumption as the person becomes more and more hooked on cigarettes. As with the first two stages, a key factor in transforming the person from an experimenter with cigarettes to a regular smoker is peer pressure. In a longitudinal study of adolescent smoking, David Ary and Anthony Biglan (1988)

BOX 13.2 **Is the Use of Smokeless Tobacco Less Harmful Than Smoking?**

Because of increased public awareness of the dangers of smoking, the tobacco industry has attempted to promote smokeless tobacco (chewing tobacco, snuff) as a relatively safe alternative to smoking (Venitt, 1990). Since smokeless tobacco is not associated with lung cancer, a major danger from smoking, some have argued that smokeless tobacco is safer than smoking. The use of smokeless tobacco has recently increased; an estimated 6% of American adult men now use it in one form or another. As a reflection of youth-oriented advertising and the association of smokeless tobacco with professional sports figures, young men are particularly likely to use smokeless tobacco. Recent survey evidence indicates that 16% of males between 12 and 25 use snuff, chewing tobacco, or both. Smokeless tobacco use among girls and women is much lower: less than 2% using either snuff or chewing tobacco (Centers for Disease Control, 1989b; Cullen et al., 1986).

How safe is smokeless tobacco? Smokeless tobacco may not be a significant cause of lung cancer, but it is strongly related to cancers of the oral cavity, prostate, and, possibly, kidney. For example, current evidence indicates that users of smokeless tobacco are twice as likely to develop cancer of the prostate, and up to fifty times more likely to develop cancer of the mouth than are non-users (Cullen et al., 1986; Hsing et al., 1990). Smokeless tobacco also causes gum disease, tooth decay, and inflammation of the salivary glands (Connolly, 1990; Cullen et al., 1986; Cummings, Michalek, Carl, Wood, & Haley, 1989). Further, smokeless tobacco has a nicotine content similar to that of cigarettes, and strong evidence indicates that its use is addictive.

Because of these effects, health experts have warned that smokeless tobacco is not a safe alternative to smoking and have called for programs to discourage its use, particularly among young people (Cullen et al., 1986). At least one country, the United Kingdom, has gone so far as to ban smokeless tobacco altogether (West & Krafona, 1990).

found that the best predictors of continued smoking were peer smoking and the number of cigarettes offered by peers. Smokers had more friends who smoked and received 26 times as many offers of cigarettes as did nonsmokers.

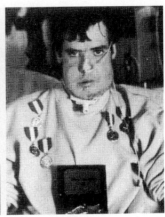

Sean Marsee, a popular student and athlete, began dipping snuff at 13, thinking it was safer than smoking. After five years of dipping one or more cans a day, he developed mouth cancer. He died at 19, after writing out the message "Don't dip snuff."

Among the most important factors in the development of the smoking habit is having peers who smoke.

After cigarette smoking becomes a regular habit, the person enters the stage of *maintenance*. During this stage, which lasts as long as the person continues smoking, psychological and physiological factors keep the person smoking. Evidence suggests that smoking is often used to regulate emotional states. Studies of the reasons smokers give for continuing include relaxation, the pleasure derived from smoking, use of smoking to reduce anxiety or tension, and habit. These reasons differ significantly from person to person and are, in turn, related to the effectiveness of different techniques for stopping smoking. For example, experimental studies have found that smokers who smoke for pleasure show a sharp drop in number of cigarettes smoked after those cigarettes have been dipped in vinegar, whereas those who smoke for other reasons do not. Smokers who smoke primarily from habit show a significant reduction in smoking when asked to keep a record of cigarettes smoked, whereas this is not the case for those who smoke for pleasure (Leventhal & Cleary, 1980).

But smoking is also a physiological addiction. Once they begin smoking regularly, smokers become physiologically dependent on the nicotine in cigarettes. Although substantial evidence demonstrates that nicotine is addictive, the exact nature of this addiction is not entirely clear (Leventhal & Cleary, 1980; Pomerleau et al., 1986). The *nicotine fixed effects model* argues that nicotine produces addiction by stimulating specific reward centers in the central nervous system. According to this theory, the increased heart rate, feelings of mental alertness, and relaxation produced by nicotine reinforce smoking behavior (Hall, Rappaport, Hopkins, & Griffin, 1973). By contrast, the *nicotine regulation model* contends that smokers develop an optimal level of nicotine in their bodies and then smoke to maintain this level and avoid withdrawal symptoms (Jarvik, 1973; McMorrow & Foxx, 1983). Both these models suffer by focusing entirely on the physiological aspects of addiction to the exclusion of psychological factors.

A more comprehensive model has been proposed by Howard Leventhal and Paul Cleary (1980). The *multiple regulation model* argues that the physiological effects of nicotine interact with the psychological functions of smoking to produce addiction. According to this model, the key to smoking is emotional regulation, with nicotine levels being regulated because they have become conditioned to various emotional states. For example, many people smoke in social situations where they feel anxious. Having a cigarette to smoke gives them a sense of security that temporarily masks their feelings of social anxiety. When the cigarette is done, the level of nicotine in the blood begins to decline. At the same time, their anxiety returns. As this is repeated over time, an increase in anxiety becomes conditioned to the decline in nicotine levels. This reinforces smoking as a way of increasing nicotine level and avoiding anxiety. Although this model seems to account for the addictive nature of smoking better than theories that focus exclusively on either psychological or physiological aspects, whether it can adequately account for the various aspects of nicotine addiction remains to be seen. Whatever the actual reasons, smoking is a powerful addiction that many consider more difficult to break than addiction to even drugs or alcohol (Kozlowsky et al., 1989).

Stopping smoking. Because of smoking's extremely negative health effects, massive efforts have been mounted to reduce the number of people who smoke. Public health officials have repeatedly urged people to stop smoking, as have organizations such as the American Cancer Society and the American Lung Association. In addition, numerous treatment programs have been developed to help smokers quit. What kinds of strategies have been used, and how successful have these been?

One strategy that holds out the hope of reaching a large number of people at relatively low cost is the use of mass media campaigns (Flay, 1987; Leventhal & Cleary, 1980). Unfortunately, mass media campaigns have been only moderately successful in reducing smoking. In general, mass media campaigns have been successful in alerting people to the dangers of smoking and changing attitudes. However, the number of smokers who actually quit in response to such campaigns is relatively small. For example, in four large-scale community-based interventions using mass media and other techniques for health promotion, communities exposed only to mass media campaigns showed an average 15% reduction in the number of smokers. This figure is only 8% higher than the number of people who quit in communities without the campaign, and is very close to the number of people who quit using the American Lung Association's self-help program. By comparison, communities receiving mass media plus more intensive community interventions, such as face-to-face appeals and group meetings, showed an average 34% reduction in smoking (Flay, 1987).

This is not to denigrate the role of informational campaigns in the fight against smoking. Even though a relatively small number of smokers quit in response to them, media campaigns spread awareness of the dangers of smoking and the need to quit or, better yet, never start. Therefore, they lay the essential groundwork in the fight against smoking and can significantly enhance the effectiveness of other efforts, such as smoking cessation clinics (Mogielnicki et al., 1986).

For many smokers, the route to quitting includes some kind of antismoking therapy. Clinics to help people stop smoking have become prevalent. Although some programs include pharmacological treatments such as nicotine gum (Fagerstrom, 1982), most are based on the principles of behavior modification. Among the more common techniques are those based on aversion, operant conditioning, and self-control techniques.

Aversion techniques attempt to reduce smoking by pairing the act of smoking with some sort of noxious stimulus so that smoking itself becomes perceived as unpleasant. For example, the technique of *rapid smoking* instructs patients to smoke rapidly and continuously so as to exceed their tolerance for cigarette smoke, producing unpleasant sensations. Treatments using this method have typically had good success, ranging as high as 60% to 90% by the end of the treatment. However, many of the patients relapse over time, and enthusiasm for the method has been diminished by the fact that it can significantly aggravate existing health problems (Leventhal & Cleary, 1980; Lichtenstein & Mermelstein, 1984). Other aversion therapies such as the pairing of smoking with electrical shocks or the pairing of smoking with aversive images have generally been unsuccessful (Lichtenstein & Mermelstein, 1984).

Operant strategies for smoking cessation are designed to detect the environmental stimuli that promote smoking and then to extinguish the control of these stimuli over the smoking response. For example, one technique requires smokers to carry a timer that sounds a buzzer at random intervals. When the buzzer sounds, the person is required to smoke a cigarette. After smoking is conditioned to the buzzer, the buzzer is eliminated, and, presumably, with it the smoking. Other techniques, such as awarding points for stopping smoking or the use of praise, have also been tried. These techniques can be effective in reducing smoking, but, as with aversion therapy, relapse is a major problem (Leventhal & Cleary, 1980). For example, one study found a 75% success rate in stopping smoking by pairing it with a random buzzer. However, six weeks later the success rate had declined to 43% (Shapiro, Tursky, Schwartz, & Shnidman, 1971).

Self-control strategies view smoking as a learned habit associated with specific situations. Therapy is aimed at identifying those situations and teaching smokers the skills necessary to resist smoking. These strategies often involve various techniques that address different aspects of smoking. For example, in the initial stages of a program, the emphasis is on strengthening the motivation to quit, setting a target date, and the self-monitoring of smoking behavior. Self-monitoring is particularly important for providing a baseline for later comparison and increasing self-awareness of smoking patterns. In fact, self-monitoring itself can lead to a reduction in smoking, though this is often temporary (Lichtenstein & Mermelstein, 1984).

Once past these preliminaries, other techniques are used to reduce smoking behavior. For instance, contingency contracting might be used to provide additional motivation to stop smoking. For example, a smoker might deposit a sum of money with the therapist, on the understanding that the money would be returned on the completion of six months without smoking, but otherwise would be forfeited. Studies of contingency contracting have found that it can be effective, at least in the short term. For example, one study obtained an 84% abstinence rate at the end of treatment using contingency contracting. However, this dropped to 38% at follow-up (Elliot & Tighe, 1968).

Other techniques that might be used include stimulus control and response substitution. Stimulus control asks the person to identify the situations in which smoking occurs and then to change the environment so as to alter or remove the stimuli that lead to smoking. For example, a smoker might remove all the ash trays in the house so as not to be reminded of smoking. Many smokers sit in a favorite chair to smoke and read or watch TV. Simply sitting in another chair or lying down while reading or watching TV can help the person to break the cigarette habit. Response substitution teaches the person to substitute other activities for smoking. For example, to overcome the temptation to smoke, the person might take a walk instead. Or a person who uses smoking to relax might be taught other ways to relax.

Most therapeutic techniques for smoking cessation are effective to some degree. Initially, most produce a fairly high rate of abstinence. However, over time a significant number of participants return to smoking. Reviews of smoking cessation studies have found roughly equivalent rates of success for different programs, indicating that the type of program is not all that critical. However, relapse is a serious problem for all the programs (Leventhal & Cleary, 1980; Lichtenstein & Mermelstein, 1984; Lichtenstein et al., 1986; Shiffman, 1989).

Interestingly, the majority of people who finally quit smoking do so on their own and often without professional help. In fact, of the millions of people in the United States who have successfully quit smoking, as many as 95% of them may have done so on their own (Cohen et al., 1989). From what we know about successful self-quitters, quitting is often a lengthy process involving several unsuccessful attempts before success is finally achieved. In general, the number of previous attempts at quitting does not predict whether a person will be successful on any given try. Rather, success appears to be a matter of trying different methods until one is found that works. Not surprisingly, heavy smokers have a harder time stopping than do light smokers. Factors that appear to be related to success at self-quitting are self-confidence, good self-control skills, strong beliefs in the health benefits of quitting, and a socially supportive environment (Cohen et al., 1989; Katz & Singh, 1986; Schacter, 1982). But even successful quitters suffer occasional slips—which emphasizes the fact that quitting smoking is a dynamic process that occurs over time, not a discrete event (Cohen et al., 1989).

Preventing smoking. Because of the difficulty in quitting smoking, the current emphasis is on preventing people from taking up the habit in the first place. As noted earlier, smokers tend to begin early, often during early adolescence. Therefore, prevention efforts have typically been carried out in schools and emphasize the psychosocial factors that tend to lead to smoking among young people (Biglan et al., 1987; Botvin, Dusenbury, Baker, James-Ortiz, & Kerner, 1989; Flay et al., 1985; Hirschman & Leventhal, 1989; Johnson, Hansen, Collins, & Graham, 1986; Luepker, Johnson, Murray, & Pechacek, 1983).

A typical prevention program includes several different components (Flay, 1985). One important goal is presenting young people with the facts about smoking. Although most programs include information about long-term health effects, they also emphasize the immediate physiological and social effects of smoking. This is particularly important because young people are likely to be influenced more by the immediate consequences of smoking than by its long-term effects. The heart of prevention programs, however, lies in helping young people to resist social pressures to smoke. Thus particular attention is paid to teaching students about those pressures and helping them to develop the skills to resist them. In addition, some programs focus on helping the participants to develop more general personal and social skills.

The Waterloo Smoking Prevention Project (Flay et al., 1985), involving nearly 700 Canadian sixth graders, provides a good example of the kinds of methods used. This program consisted of three main components. First, the participants were engaged in activities designed to elicit their beliefs about smoking and get them actively involved in seeking out smoking-related information; this was designed to set the stage for the other components. The second component focused on making the children aware of social influences to smoke and teaching specific skills for resisting those pressures. For example, specific social coping skills, such as saying "No, thank you, I don't smoke," were taught, role played, and practiced. Finally, the children were encouraged to consider carefully what they had learned and to make a commitment as to whether or not they would smoke. This commitment, along with the main reason for it, was then announced to the class. After completing the program, the participants also received "booster sessions" for the next two years.

The program appears to have been successful. Fewer students in the program began smoking, and more quit than was the case in schools not participating in the program. The effect of the program on experimentation with smoking is shown in Figure 13.3. Although these results are very encouraging, the program followed students only through the eighth grade. Longer term follow-up of prevention programs has found that many of the benefits of such programs have dissipated by the end of high school, suggesting the need for continued booster sessions (Murray, Pirie, Luepker, & Pallonen, 1989).

Diet

Although smoking is undoubtedly the most intensely studied life-style factor in cancer, it is by no means the only one. A second major cause of cancer can be found in the foods we eat. In fact, diet is estimated to be responsible for more cancer deaths than is smoking, approximately 35% (Doll & Peto, 1981).

The role of diet in cancer. Although diet has long been suspected to be important in the development of cancer, not until the early 1980s was scientific evidence for the link widely recognized. Further, only in the mid-1980s did bodies like the National Cancer Institute and American Cancer Society issue dietary recommendations for avoiding cancer (DiSogra & DiSogra, 1988a).

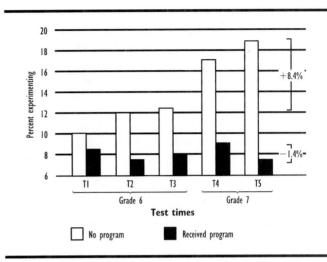

FIGURE 13.3

Effects of the Waterloo Smoking Prevention Project on experimentation with smoking.

Note. Five measurements were taken: T1, one week before the beginning of the program; T2, immediately after; T3, at the end of 6th grade; T4, at the beginning of 7th grade; and T5, at the end of 7th grade. From "Are social-psychological smoking prevention programs effective? The Waterloo Study" by B. R. Flay, K. B. Ryan, J. A. Best, K. S. Brown, M. W. Kersell, J. R. d'Avernas, and M. P. Zanna, 1985, *Journal of Behavioral Medicine, 8*, p. 47.

What is it about what we eat that leads to cancer? Current evidence suggests that several elements of a person's diet can act either to promote the development of cancer or inhibit it. A key factor in the promotion of cancer is dietary fat. Both epidemiological and laboratory studies indicate that a high-fat diet promotes cancer of the breast, colon, prostate, testes, uterus, and ovary (Byers, 1988; Cohen, 1987; DiSogra & DiSogra, 1988b). These cancers are most prevalent in countries with diets high in fats, particularly animal fats such as beef, and least frequent in countries where fats make up a smaller portion of the diet. An estimated 36% to 41% of the calories in the American diet come from fats. In its dietary guidelines for avoiding cancer, the National Cancer Institute recommends that this proportion be reduced to 30% or less (DiSogra & DiSogra, 1988b).

Cancer may also be promoted by the way in which food is prepared (Doll & Peto, 1981). Grilling or charcoal-broiling foods leads to the formation of polycyclic aromatic hydrocarbons on the food surface. Some of these compounds are known to be carcinogenic, and one, benzopyrene, is actually used in laboratory experiments to induce tumor growth. No epidemiological studies as yet have examined the association between grilled or charcoal-broiled foods and cancer in humans. However, the effects of polycyclic aromatic hydrocarbons on animals has led the National Cancer Institute to recommend that people consume such foods in moderation and use other cooking methods such as baking, roasting, steaming, or wrapping foods in foil to reduce contact with smoke and flame (DiSogra & DiSogra, 1988b).

Chapter 5 discussed the problem of alcohol abuse and how it can be treated. Although the primary concern for many people is the behavioral effect of alcohol and its effect on the liver, alcohol also plays a significant role in promoting cancer. The consumption of alcoholic beverages has been associated with cancer of the mouth, tongue, throat, esophagus, lung, stomach, colon, and rectum (DiSogra & DiSogra, 1988b). For example, one study estimated that men who drink an average of 3.5 cans of beer a day have three times the risk of developing rectal cancer than do nondrinkers; consumption of 50 or more ounces of wine or whiskey per month doubles the likelihood of lung cancer (Pollack, Nomura, Heilbrun, Stemmermann, & Green, 1984).

But certain dietary elements can protect against cancer. In particular, diets high in fiber are believed to be protective against cancer of the colon. Both epidemiological studies and studies in animals have shown that increased fiber consumption is associated with reductions in colon cancer (Cohen, 1987). Fiber is a structural component of plant cell walls and is not digested by the enzymes in the digestive tract. Rather, it enters the large intestine mostly intact and adds bulk to the stool. One possibility is that it prevents colon cancer both by diluting the concentration of carcinogenic bile acids in the stool and speeding the passage of fecal matter through the colon, thus cutting down the amount of time that the colon walls are exposed to these carcinogens (Cohen, 1987; DiSogra & DiSogra, 1988b).

Certain vegetables and vitamins may also play a role in preventing cancer. Specifically, cruciferous vegetables—members of the cabbage family such as brussels sprouts, cabbage, broccoli, kale, and turnips—appear to be protective against colon cancer. In addition, some evidence shows that vitamin A can help to protect against cancer of the lung, bladder, colon, larynx, stomach, and esophagus, whereas vitamin C may be protective against cancer of the stomach, esophagus, larynx, and cervix (Byers, 1988; DiSogra & DiSogra, 1988b). Although the evidence for these effects is still tentative, both the American Cancer Society and National Cancer Institute recommend increases in the consumption of fruits and vegetables rich in these vitamins. Vitamin supplements, however, do not appear useful in reducing cancer risk (DiSogra & DiSogra, 1988b).

Accomplishing dietary change. The evidence linking diet to cancer strongly argues for changes in dietary practices. As a first step toward such changes, guidelines on dietary changes to reduce cancer risk have been issued by such groups as the National Academy of Sciences, the National Cancer Institute, and American Cancer Society. Chief among the recommendations are reductions in the intake of fats, alcohol, and charred or smoked foods, along with increases in the consumption of foods high in fiber and vitamins A and C. Table 13.1 summarizes these recommendations.

Although these guidelines are an essential first step, achieving these changes is quite another matter. Dietary practices are established early in life, and are embedded in cultural traditions and personal preferences. In addition, efforts to encourage healthier eating have been hampered by disagreement among health experts as to specific recommendations, inadequate food labeling, and the fact that many foods are

TABLE 13.1   *Summary of Dietary Recommendations for Reducing Cancer Risk*

Risk Factor	Agency (Year)		
	NAS (1982)	NCI (1984)	ACS (1984)
Total fat (% of calories)	Reduce to 30%	Reduce to 30% or below	Reduce to 30%
Fiber (vegetables, fruit, whole grains)	Daily	Increase to 25–35 g/day (several servings per day)	Eat more
Vitamin A/β-carotene foods	Frequently	Daily	Daily
Vitamin C foods	Frequently	Daily	Daily
Cruciferous vegetables (indoles)	Frequently	Several servings per week	Include in diet
Charred or smoked foods (benzopyrene)	Minimize	Choose less often	Moderation in smoked foods only
Alcohol	Moderation	Moderation	Moderation
Nitrites (cured/preserved foods)	Minimize	—	Moderation
Obesity	—	—	Avoid

A dash (—) indicates that no recommendation has been made.

Note. From "Diet and cancer" by L. K. DiSogra and C. A. DiSogra, 1988 (p. 84), in *Understanding cancer* (3d ed.) by M. Renneker, Palo Alto, CA: Bull Publishing Co.

processed, which makes it difficult to determine and state their nutritional characteristics (Wadden & Brownell, 1984).

Despite these difficulties, many programs have been developed for encouraging dietary change. Most of these have been directed toward weight reduction or changes in cardiovascular risk (see Chapter 14). However, they point to ways in which eating habits might be changed to reduce cancer risk.

One approach targets the eating habits of individuals and families, relying heavily on the cognitive-behavioral approaches discussed in Chapter 5. Typically these programs attempt to bring about dietary change first by making people aware of their own eating habits and the foods that increase disease risk, and then by encouraging individuals to make gradual changes in their diets by substituting healthy foods for unhealthy ones. Key elements in such programs include self-monitoring, gradual modification of diet over time so as to prevent participants from feeling overwhelmed, and social rewards for appropriate food choices (Wadden & Brownell, 1984). Since eating often takes place in a family context, the success of such programs is likely to depend on enlisting the cooperation of all family members (Weidner, Archer, Healy, & Matarazzo, 1985). Programs focusing on individuals and families often produce short-term changes, but the programs tend to be costly in relation to their effects and the changes short-lived (Jeffery, 1988).

A second approach targets the purchasing of food in supermarkets and restaurants (Wadden & Brownell, 1984). The rationale in these programs is that dietary changes will be facilitated when people are offered attractively packaged or prepared healthy foods in place of less healthy ones. In one program, for example, the menu of the cafeteria at a large aircraft manufacturing company was modified to include low-calorie foods that were identified by tags bearing a rainbow and listing their caloric content. Approximately 12% of the cafeteria's clientele regularly selected these items (Farnon, 1981). Similar campaigns have been mounted in supermarkets: health education materials have been made available to customers, and healthy foods have been highlighted in store promotions. The results of these campaigns have been mixed. One study, for example, found that nutrition knowledge increased in both the control and experimental stores, but that sales data for targeted products did not change (Wadden & Brownell, 1984).

The most comprehensive approach to dietary change is through mass public health campaigns (Celentano, 1991; Wadden & Brownell, 1984). These programs typically target several aspects of life-styles within an entire community, including diet, smoking, alcohol consumption, and exercise. Examples of this type of program were described in Chapter 5. These programs have been reasonably successful in altering several aspects of life-style, including diet. For example, in the Stanford Three Community Study (Farquhar et al., 1977; Maccoby, Farquhar, Wood, & Alexander, 1977), residents of communities receiving a mass media campaign showed significant reductions in smoking and the consumption of high-cholesterol foods as compared to a community not receiving the campaign. As noted in Chapter 5, these effects were enhanced when the media campaign was supplemented with face-to-face instruction.

Other Life-style Factors

In addition to the major life-style factors of smoking and diet, the likelihood of developing cancer is also influenced significantly by such factors as occupation and exposure to ultraviolet light.

Occupation. People in certain occupations have long been known to be more likely to develop cancer than those in others because of the presence of various carcinogens in the workplace. For example, people who work with asbestos and are exposed to asbestos fibers in the air have a significantly increased risk of developing lung cancer. Workers exposed to benzene, a chemical commonly used in the chemical and drug industries, are significantly more likely to develop leukemia; people who work with chromium and chromium compounds are at higher risk for developing lung cancer. Altogether an estimated 4% of cancers can be traced to occupational exposure (Doll & Peto, 1981).

Exposure to ultraviolet light. Every year more than 400,000 cases of skin cancer are diagnosed in the United States alone. Skin cancer has a high cure rate (over 90%), but can still exact a high price in health care costs and possible disfigurement. Skin cancer is also easily prevented. Exposure to ultraviolet (UV) light, in the form of sunlight, accounts for an estimated 90% of skin cancer cases (Keesling & Friedman, 1987; Page & Asire, 1988). In line with this, skin cancer tends to be more prevalent in tropical regions of the world near the equator, where sunlight is stronger (O'Rourke & Emmett, 1991). Although one would certainly not want to avoid sunlight altogether, its negative effects can be minimized. For example, wearing a hat or covering the skin with clothing blocks out harmful UV radiation. When skin is exposed to the sun, such as while a person is sunbathing or playing outdoor sports, sunscreens can be used to reduce the effects of harmful radiation. Despite these relatively simple ways of avoiding exposure, the rates of skin cancer have been increasing, partly because of the social benefits of having a suntan (Keesling & Friedman, 1987).

The evidence is clear that a large proportion of cancers are directly related to life-style and could be prevented through changes in smoking, diet, UV radiation exposure, and reduced carcinogen exposure on the job. Even though a significant number of Americans still smoke, anti-smoking campaigns saved an estimated 200,000 lives between 1964 and 1978 alone (Warner & Murt, 1983). Despite such efforts, however, cancer remains a leading health problem: Nearly a third of people living in industrialized countries can expect to develop cancer during their lifetimes (Renneker, 1988). We now turn from primary prevention to questions concerning the detection and treatment of cancer.

DETECTING CANCER AND SEEKING HELP

The best way to control cancer is, clearly, to prevent it from ever occurring. However, when cancer does develop, its impact can often be blunted through early detection and treatment. As noted earlier, cancer develops over time, starting with a few cells and developing into tumors that invade surrounding tissue and may eventually metastasize to other parts of the body. Detecting and treating cancer early, before it has seriously invaded surrounding tissues or metastasized, can significantly improve the person's chances of survival (Spencer, 1988). The impact of early detection and treatment can be seen in the dramatic changes in cancer survival rates over the last several decades. A person who developed cancer in 1930 had only a one in five chance of living for five years or more. Currently, approximately half of all cancer patients survive for five or more years, and the American Cancer Society has set the goal of increasing this percentage to 75% by the year 2000 (Hutter, 1988; McKenna, 1988).

The Problem of Delay

Despite the evidence that early treatment significantly increases longevity, many cancer patients delay seeking help for significant periods of time. Studies of delay behavior have found that between 35% and 55% of patients with cancer symptoms delay three or more months before seeking medical attention—delays that can seriously affect their chances of survival (Antonovsky & Hartman, 1974; Singer, 1988).

What accounts for this delay? As seen in Chapter 8, delay in seeking medical attention is often a function of the type of symptoms involved, the person's cognitive illness representations, and various situational factors. With specific respect to cancer, key factors appear to be the nature of early cancer symptoms and how people interpret them, people's beliefs and fears about cancer, past experience with the disease, and the person's age and socioeconomic status.

In its early stages, cancer is rarely, if ever, painful. Rather, tumors develop silently, generally without immediately noticeable symptoms. The first indication a person has of cancer is often the gradual development of a lump, a change in the color of a wart or mole, or other relatively subtle symptom. This should prompt people to seek medical attention, but most wait until they feel pain or have other noticeable symptoms before asking for help (Mechanic, 1978; Safer, Tharps, Jackson, & Leventhal, 1979). Studies of delay behavior in cancer have found that many people delay seeking help because they are unaware of the significance of their symptoms (Antonovsky & Hartman, 1974). The absence of dramatic symptoms for cancer requires that the person be aware of signs of potential cancer and be on the lookout for them constantly. For this reason, efforts have been focused on alerting people to cancer symptoms. Table 13.2 lists seven early signs of cancer that should be closely monitored. These are only general signs of cancer; the symptoms for specific cancers depend on the site and type of cancer involved. For detailed descriptions of self-examination techniques designed to help people detect early symptoms of specific cancers, see Renneker (1988).

Although knowledge of cancer symptoms is a critical first step, it does not ensure prompt help-seeking, and under some circumstances may even work against it. In particular, patients who promptly seek medical attention seem to be those who are knowledgeable about cancer and have a low level of anxiety, whereas patients who are knowledgeable but fearful of cancer delay longer. The type of fear also makes a difference in that patients who fear a cancer diagnosis tend to delay longer than those who fear the consequences of the disease (Antonovsky & Hartman, 1974). Apparently, fearing a cancer diagnosis prompts the person to deny that possibility, whereas concern over cancer's effects leads the person to attempt to avoid those outcomes by seeking treatment. Relatedly, prior experience with cancer, whether from past personal history or knowing someone who has had cancer, tends to lead to more rapid help-seeking (Singer, 1988).

Finally, age and socioeconomic status influence the speed with which help is sought. In general, older people delay more than do those who are younger

TABLE 13.2 *Early Warning Signs of Cancer*

1. A change in bowel or bladder habits

2. A sore that does not heal

3. Unusual discharge or bleeding from genital, urinary, or digestive tract

4. A thickening or lump in a breast or elsewhere

5. Indigestion or difficulty swallowing

6. An obvious change in a wart or mole

7. A persistent cough or hoarseness

Note. From *The American Cancer Society cancer book: Prevention, detection, diagnosis, treatment, rehabilitation, cure,* ed. by A. I. Holleb, 1986, Garden City, NY: Doubleday.

(Antonovsky & Hartman, 1974; Singer, 1988). Further, perhaps because of a relative lack of education or concerns about treatment costs, people with low socioeconomic status have a greater tendency to delay than those who are more affluent (Antonovsky & Hartman, 1974).

Promoting Early Detection

Because of the importance of early detection in saving lives, public education about cancer and encouraging the detection of cancer symptoms through various self-examination techniques and medical screening procedures are receiving strong emphasis (Hutter, 1988; McKenna, 1988; Smart, 1990). Easily learned self-examination techniques are available for detecting cancer of the skin, thyroid, breast, and testes, as well as for detecting swollen lymph nodes that may reflect the presence of cancer (Renneker, 1988). In addition, screening procedures can evaluate potential cancer symptoms and detect cancers, such as those of the lung, cervix, and colon, that cannot be easily identified through self-examination (Smart, 1990).

The key, of course, is persuading people to perform self-examinations regularly and to seek cancer screening. Research studies suggest that only 20% to 40% of women practice monthly breast self-examination (BSE; Strauss, Solomon, Costanza, Worden, & Foster, 1987), probably fewer than 15% of young men perform testicular self-exams (TSE; Brubaker & Wickersham, 1990), and less than 40% of adults have ever had a stool blood examination for colorectal cancer (McKenna, 1988). In all these cases, regular practice of the procedure in question would significantly reduce cancer mortality.

What can be done to encourage greater use of early detection measures? Many measures have been tried that draw on research in persuasive communication and behavioral techniques. Among these are the use of persuasive messages, prompts and external rewards, increases in recommended examination frequency, and community education programs.

Perhaps the most straightforward method is to present people with persuasive messages containing information about the procedure in question and urging them to perform it regularly. Although, as seen in Chapter 5, mass media campaigns are often less effective than we would like at producing behavioral change, such appeals can work. For example, an experiment by Valerie Steffen (1990) found that reading a brochure about TSE resulted in more positive attitudes and greater intentions to perform TSE, particularly among men who previously knew little about testicular cancer. Another experiment relating to TSE found that male college students who listened to a taped message about testicular cancer were significantly more likely to report TSE one month later than were those not exposed to the message (Brubaker & Fowler, 1990). Interestingly, serendipitous messages, such as news reports of a celebrity with cancer, may be among the most persuasive. Significant increases in the number of people performing BSE were noted after the news that Betty Ford (wife of then American President Gerald Ford) and Happy Rockefeller (wife of then American Vice President Nelson Rockefeller) had breast cancer. Similarly, a significant increase was seen in the incidence of colorectal cancer, presumably from increased screening, after the news of former President Ronald Reagan's colon cancer. Mortality from colorectal cancer subsequently showed a significant decline in the United States (Smart, 1990).

Another relatively simple means of increasing the use of early detection procedures is through the use of prompts. Techniques such as BSE and TSE are generally done only periodically, most often monthly, and are easily forgotten. To deal with this problem, the person can be prompted through reminder postcards or telephone calls when it is time to perform the procedure. For example, one study (Craun & Deffenbacher, 1987) used three approaches in an attempt to increase the frequency of BSE. An educational format provided information about breast cancer and BSE, whereas a demonstration format demonstrated BSE techniques and provided participants with practice. Finally, in the prompt procedure women were mailed monthly reminders that simply said, "Remember to practice a breast self-examination this month." The use of prompts was the most effective in increasing BSE frequency (see also Grady, 1984). Similar results have been found with telephone reminders (Mayer & Frederiksen, 1986).

Rewards are a third means of increasing early detection. For example, one study (Grady, Goodenow, & Borkin, 1988) divided participants into three groups: groups received an extrinsic reward (a $1 lottery ticket or a Susan B. Anthony silver dollar) for each BSE, were instructed to give themselves a reward of their own choice, or received no reward for performing BSE. Half the participants in each group were also sent reminders, whereas the other half were not. Women who received the extrinsic reward performed BSE nearly 50% more often than those in the self-reward or no reward condition, regardless of whether they received a reminder.

In addition, increasing the recommended frequency of screening procedures appears to lead to increased adherence, perhaps because actions that are performed more often are more easily remembered. One study, for example, instructed women to perform BSE weekly, biweekly, or monthly (Kemeny, Hovell, Mewborn, Dockter, & Chin, 1988). Those instructed to perform the procedure more often showed higher levels of BSE than those advised to do it less frequently.

The programs discussed so far have generally involved a relatively small number of participants. Significantly increasing the use of self-exams and screening procedures requires reaching many more people than can be reached through small-scale programs. To overcome this difficulty, community-wide programs have been developed, which attempt to influence a large number of people and to teach them the skills necessary to perform self-examinations effectively. A good example of this type of effort is a community program in Vermont for increasing BSE (Worden & Foster, 1987). Home health agency nurses in this program made presentations to groups of women in which they evoked discussion about the need for BSE and then taught them techniques for performing it effectively. In addition, radio and television announcements and newspaper stories publicized the training sessions and created positive norms for practicing BSE. Evaluation of this program found that over a one-year period, the frequency of BSE increased significantly compared with communities not receiving the program. Equally important was an increase in the effectiveness of BSE procedures used by participants who received the training sessions.

COPING WITH CANCER

For the hundreds of thousands of people who are diagnosed every year with cancer, that diagnosis brings with it a whole new set of challenges. Now they must confront not only the physical aspects of cancer but also the psychological and social impact of the disease.

The Physical Impact of Cancer

Depending on its location, type, and stage of development, cancer can have a devastating physical impact on its victims. Some of this impact comes from the direct effects of the cancer itself in the form of pain, physical changes, and reduced physical abilities. In addition, therapeutic efforts to control the disease and its spread can often be at least as distressing and debilitating as the disease itself.

Physical symptoms and changes. Cancer may begin insidiously without pain or other overt symptoms. However, as it progresses, it begins to produce unmistakable physical symptoms and changes. In some cases, the cancer may lead to disability, such as the difficulty in breathing that comes with lung cancer or sexual dysfunction that is often associated with cancer of the sexual organs (Anderson & Hacker, 1983; Renneker, 1988). In other cases, the person may be disfigured by the cancer or its treatment (Mages & Mendelsohn, 1979). In addition, the person with cancer in the terminal stages may experience cachexia, a symptom complex involving weight loss, serious metabolic changes, kidney and liver problems, and other biochemical changes (Calman & Welsh, 1984).

One symptom that seems to stand out, particularly in the later stages, is pain. For many people, the very concept of cancer is inextricably bound up with the idea of a slow and painful death. In reality, only about two thirds of cancer patients experience significant pain in the months and weeks leading up to their deaths (Twycross, 1984). However, for these patients, pain can be an excruciating and constant companion unless steps are taken to relieve it.

What can be done to help cancer patients deal with pain? Contrary to popular opinion, cancer pain is rarely intractable (Laszlo, 1987; Twycross, 1984). In most cases, the pain can be managed with a combination of pharmacological and behavioral methods. Analgesics, ranging from aspirin to morphine, are available for relieving pain. These drugs may be used either separately or in combination, with the dosage and frequency tailored to the particular patient (Twycross, 1984). In addition, various behavioral techniques, such as hypnosis, relaxation, massage, and distraction, can be used to help patients cope (Dalton, 1987; Katz, Kellerman, & Ellenberg, 1987). These and other techniques for pain control are discussed in more detail in Chapter 15.

Treatment effects. Treatment for cancer generally takes one of three forms: surgery to remove the cancerous tissues, radiation to obstruct the division and growth of cancer cells, and chemotherapy to destroy cancer cells or keep them from reproducing. Different combinations of these three forms of therapy are often used to provide more effective treatment than any one of them could alone. Although the various methods for treating cancer significantly improve the prognosis for most patients and, in many cases, are essential for preserving life, they can also take a heavy toll.

The goal of the surgical treatment of cancer is to remove as much of the cancer as possible, while leaving healthy tissue intact. However, to be on the safe side, surgeons generally remove healthy tissue from around the tumor site to ensure that they have all the cancer cells. In general, surgery is most effective when the tumor is localized and has not yet metastasized to other parts of the body. The surgeon must be able to remove the cancer without destroying essential life-sustaining tissue. In cases where removal of the tumor would require destruction of critical tissue, such as a tumor buried in delicate brain tissue, the tumor is said to be inoperable. A major problem of surgery is that it often results in disability or disfigurement for the patient. For example, treatment of bone cancer frequently requires amputation of the affected limb; treatment of breast cancer often involves removal of all or part of the breast, and treatment of testicular cancer requires removal of the testis involved (Laszlo, 1987; Renneker, 1988). In addition, some types of cancer surgery require a major change in bodily functions: Colon cancer patients may be required to excrete wastes through a colostomy, or surgical opening, in the abdomen.

Radiation therapy also works best with localized tumors. Ionizing radiation aims to kill tumor cells by damaging vital cell components such as DNA and proteins (Laszlo, 1987; Odell, 1988). This radiation is most often applied from outside of the body in the form of *external radiation,* in which a radiation beam from a large machine is directed at the tumor site. In some cases, however, radioactive pellets may be injected into the tumor or surrounding tissues to destroy the tumor through *internal radiation.* Although radiation therapy can be used alone as an alternative to surgery or chemo-therapy, it is frequently used in combination with other treatments. For example, surgery may be used to remove as much of a tumor as possible, and then radiation is used to destroy any cancer cells left behind. Radiation therapy is often highly effective in reducing or eliminating tumors, but also has side effects. The radiation cannot be directed solely at the cancerous cells, and, since radiation is equally effective in killing healthy and cancerous cells, healthy tissue is invariably damaged. Even though the radiation is painless, patients undergoing radiation therapy often experience nausea, vomiting, hair loss, loss of appetite, and reduced bone marrow functioning. In addition, the radiation can itself lead to new cancers that may not be detected until years later (Holm, 1990; Odell, 1988).

chemotherapy
Treatment using drugs or chemicals.

Of all of the types of cancer treatment, **chemotherapy** is the most rapidly developing. Thousands of substances have been tested as potential cancer treatments (McWaters & Renneker, 1988). Chemotherapy uses various drugs to destroy cancer cells by disrupting their functioning and reproduction. In addition, chemical agents known as *biological response modifiers,* such as interferons and interleukins, are now being used to fight cancer by boosting the effectiveness of the patient's immune system. One advantage of chemotherapy is that it can be used in cases where the tumor either is not localized or has already metastasized.

Like radiation, however, chemotherapy of necessity destroys many healthy cells and has often distressing side effects, including loss of appetite, hair loss, frequent

anticipatory nausea and vomiting
A classically conditioned response in which cancer patients experience nausea and vomiting before chemotherapy is administered.

nausea and vomiting, damage to various bodily organs, sores in the mouth, and increased susceptibility to infection (Laszlo, 1987). Because nausea and vomiting occur soon after the chemotherapy is administered, an estimated 18% to 50% of cancer patients have **anticipatory nausea and vomiting,** that is, they experience these side effects before the treatment is even administered (Nicholas, 1982; Redd & Andrykowski, 1982; van Komen & Redd, 1985). These effects are sometimes so severe that patients will forego chemotherapy to avoid them. Several techniques are now used to help patients deal with these anticipatory reactions, including hypnosis, guided imagery, progressive muscle relaxation, biofeedback, and systematic desensitization (Carey & Burish, 1988; Redd & Andrykowski, 1982).

The Psychosocial Impact of Cancer

In reality, the physical impact of cancer is only the beginning. The physical characteristics of cancer may define the objective situation that the patient is faced with, but cancer also has far-reaching effects on the person's psychological and social functioning.

Emotional distress. Given the common images attached to cancer as a disease, a diagnosis of cancer can produce considerable emotional distress. Studies of the emotional effects of cancer have found that cancer patients exhibit emotional responses including feelings of anxiety, depression, anger, shame, and worthlessness. In addition, cancer patients may experience insomnia, lack of concentration, and thoughts of suicide (Taylor, Lichtman, & Wood, 1984). These reactions, however, should be kept in perspective. Such responses appear to be most troublesome immediately after the diagnosis (Cassileth et al., 1984), and reach clinical proportions for only a portion of patients. For example, not more than 25% to 50% of cancer patients exhibit clinical depression (Burish, Meyerowitz, Carey, & Morrow, 1987; Massey & Holland, 1990). Further, one study comparing the mental health of five groups of medical patients with that of the general public found that, on average, the mental health of the medical patients, including those with cancer, was essentially equivalent to healthy members of the general public (Cassileth et al., 1984).

How do cancer patients cope with the emotional impact of cancer? As seen in Chapter 10, people who develop chronic illness employ different mechanisms for coping with their disease. Key mechanisms used by cancer patients include devising an explanation for the occurrence of the cancer, developing a sense of control over the disease, and maintaining a positive sense of self-esteem and meaning (Taylor, 1983). For example, studies with cancer patients have found that nearly all of them have some kind of explanation as to why they developed the disease. These explanations may have nothing to do with the actual causes of the cancer (such as attributing breast cancer to being hit in the chest with a frisbee), but appear to provide comfort for the person (Taylor et al., 1984).

Developing a sense of control over the disease also appears to facilitate coping. Patients who believe that they or their doctors can control the recurrence of the cancer show more positive psychological adjustment than do patients without those beliefs (Marks, Richardson, Graham, & Levine, 1986; Taylor et al., 1984; Timko & Janoff-

Bulman, 1985). This sense of control helps reduce the person's sense of vulnerability to recurrence and is associated with more constructive coping strategies. Ann Hilton (1989), for example, has found that cancer patients with a high sense of control are more likely to seek social support and engage in planned problem-solving and positive reappraisal than are those with less perceived control.

Finally, maintenance of a positive sense of self-esteem appears to be closely related to the kinds of social comparisons the person makes with others. Interviews with cancer patients have found that those who cope well maintain a positive sense of self by engaging in downward comparison in which they compare themselves with others who are faring less well, even if they have to construct such a person (Taylor, 1983; Wood, Taylor, & Lichtman, 1985). At the same time, however, they appear to seek information and affiliation from those who are more fortunate (Taylor & Lobel, 1989).

Interpersonal relations. Cancer's impact is not limited to the patient alone. Family members, friends, and acquaintances are also affected when a person is diagnosed with cancer. Family members, in particular, are likely to experience feelings of tension and depression as they watch their loved one struggle with cancer (Lewis, 1990). In fact, one study has suggested that the emotional impact of cancer on spouses may be even greater than it is on the patients themselves (Mathieson, Stam, & Scott, 1991).

This impact on others also has effects on patients and, in particular, their interpersonal relationships. Camille Wortman and Christine Dunkel-Schetter (1979) argue that cancer patients are in a particularly difficult situation with respect to interpersonal relationships. A diagnosis of cancer is likely to increase the patient's need for social support as he or she grapples with the emotional and physical impact of the disease and its treatment. However, feelings aroused by the disease in friends and family members may reduce their ability to provide needed support just when patients need it the most. In particular, Wortman and Dunkel-Schetter indicate that friends and family members are likely to experience conflicts between their positive feelings for the patient, negative feelings about cancer, and uncertainty about how best to interact with the patient. The result may be conflicting behavior toward the patient or even physical avoidance, which then can further increase the patient's emotional distress.

Studies of cancer patients have found that patients experience difficulty with interpersonal relationships. For example, cancer patients may find that they are avoided by others, or that others find it difficult to discuss their illness or exhibit nonverbal cues of rejection (Dunkel-Schetter, 1984; Wortman & Dunkel-Schetter, 1979). However, other evidence shows that Wortman and Dunkel-Schetter's analysis may be overly pessimistic. For example, a recent study in the Netherlands (Tempelaar et al., 1989) found that cancer patients had more experiences of positive social support and fewer instances of negative support than did a random sample from a healthy population. Further, patients with a poorer medical prognosis also indicated greater social support, a finding that has also been reported in other studies (Dunkel-Schetter, 1984).

The types and sources of social support received by the patient should be distinguished. Not all efforts at social support are positive. For example, when a family member or friend expresses too much worry about the patient or is critical of the patient's response to the cancer, such actions, though possibly well-meant, are likely to be perceived negatively. Interviews with cancer patients have found that, fortunately, helpful actions from others appear to outnumber unhelpful ones. Further, patients look to friends and family members to provide them with emotional support, but rely on physicians and other cancer patients for informational support (Dakof & Taylor, 1990; Dunkel-Schetter, 1984).

All these studies demonstrate that social support is an extremely important component of dealing with cancer and that patients who receive higher levels of positive social support show better adjustment (Dunkel-Schetter, 1984; Tempelaar et al., 1989).

Helping people cope. At this point, the question naturally arises as to what can be done to help cancer patients cope better. As with other chronic conditions (see Chapter 10), various techniques can be used. One important aspect of helping cancer patients cope is providing them with appropriate factual information about their disease and what they can expect. Information of this type is among the helpful actions frequently listed by cancer patients (Dakof & Taylor, 1990) and can be obtained from health practitioners, written materials, or through call-in information services (Meissner, Anderson, & Odenkirchen, 1990).

Psychotherapy can also be used to help patients cope. When used with cancer patients, psychotherapy is often of relatively short duration and aims at dealing with specific problems, such as cancer-related anxieties or fears of death or disfigurement, that the patient is encountering rather than more general psychological issues (Wellisch, 1981). Studies of psychotherapy with cancer patients have found that it can significantly improve the quality of life for patients and may even be a factor in extending their longevity. One study (Gordon et al., 1980) randomly assigned 308 cancer patients to either a standard care condition, in which they received their usual medical care but no additional intervention, or a psychosocial intervention in addition to their usual care. In the latter case, they received information about their cancer and counseling concerning their feelings and reactions to cancer, as well as referrals to other practitioners and agencies that might be helpful for particular patient needs. This intervention was provided for the patients while they were hospitalized and up to six months afterward. Overall, patients receiving the psychosocial intervention coped better with their disease in that their negative emotional states declined more rapidly and they were more likely to return to their former occupational status than was the case for control patients.

The possibility that psychotherapy may actually help patients live longer is suggested in a study by David Spiegel and his coworkers (Spiegel, Bloom, Kraemer, & Gottheil, 1989). In this study, 86 women with advanced breast cancer were randomly assigned either to a group that received a weekly 90-minute group therapy session for one year or a control group that did not receive this intervention. To determine the effects of the treatment on longevity, these patients were then followed for ten years. Analysis of the survival times for the patients indicated that those receiving the group therapy lived nearly twice as long as did patients in the control condition. These results

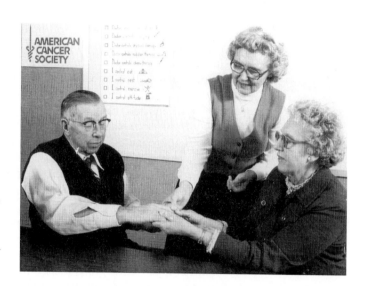

Cancer support groups can play an important role in helping cancer patients deal with the psychosocial impact of their disease.

suggest that psychotherapy can slow the progression of cancer, but—in view of the fact that all but three of the patients died during the follow-up period—it certainly does not cure it.

Help for cancer patients need not come from professionals only; patients can also help each other. Many self-help programs, such as Reach for Recovery (for breast cancer patients) or Ostomy Club (for patients with ostomies), have developed, in which patients get together to exchange information and experiences and provide each other with social support. Since the others in the group are also dealing with cancer, participants in self-help groups are likely to perceive the information as more relevant and the support as more meaningful than would be the case if they came from others not experiencing cancer. Although little controlled research has been done on the effectiveness of self-help groups, the available evidence suggests that they are effective in decreasing negative feelings and increasing feelings of self-esteem among patients (Lieberman, 1988; Van den Borne, Pruyn, & Van den Heuvel, 1987).

SUMMARY

The term cancer refers to a large group of diseases that are distinguished by the uncontrolled growth and abnormal spread of cells. Cancer, which can occur throughout the body, is initiated when carcinogenic substances or viruses cause alterations in cell DNA, which lead to changes in cell function and are passed on to daughter cells when the cell divides. Although many instances of

DNA damage are detected and repaired before they can cause cancer, some slip by immunological defenses and lead to the development of malignant tumors.

Current evidence indicates that both personality and stress are related to cancer development. People most likely to develop cancer are those who are passive, cooperative, suppress negative emotions, and respond to stress with helplessness. In addition, high levels of stress are associated with tumor development, particularly when the person does not cope with the stress effectively. Current evidence suggests that psychological variables have their influence on cancer via the immune system. Recent studies suggest that stress has the effect of decreasing the effectiveness of DNA repair as well as reducing the immune system's ability to destroy cancerous cells.

The development of cancer is closely related to life-style variables such as smoking, diet, occupation, and sunbathing. Because these factors are largely modifiable, there is currently a strong emphasis on encouraging people to adopt healthier life-styles. Particular emphasis has been placed on finding ways to discourage people from smoking and to help them quit once they begin.

The percentage of cancer patients who survive for five years or more after their diagnosis has dramatically increased over the last several decades, a result of improved methods of treatment as well as early diagnosis and treatment. Despite the importance of detecting cancer early, a substantial proportion of patients with cancer symptoms delay three or more months before seeking medical attention because of the nonpainful and subtle nature of early cancer symptoms, ignorance of the significance of symptoms, fear of cancer, and other factors. Many self-examination techniques have been developed and programs launched to encourage people to use them in order to reap the benefits of early detection. Use of early detection procedures can be encouraged through informational materials, the use of prompts and rewards, and community education programs.

Cancer can have a devastating impact, both physical and psychological. Patients diagnosed with cancer confront physical changes brought about by the disease and its treatment, as well as the psychosocial effects of the disease. Cancer patients often experience a great deal of emotional distress and difficulties in interpersonal relationships as a result of their disease. Many psychological interventions have been developed to help people cope with cancer, including behavioral techniques, psychotherapy, and self-help groups. Current evidence indicates that these interventions can be useful in helping patients to deal with both the physical and psychological aspects of cancer and, in at least some cases, may also be effective in prolonging life.

KEY TERMS

tumor (323)
benign tumor (323)
malignant tumor (323)
metastasis (323)
carcinogen (324)

DNA (deoxyribonucleic acid) (324)
oncogene (325)
chemotherapy (348)
anticipatory nausea and vomiting (349)

SUGGESTED READINGS

Cohen, L. A. (1987). Diet and cancer. *Scientific American, 257*(5), 42–48. This is a very lucid and readable discussion of the relationship between cancer and diet.

Levy, S. M. (1983). Host differences in neoplastic risk: Behavioral and social contributors to disease. *Health Psychology, 2,* 21–44. In this article, Sandra Levy discusses the behavioral and social variables that are associated with the development and course of cancer.

Renneker, M. (1988). *Understanding cancer.* (3d ed.). Palo Alto, CA: Bull Publishing Co. In this book, physician Mark Renneker and other cancer specialists provide a readable introduction to various aspects of cancer.

Taylor, S. E. (1983). Adjustment to threatening events: A theory of cognitive adaptation. *American Psychologist, 38,* 1161–73. On the basis of interviews with breast cancer patients, Shelley Taylor identifies some of the key factors involved in psychologically adapting to cancer.

Coronary Heart Disease

Throughout the world, more people die from diseases of the cardiovascular system than from any other cause. According to the World Health Organization, heart disease kills 12 million people annually; it is the leading cause of death in industrial countries and the third leading cause in developing countries ("Heart disease is public health enemy No. 1: WHO," 1992). In the United States, more people die from diseases of the cardiovascular system than the next four leading causes of death combined. Diseases of the cardiovascular system, including diseases of the heart and atherosclerosis, account for more than 37% of all deaths in the United States (National Center for Health Statistics, 1988). The good news, however, is that death rates from heart disease have been falling in many countries. Age-adjusted mortality from heart disease fell roughly 30% in the United States from the mid-1960s to the early 1980s (Jenkins, 1988). Rates have also fallen in Japan, Canada, Australia, Finland, and other countries. Unfortunately, these reductions are countered by rises, particularly in eastern Europe and developing countries (World Health Organization, 1982; "Heart disease is public health enemy No. 1: WHO," 1992).

Important though they are, mortality statistics provide only one indicator of the tremendous toll of coronary heart disease (CHD). CHD is also a chronic condition that can produce significant distress and incapacitation over long periods of time. A diagnosis of CHD is often traumatic for patients and their families, and may require significant psychosocial intervention to help them cope. This chapter examines CHD as a health problem by first exploring the ways in which biological and psychological factors interact in the development of heart disease, and then considers the role of life-style in CHD and preventive measures that can be taken. The chapter ends with a discussion on the psychosocial impact of CHD and what can be done to help people cope better.

MIND AND BODY: THE PHYSIOLOGY AND PSYCHOLOGY OF CORONARY HEART DISEASE

The interplay of biological and psychological factors in the development of CHD has long been suspected, but only recently has scientific evidence supported these suspicions. A growing number of recent research studies has provided convincing evidence of a strong link between psychosocial factors such as stress, personality, and life-style and the development of CHD (Krantz, Grunberg, & Baum, 1985). What are these linkages, and what are the mechanisms involved? To answer this question, we turn first to a consideration of the physiology of the cardiovascular system.

The Cardiovascular System and Heart Disease

The cardiovascular system is an intricate web containing some 60,000 miles of arteries, veins, and capillaries, with the heart as its center. This system plays a critical role in the body's physiology by transporting oxygen, hormones, and nutrients to body cells, and removing from those same cells carbon dioxide and other waste products (Tortora & Anagnostakos, 1984). The vehicle by which this is accomplished is the blood. Without an efficient system for circulating blood, the body's cells would die from lack of nourishment and dangerous waste products would quickly accumulate. A diagram of the circulatory system showing the heart and illustrating the flow of blood is given in Figure 14.1.

atrium (pl., atria)
One of the two upper chambers of the heart into which blood flows from the veins.

The heart. The heart itself is a hollow muscular organ that weighs roughly 300 grams (about 11 oz) and beats more than 100,000 times a day as it moves the blood through the body. As is shown in Figure 14.1, the interior of the heart consists of four chambers. The upper two chambers are called the left and right **atria,** whereas the lower chambers are the left and right **ventricles.** The atria and ventricles act as four separate but well-coordinated pumps that deftly move the blood through the blood vessels in a continuous closed cycle.

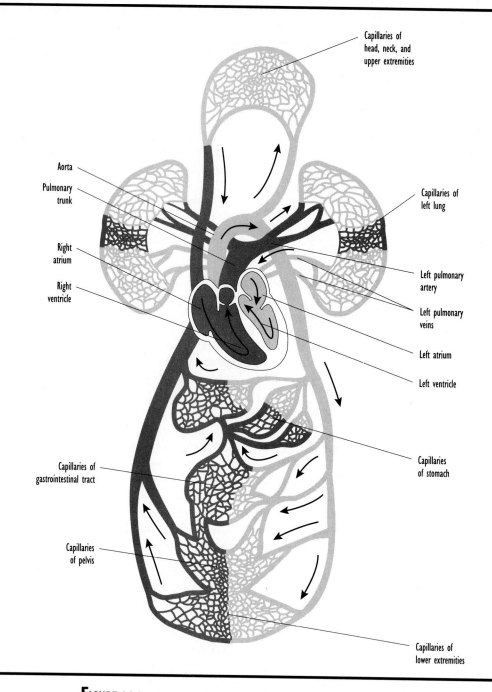

FIGURE 14.1 *Diagram of the heart and circulatory system showing the routes of blood flow.*

ventricle
The lower chamber of the heart, which pumps blood into either the pulmonary artery (right ventricle) or the aorta (left ventricle).

Blood begins its journey through the body with the contraction of the left ventricle, which expels oxygen-rich blood from the heart into the main artery of the body known as the *aorta*. From there it moves through the arteries and capillaries of the various parts of the body, supplying the cells with oxygen and nutrients and removing carbon dioxide and other waste products. It then returns via the veins to the right atrium of the heart, where it is pumped into the right ventricle. The contraction of the right ventricle causes the blood to move through the pulmonary arteries into the lungs, where it releases its accumulated carbon dioxide and takes on oxygen. The blood then returns to the left atrium via the pulmonary veins and is pushed into the left ventricle to begin another cycle.

myocardium
The muscle cells making up the wall of the heart.

The pumping action of the heart is accomplished by the regular contraction and relaxation of the **myocardium,** the muscle that makes up the wall of the heart. In the normal heartbeat, the two atria contract first, pushing the blood into the ventricles, which are relaxed. Then the atria relax while the ventricles contract, pushing the blood through the blood vessels. This alteration of contraction with relaxation is referred to as the *cardiac cycle.* A full cardiac cycle consists of a *systole* (contraction) and *diastole* (relaxation) of the atria, plus a systole and diastole of the ventricles. During the diastole of the ventricles, blood is being taken into the heart and blood pressure drops. In the systolic phase of the ventricles, blood is being pushed out of the heart through the blood vessels and blood pressure rises. The two numbers given as measures of blood pressure correspond to these two phases of the cardiac cycle. The first, higher number, known as **systolic pressure,** indicates the pressure (measured in millimeters of mercury or mmHg) exerted on the arteries when the ventricles contract and push blood out of the heart. The second, lower number, called **diastolic pressure,** indicates the pressure on arteries when the ventricles are in their relaxation phase. The average blood pressure is 120/80 mmHg for young adult males, and 8–10 mmHg less for young adult females.

systolic blood pressure
Pressure on the arteries when the ventricles are in their contraction phase.

diastolic blood pressure
Pressure on the arteries when the ventricles are in their relaxation phase.

When a person is at rest, the heart beats an average of 75 times per minute. However, when people exercise, experience stress, or feel strong emotion, the heart speeds up. These increases in heart rate occur mostly in the diastolic phase, meaning that the heart is taking less time to rest and refill with blood before expelling that blood into the arteries. Thus, even though overall cardiac output increases with increased heart rate, the heart tends to function less efficiently. Over time, a chronically rapid heart rate can lead to a reduction in the heart's strength. Regular exercise, however, strengthens the heart and leads to a reduction in heart rate when the person is at rest.

Diseases of the heart. Every year millions of people have heart attacks, and many more experience other forms of heart disease. In the United States, for example, an estimated one in five Americans who reach the age of 60 will have had a heart attack, and one in four persons between the ages of 30 and 60 has the potential to have one (Tortora & Anagnostakos, 1984). What are the major forms of heart disease, and what leads to their occurrence?

Heart disease comes in several forms and has several antecedents. In general, however, most heart problems can be traced almost immediately to either an inade-

atherosclerosis
The process through which cholesterol and other fats accumulate on artery walls, potentially impeding blood flow.

angina pectoris
A cramping pain felt in the chest that may indicate a shortage of oxygen to the heart muscle.

myocardial infarction (MI)
A blockage of a coronary artery, commonly referred to as a heart attack, leading to the destruction of heart muscle.

quate supply of blood to the heart muscle or faulty electrical conduction in the heart (Tortora & Anagnostakos, 1984).

Like all other body tissues, heart muscle requires the circulation of blood to supply it with nutrients and remove waste products. Blood to the heart muscle is supplied through the *coronary arteries,* so-called because their configuration was thought to resemble a crown (see Figure 14.2). Over time, these arteries may become clogged with fatty substances, particularly cholesterol and triglycerides (ingested fats), which results in the obstruction of blood flow to the myocardium. This process, known as **atherosclerosis,** may do considerable damage to the heart as it deprives the heart muscle of essential nutrients. Clinically, atherosclerosis manifests itself in **angina pectoris,** in which the person experiences pain and tightness in the chest as the heart is deprived of oxygen. In more serious cases, the person may experience a **myocardial infarction** (MI), or "heart attack," in which a part of the heart muscle dies because of the obstructed blood flow. MIs often occur because a blood clot formed around built-up cholesterol breaks free and blocks the passage of blood through the coronary arteries. When blood flow is not restored and the area affected is large enough, the MI results in death (Shillingford, 1981).

Faulty electrical conduction in the heart also plays a critical role. At least half of all deaths from MI occur before the person reaches the hospital for treatment. These deaths may be brought on by an irregular heartbeat, or *arrhythmia,* in which the

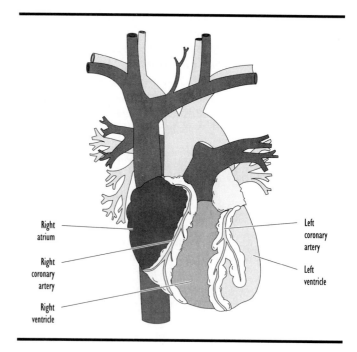

Right
atrium

Right
coronary
artery

Right
ventricle

Left
coronary
artery

Left
ventricle

FIGURE 14.2
Diagram of the exterior of the heart showing the coronary arteries.

heart's contractions are no longer synchronized properly. In serious cases, arrhythmia may progress to the point where the heart stops functioning altogether and death results. Arrhythmias are caused by disturbances in the electrical conduction system, the heart's mechanism for keeping the heartbeat regular. These disturbances can be controlled and corrected when they are detected and treated early enough, but left untreated can lead to death. For example, in cases of *ventricular fibrillation,* which involves haphazard contractions of the ventricles, a strong electrical current can be applied for short periods to stop the fibrillation in hopes that a normal heartbeat can be restored.

Although it is not possible to predict with absolute certainty who will fall victim to coronary heart disease and who will not, several factors significantly influence that likelihood (Jenkins, 1988). **Coronary risk factors** are characteristics of a person that influence the probability of developing CHD. Some of these, in particular age, sex, and family history, cannot be controlled. Like cancer, CHD is a disease of aging. The longer people live the more likely they are to develop CHD; not because aging per se causes heart disease, but because over the years deposits of cholesterol and triglycerides have more opportunity to build up in blood vessels. In addition, regardless of age, males are more likely than females to develop heart problems. Further, CHD tends to run in families. The fact that a person's parents or grandparents suffered from CHD increases the likelihood that the person will also be afflicted. But other risk factors can be altered. Voluntary behaviors such as cigarette smoking, dietary practices, and physical exercise significantly influence a person's likelihood of developing CHD (see discussion of life-style and coronary risk below).

coronary risk factors
Factors that increase the likelihood that the person will experience clinical coronary heart disease.

Hypertension. A cause of major concern in CHD is **hypertension,** or high blood pressure. Although some controversy exists as to exactly what constitutes abnormally high blood pressure, a common rule of thumb defines hypertension as systolic pressure above 140 mmHg or a diastolic pressure of more than 90 mmHg. Although hypertension has no overt symptoms and is not by itself lethal, it is a major health concern because of its relationship to other diseases. High blood pressure can result in abnormal hardening of artery walls, and is a major risk factor for diseases such as MI, stroke, and kidney failure. Fortunately, effective control of hypertension can substantially reduce these potential effects.

In about 15% of cases, hypertension is the result of an identifiable disease process such as atherosclerosis or kidney disease. For the remaining 85%, however, no organic cause can be identified, a condition known as *essential hypertension* (Epstein & Oster, 1984). In these cases, blood pressure remains abnormally high, but for unknown reasons. One particularly important issue with hypertension in the United States concerns racial differences. Although a significant number of both black and white Americans show elevated blood pressure, hypertension is a particular problem among black Americans. An estimated 16% of white Americans suffer from essential hypertension as compared to 25% of black Americans (Armstead, Lawler, Gorden, Cross, & Gibbons, 1989). At present, there are no clear answers as to why this difference exists. One possibility is that black Americans may show greater physiological reac-

hypertension
Blood pressure that is persistently above 140/90 mmHg.

BOX 14.1 Blood Pressure in Black Americans: The Role of John Henryism

John Henry, the legendary black steeldriver, is a symbol of the belief that a person can overcome any obstacle through enough hard work. According to the legend, John Henry was a champion steeldriver (a person who uses a steel stake and sledgehammer to make holes for explosives) on the C&O Railroad when he bragged that he could drive more steel than a steam-driven machine being used by a competing contractor. A contest was arranged in which John Henry indeed beat the machine, but afterward died from his efforts (Botkin, 1944). In their work on "John Henryism," Sherman James and his colleagues (James, Hartnett, & Kalsbeek, 1983; James, LaCroix, Kleinbaum, & Strogatz, 1984) draw an analogy between John Henry's efforts and those of black Americans who have worked to overcome daunting odds in their struggle for economic self-sufficiency. According to this reasoning, the belief that any obstacle can be overcome by hard work and determination can lead to chronic, excessive arousal when the person is continually required to overcome obstacles such as discrimination or lack of formal education. In turn, this excessive arousal may be one of the factors leading to hypertension among black Americans, particularly those with limited education.

To test this hypothesis, James and his colleagues (James et al., 1983) developed an eight-item scale for John Henryism including such items as "Once I make up my mind to do something, I stay with it until the job is completely done" and "I feel I am the kind of man who stands up for what he believes in, regardless of the consequences." This scale was then administered to a group of Southern, working-class black men during an interview in which they answered questions about educational background, life aspirations, and various health issues. In addition, blood pressure measures were obtained. The results showed that men who were high on John Henryism and had fewer than 11 years of education had significantly higher diastolic blood pressure than did those who were either low in John Henryism or had more education. Differences for systolic blood pressure were in the predicted direction, but were not statistically significant.

A later set of analyses (James et al., 1984) explored the role of John Henryism in the relationship between occupational stress and blood pressure. These analyses showed that although black men who perceived themselves as being successful tended to have lower diastolic blood pressure, this was not true for those who were also high in John Henryism. In addition, diastolic blood pressure was particularly high for men who were successful but high in John Henryism and felt that they had been hindered by being black. These data lend support to the hypothesis that hypertension in black Americans may, at least in part, be a function of barriers faced by black Americans and beliefs about how those barriers can be overcome.

tions to certain kinds of stressors, which may, in turn, lead to increased blood pressure (Anderson, 1989). Two types of stressors that appear to be particularly important are those relating to occupation and racial discrimination (Armstead et al., 1989; James, LaCroix, Kleinbaum, & Strogatz, 1984). Box 14.1 explores one aspect of this in more detail.

Hypertension cannot currently be cured, but it can be controlled using various methods. Overweight persons with hypertension are advised to lose weight, because blood pressure tends to fall with weight loss. In addition, hypertensives are often advised to reduce their sodium intake and engage in more exercise. Drugs are used to reduce blood pressure in many cases. Whatever the prescription, hypertension requires life-long treatment.

Stress, Personality, and Coronary Heart Disease

The risk factors discussed thus far (often termed "traditional risk factors") are useful in predicting CHD, but, even taken together, account for only about half the differences between groups in CHD (Jenkins, 1988). Researchers have therefore increasingly turned to the study of stress and personality for clues in understanding heart disease.

Stress. Emotional stress has long been popularly believed to be related to heart disease. In fact, reports of sudden cardiac death after emotional trauma go back to the time of the Egyptian pharaohs. According to ancient records, the chief architect to Pharaoh Nepherirke was so stunned when the divine pharaoh spoke directly to him that he fell to the ground, dead, and could not be revived (Siltanen, 1987). Even today numerous reports describe people experiencing cardiac arrest after traumatic experiences (Kamarck & Jennings, 1991).

Fortunately, in most people emotional stress does not lead directly to cardiac arrest. But evidence is mounting that stress plays an important role in the development of CHD. Studies of the role of life stress in sudden cardiac death, for example, have found significantly higher levels of life stress among victims of sudden cardiac death in the months before death than was the case for matched controls (Kamarck & Jennings, 1991). Other studies have found significant relationships between work stress and the occurrence of CHD. In particular, people in occupations with high levels of psychological demand but low decision control (such as firefighters) tend to have higher rates of CHD than do those in less demanding jobs (Krantz, Contrada, Hill, & Friedler, 1988).

Why is this the case? Recalling that changes in cardiovascular functioning play a prominent role in people's response to stress is helpful in understanding the role of stress in CHD. As noted in Chapter 6, the perception of an event as threatening leads to an acceleration of the heartbeat and a strengthening of the heart's contractions. In addition, the release of epinephrine and norepinephrine decreases the time needed for blood to coagulate and raises blood pressure, in part by causing blood vessels to constrict. In most cases of transitory stress, these responses pose no particular difficulty. However, when stress is chronic, the cumulative effect over time can be excessive wear on the cardiovascular system, leading to CHD (Krantz et al., 1988; Siltanen, 1987).

By contrast, when stress is especially acute, particularly in individuals who already show signs of heart disease, the results can be catastrophic. Research on sudden cardiac deaths (those occurring within 24 hours of the first symptoms) indicates that the impact of stress on the autonomic nervous system can set off a series of events resulting in cardiac arrest. These events are shown in Figure 14.3. Cardiac arrest itself results from lethal arrhythmias such as those occurring in fibrillation. These arrhythmias are, in turn, made more likely by the impact of stress in causing changes such as the constriction of coronary arteries, changes in blood clotting, and the rupturing of cholesterol plaques from arterial walls. These processes can lead to a clogging of

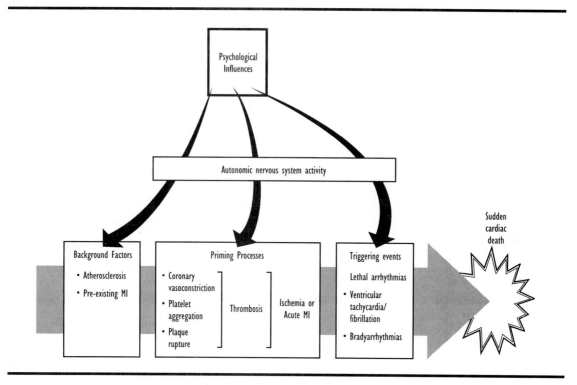

FIGURE 14.3   *Pathways of psychological influences in sudden cardiac death.*

Note. Adapted from "Biobehavioral factors in sudden cardiac death" by T. Kamarck and J. R. Jennings, 1991, *Psychological Bulletin, 109,* p. 46.

coronary arteries (thrombosis), resulting in the death of heart muscle, and MI. Although sudden cardiac death can and does occur among individuals without a history of heart disease, most such deaths occur among people with significant atherosclerosis or who have previously had an MI (Kamarck & Jennings, 1991).

Type A behavior pattern. The occurrence of CHD has also been related to personality. As early as the 1890s, physician William Osler described the heart patient as "not the delicate, neurotic person . . . but the robust, the vigorous in mind and body, the keen and ambitious man, the indicator of whose engine is always at full speed ahead" (quoted in Williams, 1989, p. 19). More recently, cardiologists Meyer Friedman and Ray Rosenman (1959, 1974) have proposed the concept of the **Type A behavior pattern,** which is described as "an action-emotion complex that can be observed in any person who is aggressively involved in a chronic, incessant struggle to achieve more and more in less and less time" (Friedman & Rosenman, 1974, p. 84). According to this formulation, CHD is most likely to develop in people who are characterized by

Type A behavior pattern
A behavior pattern characterized by high levels of competitive drive, time urgency, vigorous speech characteristics, and hostility.

high competitive drive, impatience, vigorous speech characteristics, and hostility, as well as a general hyperalertness and restlessness. By contrast, people exhibiting a Type B behavior pattern are described as having a lower level of competitive drive, being more relaxed and less hostile and less likely to develop CHD.

Initial evidence of the relationship between Type A behavior and CHD was obtained in two large-scale epidemiological studies conducted during the 1960s and 1970s. In the Western Collaborative Group Study (WCGS), more than 3,000 initially healthy men between the ages of 39 and 59 were followed for a period of 8½ years. As part of the data gathered at the beginning of the study, the participants were interviewed concerning Type A behaviors through the use of the Structured Interview (SI), developed specifically for that purpose. Comparison of Type A and Type B participants after 8½ years indicated that those classified as Type A were more than twice as likely to develop clinically significant CHD than were those classified as Type B. Since much of this difference remained after statistically controlling for other risk factors such as smoking, blood pressure, and cholesterol levels, these data strongly implicated Type A behavior as a significant risk factor for CHD (Rosenman et al., 1975).

These results were corroborated by the Framingham Heart Study, which followed a group of both men and women, aged 45 to 77, for a period of eight years. At the beginning of the study, more than 1,600 participants were asked to complete a lengthy questionnaire including questions on reactions to anger, stress, occupational mobility, and Type A behaviors. Comparisons of Type A and B individuals at the end of the study found a significant association between Type A and CHD for both men and women. Type A women were twice as likely to develop CHD and three times as likely to experience angina pectoris than were Type B women. Among men, Type A behavior was associated with a nearly 200% greater risk of both CHD and angina. These associations were found only among men in white-collar occupations and women working outside the home. As in the WCGS, the association of Type A with CHD was mostly independent of other risk factors (Haynes & Feinleib, 1980; Haynes, Feinleib, & Kannel, 1980).

These initial studies and others that followed, both in the United States and Europe, provided strong evidence that Type A is a significant risk factor in CHD (see Booth-Kewley & Friedman, 1987; Matthews, 1988; Matthews & Haynes, 1986; Rhodewalt & Smith, 1991, for reviews). However, later studies, particularly those in populations already at high risk for CHD, have raised important questions about the extent of the Type A-CHD connection. For example, in the Multiple Risk Factor Intervention Trial (MRFIT) (MRFIT Study Group, 1982; Shekelle, Gale, & Norusis, 1985) more than 3,000 men at high risk for CHD were followed for an average of seven years. All the participants were healthy at the beginning of the study, but were in the upper 10% of the population with respect to CHD risk because of cigarette smoking, high serum cholesterol levels, and blood pressure. Participants were randomly assigned to either an intervention designed to reduce CHD risk or a control group. Regardless of group assignment, Type A was unrelated to the development of CHD. Similar findings were obtained in the Aspirin Myocardial Infarction Study (Shekelle et al., 1985), and in a smaller study of patients undergoing cardiac catheterization,

Type B individuals actually showed more evidence of CHD than did Type As (Dimsdale, Gilbert, Hutter, Hackett, & Block, 1981).

How can these discrepancies be explained? One strong possibility is that Type A predicts CHD in some populations, but not others. The strongest results for Type A have been obtained when attempting to predict CHD in relatively broad populations. Both the WGCS and the Framingham Study looked at initially healthy individuals who were selected without reference to their risk for CHD. But studies questioning the validity of Type A have tended to focus on high-risk populations. Thus Type A might be related to CHD in the general population, but not in populations specifically at high risk for CHD (Matthews & Haynes, 1986; Rhodewalt & Smith, 1991).

Some of the discrepancies may also be the result of the methods by which Type A is assessed. Different studies often use different measures, which may or may not be measuring the same construct. Based on their original formulation of the Type A concept, Friedman and Rosenman developed the Structured Interview (SI), designed to obtain information on Type A behavior as well as to elicit Type A behavior by challenging the interviewee (Rosenman, 1978). In the SI, the person is asked about characteristic ways of responding to situations involving potential impatience, competitiveness, and hostility. In addition, the SI format allows the interviewer to assess the interviewee's response to challenges in the interview as well as aspects of expressive style such as vocal speed, volume, and explosiveness. Based on all these factors, the person is then categorized as to the extent of Type A or Type B behavior.

Type A is also assessed through self-report questionnaires. The Jenkins Activity Survey (JAS) was developed as a written alternative to the SI (Jenkins, Zyzanski, & Rosenman, 1971). Based on the SI, 52 questions were developed that were thought to capture the essence of the Type A pattern. Using data from participants in the WGCS, these items were then statistically analyzed to find the items that best separated Type As and Type Bs as determined from the SI. Other self-report measures include the Framingham Type A Scale used in the Framingham Heart Study (Haynes, Levine, Scotch, Feinleib, & Kannel, 1978) and the Bortner Rating Scale, which has been used primarily in European studies (Bortner, 1969). These scales ask about similar types of behaviors, but are shorter (10 to 14 items) and use different question formats. Sample questions from three Type A measures are given in Table 14.1.

All these measures purport to measure the same construct, but are actually only partly related to each other. For example, although the JAS was designed to predict classification on the SI, it agrees with the SI for only 60–70% of the respondents. Moreover, the Framingham and Bortner scales are only modestly correlated with other measures of Type A (Matthews & Haynes, 1986; Rhodewalt & Smith, 1991). This lack of agreement between measures of Type A may help to explain some of the discrepancy in study results. Meta-analysis indicates that the SI produces more consistent results than does the JAS (Booth-Kewley & Friedman, 1987). Too few studies have been done using the Framingham and Bortner scales to pass judgment on them.

Closely related to the problem of measuring Type A are questions about what Type A actually represents. The original concept was of a global set of traits that predisposes

TABLE 14.1 *Sample Questions Used to Measure Type A*

Structured Interview

Would you describe yourself as a HARD-DRIVING, AMBITIOUS type of person in accomplishing things you want, OR would you describe yourself as a relatively RELAXED and EASY-GOING person?

When you play games with people YOUR OWN age, do you play for the FUN of it, or are you REALLY in there to WIN?

Do you ALWAYS feel anxious to GET GOING and FINISH whatever you have to do?

Framingham Type A Scale

Traits and qualities that describe you: Being hard-driving and competitive, usually pressed for time, being bossy and domineering, having a strong need to excel in most things, eating too quickly.

Do you get upset when you have to wait for anything?

Jenkins Activity Survey

When you listen to someone talking and this person takes too long to come to the point, how often do you feel like hurrying the person along?

Would people you know well agree that you tend to get irritated easily?

Do you ever set deadlines or quotas for yourself at work or at home?

Note. From "Type A behavior: Assessment and intervention" by M. A. Chesney, J. R. Eagleston, and R. H. Rosenman, 1981, in *Medical psychology: Contributions to behavioral medicine,* ed. by C. K. Prokop and L. A. Bradley, New York: Academic Press; "Progress toward validation of a computer-scored test for the Type A coronary-prone behavior pattern" by C. D. Jenkins, S. J. Zyzanski, and R. H. Rosenman, 1971, *Psychosomatic Medicine, 33,* 193–202; and *Type A behavior pattern: A model for research and practice* by V. A. Price, 1982, New York: Academic Press.

people to CHD. However, later studies have made it clear that Type A actually involves several components, only some of which may be predictive of CHD. For example, the JAS consists of three subscales, speed and impatience, job involvement, and hard-driving. Of these, the hard-driving subscale best predicts CHD, whereas job involvement shows little relationship to it (Booth-Kewley & Friedman, 1987).

This raises the possibility that one or more components of the overall Type A construct are the toxic elements, and the others are, at best, unrelated or, at worst, may obscure the relationship of the toxic elements to CHD. A prime candidate for the key toxic element is hostility. Studies separating the different components of Type A have found that measures of hostility show the most consistent relationship to CHD (Booth-Kewley & Friedman, 1987; Rhodewalt & Smith, 1991). In line with this, several studies explicitly focusing on hostility have found that individuals who express a great deal of hostility toward others tend to have higher levels of CHD. Other possible candidates for toxic elements in Type A are antagonism and self-involvement. Current evidence suggests that people who are more antagonistic than agreeable toward others tend to have more CHD, as do those who are more self-involved (Rhodewalt & Smith, 1991).

Finally, Type A may be predictive of CHD in some cultures, but not in others. Although most studies of Type A in the American general population have supported its relationship to CHD, a study among men of Japanese descent in Hawaii found only inconsistent evidence relating Type A to CHD (Cohen & Reed, 1985). Although Type A was associated with overall CHD in some of the analyses done, Type A showed no relationship to clinically manifested CHD, such as MI, nor to the degree of coronary atherosclerosis among men who died and were later autopsied (see also Cohen, Syme, Jenkins, Kagan, & Zyzanski, 1979).

Explaining the relationship between Type A and CHD. Despite the questions that have been raised about Type A, at least some aspect of this behavior pattern has been shown to be related to CHD. What are the mechanisms involved in this relationship? Answers are still being sought to this question, but the best evidence at this time argues that Type As respond differently to stress, at both a psychological and a physiological level, than do others. Specifically, evidence is growing that Type A individuals appraise challenging situations as more stressful and may well behave in ways that increase their stress levels, relative to Type Bs (Smith & Anderson, 1986). For example, Type As report greater involvement in academic and extracurricular activities in school (Glass, 1977), and, when playing games, view their opponents as more hard-driving and competitive than do Type Bs (Smith & Brehm, 1981). In addition, Type As increase their exposure to stressful situations by denying and suppressing aversive emotions as well as by evaluating their task performances more harshly (Smith & Anderson, 1986). Not surprisingly, they also elicit more competitive and aggressive responses from others (Van Egern, Abelson, & Sniderman, 1983).

This increased reactivity to stress on the part of Type As is also seen in their physiological responses. As noted earlier, stress produces significant changes in cardiovascular functioning, changes that, particularly when chronic, can increase the chances of developing clinical CHD. Even though these changes occur in everyone, evidence demonstrates that they occur more strongly in Type As than they do in Type Bs. In other words, Type As appear to show physiological **hyperreactivity** in response to stress (Krantz & Manuck, 1984; Matthews & Haynes, 1986; Rhodewalt & Smith, 1991). Specifically, when Type As are placed in situations where they feel threatened or challenged (or when they create such situations), they show greater changes in heart rate, blood pressure, and catecholamine levels than do Type Bs. For example, in one experiment (Ward et al., 1986) subjects were assessed for Type A using the SI and then engaged in a series of potentially stressful tasks. The results showed that for four of the tasks, those involving time urgency, Type A subjects experienced significantly greater increases in blood pressure and heart rate than did Type B subjects. No differences were found for tasks that involved passive waiting or endurance of discomfort. Other studies have found that Type As also show higher catecholamine excretion in response to stress, and have a slower return to baseline levels of cardiovascular functioning (Dembroski, MacDougall, Shields, Pettito, & Lushene, 1978; Jamieson & Lavoie, 1987; Krantz & Manuck, 1984; Muranaka et al., 1988).

hyperreactivity
An exaggerated physiological response to challenging situations.

Differences in physiological responses between Type As and Type Bs seem to be particularly pronounced under conditions of harassment (Diamond et al., 1984).

The significance of these differences for CHD becomes clear when we consider the impact of these changes on the cardiovascular system. As noted earlier, most heart problems in adults are the result of atherosclerosis of the coronary arteries or problems with arrhythmias. Current evidence indicates that the kind of hyperreactivity shown by Type As can significantly increase the likelihood of these problems (Krantz & Manuck, 1984; Matthews & Haynes, 1986). In particular, heightened levels of catecholamines may elevate blood pressure, accelerate the rate of damage of coronary arteries, induce damage to the heart muscle, and increase the likelihood of fatal arrhythmias. Moreover, catecholamines appear to increase the aggregation (clumping) of blood platelets, an important process in atherosclerosis and coronary thrombosis, as well as promote increased serum cholesterol, another risk factor for CHD. Temporary increases in blood pressure may also be an important factor in injury to blood vessels, which can then lead to an increase in the development of atherosclerosis. The end result of all of this is that through both their psychological and physiological responses to stress, Type As tends to accelerate damage to the cardiovascular system and increase their likelihood of CHD. The Type A-CHD relationship is summarized in Figure 14.4.

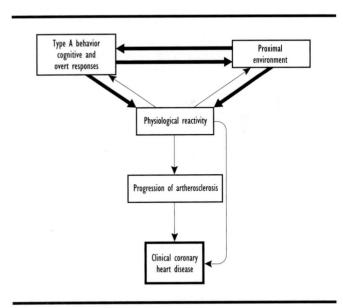

FIGURE 14.4

A transactional model of Type A behavior and heart disease.

Note. From "Models of personality and disease: An interactional approach to Type A behavior and cardiovascular risk" by T. W. Smith and N. B. Anderson, 1986, *Journal of Personality and Social Psychology, 50,* p. 1168.

The development of Type A behavior. The kinds of responses exhibited by Type As do not suddenly appear when the person reaches adulthood. Rather, they are the result of a developmental history that begins in childhood. Understanding this development can provide clues as to possible interventions for reducing Type A responses and its associated coronary risk.

That children exhibit Type A behavior has been amply demonstrated in many studies assessing Type A characteristics in children and adolescents (Matthews & Woodall, 1988). One of the most common instruments for measuring Type A in children is the Matthews Youth Test for Health (MYTH), in which observers (often teachers) are asked to rate the child on several Type A–related characteristics such as "gets irritated easily" and "does things in a hurry" (Matthews & Angulo, 1980). Children who score high on the MYTH, like their adult counterparts, have been found to respond to threats to control by increasing their efforts to exert control (Matthews, 1979). In addition, they have higher achievement scores, regardless of IQ (Matthews, Stoney, Rakaczky, & Jamison, 1986), and are more talkative and outgoing than Type B children (Matthews & Woodall, 1988). Of particular importance is the fact that they show the same heightened level of physiological activity in response to stress as do adult Type As (Houston, 1983; Lundberg, 1983; Matthews & Jennings, 1984). Thus the psychological and physiological processes that put Type As at risk for CHD appear to start early.

Studies of the origins of Type A in children indicate that some of the predisposing characteristics are identifiable in children as young as 12 to 18 months of age. For example, one study found that infants who responded to their mothers with avoidance after the mother had been away for a brief time were likely to display Type A characteristics, specifically anger and hostility, when followed up seven years later (Rhodewalt & Smith, 1991). Beyond this, Type A characteristics seem to run in families and be encouraged by certain child-rearing practices. Young Type A boys, but not girls, tend to have Type A parents, suggesting that boys acquired it through modeling (Matthews et al., 1986). In addition, studies of parents of Type A children indicate that they tend to place a high value on performance and achievement, but, at the same time, do not provide clear performance standards. Parents respond to Type A children by encouraging them to do better, but make fewer positive remarks about their performance (Matthews et al., 1986; Matthews & Woodall, 1988). Thus Type A children are placed in the position of being pushed to improve their performance, but never receiving the positive feedback that would indicate that their performance has improved. Longitudinal research indicates that children who exhibit Type A behaviors are likely to develop into Type A adults (Keltikangas-Jarvinen, 1989).

LIFE-STYLE AND CORONARY RISK

CHD is also a life-style disease, influenced by several important modifiable behavioral factors. Whether a person develops CHD is, in part, a function of such life-style variables as smoking, diet, physical exercise, and interpersonal relationships.

Smoking

One of the most important of these is cigarette smoking. People, especially males, who smoke are almost twice as likely to experience heart disease as are those who do not, even after controlling for other risk factors (Jenkins, 1988). Among smokers, the amount of smoking appears to be an important factor. Epidemiological studies have found a linear relationship between the number of cigarettes smoked and the incidence of CHD, a relationship that appears to be particularly strong for sudden cardiac death. Further, current evidence suggests that stopping smoking may have a greater effect in reducing cardiovascular risk than changes in any other risk factor. Men who quit smoking before the age of 65 can reduce their risk of heart attacks by up to 50%. In addition, the longer the person abstains from smoking, the greater is the risk reduction (Epstein & Perkins, 1988).

Why should smoking be related to CHD? Answers to this question are still being sought, but available evidence demonstrates specific effects of smoking, in particular those of nicotine, on the heart and circulatory system. For one thing, smoking produces stresslike changes in autonomic activity, including increases in heart rate, blood pressure, catecholamines, and constriction of blood vessels (Epstein & Perkins, 1988; Velican & Velican, 1989). As noted earlier, when changes like these become chronic they can increase the likelihood of CHD. Recent studies indicate that the effects of smoking combine additively with stress: People who smoke while under stress experience particularly large cardiovascular changes. For example, in one study women who both smoked and were exposed to an experimental stressor showed significantly greater cardiovascular arousal than did those who either only smoked or were only exposed to stress (Dembroski, MacDougall, Cardozo, Ireland, & Krug-Fite, 1985).

In addition, smoking affects serum cholesterol levels and the clotting of blood (Velican & Velican, 1989). Smoking increases the formation of low-density cholesterol, which is associated with increased atherosclerosis, while it decreases the production of high-density cholesterol, which protects against CHD. Smoking also increases the blood's ability to coagulate and form blood clots. Together, these processes increase wear on the heart and blood vessels, and accelerate atherosclerosis, making it more likely that the person will develop heart disease. Stopping smoking improves heart functioning, slows the rate of atherosclerosis, and reduces the likelihood of the formation of blood clots that can clog coronary arteries (Velican & Velican, 1989).

Diet

Diet is also considered to play a significant role in the development of CHD. Epidemiological studies have shown that rates of CHD are significantly correlated with various aspects of diet, suggesting that changes in diet may be effective in reducing CHD (Jeffery, 1988). In particular, current evidence suggests that what people eat has a significant impact on CHD through its effects on the physiological risk factors of hypertension, elevated cholesterol levels, and obesity.

As mentioned earlier, hypertension is a significant precursor of heart and other diseases. People with high blood pressure may develop greater hardening of artery walls and are more likely to experience MI, stroke, and other problems. Although the exact causes of hypertension are often not known, blood pressure can be influenced by diet (Jeffery, 1988). In particular, two major determinants of blood pressure are body weight and sodium intake, both of which are diet related. Epidemiological studies have consistently shown that greater body weight is associated with higher blood pressure (Gillum, Taylor, Brozek, Polansky, & Blackburn, 1982; Harlan, et al., 1984). Body weight, in turn, is closely related to both the amount and types of foods that a person eats. Although the evidence is not as strong, sodium intake has also been shown to correlate with blood pressure. On the basis of this evidence, people with hypertension are commonly recommended to lose weight and cut down on their consumption of salt (Jeffery, 1988).

A second means by which diet affects CHD is through its influence on levels of cholesterol in the blood. High levels of serum cholesterol are known to accelerate the build-up of cholesterol deposits on blood vessel walls and increase the person's chances of developing clinical heart disease (Velican & Velican, 1989). However, not all cholesterol is created equal. Whereas a high level of low-density lipoprotein cholesterol (LDLC) puts a person at greater risk for CHD, a high level of high-density lipoprotein cholesterol (HDLC) is inversely related to CHD (Jeffery, 1988; Velican & Velican, 1989). Thus having both a high level of HDLC and a low level of LDLC is most desirable. When physicians and others say that a person has a high cholesterol level, they are generally referring to a high level of LDLC. LDLC is also the type of cholesterol that is most influenced by diet. Diets that are high in animal fats and cholesterol increase the person's serum cholesterol level, whereas diets whose fat content is in the form of polyunsaturated fats, usually derived from vegetable sources, reduce serum cholesterol. People with high levels of LDLC are therefore advised to reduce their intake of animal fats and cholesterol, and replace these with fats that are polyunsaturated (National Institutes of Health, 1984). One component of diet that influences the level of HDLC is alcohol. Recent studies have shown that moderate consumption of alcohol (two or three drinks per week) increases HDLC levels and may also protect against CHD (Jeffery, 1988).

Finally, diet influences CHD through its effects on obesity. Although obesity has usually been thought of as a risk factor for CHD primarily because of its association with hypertension and serum cholesterol, evidence now indicates that obesity may be an independent risk factor in its own right. For example, data from two large longitudinal heart studies (The Framingham Study; Hubert, Feinleib, McNamara, & Castelli, 1983; and the Manitoba Heart Study; Rabkin, Mathewson, & Hsu, 1977) have found that, over a 26-year period, people who were fat had a higher incidence of CHD, regardless of other risk factors. New evidence shows that CHD may be related to body fat distribution. Individuals who have excess levels of fat in the hips appear to be at lower risk for CHD than those who have a similar amount of fat in the abdominal region. Further, individuals who put on their excess weight as adults appear to be at higher risk for CHD than those who have always been heavy (Jeffery, 1988). This argues that one means of reducing CHD risk is for obese individuals to shed extra pounds by either eating less, exercising more, or both.

Exercise

People who live sedentary lives have long been recognized as more likely to suffer from CHD. Epidemiological studies comparing people with different levels of both occupational and leisure activity have confirmed that lower levels of physical activity are associated with increased likelihood of developing heart disease (Jenkins, 1988; Wenger, 1983). For example, studies examining the amount of physical exertion required in a person's occupation have found that higher levels of exertion reduce CHD, whereas more sedentary jobs place people at higher risk (Jenkins, 1988). Other studies examining leisure-time physical activities have found that people who regularly participate in moderately strenuous activities such as jogging, swimming, and bicycling have 20% to 50% less CHD than those who are more sedentary (Paffenbarger, 1985). Further, regular and moderately strenuous aerobic exercise is associated not only with lower rates of CHD overall but also reduces the chances that any given heart attack will be fatal (Jenkins, 1988).

Why should this be the case? Current evidence suggests that physical activity is protective against CHD for several reasons (Jenkins, 1988; Wenger, 1983). First, people who are physically active are less likely to accumulate excess bodily fat, which, as seen earlier, reduces the likelihood that they will have elevated blood pressure or serum cholesterol. Second, regular exercise increases cardiopulmonary efficiency such that the heart is more efficient in pumping blood through the circulatory system and the lungs have an increased capacity for extracting oxygen from the air. The effect of this increased efficiency is to expand cardiovascular capacity and reduce blood pressure. People with higher levels of fitness also appear to show less cardiovascular reactivity in response to stress (Czajkowski et al., 1990). In addition, exercise influences the person's serum cholesterol levels. People who engage in regular exercise have lower levels of LDLC, and some evidence indicates that exercise may promote higher

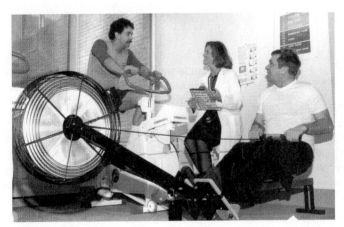

Physical exercise reduces coronary risk by strengthening the heart as well as reducing body weight, blood pressure, and reactivity to stress.

levels of HDLC (Wenger, 1983). Finally, exercise appears to have an indirect effect on CHD through other behavioral risk factors such as smoking and alcohol consumption. Specifically, people who exercise regularly are less likely to smoke and consume high levels of alcohol.

Interpersonal Relationships

Evidence also demonstrates that the person's social relationships influence the development of heart disease. In particular, epidemiological studies have found that marital status is linked to the likelihood that a person will die of heart disease (Lynch, 1977; Venters, 1986). For example, death rates for CHD in the United States are significantly higher for individuals who are single, divorced, or widowed than they are for those who are married. These differences, which tend to be greater for younger age groups, are found for both males and females, as well as across ethnic groups (Lynch, 1977). Marital status is also a significant predictor of survival after a heart attack. In one study, 1,400 patients who had experienced a myocardial infarction were followed for up to ten years after their initial hospitalization. Analysis of mortality data by marital status showed that unmarried individuals were more likely to die in the hospital and showed higher death rates at both the five- and ten-year follow-up than did married patients (Chandra, Szklo, Goldberg, & Tonascia, 1983; see also Box 1.1).

Why should marital status affect CHD? One possibility is that people who are married differ from their unmarried counterparts with respect to other CHD risk factors. The data in support of this notion, however, are inconsistent. For example, one study found that separated/divorced males and females were more likely to smoke and less likely to quit smoking than were either those who were single or married. Rates for widowed individuals were in between. Married individuals below the age of 55 reported less alcohol use than their formerly married counterparts. Yet married men and women were less likely to report getting regular exercise (Venters et al., 1986). Although such differences may be part of the reason for the differences in CHD by marital status, differences in CHD rates remain significant when these and other risk factors are statistically controlled (Chandra et al., 1983).

The differences in CHD rates are more likely related to differences between the groups in levels of stress and social support. Separation, divorce, and the death of a spouse are all generally considered stressful events. People who are not married may be less likely to have companions readily available to provide social support in times of distress (Venters, 1986). As seen earlier, stress plays a significant role in the development of CHD, and differences between marital status groups in stress may well lead to differences in CHD. However, marital status is only one aspect of interpersonal relations, and one's marital status by itself says nothing about the quality of the relationship. The data linking marital status to CHD suggest that future research could fruitfully investigate the role of interpersonal relations in CHD, particularly focusing on the nature of those relationships and the mechanisms linking them to CHD.

INTERVENTIONS FOR REDUCING CORONARY HEART DISEASE

The close relationship of Type A behavior and life-style factors to CHD raises the possibility of reducing cardiovascular risk through behavioral means. If, indeed, CHD risk is influenced by how one handles stress, as well as by smoking, diet, and exercise, to what degree is it possible to reduce CHD incidence and death by altering these behaviors? How might that be accomplished? Data on the actual reduction of CHD through behavioral means are still sketchy and somewhat controversial. However, strategies have been developed that show promise for changing behavioral CHD risk factors and, potentially, reducing CHD itself.

Modifying Type A Behavior

The evidence linking Type A behavior to CHD suggests that one means of reducing CHD risk is the modification of this behavior pattern. Indeed, several studies have been initiated to do just that. How might Type A behavior be modified? Because the Type A pattern seems to involve an overreaction to challenging situations, one possibility is to teach people more adaptive ways of dealing with such situations (Levenkron & Moore, 1988; Rhodewalt & Smith, 1991). For example, in the Montreal Type A Intervention Project (Roskies et al., 1986), Type A individuals in a cognitive-behavioral intervention group were taught strategies for coping with different kinds of stress including muscle relaxation, communication skills, problem solving, and cognitive relabeling, which involves learning how to think about stressful situations in less stressful ways. To determine the effects of this training, measures of Type A behavior and cardiovascular reactivity were obtained both before the training began and after completion of the 10-week program. The results showed that, compared with one group that engaged in aerobic exercise and another that received weight training, participants in the cognitive-behavioral intervention group showed lower levels of Type A behaviors after treatment. The groups did not differ, however, with respect to changes in physiological reactivity, raising possible questions about the clinical significance of the behavioral changes.

In another study officer-students at the U.S. Army War College received a nine-month treatment program involving group therapy, in which they were taught relaxation techniques and methods for changing Type A cognitions, behaviors, and emotional responses (Gill et al., 1985). As a part of this treatment, participants were taught to observe their own behavior and to modify their Type A assumptions and values. At the end of the treatment, 40% of the participants in the program showed a significant reduction in Type A scores compared with 9% of the participants in a no-treatment control group. In addition, those who showed a significant reduction in Type A scores showed greatly reduced serum cholesterol levels.

Some evidence also indicates that reductions in Type A behavior can decrease the likelihood of recurrent heart attacks. The Recurrent Coronary Prevention Project (Friedman et al., 1986) randomly assigned more than 1,000 heart patients who had already had one heart attack to one of four groups: a Type A intervention group that received the same intervention program received by the army officers discussed above, a cardiac counseling group, a group receiving both treatments, or a no-treatment control. Cardiac counseling included information about the diagnosis and treatment of heart disease, along with counseling on recommended diet, medications, and exercise. At the end of 4.5 years, only 12.9% of the patients receiving both cardiac counseling and Type A intervention had had second heart attacks as compared to 21.2% of those receiving only cardiac counseling. Supporting the importance of Type A reduction in preventing cardiac recurrence was the finding that, regardless of treatment group, patients who showed reductions in Type A scores suffered only one fourth as many heart attacks as those who showed no change.

Controlling Hypertension

A second essential component in efforts to prevent CHD is the control of hypertension. As we have seen, hypertension is a key risk factor in predicting CHD. The critical question then is what can be done to reduce it. Current treatments for hypertension fall into two categories: those that use medications to reduce blood pressure and those that attempt to control blood pressure through behavioral means.

Pharmacological treatments. The most common method of treating hypertension is through the use of various types of medication. Several major classes of drugs are currently used to lower blood pressure, each operating through different physiological mechanisms (Epstein & Oster, 1984; Laragh, 1988). The most commonly prescribed medications, at least in the initial phases of treatment, are diuretics. Blood pressure is in part dependent on the volume of blood in the circulatory system. Diuretics influence blood pressure by decreasing blood volume through the excretion of sodium from the body. The decrease in sodium leaves less fluid in the body, and more is excreted through the urine. Whereas diuretics operate through reducing blood volume, beta-adrenoceptor blockers (also known as simply beta-blockers) influence blood pressure through several other mechanisms, including the reduction of cardiac output and peripheral resistance to blood flow. In addition, beta-blockers influence the level of the hormone renin, which is involved in the regulation of blood pressure. Less commonly used are alpha-adrenoceptor blockers (alpha-blockers), vasodilators, converting enzyme inhibitors, and calcium channel blockers. These drugs work by a variety of mechanisms, including reduction of peripheral resistance to blood flow, reducing cardiac output, and altering the level of hormones involved in blood pressure regulation.

Although pharmacological treatment of hypertension has proven effective in reducing blood pressure, it is also controversial. On the one hand, blood pressure medications often produce side effects that can be distressing to patients and reduce cooperation with treatment. Among the common side effects are weakness, fatigue, drowsiness, dizziness, depression, headaches, adverse metabolic effects, and sexual dysfunction (Epstein & Oster, 1984). Since hypertension itself is a symptomless condition, the production of symptoms by the medications used to treat it can be a serious disincentive to continuing with treatment.

On the other hand, questions have arisen about the effects of some of the medications on heart disease itself. Although lowering blood pressure is an important goal, achieving this goal through pharmacological means may not have as much effect on heart disease as is commonly assumed. For example, recent reviews of long-term outcome studies on the treatment of hypertension found that treating hypertension with drugs is highly effective in reducing the incidence of hypertension-related diseases such as stroke and congestive heart failure, but has less certain effects on CHD. Although most studies have found that overall death rates from CHD are reduced through drug treatments for hypertension, several studies have found little or no impact on nonfatal MI (Berglund, 1988; Tifft & Chobanian, 1991). Why is this the case? It turns out that some of the drugs used to fight hypertension, particularly diuretics, also increase sympathetic activity, which may then reduce favorable changes in cardiovascular risk obtained by lowering blood pressure. This argues for using considerable care in controlling hypertension through drugs and for selecting drugs that do not result in sympathetic activation (Lee et al., 1988).

Behavioral treatments. Because of the problems associated with treating hypertension through drugs and the association of hypertension with behavior and other psychosocial factors, attention has increasingly turned to the use of behavioral methods for treating this problem. These methods range from changes in diet and exercise through the use of stress management and biofeedback and may be used either in conjunction with or instead of drug treatments.

Among the most common behavioral methods for the treatment of hypertension are those aimed at weight reduction, dietary change, and increases in exercise (Epstein & Oster, 1984; Horan & Roccella, 1988; Jeffery, 1991; Siegel & Blumenthal, 1991). Of these, weight reduction is probably the most commonly prescribed. As seen earlier, people who are obese are more likely to show elevated blood pressure. Further, weight reduction often leads to blood pressure reductions. For example, one study found that among 81 hypertensives who lost an average of 9.5 kg in a four-month weight reduction plan, 79 showed significant reductions in blood pressure (Epstein & Oster, 1984). Unfortunately, treatment of obesity is often difficult. As noted in Chapter 5, many methods have been successfully used to help people lose weight, but long-term maintenance of this weight loss is a problem. Many patients who are able to take off pounds show weight gains after the intervention is completed (Jeffery, 1991); therefore, weight loss programs should focus on ways of keeping weight off, not just on losing it.

Patients are also generally advised to change their diets. In particular, they are usually advised to cut down on sodium (salt) intake and to restrict their use of alcohol. Some have suggested that increases in potassium, calcium, and magnesium may be beneficial. Despite the frequency with which dietary changes are prescribed, however, their effectiveness is controversial (Berglund, 1984; Horan & Roccella, 1988). Studies

Recent research has shown that relaxation training can significantly reduce blood pressure and the need for medications to control hypertension.

of sodium reduction, for example, have found that reducing sodium intake can have a significant impact on blood pressure in some people, but very little, if any, in others. At present, there is no way of reliably differentiating those who respond to sodium reduction and those who do not. However, because reducing sodium intake generally has no negative effects, most patients have been recommended to reduce their use of salt. The roles of potassium, calcium, and magnesium are even more controversial and less established, though increases in consumption of these minerals may be beneficial for some individuals. Alcohol use, however, has been reliably shown to increase blood pressure, and patients who drink alcohol are generally advised to reduce their consumption to less than 1 oz of ethanol per day (the equivalent of 2 oz of 100 proof whiskey or 24 oz of beer) (Horan & Roccella, 1988).

A third behavioral means of reducing blood pressure is through physical exercise. As was noted earlier, people living sedentary life-styles have more problems with hypertension. Therefore, hypertension patients are often recommended to begin a physical exercise program. Does physical exercise lead to blood pressure reduction? Evidence shows that it can, at least for some patients (Siegel & Blumenthal, 1991). For example, one study randomly assigned 56 hypertensive men to either an exercise group in which they received four months of exercise or a sedentary control group. Among the exercising subjects, blood pressure declined significantly, whereas for the control group only minor changes occurred (Duncan et al., 1985). Despite such encouraging results, however, exercise leads to relatively modest reductions in blood pressure and appears to be more useful for older than younger patients (Herd & Hartley, 1984).

Beyond changes in weight, diet, and exercise, interest is also growing in the use of stress reduction techniques for fighting hypertension. Along these lines, relaxation techniques including muscle relaxation, biofeedback, **autogenic training,** meditation, and hypnosis have been used with hypertensive patients under the assumption that

autogenic training
A type of self-hypnosis that produces relaxation through concentration on bodily sensations of warmth and heaviness.

blood pressure will be lowered by reducing overall arousal. Does it work? At present, the evidence is mixed (see Jacob, Chesney, Williams, Ding, & Shapiro, 1991; Kaufmann et al., 1988, for reviews). Some studies have shown significant reductions in blood pressure after relaxation. For example, one study in the former Soviet Union randomly assigned 117 mildly hypertensive patients to one of three types of relaxation (autogenic training, biofeedback, or breathing relaxation training) or one of two untreated control groups. At the end of a one-year follow-up, subjects given the relaxation training showed significant reductions in blood pressure, reductions that were significantly larger than those obtained in the control conditions (Aivazyan, Zaitsev, Salenko, Yurenev, & Patruskeva, 1988). Not all studies, however, have obtained such favorable results. For instance, a meta-analysis of 12 independent investigations of various behavioral interventions for hypertension, most of which involved relaxation, found that although these techniques produced a reliable reduction in diastolic blood pressure for patients not receiving medication, no effect was detectable for systolic blood pressure or for medicated patients (Kaufmann et al., 1988). Further, at least some of the blood pressure reduction in some studies may be an artifact of study design rather than a result of treatment (Jacob et al., 1991).

Taken as a whole, the results of behavioral treatments for hypertension indicate that they can be effective in reducing blood pressure, but generally result in only modest reductions. Some patients with mild hypertension might be able to control their blood pressure solely through behavioral means. However, the control of seriously elevated blood pressure is still likely to require medication. Moreover, all hypertension treatments suffer from relatively high levels of noncooperation. On the average, more than a third of hypertensive patients fail to cooperate with treatment (Dunbar-Jacob, Dwyer, & Dunning, 1991). Even the most effective treatment loses its effectiveness when people do not follow it. Thus an important challenge in treating hypertension is improving patient cooperation.

Changing Life-style

The thread running through all the efforts to reduce CHD risk is the need for people to adopt a healthier life-style. How can this best be accomplished? Chapter 5 examined different techniques to change life-style and promote more positive health behaviors; some of these concentrated on changing the behavior of individuals, whereas others focused on whole communities. Which of these approaches is most useful in reducing CHD risk?

The most successful programs for reducing CHD risk are those that target whole communities (Perry, Klepp, & Shultz, 1988). In many countries, particularly in the industrialized world, the major risk factors for CHD are common in the population at large because a significant number of people smoke, have elevated cholesterol, and live sedentary lives. Attempting to change these risk factors through individually oriented programs would be an expensive and time-consuming task. Programs oriented toward individuals typically target those at particularly high risk, and, although they may be effective in producing significant risk reduction for those individuals, they generally ignore those at more moderate risk. In reality, it is people at moderate risk who by their sheer numbers account for the bulk of CHD mortality and morbidity. Community-based programs, which typically target more moderate changes in a larger number of people, thus provide a more efficient and cost-effective means for CHD prevention. Given that some people are at particularly high risk, however, those people should be targeted for special attention.

Programs for reducing CHD should also consider the age groups to be targeted. As noted earlier, CHD is a disease of aging. Deaths from CHD are relatively infrequent among the young, but become increasingly more frequent in people over the age of 45 (National Center for Health Statistics, 1989). However, the process of atherosclerosis that leads up to heart disease begins early. Autopsies have found the build-up of atherosclerotic plaques in children as young as 10 years old (Strasser, 1980). Further, the development of food preferences, exercise habits, and other health behaviors begins during childhood (see Chapter 4). All this argues that the programs for reducing CHD are likely to be most effective when they place particular emphasis on school-age children (Harlan, 1984; Perry et al., 1988). Interventions for changing life-style can be useful at any age, but are likely to have their maximal impact among young people.

To date, no major community-based CHD risk reduction program has targeted young people exclusively, but virtually all the major community-based programs have a component specifically for youth (Perry et al., 1988). A good example is the Minnesota Heart Health Program (MHHP) conducted in three cities in Minnesota over a ten-year period (Blackburn et al., 1984; Perry et al., 1988). Although the program was community-wide, particular attention was given to altering CHD risk among children and adolescents. Materials were developed for reaching children and adolescents both individually and through their peer groups, families, schools, and the community at large. For example, correspondence materials were developed and given to children for use on their own. In addition, young people were invited with their families to attend the community risk-factor screening center so that they could be recognized as important members of their families in bringing about life-style change. Further, age-appropriate educational programs were developed for use in schools, including materials on diet, smoking, physical activity, and drug use. Preliminary results from these interventions indicate that, compared to young people from other cities not participating in the program, rates of smoking as well as fat and sodium intake were significantly reduced for program participants (Perry et al., 1988). Only time will tell whether these changes ultimately result in reduced CHD. Other community-wide intervention programs are discussed in Chapter 5.

LIVING WITH HEART DISEASE

Even though rates of CHD are falling in many countries, millions of people every year experience myocardial infarction and other forms of heart disease. More than 4,000 people experience heart attacks every day in the United States alone (Blumenthal &

Emery, 1988). Of these, approximately half will die within an hour of the onset of symptoms, and another 15% will die in the hospital (Sheps, 1987). Those who survive are faced with daunting challenges that will significantly shape the rest of their lives. What are these challenges, and what can be done to help cardiac patients cope and lead productive lives?

The Physical and Psychosocial Impact of a Heart Attack

For many MI patients, the first indication of trouble comes in the form of severe chest pain, often described as gripping or vicelike, which may continue for several hours. In some cases, the pain may feel like indigestion and is generally felt most intensely behind the breastbone, though it may radiate from there to the arms, neck, back, or upper abdomen. In addition, during a heart attack, the person may experience restlessness and cold sweating, and is almost certain to turn pale (Mulcahy, 1983).

These initial symptoms are only the very beginning. Once they begin, the person enters a life or death struggle with substantial physical and psychological impact. The initial hurdle is simply to survive the first few hours after the attack. Because immediate medical attention is often critical for survival, the person is likely to be rushed to a hospital via ambulance and immediately placed in a coronary care unit (CCU), where cardiac functioning can be continuously monitored and needed interventions applied. This experience alone is likely to be traumatic because it underscores the seriousness of the person's condition. Not surprisingly, a significant number of patients experience considerable emotional distress while in the CCU, and more than a third require psychiatric consultation. Despite the negative psychological effects of hospitalization (see Chapter 9), some patients find the CCU reassuring because of the constant monitoring and ready availability of medical attention (Doehrman, 1977).

Most common complications of an acute MI occur during the first few days after onset. If the person is able to survive this initial period, the prospects for recovery are favorable: 90% survive for at least one year and 85% for two or more years (Sheps, 1987). Life, however, is unlikely to be the same. MI patients are likely to find that they are required to cut down on their activities, change their life-style, and have considerably less overall stamina than they did before. These changes can be extremely disruptive for some patients. Heart patients are generally advised to avoid stressful situations, strenuous activities, and heavy lifting. These restrictions can be particularly difficult for individuals in high-stress occupations or those that require lifting and other exertion. Although roughly three fourths of the previously employed MI patients return to some form and amount of work within six months and about 85% within a year, white-collar workers return more quickly and frequently than do patients in blue-collar occupations. In addition, many patients returning to work either change jobs or reduce their hours (Croog & Levine, 1982; Doehrman, 1977). Further, MI patients are often required to make significant changes in life-style and may be forced to give up valued activities.

The physical impact of an MI and its effects on the person's activities and life-style often take a significant emotional toll. MI patients frequently report bouts of depression and anxiety, and may experience insomnia, nervousness, social withdrawal, and a sense of uselessness and pessimism about the future. Further, many patients do not return to their previous levels of sexual activity for fear of aggravating their condition (Hackett & Cassem, 1984; Stern, 1984). These problems appear to be most acute in the weeks immediately after the patient returns home from the hospital. During this period, the person may have high expectations about recovery and return to former activities, only to find that these are contradicted by lack of physical stamina, weakness, and limitations placed on activities (Stern, 1984).

Fortunately, most patients are able to resume many of their activities, and the psychological effects of the MI dissipate with time. One study that followed MI patients for eight years after their attack found that of those surviving for eight years nearly two thirds were rated by their physicians as having no significant physical impairment. In addition, although nearly half the patients showed a depressive reaction to their illness one year after their heart attack, this proportion was reduced to a fourth after eight years (Croog & Levine, 1982).

Cardiac Rehabilitation

cardiac rehabilitation
Interventions with heart patients designed to help them recover from a heart attack or other heart disease and return to optimal functioning.

Recovering from a heart attack is a long-term process that requires both medical and psychosocial interventions. In the period immediately after the attack, the most critical interventions are medical and surgical. However, the prevention of future attacks may well require changes in activities and life-style, and the person's overall well-being may depend on the kinds of psychological and social support received.

Medical and surgical treatment. In the minutes and hours immediately after the onset of an MI, the goal of treatment is to stabilize the patient and limit the amount of damage to the heart. On diagnosis of an acute MI, the patient is generally transferred to a CCU, where cardiac monitors are attached and initial interventions are begun. Analgesics, such as morphine sulfate or nitrous oxide, may be administered to relieve chest pain or discomfort. In addition, anticoagulants may be given to reduce blood clotting, anti-arrhythmics administered to reduce the likelihood of dangerous arrhythmias, and beta-blockers given to reduce the chances of a sudden cardiac arrest and the amount of damage to the heart muscle. In general, patients are also ordered to strict bed rest and, because of the high incidence of nausea and vomiting associated with an acute MI, placed on a liquid diet for the first 24 hours (Leon & Cohen, 1984).

Once the initial crisis has passed, planning can begin for the patient's long-term rehabilitation. Medical tests are performed to determine the extent and location of the damage and to provide a basis for future therapy. For some patients, therapy will involve primarily medical intervention, such as the use of anticoagulants, beta-blockers, and anti-arrhythmics. For others, however, surgical intervention may be required. Among the most common surgical interventions is *coronary artery bypass graft surgery,* which can be used to deal with extensive blockage of one or more of the coronary arteries (Wenger & Hurst, 1984). In this procedure, blood vessels from another part of the body, often the leg, are grafted onto the affected coronary arteries to restore

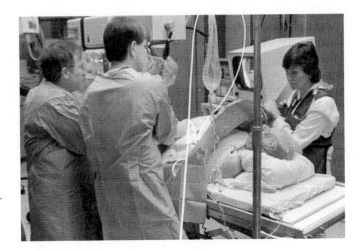

Percutaneous trans-lumenal coronary angioplasty can be used to open clogged coronary arteries without surgery through the use of a balloon-tipped catheter.

blood flow. Although this has become a common procedure for treating CHD, questions have been raised about its effectiveness in improving patients' functional status and reducing mortality. Early studies found little or no benefit for bypass surgery. However, more recent studies indicate that it does improve survival rates for carefully selected patients (Blumenthal & Emery, 1988; Wenger & Hurst, 1984).

Bypass surgery is clearly a serious undertaking, entailing all the risks of major open-heart surgery. Fortunately, some blocked coronary arteries can be opened without surgery. In *percutaneous translumenal coronary angioplasty* (PTCA) a tiny, balloon-tipped catheter is threaded through the person's blood vessels into the affected coronary artery. After it reaches the point of the blockage, it is inflated, widening the artery and restoring blood flow. PTCA is an attractive alternative for some patients who might otherwise need bypass surgery because it can be as effective as bypass surgery in restoring blood flow and avoids the necessity of open-heart surgery (Blumenthal & Emery, 1988; Tommaso, Lesch, & Sonnenblick, 1984).

Life-style interventions. Medical and surgical interventions deal with the patient's immediate physical problems, but to be maximally effective, they should be accompanied by life-style changes to reduce the likelihood of future MIs. Among the important life-style changes for cardiac patients are appropriate physical exercise, changes in diet, elimination of smoking, and effective management of stress.

In the past, patients who experienced MIs were immobilized for a minimum of six to eight weeks in the belief that physical exertion would increase the likelihood of further damage to the heart. In addition, patients were advised to avoid any strenuous activity for at least a year and sometimes for life (Blumenthal & Emery, 1988). More recently, physicians have become aware that such restrictions are unnecessary and may even be harmful, causing "cardiac invalidism." Now, once out of the CCU, MI patients are advised to begin gradually resuming physical activity, even while still hospitalized (Young, 1987). After they leave the hospital, patients are advised to engage in regular aerobic exercise within the limits of their capacity and to return to a moderate level of sexual activity. Studies of exercise in MI patients have found that not only can most patients tolerate exercise well, but patients who engage in regular exercise show improved cardiovascular functioning, as indexed by resting heart rate, blood pressure, and treadmill exercise performance, as well as more positive self-perceptions and psychosocial functioning (Blumenthal & Emery, 1988; Roviaro, Holmes, & Holmsten, 1984). One study, for example, found that, in addition to improved cardiac function-ing, patients randomly assigned to an exercise-based rehabilitation program showed more positive perceptions of their health, body, and self than did patients receiving standard care. In addition, patients in the rehabilitation program reported reduced job-related stress and increased physical and sexual activity (Roviaro et al., 1984). Despite these improvements, whether or not exercise programs by themselves increase longevity or reduce the risk of subsequent heart attacks is not clear. Several studies have shown reduced mortality for MI patients engaging in exercise, but these differ-ences have generally been small and not statistically significant (Blumenthal & Emery, 1988). Regardless of its effect on mortality, however, exercise does appear to improve patients' quality of life.

Coronary patients are also advised to alter their dietary and smoking habits and to avoid stress. As seen earlier, both diet and smoking are major risk factors for CHD. After an MI, patients are advised to reduce their intake of both salt and calories if they are overweight and to avoid saturated fats and cholesterol. Smokers are advised to stop smoking; patients who drink alcohol are urged to reduce their consumption or eliminate it altogether (Argondizzo, 1984; Burling, Singleton, Bigelow, Baile, & Gottlieb, 1984). Further, because of the potential effects of stress on cardiac function-ing, patients are generally counseled to avoid stressful situations and to practice stress management.

What are the cumulative effects of these life-style changes? Are they effective in halting or possibly even reversing the damage done by CHD? Empirical data address-ing these questions are hard to come by, but recent evidence from a clinical trial of an intensive life-style modification program is promising (Gould et al., 1992; Ornish et al., 1990). In this trial, 48 patients with documented stenosis (narrowing) of the coronary arteries were randomly assigned either to a group receiving an intensive life-style intervention or to a control group receiving the usual medical care for this condition but no life-style modifications. Patients in the life-style modification group were placed on a low-cholesterol, low-fat diet, received training in stress management techniques, and were instructed to engage in moderate levels of physical exercise. In addition, they met twice a week to provide each other with social support for adhering to the regimen. Compared to measurements taken at the beginning of the study, follow-up an average of 15 months later found that patients in the life-style modifica-tion condition reported a 91% reduction in the frequency of angina pectoris, a 42% reduction in the duration of the angina, and a 28% reduction in its severity. By comparison, patients in the control group showed a 165% rise in frequency, a 95% rise in duration, and a 39% rise in severity of their angina. More important, quantitative measurement of the extent of coronary stenosis found that whereas the amount of stenosis increased significantly for patients in the control condition, stenosis was significantly reduced and coronary blood flow improved for the patients in the life-style modification condition. Although the number of patients in this trial is small, these results suggest that life-style modifications may successfully reverse at least some aspects of CHD.

Psychological and social support. Recovery from a heart attack is also hastened by support from other people, including family, friends, and health care staff. Psychological support begins early in the patient's hospitalization as members of the health care team explain what has happened, and begin educating patients and their families about heart disease and what can be expected during recovery (Argondizzo, 1984). During this time, the patient's mental state can be assessed and psychological concerns addressed. Problems of anxiety, depression, and low morale, which are common among MI patients, are significant predictors of mortality (Blumenthal & Emery, 1988).

Psychological interventions hold the promise of not only improving the person's psychological state but also increasing longevity. In fact, several studies have shown that psychotherapy may be effective in reducing CHD morbidity and mortality. For example, one study found that even though group psychotherapy did not alter traditional CHD risk factors such as obesity and smoking, patients receiving the therapy had fewer heart attacks and significantly lower mortality than did a control group (Rahe, Ward, & Hayes, 1979). Other studies have found that patients receiving psychotherapy return to work sooner and have shorter hospitalization and less depression than those receiving no psychological treatment (Blumenthal & Emery, 1988).

Support from family members and others is also an important ingredient in cardiac rehabilitation. As seen in Chapter 10, chronic illness often exerts considerable strain on both the patient and members of the patient's family, and CHD is no exception. Studies of MI patients and their families have shown that the strains associated with the disease can result in significant disruption and marital strife (Michela, 1987). Patients may become irritable over the extent of their disability or may find it difficult to adhere to recommended life-style changes. In addition, concerns over the potential effects of sexual activity on cardiac function may lead to marital disharmony. Dealing with these problems is an important aspect of cardiac rehabilitation. Research on social support among cardiac patients has shown that social support from family and friends reduces feelings of distress and cardiac symptoms, particularly in the months directly after hospitalization (Fontana, Kerns, Rosenberg, & Colonese, 1989). In addition, a recent study of social support among coronary artery bypass patients found that patients receiving higher levels of social support recovered more rapidly from their surgery and required less pain medication than those with less support (Kulik &

Mahler, 1989). Results like these reinforce the need to assess the social support received by the cardiac patients and work with patients' families to help them deal effectively with the patient's illness.

SUMMARY

Coronary heart disease is a major killer throughout the world. Even though CHD mortality is declining in some countries, it remains the leading cause of death and disability in the United States and other industrialized countries.

The heart is a small muscular organ responsible for maintaining the circulation of blood through the body. Although for most people the heart continues to function faithfully for years, heart problems can develop from inadequate blood supply to the heart muscle or faulty electrical conduction in the heart. The most common difficulties come from the process of atherosclerosis, in which the arteries supplying blood to the heart muscle become clogged with cholesterol and other fatty substances. When this happens, the blood supply to the heart muscle may be significantly reduced or cut off. In serious cases, this can lead to a myocardial infarction, or heart attack, resulting in dangerous destruction of heart tissue. Although atherosclerosis occurs in everyone, those likely to find it particularly problematic are people with a family history of heart disease or who smoke, have high blood pressure, live sedentary lives, are obese, and have diets high in sodium, fat, and cholesterol.

Psychological stress also plays a significant role in CHD. Through its role in activating the sympathetic nervous system, stress can produce wear and tear on the cardiovascular system and, in some cases, lead to sudden cardiac death. The effects of stress on CHD appear to be particularly pronounced for individuals with a Type A behavior pattern. Although questions have been raised as to the actual relationship between Type A and CHD, current evidence suggests that in the general population persons exhibiting the Type A behavior pattern have roughly twice the risk of CHD as do those with the more placid Type B pattern. Among persons already at high risk for CHD, Type A is not predictive of heart disease. Exactly what aspects of the Type A pattern predispose people to CHD is unclear; Type A apparently represents both a psychological and a physiological hyperreactivity to challenge, which may produce excess wear on the heart and hasten the process of atherosclerosis. Hostility is a prime candidate for the toxic ingredient in Type A.

CHD is definitely a life-style disease, influenced by modifiable behavioral factors. Cigarette smoking significantly increases CHD risk, most likely because it produces stresslike effects on the cardiovascular system and affects serum cholesterol and blood clotting. Diet affects CHD by influencing serum cholesterol, blood pressure, and obesity, all of which are CHD risk factors on their own. Regular physical exercise reduces CHD risk by reducing body fat, increasing cardiopulmonary efficiency, and reducing serum cholesterol. Finally, CHD risk is influenced by one's interpersonal relationships; married individuals experience less CHD than their unmarried counterparts.

Because of the close relationship between CHD and psychosocial factors, efforts are currently being made to reduce coronary risk by altering Type A behavior, controlling hypertension, and modifying life-style. Although the long-term effectiveness of such interventions in reducing CHD mortality is controversial, the results of these efforts thus far are promising. In particular, efforts to change Type A behavior and reduce hypertension have been successful. Community-wide interventions to reduce CHD risk through changing life-style have met with at least initial success.

Despite efforts to reduce CHD risk, every year millions of people experience heart attacks. Of these, roughly two thirds die within the first few hours or days of the attack. Those who survive are faced with daunting challenges and generally require cardiac rehabilitation to resume normal lives. Cardiac rehabilitation includes medical and surgical treatment as well as life-style modification and psychological and social support.

KEY TERMS

atrium (355)
ventricle (357)
myocardium (357)
systolic blood pressure (357)
diastolic blood pressure (357)
atherosclerosis (358)
angina pectoris (358)

myocardial infarction (MI) (358)
coronary risk factors (359)
hypertension (359)
Type A behavior pattern (362)
hyperreactivity (366)
autogenic training (377)
cardiac rehabilitation (380)

SUGGESTED READINGS

Cousins, N. (1983). *The healing heart: Antidotes to panic and helplessness.* New York: W. W. Norton. This is a first-person account of having a heart attack and the problems of panic and helplessness that heart attacks can cause. In his discussion, Norman Cousins explores the patient's role in recovery.

Heaton, R. K. (ed.) (1988). Special series: Cardiovascular disease. *Journal of Consulting and Clinical Psychology, 56,* 323–92. This special series includes eight articles exploring various aspects of cardiovascular disease including its epidemiology, the role of stress, Type A behavior, life-style change, and cardiac rehabilitation.

Williams, R. (1989). *The trusting heart: Great news about Type A behavior.* New York: Times Books. In this book, cardiologist Redford Williams discusses the Type A behavior pattern and ways in which it can be changed.

CHAPTER **15**

Pain

Pain is one of the great enigmas of life. The experience of pain plays an essential role in warning us about dangers in our environment. Pain sensations tell us to stay away from hot stoves or sharp objects that can injure us, and provide signals for the presence of disease or injury. At other times, however, pain seems totally gratuitous, such as when a person continues to experience pain long after an injury has healed or experiences pain in a limb that has long since been amputated. Often pain seems like just a nuisance, one of the prices we pay for being alive. More than that, pain is one of the great health problems of modern society—tens of billions of dollars are spent annually in search of pain relief. But what is pain, and how are we to understand these phenomena? This chapter takes up these issues, along with the question of what can be done to control and alleviate pain.

MIND AND BODY: THE PROBLEM OF PAIN

On the surface, the experience of pain seems so simple: physical injury or disease causes the experience of discomfort. A child stubs a toe and immediately experiences pain. A football player sprains a muscle or breaks a leg during a game and feels discomfort that necessitates leaving the game. Or so it seems. When we examine the phenomena of pain more closely, however, we find that the relationship between physical injury or disease and the experience of pain is far more variable than it seems on the surface. Indeed, a person can experience significant tissue damage without feeling pain or, conversely, experience considerable pain in the absence of any discernable physical abnormality.

But what is pain? Even though virtually everyone has experienced pain at one time or another, a clear definition of pain is elusive. Pain might be defined as the discomfort a person experiences as a result of injury or tissue damage, but such a definition excludes important categories of pain phenomena. More accurately, pain can be defined as the subjective experience of discomfort that often, but not always, results from disease or injury. The key phrase here is "subjective experience." Pain is a private experience. Although pain has many outward manifestations, such as limping, wincing, crying, or restriction of activity, the experience itself is internal and available to no one but the sufferer. This subjective nature of pain is critical in understanding pain phenomena and is reflected in techniques used to measure pain, as discussed in Box 15.1.

BOX 15.1   Measuring Pain

The elusive and subjective nature of pain presents important problems for measurement. How can we accurately measure a subjective experience that has a highly variable connection to physical stimuli? As yet, no universally accepted means of measuring pain has been developed, but many different pain measures have been proposed (Karoly, 1985; Melzack & Wall, 1982; Reading, 1989; Turk et al., 1983). Current attempts to measure pain can be classified into three basic groups: self-report measures, measures of pain behaviors, and measures of physiological concomitants of pain.

Self-report measures are based on the assumption that if you want to know how people feel, you should ask them. Thus self-report measures ask patients to describe their pain. For example, the *visual analog scale* (Huskisson, 1974) asks the person to rate experienced pain on a 10-cm line anchored on the left by the phrase "no pain" and on the right by "pain as bad as it could be." Pain is rated by drawing a line at the point indicating the intensity of the experienced pain. Although this method has the virtue of simplicity, it deals with only one aspect of the pain experience (Karoly, 1985).

To get a more detailed description of pain, Ronald Melzack (1975) has developed the McGill-Melzack Pain Questionnaire (Figure 15.1), which attempts to quantify the "language of pain." In this questionnaire, patients are asked to select from a structured list the words that best describe their pain experience. Words on the list are grouped into four major categories (sensory, affective, evaluative, and miscellaneous) and ranked according to intensity. Scoring of the questionnaire then provides the clinician with an indication of both the quality of the pain and its intensity.

Patients' reports of pain may also be obtained in clinical interviews. During the interview, patients may be questioned about the history of their pain as well as its intensity and quality. Such interviews can provide

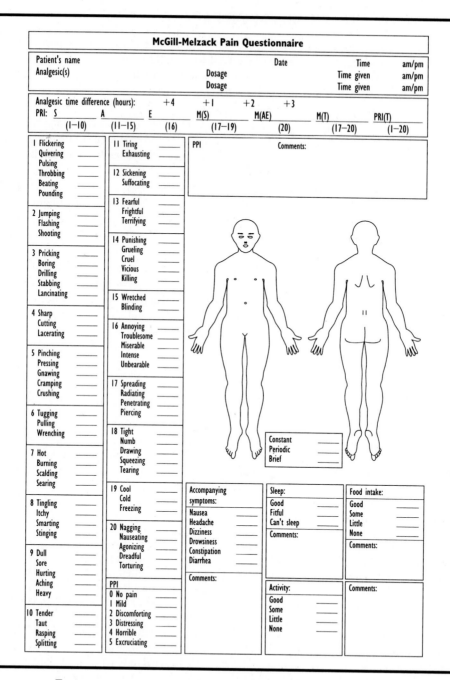

FIGURE 15.1   *The McGill-Melzack Pain Questionnaire.*

Note. From *The challenge of pain* by R. Melzack and P. D. Wall, 1982, New York: Basic Books.

valuable information about the development of the pain and its source (Karoly, 1985; Turk et al., 1983).

Whereas self-report measures of pain focus on the subjective experience itself, behavioral pain measures assess pain's outward manifestations. In these measures, an observer, such as a health professional or the patient's spouse, observes the patient's behavior and records the frequency of various behaviors indicative of pain. For example, one study designed to evaluate the pain behavior concept (Turk, Wack, & Kerns, 1985) had two groups of health professionals observe and record the pain behaviors of chronic pain patients. Analysis of these observations indicated a high level of consistency in the rating of pain behaviors and revealed four primary clusters of pain behaviors. Pain behaviors could be generally classified into those relating to (1) distorted ambulation or posture (such as limping or stooping), (2) negative affect (such as irritability or questioning the cause of

the pain), (3) facial/audible expressions of distress, and (4) avoidance of activity.

Finally, psychophysiological measures of pain tap the physiological concomitants of the pain experience. For example, the muscle tension that often accompanies headaches or lower back pain can be measured with an *electromyograph* (EMG) (Cohen et al., 1983; Hovanitz, Chin, & Warm, 1989) or an *electroencephalograph* (EEG) can be used to measure electrical activity in the brain (Chapman et al., 1985). In addition, the person's overall physiological arousal may be assessed through the measurement of heart rate or skin conductance. Although these measures often correlate poorly with subjective reports of pain, they can be useful in identifying subgroups of patients experiencing pain for different reasons and who may respond differently to different treatments (Dolce & Raczynski, 1985).

The Puzzling Phenomena of Pain

Imagine a life without pain. You would feel no pain when stubbing your toe or hitting your finger with a hammer; no headaches; no itches; no pain when having teeth drilled for fillings. Sound attractive? Before you conclude that such a life would be ideal, consider the case of Miss C., a student at McGill University (Melzack & Wall, 1982). Miss C. was highly intelligent and appeared normal in every way except that she was incapable of experiencing pain. As a young child, she had bitten off the tip of her tongue while chewing food and had gotten third degree burns on her legs after kneeling on a hot radiator to look out the window. Further, she felt no pain when subjected to strong electrical shocks, hot water, or other normally noxious stimuli. As a result, Miss C. had severe medical problems, including pathological changes in her knees, hip, and spine, as well as infections. These problems were attributed to the fact that she failed to turn over when sleeping, shift her weight when standing, or take other measures that people normally take to protect their joints and avoid inflammation. She died at the age of 29 from massive and uncontrollable infections.

Miss C. is not alone in her affliction. Although the condition is rare, numerous people have been reported with varying degrees of insensitivity to pain. In some cases, this insensitivity can be attributed to identifiable neurological abnormalities, but in others the nervous system appears completely normal. Regardless of the source of the insensitivity, such people are at risk for serious medical problems and have to learn, often with great difficulty, to avoid seriously injuring themselves in their everyday activities (Melzack & Wall, 1982). Whereas most people instinctively learn to avoid falls, sharp or hot objects, and bruises, individuals insensitive to pain must be continually and consciously aware of these dangers.

More common than pain insensitivity are cases where people experience considerable, and sometimes excruciating, pain without a clear physical source. A dramatic and puzzling example of this is phantom limb pain, pain felt by amputees in amputated limbs. Research reports indicate that the majority (as much as 90–100% in some studies) of amputees report experiencing sensations in limbs that have been severed from their bodies (Jensen & Rasmussen, 1989). Most of these sensations involve feelings of presence, movement, touch, temperature, or pressure, but many patients report pain in the amputated limb, with the pain being severe for more than 5% of the patients. This pain is often present soon after the amputation and may last for years. In addition, phantom pain may occur in other cases where body parts are removed. For example, among women who have had mastectomies 10% to 15% report phantom pain sensations in the removed breast (Kroner, Krebs, Skov, & Jorgensen, 1989).

Pain may also continue long after wounds are healed. For example, in a condition known as *causalgia*, a person continues to feel "burning" pain in a wound, often in the foot or hand, well after the wound itself has healed. The pain appears completely out of proportion to the injury, and, though it generally starts in the injured area, often moves into other areas as well (Tasker & Dostrovsky, 1989). Observations of patients with continuing pain after healing indicate that pain can be triggered by stimuli as innocuous as a gentle touch or a puff of air and that relatively minor injuries can give rise to extreme pain (Melzack & Wall, 1982).

Pain Physiology

Phenomena like these raise many questions about the nature of pain and where it comes from. To begin exploring these, we first consider the physical side of pain. How do pain sensations originate? What are the physiological processes by which physical damage to body tissue is converted into the experience of pain?

Careful study of the nervous system has revealed a series of physical structures involved in pain sensations (Campbell et al., 1989; Chapman, 1984; Melzack & Wall, 1982). These structures convert noxious stimuli into nerve impulses and then transmit these impulses to the brain, where they are processed and interpreted. To begin, when body tissues are injured, such as when a person receives a cut or scrape, **algogenic substances** are released, which signal injury, producing inflammation and stimulating nerve endings in the affected area. The nerves stimulated, known as **nociceptors,** then produce nerve impulses that are transmitted to the spinal cord and up to the brain. These nociceptors respond to a variety of stimuli, only some of which may result in pain. Thus they cannot properly be termed "pain receptors," even though they are an integral part of the pain experience.

In general, three major groups of nerve fibers are involved in pain sensations (Campbell et al., 1989; Melzack & Wall, 1982). **A-delta fibers** are small diameter nerve fibers encased in a sheath of myelin, a fatty substance that acts as an insulator. A-delta fibers conduct impulses rapidly and respond to light and heavy pressure as well as heat, cooling, and various chemicals. These fibers appear to be responsible for

algogenic substances
Chemical substances occurring naturally in body tissues that are released when the tissue is injured.

nociceptors
Free nerve endings that respond to pain and signal injury.

A-delta fibers
Small myelinated nerve fibers that project to the dorsal horn and are associated with sharp, prickling pains.

C fibers
Small unmyelinated nerve fibers that project to the dorsal horn and are associated with dull, aching pains.

A-beta fibers
Large myelinated nerve fibers that project both to the dorsal horn and the brain.

endogenous opioids
Opiate-like substances produced by the body that act as natural pain relievers.

pains that are localized, sharp, and distinct. **C fibers** are even smaller nerve fibers that have no myelin sheath and conduct impulses more slowly. Like the A-delta fibers, C fibers respond to various stimuli but are associated with more diffuse, dull, or aching pains. About 60% to 70% of sensory afferent fibers are C fibers. A third group of fibers, a set of large, rapidly conducting, myelinated fibers known as **A-beta fibers,** are involved in transmitting sensations that are more innocuous in nature, but also appear to play a role in modulating pain sensations.

From the site of stimulation, the impulses involved in pain travel along the different nerve fibers to an area known as the *dorsal horn,* where they enter the spinal cord. In the dorsal horn, the impulses are considerably modified and then transmitted up the spinal cord, where they pass through the reticular formation, an area of the brain involved in arousal and attention. The impulses then travel through the thalamus, where they are further modified (Andersen, 1986), and into the cortex, where they are consciously interpreted. The pathways taken by pain impulses are shown in Figure 15.2. Available evidence does not indicate any specific area of the cortex that can be considered to be a "pain center." Rather, several areas appear to be involved in pain perception, and recent studies show that pain sensations may be represented in multiple areas of the cortex simultaneously (Talbot et al., 1991).

The transmission of pain signals along these pathways is strongly influenced by a group of neurochemicals known as **endogenous opioids,** of which the best known are *endorphins* and *enkephalins* (Fields & Basbaum, 1989). These are naturally occurring substances in the brain, spinal cord, and other organs of the body that significantly reduce pain. Although a great deal remains to be learned about these substances, current evidence indicates that they act as an internal pain relief system by slowing or blocking the transmission of nerve impulses, in much the same way as morphine and other opiates. What triggers this pain relief system? Research studies with animals demonstrate that endogenous opioids can be released in response to electrical and other stressful stimulation and can also be classically conditioned. For example, pairing a painful stimulus, such as a prolonged electrical shock to the foot, to a neutral stimulus, such as a light or tone, can lead to the release of endorphins and enkephalins (Watkins & Mayer, 1982). As seen in Chapter 2, endorphins may also be released in response to the administration of placebos. Thus, physiologically, the experience of pain depends on the transmission of nerve impulses to the brain from the site of injury as well as on neurochemical pain regulation systems in the body.

Psychosocial Factors in the Experience of Pain

These physiological mechanisms explore one side of the puzzle of pain, but other processes operate as well. Psychosocial factors play a significant role in modulating pain. In particular, the experience of pain is significantly influenced by a person's culture, previous experiences, emotional needs, and cognition.

Culture. Although the physiology of pain is the same for all humans, cultures differ in the experience and response to pain. For example, one study comparing pain response among ethnic groups in the United States found that whereas Italian and

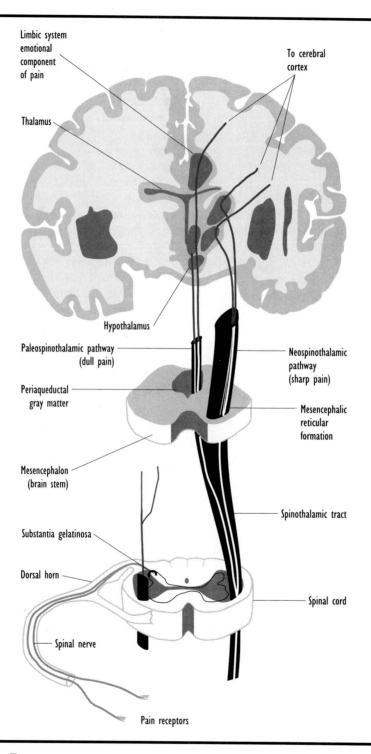

FIGURE 15.2 *Pain pathways.*

Jewish patients were highly emotional about their pain and complained vociferously, Irish patients denied their pain and white New Englanders (referred to as "Old Americans") were more objective and stoical (Zborowski, 1952).

Particularly dramatic illustrations of cultural differences in pain can be found in various cultural practices. For example, in East Africa both men and women undergo an operation known as "trepanation" for the relief of chronic pain. In this operation, a large area of the skull is exposed by cutting back the scalp and underlying muscles. The operation is performed by a "doktari" using no anesthetic as the person sits calmly without flinching, holding a pan under the chin to catch the dripping blood. Ronald Melzack and Patrick Wall note that "films of this procedure are extraordinary to watch because of the discomfort they induce in the observers which is in striking contrast to the lack of discomfort in the people undergoing the operation" (1982, pp. 30–31). Another example of apparently painful procedures endured without visible discomfort is described in Box 15.2.

These cultural differences in pain response are striking in light of data that indicate few ethnic differences in sensation thresholds. Measurements of sensation thresholds using electrical shock, for example, found that Italian, Jewish, Irish, and "Old American" women did not differ as to when they first detected electrical shocks. On average, the women in all four groups reported feeling the shock at the same level of stimulus intensity (Sternbach & Tursky, 1965). This suggests a basic equivalence between groups in stimulus sensitivity. The real differences seem to occur in what constitutes pain as well as when that pain becomes intolerable. For example, studies using radiant heat have found significant differences between ethnic groups in both their pain perception thresholds and the point at which they behaviorally reacted to pain. Overall, these studies suggest that Americans of Northern European descent have higher pain perception and reaction thresholds than do black Americans, Russian Jews, and Italians (Wolff & Langley, 1977). Similar differences have been observed in pain tolerance levels. Even though they have similar sensation thresholds, Italian women tolerate less shock than do "Old American" or Jewish women (Sternbach & Tursky, 1965). Interestingly, one study found that Jewish, but not Protestant, women showed an increase in pain tolerance when they were told that their ethnic group did not tolerate pain as well as others (Lambert, Libman, & Poser, 1960).

Past experience. Phenomenologically, reaction to pain seems automatic and inborn. However, evidence demonstrates that early experiences influence pain perception. Such influences can be seen in animals that have been raised in isolation. For example, Scottish terriers in one study were raised in isolation from infancy to maturity and were prevented from experiencing the usual knocks and scrapes of young animals. In contrast to their litter-mates, who were raised normally and responded quickly to painful stimuli, these animals repeatedly poked their noses into flames and endured pinpricks with little indication of pain (Melzack & Wall, 1982). Similar findings have been obtained with monkeys. Monkeys raised in isolation away from damaging objects or other monkeys who might bite or slap them often behaved in seemingly self-destructive ways. When placed with other monkeys, they would engage in suicidal

BOX 15.2 **Pain and Culture: The Hindu Festival of Thaipusam**

Cultural influences on pain are vividly demonstrated in cultural practices that involve the application of noxious stimuli to the body without the apparent experience of pain. One example of this is found in the Hindu festival of Thaipusam, celebrated annually as a tribute to the Hindu god Lord Murugan. According to Hindu mythology, Lord Murugan rendered assistance to the *devas* (celestial beings) and achieved a martial victory over the forces of evil. In honor of this, every year during the tenth month of the Tamil calendar, Indian Hindus have a three-day celebration in which the image of Murugan is paraded through the streets, offerings are made, and devotees fulfill vows by piercing themselves with skewers and carrying a *kavadi,* a heavy metal structure weighing up to 100 lbs. that is adorned with pea-

cock feathers. *Kavadi* carriers generally have sharp metal rods piercing the cheeks and tongue (to prevent speaking) and may also be pierced with small needles in the forehead. In addition, some *kavadi* carriers have 100 or more skewers extending from the *kavadi* itself and embedded in the skin of the devotee's back, chest, and abdomen. A few *kavadi* carriers even pull small carts from hooks implanted in their back (Babb, 1976; Ward, 1984). During the 3-km (approximately 1¼ mile) procession, which the author observed in Singapore, *kavadi* carriers, urged on by the clapping and singing of their companions and supporters, would frequently break into vigorous dancing, one effect of which was to agitate the skewers embedded in the back, chest, and abdomen.

Kavadi *carrier with skewers in the chest, back and abdomen.*

Despite what strikes observers as being a painful form of self-mortification, the *kavadi* carriers themselves show little sign of being in pain. How is this? In her analysis of Thaipusam, Colleen Ward (1984) notes several psychosocial and psychophysiological processes that appear to mitigate against pain. First, the carrying of a *kavadi* and its associated body piercing are motivated by a religious vow, often in pursuit of some favor from Murugan or in thanksgiving for a favor received. Therefore, it carries considerable personal and religious meaning. In preparation for *kavadi* carrying, the devotee engages in rigorous self-discipline, including restrictions on diet, smoking, alcohol use, sexual activity, and sleeping. Thus the period before taking up the *kavadi* is spent in spiritual preparation and purification as the devotee seeks to attain an appropriate state of mind.

Second, body piercing is preceded by the induction of a ritual trance as the devotee seeks protection from the gods. As a part of this, *kavadi* carriers experience intense stimulus bombardment from the chanting of prayers and the inhalation of pungent incense. Devotees are instructed to engage in fervent prayer, eliminating all extraneous thoughts and focusing their attention away from the body and onto Lord Murugan. The result is an ecstatic trance with the subjective experience of peace, lightness, purity, euphoria, and detachment and the outward manifestations of trembling, temporary loss of muscle control, pupil dilation, and spatial disorientation. It is during this trance that the piercing takes place. The dissociative state achieved with the trance appears to be a key factor in modifying pain sensations.

Third, *kavadi* carriers are urged on by their companions and supporters in a procession with a carnival atmosphere. The path of the procession is lined with spectators as well as food and drink sellers and stalls playing religious or popular music. As devotees fulfill their vows, they are generally accompanied by family, friends, and supporters who urge them on, provide drinks, massage tired muscles, chant, and sing. This social support further helps to focus the person's attention on the religious and social aspects of the occasion and away from physical pain sensations.

Taken together, these factors illustrate the extent to which the experience of pain is a function of not only the physiological input from nerve endings but also the person's beliefs, state of mind, and support from others.

attacks against older and stronger monkeys, and would at times brutally bite their own limbs. Even after experiencing the negative results of such actions, they would still continue to bite themselves or attack larger animals (Lichstein & Sackett, 1971).

Evidence on humans as well demonstrates that pain responses change with development and experience. For example, a few hours after birth, infants show virtually no response to pinpricks. By one week, they respond with diffuse body movements, crying, and withdrawal. At one month, their responses are more organized and specific to the stimulus (McGraw, 1963). This indicates the necessity of a certain level of neurological maturity for the experience of pain. Studies beyond early infancy show that pain thresholds tend to increase over the course of childhood and that the experience of pain is related to both cognitive and psychosocial development (Bush, 1987).

Emotions and stress. The experience of pain is also significantly influenced by the person's emotional needs and level of stress. This is particularly noticeable in cases of **psychogenic pain,** chronic pain that has no identifiable physical basis. In such cases, the person experiences pain not because of physical injury, but because of psychological needs. For example, patients with pain that is hysterical or hypochon-

psychogenic pain
Chronic pain that appears to have no physical basis but develops in response to psychological needs.

driacal in origin generally have an excessive concern or fear of symptoms and are convinced that they are ill despite the absence of physical evidence (Craig, 1989). Many patients with psychogenic pain are depressed and have other emotional problems, but it is often unclear whether these problems produce the pain or are a result of it (Ackerman & Stevens, 1989; Gamsa, 1990; Pearce, 1987). Other patients may be either consciously or unconsciously using their pain to manipulate others (Melzack & Wall, 1982).

Regardless of its source, pain can also be influenced by stress. Reports of daily hassles, for example, are associated with increased pain (Sternbach, 1986), as are environmental stressors such as family conflict, marital problems, and major life events (Feurstein, Salt, & Houle, 1985; Merskey & Boyd, 1978). Further, some evidence indicates that the anxiety caused by stress can increase the experience of pain (Romano & Turner, 1985). One plausible explanation for these phenomena is that emotional stress may augment pain by increasing anxiety, which, in turn, produces prolonged muscle spasms and other physiological responses, leading to painful sensations (Craig, 1989).

Cognition. How people think about pain is among the more potent influences on the pain experience. Consider the observations of physician Henry Beecher (1959) during and after World War II. During the war, Beecher observed numerous severely wounded soldiers brought to combat hospitals. Despite the severity of their wounds, many denied being in pain, and only one in three complained of enough pain to require morphine. By contrast, in his postwar surgical practice, Beecher noted that four fifths of his patients complained loudly about their pain and requested morphine, even though they had far less tissue damage than the soldiers. Beecher attributed these discrepancies to differences in the meaning of the pain. Whereas the surgical patients often considered surgery a depressing calamitous event to be endured, the soldiers were thankful to be alive and saw their wounds as their ticket away from the horrors of the battlefield. Similar observations came from Israel, where soldiers undergoing traumatic amputation during the October 1973 Yom Kippur War described their initial wounds as painless (Melzack & Wall, 1982).

Feelings of control and self-efficacy also play a significant role in modulating the pain experience. As seen in Chapter 7, feelings of control can help people cope with stressful situations. Similarly, perceptions of control can reduce the painfulness of noxious stimuli (Thompson, 1981). For example, subjects who were told how to respond to electrical shocks reported that the shocks were less painful than subjects who were told that there was nothing that could be done about them (Bowers, 1968). Similarly, a strong feeling of self-efficacy, in this case the belief that a person can effectively control pain sensations, has been shown to reduce experimentally induced pain (Litt, 1988). These feelings of control and self-efficacy appear to have important practical applications. In another study, surgical patients encouraged in the use of cognitive control through cognitive reappraisal, calming self-talk, and selective attention reported less pain, required fewer pain relievers and sedatives, and left the hospital on average two to three days sooner than patients given standard care (Langer, Janis, & Wolfer, 1975).

The pain experience is also influenced by the person's focus of attention. Specifically, when the person's attention is focused away from the injury, such as when engrossed in a game or other activity, pain is experienced as less severe and may, in fact, not be noticed at all. For example, a child may not notice scrapes or bruises obtained in the course of play until they are pointed out by a parent or playmate. Experimentally, this can be seen in the effect of attention instructions on perceived pain in the laboratory. For example, one study exposed subjects to pain by pressing a football cleat against leg muscles. Subjects instructed to focus on a poster over their heads reported experiencing less pain than subjects told to concentrate on body sensations (Brewer & Karoly, 1989). Similarly, subjects who had their hands immersed in ice water and were given the opportunity to listen to either music or white noise found that they could control their pain by tapping their feet, singing out loud, or altering the volume of the sound (Melzack, Weisz, & Sprague, 1963). But instructing patients to focus on concrete and objective aspects of pain sensations can also increase pain tolerance. For example, instructing mothers to focus on concrete and objective aspects of pain sensations during child birth can reduce the experience of child birth pain (Leventhal, Leventhal, Shacham, & Easterling, 1989).

THEORIES OF PAIN

The highly variable link between injury and pain raises the question of how we are to understand these phenomena. Pain is clearly both a physiological and a psychological phenomenon, but how can these different aspects be brought together? To address this question, we now turn to a consideration of some of the major pain theories.

Early Pain Theories

Early theories of pain focused primarily on pain as a sensory modality and explored the generation and transmission of pain sensations. Therefore, they were primarily biomedical in orientation and paid little attention to psychosocial aspects of pain.

Specificity theory. The earliest scientific theories of pain can be grouped under what is known as "specificity theory," so called because of the emphasis on a specific pain system carrying pain messages from pain receptors to a pain center in the brain. This theory, described in almost all textbooks on neurophysiology, neurology, and neurosurgery, until recently was often presented more as fact than theory (Melzack & Wall, 1982), and thus has had a tremendous impact on medical approaches to pain.

Specificity theory has its origins in the description of pain made by the French philosopher René Descartes in the mid-seventeenth century. Descartes considered the pain system a straightforward channel between physical injury and the brain. According to this view, a person's injuries intiate a chain of events, somewhat like a person pulling a string to ring a bell, in which the stimulation goes directly to the brain, where it sets off an alarm, and the person feels pain.

This description was simple and had no basis in physiology, but provided the foundation for later, more scientifically based descriptions. In the nineteenth century, physiologists such as Johannes Müller and Max von Frey developed theories arguing that pain could be understood in the same way as other body senses, such as sight and hearing. These senses have specialized receptors that convert physical energy into nerve impulses, which are then transmitted to a specific area of the brain for interpretation. Likewise, it was argued, pain has specific receptors that transmit impulses to a pain center in the brain. Free nerve endings were identified as being pain receptors and a search was made for the brain center responsible for pain interpretation (Melzack & Wall, 1982).

Although this approach seems logically appealing and seems to fit at least some aspects of the pain experience, it fails to account for important pain phenomena. In particular, specificity theory postulates a one-to-one correspondence between physical stimulation and the experience of pain. As we have seen, the connection between tissue damage and the experience of pain is not nearly that direct, and one can have pain without tissue damage and tissue damage without pain. Further, an important implication of this approach is that pain can be controlled by severing the pain pathways. Although surgically cutting the nerves associated with pain can provide temporary pain relief, that relief is rarely permanent (Melzack & Wall, 1982).

Pattern theory. In an effort to overcome some of the difficulties of specificity theory, pattern theory proposes that the experience of pain is the result of certain patterns of nerve stimulation. Several versions of this theory have been developed, which differ primarily in the particular patterns of stimulation believed to be important. For example, peripheral pattern theory argues that pain is due to excessive stimulation in peripheral areas which produces a pattern of stimulation that is interpreted by the brain as pain. Central summation theory, by contrast, proposes that abnormal stimulation of sensory nerves, such as occurs after damage to peripheral nerves, results in the excitation of reverberation circuits in the spinal cord. These reverberation circuits then bombard the transmission cells of the spinal cord with intense stimulation and produce the sensation of pain (Melzack & Wall, 1982). Although these theories are more sophisticated than specificity theory, they too fail to account for important pain phenomena such as the role of culture or cognitive factors.

Gate Control Theory

A major breakthrough in the understanding of pain came with the development of the Gate Control Theory by Ronald Melzack and Patrick Wall (1965, 1982). This theory argues that the perception of pain is determined by three essential factors. First, the stimulation of free nerve endings gives rise to the physical input for pain sensations. These pain sensations are then significantly modified by a spinal gating mechanism that controls the transmission of pain sensations up the spinal cord. Finally, a central control mechanism in the brain interprets pain sensations and exerts influence on which pain signals are allowed through the spinal gate.

The key to this conception is the spinal gate. Melzack and Wall (1965, 1982) note that the nerve impulses from the stimulation of the A-beta, A-delta, and C fibers feed into the dorsal horn area of the spinal cord. In the dorsal horn, all these fibers project into the *substantia gelatinosa,* a group of densely packed cells that extend the length of the spinal cord. These cells are hypothesized to act as a gate for incoming stimuli and to determine which nerve impulses are then transmitted up the spinal cord to the brain. A diagram of this mechanism is given in Figure 15.3.

As seen earlier, the A-delta and C fibers are associated with different types of pain, whereas the A-beta fibers transmit more innocuous sensations. Melzack and Wall

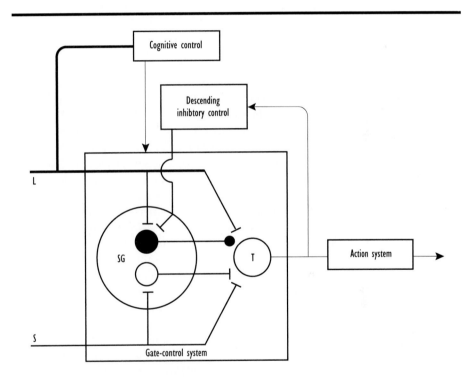

FIGURE 15.3

The gate control theory: Stimulation of the small fibers keeps the gate open, allowing pain signals to ascend the spinal cord. Conversely, stimulation of the large fibers closes the gate. The opening and closing of the gate is also influenced by central control mechanisms and descending inhibitory control.

Note: A white circle indicates an excitatory effect whereas a black circle indicates an inhibitory effect.

SG - Spinal gate (substantia gelitinosa)

L - Large fibres

S - Small fibres

T - Transmission cells

Note. From *The challenge of pain* by R. Melzack and P. D. Wall, 1982, New York: Basic Books.

believe that the balance of stimulation between these different sets of fibers is crucial in pain sensations. Specifically, stimulation of the small A-delta and C fibers has an excitatory effect on the substantia gelatinosa and tends to keep the spinal gate open, allowing the pain signals from these fibers to be transmitted up the spinal cord. Conversely, stimulation of the larger A-beta fibers has an inhibitory effect on the substantia gelatinosa, tending to close the spinal gate. When this happens, the transmission of pain signals up the spinal cord is blocked. Thus, at a purely physiological level, the experience of pain is a function of the relative activity in the A-delta and C fibers, on the one hand, and the A-beta fibers, on the other, as they influence the extent to which pain signals are allowed to pass up the spinal cord.

However, the spinal gate is not influenced solely by afferent (incoming) nerve stimulation. In addition, the extent to which the gate is open or closed is influenced by messages descending from the brain. Some of the largest and most rapidly conducting A-beta fibers actually bypass the spinal gate and project directly to the brain. These fibers carry information about stimulation to the brain, where it is interpreted and evaluated. Nerve fibers descending from these central control mechanisms in the brain then influence the opening and closing of the gate. For example, in the case of the soldiers observed by Beecher (1959), signals about the wound would be sent both to the spinal gate as well as directly to the brain. Evaluation of the wound as providing the person with escape from the battlefield and the person's relief at still being alive would then lead to signals resulting in the closure of the gate. But in surgical patients who view their surgery as a calamity, the descending signals would result in keeping the gate open and thus increase transmission of pain signals.

Pain includes not only the sensations involved but also the person's responses to those sensations. People not only feel pain sensations, they react to the pain both on a behavioral and a cognitive-affective level. In recognition of the importance of these dimensions of pain, the gate control theory incorporates an action system as well as cognitive and affective components (Melzack & Wall, 1982). This is illustrated in Figure 15.4. After the level of stimulation in the transmission cells of the spinal cord reaches a critical level, pain signals are transmitted to the brain, where they are evaluated by the motivational-affective and sensory-discriminative systems. These systems analyze the sensations in terms of their intensity and spatiotemporal aspects. This then provides the basis for the person's behavioral response. For example, suppose that you accidentally touch a hot stove. The pain signals from that event are transmitted up the spinal cord to the brain, where they are analyzed in terms of their intensity and cause; you are likely to respond by withdrawing your hand and by taking actions to soothe the burn. As indicated in Figure 15.4, the various processes involved are highly interactive—which helps to account for the complexity of people's pain responses.

Since its introduction in 1965, the gate control theory has been the subject of intense discussion and research (Weisenberg, 1977). Research results have mostly been supportive, and the gate control theory is generally consistent with physiological evidence (Wall & Melzack, 1989). However, not all studies have been supportive;

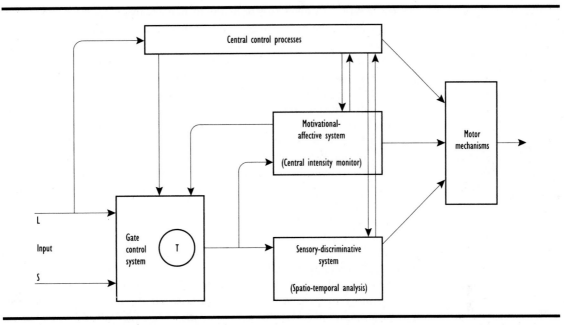

FIGURE 15.4 *Further elaboration of the gate control theory including the motivational-affective and sensory-discriminative systems and their interactions with other processes in the pain experience.*

Note. From *The challenge of pain* by R. Melzack and P. D. Wall, 1982, New York: Basic Books.

disagreement has arisen over the technical details of the gating mechanism. Despite these disagreements, the gate control theory has had tremendous influence on pain research and the understanding of pain in general. One of its key contributions is the explicit incorporation of psychosocial aspects of the pain experience and the description of a plausible mechanism by which they operate. As seen below, the gate control theory has also had an important impact on the development of methods for controlling pain.

PAIN AS A HEALTH PROBLEM

Pain is easily one of the most common health problems. Up to 80% of all visits to physicians involve pain-related complaints (Bresler, 1979); of all of the demands made of physicians, pain relief is the most frequent (Black, 1975). In the United States alone, 20 to 50 million people suffer from arthritis, 25 million people are afflicted with migraine headaches, and 7 million are disabled with low back pain. Tens of billions of dollars are spent on pain relief every year, and, by one estimate, the average American takes 225 aspirin tablets annually (Turk, Meichenbaum, & Genest, 1983).

acute pain
Intense but time-limited pain that is generally the result of tissue damage or disease.

chronic pain
Pain that may originally have been associated with an injury but that persists and does not respond to usual treatments.

Different types of pain should be distinguished when approaching pain as a health problem. Virtually everyone at one time or another has experienced **acute pain.** Acute pain is generally the result of tissue damage or disease and is usually self-limiting in nature. Thus the pain experienced during dental procedures or after surgery may be very intense at the time, but it subsides with healing. **Chronic pain,** however, continues for long periods of time and, even though it may originally have been the result of bodily injury or disease, seems to take on a life of its own. Whereas acute pain generally varies with the extent of the injury, chronic pain persists long after the injury is healed and often bears little relation to the amount of tissue damage. Acute pain usually responds to standard treatment procedures, whereas chronic pain does not. A person with chronic pain thus experiences pain that appears to have little or no physical basis and seems endless. As Wilbert Fordyce (1988) points out, the prime characteristic of such cases is unrelieved suffering. Chronic pain presents major challenges as a health problem.

Chronic pain can be further categorized into three predominant types (Turk et al., 1983). The person with *chronic periodic pain* suffers from pain that is acute but intermittent. For example, a person who suffers from migraine headaches may have excruciating headaches lasting from hours to days, but then may have several painfree weeks or months. By comparison, the person with *chronic, intractable benign pain* has pain that is present most of the time with varying intensity. One of the most common examples of this category is lower back pain. People who suffer from lower back pain generally experience their pain continually and find that they can do little to reduce it. Finally, *chronic progressive pain,* such as that found in cancer patients, means that the person experiences continuous pain that becomes worse as the disease progresses.

What leads to chronic pain? The answer to this question depends on the type of chronic pain. Chronic progressive pain derives primarily from the disease process. For example, cancer patients frequently experience severe bouts of pain that become more frequent and more intense as the cancer progresses. Even in these cases, however, psychological variables play a role with patients' assumptions about the nature of cancer and expectations of pain, influencing pain reports (Turk & Fernandez, 1990).

For other types of chronic pain, the picture is different. In these cases, tissue damage may well have produced the first acute pain that the person experienced. However, over time psychosocial factors play a more prominent role. Distinguishing between respondent and operant pain will help clarify this process (Fordyce, 1976, 1978). **Respondent pain** refers to pain that occurs in response to noxious stimulation or tissue damage. Acute pain and chronic progressive pain generally fall into this category. **Operant pain,** however, is pain that is reinforced by the person's environment. People in pain typically alter their behavior so as to try to reduce the pain. For example, a person may limp, guard a painful arm, avoid exercise, or even stay in bed to avoid pain. When such **pain behaviors** either reduce the pain or prevent it from getting worse, the tendency to continue the behavior is reinforced. These behaviors are particularly resistant to extinction because they are specifically aimed at avoidance. Since the behaviors are successful at preventing or reducing pain the person is unlikely

respondent pain
Pain in response to noxious stimulation or tissue damage.

operant pain
Pain that is maintained through the reinforcement of pain behavior.

pain behavior
Behavior that develops in response to pain, such as limping, lying down, or reducing physical

to change them for fear that the pain will return: Normal behavior may be discouraged by the actual or feared recurrence of pain.

In addition, verbal and behavioral expressions of pain often have a powerful effect on other people. Thus a person's pain complaints, pained facial expressions, or abnormal gait or posture are likely to gain attention as well as concern and assistance from others—which can further reinforce pain behavior (von Baeyer, Johnson, & McMillan, 1984). Along these lines, a recent study of chronic pain patients found that patients reporting higher levels of satisfaction with social support also exhibited higher levels of pain-related behaviors (Gil, Keefe, Crisson, & Van Dalfsen, 1987). Responses of family members to expressions of pain seem to play a particularly important role in maintaining pain behaviors. For example, one study found that among a group of chronic pain patients the best predictor of pain and activity level was the patients' perception of their spouses' solicitousness in response to the expression of pain. Patients whose spouses showed greater levels of concern reported higher levels of pain and lower activity levels than those whose spouses showed less concern (Flor, Kerns, & Turk, 1987).

The reinforcement of pain behaviors also has the effect of reinforcing the experience of pain. People with operant pain experience real suffering. As seen earlier, the experience of pain is influenced by how the person thinks about pain as well as rewards for pain behavior. Thus the reinforcement of pain expressions and behavior may well open the spinal gate and make the person more sensitive to discomfort. Although these factors influence all types of pain, they are particularly influential in the case of operant pain, and provide important clues to techniques for the effective management of chronic pain.

Chronic pain may also be related to personality. Studies of chronic pain patients have consistently found that individuals experiencing chronic pain tend to have particularly high scores for the hypochondriasis, depression, and hysteria scales of the Minnesota Multiphasic Personality Inventory (MMPI) (Rappaport, McAnulty, Waggoner, & Brantley, 1987; Rosen, Grubman, Bevins, & Frymoyer, 1987; Weisenberg, 1977). This pattern of scores indicates that chronic pain patients become preoccupied with concerns about bodily symptoms and health, have feelings of sadness, pessimism, and hopelessness, and cope with distress through the development of physical symptoms.

These findings are merely suggestive because they represent only correlations between personality variables and chronic pain. Whether the personality characteristics preceded the pain or developed in response to it cannot be determined based on these relationships alone. For example, the experience of chronic intractable pain might produce feelings of frustration and helplessness, which, in turn, lead to the psychological disturbances shown on the MMPI. Personality factors do, however, have potential implications for therapy. One useful approach appears to be the identification of subgroups of patients based on personality profiles. For example, studies of headache and lower back pain patients have identified subgroups of patients with different personality profiles (Rappaport et al., 1987; Rosen et al., 1987). These different subgroups of patients may well experience pain for different reasons and respond to different types of treatment (Curtiss, Kinder, Kalichman, & Spana, 1988; Love & Peck, 1987).

Although different chronic pain syndromes and patients share some commonalities, the unique aspects of different syndromes should also be recognized. We now turn to a consideration of two of the more common chronic pain conditions. Recurrent headaches are a prime example of chronic periodic pain, and back pain is the most common variety of chronic, intractable benign pain.

Chronic Headache

Who has not, at one time or another, suffered from a headache? Headaches are an extremely common affliction that can result from many different causes. Although headaches can be caused by tumors, infections, allergies, or concussions, most headaches are believed to be, at least in part, the result of psychological factors (Raskin, 1988; Wolman, 1988). Occasional mild headaches are common, but an estimated 20% of people suffer from painful chronic headaches (Bakal, 1975; Blanchard & Andrasik, 1985).

Chronic headaches can be divided into three general categories: migraine, tension, and a mixed category, in which the person experiences symptoms of both migraine and tension headaches. **Migraine headaches** are the result of constriction and dilation of the arteries both inside and outside the skull. They are characterized by intense sharp pain that may begin in the temple, eyeball, or forehead, and can last from an hour to a week or more. Such headaches typically affect one side of the head, but some migraine sufferers report pain throughout the entire face and neck. In addition, these headaches are often periodic in their recurrence and may be hereditary. In some migraines, known as *classic migraines,* the headache is preceded by certain warning signs such as visual blind spots or flashing lights, nausea, vertigo, or sensitivity to noise (Bakal, 1975; Wolman, 1988).

Tension headaches, which are generally more common than migraines, were long believed to be caused by sustained contraction of the skeletal muscles about the face, scalp, neck, and shoulders. The role of muscle contractions, however, has been called into question by recent studies that have found little or no relationship between muscle contractions and pain from tension headaches (Holroyd et al., 1984; LaCroix & Corbett, 1990; Pikoff, 1984). Although muscle contractions can lead to headaches, recent research suggests that other factors—such as cephalic blood flow or psychosocial stressors—may be more important (Haynes, Gannon, Bank, Shelton, & Goodwin, 1990). Tension headaches do not have the warning signs associated with classic migraines, and the pain experienced is generally that of a dull, steady ache that affects both sides of the head. People suffering from tension headaches often describe the sensation as that of a tight band around the head (Bakal, 1975; Wolman, 1988).

Headaches can be triggered by certain foods, alcohol, noise, extended exercise, or lack of sleep, as well as psychosocial factors such as stress (Bakal, 1975). The exact role of stress in causing headaches has, until recently, been mostly a matter of

migraine headache
A throbbing headache characterized by intense sharp pain that is the result of constriction and dilation of the arteries inside and outside the skull.

tension headache
A headache generally described as a dull, steady ache affecting both sides of the

speculation. Although most people believe that stress can cause headaches, the evidence for this relationship has been primarily correlational. Recently, however, research studies have provided more definitive evidence for the causal role of stress in headaches (Cohen et al., 1983; Gannon, Hayes, Ceuvas, & Chavez, 1987; Haynes et al., 1990; Lehrer & Murphy, 1991). For example, in one study (Gannon et al., 1987), 16 headache (8 migraine, 8 tension) sufferers and 8 individuals not suffering from chronic headaches were first asked to sit quietly and relax for 15 minutes and then, for an hour, were given a series of arithmetic problems as a cognitive stressor. During this time and for 10 minutes after completion of the task, several physiological measures were taken, and subjects were asked to report periodically on their headache pain. Eleven of the 16 headache subjects developed headaches, as did two of the non-headache subjects. The researchers examining the data found that stress produced changes in several physiological measures (heart rate, cephalic blood flow, and muscle tension in the forehead, neck, and forearm), which, in turn, preceded and predicted the occurrence and severity of headaches.

Back Pain

Back pain, particularly pain in the lower back, is another major pain syndrome causing substantial suffering and disability. An estimated 80% of the general United States population experiences problems with back pain sometime during their lives; 50 out of 1,000 American workers report lower back pain during any given year (Dolce & Raczynski, 1985). Back pain complaints account for three fourths of total days absent from work, as well as untold billions of dollars annually in medical costs, lost productivity, and disability compensation (Tunks & Bellissimo, 1991).

What causes back pain? Many physical conditions can cause tenderness and pain in the back (Kirwan, 1989; Parry, 1989), as can physical strain and overuse. However, a majority of all cases of low back pain (as much as 85%, by some estimates) have been described as having no identifiable physical basis. This high rate of back pain without apparent cause, and the fact that many people experience degenerative changes in the spine and back without pain, demonstrate the importance of psychological factors (Dolce & Raczynski, 1985; Schmidt & Arntz, 1987).

Several models are currently competing to explain the role of psychosocial factors in back pain. One group of models focuses on neuromuscular activity and the role of psychosocial factors in influencing that activity (Dolce & Raczynski, 1985). The underlying concept of these models is that painful backs are caused by tension or spasms in the back muscles, which, in turn, are related to activity or psychological variables. For example, the *physical stressor model* argues that back pain originates from mechanical or organic stress on the back, which triggers painful reflexive muscle spasms. These spasms then become self-sustaining through a pain-spasm-pain cycle, in which protective actions taken to reduce pain cause further irritation of back muscles, which then lead to more spasms and pain. By contrast, the *psychosocial stressor model* contends that ineffective coping with environmental and emotional stress produces heightened tension in back muscles, which leads to spasms and back pain.

A second approach to back pain emphasizes the role of learning variables (Fordyce, 1978, 1988; Schmidt & Arntz, 1987). In line with the concept of operant pain discussed earlier, this approach argues that back pain and disability are reinforced by environmental contingencies. Back pain may originate in physical injury or muscle spasms, but is maintained because of the concern and assistance provided by others. One study found that the pain reports of back pain patients differed depending on the solicitousness of their spouses and who they thought was observing them. Patients with solicitous spouses reported higher levels of pain when they thought the spouse was behind a one-way mirror than when they were told that the person behind the mirror was a ward clerk. But patients whose spouses were less solicitous complained of greater pain when they thought they were being observed by a ward clerk (Block, Kremer, & Gaylor, 1980, cited in Flor et al., 1987). In addition, disability from back pain appears to be closely related to government disability policies—more generous disability policies appear to lead to greater disability (Fordyce, 1988). This relationship between policy and disability levels prompted one observer to remark that "physicians should not treat back pain; nor should psychologists. Politicians should" (Nachemson quoted in Fordyce, 1988, p. 278).

Back pain has also been linked to personality and cognition. For example, James Rosen and his colleagues (Rosen et al., 1987) identified five groups of back pain patients based on their scores on the MMPI who differ in the source of their pain as well as level of disability. For two of these groups, the MMPI profiles were within normal limits. Although they differed from each other with respect to duration of their pain and the frequency of physical abnormalities, of all the groups they were the least likely to show physical abnormalities and were the least disabled. The third group of patients had significantly elevated scores for the hypochondriasis and hysteria scales, and had moderately high scores for depression. This group had experienced their pain the longest, were the most likely to have physical abnormalities, and showed a high level of disability. The fourth group also had high scores for hypochondriasis, hysteria, and depression, but had relatively little physical pathology. This group, however, had the highest rate of unemployment, the longest time away from work, and the lowest likelihood of returning to their jobs. The fifth group showed significantly elevated scores on most of the clinical scales of the MMPI and was judged to have the most psychopathology. Interestingly, this group comprised mostly acute back pain patients and had relatively low levels of physical impairment or disability.

Beyond psychopathology, evidence also exists of the importance of specific cognitions. Current evidence suggests that back patients have characteristic beliefs and ways of explaining things that are related to their pain and disability. One recent study, for instance, found significant correlations between pain and disability, on the one hand, and cognitive measures of catastrophizing, hopelessness, and control, on the other. Interestingly, similar relationships were found for both back pain patients with only minimal physical pathology, as well as patients with rheumatoid arthritis.

Cognitive variables accounted for more of the variance in pain and disability than did disease-related ones (Flor & Turk, 1988).

CONTROLLING PAIN

The key questions for anyone who has ever been in pain are when it will be over and what can be done to relieve it. Pain control has been a preoccupation of medicine since time immemorial and will certainly continue to be a major concern in the future. A more sophisticated understanding of pain now allows for a wide variety of available treatments. This section examines physical and psychological techniques for the relief of pain.

Physical Methods of Pain Control

Physical methods for the control of pain focus on altering the process of nociception, or blocking the nerve impulses that carry pain signals. This may be done through the use of drugs, surgical intervention, or the use of physical stimulation techniques.

Medical pain control. Nearly all of us at one time or another have used medications for controlling pain. Most of these probably fell under the heading of *peripherally acting analgesics,* also known as non-narcotic analgesics (Melzack & Wall, 1982; Sunshine & Olson, 1989). Included in this group are such common pain relievers as aspirin, ibuprophen (Nuprin, Advil), acetaminophen (Tylenol), and naproxen (Naprosyn). These drugs work by interrupting the process of nociception at sites of injury and thus reducing pain sensations. For example, aspirin works by inhibiting the synthesis of algogenic substances, reducing inflammation, and lowering fever. Although peripherally acting analgesics are generally readily available without prescription, they do have side effects and may interact with other drugs. Used in recommended amounts, however, they are generally safe and are effective when dealing with mild to moderate pain.

A second family of drugs used in pain control are the narcotics, or *centrally acting analgesics* (Melzack & Wall, 1982; Twycross & McQuay, 1989). Examples of narcotics are morphine and codeine, both derived from the opium poppy, as well as heroin, Demerol, and Dilaudid, which are synthetically produced but based on opium molecules. These drugs operate on the central nervous system by imitating the effects of the body's endogenous pain relief system, described earlier. Specifically, the molecules in these drugs bind to receptors for endorphins and enkephalins in the brain and spinal cord, blocking the transmission of pain signals. Thus they are considered the most potent pain relievers available and are commonly used in emergency cases involving the rapid onset of extreme pain or to control intractable cases of chronic progressive pain such as that found in some terminal cancer patients. They are also frequently used to alleviate labor pain and postoperative pain.

Narcotics are extremely effective for relieving some types of pain, but they also have some serious disadvantages. In addition to their analgesic qualities, they are also psychoactive, depress respiration, and can be addictive. Further, patients may develop tolerance to their effects with repeated use. Of particular concern to many is the possibility that repeated use of narcotics may cause patients to require increasing dosages to achieve pain relief and may make them addicted (Aronoff, Wagner, & Spangler, 1986; Melzack & Wall, 1982). Although these drugs are undeniably addicting, considerable debate rages as to the extent to which this is a problem in actual practice. Whereas some researchers argue that it is a serious problem (Aronoff et al., 1986), others believe that it has been blown out of proportion (Melzack & Wall, 1982). Studies of both acute and chronic pain patients have found that few patients actually become addicted (Twycross & McQuay, 1989). One study found that when allowed to self-administer narcotics, patients recovering from surgery, in fact, used *less* medication than they would have been given by hospital staff (Hill et al., 1990).

Surgical pain control. Given the neural pathways by which pain sensations travel to the brain, one seemingly obvious solution to intractable pain is simply to sever the nerves by which the pain is transmitted. Indeed, many different surgical interventions have been used for pain control (Melzack & Wall, 1982; Wall & Melzack, 1989). For example, the peripheral nerves leading from the pain site to the spinal cord might be cut, nerve tracts in the spinal cord might be severed (cordotomy), or a lobotomy might be performed to destroy portions of the cerebral cortex thought to be involved in pain. These are extreme measures to be used only when the pain is severe and intractable. Although they might be justified in a few cases, such as with a terminally ill patient whose pain cannot be controlled otherwise, these procedures result in serious and often irreversible side effects and are frequently ineffective for

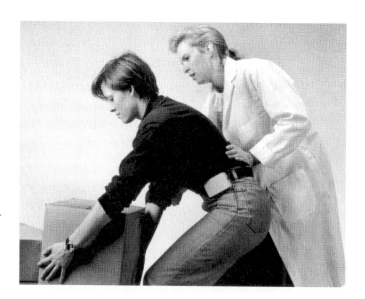

Transcutaneous electrical nerve stimulation achieves pain relief through counterirritation using electrical current.

pain relief. Severing the nerves to a particular area of the body cuts not only those fibers associated with pain but many other fibers as well. The result is often a general numbness and, depending on the nerves involved, paralysis in the area affected. In addition, nerve fibers can regenerate, leading to a resumption of the pain signals. Thus although the person may experience temporary relief, the pain often returns, sometimes more intensely than before. Because of these serious drawbacks, invasive surgical interventions strictly for pain relief are now rarely used, and then only in extreme cases.

nerve block
The use of local anesthetic to interrupt the transmission of pain signals.

Some less invasive procedures are used, however. For instance, **nerve blocks** are used for the treatment of pain syndromes including regional and localized pain (Bonica, 1989). Nerve blocks are created by injecting a local anesthetic into painful tissues or neural pathways so as to interrupt the transmission of pain signals. For example, a patient with myofacial pain might have anesthetic injected into the affected muscles, whereas a patient experiencing pain in the abdomen or thorax might receive an intercostal block, that is, an anesthetic is injected into nerves along the ribs. Nerve blocks have the advantage of interrupting neural transmission without permanent destruction of the nerves themselves. Since the anesthetic wears off, these solutions are only temporary, but they can provide meaningful relief, particularly for acute pain.

Physical stimulation. Irritating body tissue to reduce pain may at first seem counterintuitive, but, in fact, we do it frequently. Who, for example, has not scratched an itch, rubbed a wound, or used a hot compress to relieve pain? From our discussion of the gate control theory, we know that only certain nerve endings are involved in producing pain sensations, whereas the stimulation of other nerves can close the pain gate. Apparently scratching, rubbing, and other stimulation techniques produce their effects through stimulating nerves that close the gate.

transcutaneous electrical nerve stimulation
A method of pain control using electrical stimulation of nerve endings through electrodes placed on the skin.

This basic principle is behind physical stimulation techniques for pain control. Known as *counterirritation,* these techniques relieve pain through the application of such stimuli as heat, pressure, rubbing, and electrical current (Melzack & Wall, 1982; Melzack, 1989). For example, various types of physical therapy use massage, manipulation, heat, or cold to counteract aches and pains. In addition, the technique of **transcutaneous electrical nerve stimulation** (TENS) uses electrodes placed on the skin to stimulate nerve endings near the surface using current from a battery-operated stimulator. Clinical evaluations have shown this technique to be effective in relieving certain kinds of both acute and chronic pain, particularly when there is localized nerve damage (Johnson, Aston, & Thompson, 1991; Melzack & Wall, 1982; Wolff, 1989). Stimulation can also be applied to the nerves in the spinal cord (Melzack & Wall, 1982). For example, patients with chronic back pain might have electrodes implanted in the spinal cord, which would then stimulate spinal nerves when the person experienced pain. Studies of spinal stimulation have shown it to be an effective method for pain relief, particularly when the pain is localized and the person is receiving no secondary gain (such as disability payments) from being in pain (Krainick & Thoden, 1989).

One treatment that long predates the gate control theory, but which also apparently uses these principles, is *acupuncture*. Based on principles of traditional Chinese medicine, acupuncture involves the insertion of fine needles into selected acupuncture points specified by traditional charts and then twirling them slowly for a period of time. In some cases, a weak electrical current may be applied to the needles for further stimulation (Macdonald, 1989; Melzack, 1989; Porkert & Ullmann, 1988). Does acupuncture work? Although rigorous evaluation of therapy trials is hard to carry out because of ambiguities in some of the technical aspects of the technique, acupuncture can be effective in relieving pain. Recent reviews of acupuncture trials involving chronic pain from different sources indicate that between 20% and 80% of patients treated with acupuncture obtain relief (Macdonald, 1989; Richardson & Vincent, 1986). Studies producing results near the low end of this range tend to be those using acupuncture as a last resort, whereas those using a broader selection of patients tend to find improvement in a majority of cases.

Psychological Approaches to Pain Control

Physical methods of pain control attempt to reduce pain by manipulating stimulus input. As we have seen, however, this stimulus input is only part of the pain process. Psychological methods address the behavioral, cognitive, and motivational aspects of pain. These methods, which are based largely on learning principles, attempt to change the reinforcement that a person receives from pain behavior as well as deal with the emotional aspects of pain and help the person to exercise control over the pain experience.

Operant methods. Rooted in the distinction Fordyce (1976, 1978) made between respondent and operant pain, operant techniques focus on reducing pain behaviors and complaints. Since behaviors are considered the primary feature of chronic pain, relatively little concern is given to the experience of pain itself. Rather, the goal of therapy is to reduce pain behaviors and encourage well behaviors. The assumption is that as the patient engages in a greater proportion of well behaviors the subjective experience of pain will decline.

The program itself consists of measures aimed at eliminating the contingencies between pain behavior and environmental rewards. One aspect of this is the relationship between expressed pain and the receipt of pain medication. Instead of being given medication in response to expressed pain, a procedure believed to reinforce the expression of pain, patients are given medication only at fixed intervals. Over time, with the patient's permission, the amount of analgesic is reduced and eventually eliminated. Further, during treatment, concerted efforts are made to ignore pain behaviors and only reinforce well behaviors.

Does this approach work? Unfortunately, most of the evaluations of this technique have been in the form of case studies; few controlled investigations have been done. However, available evidence supports its effectiveness. Use of these procedures with both chronic and acute pain patients has led to significant reductions in disability and at least moderate reductions in expressed pain (Fordyce, Brockway, Bergman, & Spengler, 1986; Fordyce, Shelton, & Dundore, 1982). Despite these successes, this approach has been criticized because it is unconcerned with experienced pain and because it often requires a hospital stay of several weeks, which can make it expensive (Melzack & Wall, 1982).

Biofeedback. Biofeedback is another technique based on operant conditioning. As seen in Chapter 7, this technique aims to train people to monitor and change selected physiological functions with the aid of electronic monitors. Studies have shown that people can be successful in using biofeedback to alter such physiological functions as heart rate, finger temperature, muscle activity, and brain wave patterns. In addition, it can be used to help reduce blood pressure and manage stress (Andrasik, Blanchard, & Edlund, 1985; McGrady, Woerner, Bernal, & Higgins, 1987).

Can biofeedback be used to relieve pain? The evidence so far looks promising. Studies using biofeedback to treat pain syndromes including headaches and back pain have found that patients are able to learn how to reduce muscle tension and alter the vascular tension associated with back pain and headaches. Further, biofeedback can reduce the intensity and frequency of experienced pain (Jessup, 1989; Turk et al., 1983). However, important caveats should be noted. First, the improvements obtained with biofeedback are often modest and generally no greater than those obtained through other techniques involving relaxation (Jessup, 1989; Melzack & Wall, 1982; Sargent, Solbach, Coyne, Spohn, & Segerson, 1986). Since relaxation is an important ingredient in biofeedback, the results of biofeedback on pain might be primarily the result of relaxation, not the training in controlling physiological functions. Second, biofeedback is an expensive procedure, requiring expensive machinery and considerable time commitment. Unless the results are substantially better than those obtained with less expensive procedures, the additional cost incurred in using biofeedback is hard to justify.

Hypnosis. Among the oldest psychological treatments for pain is hypnosis. Although modern hypnotic techniques originated in the eighteenth century, the rhythmic drumming and incantations used as part of healing ceremonies in so-called primitive societies may well have hypnotic effects and produce pain relief though processes similar to those of modern hypnosis (Melzack & Wall, 1982).

What is hypnosis, and how does it influence pain? The nature of hypnosis has long been the subject of considerable controversy. The hypnotic state has been described variously as being an altered state of consciousness, believed-in imagining, focused attention, and role enactment. However, in general hypnosis can be defined as "that state or condition which occurs when appropriate suggestions elicit distortions of perception, memory or mood" (Orne & Dinges, 1989, p. 1021). This state can be induced in different ways; hypnotic induction generally involves instructing the person to focus attention on the hypnotist, relax, eventually close one's eyes, and imagine what the hypnotist is suggesting. Unlike biofeedback, which requires special equipment and training, hypnosis is a simple procedure requiring no specialized equipment (Orne & Dinges, 1989).

Reports of hypnotic effects on pain are often quite dramatic. For example, reports have been made of people undergoing cardiac surgery, appendectomies, Caesarean sections, and other major surgeries using no anesthesia other than hypnosis (Melzack & Wall, 1982; Orne & Dinges, 1989). These are particularly dramatic cases, which come to our attention because of their rarity. Although most people can be hypnotized to some degree, the percentage of people who are highly hypnotizable and thus able to reach the depth of trance required for surgery is very small (Melzack & Wall, 1982).

Controlled studies provide substantiation for the role of hypnosis in relieving pain, but also suggest important limitations. Studies of the effects of hypnosis on experimentally induced pain indicate significant pain reduction in people who are highly susceptible to hypnosis (Wadden & Anderton, 1982). For example, one recent study examined the effectiveness of hypnosis on ischemic pain, which is induced through using a tourniquet to cut off the blood supply to the subject's arm. Subjects exposed to ischemic pain while hypnotized showed greater tolerance for pain than they did during a waking state. The amount of pain relief obtained was significantly correlated with the subjects' hypnotizability (DeBenedittis, Panerai, & Villamira, 1989). Similar findings have been obtained for various types of clinical pain (Orne & Dinges, 1989). For instance, hypnosis has been shown to provide significant pain relief during dental procedures (Kent, 1986), burn debridement (Patterson, Questad, & de Lateur, 1989), bone marrow aspiration, and lumbar puncture (Wall & Womack, 1989), as well to reduce cancer and arthritis pain (Orne & Dinges, 1989). Hypnosis does not appear to be useful, however, for headaches, back pain, or pain from which the person is receiving significant secondary gains (Orne & Dinges, 1989). Further, the amount of pain relief obtained from hypnosis is generally equivalent to other psychological treatments, and in some cases is no greater than that obtained from placebos (Melzack & Wall, 1982).

How does hypnosis achieve pain relief? A great deal of controversy surrounds the question of how hypnosis actually operates. Some argue that hypnotic effects are primarily the result of suggestibility, whereas others argue that pain reduction is the result of more complex processes at a high level in the central nervous system (Orne & Dinges, 1989). One possibility is that hypnosis achieves its effects through a process of dissociation, in which the person is able to separate the sensory information about pain from conscious awareness. Evidence for this comes from experiments with highly hypnotizable subjects, who are able to engage in a phenomenon known as automatic writing. While in a hypnotic trance, these subjects are able to use a "hidden observer" to write out reports on events outside conscious awareness. When subjected to experimental pain, these subjects verbally deny pain, while the "hidden observer" reports pain sensations at normal or near normal levels (Hilgard, 1977). This interpretation of hypnosis, however, is controversial (Wadden & Anderton,

1982), and the actual mechanisms by which hypnosis operates are still unclear (Orne & Dinges, 1989).

Relaxation. Common to both biofeedback and hypnosis is relaxation. In both these procedures, the person is generally required to relax as part of the treatment. Might relaxation provide effective pain relief on its own? The answer appears to be yes. As seen in Chapter 7, different methods can be used for producing relaxation. However, all of them can be successful in generating a reduction in muscle tension and overall stress, which can significantly influence the experience of pain (Melzack & Wall, 1982). For example, Jon Kabat-Zinn and his colleagues (Kabat-Zinn, Lipworth, & Burney, 1985) trained chronic pain patients to relax through meditation. Compared to a control group of pain patients, who were receiving treatment but were not trained in meditation, patients in the meditation condition showed significant improvements in their levels of pain and pain-related activity reduction, as well as reduction in negative psychological states such as anxiety and depression. Follow-up showed that these improvements were maintained at 15 months, with the exception that the reduction in pain level was no longer statistically significant. Other studies have shown that relaxation can provide significant relief for back pain (Stuckey, Jacobs, & Goldfarb, 1986), headaches (Larsson, Melin, Lamminen, & Ullstedt, 1987), ulcerative colitis (Shaw & Ehrlich, 1987), and other chronic pain conditions (Jessup, 1989; Ost, 1987).

Cognitive-behavioral methods. Recognizing that pain is related to people's behavior as well as their cognitions, the cognitive-behavioral approach has been developed as an overarching psychological framework for pain control (Turk et al., 1983; Turk & Meichenbaum, 1989). This approach argues that pain control requires both a consideration of pain behaviors and their reinforcement and an understanding of patients' thoughts, feelings, and beliefs. Therefore, this approach has a close relationship with the cognitive-behavioral approach to health behaviors discussed in Chapters 4 and 5, as well as stress inoculation training, discussed in Chapter 7. When applied to pain, cognitive-behavioral treatment is designed to help the patient constructively deal with pain and live a more effective and satisfying life. The reduction of pain sensations is a desirable result of the treatment, but is not its primary focus (Turk & Meichenbaum, 1989).

Cognitive-behavioral treatment consists of six basic stages. The sequence begins with *assessment,* in which the therapist attempts to establish the extent of physical inpairment and gather information from the patient and significant others about the pain problem and the factors that influence it. Particular attention is paid to ways in which pain behaviors are maintained and to establishing goals for treatment. This information then provides the basis for moving on to the second stage of *reconceptualization.* During this stage, the therapist works with the patient to help him or her understand the multidimensional nature of pain and how pain is influenced by both physical and psychological factors. Reconceptualization prepares the patient for the treatment methods to be used and also facilitates the setting of realistic treatment goals. In this stage the patient is encouraged to become more physically active and to develop outside interests to focus attention away from pain sensations and disability. In addition, to the extent possible, patients are weaned from pain medications.

During Stage 3, *skills acquisition and consolidation,* the therapist helps the patient to develop new ways of dealing with pain. Specifically, the patient is provided training in different pain control techniques and is urged to practice them so that they can be used when needed. Particular emphasis is placed on relaxation and the conscious focusing of attention. Patients are taught to use a relaxation technique and to practice controlled breathing exercises; both help the patient to relax and to develop a sense of control over pain and stress. Training in the focusing of attention is designed to help the patient develop cognitive controls over pain sensations. Depending on the particular patient, this training might include avoidance strategies involving the diversion of attention away from pain to external stimuli, attentional strategies, in which the person focuses on specific aspects of the pain, or guided imagery, in which the patient is instructed to imagine pleasant diverting scenes (Fowler-Kerry & Lander, 1987; Holmes & Stevenson, 1990; McCaul & Malott, 1984; Turk & Meichenbaum, 1989).

After the patient has been taught specific treatment procedures, the emphasis changes to rehearsing those techniques and applying them to specific situations. In Stage 4, *rehearsal and application,* role playing is used to help the patient better understand the treatment techniques and how they might be applied in everyday settings. This emphasis on practical application is continued during Stage 5, *generalization and maintenance,* in which patients are given homework assignments and encouraged to try out their new skills in various situations. Particular attention is paid to problems encountered by the patient and to the development of solutions for overcoming them. During this stage, the patient is encouraged to evaluate the progress that has been made and, most important, to attribute that progress and success to personal efforts. Finally, the long-term effects of treatment are assessed during Stage 6, *treatment follow-up,* in which patients are contacted at selected intervals after the completion of therapy to review progress and encourage the maintenance of skills.

Are these procedures effective in pain management? The evidence indicates that they are. Studies with different pain syndromes have indicated that the cognitive-behavioral approach can be used effectively with headaches, back pain, temporo-mandibular pain, and debridement of burns, to mention a few (Basler & Rehfisch, 1990; Graff-Radford, Reeves, & Jaeger, 1987; Turk & Meichenbaum, 1989; Turk et al., 1983; Turner & Clancy, 1988; Turner, Clancy, McQuade, & Cardenas, 1990). However, this approach includes many different procedures, and the success of the program is likely to hinge on successfully matching treatment procedures with specific patients.

Pain Clinics

Pain derives from many sources, both physical and psychological, and no one approach to treatment is effective for all types of pain or for all patients. The growing appreciation of the multidimensional nature of pain and pain management, and, in particular, the failure of purely medical means to control chronic pain effectively, have led to the development of multidisciplinary pain clinics (Kanner, 1986; Turk & Meichenbaum, 1989). These pain clinics, often associated with hospitals or universities, attempt to address the broad spectrum of causes for pain and involve medical, psychological, social, physical therapy, and vocational elements in their programs. Evaluation of the effectiveness of these clinics has generally been favorable with both short- and long-term reduction of pain, as well as improvements in activity levels, psychological functioning, and employment (Cinciripini & Floreen, 1982; Maruta, Swanson, & McHardy, 1990; Peters & Large, 1990).

A good illustration of a multidisciplinary pain clinic is one developed at the Miller-Dwan Hospital in Duluth, Minnesota (Cinciripini & Floreen, 1982). This is a four-week program involving medicine reduction, biofeedback/relaxation, behavioral group therapy, physical therapy, self-monitoring, contracting, family training, and follow-up meetings. Staff members involved in the program include psychologists, nurses, a biofeedback technician, physical therapists, and occupational therapists. Patients are referred by their physicians and are initially screened by a consortium of medical and psychological practitioners. The first three days of the treatment are an observation period during which baseline measures are taken of various behaviors, pain level, activity, physical performance, and medicine intake. This is followed by a systematic reduction of pain medication and the application of the various treatment modalities. Evaluation of this program found significant reductions in medicine use, self-reported pain levels, pain complaints, and pain behaviors, as well as increases in functional mobility, positive health talk, and physical fitness. Further, these gains were maintained at six- and twelve-month follow-ups.

SUMMARY

Pain can be defined as the subjective experience of physical discomfort, which is often, but not always, related to tissue damage or disease. Although pain may at first seem to be a relatively simple phenomenon, the complexity of pain is seen in phenomena—such as congenital pain insensitivity, causalgia, and phantom limb pain—that illustrate the variable connection between tissue damage and pain experience.

The experience of pain includes both physical and psychological components. Physiologically, pain sensations are generated by the stimulation of free nerve endings, particularly in A-delta and C fibers, which produces nerve impulses that are transmitted through the spinal cord to the brain. These impulses are then modified as they pass through the dorsal horn of the spinal column and the thalamus on their way to the cerebral cortex, where they are interpreted. Transmission of pain signals is also strongly influenced by endogenous opioids, neurochemicals that can slow or block the impulses.

The experience of pain is also a function of psychosocial factors. Culture influences the pain experience as does prior experience. Although sensation thresholds are relatively constant across cultures, different cultures vary widely in how they respond to pain. Moreover, developmental experience influences responses to noxious stimuli. Pain responses are further influenced by emotions and stress as well as the meaning of the situation, feelings of control and self-efficacy, and the person's focus of attention.

Pain theories such as specificity theory and pattern theory have generally overlooked psychosocial influences on pain. However, the gate control theory attempts to integrate physiological and psychosocial aspects of pain. This theory proposes that cells in the dorsal horn act as a gate for incoming stimuli and determine which nerve impulses are transmitted up the spinal cord. Whether the gate allows pain signals to be transmitted to the brain depends on (1) the balance of stimulation between small (A-delta and C) and large (A-beta) fibers and (2) signals descending from central control mechanisms in the brain. In addition, pain signals to the brain are evaluated by motivational-affective and sensory-discriminative systems, which play a critical role in pain responses.

Although acute pain plays an important role in signaling tissue damage and disease, chronic pain constitutes a major health problem. Millions of people suffer from chronic pain, and every year tens of billions of dollars are spent on pain relief. Two chronic pain syndromes that are particularly troublesome are chronic headaches and back pain. Chronic headaches are a good example of chronic periodic pain, whereas back pain exemplifies chronic, intractable benign pain. Chronic pain generally begins as acute pain, but then becomes chronic, often because pain behaviors are reinforced.

The close interaction of physiological and psychosocial factors in pain argues for a multidimensional approach to pain control. Physical methods of pain control attempt to reduce pain through the use of medicines that reduce or block pain signals, surgical severing of nerve pathways, or counterirritation to stimulate the closing of the spinal gate. By contrast, psychological pain control is concerned with the behavioral, cognitive, and motivational aspects of pain. Operant methods focus on removing rewards for pain behaviors; biofeedback attempts to teach patients to control physiological processes that contribute to pain. Hypnosis uses hypnotic induction techniques along with suggestion to alter the pain experience. Common to both biofeedback and hypnosis is relaxation, which can be used on its own to produce pain reduction. The cognitive-behavioral approach developed as an overarching strategy for pain control includes the use of relaxation and various cognitive strategies for helping people deal with chronic pain. Recognizing the multidimensional nature of pain, specialized pain clinics have been developed that attempt to integrate physical and psychological evaluation and methods in a holistic approach to pain control.

KEY TERMS

algogenic substances (390)
nociceptors (390)
A-delta fibers (391)
C fibers (391)
A-beta fibers (391)
endogenous opioids (391)
psychogenic pain (396)
acute pain (402)

chronic pain (402)
respondent pain (402)
operant pain (402)
pain behavior (403)
migraine headache (404)
tension headache (404)
nerve block (409)
transcutaneous electrical nerve stimulation (409)

SUGGESTED READINGS

Fordyce, W. E. (1988). Pain and suffering: A reappraisal. *American Psychologist, 43,* 276–83. Leading pain clinician William Fordyce discusses the important distinction between pain and suffering and its implications for treating chronic pain.

Melzack, R., & Wall, P. D. (1982). *The challenge of pain.* New York: Basic Books. In this book, Ronald Melzack and Patrick Wall provide a readable and comprehensive discussion of the various phenomena of pain, pain theories, and pain control.

Turk, D. C., Meichenbaum, D., & Genest, M. (1983). *Pain and behavioral medicine: A cognitive-behavioral perspective.* New York: Guilford Press. This book presents a cognitive-behavioral approach to the problem of chronic pain and its treatment.

16

Health Psychology:
Critical Issues
for the Future

As we have seen throughout this text, health psychology is a rapidly developing field that addresses many key health concerns. Despite its relative youth, health psychology has made important contributions to understanding the nature of health and illness and has provided new methods for enhancing health and well-being. But where does health psychology go from here? What critical issues face health psychology as it moves into the twenty-first century? No one can forecast with total accuracy how health psychology will develop. However, consideration of the current state of the field suggests some key issues that are likely to occupy center stage. For purposes of exposition, these are classified into issues concerned with research, clinical application, and health psychology as a profession. These are broad issues, many of which have relevance for more than one category.

CRITICAL RESEARCH ISSUES

Research provides the backbone for health psychology by providing an empirical basis for understanding health issues and the development of treatment modalities. Research activity in health psychology has recently burgeoned as more psychologists have turned their attention to health issues. This research has provided many new insights and promises to provide many more in the years to come. Three aspects of research that are critical for the continued development of health psychology are the continued documentation of the mind-body link, the development of better theoretical frameworks, and the careful evaluation of the effectiveness of interventions.

Documenting the Mind-Body Link

The discussions of the various topics in this text illustrate that the mind-body link is a strong one. On the one hand, psychological states and behavior influence people's physical well-being. As we have seen, psychological states such as emotions and feelings of stress are strongly implicated in the development of disease. In addition, health behaviors such as smoking, alcohol use, exercise, and sexual behavior are significant risk factors for various diseases and for well-being in general. On the other hand, a person's physical health has important psychosocial effects. The discussion of chronic illness in general and specific health problems in particular demonstrate that illness can have profound effects on psychological and social well-being.

Research studies are now providing the empirical evidence for links that not long ago were only speculation. Yet, in reality, we are only beginning to explore the intricacies of the mind-body link. Key questions for the future include the details of the ways in which behaviors and psychological states influence health outcomes as well as the ways in which people defend themselves against these effects. For example, current evidence suggests that stress affects the development of cancer through its impact on immune functioning. However, we are still in the dark about exactly how this operates. It might operate by suppressing DNA repair and the functioning of natural killer (NK) cells (Glaser, Thorn, Tarr, Kiecolt-Glaser, & D'Ambrosio, 1985; O'Leary, 1990), but many of the details of these mechanisms are still unknown. Similarly, some evidence indicates that the Type A behavior pattern, and in particular the anger component of that pattern, is associated with CHD. However, as we have seen, many questions about this relationship and the mechanisms involved (Glass, 1989; Rhodewalt & Smith, 1991) remain to be answered by future research. Strong evidence exists about the role of expectations and beliefs in the healing process (Ornstein & Sobel, 1987; White, Tursky, & Schwartz, 1985), but we know little about how they exert their influence. Finally, how people perceive and cope with stressful situations clearly has critical implications for their health. As yet, however, we are only beginning to understand the different ways in which people cope and the ways in which these coping strategies affect health outcomes (Taylor, 1990). These are only a few of the research questions facing health psychologists in the future, but they illustrate the types of issues that are likely to be major foci of attention.

Questions concerning the mind-body link are by their very nature extremely complex, and require an understanding of both the biological and the psychosocial processes involved. Therefore, future research on these issues is likely to be strongly interdisciplinary, involving not just psychologists but medical and other researchers as well (Carmody & Matarazzo, 1991; Taylor, 1987). The research will thus require that health psychologists forge collaborative relationships with other disciplines. For example, research on the mind-body link in heart disease requires input from such diverse professionals as epidemiologists, cardiologists, psychologists, physiologists, and nutritionists. Each of these disciplines takes a different perspective and brings different skills to the issues involved. None of these disciplines is able to address the entire problem on its own. Rather, each has its own perspective, which, when taken with the others, can contribute to a more comprehensive approach. So health psychologists seriously interested in addressing important health issues should be prepared to develop collaborative relationships across discipline lines and to work as a part of multidisciplinary teams. Such collaboration often requires that the researchers overcome basic differences in assumptions, methods, and general approach, but this is critical for real advancement to take place (Glass, 1989).

Developing Theory

Future progress in health psychology also depends on the development of strong theoretical frameworks for understanding empirical findings. The biopsychosocial model and its variants provide a general theoretical framework for efforts in health psychology (Schwartz, 1982). However, this model can offer only a general framework and does not address specific health issues. At present, theoretical models for specific issues are often tentative or seriously underdeveloped. For example, David Glass (1989) writes that despite voluminous research on the Type A behavior pattern, a systematic theoretical understanding of this pattern and its relationship to CHD is still lacking. The same can be said for almost every topic discussed in this text. A particularly troubling aspect of this is that interventions are often developed and used without a clear understanding of what the intervention actually does, why it works (or doesn't), and what components are critical for its success. The interventions for treating chronic pain, for instance, often involve multiple components (Turk, Meichenbaum, & Genest, 1983; Wall & Melzack, 1989); but exactly what it is about the treatment that leads to the reduction of pain and disability is often unclear. Future progress requires that we not only provide empirical evidence on the issues in question, but also pay close attention to the development of viable theoretical models.

Evaluating Interventions

Research in health psychology is not only directed at basic issues but is also concerned with the practical application of the findings. But how effective are the interventions we develop? Assuming that an intervention will be effective because it is based on solid research findings would be all too easy. However, this is clearly an assumption that should be subjected to empirical testing. An assumption that because life-style has been closely and consistently related to the development of such diseases as cancer

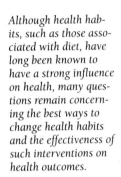

Although health habits, such as those associated with diet, have long been known to have a strong influence on health, many questions remain concerning the best ways to change health habits and the effectiveness of such interventions on health outcomes.

and heart disease, interventions to modify life-style will successfully reduce the risk of contracting these diseases is tempting. But, as we have seen repeatedly, life-style variables are difficult to change. Further, many factors are involved in these diseases, so changes in life-style alone may not be so effective as one might think in reducing disease incidence. The results of major intervention trials for reducing cardiovascular risk have generally produced smaller than expected changes in disease incidence (Kaplan, 1984). This argues strongly for research efforts to rigorously evaluate interventions, efforts that examine ultimate health outcomes as well as changes in risk factors.

DIRECTIONS IN CLINICAL APPLICATIONS

Health psychology also faces important clinical challenges. As we learn more about the nature of the mind-body link, the question arises as to how we can best apply that knowledge in improving people's lives. An impressive arsenal of intervention techniques has already been developed, but more needs to be done. The next section considers, first, three general areas of future clinical challenge and, then, the question of cost effectiveness.

Stress Management

Modern life is unquestionably filled with stress. Whether as major life events or daily hassles, numerous challenges confront each of us every day. We now know that how people deal with those challenges is at least as important as the events themselves in producing the experience of stress. We also know that how people cope with stress has critical implications for their health in general as well as for their likelihood of contracting specific diseases. A major challenge for health psychology is the development and application of effective stress management techniques. Numerous interventions are already available. In addition, overarching frameworks, such as stress inoculation training (SIT), provide useful guidance for their application (Meichenbaum, 1985). The future challenge is to refine the available techniques further, develop new ones, and make these interventions available to those who need them.

A good example of this can be found in interventions to change Type A behavior. The goal in Type A interventions is to help Type A individuals to deal better with daily challenges and thus reduce their feelings of stress and the effects of that stress on their health. As seen in Chapter 14, several promising interventions have been developed (Rhodewalt & Smith, 1991; Roskies et al., 1986). However, these interventions often involve several different components, only some of which may actually be effective, and may require intensive treatment over a period of months. Moreover, they often work for some individuals but not for others. A major challenge in dealing with Type A is to refine these programs, selecting only those components that are effective in reducing stress, and finding ways to help those who do not respond to current programs. Further, these interventions must be cost effective. If we develop interventions that are effective in reducing stress but so expensive that they add to health care costs rather than help reduce them, those interventions are unlikely to be taken seriously. These challenges are certainly not exclusive to interventions for Type A, but apply to any intervention program.

Disease Prevention

A second major clinical challenge is in applying our knowledge of behavior change to the prevention of disease. From our discussion of health promotion (Chapters 4 and 5), we know that health behaviors have many different determinants. Further, various interventions are available for promoting positive health behaviors. The development of intervention programs that are effective and can be feasibly applied to large numbers of people is therefore a necessary task. The most effective current methods for changing health behaviors use a cognitive-behavioral approach, but these may also be the most expensive to use because they are often applied either individually or in small groups. Efforts to alter health behaviors through the mass media can reach many people at relatively low cost, but often have relatively weak effects (Lau, Kane, Berry, Ware, & Roy, 1980).

One possible solution is the development of multifaceted programs, drawing on the full spectrum of intervention techniques and applied to whole communities. Several recently developed programs show considerable promise (Perry, Klepp, & Shultz, 1988; Puska, 1984; Stunkard, Felix, & Cohen, 1985) and offer many advantages including the ability to reach large numbers of people in the environments in which they live for a relatively low per capita cost. However, they also present several challenges. By their very nature, they are highly complex undertakings, requiring the involvement of professionals from several different disciplines and lay community leaders. Further, the specific intervention techniques to be used, as well as their mode and site of presentation, should be selected carefully, and maximum effectiveness requires that the interventions be applied over a period of years. Data on the long-term effectiveness of early community interventions are only just becoming available; the successes and failures of these programs offer valuable lessons for designing more effective ones in the future.

The prevention of relapse represents a key challenge in any program for changing health behaviors, whether focused on individuals or whole communities. Many interventions show encouraging behavior changes early on. However, follow-up data often show that many subjects revert to their previous negative health habits as time goes on. For example, studies of interventions to help people stop smoking often show short-term success rates of up to 90% (Leventhal & Cleary, 1980). But over time, a high proportion of people go back to smoking. Similar observations have been made of other negative health habits such as alcohol use, overeating, and drug use (Hunt, Barnett, & Ranch, 1971; Marlatt, 1985). Health psychologists therefore need to develop methods for maintaining behavior changes and preventing reversion to negative health habits.

Treating Health Problems

Health psychologists also face important challenges in the treatment of health problems. As we have seen repeatedly throughout this text, healing involves far more than just ministrations to the person's physical needs. Recovery from illness or, in the case of chronic conditions, effectively coping with it, has behavioral, psychological, and social dimensions. For example, recovering from cancer or a heart attack requires not only good medical treatment but also effectively coping with the emotions involved, the physical changes that these diseases bring, and the strain that they can place on

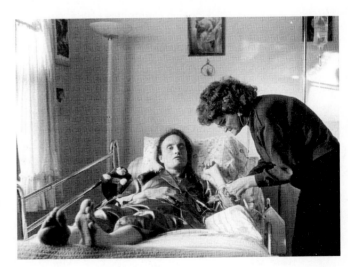

One of the important future challenges for health psychology is the development and implementation of interventions to help people deal more effectively with serious health problems such as AIDS.

relationships. In addition, significant behavioral change may be required if the person is to prevent recurrence of disease. Thus heart patients may be required to alter their dietary or work habits substantially or risk another heart attack. Similarly, AIDS is not just a disease of the body; it also has profound effects on persons with AIDS and their loved ones. In cases like these, health psychologists are challenged to develop and implement interventions that help people adhere to recommended behavior changes and treatment regimens, as well as deal with the psychosocial dimensions of their illness. When properly implemented, such interventions can significantly enhance the quality of life for patients and increase their longevity (Gordon et al., 1980; Ornish et al., 1990; Spiegel, Bloom, Kraemer, & Gottheil, 1989).

In other cases, health psychologists are directly involved in the treatment of the health problem itself. For example, evidence is growing that chronic pain syndromes respond well to psychological and behavioral treatments (Turk et al., 1983). Similarly, diseases in which stress plays a prominent role may be treatable through the application of stress reduction techniques. Health psychologists are charged with developing and refining psychological methods of treatment, and then demonstrating their effectiveness in medical settings.

Demonstrating Cost Effectiveness

Our interventions obviously must be effective in achieving their aims, but, equally important, they must be cost effective. The discussion of the origins of health psychology at the beginning of this book noted the dramatic rise in health care costs in recent years. By the year 2000, some have estimated that health care costs in the United States will consume 14% of GNP, up from only 5.2% in 1960 (Carmody & Matarazzo, 1991). One hope in developing health psychology has been that the use of psychological interventions would help to contain or reduce treatment costs. Some evidence demonstrates that this is occurring, at least in some cases. For example, Nicholas Cummings (1985, cited in Taylor, 1987) claims that even one session with a clinical psychologist can markedly reduce the use of health care services by individuals whose symptoms are primarily psychological in origin. Similarly, simple interventions designed to provide information to surgical patients and help them develop a sense of control have resulted in diminished use of pain relievers and tranquilizers, as well as shorter hospital stays (Anderson & Masur, 1983; Langer, Janis, & Wolfer, 1975). Further, the development of pain clinics has provided effective treatment for patients who might otherwise visit many different health care providers in a futile effort to deal with intractable pain. Even though pain clinics are often expensive, they are generally less expensive and more effective than the treatment the patient would otherwise receive (Taylor, 1987; Turk et al., 1983).

These examples demonstrate that psychological interventions can be cost effective. However, the cost effectiveness of many interventions remains unproven. Although logically it seems that interventions to improve health habits, reduce stress, improve medical compliance, and help people better cope with illness ought to be cost effective, this proposition must still be conclusively demonstrated if the interventions are to be fully accepted.

HEALTH PSYCHOLOGY AS A PROFESSION

The future of health psychology also depends on providing high quality and relevant training to future health psychologists, as well as placing them in positions where they can have the most impact.

Training in Health Psychology

The challenges for health psychologists are clearly complex, dealing as they do with the intersection of psychology and biomedicine. To meet these challenges, health psychologists should have a solid grounding in psychology as well as a thorough understanding of the health problems involved. So what type of training should health psychologists receive? To address this question and chart a future course for health psychology, the Arden House Training Conference was convened in May 1983 (Olbrisch, Weiss, Stone, & Schwartz, 1985; Stone, 1983). During this conference, 54 selected delegates attempted to develop an ideal curriculum for training health psychologists. Although delegates debated the exact contents of the desired training, they endorsed the concept of health psychologists as both scientists and practitioners, meaning that health psychologists should be trained both in scientific research and in the use of clinical interventions. In addition, they recommended that an earned Ph.D., based in part on a research-based dissertation, be the minimum entry degree for health psychologists.

Precisely what should training in health psychology entail? The conferees at the Arden House Conference determined three general levels of training: predoctoral, apprenticeship, and postdoctoral. Predoctoral training is designed to provide new health psychologists with basic background and skills. At this level, the curriculum is designed to provide a grounding in general psychological principles as well as specialized training in health psychology and professional issues. The conferees recommended that students should take core courses in the biological, cognitive-affective, social, and individual bases of behavior, and research methodology, as a part of their training in generic psychology. With these courses as background, specialized courses in health psychology would then teach students to apply these basic principles to issues concerned with health systems and behavior. Finally, course work on professional issues aims to develop students' skills in assessment, intervention, consultation, and services evaluation (Working Group on Predoctoral Education/Doctoral Training, 1983).

In order to further hone students' skills and prepare them to make meaningful contributions to both research and practice, the Arden House conferees also recommended that students have apprenticeship experiences in which they apply their knowledge and skills to practical health issues. For students planning to provide clinical services, these apprenticeship experiences would take the form of field placements, such as externships or internships, in which the student would engage in supervised delivery of clinical services. For students planning a research career, the apprenticeship would provide experiences in designing, conducting, and publishing research, as well as in preparing grant proposals to obtain funding. In each case, the conferees agreed that apprenticeship experiences should begin early in the student's training and be conducted under the supervision of experienced health psychologists (Working Group on Apprenticeship, 1983).

Finally, in recognition of the complexity of many of the issues in health psychology, the Arden House delegates proposed that fully trained health psychologists should receive an additional two years of postdoctoral training. During this training, students planning a research career would work under the tutelage of established researchers to develop the specialized skills required for doing research on particular health problems, such as coronary heart disease, stress, or cancer (Working Group on Postdoctoral Research Training, 1983). Those looking to careers as service providers would receive additional training aimed at developing their understanding of specific health issues as well as refining their clinical skills for dealing with those issues (Working Group on Postdoctoral Training for the Health Psychology Service Provider, 1983).

This describes the ideal training program. Although most of the delegates agreed on the desirability of the basic elements, some were also concerned that the requirement of two years of postdoctoral training was excessive and could price health psychologists out of the market (Taylor, 1987).

Where can one obtain health psychology training? Approximately 40 Ph.D. programs in the United States currently offer training labeled as health or medical psychology (American Psychological Association, 1990), in addition to an undetermined number of programs in other countries. A survey of program orientation and content in American programs found two major approaches (Belar, Wilson, & Hughes, 1982). A few programs described health psychology as the main focus of the program. For example, the University of California (San Francisco), Albert Einstein College of Medicine, and the Uniformed Services University of the Health Sciences offer Ph.D.'s in health psychology. Most programs, however, offered health psychology as a track within another specialty in psychology, for instance, clinical, social, school, community, or experimental. Half the programs surveyed reported that health psychology training was given within a clinical psychology program. Along these lines, a recent survey of programs in clinical psychology found behavioral medicine/health psychology to be the most popular area for clinical research and training among the various clinical specialties (Sayette & Mayne, 1990).

Students also have numerous opportunities for apprenticeship and postdoctoral training. A survey of health-related clinical internship opportunities found that of the 65 internship programs surveyed nearly three fourths offered training in health psychology, and nearly 40% indicated that health psychology training was required (Doyle, Street, Masur, & Asken, 1981). In addition, a survey of postdoctoral training programs in 1982 identified 43 facilities with a total of 105 positions. These programs were strongly application-oriented, with 90% indicating an emphasis on applied research and 70% reporting emphasis on clinical applications. In addition, 44% reported that all or part of their program focused on basic research, while 32% reported a public health or community focus, and 12% had a public policy emphasis (Belar & Siegel, 1983).

Careers in Health Psychology

Once trained, where are health psychologists employed? As was mentioned at the beginning of this book, health psychologists are actively involved in research, education, clinical services delivery, administration, and policy-making. The Arden House conferees indicated many potential job settings (Altman & Cahn, 1983). Health psychologists engaged in research and education may be found in academic settings such as psychology and sociology departments, and schools of medicine, nursing, public health, dentistry, and pharmacy. In addition, research- and policy-oriented health psychologists are found in university policy and research centers, such as the Institute for Social Science Research at UCLA or the Institute of Social Research at the University of Michigan, or in private think tanks and consulting firms. Clinical health psychologists are employed in hospitals, HMOs, and other health-related organizations, or in private practice. Beyond this, health psychologists may be employed by governmental agencies such as the U.S. Food and Drug Administration, the National Institutes of Health, or the military. One survey of graduates from health psychology programs (Belar et al., 1982) found that 41% were employed by university medical centers, 25% were in colleges and universities, 17% in clinical settings, 7% in private practice, and the rest in the federal government, private industry, or a combination of settings.

SUMMARY

Health psychology has made important strides in its short existence. However, it also faces important challenges in the future. Among the critical research challenges are the continued documentation of the mind-body link, the development of viable theoretical frameworks, and the evaluation of interventions. Important clinical challenges include stress and stress management, disease prevention, and the treatment of health problems. In addition, the future of health psychology demands that clinical interventions be cost effective.

The future of health psychology also depends on the availability of quality training programs and placing health psychology graduates in positions where they can make their best contributions. The Arden House Conference in May 1983 has laid out a basic framework for health psychology training. Many opportunities for training in health psychology exist, and health psychology graduates are employed in a variety of academic, clinical, and policy settings.

SUGGESTED READINGS

Glass, D. C. (1989). Psychology and health: Obstacles and opportunities. *Journal of Applied Social Psychology, 19,* 1145–63. David Glass briefly reviews the achievements of health psychology, and discusses obstacles to future progress and what can be done to overcome them.

Taylor, S. E. (1990). Health psychology: The science and the field. *American Psychologist, 45,* 40–50. In this article, Shelley Taylor discusses the critical issues facing health psychology and outlines what she sees as health psychology's agenda for the future.

Glossary

A-beta fibers Large myelinated nerve fibers that project both to the dorsal horn and the brain.

A-delta fibers Small myelinated nerve fibers that project to the dorsal horn and are associated with sharp, prickling pains.

Accidental (convenience) sample A sample consisting of individuals who happen to be available and willing to participate in the survey.

Acquired immunodeficiency syndrome (AIDS) A disease, caused by the human immunodeficiency virus (HIV), which causes severe impairment of immune functioning.

Acute pain Intense but time-limited pain that is generally the result of tissue damage or disease.

Adrenal cortex The outer layer of the adrenal gland, which produces corticosteroids when stimulated by adrenocorticotrophic hormone.

Adrenal medulla The inner portion of the adrenal gland, which produces the catecholamines epinephrine and norepinephrine when stimulated by the sympathetic nervous system.

AIDS-related complex (ARC) A medical syndrome that is similar to AIDS, but does not involve the same degree of impairment in immune functioning or as severe symptoms as AIDS.

Alcoholism Compulsive, addictive, or habitual consumption of alcohol that poses a serious threat to the person's well-being.

Algogenic substances Chemical substances occurring naturally in body tissues that are released when the tissue is injured.

Allergic (extrinsic) asthma Asthma that results from failure of immunological defenses or from allergies.

Alzheimer's disease A degenerative brain disease producing progressive and irreversible loss of cognitive function.

Angina pectoris A cramping pain felt in the chest that may indicate a shortage of oxygen to the heart muscle.

Antibodies Protein molecules produced by activated B cells that act to protect the body against specific antigens.

Anticipatory grief Grieving that takes place before a death actually occurs.

Anticipatory nausea and vomiting A classically conditioned response in which cancer patients experience nausea and vomiting before chemotherapy is administered.

Antigen Any substance from inside or outside the body that is recognized as foreign and induces a response from the immune system.

Applied behavior analysis A strategy for modifying behavior in which the behavior is carefully specified and observations are made of the antecedents and consequences of the behavior. Following these observations, attempts are made to alter the conditions that control the behavior.

Appraisal delay The amount of time that it takes a person after experiencing symptoms to decide that he or she is ill.

Atherosclerosis The process through which cholesterol and other fats accumulate on artery walls, potentially impeding blood flow.

Atrium (pl., atria) One of the two upper chambers of the heart into which blood flows from the veins.

Autogenic training A type of self-hypnosis that produces relaxation through concentration on bodily sensations of warmth and heaviness.

Autonomic nervous system The branch of the nervous system that relays messages from the central nervous system to the internal organs of the body.

Aversion therapy The use of respondent conditioning to pair an undesirable health behavior, such as alcohol abuse, with a noxious stimulus.

B cells Circulating white blood cells also known as B lymphocytes that, when activated by an antigen, produce antibodies.

Behavioral control The belief that a person has the ability to influence the aversiveness of a situation.

Behavioral health An interdisciplinary field that focuses on behaviorally promoting good health habits and preventing disease among those who are currently healthy.

Behavioral immunogens Behaviors that reduce a person's risk for disease.

Behavioral medicine An interdisciplinary field that applies theories and techniques from the behavioral sciences to the treatment and prevention of illness.

Behavioral pathogens Behaviors that increase a person's risk for disease.

Benign tumor An abnormal growth that is not cancerous and generally not considered to be threatening to health.

Bereavement The experience of losing a loved one to death.

Biofeedback A technique in which a person learns to exert control over a specific physiological function by responding to feedback from that function.

Biomedical model The currently dominant medical model, which emphasizes the separation of mind and body and the physical causation of disease.

Biopsychosocial model A systems approach to illness that emphasizes the interconnectedness of mind and body and the importance of understanding disease at the psychological and social as well as physical levels.

Brain death The definition of biological death based on the lack of brain wave activity and circulation in and to the brain.

Bronchial asthma A respiratory disorder in which the bronchial airways become blocked and the person experiences wheezing, coughing, and shortness of breath.

C fibers Small unmyelinated nerve fibers that project to the dorsal horn and are associated with dull, aching pains.

Carcinogen Any substance capable of converting normal cells into cancerous ones.

Cardiac rehabilitation Interventions with heart patients designed to help them recover from a heart attack or other heart disease and return to optimal functioning.

Case control study A study matching patients already diagnosed with the target disease to healthy individuals (or patients with another disease) so as to identify factors associated with the occurrence of the target disease.

Catecholamines A group of chemicals produced by the body that act as neurotransmitters. Two important catecholamines are epinephrine and norepinephrine.

Cell-mediated immunity Immunity based on sensitized lymphocytes (a type of white blood cell) known as T cells, which attack invading foreign substances in the body.

Chemotherapy Treatment using drugs or chemicals.

Chronic pain Pain that may originally have been associated with an injury but that persists and does not respond to usual treatments.

Clinical health promotion The application of health promotion principles in a clinical setting, often for a fee.

Clinical thanatology Counseling techniques used with dying patients.

Coding A medical decision about the amount of effort to be expended in reviving the patient in the event of cardiopulmonary failure.

Cognitive control Having a cognitive strategy for reducing the effects of a stressful situation.

Cohort study A study comparing the rates at which persons with and without a specified risk factor develop given diseases.

Concomitant treatment Any clinical intervention that is received by patients in addition to the experimental intervention.

Confidentiality The shielding of individual subjects' data from unauthorized disclosure.

Contingency contracting A treatment procedure in which the person contracts with the therapist or other person specifying the behavior change desired and the consequences for failure to adhere to those changes.

Coping Efforts taken to deal with stressful situations.

Coronary risk factors Factors that increase the likelihood that the person will experience clinical coronary heart disease.

Correlation Any relationship between two variables, whether causal or not.

Corticosteroids A group of hormones produced by the adrenal cortex that are involved in the regulation of bodily functions.

Crisis A situation so novel or so major that a person's usual methods of coping are insufficient.

Deception Misleading subjects concerning the purpose(s) or procedure(s) of a research study.

Dependent variable The outcome variable for a research study.

Diabetes mellitus A metabolic disorder in which the body is unable to properly convert glucose into usable energy.

Diastolic blood pressure Pressure on the arteries when the ventricles are in their relaxation phase.

Discriminative stimulus A stimulus that acts as a cue, releasing a given behavior.

Disease The occurrence of objective pathological abnormalities in the body—which may or may not be clinically apparent.

Disequilibrium A state of physical, psychological, or social imbalance.

DNA (deoxyribonucleic acid) A large molecule found primarily in cell nuclei, which carries the cell's genetic information and controls cell functioning.

Double blind study A clinical study procedure in which neither the patients nor the researchers know which treatment condition a particular patient is in.

Emotion-focused coping Coping that focuses on controlling the emotional effects of stress.

Endogenous opioids Opiate-like substances produced by the body that act as natural pain relievers.

Epinephrine (adrenaline) A catecholamine produced by the adrenal medulla that has effects similar to arousal of the sympathetic nervous system.

External validity The degree to which the results of a study can be applied outside the original research setting.

Feedback loop A means of system regulation in which the results of system actions are returned to the system and influence its future behavior. Feedback loops can be either negative, in which case they reduce the discrepancy between the state of the system and reference values, or positive, in which case the discrepancy is increased.

Fight-or-flight response Arousal of the body either to fight off or flee from a perceived threat. This involves a significant rise in epinephrine and norepinephrine in the blood along with increases in heart rate, blood pressure, respiration, and blood sugar as well as a movement of blood away from the skin and toward the muscles.

General Adaptation Syndrome (GAS) The body's generalized response to threat that includes the phases of alarm, resistance, and exhaustion.

Gradient of reinforcement The behavioral principle stating that immediate rewards and punishments are much more effective than are delayed rewards and punishments.

Grief Emotional responses to bereavement.

Guided imagery A counseling technique in which bereaved individuals are taken through exercises in which they relive aspects of their relationship with the deceased.

Health behavior Behaviors that a person engages in while healthy so as to prevent disease.

Health psychology The subfield of psychology concerned with the dynamic interrelationship of behavior and psychological states with physical health.

Hospice An approach to care for the dying that emphasizes patient comfort and death with dignity.

Human immunodeficiency virus (HIV) A retrovirus that causes AIDS and ARC by invading and taking over helper T cells.

Humoral immunity Immunity based on antibodies that circulate in the blood and attack foreign substances before they enter body cells.

Hyperglycemia A condition of having too much sugar in the blood.

Hyperreactivity An exaggerated physiological response to challenging situations.

Hypertension Blood pressure that is persistently above 140/90 mmHg.

Hypochondriasis A false belief, also known as hypochondria, in having a disease or an exaggerated fear of contracting disease.

Iatrogenic illness Illness that is the result of medical intervention.

Idiosyncratic (intrinsic) asthma Asthma that is not related to allergies and may be related to psychological factors.

Illness The experience of suffering and discomfort, which may or may not be related to objective physical pathology.

Illness behavior The reaction component of illness, specifically the behavior that a person exhibits in response to experienced suffering and discomfort.

Illness delay The time required for a person to decide that professional help is required after deciding that he or she is ill.

Immunity The body's ability to protect itself from a disease, particularly one that is infectious.

Immunocompetence The extent to which the immune system is able to fight off disease.

Incidence The number of new cases of a disease that occur within a specified population during a given period.

Independent variable The variable manipulated by the researcher in an experimental study.

Informed consent Agreeing to participate in a research study after receiving an accurate description of the purpose(s) and procedure(s) of the study as well as any risk that might be involved.

Institutional review The review of research plans for ethical concerns by an institutional ethics panel before the performance of a study.

Insulin A hormone produced by the pancreas that regulates the body's use of sugar.

Intermittent reinforcement Reinforcement that is given for only some occurrences of a response. This is contrasted to continuous reinforcement that is given for every occurrence of the response.

Internal validity The degree to which one can validly draw conclusions about the effects of the independent variable.

Lay referral Informal discussion of symptoms and physical concerns with friends, family, or other nonprofessional individuals.

Locus of control Beliefs that people have about what determines their outcomes. Individuals who believe that their outcomes are determined by their own efforts have an internal locus of control, while those who believe that their outcomes are controlled by forces outside of themselves have an external locus of control.

Macrophage A large cell, part of nonspecific immunity, that surrounds an antigen and digests it.

Malignant tumor An abnormal growth that is cancerous and has the capacity to spread to other parts of the body.

Medical anthropology The specialty within anthropology that studies cultural aspects of health and illness.

Medical psychology The application of clinical psychological methods to problems of physical illness.

Medical sociology The specialty within sociology that studies the social aspects of health and illness.

Meditation Techniques in which the person focuses inwardly in a nonanalytical way and attempts to become aware of the process of thoughts coming and going.

Metastasis The process by which malignant tumors spread to distant parts of the body.

Migraine headache A throbbing headache characterized by intense sharp pain that is the result of constriction and dilation of the arteries inside and outside the skull.

Mind-body dualism The doctrine that the mind and body are two separate entities with only limited interaction.

Monocyte The largest of the white blood cells. Monocytes participate in the nonspecific immune response.

Morbidity The occurrence of disease.

Mourning Socially prescribed ways of expressing grief.

Multimodal approach A treatment approach that combines the use of several different techniques.

Myocardial infarction (MI) A blockage of a coronary artery, commonly referred to as a heart attack, leading to the destruction of heart muscle.

Myocardium The muscle cells making up the wall of the heart.

Natural experiment An experiment in which the manipulation of interest occurs without the experimenter's intervention.

Natural killer (NK) cell Leukocytes that play a role in nonspecific immunity by destroying cancer cells and cells infected with viruses.

Nerve block The use of local anesthetic to interrupt the transmission of pain signals.

Neuroticism A broad personality trait including self-consciousness, inability to inhibit cravings, vulnerability to stress, and a tendency to experience negative emotions.

Nociceptors Free nerve endings that respond to pain and signal injury.

Non-sampling error Errors or biases in survey results from factors other than sampling, such as question wording, interviewer bias, and requesting information the respondent cannot accurately give.

Nonspecific immunity Immune responses to any antigen without concern for its identity.

Norepinephrine (noradrenaline) A catecholamine produced by the adrenal medulla as well as the neurons of the sympathetic nervous system that serves as a neurotransmitter in the SNS and has effects generally similar to those of epinephrine.

Observational learning Learning that takes place through watching another's behavior.

Obsessional review The continuous review of the events surrounding the death of a loved one.

Oncogene Genes that control cell growth and reproduction and may play a pivotal role in the development of cancer.

Operant conditioning Learning in which behavioral responses are increased through reward.

Operant pain Pain that is maintained through the reinforcement of pain behavior.

Osteoarthritis A degenerative joint disease characterized by the progressive loss of cartilage and other changes in the joints.

Pain behavior Behavior that develops in response to pain, such as limping, lying down, or reducing physical activity.

Parasympathetic nervous system The section of the autonomic nervous system concerned with normal and restorative functions.

Peptic ulcer A lesion (wound) in the wall of the stomach or upper part of the small intestine (duodenum). Ulcers in the stomach are referred to as gastric ulcers, while those in the duodenum are duodenal ulcers.

Phagocytes A cell, such as a macrophage, with the ability to ingest micro-organisms and cell debris.

Placebo A treatment with no action specific for the condition being treated but that is used for its nonspecific psychological or psychophysiological effects.

Prevalence The number of people in a given population who have a specific disease at a given time.

Primary appraisal The initial appraisal of a threat in which the person assesses the amount of danger involved.

Primary prevention Efforts taken to prevent disease in currently healthy individuals.

Problem-focused coping Coping concerned with changing the objective situation.

Progressive relaxation A relaxation technique in which the person is taught to relax by successively tensing and relaxing different muscle groups.

Prototype An idealized or typical instance of a category. Disease prototypes are idealized conceptions of specific diseases.

Psychogenic pain Chronic pain that appears to have no physical basis but develops in response to psychological needs.

Psychoneuroimmunology The study of the interrelationships between psychosocial factors and the immune, nervous, and endocrine systems.

Psychosomatic medicine The specialty within biomedicine that is concerned with psychological factors in the development and course of physical illness.

Quasi-experiment A research study in which, for practical or ethical reasons, subjects cannot be randomly assigned to conditions but the experimenter still retains control over the independent variable.

Random assignment The assignment of subjects to experimental conditions such that each subject has an equal likelihood of being in a given experimental condition.

Random sample A sample selected by the rule that every person in the population has an equal likelihood of being selected.

Reactance A patient's psychological motive to preserve a sense of freedom that is being threatened.

Reductionism The doctrine that the phenomena of health and illness are best understood at the level of physics and chemistry.

Relative risk The incidence of a disease among individuals having a particular characteristic divided by the incidence of disease among individuals not having the characteristic.

Respondent learning Learning in which a previously neutral stimulus comes to evoke the same response as another stimulus with which it is paired.

Respondent pain Pain in response to noxious stimulation or tissue damage.

Retrovirus A type of virus that carries its genetic information in the form of ribonucleic acid (RNA).

Rheumatoid arthritis A chronic, systemic, inflammatory condition causing pain and swelling of the joints.

Sampling error Errors in survey results attributable to the manner in which the sample of respondents was selected.

Schema (pl., schemata) An organized "bundle" of information about a specific object, idea, or event.

Secondary appraisal Appraisal of a threat in terms of what the person believes that he or she can do about it.

Secondary gain Gain or advantage that a person obtains by being ill.

Secondary prevention Measures taken to stop the progress of a disease in its early stages.

Self-complexity The extent to which people make and maintain cognitive distinctions between different aspects of their lives.

Self-efficacy A person's beliefs about his or her ability to attain particular goals in a particular situation.

Self-esteem A person's sense of self-worth.

Self-monitoring A self-control technique in which the person keeps detailed records of the behavior in question and the circumstances in which it occurs.

Self-reinforcement A treatment technique in which the person is trained to give self-rewards for desired behavior.

Separation anxiety Anxiety felt by a child when separated from parents or primary caretakers.

Shaping Teaching a response by reinforcing successive approximations to the desired behavior.

Sick role The role taken by a person who is defined as sick.

Single blind study A clinical study procedure in which the researcher knows which treatment condition the patient is in, but the patient is kept blind to this information.

Skills training A treatment procedure in which the person is given training in dealing with interpersonal situations that tend to result in poor health behaviors such as overeating or alcohol abuse, and training for dealing with situations involving temptation.

Social support The aid and support that people receive from their interactions with others.

Specific immunity An immune response to a specific antigen.

Stimulus control Arranging the environment so as to minimize or eliminate the stimuli that tend to trigger problem health behaviors.

Stress A transaction between a person and the environment that includes the person's appraisal of the challenges posed by the situation and available coping resources, along with the psychological and physiological responses to those perceived challenges.

Stress inoculation training An approach to stress management designed to help people build their coping skills and enhance their resistance to stress.

Sympathetic nervous system The branch of the autonomic nervous system responsible for arousing the body to action.

Symptom Subjective experience of a physiological state.

Systematic desensitization A relaxation technique in which the person is taught to relax while imagining encounters with feared objects or situations.

Systolic blood pressure Pressure on the arteries when the ventricles are in their contraction phase.

T cells White blood cells that originate in the bone marrow but mature in the thymus gland.

Tension headache A headache generally described as a dull, steady ache affecting both sides of the head.

Tertiary prevention Procedures for the treatment and rehabilitation of persons with fully developed diseases.

Thanatology The study of death and dying. Professionals who study death and dying are known as thanatologists.

Thymus gland An organ located above the heart and behind the breastbone, where T cells mature and differentiate into several different varieties.

Token economy A behavioral modification technique in which patients are given points for exhibiting desired behavior, which can later be exchanged for various rewards.

Total institution An institution that takes control of virtually every aspect of a person's life.

Tracer A substance added to a medication that can be used as a marker of whether and how much of it has been ingested.

Transcutaneous electrical nerve stimulation A method of pain control using electrical stimulation of nerve endings through electrodes placed on the skin.

Tumor An abnormal growth of tissue, which may be either benign or malignant.

Type A behavior pattern A behavior pattern characterized by high levels of competitive drive, time urgency, vigorous speech characteristics, and hostility.

Utilization delay The time it takes a person to decide to seek professional help after deciding that such help is needed.

Ventricle The lower chamber of the heart, which pumps blood into either the pulmonary artery (right ventricle) or the aorta (left ventricle).

Vicarious counterconditioning A treatment method for helping people deal with fear in which the patient repeatedly observes a model engaging in a feared behavior.

Vicarious reinforcement Reinforcement of a behavior through seeing another person being rewarded.

Vicarious systematic desensitization A treatment technique, also known as contact desensitization, in which the patient observes a model successfully dealing with a hierarchy of anxiety-arousing situations.

References

Abbott, B. B., Schoen, L. S., & Badia, P. (1984). Predictable and unpredictable shock: Behavioral measures of aversion and physiological measures of stress. *Psychological Bulletin, 96,* 45–71.

Abramson, E. E. (1982). Behavioral approaches to the treatment of obesity. In B. B. Wolman (Ed.), *Psychological aspects of obesity: A handbook.* New York: Van Nostrand Reinhold.

Abramson, M., & Torghele, J. R. (1961). Weight, temperature change and psychosomatic symptomatology in relation to the menstrual cycle. *American Journal of Obstetrics and Gynecology, 81,* 223–232.

Ackerknecht, E. H. (1955). *A short history of medicine.* New York: Roland.

Ackerman, M. D., & Stevens, M. J. (1989). Acute and chronic pain: Pain dimensions and psychological status. *Journal of Clinical Psychology, 45,* 223–228.

Ader, R., & Cohen, N. (1975). Behaviorally conditioned immunosuppression. *Psychosomatic Medicine, 37,* 333–340.

Ader, R., & Cohen, N. (1981). Conditioned immunopharmacologic responses. In R. Ader (Ed.), *Psychoneuroimmunology* (pp. 281–319). Orlando, FL: Academic Press.

Ader, R., & Cohen, N. (1982). Behavioral conditioned immunosuppression and murine systemic lupus erythematosus. *Science, 215* (4539), 1534–1536.

Ad Hoc Committee of the Harvard Medical School to Examine the Definition of Brain Death (1968). A definition of irreversible coma. *Journal of the American Medical Association, 205,* 337–340.

Adler, N. E., Cohen, F., & Stone, G. C. (1979). Themes and professional prospects in health psychology. In G. C. Stone, F. Cohen, N. E. Adler, & Associates (Eds.), *Health Psychology—A handbook.* San Francisco: Jossey-Bass.

Adler, T. (1989a). For misconduct, best medicine is prevention: IOM. *APA Monitor, 20*(4), 6.

Adler, T. (1989b). Scientific fraud: How to handle it? *APA Monitor, 20*(6), 5.

Affleck, G., Tennen, H., Pfeiffer, C., & Fifield, J. (1987). Appraisals of control and predictability in adapting to a chronic disease. *Journal of Personality and Social Psychology, 53,* 273–279.

Agras, W. S. (1982). Behavioral medicine in the 1980s: Nonrandom connections. *Journal of Consulting and Clinical Psychology, 50,* 797–803.

Ahmed, P. I., Kolker, A., and Coehlo, G. V. (1979). Toward a new definition of health: An overview. In P. I. Ahmed and G. V. Coehlo (Eds.), *Toward a new definition of health: Psychosocial dimensions.* New York: Plenum.

Aiken, L. H. (1983). Nurses. In D. Mechanic (Ed.), *Handbook of health, health care, and the health professions.* New York: Free Press.

Aiken, L. H., & Marx, M. M. (1982). Perspectives on the public policy debate. *American Psychologist, 37,* 1271–1279.

Aiken, L. R. (1985). *Dying, death, and bereavement.* Boston: Allyn & Bacon.

Ainsworth, M. D. S. (1979). Infant-mother attachment. *American Psychologist, 34,* 932–937.

Aivazyan, T. A., Zaitsev, V. P., Salenko, B. B., Yurenev, A. P., & Patrusheva, I. F. (1988). Efficacy of relaxation techniques in hypertensive patients. *Health Psychology, 7,* 193–200.

Ajzen, I., & Fishbein, M. (1977). Attitude-behavior relations: A theoretical analysis and review of empirical research. *Psychological Bulletin, 84,* 888–918.

Ajzen, I., & Fishbein, M. (1980). *Understanding attitudes and predicting social behavior.* Englewood Cliffs, NJ: Prentice-Hall.

Alonzo, A. A. (1979). Everyday illness behavior: A situational approach to health status deviations. *Social Science and Medicine, 13A,* 397–404.

Altman, D. G., & Cahn, J. (1983). The rest of the challenge: Position statement on employment opportunities. *Health Psychology, 2*(Suppl. 5), 119–122.

Altman, H. J. (1987). *Alzheimer's disease: Problems, prospects, and perspectives.* New York: Plenum.

American Cancer Society (1989). *1989 Cancer facts and figures.* New York: author.

American Psychological Association (1990). *Graduate study in psychology and associated fields, 1990 edition.* Washington, DC: author.

American Psychological Association, Task Force on Health Research (1976). Contributions of psychology to health research: Patterns, problems, and potentials. *American Psychologist, 31,* 263–274.

Andersen, E. (1986). Periaqueductal gray and cerebral cortex modulate responses of medial thalamic neurons to noxious stimulation. *Brain Research, 371,* 30–36.

Anderson, B. L., & Hacker, N. F. (1983). Treatment for gynecologic cancer: A review of the effects on female sexuality. *Health Psychology, 2,* 203–221.

Anderson, C. A., & Arnoult, L. H. (1989). An examination of perceived control, irrational beliefs, and positive stress as moderators of the relation between negative stress and health. *Basic and Applied Social Psychology, 10,* 101–107.

Anderson, C. R. (1977). Locus of control, coping behaviors and performance in a stress setting: A longitudinal study. *Journal of Applied Psychology, 62,* 446–451.

Anderson, K. O., Bradley, L. A., Young, L. D., McDaniel, L. K., & Wise, C. M. (1985). Rheumatoid arthritis: Review of psychological factors related to etiology, effects, and treatment. *Psychological Bulletin, 98,* 358–387.

Anderson, K. O., & Masur, F. T. (1983). Psychological preparation for invasive medical and dental procedures. *Journal of Behavioral Medicine, 6,* 1–40.

Anderson, N. B. (1989). Racial differences in stress-induced cardiovascular reactivity and hypertension: Current status and substantive issues. *Psychological Bulletin, 105,* 89–105.

Anderson, O. W., & Gevitz, N. (1983). The general hospital: A social and historical perspective. In D. Mechanic (Ed.), *Handbook of health, health care, and the health professions.* New York: Free Press.

Andrasik, F., Blanchard, E. B., & Edlund, S. R. (1985). Physiological responding during biofeedback. In S. R. Burchfield (Ed.), *Stress: Psychological and physiological interactions.* Washington, DC: Hemisphere.

Andrasik, F., Coleman, D., & Epstein, L. (1982). Biofeedback: Clinical and research considerations. In D. M. Doleys, R. L. Meredith, & A. R. Ciminero (Eds.), *Behavioral medicine: Assessment and treatment strategies.* New York: Plenum.

Antoni, M. H. (1987). Neuroendocrine influences in psychoimmunology and neoplasia: A review. *Psychology and Health, 1,* 3–24.

Antonovksy, A. (1979). *Health, stress, and coping.* San Francisco: Jossey-Bass.

Antonovksy, A. (1987). *Unraveling the mystery of health: How people manage stress and stay healthy.* San Francisco: Jossey-Bass.

Antonovsky, A., & Hartman, H. (1974). Delay in the detection of cancer: A review of the literature. *Health Education Monographs, 2,* 98–128.

Argondizzo, N. T. (1984). Education of the patient and family. In N. K. Wenger & H. K. Hellerstein (Eds.), *Rehabilitation of the coronary patient* (2d ed.). New York: Wiley.

Arluke, A., Kennedy, L., & Kessler, R. C. (1979). Reexamining the sick-role concept: An empirical assessment. *Journal of Health and Social Behavior, 20,* 30–36.

Armstead, C. A., Lawler, K. A., Gorden, G., Cross, J., & Gibbons, J. (1989). Relationship of racial stressors to blood pressure responses and anger expression in black college students. *Health Psychology, 8,* 541–556.

Armstrong, B. K., & Doll, R. (1975). Environmental factors and cancer incidence in different countries with special reference to dietary practices. *International Journal of Cancer, 15,* 617–631.

Arnetz, B. B., Wasserman, J., Petrini, B., Brenner, S.-O., Levi, L., Eneroth, P., Salovaara, H., Hjelm, R., Salovaara, L., Theorell, T., & Petterson, I.-L. (1987). Immune function in unemployed women. *Psychosomatic Medicine, 49,* 3–12.

Aronoff, G. M., Wagner, J. M., & Spangler, A. S. (1986). Chemical interventions for pain. *Journal of Consulting and Clinical Psychology, 54,* 769–775.

Ary, D. V. & Biglan, A. (1988). Longitudinal changes in adolescent cigarette smoking behavior: Onset and cessation. *Journal of Behavioral Medicine, 11,* 361–382.

Asterita, M. F. (1985). *The physiology of stress.* New York: Human Sciences Press.

Auerbach, S. M., Martelli, M. F., & Mercuri, L. G. (1983). Anxiety, information, interpersonal impacts, and adjustment to a stressful health care situation. *Journal of Personality and Social Psychology, 44,* 1284–1296.

Averill, J. R. (1973). Personal control over aversive stimuli and its relationship to stress. *Psychological Bulletin, 80,* 286–303.

Babb, L. A. (1976). *Thiapusam in Singapore: Religious individualism in a hierarchical culture* (Sociology Working Paper No. 49, Department of Sociology, University of Singapore). Singapore: Chopmen Enterprises.

Babiker, I. E., Cooke, P. R., Gillett, M. G. (1989). How useful is riboflavin as a tracer of medication compliance? *Journal of Behavioral Medicine, 12,* 25–38.

Bachrach, W. H. (1982). Psychological elements of gastro-intestinal disorders. In W. E. Fann, I. Karacan, A. D. Pokorny, & R. L. Williams (Eds.), *Phenomenology and treatment of psychophysiological disorders.* New York: Spectrum.

Backer, T. E., Batchelor, W. F., Jones, J. M., & Mays, V. M. (Eds.) (1988). Special issue: Psychology and AIDS. *American Psychologist, 43,* 835–987.

Baekeland, F., & Lundwall, L. (1975). Dropping out of treatment: A critical review. *Psychological Bulletin, 82,* 738–783.

Bakal, D. A. (1975). Headache: A biopsychological perspective. *Psychological Bulletin, 82,* 369–382.

Ball, J. F. (1977). Widow's grief: The impact of age and mode of death. *Omega, 7,* 307–333.

Bandura, A. (1969). *Principles of behavior modification.* New York: Holt, Rinehart, & Winston.

Bandura, A. (1977a). Self-efficacy: Toward a unifying theory of behavioral change. *Psychological Review, 84,* 191–215.

Bandura, A. (1977b). *Social learning theory.* Englewood Cliffs, NJ: Prentice-Hall.

Bandura, A. (1986). *Social foundations of thought and action: A social cognitive theory.* Englewood Cliffs, NJ: Prentice-Hall.

Bandura, A., O'Leary, A., Taylor, C. B., Gauthier, J., & Gossard, D. (1987). Perceived self-efficacy and pain control: Opioid and nonopioid mechanisms. *Journal of Personality and Social Psychology, 53,* 563–571.

Barefoot, J. C., Dahlstrom, G., & Williams, R. B. (1983). Hostility, CHD incidence, and total mortality: A 25-year follow-up study of 255 physicians. *Psychosomatic Medicine, 45,* 59–63.

Barker, D. J. P. & Rose, G. (1984). *Epidemiology in medical practice* (3d ed.). Edinburgh: Churchill Livingstone.

Baron, R. S., Cutrona, C. E., Hicklin, D., Russell, D. W., & Lubaroff, D. M. (1990). Social support and immune function among spouses of cancer patients. *Journal of Personality and Social Psychology, 59,* 344–352.

Barondess, J. A. (1979). Disease and illness—A crucial distinction. *American Journal of Medicine, 66,* 375–376.

Barsevick, A. M., & Johnson, J. E. (1990). Preference for information and involvement, information seeking and emotional responses to women undergoing colposcopy. *Research in Nursing and Health, 13,* 1–7.

Barsky, A. J., & Klerman, G. L. (1983). Overview: Hypochondriasis, bodily complaints, and somatic styles. *American Journal of Psychiatry, 140,* 273–283.

Basler, H. E., & Rehfisch, H. P. (1990). Follow-up results of a cognitive-behavioral treatment for chronic pain in a primary care setting. *Psychology and Health, 4,* 293–304.

Baum, A., Gatchel, R. J., Fleming, R., & Lake, C. R. (1981). *Chronic and acute stress associated with the Three Mile Island accident and decontamination: Preliminary findings of a longitudinal study.* Technical report submitted to the U.S. Nuclear Regulatory Commission, Washington, DC. Cited in Baum et al. (1982).

Baum, A., Grunberg, N. E., & Singer, J. E. (1982). The use of psychological and neuroendocrinological measurements in the study of stress. *Health Psychology, 1,* 217–236.

Baumann, L. J., & Leventhal, H. (1985). "I can tell when my blood pressure is up, can't I?" *Health Psychology, 4,* 203–218.

Bayer, R., & Gostin, L. (1990). Legal and ethical issues relating to AIDS. *Bulletin of the Pan American Health Organization, 24,* 454–468.

Becker, M. H., & Joseph, J. G. (1988). AIDS and behavioral change to reduce risk: A review. *American Journal of Public Health, 78,* 394–410.

Becker, M. H., & Maiman, L. A. (1975). Sociobehavioral determinants of compliance with health and medical care recommendations. *Medical Care, 13,* 10–24.

Becker, M. H., Maiman, L. A., Kirscht, J. P., Haefner, D. P., & Drachman, R. H. (1977). The health belief model and prediction of dietary compliance: A field experiment. *Journal of Health and Social Behavior, 18,* 348–365.

Beecher, H. K. (1955). Powerful placebo. *Journal of the American Medical Association, 159,* 1602–1606.

Beecher, H. K. (1959). *Measurement of subjective responses.* New York: Oxford University Press.

Beecher, H. K. (1960). Increased stress and effectiveness of placebos and "active" drugs. *Science, 132,* 91–92.

Belar, C. D., & Siegel, L. J. (1983). A survey of postdoctoral training programs in health psychology. *Health Psychology, 2,* 413–425.

Belar, C. D., Wilson, E., & Hughes, H. (1982). Health psychology training in doctoral psychology programs. *Health Psychology, 1,* 289–299.

Belli, M. M., & Carlova, J. (1986). *Belli for your malpractice defense.* Oradell, NJ: Medical Economics Books.

Belloc, N. B. (1973). Relationship of health practices and mortality. *Preventive Medicine, 2,* 67–81.

Belloc, N. B., & Breslow, L. (1972). Relationships of physical health status and health practices. *Preventive Medicine, 1,* 409–421.

Ben-Sira, Z. (1976). The function of the professional's affective behavior in client satisfaction: A revised approach to social interaction theory. *Journal of Health and Social Behavior, 17,* 3–11.

Ben-Sira, Z. (1980). Affective and instrumental components in the physician-patient relationship: An additional dimension of interaction theory. *Journal of Health and Social Behavior, 21,* 170–180.

Benedek, T. G. (1988). History of the rheumatic diseases. In H. R. Schumacher, J. H. Klippel, & D. R. Robinson (Eds.), *Primer on the rheumatic diseases* (9th ed.). Atlanta: Arthritis Foundation.

Bennett, H. L., Davis, H. S., & Giannini, J. A. (1985). Non-verbal response to intraoperative conversation. *British Journal of Anaesthesiology, 57,* 174–179.

Bennett, J. C. (1988). Rheumatoid arthritis: Clinical features. In H. R. Schumacher, J. H. Klippel, & D. R. Robinson (Eds.), *Primer on the rheumatic diseases* (9th ed.). Atlanta: Arthritis Foundation.

Bennett, W., & Gurin, J. (1982). *The dieter's dilemma: Eating less and weighing more.* New York: Basic Books.

Benson, H. (1984). *Beyond the relaxation response.* New York: Times Books.

Benson, H., & Epstein, M. D. (1975). The placebo effect: A neglected aspect in the care of patients. *Journal of the American Medical Association, 232,* 1225–1227.

Bentler, P. M., & Speckart, G. (1979). Models of attitude-behavior relationships. *Psychological Review, 86,* 451–464.

Benzer, D. G. (1987). Medical complications of alcoholism. In R. E. Herrington, G. R. Jacobson, & D. G. Benzer (Eds.), *Alcohol and drug abuse handbook.* St. Louis: Warren H. Green.

Berenson, M., Groshen, S., Miller, H., & DeCosse, J. (1989). Subject-reported compliance in a chemoprevention trial for familial adenomatous polyposis. *Journal of Behavioral Medicine, 12,* 233–247.

Berger, B. (1984). Running away from anxiety and depression. A female as well as a male rat race. In M. Sachs & G. Buffone (Eds.), *Running as therapy: An integrated approach.* Lincoln: University of Nebraska Press.

Berglund, G. (1984). Sodium excretion and blood pressure. In J. D. Matarazzo, S. M. Weiss, J. A. Herd, N. E. Miller, & S. M. Weiss (Eds.), *Behavioral health: A handbook of health enhancement and disease prevention.* New York: Wiley.

Berglund, G. (1988). Experiences from hypertension trials—Effects on stroke and coronary heart disease. *Drugs, 36*(Suppl. 3), 5–8.

Berman, S. H., & Wandersman, A. (1990). Fear of cancer and knowledge of cancer: A review and proposed relevance to hazardous waste sites. *Social Science and Medicine, 31,* 81–90.

Bernstein, D. A., & Glasgow, R. E. (1979). Smoking. In O. F. Pomerleau & J. P. Brady (Eds.), *Behavioral medicine: Theory and practice.* Baltimore: Williams and Wilkins.

Bibace, R., & Walsh, M. E. (1979). Developmental stages in children's conceptions of illness. In G. C. Stone, F. Cohen, & N. E. Adler (Eds.), *Health psychology—A handbook.* San Francisco: Jossey-Bass.

Biglan, A., McConnell, S., Severson, H. H., Bavry, J., & Ary, D. (1984). A situational analysis of adolescent smoking. *Journal of Behavioral Medicine, 7,* 109–114.

Biglan, A., Metzler, C. W., Wirt, R., Ary, D., Noell, J., Ochs, L., French, C., & Hood, D. (1990). Social and behavioral factors associated with high-risk sexual behavior among adolescents. *Journal of Behavioral Medicine, 13,* 245–261.

Biglan, A., Severson, H., Ary, D., Faller, C., Gallison, C., Thompson, R., Glasgow, R., & Lichtenstein, E. (1987). Do smoking prevention programs really work? Attrition and the internal and external validity of an evaluation of a refusal skills program. *Journal of Behavioral Medicine, 10,* 159–171.

Billings, A. G., Moos, R. H., Miller, J. J., III, & Gottlieb, J. E. (1987). Psychosocial adaptation in juvenile rheumatic disease: A controlled evaluation. *Health Psychology, 6,* 343–359.

Binik, Y. M., Devins, G. W., & Orme, C. M. (1989). Psychological stress and coping in end-stage renal disease. In R. W. J. Neufeld (Ed.), *Advances in the investigation of psychological stress.* New York: Wiley.

Birenbaum, L. K., Robinson, M. A., Phillips, D. S., Stewart, B. J., & McCown, D. E. (1989). *Omega, 20,* 213–228.

Biringer, F., Anderson, J. R., & Strubel, D. (1988). Self-recognition in senile dementia. *Experimental Aging Research, 14,* 177–180.

Birren, J. E., & Schaie, K. W. (Eds.) (1990). *Handbook of the psychology of aging.* (3d ed.). San Diego: Academic Press.

Bishop, G. D. (1984). Gender, role and illness behavior in a military population. *Health Psychology, 3,* 519–534.

Bishop, G. D. (1987). Lay conceptions of physical symptoms. *Journal of Applied Social Psychology, 17,* 127–146.

Bishop, G. D. (1991a). Lay disease representations and responses to victims of disease. *Basic and Applied Social Psychology, 12,* 115–132.

Bishop, G. D. (1991b). Understanding the understanding of illness: Lay disease representations. In J. A. Skelton & R. T. Croyle (Eds.), *Mental representation in health and illness.* New York: Springer-Verlag.

Bishop, G. D., Alva, A. K., Cantu, L., & Rittiman, T. K. (1991). Responses to persons with AIDS: Fear of contagion or stigma? *Journal of Applied Social Psychology, 21,* 1877–1888.

Bishop, G. D., Briede, C., Cavazos, L., Grotzinger, R., & McMahon, S. (1987). Processing illness information: The role of disease prototypes. *Basic and Applied Social Psychology, 8,* 21–43.

Bishop, G. D., & Converse, S. A. (1986). Illness representations: A prototype approach. *Health Psychology, 5,* 95–114.

Bishop, G. D., Madey, S., Salinas, J., Massey, J., & Tudyk, D. (1992). The role of the availability heuristic in disease perception. *International Journal of Psychology, 27, 637.* (Abstract)

Bishop, G. D., Sikes, L., Schroeder, D., McGregor, U. K. & Holub, D. (1985, August). *Behavior in response to physical symptoms.* Paper presented at the American Psychological Association Convention.

Black, R. G. (1975). The chronic pain syndrome. *Surgical Clinics of North America, 55,* 999–1011.

Blackburn, H., Luepker, R. V., Kline, F. G., Bracht, N., Carlaw, R., Jacobs, D., Mittelmark, M., Stauffer, L., & Taylor, H. L. (1984). The Minnesota Heart Health Program: A research and demonstration project in cardiovascular disease prevention. In J. D. Matarazzo, S. M. Weiss, J. A. Herd, N. E. Miller, & S. M. Weiss (Eds.), *Behavioral health: A handbook of health enhancement and disease prevention.* New York: Wiley.

Blair, S. N., Kohl, H. W., Paffenbarger, R. S., Clark, D. G., Cooper, K. H., & Gibbons, L. W. (1989). Physical fitness and all-cause mortality: A prospective study of healthy men and women. *Journal of the American Medical Association, 262,* 2395–2401.

Blanchard, E. B., & Andrasik, F. (1985). *Management of chronic headaches: A psychological approach.* New York: Pergamon.

Blondis, M. N., & Jackson, B. E. (1977). *Nonverbal communication with patients.* New York: Wiley.

Bloom, G., Euler, U. S. V., & Frankenhaeuser, M. (1963). Catecholamine excretion and personality in paratroop trainees. *Acta Physiologica Scandinavica, 58,* 77–89.

Bloom, S. W. (1963). *The doctor and his patient: A sociological interpretation.* New York: Russell Sage Foundation.

Bluebond-Langner, M. (1977). Meanings of death to children. In H. Feifel (Ed.), *New meanings of death.* New York: McGraw-Hill.

Blumenthal, J. A., & Emery, C. F. (1988). Rehabilitation of patients following myocardial infarction. *Journal of Consulting and Clinical Psychology, 56,* 374–381.

Bok, S. (1974). The ethics of giving placebos. *Scientific American, 231,* 17–23.

Bonica, J. J. (1989). Local anaesthesia and regional blocks. In P. D. Wall & R. Melzack (Eds.), *Textbook of pain* (2d ed.). Edinburgh: Churchill Livingstone.

Booth-Kewley, S., & Friedman, H. S. (1987). Psychological predictors of heart disease: A quantitative review. *Psychological Bulletin, 101,* 343–362.

Borman, L. D., Borck, L. E., Hess, R., & Pasquale, F. L. (Eds.) (1982). *Helping people to help themselves: Self-help and prevention.* New York: The Hawthorne Press.

Bortner, R. W. (1969). A short rating scale as a potential measure of Pattern A behavior. *Journal of Chronic Disease, 22,* 87–91.

Bosley, F., & Allen, T. W. (1989). Stress management training for hypertensives: Cognitive and physiological effects. *Journal of Behavioral Medicine, 12,* 77–89.

Botkin, B. A. (1944). *A treasury of American folklore.* New York: Crown Publishers.

Botvin, G. J., Dusenbury, L., Baker, E., James-Ortiz, S., & Kerner, J. (1989). A skills training approach to smoking prevention among Hispanic youth. *Journal of Behavioral Medicine, 12,* 279–296.

Boulanger, G. (1985). Post-traumatic stress disorder: An old problem with a new name. In S. M. Sonnenberg, A. S. Blank, & J. A. Talbott (Eds.), *The trauma of war: Stress and recovery in Vietnam veterans.* Washington, DC: American Psychiatric Press.

Bourne, P. G., Rose, R. M., & Mason, J. W. (1967). Urinary 17-OHCS levels: Data on seven helicopter ambulance medics in combat. *Archives of General Psychiatry, 17,* 104–110.

Bovbjerg, D. H. (1991). Psychoneuroimmunology: Implications for oncology? *Cancer, 67,* 828–832.

Bowen, D. L., Lane, M. D., & Fauci, A. S. (1985). Immunopathogenesis of the acquired immunodeficiency syndrome. *Annals of Internal Medicine, 103,* 704–709.

Bowers, K. (1968). Pain, anxiety, and perceived control. *Journal of Clinical and Consulting Psychology, 32,* 596–602.

Bowers, M., Jackson, E., Knight, J., & LaShan, L. (1964). *Counseling the dying.* New York: Thomas Nelson & Sons.

Bowlby, J. (1973). *Attachment and loss. Vol. 2: Separation.* New York: Basic Books.

Bowling, A. (1988). Who dies after widow(er)hood? A discriminant analysis. *Omega, 19,* 135.

Bram, P. J., & Katz, L. F. (1989). A study of burnout in nurses working in hospice and hospital oncology settings. *Oncology Nursing Forum, 16,* 555–560.

Bramwell, S. T., Masuda, M., Wagner, N. N., & Holmes, T. H. (1975). Psychological factors in athletic injuries: Development and application of the Social and Athletic Readjustment Rating Scale. *Journal of Human Stress, 1*(2), 6–20.

Brandsma, J. M., Maultsby, M. C., & Welch, R. J. (1980). *The outpatient treatment of alcoholism: A review and comparative study.* Baltimore: University Park Press.

Branthwaite, A., & Cooper, P. (1981). Analgesic effect of branding in treatment of headaches. *British Medical Journal, 282,* 1576–1578.

Bray, G. A. (1984). The role of weight control in health promotion and disease prevention. In J. D. Matarazzo, S. M. Weiss, J. A. Herd, N. E. Miller, & S. M. Weiss (Eds.), *Behavioral health: A handbook of health enhancement and disease prevention.* New York: Wiley.

Brehm, J. W. (1966). *A theory of psychological reactance.* New York: Academic Press.

Bresler, D. E. (1979). *Free yourself from pain.* New York: Simon & Schuster.

Breslow, L., & Enstrom, J. E. (1980). Persistence of health habits and their relationship to mortality. *Preventive Medicine, 9,* 469–483.

Brett, E. A., Spitzer, R. L., & Williams, J. B. W. (1988). DSM-III-R criteria for posttraumatic stress disorder. *American Journal of Psychiatry, 145,* 1232–1236.

Brewer, B. W., & Karoly, P. (1989). Effects of attentional focusing on pain perception. *Motivation and Emotion, 13,* 193–203.

Brody, D. S., Miller, S. M., Lerman, C. E., Smith, D. G., & Caputo, G. C. (1989). Patient perception of involvement with medical care: Relationship to illness attitudes and outcomes. *Journal of General Internal Medicine, 4,* 506–511.

Brody, H. (1973). The systems view of man: Implications of medicine, science, and ethics. *Perspectives in Biology and Medicine, 17*(1), 71–91.

Brooks, F. P. (1985). The pathophysiology of peptic ulcer disease. *Digestive Diseases and Sciences, 30* (Suppl. 11), 15S–29S.

Brown, G. K., Wallston, K. A., & Nicassio, P. M. (1989). Social support and depression in rheumatoid arthritis: A one-year prospective study. *Journal of Applied Social Psychology, 19,* 1164–1181.

Brown, J. D., & Siegel, J. M. (1988). Exercise as a buffer of life stress: A prospective study of adolescent health. *Health Psychology, 7,* 341–353.

Brown, N. K., & Thompson, D. J. (1979). Nontreatment of fever in extended-care facilities. *New England Journal of Medicine, 300,* 1246–1250.

Brownell, K. D. (1982). The addictive disorders. In C. M. Franks, G. T. Wilson, P. C. Kendall, & K. D. Brownell (Eds.), *Annual review of behavior therapy: Theory and practice* (Vol. 8). New York: Guilford Press.

Brownell, K. D., Stunkard, A. J., & Albaum, J. M. (1980). Evaluation and modification of exercise patterns in the natural environment. *American Journal of Psychiatry, 137,* 1540–1545.

Brubaker, R. G., & Fowler, C. (1990). Encouraging college males to perform testicular self-examination: Evaluation of a persuasive message based on the Revised Theory of Reasoned Action. *Journal of Applied Social Psychology, 20,* 1411–1422.

Brubaker, R. G., & Wickersham, D. (1990). Encouraging the practice of testicular self-examination: A field application of the theory of reasoned action. *Health Psychology, 9,* 154–163.

Bruhn, J. G., & Philips, B. U. (1984). Measuring social support: A synthesis of current approaches. *Journal of Behavioral Medicine, 7,* 151–169.

Buckalew, L. W., & Ross. S. (1981). Relationship of perceptual characteristics to efficacy of placebos. *Psychological Reports, 49,* 955–961.

Buie, J. (1990a). Medicare victory caps 25-year political effort. *APA Monitor, 21*(1), 18.

Buie, J. (1990b). President signs Medicare bill: Victory caps uphill trek. *APA Monitor, 21*(1), 1, 17–19.

Buller, M. K., & Buller, D. B. (1987). Physicians' communication style and patient satisfaction. *Journal of Health and Social Behavior, 28,* 375–388.

Burbach, D. J., & Peterson, L. (1986). Children's concepts of physical illness: A review and critique of the cognitive-developmental literature. *Health Psychology, 5,* 307–325.

Burish, T. G., Meyerowitz, B. E., Carey, M. P., & Morrow, G. R. (1987). The stressful effects of cancer in adults. In A. Baum & J. E. Singer (Eds.), *Handbook of psychology and health* (Vol. 5). Hillsdale, NJ: Erlbaum.

Burks, N., & Martin, B. (1985). Everyday problems and life change events: Ongoing versus acute sources of stress. *Journal of Human Stress, 11*(1), 27–35.

Burling, T. A., Singleton, E. G., Bigelow, G. E., Baile, W. F., & Gottlieb, S. H. (1984). Smoking following myocardial infarction: A critical review of the literature. *Health Psychology, 3,* 83–96.

Burton, D., Sussman, S., Hansen, W. B., Johnson, C. A., & Flay, B. R. (1989). Image attributions and smoking intentions among seventh grade students. *Journal of Applied Social Psychology, 19,* 656–664.

Bush, J. P. (1987). Pain in children: A review of the literature from a developmental perspective. *Psychology and Health, 1,* 215–236.

Butterfield-Picard, H., & Magno, J. B. (1982). Hospice the adjective, not the noun: The future of a national priority. *American Psychologist, 37,* 1254–1259.

Byers, T. (1988). Diet and cancer: Any progress in the interim? *Cancer, 62,* 1713–1724.

Calman, K. C., & Welsh, J. (1984). Physical aspects. In C. Saunders (Ed.), *The management of terminal malignant disease* (2d ed.). London: Edward Arnold.

Calnan, M. (1988). Images of general practice: The perceptions of the doctor. *Social Science and Medicine, 27,* 579–586.

Calnan, M. (1989). Control over health and patterns of health-related behaviour. *Social Science and Medicine, 29,* 131–136.

Calnan, M. W., & Moss, S. (1984). The health belief model and compliance with education given at a class in breast self-examination. *Journal of Health and Social Behavior, 25,* 198–210.

Campbell, J. N., Raja, S. N., Cohen, R. H., Manning, D. C., Khan, A. A., & Meyer, R. A. (1989). Peripheral neural mechanisms of nociception. In P. D. Wall & R. Melzack (Eds.), *Textbook of pain* (2d ed.). Edinburgh: Churchill Livingstone.

Campbell, P. A., & Cohen, J. J. (1985). Effects of stress on the immune response. In T. M. Field, P. M. McCabe, & N. Schneiderman (Eds.), *Stress and coping.* Hillsdale, NJ: Erlbaum.

Cannon, W. B. (1929). *Bodily changes in pain, hunger, fear and rage* (2d ed.). New York: Appleton.

Cannon, W. B. (1935). Stresses and strains of homeostasis. *American Journal of Medical Sciences, 189,* 1–14.

Cannon, W. B. (1942). "Voodoo" death. *American Anthropologist, 44,* 169–181.

Carey, M. P., & Burish, T. G. (1988). Etiology and treatment of the psychological side effects associated with cancer chemotherapy: A critical review and discussion. *Psychological Bulletin, 104,* 307–325.

Carey, R. G. (1975). Living with death: A program of service and research for the terminally ill. In E. Kübler-Ross (Ed.), *Death: The final stage of growth.* Englewood Cliffs, NJ: Prentice-Hall.

Carmody, T. P., & Matarazzo, J. D. (1991). Health psychology. In M. Hersen, A. E. Kazdin, & A. S. Bellack (Eds.), *The clinical psychology handbook* (2d ed.). New York: Pergamon.

Carver, C. S. (1989). How should multifaceted personality constructs be tested? Issues illustrated by self-monitoring, attributional style, and hardiness. *Journal of Personality and Social Psychology, 56,* 577–585.

Carver, C. S., Coleman, A. E., & Glass, D. C. (1976). The coronary-prone behavior pattern and the suppression of fatigue on a treadmill test. *Journal of Personality and Social Psychology, 33,* 460–466.

Carver, C. S., & Scheier, M. F. (1981). *Attention and self-regulation: A control-theory approach to human behavior.* New York: Springer-Verlag.

Carver, C. S., & Scheier, M. F. (1982). Control theory: A useful conceptual framework for personality—social, clinical, and health psychology. *Psychological Bulletin, 92,* 111–135.

Carver, C. S., Scheier, M. F., & Weintraub, J. K. (1989). Assessing coping strategies: A theoretically based approach. *Journal of Personality and Social Psychology, 56,* 267–283.

Case, R. B., Moss, A. J., Case, N., McDermott, M., & Eberly, S. (1992). Living alone after myocardial infarction: Impact on prognosis. *Journal of the American Medical Association, 267,* 515–519.

Cassell, S. (1965). Effects of brief puppet therapy upon the emotional responses of children undergoing cardiac catheterization. *Journal of Consulting Psychology, 29,* 1–8.

Cassileth, B. R., Lusk, E. J., Miller, D. S., Brown, L. L., & Miller, C. (1985). Psychosocial correlates of survival in advanced malignant disease? *New England Journal of Medicine, 312,* 1551–1555.

Cassileth, B. R., Lusk, E. J., Strouse, T. B., Miller, D. S., Brown, L. L., Cross, P. A., & Tenaglia, A. N. (1984). Psychosocial status in chronic illness: A comparative analysis of six diagnostic groups. *New England Journal of Medicine, 311,* 506–511.

Catalan, J. (1988). Psychosocial and neuropsychiatric aspects of HIV infection: Review of their extent and implications for psychiatry. *Journal of Psychosomatic Research, 32,* 237–248.

Caughill, R. E. (1976). *The dying patient: A supportive approach.* Boston: Little, Brown.

Cavanagh, J., & Clairmonte, F. F. (1985). *Alcoholic beverages: Dimensions of corporate power.* New York: St. Martin's Press.

Celentano, D. D. (1991). Epidemiologic perspectives on life-style modification and health promotion in cancer research. *Cancer, 67,* 808–812.

Centers for Disease Control (1987). Smoking-attributable mortality and years of potential life lost—United States, 1984. *Morbidity and Mortality Weekly Report, 36,* 693–697.

Centers for Disease Control (1989a). *Surgeon General's report on smoking: Reducing health consequences of smoking: 25 years of progress, 1964–1989.* Washington, DC: Central Office of Health Promotion and Education on Smoking and Health, U.S. Government Printing Office.

Centers for Disease Control (1989b). Tobacco use by adults—United States, 1987. *Morbidity and Mortality Weekly Report, 38,* 685–687.

Centers for Disease Control (1990). World No-Tobacco Day. *Morbidity and Mortality Weekly Report, 39,* 218.

Centers for Disease Control (1991a). CDC update: Transmission of HIV during an invasive dental procedure—Florida. *Morbidity & Mortality Weekly Report, 40,* 21–33.

Centers for Disease Control (1991b). Mortality attributable to HIV infection/AIDS—United States, 1981–1990. *Morbidity and Mortality Weekly Report, 40,* 41–44.

Centers for Disease Control (1991c). Smoking-attributable mortality and years of potential life lost—United States, 1988. *Morbidity and Mortality Weekly Report, 40,* 62–63, 69–71.

Centers for Disease Control (1991d). The HIV/AIDS epidemic: The first 10 years. *Morbidity and Mortality Weekly Report, 40,* 357–369.

Centers for Disease Control (1992). *HIV/AIDS Surveillance Report, July, 1992.* Atlanta: author.

Chaiken, S. (1979). Communicator physical attractiveness and persuasion. *Journal of Personality and Social Psychology, 37,* 1387–1397.

Champion, V. L. (1990). Breast self-examination in women 35 and older: A prospective study. *Journal of Behavioral Medicine, 13,* 523–538.

Chandra, V., Szklo, M., Goldberg, R., & Tonascia, J. (1983). The impact of marital status on survival after an acute myocardial infarction: A population-based study. *American Journal of Epidemiology, 117,* 320–325.

Chapman, C. R. (1984). New directions in the understanding and management of pain. *Social Science and Medicine, 19,* 1261–1277.

Chapman, C. R., Casey, K. L., Dubner, R., Roley, K. M., Gracely, R. H., & Reading, A. E. (1985). Pain measurement: An overview. *Pain, 22,* 1261–1277.

Chassin, L., Presson, C. C., Sherman, S. J., Corty, E., & Olshavsky, R. W. (1981). Self-images and cigarette smoking in adolescence. *Personality and Social Psychology Bulletin, 7,* 670–676.

Chassin, L., Presson, C. C., Sherman, S. J., & Edwards, D. A. (1990). The natural history of cigarette smoking: Predicting young-adult smoking outcomes from adolescent smoking patterns. *Health Psychology, 9,* 701–716.

Chassin, L., Presson, C. C., Sherman, S. J., & McGrew, J. (1987). The changing smoking environment for middle and high school students: 1980–1983. *Journal of Behavioral Medicine, 10,* 581–593.

Chesney, M. A. (1984). Behavior modification and health enhancement. In J. D. Matarazzo, S. M. Weiss, J. A. Herd, N. E. Miller, & S. M. Weiss (Eds.), *Behavioral health: A handbook of health enhancement and disease prevention.* New York: Wiley.

Chesney, M. A., Eagleston, J. R., & Rosenman, R. H. (1981). Type A behavior: Assessment and intervention. In C. K. Prokop & L. A. Bradley (Eds.), *Medical psychology: Contributions to behavioral medicine.* New York: Academic Press.

Christensen, A. J., Turner, C. W., Slaughter, J. R., & Holman, J. M. Jr. (1989). Perceived family support as a moderator of psychological well-being in end-stage renal disease. *Journal of Behavioral Medicine, 12,* 249–265.

Chuan, H. T., Devins, G. M., Hunsley, J., & Gill, M. J. (1989). Psychosocial distress and well-being among gay and bisexual men with human immunodeficiency virus infection. *American Journal of Psychiatry, 146,* 876–880.

Cinciripini, P. M., & Floreen, A. (1982). An evaluation of a behavioral program for chronic pain. *Journal of Behavioral Medicine, 5,* 375–389.

Cioffi, D. (1991). Beyond attentional strategies: A cognitive-perceptual model of somatic interpretations. *Psychological Bulletin, 109,* 25–41.

Citrin, W. S., Kleinman, G. A., Skyler, J. S. (1986). In M. B. Davidson (Ed.), *Diabetes mellitus: Diagnosis and treatment* (2d ed.). New York: Wiley.

Clark, S. J., Saag, M. S., Decker, W. D., Campbell-Hill, S., Roberson, J. L., Veldcamp, P. J., Kappes, J. C., Hahn, B. H., & Shaw, G. M. (1991). High titers of cytopathic virus in plasma of patients with symptomatic primary HIV-1 infection. *New England Journal of Medicine, 324,* 954–960.

Clark, W. R. (1988). Introduction to immunology. In M. Renneker (Ed.), *Understanding cancer* (3d ed.). Palo Alto, CA: Bull Publishing Co.

Clarke, J. H., MacPherson, B. W., & Holmes, D. R. (1982). Cigarette smoking and external locus of control among young adolescents. *Journal of Health and Social Behavior, 23,* 253–259.

Coates, T. J., Stall, R. D., Kegeles, S. M., Lo, B., Morin, S. F., & McKusick, L. (1988). AIDS antibody testing: Will it stop the AIDS epidemic? Will it help people infected with HIV? *American Psychologist, 43,* 859–864.

Cochran, S. D., & Mays, V. M. (1989). Women and AIDS-related concerns: Roles for psychologists in helping the worried well. *American Psychologist, 44,* 529–535.

Cochrane, R., & Robertson, A. (1973). The Life Events Inventory: A measure of the relative severity of psychosocial stressors. *Journal of Psychosomatic Research, 17,* 135–139.

Cockerham, W. C., Lueschen, G., Kunz, G., & Spaeth, J. L. (1986). Social stratification and self-management of health. *Journal of Health and Social Behavior, 27,* 1–14.

Cohen, F., & Lazarus, R. S. (1979). Coping with the stresses of illness. In G. Stone, F. Cohen, & N. E. Adler (Eds.), *Health psychology—A handbook.* San Francisco: Jossey-Bass.

Cohen, J. B., & Reed, D. (1985). The type A behavior pattern and coronary heart disease among Japanese men in Hawaii. *Journal of Behavioral Medicine, 8,* 343–352.

Cohen, J. B., Syme, S. L., Jenkins, C. D., Kagan, A., & Zyzanski, S. J. (1979). Cultural context of type A behavior and risk for CHD: A study of Japanese American males. *Journal of Behavioral Medicine, 2,* 375–384.

Cohen, L. A. (1987). Diet and cancer. *Scientific American, 257*(5), 42–48.

Cohen, R. A., Williamson, D. A., Monguillot, J. E., Hutchinson, P. C., Gottlieb, J., & Waters, W. F. (1983). Psychophysiological response patterns in vascular and muscle-contraction headaches. *Journal of Behavioral Medicine, 6,* 93–107.

Cohen, S. (1980). Aftereffects of stress on human performance and social behavior: A review of research and theory. *Psychological Bulletin, 88,* 82–108.

Cohen, S., & Edwards, J. R. (1989). Personality characteristics as moderators of the relationship between stress and disorder. In R. W. J. Neufeld (Ed.), *Advances in the investigation of psychological stress.* New York: Wiley.

Cohen, S., Evans, G. W., Krantz, D. S., & Stokols, D. (1980). Physiological, motivational and cognitive effects of aircraft noise on children: Moving from the laboratory to the field. *American Psychologist, 35,* 231–243.

Cohen, S., Lichtenstein, E., Prochaska, J. O., Rossi, J. S., Gritz, E. R., Carr, C. R., Orleans, C. T., Schoenbach, V. J., Biener, L., Abrams, D., DiClemente, C., Curry, S., Marlatt, G. A., Cummings, K. M., Emont, S. L., Giovino, G., & Ossip-Klein, D. (1989). Debunking myths about self-quitting: Evidence from 10 prospective studies of persons who attempt to quit smoking by themselves. *American Psychologist, 44,* 1355–1365.

Cohen, S., & Wills, T. A. (1985). Stress, social support, and the buffering hypothesis. *Psychological Bulletin, 98,* 310–357.

Cole, P. (1974). Morbidity in the U.S. In C. L. Erhardt & J. Berlin (Eds.), *Mortality and morbidity in the U.S.* Cambridge: Harvard University Press.

Collins, D. L., Baum, A., & Singer, J. E. (1983). Coping with chronic stress at Three Mile Island: Psychological and biochemical evidence. *Health Psychology, 2,* 149–166.

Condiotte, M. M., & Lichtenstein, E. (1981). Self-efficacy and relapse in smoking cessation programs. *Journal of Consulting and Clinical Psychology, 49,* 648–658.

Connolly, G. N. (1990). Back to the future with oral snuff. *British Journal of Addiction, 85,* 1102–1104.

Conrad, P. (1986). The social meaning of AIDS. *Social Policy, 17,* 51–56.

Converse, P. E. (1964). The nature of belief systems in mass publics. In D. E. Apter (Ed.), *Ideology and discontent.* New York: Free Press of Glencoe.

Conway, T. L., Vickers, R. R., Ward, H. W., & Rahe, R. H. (1981). Occupational stress and variation in cigarette, coffee, and alcohol consumption. *Journal of Health and Social Behavior, 22,* 155–165.

Cooper, E. L. (1982). *General immunology.* Oxford: Pergamon.

Costa, P. T., & McCrae, R. R. (1980). Somatic complaints in males as a function of age and neuroticism: A longitudinal analysis. *Journal of Behavioral Medicine, 3,* 245–257.

Costa, P. T., & McCrae, R. R. (1985). Hypochondriasis, neuroticism, and aging: When are somatic complaints unfounded? *American Psychologist, 40,* 19–28.

Cousins, N. (1979). *Anatomy of an illness.* New York: W. W. Norton.

Cousins, N. (1983). *The healing heart: Antidotes to panic and helplessness.* New York: W. W. Norton.

Cousins, N. (1985). How patients appraise physicians. *New England Journal of Medicine, 313,* 1422–1423.

Coyne, J. C., & Holroyd, K. (1982). Stress, coping, and illness: A transactional perspective. In T. Millon, C. Green, & R. Meagher (Eds.), *Handbook of clinical health psychology.* New York: Plenum.

Craig, K. E. (1989). Emotional aspects of pain. In P. D. Wall & R. Melzack (Eds.). *Textbook of pain* (2d ed.). Edinburgh: Churchill Livingstone.

Crandall, C., & Biernat, M. (1990). The ideology of anti-fat attitudes. *Journal of Applied Social Psychology, 20,* 227–243.

Craun, A. M., & Deffenbacher, J. L. (1987). The effects of information, behavioral rehearsal, and prompting on breast self-exams. *Journal of Behavioral Medicine, 10,* 351–365.

Creer, T. L. (1982). Asthma. *Journal of Consulting and Clinical Psychology, 50,* 912–921.

Croog, S. H., & Levine, S. (1977). *The heart patient recovers.* New York: Human Sciences Press.

Croog, S. H., & Levine, S. (1982). *Life after a heart attack: Social and psychological factors eight years later.* New York: Human Sciences Press.

Crowther, J. H. (1983). Stress management training and relaxation imagery in the treatment of essential hypertension. *Journal of Behavioral Medicine, 6,* 169–187.

Croyle, R. T., & Uretsky, M. B. (1987). Effects of mood on self-appraisal of health status. *Health Psychology, 6,* 239–253.

Cullen, J. W., Blot, W., Henningfield, J., Boyd, G., Mecklenburg, R., & Massey, M. M. (1986). Health consequences of using smokeless tobacco: Summary of the Advisory Committee's report to the Surgeon General. *Public Health Reports, 101,* 355–373.

Cummings, K. M., Michalek, A. M., Carl, W., Wood, R., & Haley, N. J. (1989). Use of smokeless tobacco in a group of professional baseball players. *Journal of Behavioral Medicine, 12,* 559–567.

Curtiss, G., Kinder, B. N., Kalichman, S., & Spana, R. (1988). Affective differences among subgroups of chronic pain patients. *Anxiety Research, 1,* 65–73.

Czajkowski, S. M., Hindelang, R. D., Dembroski, T. M., Mayerson, S. E., Parks, E. B., & Holland, J. C. (1990). Aerobic fitness, psychological characteristics, and cardiovascular reactivity to stress. *Health Psychology, 9,* 676–692.

Daar, E. S., Moudgil, T., Meyer, R. D., & Ho, D. D. (1991). Transient high levels of viremia in patients with primary human immunodeficiency virus type 1 infection. *New England Journal of Medicine, 324,* 961–964.

Dahlstrom, L., Carlsson, S. G., Gale, E. N., & Jansson, T. G. (1985). Stress-induced muscular activity in mandibular dysfunction: Effects of biofeedback training. *Journal of Behavioral Medicine, 8,* 191–200.

Dakof, G. A., & Mendelsohn, G. A. (1989). Patterns of adaptation to Parkinson's disease. *Health Psychology, 8,* 355–372.

Dakof, G. A., & Taylor, S. E. (1990). Victims' perceptions of social support: What is helpful from whom? *Journal of Personality and Social Psychology, 58,* 80–89.

Dalton, J. A. (1987). Education for pain management: A pilot study. *Patient Education and Counseling, 9,* 155–165.

DaSilva, A., & Schork, M. S. (1984). Gender differences in attitudes to death among a group of public health students. *Omega, 15,* 77–84.

Dattore, P. J., Shontz, R. C., & Coyne, L. (1980). Premorbid personality differentiation of cancer and noncancer groups: A test of the hypothesis of cancer proneness. *Journal of Consulting and Clinical Psychology, 48,* 388–394.

Davidson, M. B. (1986). *Diabetes mellitus: Diagnosis and treatment* (2d ed.). New York: Wiley.

Davis, D. L., Hoel, D., Fox, J., & Lopez, A. D. (1990). International trends in cancer mortality in France, West Germany, Italy, Japan, England and Wales, and the United States. *Annals of the New York Academy of Sciences, 609,* 5–48.

Davis, J. (1989). *Defending the body: Unraveling the mysteries of immunology.* New York: Atheneum.

Davis, M. S. (1966). Variation in patients' compliance with doctors' orders: Analysis of congruence between survey responses and results of empirical investigations. *Journal of Medical Education, 41,* 1037–1048.

Dawson, D. A. (1990). AIDS knowledge and attitudes for January–March 1990: Provisional data from the National Health Interview Survey. *Advance Data from the National Health Interview Survey, No. 193.* Hyattsville, MD: National Center for Health Statistics.

DeBenedittis, G., Panerai, A. A., & Villamira, M. A. (1989). Effects of hypnotic analgesia and hypnotizability on experimental ischemic pain. *International Journal of Clinical and Experimental Hypnosis, 37,* 55–69.

DeGood, D. E., & Redgate, E. S. (1982). Interrelationship of plasma cortisol and other activation indices during EMG biofeedback training. *Journal of Behavioral Medicine, 5,* 213–223.

Delaney, J., Lupton, M. J., & Toth, E. (1988). *The curse: A cultural history of menstruation.* Urbana: University of Illinois Press.

DeLeon, P. H., Kjervik, D. K., Kraut, A. G., & VandenBos, G. R. (1985). Psychology and nursing: A natural alliance. *American Psychologist, 40,* 1153–1164.

DeLeon, P. H., & Pallak, M. S. (1982). Public health and psychology: An important, expanding interaction. *American Psychologist, 37,* 934–935.

DeLongis, A., Coyne, J. C., Dakof, G., Folkman, S., & Lazarus, R. S. (1982). Relationship of daily hassles, uplifts, and major life events to health status. *Health Psychology, 1,* 119–136.

DeLongis, A., Folkman, S., & Lazarus, R. S. (1988). The impact of daily stress on health and mood: Psychological and social resources as mediators. *Journal of Personality and Social Psychology, 54,* 486–495.

Dembroski, T. M., Lasater, T. M., & Ramirez, A. (1978). Communicator similarity, fear arousing communications, and compliance with health care recommendations. *Journal of Applied Social Psychology, 8,* 254–269.

Dembroski, T. M., MacDougall, J. M., Cardozo, S. R., Ireland, S. K., & Krug-Fite, J. (1985). Selective cardiovascular effects of stress and cigarette smoking in young women. *Health Psychology, 4,* 153–167.

Dembroski, T. M., MacDougall, J. M., Shields, J., Pettito, J., & Lushene, R. (1978). Components of the type A coronary-prone behavior pattern and cardiovascular responses to psychomotor performance challenge. *Journal of Behavioral Medicine, 1,* 159–176.

Descartes, R. (1955). Selections. (Edited by R. Eaton). New York: Scribner's.

Des Jarlais, D. C., Casriel, C., & Friedman, S. (1989). The new death among IV drug users. In I. B. Corless & M. Pittman-Lindeman (Eds.), *AIDS: Principles, practices, & politics* (Ref. ed.). New York: Hemisphere.

Des Jarlais, D. C., & Friedman, S. R. (1988). HIV infection among persons who inject illicit drugs: Problems and prospects. *Journal of Acquired Immune Deficiency Syndromes, 1,* 267–273.

Des Jarlais, D. C., Friedman, S. R., Casriel, C., & Kott, A. (1987). AIDS and preventing initiation into intravenous (IV) drug use. *Psychology and Health, 1,* 179–194.

Desowitz, R. S. (1987). *The thorn in the starfish: How the human immune system works.* New York: W. W. Norton.

Devins, G. M., & Seland, T. P. (1987). Emotional impact of multiple sclerosis: Recent findings and suggestions for future research. *Psychological Bulletin, 101,* 363–375.

Deyo, R. A., Inui, T. S., Leininger, J., & Overman, S. (1982). Physical and psychosocial function in rheumatoid arthritis. *Archives of Internal Medicine, 142,* 879–882.

Diamond, E. L., Schneiderman, N., Schwartz, D., Smith, J. C., Vorp, R., & Pasin, R. D. (1984). Harassment, hostility, and type A as determinants of cardiovascular reactivity during competition. *Journal of Behavioral Medicine, 7,* 171–189.

Diefenbach, M. A., Leventhal, H., Patrick-Miller, L. (1990, August). *Cognitions and procedures in response to illness.* Paper presented at the American Psychological Association Convention, Boston, MA.

Diener, E., & Crandall, R. (1978). *Ethics in social and behavioral research.* Chicago: University of Chicago Press.

DiMatteo, M. R. (1979). A social-psychological analysis of physician-patient rapport: Toward a science of the art of medicine. *Journal of Social Issues, 35,* 12–33.

DiMatteo, M. R., & DiNicola, D. D. (1982). *Achieving patient compliance: The psychology of the medical practitioner's role.* New York: Pergamon.

DiMatteo, M. R., Hays, R. D., & Prince, L. M. (1986). Relationship of physicians' nonverbal communication skill to patient satisfaction, appointment noncompliance, and physician workload. *Health Psychology, 5,* 581–594.

DiMatteo, M. R., Linn, L. S., Chang, B. L., & Cope, D. W. (1985). Affect and neutrality in physician behavior: A study of patients' values and satisfaction. *Journal of Behavioral Medicine, 8,* 397–409.

Dimond, M., & Jones, S. L. (1983). *Chronic illness across the life span.* Norwalk, CT: Appleton-Century-Crofts.

Dimsdale, J. E. (1987). Measuring human sympathoadrenomedullary responses to stressors. In A. Baum & J. E. Singer (Eds.), *Handbook of psychology and health, Vol. V: Stress.* Hillsdale, NJ: Erlbaum.

Dimsdale, J. E., Gilbert, J., Hutter, A. M., Hackett, T. P., & Block, P. C. (1981). Predicting cardiac morbidity based on risk factors and coronary angiographic findings. *American Journal of Cardiology, 47,* 73–76.

DiNicola, D. D., & DiMatteo, M. R. (1984). Practitioners, patients, and compliance with medical regimens: A social psychological perspective. In A. Baum, S. E. Taylor, & J. E. Singer (Eds.), *Handbook of psychology and health: Vol. IV: Social psychological aspects of health.* Hillsdale, NJ: Erlbaum.

DiPasquale, J. A. (1990). The psychological effects of support groups on individuals infected by the AIDS virus. *Cancer Nursing, 13,* 278–285.

Dishman, R. K. (1982). Compliance/adherence in health-related exercise. *Health Psychology, 1,* 237–267.

DiSogra, L. K., & DiSogra, C. A. (1988a). Diet and cancer. In M. Renneker, *Understanding cancer.* (3d ed.). Palo Alto, CA: Bull Publishing Co.

DiSogra, L. K., & DiSogra, C. A. (1988b). Diet and cancer prevention. In M. Renneker, *Understanding cancer.* (3d ed.). Palo Alto, CA: Bull Publishing Co.

Doehrman, S. R. (1977). Psycho-social aspects of recovery from coronary heart disease: A review. *Social Science and Medicine, 11,* 199–218.

Dohrenwend, B. S., Dohrenwend, B. P., Dodson, M., & Shrout, P. E. (1984). Symptoms, hassles, social supports and life events: The problem of confounded measures. *Journal of Abnormal Psychology, 93,* 222–230.

Dohrenwend, B. S., Kasnoff, L., Askenasy, A. R., & Dohrenwend, B. P. (1978). Exemplification of a method for scaling life events: The PERI life events scale. *Journal of Health and Social Behavior, 19,* 205–229.

Doka, K. J., Schwarz, E. E., & Schwarz, C. (1990). Risky business: Observations on the nature of death in hazardous sports. *Omega, 21,* 215–223.

Dolce, J. J., & Raczynski, J. M. (1985). Neuromuscular activity and electromyography in painful backs: Psychological and biomechanical models in assessment and treatment. *Psychological Bulletin, 97,* 502–520.

Doll, L. S., O'Malley, P. M., Pershing, A. L., Darrow, W. W., Hessol, N. A., & Lifson, A. R. (1990). High-risk sexual behavior and knowledge of HIV antibody status in San Francisco city clinic cohort. *Health Psychology, 9,* 253–265.

Doll, R., & Peto, R. (1981). *The causes of cancer: Quantitative estimates of avoidable risks of cancer in the United States today.* Oxford: Oxford University Press.

Donne, J. (1624/1972). *Devotions upon emergent occasions.* Cambridge: Cambridge University Press.

Doyle, W. D., Street, W. J., Masur, F. T., & Asken, M. J. (1981). Training in medical psychology: A survey of graduate and internship training programs. *Professional Psychology, 12,* 224–228.

Dranov, P. (1987). Serious breakfast. *Health, 19*(March), 57–58, 77.

Dubbert, P. M., King, A., Rapp, S. R., Brief, D., Martin, J. E., & Lake, M. (1985). Riboflavin as a tracer of medication compliance. *Journal of Behavioral Medicine, 8,* 287–299.

Dunbar-Jacob, J., Dwyer, K., Dunning, E. J. (1991). Compliance with antihypertensive regimen: A review of the research in the 1980s. *Annals of Behavioral Medicine, 13,* 31–39.

Duncan, J. J., Farr, J. E., Upton, J., Hogan, R. D., Oglesby, M. E., & Blair, S. N. (1985). The effects of aerobic exercise on plasma catecholamines and blood pressure in patients with mild essential hypertension. *Journal of the American Medical Association, 254,* 2609–2613.

Dunkel-Schetter, C. (1984). Social support and cancer: Findings based on patient interviews and their implications. *Journal of Social Issues, 40*(4), 77–98.

Dunkel-Schetter, C., & Wortman, C. (1982). The interpersonal dynamics of cancer. In H. S. Friedman & M. R.

DiMatteo (Eds.), *Interpersonal issues in health care*. New York: Academic Press.

Earle, J. R., Perricone, P. J., Maultsby, D. M., Perricone, N., Turner, R. A., & Davis, J. (1979). Psychosocial adjustment of rheumatoid arthritis patients from two alternative treatment settings. *Journal of Rheumatology, 6,* 80–87.

Egbert, L. D., Battit, G. E., Welch, C. E., & Bartlett, M. K. (1964). Reduction of postoperative pain by encouragement and instruction of patients. *New England Journal of Medicine, 270,* 825–827.

Eisen, H. N. (1990). *General immunology*. Philadelphia: J. B. Lippincott.

Eisenberg, M. G., Sutkin, L. C., & Janssen, M. A. (1984). *Chronic illness and disability through the life span: Effects on self and family*. New York: Springer.

Eiser, C. (1985). *The psychology of childhood illness*. New York: Springer-Verlag.

Eiser, C. (1988). Do children benefit from psychological preparation for hospitalization? *Psychology and Health, 2,* 133–138.

Ellerbrock, T. V., Bush, T. J., Chamberland, M. E., & Oxtoby, M. J. (1991). Epidemiology of women with AIDS in the United States, 1981 through 1990. *Journal of the American Medical Association, 265,* 2971–2975.

Elliot, R., & Tighe, T. (1968). Breaking the cigarette habit: Effects of a technique involving loss of money. *Psychological Record, 18,* 503–513.

Emrick, C. D., & Hansen, J. (1983). Assertions regarding effectiveness of treatment for alcoholism: Fact or fantasy? *American Psychologist, 38,* 1078–1088.

Engel, G. L. (1961). Is grief a disease? A challenge for medical research. *Psychosomatic Medicine, 23,* 18–22.

Engel, G. L. (1977). The need for a new medical model: A challenge for biomedicine. *Science, 196,* 129–136.

Engel, G. L. (1980). The clinical application of the biopsychosocial model. *American Journal of Psychiatry, 137,* 535–544.

Engel, G. L., Reichsman, R., & Segal, H. L. (1956). A study of an infant with a gastric fistula: I. Behavior and the rate of total hydrochloric acid secretion. *Psychosomatic Medicine, 18,* 374–398.

Epstein, L. H. (1984). The direct effects of compliance on health outcome. *Health Psychology, 3,* 385–393.

Epstein, L. H., Beck, S., Figueroa, J., Farkas, G., Kazdin, A. E., Danenman, D., & Becker, D. (1981). The effects of targeting improvements in urine glucose on metabolic control. *Journal of Applied Behavior Analysis, 14,* 365–375.

Epstein, L. H., & Cluss, P. A. (1982). A behavioral medicine perspective on adherence to long-term medical regimens. *Journal of Consulting and Clinical Psychology, 50,* 950–971.

Epstein, L. H., & Perkins, K. A. (1988). Smoking, stress, and coronary heart disease. *Journal of Consulting and Clinical Psychology, 56,* 342–349.

Epstein, L. H., & Wing, R. R. (1987). Behavioral treatment of childhood obesity. *Psychological Bulletin, 101,* 331–342.

Epstein, M., & Oster, J. R. (1984). *Hypertension: A practical approach*. Philadelphia: W. B. Saunders.

Erickson, B., Lind, E. A., Johnson, B. C., & Barr, W. M. (1978). Speech style and impression formation in a court setting: The effects of powerful and powerless speech. *Journal of Experimental Social Psychology, 14,* 266–279.

Evans, C., & Richardson, P. H. (1988). Improved recovery and reduced postoperative stay after therapeutic suggestions during general anaesthesia. *Lancet, 2,* 491–493.

Evans, D. A., Funkenstein, H. H., Albert, M. S., Scherr, P. A., Cook, N. R., Crown, M. J., Hebert, L. E., Hennekens, C. H., & Taylor, J. O. (1989). Prevalence of Alzheimer's disease in a community population of older persons: Higher than previously reported. *Journal of the American Medical Association, 262,* 2551–2556.

Evans, F. J. (1985). Expectancy, therapeutic instructions and the placebo response. In L. White, B. Tursky, & G. E. Schwartz (Eds.), *Placebo: Theory, research and mechanisms*. New York: Guilford Press.

Evans, G. W., Palsane, M. N., Lepore, S. J., & Martin, J. (1989). Residential density and psychological health: The mediating effects of social support. *Journal of Personality and Social Psychology, 57,* 994–999.

Evans, R. I. (1984). A social inoculation strategy to deter smoking in adolescents. In J. D. Matarazzo, S. M. Weiss, J. A. Herd, N. E. Miller, & S. M. Weiss (Eds.), *Behavioral health: A handbook of health enhancement and disease prevention*. New York: Wiley.

Everly, G. S. (1984). Time management: A behavioral strategy for disease prevention and health enhancement. In J. D. Matarazzo, S. M. Weiss, J. A. Herd, N. E. Miller, & S. M. Weiss (Eds.), *Behavioral health: A handbook of health enhancement and disease prevention*. New York: Wiley.

Ewart, C. K., Harris, W. L., Iwata, M. M., Coates, T. J., Bullock, R., & Simon, B. (1987). Feasibility and effectiveness of school-based relaxation in lowering blood pressure. *Health Psychology, 6,* 399–416.

Eysenck, H. J. (1988). Personality, stress and cancer: Prediction and prophylaxis. *British Journal of Medical Psychology, 61,* 57–75.

Fabrega, H. (1974). *Disease and social behavior: An interdisciplinary perspective*. Cambridge, MA: MIT Press.

Fagerstrom, K.-O. (1982). A comparison of psychological and pharmacological treatment in smoking cessation. *Journal of Behavioral Medicine, 5,* 343–351.

Farnon, C. (1981). Let's offer employees a healthier diet. *Journal of Occupational Medicine, 23,* 273–276.

Farquhar, J. W., Maccoby, N., Wood, P. D., Alexander, J. K., Breitrose, H., Brown, B. W., Haskel, W. L., McAlister, A. L., Meyer, A. J., Nash, J. D., & Stern, M. P. (1977). Community education for cardiovascular health. *Lancet, 2,* 1192–1195.

Fazio, R. H. (1989). On the power and functionality of attitudes: The role of attitude accessibility. In A. R. Pratkanis, S. J. Breckler, & A. G. Greenwald (Eds.), *Attitude structure and function.* Hillsdale, NJ: Erlbaum.

Feeley, N., & Gottlieb, L. N. (1988). Parents' coping and communication following their infant's death. *Omega, 19,* 51–67.

Feinberg, J. (1988). The effect of patient-practitioner interaction on compliance: A review of the literature and application in rheumatoid arthritis. *Patient Education and Counseling, 11,* 171–187.

Feinstein, A. R., Wood, H. F., Epstein, J. A. Taranta, A., Simpson, R., & Tursky, E. (1959). A controlled study of three methods of prophylaxis against streptococcal infection in a population of rheumatic children. II. Results of the first three years of the study, including methods for evaluating the maintenance of oral prophylaxis. *New England Journal of Medicine, 260,* 697–702.

Feletti, G., Firman, D., & Sanson-Fisher, R. (1986). Patient satisfaction with primary-care consultations. *Journal of Behavioral Medicine, 9,* 389–399.

Feurstein, M., Salt, S., & Houle, M. (1985). Environmental stressors and chronic low back pain: Life events, family and work environment. *Pain, 22,* 295–307.

Field, M. (1990). Testing for AIDS: Uses and abuses. *American Journal of Law and Medicine, 16,* 33–106.

Field, T. M., McCabe, P. M., & Schneiderman, N. (1985). *Stress and coping.* Hillsdale, NJ: Erlbaum.

Fielding, J. E. (1978). Successes of prevention. *Milbank Memorial Fund Quarterly, 56,* 274–302.

Fielding, J. E. (1984). Health promotion and disease prevention at the worksite. *Annual Review of Public Health, 5,* 237–265.

Fielding, J. E., & Breslow, L. (1983). Health promotion programs sponsored by California employers. *American Journal of Public Health, 73,* 538–541.

Fields, H. L., & Basbaum, A. I. (1989). Endogenous pain control mechanisms. In P. D. Wall & R. Melzack (Eds.), *Textbook of pain* (2d ed.). Edinburgh: Churchill Livingstone.

Fillingim, R. B., & Fine, M. A. (1986). The effects of internal versus external information processing on symptom perception in an exercise setting. *Health Psychology, 5,* 115–123.

Fineberg, H. V. (1988). Education to prevent AIDS: Prospects and obstacles. *Science, 239,* 592–596.

Fish, R. M., Ehrhardt, M. E., & Fish, B. (1985). *Malpractice: Managing your defense.* Oradell, NJ: Medical Economics Books.

Fishbein, M. (1980). A theory of reasoned action: Some applications and implications. In M. M. Page (Ed.), *1979 Nebraska Symposium on Motivation.* Lincoln: University of Nebraska Press.

Fishbein, M., & Ajzen, I. (1975). *Beliefs, attitudes, intention, and behavior: An introduction to theory and research.* Reading, MA: Addison–Wesley.

Fiske, S. T., & Taylor, S. E. (1991). *Social cognition* (2d ed.). New York: McGraw-Hill.

Fitzpatrick, R., Newman, S., Lamb, R., & Shipley, M. (1988). Social relationships and psychological well-being in rheumatoid arthritis. *Social Science and Medicine, 27,* 399–403.

Flay, B. R. (1985). Psychosocial approaches to smoking prevention: A review of findings. *Health Psychology, 4,* 449–488.

Flay, B. R. (1987). Mass media and smoking cessation: A critical review. *American Journal of Public Health, 77,* 153–160.

Flay, B. R., Ryan, K. B., Best, J. A., Brown, K. S., Kersell, M. W., d'Avernas, J. R., & Zanna, M. P. (1985). Are social-psychological smoking prevention programs effective? The Waterloo Study. *Journal of Behavioral Medicine, 8,* 37–59.

Fleming, R., Baum, A., & Singer, J. E. (1984). Toward an integrative approach to the study of stress. *Journal of Personality and Social Psychology, 46,* 939–949.

Flor, H., Kerns, R. D., & Turk, D. C. (1987). The role of spouse reinforcement, perceived pain, and activity levels of chronic pain patients. *Journal of Psychosomatic Research, 31,* 251–259.

Flor, H., & Turk, D. C. (1988). Chronic back pain and rheumatoid arthritis: Predicting pain and disability from cognitive variables. *Journal of Behavioral Medicine, 11,* 251–265.

Florian, V., & Kravetz, S. (1983). Fear of personal death: Attribution, structure, and relation to religious belief. *Journal of Personality and Social Psychology, 44,* 600–607.

Folkman, S. (1984). Personal control and stress and coping processes: A theoretical analysis. *Journal of Personality and Social Psychology, 46,* 839–852.

Folkman, S., & Lazarus, R. S. (1980). An analysis of coping in a middle-aged community sample. *Journal of Health and Social Behavior, 21,* 219–239.

Fontana, A. F., Kerns, R. D., Rosenberg, R. L., & Colonese, K. L. (1989). Support, stress, and recovery from coronary heart disease: A longitudinal causal model. *Health Psychology, 8,* 175–193.

Fordyce, W. E. (1976). *Behavioral methods for chronic pain and illness.* St. Louis: C. V. Mosby.

Fordyce, W. E. (1978). Learning processes in pain. In R. A. Sternbach (Ed.), *The psychology of pain.* New York: Raven Press.

Fordyce, W. E. (1988). Pain and suffering: A reappraisal. *American Psychologist, 43,* 276–283.

Fordyce, W. E., Brockway, J. A., Bergman, J. A., & Spengler, D. (1986). Acute back pain: A control-group comparison of behavioral vs. traditional management methods. *Journal of Behavioral Medicine, 9,* 127–140.

Fordyce, W. E., Shelton, J. L., & Dundore, D. E. (1982). The modification of avoidance learning pain behaviors. *Journal of Behavioral Medicine, 5,* 405–414.

Forman, S. (1982). Stress management for teachers: A cognitive-behavioral program. *Journal of School Psychology, 20,* 180–187.

Foster, G. M., & Anderson, B. G. (1978). *Medical anthropology.* New York: Wiley.

Foster, W. F., Somerville, M. A., & Duckett, M. (1990). HIV/AIDS and school boards: A policy approach. *Social Science and Medicine, 30,* 267–279.

Fowler-Kerry, S., & Lander, J. R. (1987). Management of injection pain in children. *Pain, 30,* 169–175.

Fox, B. H. (1988). Psychogenic factors in cancer, especially its incidence. In S. Maes, C. D. Spielberger, P. B. Defares, & I. G. Sarason (Eds.), *Topics in health psychology.* Chichester, England: Wiley.

Frame, P. S. (1989). Clinical prevention in primary care— The time is now! *Journal of Family Practice, 29,* 150–152.

Francis, V., Korsch, B., & Morris, M. (1969). Gaps in doctor-patient communication: Patients' response to medical advice. *New England Journal of Medicine, 280,* 535–540.

Frank, J. (1985). *Alzheimer's disease: The silent epidemic.* Minneapolis: Lerner.

Frankenhaeuser, M. (1975). Sympathetic-adrenomedullary activity, behavior and the psychosocial environment. In P. H. Venables & M. J. Christie (Eds.), *Research in psychophysiology.* New York: Wiley.

Friedman, A. L., Antoni, M. H., Ironson, G., LaPerrier, A., & Schneiderman, N. (1991, March). *Behavioral interventions, changes in perceived social support, and depression following notification of HIV-1 seropositivity.* Paper presented at the Society of Behavioral Medicine Meeting, Washington, DC.

Friedman, H. S. (1979). Nonverbal communication between patients and medical practitioners. *Journal of Social Issues, 35,* 82–99.

Friedman, H. S., & Booth-Kewley, S. (1987). The "disease-prone personality": A meta-analytic view of the construct. *American Psychologist, 42,* 539–555.

Friedman, H. S., DiMatteo, M. R., & Taranta, A. (1980). A study of the relationship between individual differences in nonverbal expressiveness and factors of personality and social interaction. *Journal of Research in Personality, 14,* 351–364.

Friedman, L. M., Furberg, C. D., & DeMets, D. L. (1985). *Fundamentals of clinical trials* (2d ed.). Littleton, MA: PSG Publishing.

Friedman, M., & Rosenman, R. H. (1959). Association of specific overt behavior pattern with blood and cardiovascular findings: Blood cholesterol level, blood clotting time, incidence of arcus senilis and clinical coronary artery disease. *Journal of the American Medical Association, 169,* 1286–1296.

Friedman, M., & Rosenman, R. H. (1974). *Type A behavior and your heart.* New York: Knopf.

Friedman, M., Thoresen, C. E., Gill, J. J., Ulmer, D., Powell, L. H., Price, V. A., Brown, B., Thompson, L., Rabin, D. D., Breal, W. S., Bourg, E., Levy, R., & Dixon, T. (1986). Alteration of type A behavior and its effect on recurrences in post-myocardial infarction patients: Summary results of the recurrent coronary prevention project. *American Heart Journal, 112,* 653–665.

Friedman, S. B., Mason, J. W., & Hamburg, D. A. (1963). Urinary 17-hydroxycorticosteroid levels in parents of children with neoplastic diseases: A study of chronic psychological stress. *Psychosomatic Medicine, 25,* 364–376.

Frumkin, L. R., & Leonard, J. M. (1987). *Questions and answers on AIDS.* Oradell, NJ: Medical Economics Books.

Fry, W. F., Jr. (1979). Humor and the human cardiovascular system. In H. Mindress & J. Turek (Eds.), *The study of humor.* Los Angeles: Antioch University.

Fuller, R. K., Branchey, L., Brightwell, D. R., Derman, R. M., Emrick, C. D., Iber, F. L., James, K. E., Lacoursiere, R. B., Lee, K. K., Lowenstam, I., Maany, I., Neiderhiser, D., Knocks, J. J., & Shaw, S. (1986). Disulfiram treatment of alcoholism: A Veterans Administration cooperative study. *Journal of the American Medical Association, 256,* 1449–1455.

Funk, S. C., & Houston, B. K. (1987). A critical analysis of the hardiness scale's validity and utility. *Journal of Personality and Social Psychology, 53,* 572–578.

Furman, E. F. (1974). *A child's parent dies.* New Haven: Yale University Press.

Galton, L. (1973). *The silent disease: Hypertension.* New York: Crown Publishers.

Gamsa, A. (1990). Is emotional disturbance a precipitator or a consequence of chronic pain? *Pain, 42,* 183–195.

Gannon, L. R., Hayes, S. N., Ceuvas, J., & Chavez, R. (1987). Psychophysiological correlates of induced headache. *Journal of Behavioral Medicine, 10*, 411–423.

Garfinkel, L., Auerbach, O., & Joubert, L. (1985). Involuntary smoking and lung cancer: A case control study. *Journal of the National Cancer Institute, 75*, 463–469.

Garrett, D. N. (1978). The needs of the seriously ill and their families: The haven concept. *Aging, 6*(1), 12–19.

Garrett, L. (1988). The biology of cancer. In M. Renneker (Ed.), *Understanding cancer* (3d ed.). Palo Alto, CA: Bull Publishing Co.

Garrison, W. T., & McQuiston, S. (1989). *Chronic illness during childhood and adolescence.* Newbury Park, CA: Sage.

Garrow, J. S. (1988). *Obesity and related diseases.* Edinburgh: Churchill Livingstone.

Gartner, A., & Riessman, F. (Eds.) (1984). *The self-help revolution.* New York: Human Sciences Press.

Geller, E. S., Kalsher, M. J., Rudd, J. R., & Lehman, G. R. (1989). Promoting safety belt use on a university campus: An integration of commitment and incentive strategies. *Journal of Applied Social Psychology, 19*, 3–19.

Genest, M. (1989). The relevance of stress to rheumatoid arthritis. In R. W. J. Neufeld (Ed.), *Advances in the investigation of psychological stress.* New York: Wiley.

Gentry, W. D., & Kobasa, S. C. O. (1984). Social and psychological resources mediating stress-illness relationships in humans. In W. D. Gentry (Ed.), *Handbook of behavioral medicine.* New York: Guilford.

Gerberding, J. L., & Sande, M. A. (1989). Human immunodeficiency virus: Issues in infection control. In I. B. Corless & M. Pittman-Lindeman (Eds.), *AIDS: Principles, practices, and politics* (Ref. ed.). New York: Hemisphere.

Gerberding, J. L., & Schecter, W. P. (1991). Surgery and AIDS: Reducing the risk. *Journal of the American Medical Association, 265*, 1572–1573.

Gerbert, B., Maguire, B., Badner, V., Altman, D., & Stone, G. (1988). Why fear persists: Health care professionals and AIDS. *Journal of the American Medical Association, 260*, 3481–3483.

Gesser, G., Wong, P. T. P., & Reker, G. T. (1987). Death attitudes across the life-span: The development and validation of the death attitude profile (DAP). *Omega, 18*, 113–128.

Gewanter, H. L., Roghmann, K. J., & Baum, J. (1983). The prevalence of juvenile arthritis. *Arthritis and Rheumatism, 26*, 599–603.

Ghanta, V. K., Hiramoto, R. N., Solvason, H. B., & Spector, N. H. (1985). Neural and environmental influences on neoplasia and conditioning of NK activity. *Journal of Immunology, 135*(Suppl. 2), 848s–852s.

Giacobini, E., & Becker, R. (1989). Advances in the therapy of Alzheimer's disease. In G. D. Miner, R. W. Richter, J. P. Blass, J. L. Valentine, & L. A. Winters-Miner (Eds.), *Familial Alzheimer's disease: Molecular genetics and clinical perspectives.* New York: Marcel Dekker.

Gibbs, N. (1989). Sick and tired: Uneasy patients may be surprised to find that their doctors are worried too. *Time,* July 31, 48–53.

Gil, K. M., Keefe, F. J., Crisson, J. E., & Van Dalfsen, P. J. (1987). Social support and pain behavior. *Pain, 29*, 209–217.

Gill, J. J., Price, V. A., Friedman, M., Thoresen, C. E., Powell, L. H., Ulmer, D., Brown, B., & Drews, F. R. (1985). Reduction of Type A behavior in healthy middle-aged American military officers. *American Heart Journal, 110*, 503–514.

Gillum, R. F., Feinleib, M., Margolis, M. D., Fabsitz, M. A., & Brasch, M. D. (1976). Delay in the prehospital phase of acute myocardial infarction: Lack of influence on incidence of sudden death. *Archives of Internal Medicine, 136*, 649–654.

Gillum, R. F., Taylor, H. L., Brozek, J., Polansky, P., & Blackburn, H. (1982). Indices of obesity and blood pressure in young men followed 32 years. *Journal of Chronic Disease, 35*, 211–219.

Ginzberg, E. (1983). Allied health resources. In D. Mechanic (Ed.), *Handbook of health, health care, and the health professions.* New York: Free Press.

Gitlow, L. E. (1973). Alcoholism: A disease. In P. G. Bourne & R. Fox (Eds.), *Alcoholism progress in research and treatment.* New York: Academic Press.

Glaser, B. G., & Strauss, A. L. (1968). *Time for dying.* Chicago: Aldine.

Glaser, R., Thorn, B. E., Tarr, K. L., Kiecolt-Glaser, J. K., & D'Ambrosio, S. M. (1985). Effects of stress on methyltransferase synthesis: An important DNA repair enzyme. *Health Psychology, 4*, 403–412.

Glass, D. C. (1977). *Behavior patterns, stress, and coronary disease.* Hillsdale, NJ: Erlbaum.

Glass, D. C. (1989). Psychology and health: Obstacles and opportunities. *Journal of Applied Social Psychology, 19*, 1145–1163.

Glick, I. O., Weiss, R. S., & Parkes, C. M. (1974). *The first year of bereavement.* New York: Wiley.

"Gloomy figures from WHO" (1991). *WorldAIDS, No. 16*, 5.

Goedert, J. J., Duliege, A. M., Amos, C. I., Felton, S., & Biggar, R. J. (1991). High risk of HIV-1 infection for first-born twins. The International Registry of HIV-exposed Twins. *Lancet, 338*(8781), 1471–1475.

Goethals, G. R. (1986). Social comparison theory: Psychology from the lost and found. *Personality and Social Psychology Bulletin, 12*, 261–278.

Goffman, E. (1961). *Asylums*. Garden City, NY: Doubleday.

Gofman, H., Buckman, W., & Schade, G. (1957). The child's emotional response to hospitalization. *American Journal of Diseases of Children, 93*, 157–164.

Goldfarb, L. A., Brotherson, M. J., Summers, J. A., & Turnbull, A. P. (1986). *Meeting the challenge of disability or chronic illness—A family guide*. Baltimore: Paul H. Brooks Publishing Co.

Goldman, L., Shah, M. V., & Hebden, M. W. (1987). Memory of cardiac anaesthesia. *Anaesthesia, 42*, 596–603.

Gonder-Frederick, L., & Cox, D. J. (1991). Symptom perception, symptom-beliefs, and blood glucose discrimination in the self-treatment of insulin-dependent diabetes. In J. A. Skelton & R. T. Croyle (Eds.), *Mental representation in health and illness*. New York: Springer–Verlag.

Gonder-Frederick, L. A., Cox, D. J., Bobbitt, S. A., & Pennebaker, J. W. (1986). Blood glucose symptom beliefs of diabetic patients: Accuracy and implications. *Health Psychology, 5*, 327–341.

Good, M.-J. D., Good, B. J., & Nassi, A. J. (1983). Patient requests in primary health care settings: Development and validation of a research instrument. *Journal of Behavioral Medicine, 6*, 151–168.

Goodenow, C., Reisine, S. T., & Grady, K. E. (1990). Quality of social support and associated social and psychological functioning in women with rheumatoid arthritis. *Health Psychology, 9*, 266–284.

Gordis, L. (1979). Conceptual and methodologic problems in measuring patient compliance. In R. B. Haynes, D. W. Taylor, & D. L. Sackett (Eds.), *Compliance in health care*. Baltimore: Johns Hopkins University Press.

Gordon, J. S. (1980). The paradigm of holistic medicine. In A. C. Hastings, J. Fadiman, & J. S. Gordon (Eds.), *Health for the whole person*. Boulder, CO: Westview Press.

Gordon, W. A., Greidenbergs, I., Diller, L., Hibbard, M., Wolf, C., Levine, L., Lipkins, R., Ezrachi, O., & Lucido, D. (1980). Efficacy of psychosocial intervention with cancer patients. *Journal of Consulting and Clinical Psychology, 48*, 743–759.

Gore, S. (1978). The effect of social support in moderating the health consequences of unemployment. *Journal of Health and Social Behavior, 19*, 157–165.

Gori, G. B., & Richter, B. J. (1978). Macroeconomics of disease prevention in the United States. *Science, 200*, 1124–1130.

Gortmaker, S. L., Eckenrode, J., & Gore, S. (1982). Stress and utilization of health services: A time series and cross-sectional analysis. *Journal of Health and Social Behavior, 23*, 25–38.

Gould, K. L., Ornish, D., Kirkeeide, R., Brown, S., Stuart, Y., Buchi, M., Billings, J., Armstrong, W., Ports, T., & Scherwitz, L. (1992). Improved stenosis geometry by quantitative coronary arteriography after vigorous risk factor modification. *American Journal of Cardiology, 69*, 845–853.

Gracely, R. H., Dubner, R., Wolskee, P. J., and Deeter, W. R. (1983). Placebo and naloxone can alter post-surgical pain by separate mechanisms. *Nature, 306*, 264–265.

Grady, K. E. (1984). Cue enhancement and the long-term practice of breast self-examination. *Journal of Behavioral Medicine, 7*, 191–204.

Grady, K. E., Goodenow, C., & Borkin, J. R. (1988). The effect of reward on compliance with breast self-examination. *Journal of Behavioral Medicine, 11*, 43–57.

Graff-Radford, S. B., Reeves, J. L., & Jaeger, B. (1987). Management of chronic head and neck pain: Effectiveness of altering factors perpetuating myofacial pain. *Headache, 27*, 186–190.

Graham, R. W. (1989). Adult day care: How families of the dementia patient respond. *Journal of Gerontological Nursing, 15*, 27–31.

Grant, D., & Anns, M. (1988). Counseling AIDS antibody-positive clients: Reactions and treatment. *American Psychologist, 43*, 72–74.

Greer, H. S., Morris, T., & Pettingale, K. W. (1979). Psychological response to breast cancer: Effect on outcome. *Lancet, 2*, 785–787.

Grevert, P., Albert, L. H., & Goldstein, A. (1983). Partial antagonism of placebo analgesia by naloxone. *Pain, 16*, 129–143.

Grevert, P., & Goldstein, A. (1985). Placebo analgesia, naloxone, and the role of endogenous opioids. In L. White, B. Turksy, and G. E. Schwartz (Eds.), *Placebo: Theory, research, and mechanisms*. New York: Guilford Press.

Grossman, M. (1989). Pediatric AIDS. In I. B. Corless & M. Pittman-Lindeman (Eds.), *AIDS: Principles, practices, & politics* (Ref. ed.). New York: Hemisphere.

Grunberg, N. E., Sibolboro, E. C., & Talmadge, S. A. (1988). *Stress and eating: Restraint, sex, and specific foods are important*. Paper presented at the American Psychological Association Convention.

Gwinn, M., Pappaioanou, M., George, J. R., Hannon, W. H., Wasser, S. C., Redus, M. A., Hoff, R., Grady, G. F., Willoughby, A., Novello, A. C., Petersen, L. R., Dondero, T. J., & Curran, J. W. (1991). Prevalence of HIV infection in childbearing women in the United States. *Journal of the American Medical Association, 265*, 1704–1708.

Hackett, T. P., & Cassem, N. H. (1984). Psychologic aspects of rehabilitation after myocardial infarction and coronary artery bypass surgery. In N. K. Wenger & H. K. Hellerstein (Eds.), *Rehabilitation of the coronary patient*. New York: Wiley.

Hall, J. A., Roter, D. L., & Rand, C. S. (1981). Communication of affect between patient and physician. *Journal of Health and Social Behavior, 22,* 18–30.

Hall, R. A., Rappaport, M., Hopkins, H. K., & Griffin, R. (1973). Tobacco and evoked potential. *Science, 180,* 212–214.

Hansen, W. B., Graham, J. W., Sobel, J. L., Shelton, D. R., Flay, B. R., & Johnson, C. A. (1987). The consistency of peer and parent influences on tobacco, alcohol, and marijuana use among young adolescents. *Journal of Behavioral Medicine, 10,* 559–579.

Hanson, C. L., Henggeler, S. W., Harris, M. A., Burghen, G. A., & Moore, M. (1989). Family system variables and the health status of adolescents with insulin-dependent diabetes mellitus. *Health Psychology, 8,* 239–253.

Hanson, S. L., & Pichert, J. W. (1986). Perceived stress and diabetes control in adolescents. *Health Psychology, 5,* 439–452.

Harburg, E., Blakelock, E. H., & Roeper, P. J. (1979). Resentful and reflective coping with arbitrary authority and blood pressure: Detroit. *Psychosomatic Medicine, 41,* 189–202.

Hardy, C. J., & Riehl, R. E. (1988). An examination of the life-stress-injury relationship among noncontact sports participants. *Behavioral Medicine, 14,* 113–118.

Hardy, J. D., & Smith, T. W. (1988). Cynical hostility and vulnerability to disease: Social support, life stress, and physiological response to conflict. *Health Psychology, 7,* 447–459.

Harlan, W. R. (1984). Rationale for intervention on blood pressure in childhood and adolescence. In J. D. Matarazzo, S. M. Weiss, J. A. Herd, N. E. Miller, & S. M. Weiss (Eds.), *Behavioral health: A handbook of health enhancement and disease prevention.* New York: Wiley.

Harlan, W. R., Hull, A. L., Schmouder, R. L., Landis, J. R., Thompson, F. E., & Larkin, F. A. (1984). Blood pressure and nutrition in adults: The National Health and Nutrition Examination Survey. *American Journal of Epidemiology, 120,* 17–28.

Harrison, J. (1978). Warning: The male role may be dangerous to your health. *Journal of Social Issues, 34,* 65–86.

Haynes, R. B. (1979a). Determinants of compliance: The disease and the mechanics of treatment. In R. B. Haynes, D. W. Taylor, & D. L. Sackett (Eds.), *Compliance in health care.* Baltimore: Johns Hopkins University Press.

Haynes, R. B. (1979b). Strategies to improve compliance with referrals, appointments, and prescribed medical regimens. In R. B. Haynes, D. W. Taylor, & D. L. Sackett (Eds.), *Compliance in health care.* Baltimore: Johns Hopkins University Press.

Haynes, S. G., & Feinleib, M. (1980). Women, work, and coronary heart disease: Prospective findings from the Framingham Heart Study. *American Journal of Public Health, 70,* 133–141.

Haynes, S. G., Feinleib, M., & Kannel, W. B. (1980). The relationship of psychosocial factors to coronary heart disease. *American Journal of Epidemiology, 3,* 37–58.

Haynes, S. G., Levine, S., Scotch, N., Feinleib, M., & Kannel, W. B. (1978). The relationship of psychosocial factors to coronary heart disease in the Framingham Study. I. Methods and risk factors. *American Journal of Epidemiology, 107,* 362–383.

Haynes, S. N., Gannon, L. R., Bank, J., Shelton, D., & Goodwin, J. (1990). Cephalic blood flow correlates of induced headaches. *Journal of Behavioral Medicine, 13,* 467–480.

Hazzard, A., Hutchinson, S. J., & Krawiecki, N. (1990). Factors related to adherence to medical regimens in pediatric seizure patients. *Journal of Pediatric Psychology, 15,* 543–555.

Health Care Information Network (1989). *Responding to HIV and AIDS.* Atlanta: Author.

Health Resources and Services Administration (1986). *Health status of the disadvantaged: Chartbook 1986.* DHHS Publication No. (HRSA) HRS-P-DV86-2. Washington, DC: U.S. Government Printing Office.

"Heart disease is public health enemy No. 1: WHO" (1992). *Straits Times,* April 9, 11.

Heaton, R. K. (Ed.) (1988). Special series: Cardiovascular disease. *Journal of Consulting and Clinical Psychology, 56,* 323–392.

Heckler, M. M. (1985). Psychology in the public forum: The fight against Alzheimer's disease. *American Psychologist, 40,* 1240–1244.

Heien, D. M., & Pittman, D. J. (1989). The economic costs of alcohol abuse: An assessment of current methods and estimates. *Journal of Studies on Alcohol, 50,* 567–579.

Heitzmann, C. A., & Kaplan, R. M. (1988). Assessment of methods for measuring social support. *Health Psychology, 7,* 75–109.

Helsing, K. J., Szklo, M., & Comstock, G. W. (1981). Factors associated with mortality after widowhood. *American Journal of Public Health, 71,* 802–809.

Hendrick, S. S. (1985). Behavioral medicine approaches to diabetes mellitus. In N. Schneiderman & J. T. Tapp (Eds.), *Behavioral medicine: The biopsychosocial approach.* Hillsdale, NJ: Erlbaum.

Hennekens, C. H., & Buring, J. E. (1987). *Epidemiology in medicine.* Boston: Little, Brown and Company.

Hennig, P., & Knowles, A. (1990). Factors influencing women over 40 years to take precautions against cervical cancer. *Journal of Applied Social Psychology, 20,* 1612–1621.

Herd, J. A., & Hartley, L. H. (1984). Hypertension and exercise: The role of physical conditioning in treatment and prevention. In J. D. Matarazzo, S. M. Weiss, J. A. Herd, N. E. Miller, & S. M. Weiss (Eds.), *Behavioral health: A handbook of health enhancement and disease prevention.* New York: Wiley.

Herd, J. A., & Weiss, S. M. (1984). Overview of hypertension: Its treatment and prevention. In J. D. Matarazzo, S. M. Weiss, J. A. Herd, N. E. Miller, & S. M. Weiss (Eds.), *Behavioral health: A handbook of health enhancement and disease prevention.* New York: Wiley.

Herek, G. M. (1989). Hate crimes against lesbians and gay men. *American Psychologist, 44,* 948–955.

Herek, G. M., & Glunt, E. K. (1988). An epidemic of stigma: Public reactions to AIDS. *American Psychologist, 43,* 886–891.

Hess, E. (1988). Rheumatoid arthritis: Treatment. In H. R. Schumacher, J. H. Klippel, & D. R. Robinson (Eds.), *Primer on the rheumatic diseases* (9th ed.). Atlanta: Arthritis Foundation.

Heyward, W. L., & Curran, J. W. (1988). The epidemiology of AIDS in the U.S. *Scientific American, 259*(4), 72–81.

Hilgard, E. R. (1977). *Divided consciousness: Multiple controls in human thought and action.* New York: Wiley-Interscience.

Hill, H. F., Chaptman, C. R., Kornell, J. A., Sullivan, K. M., Seager, L. C., & Benedetti, C. (1990). Self-administration of morphine in bone marrow transplant patients reduces drug requirement. *Pain, 40,* 121–129.

Hilton, B. A. (1989). The relationship of uncertainty, control, commitment, and threat of recurrence to coping strategies used by women diagnosed with breast cancer. *Journal of Behavioral Medicine, 12,* 39–54.

Hinrichsen, G. A., Revenson, T. A., & Shinn, M. (1985). Does self–help help? An empirical investigation of scoliosis peer support groups. *Journal of Social Issues, 41,* 65–87.

Hinkley, J. J., Craig, H. K., & Anderson, L. A. (1990). Communication characteristics of provider-patient information exchanges. In H. Giles & W. P. Robinson (Eds.), *Handbook of language and social psychology.* Chichester, England: Wiley.

Hinton, J. M. (1967). *Dying.* Baltimore: Penguin.

Hirschman, R. S., & Leventhal, H. (1989). Preventing smoking behavior in school children: An initial test of a cognitive-development program. *Journal of Applied Social Psychology, 19,* 559–583.

"HIV infects more than a million people in 8 months." (1992). *Global AIDSNews: The Newsletter of the World Health Organization Global Programme on AIDS, No. 1,* 4.

Hobfoll, S. E., & Leiberman, J. R. (1987). Personality and social resources in immediate and continued stress resistance among women. *Journal of Personality and Social Psychology, 52,* 18–26.

Holahan, C. J., & Moos, R. H. (1985). Life stress and health: Personality, coping, and family support in stress resistance. *Journal of Personality and Social Psychology, 49,* 739–747.

Holahan, C. K., Holahan, C. J., & Belk, S. S. (1984). Adjustment in aging: The roles of life stress, hassles, and self-efficacy. *Health Psychology, 3,* 315–328.

Holleb, A. I. (Ed.) (1986). *The American Cancer Society cancer book: Prevention, detection, diagnosis, treatment, rehabilitation, cure.* Garden City, NY: Doubleday.

Holm, L. E. (1990). Cancer occurring after radiotherapy and chemotherapy. *International Journal of Radiation: Oncology, Biology, and Physics, 19,* 1303–1308.

Holmes, D. S., & Houston, B. K. (1974). Effectiveness of situation redefinition and affective isolation in coping with stress. *Journal of Personality and Social Psychology, 29,* 212–218.

Holmes, J. A., & Stevenson, C. A. (1990). Differential effects of avoidant and attentional coping strategies on adaptation to chronic and recent-onset pain. *Health Psychology, 9,* 577–584.

Holmes, T. H., & Rahe, R. H. (1967). The social readjustment rating scale. *Journal of Psychosomatic Research, 11,* 213–218.

Holroyd, K. A., Penzien, D. B., Hursey, K. G., Tobin, D. L., Rogers, L., Holm, J. E., Marcille, P. J., Hall, J. R., & Chila, A. G. (1984). Change mechanisms in EMB biofeedback training: Cognitive changes underlying improvements in tension headache. *Journal of Consulting and Clinical Psychology, 52,* 1039–1053.

Horan, M. J., & Roccella, E. J. (1988). Nonpharmacologic treatment of hypertension in the United States. *Health Psychology, 7,* 267–282.

Horne, R. L., & Picard, R. S. (1979). Psychosocial risk factors for lung cancer. *Psychosomatic Medicine, 41,* 503–514.

Horowitz, M. J., Scheafer, C., Hiroto, D., Wilner, N., & Levin, B. (1977). Life event questionnaires for measuring presumptive stress. *Psychosomatic Medicine, 39,* 413–431.

Houston, B. K. (1983). Psychophysiological responsivity and the type A behavior pattern. *Journal of Research in Personality, 17,* 22–39.

Hovanitz, C. A., Chin, K., & Warm, J. S. (1989). Complexities in life stress-dysfunction relationships: A case in point—tension headaches. *Journal of Behavioral Medicine, 12,* 55–75.

Hovland, C. I., & Weiss, W. (1951). The influence of source credibility on communication effectiveness. *Public Opinion Quarterly, 15,* 635–650.

Howell, R. H., Owen, P. D., & Nocks, E. C. (1990). Increasing safety belt use: Effects of modeling and trip length. *Journal of Applied Social Psychology, 20,* 254–263.

Hsing, A. W., McLaughlin, J. K., Schuman, L. M., Bjelke, E., Gridley, G., Wacholder, S., Chien, H. T., & Blot, W. J. (1990). Diet, tobacco use, and fatal prostate cancer: Results from the Lutheran Brotherhood Cohort Study. *Cancer Research, 50,* 6836–6840.

Huber, P. S. (1980). Death and society among the Anggor of New Guinea. In R. A. Kalish (Ed.), *Death and dying: Views from many cultures.* Farmingdale, NY: Baywood Publishing Co.

Hubert, H. B., Feinleib, M., McNamara, P. M., & Castelli, W. P. (1983). Obesity as an independent risk factor for cardiovascular disease: A 26-year follow-up of participants in the Framingham Heart Study. *Circulation, 67,* 968–977.

Hudgens, R. W. (1974). Personal catastrophe and depression. In B. S. Dohrenwend & B. P. Dohrenwend (Eds.), *Stressful events: Their nature and effects.* New York: Wiley.

Hull, J. G., Van Treuren, R. R., & Virnelli, S. (1987). Hardiness and health: A critique and alternative approach. *Journal of Personality and Social Psychology, 53,* 518–530.

Hunt, L. M., Jordan, B., Irwin, S., & Browner, C. H. (1989). Compliance and the patient's perspective: Controlling symptoms in everyday life. *Culture, Medicine and Psychiatry, 13,* 315–334.

Hunt, W. A., Barnett, L. W., & Ranch, L. G. (1971). Relapse rates in addiction programs. *Journal of Clinical Psychology, 27,* 455–456.

Hunt, W. A., Matarazzo, J. D., Weiss, S. M., & Gentry, W. D. (1979). Associative learning, habit, and health behavior. *Journal of Behavioral Medicine, 2,* 111–123.

Hurst, M. W., Jenkins, C. D., & Rose, R. M. (1978). The assessment of life change stress: A comparative and methodological inquiry. *Psychosomatic Medicine, 40,* 126–141.

Huskisson, E. C. (1974). Measurement of pain. *Lancet, 2,* 1127–1131.

Hutter, R. V. P. (1988). Cancer prevention and detection: Status report and future prospects. *Cancer, 61,* 2372–2378.

Illich, I. (1975). *Medical nemesis: The expropriation of health.* London: Calder & Boyars.

Institute of Medicine (1986). *Confronting AIDS: Directions for public health, health care, and research.* Washington, DC: National Academy Press.

Irwin, M., Daniels, M., Smith, T. L., Bloom, E., & Weiner, H. (1987). Impaired natural killer cell activity during bereavement. *Brain, Behavior, and Immunity, 1,* 98–104.

Jaccard, J. J., & Davidson, A. R. (1975). A comparison of two models of social behavior: Results of a survey sample. *Sociometry, 38,* 491–517.

Jacob, R. G., Chesney, M. A., Williams, D. M., Ding, Y., & Shapiro, A. P. (1991). Relaxation therapy for hypertension: Design effects and treatment effects. *Annals of Behavioral Medicine, 13,* 5–17.

Jacobson, E. J. (1938). *Progressive relaxation.* Chicago: University of Chicago Press.

James, S. A., Hartnett, S. A., & Kalsbeek, W. D. (1983). John Henryism and blood pressure differences among black men. *Journal of Behavioral Medicine, 6,* 259–278.

James, S. A., LaCroix, A. Z., Kleinbaum, D. G., & Strogatz, D. S. (1984). John Henryism and blood pressure differences among black men. II. The role of occupational stressors. *Journal of Behavioral Medicine, 7,* 259–275.

Jamieson, J. L., & Lavoie, N. F. (1987). Type A behavior, aerobic power, and cardiovascular recovery from a psychosocial stressor. *Health Psychology, 6,* 361–371.

Janis, I. L. (1967). Effects of fear arousal on attitude change: Recent developments in theory and experimental research. In L. Berkowitz (Ed.), *Advances in experimental social psychology,* Vol. 3. New York: Academic Press.

Janis, I. L. (1984). Improving adherence to medical recommendations: Prescriptive hypotheses derived from recent research in social psychology. In A. Baum, S. E. Taylor, & J. E. Singer (Eds.), *Handbook of psychology and health,* Vol. 4. Hillsdale, NJ: Erlbaum.

Janis, I. L., & Feshbach, S. (1953). Effects of fear–arousing communications. *Journal of Abnormal and Social Psychology, 48,* 78–92.

Janis, I. L., & Rodin, J. (1979). Attribution, control, and decision making: Social psychology and health care. In G. C. Stone, F. Cohen, & N. E. Adler (Eds.), *Health psychology—A handbook.* San Francisco: Jossey–Bass.

Janssen, R. S. (1989). HIV and the nervous system. In I. B. Corless & M. Pittman-Lineman (Eds.), *AIDS: Principles, practices, & politics* (Ref. ed.). New York: Hemisphere.

Jarvik, M. E. (1973). Further observations on nicotine as the reinforcing agent in smoking. In W. L. Dunn, Jr. (Ed.), *Smoking behavior: Motives and incentives.* Washington, DC: V. H. Winston.

Jasnoski, M. L., & Schwartz, G. E. (1985). A synchronous systems model for health. *American Behavioral Scientist, 28,* 468–485.

Jeffery, R. W. (1988). Dietary risk factors and their modification in cardiovascular disease. *Journal of Consulting and Clinical Psychology, 56,* 350–357.

Jeffery, R. W. (1991). Weight management and hypertension. *Annals of Behavioral Medicine, 13,* 18–22.

Jellinek, E. M. (1960). *The disease concept of alcoholism.* New Haven: Hillhouse Press.

Jemmott, J. B., Borysenko, J. Z., Borysenko, M., McClelland, D. C., Chaptman, R., Meyer, D., & Benson, H. (1983). Academic stress, power motivation, and decrease in salivary secretory immunoglobulin A secretion rate. *Lancet, 1,* 1400–1402.

Jemmott, J. B., Jemmott, L. S., & Fong, G. T. (1990, August). *HIV infection and adolescents: A behavioral intervention.* Paper presented at the American Psychological Association Convention, Boston, MA.

Jemmott, J. B., & Locke, S. E. (1984). Psychosocial factors, immunologic mediation, and human susceptibility to infectious disease: How much do we know? *Psychological Bulletin, 95,* 78–108.

Jemmott, J. B., & Magloire, K. (1988). Academic stress, social support, and secretory immunoglobulin A. *Journal of Personality and Social Psychology, 55,* 803–810.

Jenkins, C. D. (1988). Epidemiology of cardiovascular diseases. *Journal of Consulting and Clinical Psychology, 56,* 324–332.

Jenkins, C. D., Zyzanski, S. J., & Rosenman, R. H. (1971). Progress toward validation of a computer-scored test for the type A coronary-prone behavior pattern. *Psychosomatic Medicine, 33,* 193–202.

Jenkins, C. D., Zyzanski, S. J., & Rosenman, R. H. (1979). *Jenkins Activity Survey.* Cleveland, OH: Psychological Corp.

Jennings, D. (1986). The confusion between disease and illness in clinical medicine. *Canadian Medical Association Journal, 135,* 865–870.

Jensen, T. S., & Rasmussen, P. (1989). Phantom pain and related phenomena after amputation. In P. D. Wall & R. Melzack (Eds.), *Textbook of pain* (2d ed.). Edinburgh: Churchill Livingstone.

Jessup, B. A. (1982). Psychophysiological factors in the treatment of the stress of pain: Biofeedback. In R. W. J. Neufeld (Ed.), *Psychological stress and psychopathology.* New York: McGraw-Hill.

Jessup, J. A. (1989). Relaxation and biofeedback. In P. D. Wall & R. Melzack (Eds.), *Textbook of pain* (2d ed.). Edinburgh: Churchill Livingstone.

Joasoo, A., & McKenzie, J. M. (1976). Stress and the immune response in rats. *International Archives of Allergy and Applied Immunology, 50,* 659–663.

Johnson, C. A., Hansen, W. B., Collins, L. M., & Graham, J. W. (1986). High-school smoking prevention: Results of a three-year longitudinal study. *Journal of Behavioral Medicine, 9,* 439–452.

Johnson, J. E. (1984). Psychological interventions and coping with surgery. In A. Baum, S. E. Taylor, & J. E. Singer (Eds.), *Handbook of psychology and health. Vol. IV: Social psychological aspects of health.* Hillsdale, NJ: Erlbaum.

Johnson, J. E., Lauver, D. R., & Nail, L. (1989). Process of coping with radiation therapy. *Journal of Consulting and Clinical Psychology, 57,* 358–364.

Johnson, J. E., Rice, V. H., Fuller, S. S., & Endress, M. P. (1978). Sensory information, instruction in a coping strategy, and recovery from surgery. *Research in Nursing and Health, 1,* 4–17.

Johnson, J. H., & Sarason, I. G. (1979). Moderator variables in life stress research. In I. G. Sarason & C. D. Speilberger (Eds.), *Stress and anxiety* (Vol. 6). New York: Wiley.

Johnson, M. I., Aston, C. H., & Thompson, J. W. (1991). An in-depth study of long-term users of transcutaneous electrical nerve stimulation (TENS): Implications for clinical use of TENS. *Pain, 44,* 221–229.

Johnson, S. B. (1980). Psychosocial factors in juvenile diabetes: A review. *Journal of Behavioral Medicine, 3,* 96–116.

Jones, S. L., Jones, P. K., & Katz, J. (1988). Health belief model intervention to increase compliance with emergency department patients. *Medical Care, 26,* 1172–1184.

Joseph, J. G., Montgomery, S. B., Emmons, C.-A., Kessler, R. C., Ostrow, D. G., Wortman, C. B., O'Brien, K., Eller, M., & Eshleman, S. (1987). Magnitude and determinants of behavioral risk reduction: Longitudinal analysis of a cohort at risk for AIDS. *Psychology and Health, 1,* 73–96.

Justice, A. (1985). Review of the effects of stress on cancer in laboratory animals: Importance of time of stress application and type of tumor. *Psychological Bulletin, 98,* 108–138.

Kabat-Zinn, J., Lipworth, L., & Burney, R. (1985). The clinical use of mindfulness meditation for the self-regulation of chronic pain. *Journal of Behavioral Medicine, 8,* 163–190.

Kamarck, T., & Jennings, J. R. (1991). Biobehavioral factors in sudden cardiac death. *Psychological Bulletin, 109,* 42–75.

Kandil, O., & Borysenko, M. (1987). Decline of natural killer cell activity and lytic activity in mice exposed to rotation stress. *Health Psychology, 6,* 89–99.

Kanner, A. D., Coyne, J. C., Schaefer, C., & Lazarus, R. S. (1981). Comparison of two modes of stress management: Daily hassles and uplifts versus major life events. *Journal of Behavioral Medicine, 4,* 1–39.

Kanner, R. (1986). Pain management. *Journal of the American Medical Association, 256,* 2110–2114.

Kaplan, H. (1983). *Peptic ulcer.* New York: Medical Examination Publishing Co.

Kaplan, H. I. (1975). Current psychodynamic concepts in psychosomatic medicine. In R. O. Pasnau (Ed.), *Consultation-liaison psychiatry.* New York: Grune & Stratton.

Kaplan, H. S. (1987). *The real truth about women and AIDS.* New York: Simon & Schuster.

Kaplan, R. M. (1984). The connection between clinical health promotion and health status: A critical overview. *American Psychologist, 39,* 755–765.

Karoly, P. (1985). The assessment of pain: Concepts and procedures. In P. Karoly (Ed.), *Measurement strategies in health psychology*. New York: Wiley.

Karon, J. M., & Dondero, T. J. (1990). HIV prevalence estimates and AIDS case projections for the United States: Report based on a workshop. *Morbidity and Mortality Weekly Report, 39*(No. RR-16), 1–31.

Kasl, S. V., & Cobb, S. (1964). Some psychological factors associated with illness behavior and selected illnesses. *Journal of Chronic Disease, 17*, 325–345.

Kasl, S. V., & Cobb, S. (1966). Health behavior, illness behavior, and sick role behavior. *Archives of Environmental Health, 12*, 246–266.

Kastenbaum, R. (1979). "Healthy dying": A paradoxical quest continues. *Journal of Social Issues, 35*, 185–206.

Kastenbaum, R. (1982). The psychologist and hospital policy. *American Psychologist, 37*, 1355–1358.

Kastenbaum, R. (1991). *Death, society, and human experience* (4th ed.). New York: Merrill.

Kastenbaum, R., & Aisenberg, R. (1976). *The psychology of death* (Concise edition). New York: Springer.

Katz, E. R., Kellerman, J., & Ellenberg, L. (1987). Hypnosis in the reduction of acute pain and distress in children with cancer. *Journal of Pediatric Psychology, 12*, 379–394.

Katz, E. R., Kellerman, J., & Siegel, S. E. (1980). Behavioral distress in children with cancer undergoing medical procedures: Developmental considerations. *Journal of Consulting and Clinical Psychology, 48*, 356–365.

Katz, R. C., & Singh, N. N. (1986). Reflections on the ex-smoker: Some findings on successful quitters. *Journal of Behavioral Medicine, 9*, 191–202.

Kaufmann, P. G., Jacob, R. G., Ewart, C. K., Chesney, M. A., Muenz, L. R., Doub, N., Mercer, W., & HIPP Investigators (1988). Hypertension Intervention Pooling Project. *Health Psychology, 7*, 209–224.

Kazdin, A. E. (1980). *Research design in clinical psychology*. New York: Harper & Row.

Keesling, B., & Friedman, H. S. (1987). Psychosocial factors in sunbathing and sunscreen use. *Health Psychology, 6*, 477–493.

Kellner, R. (1987). Hypochondriasis and somatization. *Journal of the American Medical Association, 258*, 2717–2722.

Kelly, J. A., St. Lawrence, J. S., & Brasfield, T. L. (1991). Predictors of vulnerability to AIDS risk behavior relapse. *Journal of Consulting and Clinical Psychology, 59*, 163–166.

Kelly, J. A., St. Lawrence, J. S., Brasfield, T. L., Lemke, A., Amidei, T., Roffman, R. E., Hood, H. V., Smith, J. E., Kilgore, H., & McNeill, C. (1990). Psychological factors that predict AIDS high-risk versus AIDS precautionary behavior. *Journal of Consulting and Clinical Psychology, 58*, 117–120.

Kelly, J. A., St. Lawrence, J. S., Hood, H. V., & Brasfield, T. L. (1989). Behavioral intervention to reduce AIDS risk activities. *Journal of Consulting and Clinical Psychology, 57*, 60–67.

Kelman, H. C. (1972). The rights of subjects in social research: An analysis in terms of relative power and legitimacy. *American Psychologist, 27*, 989–1016.

Keltikangas-Jarvinen, L. (1989). Stability of type A behavior during adolescence, young adulthood, and adulthood. *Journal of Behavioral Medicine, 12*, 387–396.

Kemeny, E., Hovell, M. F., Mewborn, C. R., Dockter, B., & Chin, L. (1988). Breast self-examination: The effects of prescribed frequency on adherence, accuracy, and detection ability. *American Journal of Preventive Medicine, 4*, 140–145.

Kendall, P. C., & Turk, D. C. (1984). Cognitive-behavioral strategies and health enhancement. In J. D. Matarazzo, S. M. Weiss, J. A. Herd, N. E. Miller, & S. M. Weiss (Eds.), *Behavioral health: A handbook of health enhancement and disease prevention*. New York: Wiley.

Kent, G. (1986). Hypnosis in dentistry. *British Journal of Experimental and Clinical Hypnosis, 3*, 103–112.

Kiecolt-Glaser, J. K., Fisher, L. D., Ogrocki, P., Stout, J. C., Speicher, C. E., & Glaser, R. (1987). Marital quality, marital disruption, and immune function. *Psychosomatic Medicine, 49*, 13–34.

Kiecolt-Glaser, J. K., & Glaser, R. (1988). Methodological issues in behavioral immunology research with humans. *Brain, Behavior, and Immunity, 2*, 67–78.

Kiecolt-Glaser, J. K., Glaser, R., Strain, E. C., Stout, J. C., Tarr, K. L., Holliday, J. E., & Speicher, C. E. (1986). Modulation of cellular immunity in medical students. *Journal of Behavioral Medicine, 9*, 5–21.

Kiecolt-Glaser, J. K., Glaser, R., Williger, D., Stout, J., Messick, G., Sheppard, S., Ricker, D., Romisher, S. C., Briner, W., Bonnell, G., Donnerberg, R. (1985). Psychosocial enhancement of immunocompetence in a geriatric population. *Health Psychology, 4*, 25–41.

Kiecolt-Glaser, J. L., Stephens, R. E., Lipetz, P. D., Speicher, C. E., & Glaser, R. (1985). Distress and DNA repair in human lymphocytes. *Journal of Behavioral Medicine, 8*, 311–320.

Kiecolt-Glaser, J. K., & Williams, D. A. (1987). Self-blame, compliance, and distress among burn patients. *Journal of Personality and Social Psychology, 53*, 187–193.

Kiesler, C. A., & Morton, T. L. (1988). Psychology and public policy in the "health care revolution." *American Psychologist, 43*, 993–1003.

Kincey, J. A., Bradshaw, P. W., & Ley, P. (1975). Patient satisfaction and reported acceptance of advice in general practice. *Journal of the Royal College of General Practitioners, 25,* 558–566.

Kindelan, K., & Kent, G. (1986). Patients' preferences for information. *Journal of the Royal College of General Practitioners, 36,* 461–463.

Kindelan, K., & Kent, G. (1987). Concordance between patients' information preferences and general practitioners' perceptions. *Psychology and Health, 1,* 399–409.

King, K., & Hanson, V. (1986). Psychosocial aspects of juvenile rheumatoid arthritis. *Pediatric Clinics of North America, 33,* 1221–1237.

Kirp, D. L. (1988). *Learning by heart.* New Brunswick, NJ: Rutgers University Press.

Kirschenbaum, D. S., Wittrock, D. A., Smith, R. A., & Monson, W. (1984). Criticism inoculation training: Concepts in search of strategy. *Journal of Sport Psychology, 6,* 77–93.

Kirscht, J. P. (1983). Preventive health behavior: A review of research and issues. *Health Psychology, 2,* 277–301.

Kirscht, J. P., Becker, M., Haefner, D., & Maiman, L. (1978). Effects of threatening communications and mothers' health beliefs on weight change in obese children. *Journal of Behavioral Medicine, 1,* 147–157.

Kirscht, J. P., & Rosenstock, I. M. (1979). Patients' problems in following recommendations of health experts. In G. C. Stone, F. Cohen, & N. E. Adler (Eds.), *Health psychology—A handbook.* San Francisco: Jossey-Bass.

Kirwan, E. O'G. (1989). Back pain. In P. D. Wall & R. Melzack (Eds.), *Textbook of pain* (2d ed.). Edinburgh: Churchill Livingstone.

Kittel, F. (1984). The Interuniversity Study on Nutrition and Health. In J. D. Matarazzo, S. M. Weiss, J. A. Herd, N. E. Miller, & S. M. Weiss (Eds.), *Behavioral health: A handbook of health enhancement and disease prevention.* New York: Wiley.

Klass, D. (1986). Marriage and divorce among bereaved parents in a self-help group. *Omega, 17,* 237–249.

Klass, D., & Marwit, S. J. (1988). Toward a model of parental grief. *Omega, 19,* 31–50.

Klatsky, A. L., Friedman, G. D., & Siegelaub, A. B. (1981). Alcohol and mortality: A ten-year Kaiser-Permanente experience. *Annals of Internal Medicine, 95,* 139–145.

Klesges, R. C., Brown, K., Pascale, R. W., Murphy, M., Williams, E., & Cigrang, J. A. (1988). Factors associated with participation, attrition, and outcome in a smoking cessation program at the workplace. *Health Psychology, 7,* 575–589.

Kline, F. G., Miller, P., & Morrison, A. (1974). Adolescents and family planning information: An exploration of audience needs and media effects. In J. Blumler & E. Katz (Eds.), *The uses of mass communications: Current perspectives on gratifications research.* Beverly Hills, CA: Sage.

Knowles, J. (1977). *Doing better and feeling worse: Health in the United States.* New York: Norton.

Kobasa, S. C. (1979). Stressful life events, personality and health: An inquiry into hardiness. *Journal of Personality and Social Psychology, 37,* 1–11.

Kobasa, S. C. (1982a). Commitment and coping in stress resistance among lawyers. *Journal of Personality and Social Psychology, 42,* 707–717.

Kobasa, S. C. (1982b). The hardy personality: Toward a social psychology of stress and health. In G. S. Sanders & J. Suls (Eds.), *Social psychology of health and illness.* Hillsdale, NJ: Erlbaum.

Kobasa, S. C., Maddi, S. R., & Kahn, S. (1982). Hardiness and health: A prospective study. *Journal of Personality and Social Psychology, 42,* 168–177.

Kobasa, S. C., Maddi, S. R., & Puccetti, M. C. (1982). Personality and exercise as buffers in the stress-illness relationship. *Journal of Behavioral Medicine, 5,* 391–404.

Kobasa, S. C., Maddi, S. R., & Zola, M. A. (1983). Type A and hardiness. *Journal of Behavioral Medicine, 6,* 41–51.

Kobasa, S. C., & Puccetti, M. C. (1983). Personality processes and individual differences: Personality and social resources in stress resistance. *Journal of Personality and Social Psychology, 45,* 839–850.

Kolbe, L. J., & Iverson, D. C. (1984). Comprehensive school health education programs. In J. D. Matarazzo, S. M. Weiss, J. A. Herd, N. E. Miller, & S. M. Weiss (Eds.), *Behavioral health: A handbook of health enhancement and disease prevention.* New York: Wiley.

Koocher, G. (1973). Childhood, death, and cognitive development. *Developmental Psychology, 9,* 369–375.

Koop, C. E. (1989). Responding to the patient who has AIDS. *Academic Medicine, 64,* 113–115.

Koplan, J. P., Caspersen, C. J., Powell, K. E. (1989). Physical activity, physical fitness, and health: Time to act. *Journal of the American Medical Association, 262,* 2437.

Korsch, B. M., Gozzi, E. K., & Francis, V. (1968). Gaps in doctor-patient communication: I. Doctor-patient interaction and patient satisfaction. *Pediatrics, 42,* 855–871.

Korsch, B. M., & Negrete, V. F. (1972). Doctor-patient communication. *Scientific American, 227*(2), 66–74.

Kozlowsky, L. T., Wilkinson, D. A., Skinner, W., Kent, C., Franklin, T., & Pope, M. (1989). Comparison of tobacco cigarette dependence with other drug dependencies: Greater or equal "difficulty quitting" and "urges to use," but less "pleasure" from cigarettes. *Journal of the American Medical Association, 261,* 898–901.

Krainick, J.-U., & Thoden, U. (1989). Spinal cord stimulation. In P. D. Wall & R. Melzack (Eds.), *Textbook of pain* (2d ed.). Edinburgh: Churchill Livingstone.

Krantz, D. S., Contrada, R. J., Hill, D. R., & Friedler, E. (1988). Environmental stress and biobehavioral antecedents of coronary heart disease. *Journal of Consulting and Clinical Psychology, 56,* 333–341.

Krantz, D. S., Grunberg, N. E., & Baum, A. (1985). Health psychology. *Annual Review of Psychology, 36,* 349–383.

Krantz, D. S., & Manuck, S. B. (1984). Acute psychophysiologic reactivity and risk of cardiovascular disease: A review and methodologic critique. *Psychological Bulletin, 96,* 435–464.

Kristiansen, C. M. (1985). Value correlates of preventive health behavior. *Journal of Personality and Social Psychology, 49,* 748–758.

Kroner, K., Krebs, B., Skov, J., & Jorgensen, H. S. (1989). Immediate and long-term phantom breast syndrome after mastectomy: Incidence, clinical characteristics and relationship to pre-mastectomy breast pain. *Pain, 36,* 327–334.

Kübler-Ross, E. (1969). *On death and dying.* New York: Macmillan.

Kuiken, D., & Madison, G. (1987). The effects of death contemplation on meaning and purpose in life. *Omega, 18,* 103–112.

Kulik, J. A., & Carlino, P. (1987). The effect of verbal commitment and treatment choice on medication compliance in a pediatric setting. *Journal of Behavioral Medicine, 10,* 367–376.

Kulik, J. A., & Mahler, H. I. M. (1989). Social support and recovery from surgery. *Health Psychology, 8,* 221–238.

Kurdek, L. A., & Siesky, G. (1990). The nature and correlates of psychological adjustment in gay men with AIDS-related conditions. *Journal of Applied Social Psychology, 20,* 846–860.

LaCroix, J. M., & Corbett, L. (1990). An experimental test of the muscle tension hypothesis of tension-type headache. *International Journal of Psychophysiology, 10,* 47–51.

LaGreca, A. M. (1982). Behavioral aspects of diabetes management in children and adolescents (Abstract). *Diabetes, 31,* 47. (Cited in LaGreca, 1987).

LaGreca, A. M. (1987). Children with diabetes and their families: Coping and disease management. In T. M. Field, P. M. McCabe, & N. Schneiderman (Eds.), *Stress and coping across development.* Hillsdale, NJ: Erlbaum.

Lambert, W. E., Libman, E., & Poser, E. G. (1960). The effect of increased salience of a membership group on pain tolerance. *Journal of Personality, 38,* 350–357.

Lancaster, H. O. (1990). *Expectations of life: A study in the demography, statistics, and history of world mortality.* New York: Springer-Verlag.

Langer, E. J. (1983). *The psychology of control.* Beverly Hills: Sage.

Langer, E. J., Janis, I. L., & Wolfer, J. A. (1975). Reduction of psychological stress in surgical patients. *Journal of Experimental Social Psychology, 11,* 155–165.

Langer, E. J., & Rodin, J. (1976). The effects of choice and enhanced personal responsibility for the aged: A field experiment in an institutional setting. *Journal of Personality and Social Psychology, 34,* 191–198.

Langman, R. E. (1989). *The immune system.* San Diego: Academic Press.

Laragh, J. H. (1988). A modern plan for treating hypertension. *Health Psychology, 7,* 253–265.

Larsson, B., Melin, L., Lamminen, M., & Ullstedt, F. (1987). A school-based treatment of chronic headaches in adolescents. *Journal of Pediatric Psychology, 12,* 553–566.

Lasater, T., Abrams, D., Artz, L., Beaudin, P., Cabrera, L., Elder, J., Ferreira, A., Knisley, P., Peterson, G., Rodrigues, A., Rosenberg, P., Snow, P., & Carleton, R. (1984). Lay volunteer delivery of a community-based cardiovascular risk factor change program: The Pawtucket experiment. In J. D. Matarazzo, S. M. Weiss, J. A. Herd, N. E. Miller, & S. M. Weiss (Eds.), *Behavioral health: A handbook of health enhancement and disease prevention.* New York: Wiley.

Laszlo, J. (1987). *Understanding cancer.* New York: Harper & Row.

Lau, R. R., Hartman, K. A., & Ware, J. E. (1986). Health as a value: Methodological and theoretical considerations. *Health Psychology, 5,* 25–43.

Lau, R. R., Kane, R., Berry, S., Ware, J., & Roy, D. (1980). Channeling health: A review of the evaluation of televised health campaigns. *Health Education Quarterly, 7,* 56–89.

Lavey, R. S., & Taylor, C. B. (1985). The nature of relaxation therapy. In S. R. Burchfield (Ed.), *Stress: Psychological and physiological interactions.* Washington, DC: Hemisphere.

Lazarus, R. S. (1980). The stress and coping paradigm. In C. Eisdorfer, D. Cohen, & A. Kleinman (Eds.), *Conceptual models for psychopathology.* New York: Spectrum.

Lazarus, R. S., & Alfert, E. (1964). Short-circuiting of threat by experimentally altering cognitive appraisal. *Journal of Abnormal and Social Psychology, 69,* 195–205.

Lazarus, R. S., Averill, J. R., & Opton, E. M., Jr. (1970). Toward a cognitive theory of emotions. In M. Arnold (Ed.), *Feelings and emotions.* New York: Academic Press.

Lazarus, R. S., & Cohen, J. B. (1977). Environmental stress. In I. Altman & J. F. Wohlwill (Eds.), *Human behavior and the environment: Current theory and research.* New York: Plenum.

Lazarus, R. S., Cohen, J. B., Folkman, S., Kanner, A., & Schaefer, C. (1980). Psychological stress and adaptation: Some unresolved issues. In H. Selye (Ed.), *Selye's guide to stress research,* Vol. 1. New York: Van Nostrand Reinhold.

Lazarus, R. S., DeLongis, A., Folkman, S., & Gruen, R. (1985). Stress and adaptational outcomes: The problem of confounded measures. *American Psychologist, 40,* 770–779.

Lazarus, R. S., & Folkman, S. (1984). *Stress, appraisal, and coping.* New York: Springer.

Lazarus, R. S., Speisman, J. C., Mordkoff, A. M., & Davidson, L. A. (1962). A laboratory study of psychological stress produced by a motion picture film. *Psychological Monographs, 76* (34, Whole No. 553).

Lee, D. D.-P., DeQuattro, V., Allen, J., Kimura, S., Aleman, E., Konugres, G., & Davison, G. (1988). Behavioral versus beta-blocker therapy in patients with primary hypertension: Effects on blood pressure, left ventricular function and mass, and the pressor surge of social stress anger. *American Heart Journal, 116,* 637–644.

Lehrer, P. M., & Murphy, A. I. (1991). Stress reactivity and perception of pain among tension headache sufferers. *Behaviour Research and Therapy, 29,* 61–69.

Leiker, M., & Hailey, B. J. (1988). A link between hostility and disease: Poor health habits. *Behavioral Medicine, 14,* 129–133.

Lennon, M. C., Martin, J. L., & Dean, L. (1990). The influence of social support on AIDS-related grief reaction among gay men. *Social Science and Medicine, 31,* 477–484.

Leon, G. R. (1979). Cognitive-behavior therapy for eating disturbances. In P. C. Kendall & S. D. Hollon (Eds.), *Cognitive behavioral intervention: Theory, research, and procedures.* New York: Academic Press.

Leon, M. B., & Cohen, L. S. (1984). Guidelines for patient management. In N. K. Wenger & H. K. Hellerstein (Eds.), *Rehabilitation of the coronary patient* (2d ed.). New York: Wiley.

Leonardo, C., & Chrisler, J. C. (in press). Women and sexually transmitted diseases. *Women and Health.*

LeShan, L. (1977). *You can fight for your life.* New York: Harcourt Brace Jovanovich.

Lessler, J., Tourangeau, R., & Salter, W. (1989). Questionnaire design in the cognitive research laboratory. *Vital and Health Statistics. Series 6: Cognition and Survey Measurement.* No. 1. National Center for Health Statistics, Hyattsville, MD.

Levenkron, J. C., & Moore, L. G. (1988). The type A behavior pattern: Issues for intervention and research. *Annals of Behavioral Medicine, 10,* 78–83.

Leventhal, E., Leventhal, H., Shacham, S., & Easterling, D. V. (1989). Active coping reduces reports of pain from childbirth. *Journal of Consulting and Clinical Psychology, 57,* 365–371.

Leventhal, E., & Prohaska, T. R. (1986). Age, symptom interpretation, and health behavior. *Journal of the American Geriatrics Society, 34,* 185–191.

Leventhal, H. (1970). Findings and theory in the study of fear communications. In L. Berkowitz (Ed.), *Advances in experimental social psychology,* Vol. 5. New York: Academic Press.

Leventhal, H. (1983). Behavioral medicine: Psychology in health care. In D. Mechanic (Ed.), *Handbook of health, healthcare, and the health professions.* New York: Free Press.

Leventhal, H., Brown, D., Shacham, S., & Engquist, G. (1979). Effects of preparatory information about sensations, threat of pain, and attention on cold pressor distress. *Journal of Personality and Social Psychology, 37,* 688–714.

Leventhal, H., & Cleary, P. D. (1980). The smoking problem: A review of the research and theory in behavioral risk modification. *Psychological Bulletin, 88,* 370–405.

Leventhal, H., & Diefenbach, M. (1991). The active side of illness cognition. In J. A. Skelton & R. T. Croyle (Eds.), *Mental representation in health and illness.* New York: Springer-Verlag.

Leventhal, H., Meyer, D. R., & Nerenz, D. (1980). The common sense representation of illness danger. In S. Rachman (Ed.), *Contributions to medical psychology* (Vol. 2). Oxford: Pergamon Press.

Leventhal, H., Nerenz, D. R., & Steele, D. J. (1984). Illness representations and coping with health threats. In A. Baum, S. E. Taylor, & J. E. Singer (Eds.), *Handbook of psychology and health. Vol. 4: Social psychological aspects of health.* Hillsdale, NJ: Erlbaum.

Leventhal, H., Nerenz, D. R., & Straus, A. (1982). Self-regulation and the mechanisms of symptom appraisal. In D. Mechanic (Ed.) *Symptoms, illness behavior, and help-seeking.* New York: Prodist.

Leventhal, H., Prohaska, T. R., & Hirschman, R. S. (1985). Preventive health behavior across the life-span. In J. C. Rosen & L. J. Solomon (Eds.), *Prevention in health psychology.* Hanover, NH: University Press of New England.

Levine, J. D., Gordon, N. C., & Fields, H. L. (1978). The mechanism of placebo analgesia. *Lancet, 2,* 654–657.

Levinson, B. W. (1965). States of awareness during general anaesthesia. *British Journal of Anaesthesiology, 37,* 544–546.

Levy, M. H. (1988). Pain control research in the terminally ill. *Omega, 18,* 265–279.

Levy, S. M. (1983). Host differences in neoplastic risk: Behavioral and social contributors to disease. *Health Psychology, 2,* 21–44.

Levy, S. M., Herberman, R. B., Lippman, M. N., & d'Angelo, T. (1987). Correlation of stress factors with sustained depression of natural killer cell activity and predicted prognosis in patients with breast cancer. *Journal of Clinical Oncology, 5,* 348–353.

Levy, S. M., Herberman, R. B., Maluish, A. M., Schlien, B., & Lippman, M. (1985). Prognostic risk assessment in primary breast cancer by behavioral and immunological parameters. *Health Psychology, 4,* 99–113.

Levy, S. M., Lee, J., Bagley, C., & Lippman, M. (1988). Survival hazards analysis in first recurrent breast cancer patients: Seven-year follow-up. *Psychosomatic Medicine, 50,* 520–528.

Lewinsohn, P. M., Mermelstein, R. M., Alexander, C., & MacPhillamy, D. J. (1985). The unpleasant events schedule: A scale for the measurement of aversive events. *Journal of Clinical Psychology, 41,* 483–498.

Lewis, F. M. (1990). Strengthening family supports. Cancer and the family. *Cancer, 65,* 752–759.

Lewis, G. (1981). Cultural influences on illness behavior: A medical anthropological approach. In L. Eisenberg & A. Kleinman (Eds.), *The relevance of social science for medicine.* Dordrecht, Holland: D. Reidel.

Lewis, G. M., Woods, N. F., Hough, E. E., & Bensley, L. S. (1989). The family's functioning with chronic illness in the mother: The spouse's perspective. *Social Science and Medicine, 29,* 1261–1269.

Ley, P., & Spelman, M. S. (1965). Communication in an outpatient setting. *British Journal of Social and Clinical Psychology, 4,* 114–116.

Lichstein, L., & Sackett, G. P. (1971). Reactions by differentially raised rhesus monkeys to noxious stimulations. *Developmental Psychobiology, 4,* 339–352.

Lichtenstein, E., & Mermelstein, R. J. (1984). Review of approaches to smoking treatment: Behavior modification strategies. In J. D. Matarazzo, S. M. Weiss, J. A. Herd, N. E. Miller, & S. M. Weiss (Eds.), *Behavioral health: A handbook of health enhancement and disease prevention.* New York: Wiley.

Lichtenstein, E., Weiss, S. M., Hitchcock, J. L., Leveton, L. B., O'Connell, K. A., & Prochaska, J. O. (1986). Patterns of smoking relapse. *Health Psychology, 5*(Suppl.), 29–40.

Lieberman, M. A. (1988). The role of self-help groups in helping patients and families cope with cancer. *CA, 38,* 162–168.

Lilienfeld, A. M. (1980). *Foundations of epidemiology.* New York: Oxford University Press.

Lin, N., Simeone, R. S., Ensel, W. M., & Kuo, W. (1979). Social support, stressful life events, and illness: A model and an empirical test. *Journal of Health and Social Behavior, 20,* 108–119.

Linville, P. W. (1987). Self-complexity as a cognitive buffer against stress-related illness and depression. *Journal of Personality and Social Psychology, 52,* 663–676.

Lipowski, Z. J. (1977). Psychosomatic medicine in the seventies: An overview. *American Journal of Psychiatry, 134,* 233–244.

Litt, M. D. (1988). Self-efficacy and perceived control: Cognitive mediators of pain tolerance. *Journal of Personality and Social Psychology, 54,* 149–160.

Littlefield, C. H., & Rushton, J. P. (1986). When a child dies: The sociobiology of bereavement. *Journal of Personality and Social Psychology, 51,* 797–802.

Lloyd, R. (1987). *Explorations in psychoneuroimmunology.* Orlando, FL: Grune & Stratton.

Locke, S. E., Kraus, L., Leserman, J., Hurst, M. W., Heisel, J. S., & Williams, R. M. (1984). Life change stress, psychiatric symptoms, and natural killer-cell activity. *Psychosomatic Medicine, 46,* 441–453.

Loftus, E. F., Feinberg, S. E., & Tanur, J. M. (1985). Cognitive psychology meets the national survey. *American Psychologist, 40,* 175–180.

Long, R. T., Lamont, J. H., Whipple, B., Bandler, L., Blom, G. E., Burgin, L., & Jessner, L. (1958). A psychosomatic study of allergic and emotional factors in children with asthma. *American Journal of Psychiatry, 114,* 890–899.

Lopez, A. D. (1990). Competing causes of death: A review of recent trends in industrialized countries with special reference to cancer. *Annals of the New York Academy of Sciences, 609,* 58–74.

Lorber, J. (1979). Good patients and problem patients: Conformity and deviance in a general hospital. In E. G. Jaco (Ed.), *Patients, physicians, and illness* (3d ed.). New York: Free Press.

Lorig, K., & Fries, J. (1980). *The arthritis helpbook.* Reading, MA: Addison-Wesley.

Lorig, K., & Fries, J. (1986). *The arthritis helpbook* (Rev. ed.). Reading, MA: Addison-Wesley.

Love, A. W., & Peck, C. L. (1987). The MMPI and psychological factors in chronic low back pain: A review. *Pain, 28,* 1–12.

Love, R., Nerenz, D., & Leventhal, H. (1983). Anticipatory nausea with cancer chemotherapy: Development through two mechanisms. *Proceedings of the American Society for Clinical Oncology, 2,* 62.

Lovibond, S. H., Birrell, P. C., & Langeluddecke, P. (1986). Changing coronary heart disease risk-factor status: The effects of three behavioral programs. *Journal of Behavioral Medicine, 9,* 415–438.

Luepker, R. V., Johnson, C. A., Murray, D. M., & Pechacek, T. F. (1983). Prevention of cigarette smoking: Three-year follow-up of an education program for youth. *Journal of Behavioral Medicine, 6,* 53–62.

Lukert, B. (1982). Biology of obesity. In B. B. Wolman (Ed.), *Psychological aspects of obesity: A handbook.* New York: Van Nostrand Reinhold.

Lund, A. K., & Kegeles, S. S. (1982). Increasing adolescents' acceptance of long-term personal health behavior. *Health Psychology, 1,* 27–43.

Lund, A. K., & Kegeles, S. S. (1984). Rewards and adolescent health behavior. *Health Psychology, 3,* 351–369.

Lundberg, U. (1983). Note on type A behavior and cardiovascular responses to challenge in 3–6-year-old children. *Journal of Psychosomatic Research, 27,* 39–42.

Lynch, J. J. (1977). *The broken heart: The medical consequences of loneliness.* New York: Basic Books.

Maccoby, N., Farquhar, J. W., Wood, P. D., & Alexander, J. K. (1977). Reducing the risks of cardiovascular disease: Effects of a community-based campaign on knowledge and behavior. *Journal of Community Health, 3,* 100–114.

Macdonald, A. J. R. (1989). Acupuncture analgesia and therapy. In P. D. Wall & R. Melzack (Eds.), *Textbook of pain* (2d ed.). Edinburgh: Churchill Livingstone.

Maddux, J. E., & Rogers, R. W. (1983). Protection motivation and self-efficacy: A revised theory of fear appeals and attitude change. *Journal of Experimental Social Psychology, 19,* 469–479.

Mages, N. L., & Mendelsohn, G. A. (1979). Effects of cancer on patients' lives: A personological approach. In G. C. Stone, F. Cohen, & N. E. Adler (Eds.), *Health psychology—A handbook.* San Francisco: Jossey-Bass.

Magrab, P., & Papadopoulou, Z. L. (1977). The effect of a token economy on dietary compliance for children on hemodialysis. *Journal of Applied Behavioral Analysis, 10,* 573–578.

Mahoney, M. J., & Arnkoff, D. B. (1979). Self-management. In O. F. Pomerleau & J. P. Brady (Eds.), *Behavioral medicine: Theory and practice.* Baltimore: Williams and Wilkins.

Mahoney, M. J., Moura, N. G. M., & Wade, T. C. (1973). The relative efficacy of self-reward, self-punishment, and self-monitoring techniques for weight loss. *Journal of Consulting and Clinical Psychology, 40,* 404–407.

Maletta, G. J., & Hepburn, K. (1986). Helping families cope with Alzheimer's: The physician's role. *Geriatrics, 41*(11), 81–90.

Malinowsky, H. R., & Perry, G. J. (Eds.) (1988). *AIDS information sourcebook.* Phoenix: Oryx Press.

Mandler, G. (1975). *Mind and emotion.* New York: Wiley.

Mann, J. M., Chin, J., Piot, P., & Quinn, T. (1988). The international epidemiology of AIDS. *Scientific American, 259*(4), 60–69.

Manne, S., Sandler, I., & Zautra, A. (1986). Coping and adjustment to genital herpes: The effects of time and social support. *Journal of Behavioral Medicine, 9,* 163–177.

Marcus, R., Kay, K., & Mann, J. M. (1989). Transmission of human immunodeficiency virus (HIV) in health-care settings worldwide. *Bulletin of the World Health Organization, 67,* 577–582.

Marks, G., Richardson, J. L., Graham, J. W., & Levine, A. (1986). Role of health locus of control beliefs and expectations of treatment efficacy in adjustment to cancer. *Journal of Personality and Social Psychology, 51,* 443–450.

Marlatt, G. A. (1979). Alcohol use and problem drinking: A cognitive-behavioral analysis. In P. C. Kendall & S. D. Hollon (Eds.), *Cognitive–behavioral interventions: Theory, research, and procedures.* New York: Academic Press.

Marlatt, G. A. (1983). The controlled-drinking controversy: A commentary. *American Psychologist, 38,* 1097–1110.

Marlatt, G. A. (1985). Relapse prevention: Theoretical rationale and overview of the model. In G. A. Marlatt & J. R. Gordon (Eds.), *Relapse prevention: Maintenance strategies in the treatment of addictive behaviors.* New York: Guilford Press.

Marshall, E. (1986). Diet advice, with a grain of salt and a large helping of pepper. *Science, 231,* 537–539.

Martelli, M. F., Auerbach, S. M., Alexander, J., & Mercuri, L. G. (1987). Stress management in the health care setting: Matching interventions with patient coping styles. *Journal of Consulting and Clinical Psychology, 55,* 201–207.

Martin, J. E., & Dubbert, P. M. (1982). Exercise applications and promotion in behavioral medicine: Current status and future directions. *Journal of Consulting and Clinical Psychology, 50,* 1004–1017.

Martin, J. L. (1988). Psychological consequences of AIDS-related bereavement among gay men. *Journal of Consulting and Clinical Psychology, 56,* 856–862.

Martin, R. A., & Lefcourt, H. M. (1983). Sense of humor as a moderator of the relation between stressors and moods. *Journal of Personality and Social Psychology, 45,* 1313–1324.

Marty, M. E. (1982). Watch your language. *Context, April 15,* 6.

Maruta, T., Swanson, D. W., & McHardy, M. J. (1990). Three year follow-up of patients with chronic pain who were treated in a multidisciplinary pain management center. *Pain, 41,* 47–53.

Marzuk, P. M., Tierney, H., Tardiff, K., Gross, E. M., Morgan, E. B., Hsu, M.-A., Mann, J. J. (1988). Increased risk of suicide in persons with AIDS. *Journal of the American Medical Association, 259,* 1333–1337.

Masironi, R., & Rothwell, K. (1988). Worldwide smoking trends. In M. Aoki, S. Hisamichi, & S. Tominaga (Eds.), *Smoking and health 1987: Proceedings of the 6th World Conference on Smoking and Health.* Amsterdam: Excerpta Medica.

Maslach, C., & Jackson, S. E. (1982). Burnout in health professions: A social psychological analysis. In G. S. Sanders & J. Suls (Eds.), *Social psychology of health and illness.* Hillsdale, NJ: Erlbaum.

Mason, J. W. (1968). A review of psychoendocrine research on the sympathetic-adrenal medullary system. *Psychosomatic Medicine, 30,* 631–653.

Mason, J. W. (1971). A re-evaluation of the concept of "non-specificity" in stress theory. *Journal of Psychiatric Research, 8,* 323–333.

Mason, J. W. (1975a). A historical view of the stress field, Part I. *Journal of Human Stress, 1*(1), 6–12.

Mason, J. W. (1975b). A historical view of the stress field, Part II. *Journal of Human Stress, 1*(2), 22–36.

Massey, M. J., & Holland, J. C. (1990). Depression and the cancer patient. *Journal of Clinical Psychiatry, 51*(Suppl.), 12–17.

Masur, F. T. (1981). Adherence to health care regimens. In C. K. Prokop & L. A. Bradley (Eds.), *Medical psychology: Contributions to behavioral medicine.* New York: Academic Press.

Matarazzo, J. D. (1980). Behavioral health and behavioral medicine: Frontiers for a new health psychology. *American Psychologist, 35,* 807–817.

Matarazzo, J. D. (1984a). Behavioral health: A 1990 challenge for the health sciences professions. In J. D. Matarazzo, S. M. Weiss, J. A. Herd, N. E. Miller, & S. M. Weiss (Eds.), *Behavioral health: A handbook of health enhancement and disease prevention.* New York: Wiley.

Matarazzo, J. D. (1984b). Behavior immunogens and pathogens in health and illness. In B. L. Hammonds & C. J. Scheirer (Eds.), *Psychology and health: The masters lecture series,* Vol. 3. Washington, DC: American Psychological Association.

Matarazzo, J. D., Weiss, S. M., Herd, J. A., Miller, N. E., & Weiss, S. M. (Eds.) (1984). *Behavioral health: A handbook of health enhancement and disease prevention.* New York: Wiley.

Mather, A. D. (1985). AIDS update: Halting the "epidemic of fear." *Infectious Disease Reports, 2,* 1–3.

Mathieson, C. M., Stam, H. J., & Scott, J. P. (1991). The impact of a laryngectomy on the spouse: Who is better off? *Psychology and Health, 5,* 153–163.

Matthews, K. A. (1979). Efforts to control by children and adults with the type A coronary prone behavior pattern. *Child Development, 50,* 842–847.

Matthews, K. A. (1988). Coronary heart disease and type A behaviors: Update on and alternative to the Booth-Kewley and Friedman (1987) quantitative review. *Psychological Bulletin, 104,* 373–380.

Matthews, K. A., & Angulo, J. (1980). Measurement of the type A behavior pattern in children: Assessment of children's competitiveness, impatience-anger, and aggression. *Child Development, 54,* 1507–1512.

Matthews, K. A., & Avis, N. E. (1982). Psychologists in schools of public health: Current status, future prospects, and implications for other health settings. *American Psychologist, 37,* 949–954.

Matthews, K. A., & Carra, J. (1982). Suppression of menstrual distress symptoms: A study of type A behavior. *Personality and Social Psychology Bulletin, 8,* 146–151.

Matthews, K. A., & Haynes, S. G. (1986). Type A behavior pattern and coronary disease risk: Update and critical evaluation. *American Journal of Epidemiology, 123,* 923–960.

Matthews, K. A., & Jennings, J. R. (1984). Cardiovascular responses of boys exhibiting the type A behavior pattern. *Psychosomatic Medicine, 56,* 484–497.

Matthews, K. A., Seigel, J. M., Kuller, L. H., Thompson, M., & Varat, M. (1983). Determinants of decisions to seek medical treatment by patients with acute myocardial infarction symptoms. *Journal of Personality and Social Psychology, 44,* 1144–1156.

Matthews, K. A., Stoney, C. M., Rakaczky, C. J., & Jamison, W. (1986). Family characteristics and school achievements of type A children. *Health Psychology, 5,* 453–467.

Matthews, K. A., & Woodall, K. L. (1988). Childhood origins of overt type A behaviors and cardiovascular reactivity to behavioral stressors. *Annals of Behavioral Medicine, 10,* 71–77.

Mayer, J. A., & Frederiksen, L. W. (1986). Encouraging long-term compliance with breast self-examination: The evaluation of prompting strategies. *Journal of Behavioral Medicine, 9,* 179–189.

Mays, V. M., & Cochran, S. D. (1988). Issues in the perception of AIDS risk and risk reduction activities by black and Hispanic/Latina women. *American Psychologist, 43,* 949–957.

Mazullo, J. M., Lasagna, L., & Griner, P. F. (1974). Variations in interpretation of prescription instructions. *Journal of the American Medical Association, 227,* 929–930.

McAlister, A. L., Perry, C., Killen, J., Slinkard, L. A., & Maccoby, N. (1980). Pilot study of smoking, alcohol, and drug abuse prevention. *American Journal of Public Health, 70,* 719–721.

McAlister, A. L., Perry, C., & Maccoby, N. (1979). Adolescent smoking: Onset and prevention. *Pediatrics, 63,* 650–657.

McCabe, P. M., & Schneiderman, N. (1985). Psychophysiologic reactions to stress. In N. Schneiderman & J. T. Tapp (Eds.), *Behavioral medicine: The biopsychosocial approach.* Hillsdale, NJ: Erlbaum.

McCaul, K. D., & Malott, J. M. (1984). Distraction and coping with pain. *Psychological Bulletin, 95,* 516–533.

McDonell, J. R., Abell, N., & Miller, J. (1991). Family members' willingness to care for people with AIDS: A psychosocial assessment model. *Social Work, 36,* 43–53.

McGrady, A., Woerner, M., Bernal, G. A. A., & Higgins, J. T. (1987). Effect of biofeedback-assisted relaxation on blood pressure and cortisol levels in normotensives and hypertensives. *Journal of Behavioral Medicine, 10,* 301–310.

McGraw, M. (1963). *The neuromuscular maturation of the human infant.* New York: Harper.

McGuire, W. J. (1969). The nature of attitudes and attitude change. In G. Lindzey & E. Aronson (Eds.), *The handbook of social psychology* (2d ed., Vol. 3). Reading, MA: Addison-Wesley.

McKenna, R. J. (1988). Applied cancer prevention and the primary care giver: A challenge to the community. *Cancer, 61,* 2365–2371.

McKinlay, J. B. (1972). Some approaches and problems in the study of the use of services—An overview. *Journal of Health and Social Behavior, 13,* 115–152.

McKinlay, J. B. (1975). Who is really ignorant—Physician or patient? *Journal of Health and Social Behavior, 16,* 3–11.

McKinnon, W., Weisse, C. S., Reynolds, C. P., Bowles, C. A., & Baum, A. (1989). Chronic stress, leukocyte subpopulations, and humoral response to latent viruses. *Health Psychology, 8,* 389–402.

McKusick, L. (1988). The impact of AIDS on practitioner and client: Notes for the therapeutic relationship. *American Psychologist, 43,* 935–940.

McLarnon, L. D., & Kaloupek, D. G. (1988). Psychological investigation of genital herpes recurrence: Prospective assessment and cognitive-behavioral intervention for a chronic physical disorder. *Health Psychology, 7,* 231–249.

McMahon, C. E. (1976). The role of imagination in the disease process: Pre-Cartesian history. *Psychological Medicine, 6,* 179–184.

McMahon, C. E., & Hastrup, J. L. (1980). The role of imagination in the disease process: Post-Cartesian history. *Journal of Behavioral Medicine, 3,* 205–217.

McMorrow, M. J., & Foxx, R. M. (1983). Nicotine's role in smoking: An analysis of nicotine regulation. *Psychological Bulletin, 93,* 302–327.

McWaters, D. S., & Renneker, M. (1988). Chemotherapy, immunotherapy, and biological treatments of cancer. In M. Renneker (Ed.), *Understanding cancer* (3d ed.). Palo Alto, CA: Bull Publishing Co.

Mechanic, D. (1962). The concept of illness behavior. *Journal of Chronic Disease, 15,* 189–194.

Mechanic, D. (1972). Social psychologic factors affecting the presentation of bodily complaints. *New England Journal of Medicine, 286,* 1132–1139.

Mechanic, D. (1976). Stress, illness, and illness behavior. *Journal of Human Stress, 2*(2), 2–6.

Mechanic, D. (1978). *Medical sociology* (2d ed.). New York: Free Press.

Mechanic, D. (1979). The stability of health and illness behavior: Results from a 16-year follow-up. *American Journal of Public Health, 69,* 1142–1145.

Mechanic, D., & Volkart, E. H. (1961). Stress, illness behavior, and the sick role. *American Sociological Review, 26,* 51–58.

Meenan, R. F., Yelin, E. H., Nevitt, M., & Epstein, R. V. (1981). The impact of chronic disease: A sociomedical profile of rheumatoid arthritis. *Arthritis and Rheumatism, 245,* 544–549.

Meichenbaum, D. (1985). *Stress inoculation training.* New York: Pergamon.

Meichenbaum, D. H., & Jaremko, M. E. (Eds.) (1983). *Stress regulation and prevention.* New York: Plenum.

Meissner, H. I., Anderson, D. M., & Odenkirchen, J. C. (1990). Meeting the needs of significant others: Use of the Cancer Information Service. *Patient Education and Counseling, 15,* 171–179.

Melamed, B. G., & Siegel, L. J. (1975). Reduction of anxiety in children facing hospitalization and surgery by use of filmed modeling. *Journal of Consulting and Clinical Psychology, 43,* 511–521.

Melges, F. T. (1982). *Time and the inner future: A temporal approach to psychiatric disorders.* New York: Wiley.

Melick, M. E., Logue, J. N., & Frederick, C. J. (1982). Stress and disaster. In L. Goldberger, & S. Breznitz (Eds.), *Handbook of stress: Theoretical and clinical aspects.* New York: Free Press.

Melzack, R. (1975). The McGill Pain Questionnaire: Major properties and scoring methods. *Pain, 1,* 277–299.

Melzack, R. (1989). Folk medicine and the sensory modulation of pain. In P. D. Wall & R. Melzack (Eds.), *Textbook of pain* (2d ed.). Edinburgh: Churchill Livingstone.

Melzack, R., & Wall, P. D. (1965). Pain mechanisms: A new theory. *Science, 150,* 971–979.

Melzack, R., & Wall, P. D. (1982). *The challenge of pain.* New York: Basic Books.

Melzack, R., Weisz, A. Z., & Sprague, L. T. (1963). Stratagems for controlling pain: Contributions of auditory stimulation and suggestion. *Experimental Neurology, 8,* 239–247.

Menke, W. G. (1975). Medical identity: Change and conflict in professional roles. In T. Millon (Ed.), *Medical behavioral science.* Philadelphia: W. B. Saunders.

Merkner, S. A. (1990). Survivors share their grief. *San Antonio Express-News,* November 10, 1–G.

Merskey, H., & Boyd, D. (1978). Emotional adjustment and chronic pain. *Pain, 5,* 173–178.

Meyer, D., Leventhal, H., & Gutmann, M. (1985). Commonsense models of illness: The example of hypertension. *Health Psychology, 4,* 115–135.

Michael, M., Boyce, W. T., and Wilcox, A. J. (1984). *Biomedical bestiary: An epidemiologic guide to flaws and fallacies in the medical literature*. Boston: Little, Brown and Co.

Michela, J. L. (1987). Interpersonal and individual aspects of a husband's heart attack. In A. Baum & J. E. Singer (Eds.), *Handbook of psychology and health*. Vol 5. Hillsdale, NJ: Erlbaum.

Miller, K., & Watkinson, N. (1983). Recognition of words presented during general anaesthesia. *Ergonomics, 26*, 585–594.

Miller, N. E. (1983). Behavioral medicine: Symbiosis between laboratory and clinic. *Annual Review of Psychology, 34*, 1–31.

Miller, N. E. (1984). Learning: Some facts and needed research relevant to maintaining health. In J. D. Matarazzo, S. M. Weiss, J. A. Herd, N. E. Miller, & S. M. Weiss (Eds.), *Behavioral health: A handbook of health enhancement and disease prevention*. New York: Wiley.

Miller, S. M., & Mangan, C. E. (1983). Interacting effects of information and coping style in adapting to gynecologic stress: Should the doctor tell all? *Journal of Personality and Social Psychology, 45*, 223–236.

Miller, W. R. (1985). Motivation for treatment: A review with special emphasis on alcoholism. *Psychological Bulletin, 98*, 84–107.

Milmoe, S., Rosenthal, R., Blane, H. T., Chafetz, M. E., & Wolf, I. (1967). The doctor's voice: Postdictor of successful referral of alcoholic patients. *Journal of Abnormal Psychology, 72*, 78–84.

Miner, G. D., Richter, R. W., Blass, J. P., Valentine, J. L., & Winters-Miner, L. A. (1989). *Familial Alzheimer's disease: Molecular genetics and clinical perspectives*. New York: Marcel Dekker.

Mishnu, B., Schaffner, W., Horan, J. M., Wood, L. H., Hutcheson, R. H., & McNabb, P. C. (1990). A surgeon with AIDS: Lack of evidence of transmission to patients. *Journal of the American Medical Association, 264*, 467–470.

Mogielnicki, R. P., Neslin, S., Dulac, J., Balestra, D., Gillie, E., & Corson, J. (1986). Tailored media can enhance the success of smoking cessation clinics. *Journal of Behavioral Medicine, 9*, 141–161.

Monjan, A., & Collector, M. (1977). Stress-induced modulation of the immune response. *Science, 96*, 307–308.

Monroe, S. M. (1983). Major and minor life events as predictors of psychological distress: Further issues and findings. *Journal of Behavioral Medicine, 6*, 189–205.

Montano, D. E., & Taplin, S. H. (1991). A test of an expanded theory of reasoned action to predict mammography participation. *Social Science and Medicine, 32*, 733–741.

Monti, P. M., Abrams, D. B., Kadden, R. M., & Cooney, N. L. (1989). *Treating alcohol dependence: A coping skills training guide*. New York: Guilford Press.

Moos, R. H. (1982). Coping with acute health crises. In T. Millon, C. Green, & R. Meagher (Eds.), *Handbook of clinical health psychology*. New York: Plenum.

Moos, R. H., & Tsu, V. D. (1977). The crisis of physical illness: An overview. In R. H. Moos (Ed.), *Coping with physical illness*. New York: Plenum.

Mor, V., Greer, D. S., & Kastenbaum, R. (1988). *The hospice experiment: Is it working?* Baltimore: Johns Hopkins University Press.

Morin, S. F., & Batchelor, W. F. (1984). Responding to the psychosocial crisis of AIDS. *Public Health Reports, 99*, 4–9.

Morris, L. A., & Halperin, J. A. (1979). Effects of written drug information on patient knowledge and compliance: A literature review. *American Journal of Public Health, 69*, 47–52.

Morrison, A. F., Kline, F. G., & Miller, P. (1976). Aspects of adolescent information acquisition about drugs and alcohol topics. In R. Ortman (Ed.), *Communication research and drug education*. Beverly Hills, CA: Sage.

Morse, E. V., Simon, P. M., Coburn, M., Hyslop, N., Greenspan, D., & Balson, P. M. (1991). Determinants of subject compliance within an experimental anti-HIV drug protocol. *Social Science and Medicine, 32*, 1161–1167.

Moskop, J. C. (1989). AIDS and public health. In I. B. Corless & M. Pittman-Lindeman (Eds.), *AIDS: Principles, practices, and politics* (Ref. ed.). New York: Hemisphere.

Moskowitz, R. W., & Goldberg, V. M. (1988). Osteoarthritis. In H. R. Schumacher, J. H. Klippel, & D. R. Robinson (Eds.), *Primer on rheumatic diseases* (9th ed.). Atlanta: Arthritis Foundation.

Moss, A. J., & Parsons, V. L. (1985). Current estimates from the National Health Interview Survey, United States, 1985. *Vital and Health Statistics*, Series 10, No. 160. DHHS Pub. No. (PHS) 86-1588.

Moss, R. B., Moss, H. B., & Peterson, R. (1989). Microstress, mood, and natural killer-cell activity. *Psychosomatics, 30*, 279–283.

Moulton, J. M., Sweet, D. M., Temoshok, L., & Mandel, J. S. (1987). Attributions of blame and responsibility in relation to distress and health behavior change in persons with AIDS and AIDS-related complex. *Journal of Applied Social Psychology, 17*, 493–506.

MRFIT Study Group (1982). Multiple Risk Factor Intervention Trial: Risk factor changes and mortality results. *Journal of the American Medical Association, 248*, 1465–1477.

Mulcahy, R. (1983). *Beat heart disease! A cardiologist explains how you can help your heart and enjoy a healthier life.* Singapore: P. G. Publishing.

Muranaka, M., Monou, H., Suzuki, J., Lane, J. D., Anderson, N. B., Kuhn, C. M., Schanberg, S. M., McCown, N., & Williams, R. B., Jr. (1988). Physiological responses to catecholamine infusions in type A and type B men. *Health Psychology, 7,* 145–163.

Murphy, J. S. (1989). Women with AIDS: Sexual ethics in an epidemic. In I. B. Corless & M. Pittman-Lindeman (Eds.), *AIDS: Principles, practices, & politics* (Ref. ed.). New York: Hemisphere.

Murphy, P. A. (1986). Parental death in childhood and loneliness in young adults. *Omega, 17,* 219–228.

Murray, D. M., Pirie, P., Luepker, R. V., & Pallonen, U. (1989). Five- and six-year follow-up results from four seventh-grade smoking prevention strategies. *Journal of Behavioral Medicine, 12,* 207–218.

Nagy, M. H. (1948). The child's theories concerning death. *Journal of Genetic Psychology, 73,* 3–27.

Nathan, P. R., & Goldman, M. S. (1979). Problem drinking and alcoholism. In O. F. Pomerleau & J. P. Brady (Eds.), *Behavioral medicine: Theory and practice.* Baltimore: Williams and Wilkins.

Nathanson, C. (1977). Sex, illness, and medical care: A review of data, theory, and method. *Social Science and Medicine, 11,* 13–25.

National Center for Health Statistics (1987). *Physician contacts by sociodemographic and health characteristics: United States, 1982–83* (DHHS Pub. No. PHS 87-1589). Washington, DC: U.S. Government Printing Office.

National Center for Health Statistics (1988a). *Adult health practices in the United States and Canada. Vital and Health Statistics,* Series 5, No. 3 (DHHS Pub. No. 88-1479). Washington, DC: Public Health Service.

National Center for Health Statistics (1988b). *Health United States 1987* (DHHS Pub. No. PHS 88-1232). Washington, DC: Public Health Service.

National Center for Health Statistics (1988c). *Prevalence of selected chronic conditions, United States, 1983–85. Advance Data from Vital and Health Statistics.* No. 155 (DHHS Pub. No. PHS 88-1250). Washington, D.C.: Public Health Service.

National Center for Health Statistics (1988d). *Vital statistics of the United States, 1986, Vol. II, Mortality Part A* (DHHS Pub. No. PHS 88-1122). Washington, DC: Public Health Service.

National Center for Health Statistics (1989). *Health, United States, 1988* (DHHS Pub. No. PHS 89-1232). Washington, DC: Public Health Service.

National Center for Health Statistics (1990). *Vital statistics of the United States, 1987, Vol. II, Mortality, Part A.* Washington, DC: Public Health Service.

National Diabetes Data Group (1985). *Diabetes in America.* Washington, DC: U.S. Government Printing Office.

National Institute on Alcohol Abuse and Alcoholism (1987). *Alcohol and health: Sixth special report to the U.S. Congress* (DHHS Pub. No. ADM 87-1519). Washington, DC: Public Health Service.

National Institutes of Health (1984). Lowering blood cholesterol: National Institutes of Health Consensus Development Conference Statement. *Journal of the American Dietetic Association, 85,* 586–588.

Neale, J. M., Cox, D. S., Valdimarsdottir, H., & Stone, A. A. (1988). The relation between immunity and health: Comment on Pennebaker, Kiecolt-Glaser, and Glaser. *Journal of Consulting and Clinical Psychology, 56,* 636–637.

Newberry, B. H., Gildow, J., Wogan, J., & Reese, R. L. (1976). Inhibition of Huggans tumors by forced restraint. *Psychosomatic Medicine, 38,* 155–162.

Newcomb, M. D., & Harlow, L. L. (1986). Life events and substance use among adolescents: Mediating effects of perceived loss of control and meaninglessness in life. *Journal of Personality and Social Psychology, 51,* 564–577.

Newman, A. S., & Bertelson, A. D. (1986). Sexual dysfunction in diabetic women. *Journal of Behavioral Medicine, 9,* 261–270.

Newton, T. L., Temoshok, L., Haviland, J., & O'Leary, A. (1991, March). *Emotional expressions and social support in men with AIDS.* Paper presented at the Society of Behavioral Medicine Meeting, Washington, DC.

Nezu, A. M., Nezu, C. M., & Blissett, S. E. (1988). Sense of humor as a moderator of the relationship between stressful events and psychological distress: A prospective study. *Journal of Personality and Social Psychology, 54,* 520–525.

N'Galy, B., & Ryder, R. W. (1988). Epidemiology of HIV infection in Africa. *Journal of Acquired Immune Deficiency Syndromes, 1,* 551–558.

Nicholas, D. R. (1982). Prevalence of anticipatory nausea and emesis in cancer chemotherapy patients. *Journal of Behavioral Medicine, 5,* 461–463.

Nichols, E. K. (1989). *Mobilizing against AIDS.* Cambridge: Harvard University Press.

Nisbett, R. E., & Schacter, S. (1966). Cognitive manipulation of pain. *Journal of Experimental Social Psychology, 2,* 227–236.

Nisbett, R. E., & Wilson, T. D. (1977). Telling more than we can know: Verbal reports on mental processes. *Psychological Review, 84,* 231–259.

Norbeck, J. S., & Tilden, V. P. (1983). Life stress, social support, and emotional disequilibrium in complications of pregnancy: A prospective, multivariate study. *Journal of Health and Social Behavior, 24,* 30–46.

Norman, N. M., & Tedeschi, J. T. (1989). Self-presentation, reasoned action, and adolescents' decisions to smoke cigarettes. *Journal of Applied Social Psychology, 19,* 543–558.

Odell, R. (1988). Radiation oncology: Principles and practice. In M. Renneker (Ed.), *Understanding cancer* (3d ed.). Palo Alto, CA: Bull Publishing Co.

Offutt, C., & LaCroix, J. M. (1988). Type A behavior pattern and symptom reports: A prospective investigation. *Journal of Behavioral Medicine, 11,* 227–237.

O'Hearn, P. B., Laperrier, A., August, S., Baggett, L., Ironson, G., Ingram, F., Schneiderman, N., & Fletcher, M. A. (1990, August). *Changes in psychological distress pre and post HIV notification.* Paper presented at the American Psychological Association Convention, Boston, MA.

Olbrisch, M. E., Weiss, S. M., Stone, G. C., & Schwartz, G. E. (1985). Report of the National Working Conference on Education and Training in Health Psychology. *American Psychologist, 40,* 1038–1041.

Oldenburg, B., & Owen, N. (1990). Health psychology in Australia. *Psychology and Health, 4,* 73–81.

O'Leary, A. (1990). Stress, emotion, and human immune function. *Psychological Bulletin, 108,* 363–382.

O'Leary, A., Shoor, S., Lorig, K., & Holman, H. R. (1988). A cognitive-behavioral treatment for rheumatoid arthritis. *Health Psychology, 7,* 527–544.

Oleson, V. L. (1975). Convergences and divergences: Anthropology and sociology in health care. *Social Science and Medicine, 9,* 421–425.

Orne, M. T., & Dinges, D. F. (1989). Hypnosis. In P. D. Wall & R. Melzack (Eds.), *Textbook of pain* (2d ed.). Edinburgh: Churchill Livingstone.

Ornish, D., Brown, S. E., Scherwitz, L. W., Billings, J. H., Armstrong, W. T., Ports, T. A., McLanahan, S. M., Kirkeeide, R. L., Brand, R. J., & Gould, K. L. (1990). Can lifestyle changes reverse coronary heart disease?: The Lifestyle Heart Trial. *Lancet, 336,* 129–133.

Ornstein, R., & Sobel, D. (1987). *The healing brain.* New York: Simon and Schuster.

Orona, C. J. (1990). Temporality and identity loss due to Alzheimer's disease. *Social Science and Medicine, 30,* 1247–1256.

O'Rourke, M. G. E., & Emmett, A. J. J. (1991). Epidemiology. In A. J. J. Emmett & M. G. E. O'Rourke (Eds.), *Malignant skin tumors* (2d ed.). Edinburgh: Churchill Livingstone.

Orth, J. E., Stiles, W. B., Scherwitz, L., Hennrikus, D., & Vallbona, C. (1987). Patient exposition and provider explanation in routine interviews and hypertensive pa-

tients' blood pressure control. *Health Psychology, 6,* 29–42.

Ost, L. G. (1987). Applied relaxation: Description of a coping technique and review of controlled studies. *Behaviour Research and Therapy, 25,* 397–409.

Pachuta, D. M. (1989). Chinese medicine: The law of five elements. In A. A. Sheikh & K. S. Sheikh (Eds.), *Eastern and Western approaches to healing: Ancient wisdom and modern knowledge.* New York: Wiley.

Paffenbarger, R. S. (1985). Physical activity as a defense against coronary heart disease. In W. E. Connor & J. D. Bristow (Eds.), *Coronary heart disease: Prevention, complications and treatment.* Philadelphia: Lippincott.

Page, H. S., & Asire, A. J. (1988). Solar radiation. In M. Renneker (Ed.), *Understanding cancer* (3d ed.). Palo Alto, CA: Bull Publishing Co.

Pagel, M. D., Erdly, W. W., & Becker, J. (1987). Social networks: We get by with (and in spite of) a little help from our friends. *Journal of Personality and Social Psychology, 53,* 793–804.

Palinkas, L. A. & Hoiberg, A. (1982). An epidemiology primer: Bridging the gap between epidemiology and psychology. *Health Psychology, 1,* 269–287.

Panlilio, A. L., Foy, D. R., Edward, J. R., Bell, D. M., Welch, B. A., Parrish, C. M., Culver, D. H., Lowry, P. W., Jarvis, W. R., & Perlino, C. A. (1991). Blood contacts during surgical procedures. *Journal of the American Medical Association, 265,* 1533–1537.

Park, L. C., & Covi, L. (1965). Nonblind placebo trial. *Archives of General Psychiatry, 12,* 336–345.

Parkes, C. M. (1988). Research: Bereavement. *Omega, 18,* 365–377.

Parkes, C. M., Benjamin, B., & Fitzgerald, R. G. (1969). Broken heart: A statistical study of increased mortality among widowers. *British Medical Journal, 1,* 740–743.

Parkes, C. M., & Weiss, R. S. (1983). *Recovery from bereavement.* New York: Basic Books.

Parkes, K. R. (1984). Locus of control, cognitive appraisal, and coping in stressful episodes. *Journal of Personality and Social Psychology, 46,* 655–668.

Parry, C. B. W. (1989). The failed back. In P. D. Wall & R. Melzack (Eds.), *Textbook of pain* (2d ed.). Edinburgh: Churchill Livingstone.

Parsons, T. (1975). The sick role and the role of the physician reconsidered. *Milbank Memorial Fund Quarterly, 53,* 257–278.

Pasquali, E. A. (1990). Learning to laugh: Humor as therapy. *Journal of Psychosocial Nursing, 28*(3), 31–35.

Patchner, M. A., & Finn, M. B. (1987). Volunteers: The life-line of hospice. *Omega, 18,* 135–144.

Patterson, D. R., Questad, K. A., & de Lateur, B. J. (1989). Hypnotherapy as an adjunct to narcotic analgesia for the treatment of pain for burn debridement. *American Journal of Clinical Hypnosis, 31,* 156–163.

Pattison, E. M. (1977). Death throughout the life cycle. In E. M. Pattison (Ed.), *The experience of dying.* Englewood Cliffs, NJ: Prentice-Hall.

Pearce, S. (1987). The concept of psychogenic pain: A psychological investigation of women with pelvic pain. *Current Psychology Research and Reviews, 6,* 219–228.

Pearlin, L. I., & Schooler, C. (1978). The structure of coping. *Journal of Health and Social Behavior, 22,* 337–356.

Peele, S. (1984). The cultural context of psychological approaches to alcoholism: Can we control the effects of alcohol? *American Psychologist, 39,* 1337–1351.

Penick, S. B., Filion, R., Fox, S., & Stunkard, A. J. (1971). Behavior modification in the treatment of obesity. *Psychosomatic Medicine, 33,* 49–55.

Pennebaker, J. W. (1980). Perceptual and environmental determinants of coughing. *Basic and Applied Social Psychology, 1,* 83–91.

Pennebaker, J. W. (1981). Stimulus characteristics influencing estimation of heart rate. *Psychophysiology, 18,* 540–548.

Pennebaker, J. W. (1982). *The psychology of physical symptoms.* New York: Springer-Verlag.

Pennebaker, J. W. (1984). Accuracy of symptom perception. In A. Baum, S. E. Taylor, & J. Singer (Eds.), *Handbook of psychology and health.* Vol. 4. Hillsdale, NJ: Erlbaum.

Pennebaker, J. W., Gonder-Frederick, L., Stewart, H., Elfman, L., & Skelton, J. A. (1982). Physical symptoms associated with blood pressure. *Psychophysiology, 19,* 201–210.

Pennebaker, J. W., Kiecolt-Glaser, J. K., & Glaser, R. (1988). Disclosure of traumas and immune function: Health implications for psychotherapy. *Journal of Consulting and Clinical Psychology, 56,* 239–245.

Pennebaker, J. W., & Lightner, J. M. (1980). Competition of internal and external information in an exercise setting. *Journal of Personality and Social Psychology, 39,* 165–174.

Pennebaker, J. W., & Skelton, J. A. (1978). Psychological parameters of physical symptoms. *Personality and Social Psychology Bulletin, 4,* 524–530.

Pennebaker, J. W., & Skelton, J. A. (1981). Selective monitoring of bodily sensations. *Journal of Personality and Social Psychology, 41,* 213–223.

Pennebaker, J. W., & Watson, D. (1988). Blood pressure estimation and beliefs among normotensives and hypertensives. *Health Psychology, 7,* 309–328.

Pentz, M. A., Dwyer, J. H., MacKinnon, D. P., Flay, B. R., Hansen, W. B., Wang, E. Y., & Johnson, C. A. (1989). A multicommunity trial for primary prevention of adolescent drug abuse. Effects on drug use prevalence. *Journal of the American Medical Association, 261,* 3259–3266.

Perry, C. L., Klepp, K.-L., & Shultz, J. M. (1988). Primary prevention of cardiovascular disease: Community wide strategies for youth. *Journal of Consulting and Clinical Psychology, 56,* 358–364.

Peters, J. L., & Large, R. G. (1990). A randomized control trial evaluating in- and outpatient pain management programmes. *Pain, 41,* 283–293.

Peterson, C. (1982). Learned helplessness and health psychology. *Health Psychology, 1,* 153–168.

Peterson, C., Seligman, M. E. P., & Vaillant, G. E. (1988). Pessimistic explanatory style is a risk factor for physical illness: A thirty-five-year longitudinal study. *Journal of Personality and Social Psychology, 55,* 23–27.

Pettingale, K. W. (1984). Coping and cancer prognosis. *Journal of Psychosomatic Research, 28,* 363–364.

Pettingale, K. W., Philalithis, A., Tee, D. E. H., & Greer, H. S. (1981). The biological correlates of psychological responses to breast cancer. *Journal of Psychosomatic Research, 25,* 453–458.

Petty, R. E., & Cacioppo, J. T. (1981). *Attitudes and persuasion: Classic and contemporary approaches.* Dubuque, IA: Wm. C. Brown.

Piaget, J. (1960). *The child's conception of the world.* Paterson, NJ: Littlefield, Adams & Co.

Pikoff, H. (1984). Is the muscular model of headache still viable? A review of conflicting data. *Headache, 24,* 186–198.

Pilowsky, I. (1978). A general classification of abnormal illness behaviors. *British Journal of Medical Psychology, 51,* 131–137.

Pincus, L. (1976). *Death and the family: The importance of mourning.* New York: Pantheon Books.

Pines, A. M., & Aronson, E. (1981). *Burnout: From tedium to personal growth.* New York: Free Press.

Pinto, R. P., & Hollandsworth, J. G. (1989). Using videotape modeling to prepare children psychologically for surgery: Influence of parents and costs versus benefits of providing preparation services. *Health Psychology, 8,* 79–95.

Plotkin, W. B. (1985). A psychological approach to placebo: The role of faith in therapy and treatment. In L. White, B. Turksy, & G. E. Schwartz (Eds.), *Placebo: Theory, research, and mechanisms.* New York: Guilford Press.

Pollack, E. S., Nomura, A. M. Y., Heilbrun, L. K., Stemmermann, G. N., & Green, S. B. (1984). Prospective study of alcohol consumption and cancer. *New England Journal of Medicine, 310,* 617–621.

Pollak, J. M. (1979). Correlates of death anxiety: A review of empirical studies. *Omega, 10,* 97–122.

Pomerleau, O. F., Bell, C., Benowitz, N. L., Best, J. A., Glassman, A., Russell, M., Russell, P., & Schneider, N. G.

(1986). Nicotine and relapse. *Health Psychology, 5* (Suppl.), 41–51.

Porkert, M., & Ullmann, C. (1988). *Chinese medicine as a scientific system: Its history, philosophy, and practice and how it fits with the medicine of the West* (M. Howson, Trans.). New York: Henry Holt.

Porter, S. F. (1984). *Arthritis care: A guide for patient education.* Norwalk, CT: Appleton-Century-Crofts.

Price, V. A. (1982). *Type A behavior pattern: A model for research and practice.* New York: Academic Press.

Prohaska, T. R., Keller, M. L., Leventhal, E., & Leventhal, H. (1987). Impact of symptoms and aging attribution on emotions and coping. *Health Psychology, 6,* 495–514.

Prokop, C. K., & Bradley, L. A. (Eds.) (1981). *Medical psychology: Contributions to behavioral medicine.* New York: Academic Press.

Pryor, J. B., Reeder, G. D., Vinacco, R., & Kott, T. L. (1989). The instrumental and symbolic functions of attitudes toward persons with AIDS. *Journal of Applied Social Psychology, 19,* 377–404.

Puska, P. (1984). Community based prevention of cardiovascular disease: The North Karelia Project. In J. D. Matarazzo, S. M. Weiss, J. A. Herd, N. E. Miller, & S. M. Weiss (Eds.), *Behavioral health: A handbook of health enhancement and disease prevention.* New York: Wiley.

Quah, S. R. (1985). The health belief model and preventive health behavior in Singapore. *Social Science and Medicine, 21,* 351–363.

Quill, T. E. (1985). Somatization disorder: One of medicine's blind spots. *Journal of the American Medical Association, 254,* 3075–3079.

Quill, T. E. (1989). Recognizing and adjusting to barriers in doctor-patient communication. *Annals of Internal Medicine, 111,* 51–57.

Rabkin, J. G., & Struening, E. L. (1976). Life events, stress, and illness. *Science, 194,* 1013–1020.

Rabkin, J. G., Williams, J. B. W., Neugebauer, R., Remien, R. H., & Goetz, R. (1990). Maintenance of hope in HIV-spectrum homosexual men. *American Journal of Psychiatry, 147,* 1322–1326.

Rabkin, S. W., Mathewson, F. A. L., & Hsu, P.-H. (1977). Relation of body weight to development of ischemic heart disease in a cohort of young North American men after a 26-year observation period: The Manitoba Study. *American Journal of Cardiology, 39,* 452–458.

Radelfinger, S. (1965). Some effects of fear-arousing communications on preventive health behavior. *Health Education Monographs, 9,* 2–.

Raether, H. C., & Slater, R. C. (1977). Immediate postdeath activities in the United States. In H. Feifel (Ed.), *New meanings of death.* New York: McGraw-Hill.

Rahe, R. H. (1972). Subjects' recent life changes and their near-future illness reports. *Annals of Clinical Research, 4,* 250–265.

Rahe, R. H., & Arthur, R. J. (1978). Life change and illness studies: Past history and future directions. *Journal of Human Stress, 4*(1), 3–15.

Rahe, R. H., Ward, H. W., & Hayes, V. (1979). Brief group therapy in myocardial infarction therapy: Three-to-four-year follow-up of a controlled trial. *Psychosomatic Medicine, 41,* 229–242.

Range, L. M., & Calhoun, L. G. (1990). Responses following suicide and other types of death: The perspective of the bereaved. *Omega, 21,* 311–320.

Rappaport, N. B., McAnulty, D. P., Waggoner, C. D., & Brantley, P. J. (1987). Cluster analysis of Minnesota multiphasic personality inventory (MMPI) profiles in a chronic headache population. *Journal of Behavioral Medicine, 10,* 49–60.

Raps, C. S., Peterson, C., Jonas, M., & Seligman, M. E. P. (1982). Patient behavior in hospitals: Helplessness, reactance, or both? *Journal of Personality and Social Psychology, 42,* 1036–1041.

Raskin, N. H. (1988). *Headache* (2d ed.). New York: Churchill Livingstone.

Ray, C. (1982). The surgical patient: Psychological stress and coping resources. In J. R. Eiser (Ed.), *Social psychology and behavioral medicine.* Chichester, England: Wiley.

Reading, A. E. (1989). Testing pain mechanisms in persons in pain. In P. D. Wall & R. Melzack (Eds.), *Textbook of pain* (2d ed.). Edinburgh: Churchill Livingstone.

Redd, W. H., & Andrykowski, M. A. (1982). Behavioral intervention in cancer treatment: Controlling aversion reactions to chemotherapy. *Journal of Consulting and Clinical Psychology, 50,* 1018–1029.

Redfield, R. R., & Burke, D. S. (1988). HIV infection: The clinical picture. *Scientific American, 259*(4), 70–78.

Reid, W. H., & Wise, M. G. (1989). *DSM-III-R training guide.* New York: Brunner/Mazel.

Renneker, M. (1988). *Understanding cancer* (3d ed.). Palo Alto, CA: Bull Publishing Co.

Rhodewalt, F., & Smith, T. W. (1991). Current issues in type A behavior, coronary proneness, and coronary heart disease. In C. F. Snyder & D. R. Forsyth (Eds.), *Handbook of social and clinical psychology: The health perspective.* New York: Pergamon Press.

Rich, S. (1992). Sharp rise in health costs projected. *Washington Post,* Jan. 20, A23.

Richardson, P. H., & Vincent, C. A. (1986). Acupuncture for the treatment of pain: A review of evaluative research. *Pain, 24,* 15–40.

Riley, V. (1981). Psychoneuroendocrine influences on immunocompetence and neoplasia. *Science, 212,* 1100–1109.

Roberts, M. C., & Fanurik, D. (1986). Rewarding elementary schoolchildren for their use of safety belts. *Health Psychology, 5,* 185–196.

Robertson, L., Kelley, A., O'Neill, B., Wixom, C., Eisworth, R., & Haddon, W., Jr. (1974). A controlled study of the effect of television messages on safety belt use. *American Journal of Public Health, 64,* 1071–1080.

Robinson, D. (1971). *The process of becoming ill.* London: Routledge & Kegan Paul.

Robinson, D. (1979). *Talking out alcoholism: The self-help process of Alcoholics Anonymous.* Baltimore: University Park Press.

Roccella, E. J., & Horan, M. J. (1988). The National High Blood Pressure Education Program: Measuring progress and assessing its impact. *Health Psychology, 7*(Suppl.), 297–303.

Rodin, J. (1981). Current status of the internal-external hypothesis for obesity: What went wrong? *American Psychologist, 36,* 361–372.

Rodin, J. (1982). Obesity: Why the losing battle? In B. B. Wolman (Ed.), *Psychological aspects of obesity: A handbook.* New York: Van Nostrand Reinhold.

Rodin, J., & Janis, I. L. (1979). The social power of health care practitioners as agents of change. *Journal of Social Issues, 35,* 60–81.

Rodin, J., & Langer, E. J. (1977). Long-term effects of a control-relevant intervention with the institutionalized aged. *Journal of Personality and Social Psychology, 35,* 897–902.

Rogentine, G. N., Van Kammen, D., Fox, B., Docherty, J., Rosenblatt, J., Boyd, S., & Bunney, W. (1979). Psychological factors in the prognosis of malignant melanoma. *Psychosomatic Medicine, 41,* 647–655.

Rogers, A. E., & Longnecker, M. P. (1988). Dietary and nutritional influences on cancer: A review of epidemiological and experimental data. *Laboratory Investigation, 59,* 729–759.

Rogers, M. P., Reich, P., Strom, T. B., & Carpenter, C. B. (1976). Behaviorally conditioned immunosuppression: Replication of a recent study. *Psychosomatic Medicine, 38,* 447–452.

Rogers, R. W. (1975). A protection motivation theory of fear appeals and attitude change. *Journal of Psychology, 91,* 93–114.

Rogers, R. W. (1983). Cognitive and physiological processes in fear appeals and attitude change: A revised theory of protection motivation. In J. Cacioppo & R. Petty (Eds.), *Social psychophysiology.* New York: Guilford Press.

Roitt, I. (1984). *Essential immunology* (5th ed.). Oxford, England: Blackwell Scientific Publications.

Romano, J. M., & Turner, J. A. (1985). Chronic pain and depression: Does the evidence support a relationship? *Psychological Bulletin, 97,* 18–34.

Rose, M. I., Firestone, P., Heick, H. M. C., & Faught, A. K. (1983). The effects of anxiety management training on the control of juvenile diabetes mellitus. *Journal of Behavioral Medicine, 6,* 381–395.

Rosen, J. C., Grubman, J. A., Bevins, T., & Frymoyer, J. W. (1987). Musculoskeletal status and disability of MMPI profile subgroups among patients with low back pain. *Health Psychology, 6,* 581–598.

Rosenblatt, D., & Suchman, E. A. (1964). Blue-collar attitudes and information about health and illness. In A. B. Shostak & W. Gomberg (Eds.), *Blue-collar world: Studies of the American worker.* Englewood Cliffs, NJ: Prentice-Hall.

Rosengren, W. R. (1964). Social class and becoming "ill." In A. B. Shostak & W. Gomberg (Eds.), *Blue-collar world: Studies of the American worker.* Englewood Cliffs, NJ: Prentice-Hall.

Rosenman, R. H. (1978). The interview method of assessment of the coronary-prone behavior pattern. In T. M. Dembroski, S. M. Weiss, J. L. Shields, S. G. Haynes, & M. Feinleib (Eds.), *Coronary-prone behavior.* New York: Springer-Verlag.

Rosenman, R. H., Brand, R. J., Jenkins, C. D., Friedman, M., Straus, R., & Wurm, M. (1975). Coronary heart disease in the Western Collaborative Group Study: Final follow-up experience of 8 1/2 years. *Journal of the American Medical Association, 233,* 872–877.

Rosenstock, I. M., Derryberry, M., & Carriger, B. (1959). Why people fail to seek poliomyelitis vaccination. *Public Health Reports, 74,* 98–103.

Roskies, E., Seraganian, P., Oseasohn, R., Hanley, J. A., Collu, R., Martin, N., & Smilga, C. (1986). The Montreal Type A Intervention Project: Major findings. *Health Psychology, 5,* 45–69.

Ross, C. E., & Duff, R. S. (1982). Returning to the doctor: The effect of client characteristics, type of practice, and experiences with care. *Journal of Health and Social Behavior, 23,* 119–131.

Ross, C. E., & Mirowsky, J. (1979). A comparison of life-event-weighting schemes: change, undesirability, and effect-proportional indices. *Journal of Health and Social Behavior, 20,* 166–177.

Ross, C. E., Mirowsky, J., & Duff, R. S. (1982). Physician status characteristics and client satisfaction in two types of medical practice. *Journal of Health and Social Behavior, 23,* 317–329.

Ross, S., & Buckalew, L. W. (1985). Placebo agentry: Assessment of drug and placebo effects. In L. White, B. Tursky, & G. E. Schwartz (Eds.), *Placebo: Theory, research and mechanisms.* New York: Guilford Press.

Rost, K., Carter, W., & Inui, T. (1989). Introduction of information during the initial medical visit: Consequences for patient follow-through with physician recommendations for medication. *Social Science and Medicine, 28,* 315–321.

Roter, D. L. (1984). Patient question asking in physician-patient interaction. *Health Psychology, 3,* 395–409.

Roth, H. P. (1987). Measurement of compliance. *Patient Education and Counseling, 10,* 107–116.

Rotter, J. B. (1966). Generalized expectancies for internal versus external control of reinforcement. *Psychological Monographs, 80*(1, Whole No. 609).

Rotter, J. B. (1975). Some problems and misconceptions related to the construct of internal versus external control of reinforcement. *Journal of Consulting and Clinical Psychology, 43,* 56–67.

Roviaro, S., Holmes, D. S., & Holmsten, R. D. (1984). Influence of a cardiac rehabilitation program on the cardiovascular, psychological, and social functioning of cardiac patients. *Journal of Behavioral Medicine, 7,* 61–81.

Ruble, D. N. (1977). Premenstrual symptoms: A reinterpretation. *Science, 197,* 291–292.

Ruble, D. N., & Brooks-Gunn, J. (1979). Menstrual symptoms: A social cognition analysis. *Journal of Behavioral Medicine, 2,* 171–194.

Rundall, T. G., & Wheeler, J. R. C. (1979). The effect of income on use of preventive care: An evaluation of alternative explanations. *Journal of Health and Social Behavior, 20,* 397–406.

Russell, M. A. H., Wilson, C., Taylor, C., & Baker, C. D. (1979). Effect of general practitioners' advice against smoking. *British Medical Journal, 2,* 231–235.

Sackett, D. L., & Snow, J. C. (1979). The magnitude of compliance and noncompliance. In R. B. Haynes, D. W. Taylor, & D. L. Sackett (Eds.), *Compliance in health care.* Baltimore: Johns Hopkins University Press.

Safer, M. A., Tharps, Q., Jackson, T., & Leventhal, H. (1979). Determinants of three stages of delay in seeking care at a medical clinic. *Medical Care, 17,* 11–29.

Saile, H., Burgmeier, R., & Schmidt, L. R. (1988). A meta-analysis of studies on psychological preparation of children facing medical procedures. *Psychology and Health, 2,* 107–132.

Salisbury, D. M. (1986). AIDS: Psychosocial implications. *Journal of Psychosocial Nursing, 24*(12), 13–16.

Saltzer, E. B. (1978). Locus of control and the intention to lose weight. *Health Education Monographs, 6,* 118–128.

Samora, J., Saunders, L., & Larson, R. F. (1961). Medical vocabulary knowledge among hospital patients. *Journal of Health and Human Behavior, 2,* 83–89.

Sanders, G. S. (1982). Social comparison and perceptions of health and illness. In G. S. Sanders & J. Suls (Eds.), *Social psychology of health and illness.* Hillsdale, NJ: Erlbaum.

Sandler, D. P., Everson, R. B., Wilcox, A. J., & Browder, J. P. (1985). Cancer risk in adulthood from early life exposure to parents' smoking. *American Journal of Public Health, 75,* 487–492.

Sarason, B. R., Shearin, E. N., Pierce, G. R., & Sarason, I. G. (1987). Interrelations of social support measures: Theoretical and practical implications. *Journal of Personality and Social Psychology, 52,* 813–832.

Sarason, I. G., Johnson, J., Berberich, J., & Seigel, J. (1979). Helping police officers to cope with stress: A cognitive-behavioral approach. *American Journal of Community Psychology, 7,* 593–603.

Sarason, I. G., Johnson, J. H., & Siegel, J. M. (1978). Assessing the impact of life changes: Development of the Life Experiences Survey. *Journal of Consulting and Clinical Psychology, 46,* 932–946.

Sargent, J., Solbach, P., Coyne, L., Spohn, H., & Segerson, J. (1986). Results of a controlled, experimental, outcome study of nondrug treatments for the control of migraine headaches. *Journal of Behavioral Medicine, 9,* 291–323.

Saunders, C. (1984). St. Christopher's Hospice. In E. S. Shneidman (Ed.), *Death: Current perspectives* (3d ed.). Palo Alto, CA: Mayfield.

Sawyer, A. (1981). Repetition, cognitive responses, and persuasion. In R. E. Petty, T. M. Ostrom, & T. C. Brock (Eds.), *Cognitive responses in persuasion.* Hillsdale, NJ: Erlbaum.

Sayette, M. A., & Mayne, T. J. (1990). Survey of current clinical and research trends in clinical psychology. *American Psychologist, 45,* 1263–1266.

Scambler, G., & Hopkins, A. (1990). Generating a model of epileptic stigma: The role of qualitative analysis. *Social Science and Medicine, 30,* 1187–1194.

Scarf, M. (1980). Images that heal: A doubtful idea whose time has come. *Psychology Today, 14*(4), 33–46.

Schacter, S. (1982). Recidivism and self-cure of smoking and obesity. *American Psychologist, 37,* 436–444.

Schaffer, H. R., & Challender, W. H. (1959). Psychologic effect of hospitalization in infancy. *Pediatrics, 24,* 528–539.

Scheier, M. F., & Carver, C. S. (1987). Dispositional optimism and physical well-being: The influence of generalized outcome expectancies on health. *Journal of Personality, 55,* 169–210.

Schifter, D. E., & Ajzen, I. (1985). Intention, perceived control, and weight loss: An application of the theory of planned behavior. *Journal of Personality and Social Psychology, 49,* 843–851.

Schlesier-Stropp, B. (1984). Bulimia: A review of the literature. *Psychological Bulletin, 95,* 247–257.

Schmidt, A. J., & Arntz, A. (1987). Psychological research and chronic low back pain: A stand-still or breakthrough. *Social Science and Medicine, 25,* 1095–1014.

Schmidt, A. J., Gierlings, R. E. H., & Peters, M. L. (1989). Environmental and interoceptive influences on chronic low back pain behavior. *Pain, 38,* 137–143.

Schroeder, D. H., & Costa, P. T., Jr. (1984). Influence of life event stress on physical illness: Substantive effects or methodological flaws? *Journal of Personality and Social Psychology, 46,* 853–863.

Schuckit, M. A. (1989). *Drug and alcohol abuse: A clinical guide to diagnosis and treatment* (3d ed.). New York: Plenum.

Schulz, R., & Decker, S. (1985). Long-term adjustment to physical disability: The role of social support, perceived control, and self-blame. *Journal of Personality and Social Psychology, 48,* 1162–1172.

Schulz, R., & Schlarb, J. (1988). Two decades of research on dying: What do we know about the patient? *Omega, 18,* 299–317.

Schwartz, G. E. (1982). Testing the biopsychosocial model: The ultimate challenge facing behavioral medicine? *Journal of Consulting and Clinical Psychology, 50,* 1040–1053.

Schwartz, G. E., & Weiss, S. M. (1977). What is behavioral medicine? *Psychosomatic Medicine, 39,* 377–381.

Seeman, M., & Evans, J. W. (1962). Alienation and learning in a hospital setting. *American Sociological Review, 27,* 772–783.

Seligman, M. E. P. (1975). *Helplessness: On depression, development, and death.* San Fransisco: W. H. Freeman

Selltiz, C., Wrightsman, L. S., & Cook, S. W. (1976). *Research methods in social relations.* (3d ed.). New York: Holt, Rinehart, and Winston.

Selye, H. (1976). *The stress of life* (rev. ed.). New York: McGraw-Hill.

Selye, H. (1982). History and present status of the stress concept. In L. Goldberger & S. Breznitz (Eds.), *Handbook of stress: Theoretical and clinical aspects.* New York: Free Press.

Shaffer, J. W., Duszynski, K. R., & Thomas, C. B. (1982). Family attitudes in youth as a possible precursor of cancer among physicians: A search for explanatory mechanisms. *Journal of Behavioral Medicine, 5,* 143–163.

Shaffer, J. W., Graves, P. L., Swank, R. T., & Pearson, T. A. (1987). Clustering of personality traits in youth and the subsequent development of cancer among physicians. *Journal of Behavioral Medicine, 10,* 441–447.

Shah, M., & Jeffery, R. W. (1991). Is obesity due to overeating and inactivity, or to a defective metabolic rate? A review. *Annals of Behavioral Medicine, 13,* 73–81.

Shanfield, S. B., Swain, B. J., & Benjamin, G. A. H. (1987). Parents' responses to the death of adult children from accidents and cancer: A comparison. *Omega, 17,* 289–297.

Shapiro, A. K. (1964). Factors contributing to the placebo effect: Their significance for psychotherapy. *American Journal of Psychotherapy, 18,* 73–88.

Shapiro, A. K., & Morris, L. A. (1978). The placebo effect in medical and psychological therapies. In S. L. Garfield & A. E. Bergin (Eds.), *Handbook of psychotherapy and behavior change: An empirical analysis* (2d ed.). New York: Wiley.

Shapiro, D., & Goldstein, I. B. (1982). Biobehavioral perspective on hypertension. *Journal of Consulting and Clinical Psychology, 50,* 841–858.

Shapiro, D., Tursky, B., Schwartz, G. E., & Shnidman, S. R. (1971). Smoking on cue: A behavioral approach to smoking reduction. *Journal of Health and Social Behavior, 12,* 108–113.

Shapiro, D. H. (1985). Meditation and behavioral medicine: Application of a self-regulation strategy to the clinical management of stress. In S. R. Burchfield (Ed.), *Stress: Psychological and physiological interactions.* Washington, DC: Hemisphere.

Shaw, L., & Ehrlich, A. (1987). Relaxation training as a treatment for chronic pain caused by ulcerative colitis. *Pain, 29,* 287–293.

Shekelle, R. B., Gale, M., & Norusis, M. (1985). Type A score (Jenkins Activity Survey) and risk of recurrent coronary heart disease in the Aspirin Myocardial Infarction Study. *American Journal of Cardiology, 56,* 221–225.

Shekelle, R. B., Gale, M., Ostfeld, A. M., & Paul, O. (1983). Hostility, risk of coronary heart disease, and mortality. *Psychosomatic Medicine, 45,* 109–114.

Shekelle, R. B., Hulley, S. B., Neaton, J. D., Billings, J. H., Bomani, M. O., Gerace, T. A., Jacobs, D. R., Lasser, N. L., Mittelmakr, M. B., & Stamler, J. (1985). The MRFIT behavioral pattern study. Type A behavior and incidence of coronary heart disease. *American Journal of Epidemiology, 122,* 559–570.

Sheps, D. S. (1987). Myocardial infarction—An overview. In D. S. Sheps (Ed.), *The management of post-myocardial infarction patients.* New York: McGraw-Hill.

Shiffman, S. (1989). Trans-situational consistency in smoking relapse. *Health Psychology, 8,* 471–481.

Shillingford, J. P. (1981). *Coronary heart disease: The facts.* Oxford: Oxford University Press.

Shilts, R. (1987). *And the band played on: Politics, people and the AIDS epidemic.* New York: St. Martin's Press.

Shimao, T. (1988). Smoking and its control in Japan. In M. Aoki, S., Hisamichi, & S. Tominaga (Eds.), *Smoking and health 1987: Proceedings of the 6th World Conference on Smoking and Health.* Amsterdam: Excerpta Medica.

Shneidman, E. S. (1980). Death work and stages of dying. In E. S. Shneidman (Ed.), *Death: Current perspectives* (2d ed.). Palo Alto, CA: Mayfield.

Shneidman, E. S. (1984). Some aspects of psychotherapy with dying persons. In E. S. Shneidman (Ed.), *Death: Current perspectives* (3d ed.). Palo Alto, CA: Mayfield.

Shneidman, E. S. (1984). *Death: Current perspectives* (3d ed.). Palo Alto, CA: Mayfield.

Sholomskas, D. E., Steil, J. M., & Plummer, J. K. (1990). The spinal cord injured revisited: The relationship between self-blame, other-blame and coping. *Journal of Applied Social Psychology, 20,* 548–574.

Shontz, F. C. (1975). *The psychological aspects of physical illness and disability.* New York: Macmillan.

Siegel, W. C., & Blumenthal, J. A. (1991). The role of exercise in the prevention and treatment of hypertension. *Annals of Behavioral Medicine, 13,* 23–30.

Siltanen, P. (1987). Stress, coronary disease, and coronary death. *Annals of Clinical Research, 19,* 96–103.

Sime, W. E. (1984). Psychological benefits of exercise training in the healthy individual. In J. D. Matarazzo, S. M. Weiss, J. Herd, N. E. Miller, & S. M. Weiss (Eds.), *Behavioral health: A handbook of health enhancement and disease prevention.* New York: Wiley.

Simon, J. M. (1988). The therapeutic value of humor in aging adults. *Journal of Gerontological Nursing, 14*(8), 9–13.

Simpson, M. A. (1989). AIDS in Africa. In I. B. Corless & M. Pittman-Lindeman (Eds.), *AIDS: Principles, practices, and politics* (Ref. ed.). New York: Hemisphere.

Sinclair-Gieben, A. H. C., & Chalmers, D. (1959). Evaluation of treatment of warts by hypnosis. *Lancet, 2,* 480–482.

Singer, E. M. (1988). Delay behavior among women with breast symptoms. In T. M. Field, P. M. McCabe, & N. Schneiderman (Eds.), *Stress and coping across development.* Hillsdale, NJ: Erlbaum.

Singer, J. E., & Lord, D. (1984). The role of social support in coping with chronic or life-threatening illness. In A. Baum, S. E. Taylor, & J. E. Singer (Eds.), *Handbook of psychology and health. Vol. IV: Social psychological aspects of health.* Hillsdale, NJ: Erlbaum.

Skelton, J. A., & Croyle, R. T. (Eds.) (1991). *Mental representation in health and illness.* New York: Springer-Verlag.

Skelton, J. A., Oppler, E., Taylor, D., & Thomas, D. (1988). *Somatic imagery and physical symptom-reporting: Explaining symptom suggestibility.* Unpublished manuscript.

Skelton, J. A., & Pennebaker. J. W. (1990). The verbal system. In J. T. Cacioppo & L. G. Tassinary (Eds.), *Principles of psychophysiology: Physical, social, and inferential elements.* Cambridge: Cambridge University Press.

Skelton, J. A., & Strohmetz, D. B. (1990). Priming symptom reports with health-related cognitive activity. *Personality and Social Psychology Bulletin, 16,* 449–464.

Skipper, J. K., Tagliacozzo, D. L., & Mauksch, H. O. (1964). Some possible consequences of limited communication between patients and hospital functionaries. *Journal of Health and Human Behavior, 5,* 34–39.

Sklar, L. S., & Anisman, H. (1979). Stress and coping factors influence tumor growth. *Science, 205,* 513–515.

Sklar, L. S., & Anisman, H. (1981). Stress and cancer. *Psychological Bulletin, 89,* 369–406.

Sloan, R. P. (1987). Workplace health promotion: A commentary on the evolution of a paradigm. *Health Education Quarterly, 17,* 182–194.

Slovic, P., Fischoff, B., & Lichtenstein, S. (1982). Facts versus fears: Understanding perceived risk. In D. Kahneman, P. Slovic, & A. Tversky (Eds.), *Judgment under uncertainty: Heuristics and biases.* New York: Cambridge University Press.

Smart, C. R. (1990). Screening and early cancer detection. *Seminars in Oncology, 17,* 456–462.

Smith, C. W. (1988). Management of Alzheimer's disease: A family affair. *Postgraduate Medicine, 83,* 118–127.

Smith, J. R. (1985). Individual psychotherapy with Vietnam veterans. In S. M. Sonnenberg, A. S. Blank, & J. A. Talbott (Eds.), *The trauma of war: Stress and recovery in Vietnam veterans.* Washington, DC: American Psychiatric Press.

Smith, R. E. (1989). Effects of coping skills training on generalized self-efficacy and locus of control. *Journal of Personality and Social Psychology, 56,* 228–233.

Smith, R. E., Smoll, F. L., & Ptacek, J. T. (1990). Conjunctive moderator variables in vulnerability and resiliency research: Life stress, social support and coping skills, and adolescent sport injuries. *Journal of Personality and Social Psychology, 58,* 360–370.

Smith, T. W., & Anderson, N. B. (1986). Models of personality and disease: An interactional approach to type A behavior and cardiovascular risk. *Journal of Personality and Social Psychology, 50,* 1166–1173.

Smith, T. W., & Brehm, S. S. (1981). Person perception and the type A coronary-prone behavior pattern. *Journal of Personality and Social Psychology, 40,* 1137–1149.

Smith, T. W., Peck, J. R., & Ward, J. R. (1990). Helplessness and depression in rheumatoid arthritis. *Health Psychology, 9,* 377–389.

Smith, T. W., Snyder, C. R., & Perkins, S. C. (1983). The self-serving function of hypochondriacal complaints: Physical symptoms as self-handicapping strategies. *Journal of Personality and Social Psychology, 44,* 787–797.

Sobel, H. (1981). *Behavioral therapy in terminal care: A humanistic approach.* Cambridge, MA: Ballinger.

Sontag, S. (1978). *Illness as metaphor.* New York: Farrar, Straus, and Giroux.

Souria, J.-C. (1990). *A history of alcoholism* (N. Hindley & G. Stanton, Trans.). Oxford: Basil Blackwell. (Original work published in 1986).

Speisman, J. C., Lazarus, R. S., Mordkoff, A., & Davison, L. (1964). Experimental reduction of stress based on ego-defense theory. *Journal of Abnormal and Social Psychology, 68,* 367–380.

Spencer, R. P. (1988). Cancer staging and survival rates: An analysis. *Anticancer Research, 8,* 685–688.

Spiegel, D., Bloom, J. R., Kraemer, H. C., & Gottheil, E. (1989). Effect of psychosocial treatment on survival of patients with metastatic breast cancer. *Lancet, 2,* 888–891.

Stachnik, T. J., Stoffelmayr, B. E., & Hoppe, R. B. (1983). Prevention, behavior change, and chronic disease. In T. G. Burish & L. A. Bradley (Eds.), *Coping with chronic disease: Research and applications.* New York: Academic Press.

Stall, R. D., Coates, T. J., & Hoff, C. (1988). Behavioral risk reduction for HIV infection among gay and bisexual men. *American Psychologist, 43,* 878–885.

Stall, R. D., Ekstrand, M., Pollack, L., McKusick, L., & Coates, T. J. (1990). Relapse from safer sex: The next challenge for AIDS prevention efforts. *Journal of Acquired Immune Deficiency Syndromes, 3,* 1181–1187.

Stallone, D. D., & Stunkard, A. J. (1991). The regulation of body weight: Evidence and clinical implications. *Annals of Behavioral Medicine, 13,* 220–230.

Steffen, V. J. (1990). Men's motivation to perform the testicle self-exam: Effects of prior knowledge and an educational brochure. *Journal of Applied Social Psychology, 20,* 681–702.

Steptoe, A., & Cox, S. (1988). Acute effects of aerobic exercise on mood. *Health Psychology, 7,* 329–340.

Stern, G. S., McCants, T. R., & Pettine, P. W. (1982). Stress and illness: Controllable and uncontrollable life events' relative contributions. *Personality and Social Psychology Bulletin, 8,* 140–145.

Stern, M. J. (1984). Psychosocial rehabilitation following myocardial infarction and coronary artery bypass surgery. In N. K. Wenger & H. K. Hellerstein (Eds.), *Rehabilitation of the coronary patient.* New York: Wiley.

Sternbach, R. A. (1964). The effects of instructional set on autonomic responsivity. *Psychophysiology, 1,* 67–72.

Sternbach, R. A. (1986). Pain and "hassles" in the United States: Findings of the Nuprin pain report. *Pain, 27,* 69–80.

Sternbach, R. A., & Tursky, B. (1965). Ethnic differences among housewives in psychophysical and skin potential responses to electric shock. *Psychophysiology, 1,* 241–246.

Stillion, J., & Wass, H. (1984). Children and death. In E. S. Shneidman (Ed.), *Death: Current perspectives* (3d ed.). Palo Alto: Mayfield.

Stone, A. A., & Neale, J. M. (1984). New measure of daily coping: Development and preliminary results. *Journal of Personality and Social Psychology, 46,* 892–906.

Stone, G. C. (1979a). Patient compliance and the role of the expert. *Journal of Social Issues, 35,* 34–59.

Stone, G. C. (1979b). Psychology and the health system. In G. C. Stone, F. Cohen, N. E. Adler, & Associates (Eds.), *Health Psychology—A handbook.* San Francisco, CA: Jossey-Bass.

Stone, G. C. (1982). Health Psychology: A new journal for a new field. *Health Psychology, 1,* 1–6.

Stone, G. C. (1983). Proceedings of the National Working Conference on Education and Training in Health Psychology. *Health Psychology, 2*(Suppl. 5).

Stone, G. C. (1990). An international review of the emergence and development of health psychology. *Psychology and Health, 4,* 3–17.

Strasser, T. (1980). Prevention in childhood of major cardiovascular diseases of adults. In F. Falkner (Ed.), *Prevention in childhood of health problems in adult life.* Geneva, Switzerland: World Health Organization.

Straus, R. (1957). The nature and status of medical sociology. *American Sociological Review, 22,* 200–204.

Strauss, A. L., Corbin, J., Fagerhaugh, S., Glaser, B. G., Maines, D., Suczek, B., & Wiener, C. L. (1984). *Chronic illness and the quality of life* (2d ed.). St. Louis: C. V. Mosby.

Strauss, L. M., Solomon, L. J., Constanza, M. C., Worden, J. K., & Foster, R. S. (1987). Breast self-examination practices and attitudes of women with and without a history of breast cancer. *Journal of Behavioral Medicine, 10,* 337–350.

Streicher, H. Z., & Heller, E. (1989). Human retroviruses and human disease. In I. B. Corless & M. Pittman-Lindeman (Eds.), *AIDS: Principles, practices, & politics.* New York: Hemisphere.

Striegel-Moore, R., & Rodin, J. (1985). Prevention of obesity. In J. C. Rosen & L. J. Solomon (Eds.), *Prevention in health psychology.* Hanover, NH: University Press of New England.

Stuckey, S. J., Jacobs, A., & Goldfarb, J. (1986). EMG biofeedback training, relaxation training, and placebo for the relief of chronic back pain. *Perceptual and Motor Skills, 63,* 1023–1036.

Strunin, L. (1991). Adolescents' perceptions of risk for HIV infection: Implications for future research. *Social Science and Medicine, 32,* 221–228.

Stunkard, A. J. (1979). Behavioral medicine and beyond: The example of obesity. In O. F. Pomerleau & J. P. Brady (Eds.), *Behavioral medicine: Theory and practice.* Baltimore: Williams & Wilkins.

Stunkard, A. J., Felix, M. R. J., & Cohen, R. Y. (1985). Mobilizing a community to promote health: The Pennsylvania County Health Improvement Program (CHIP). In J. C. Rosen & L. J. Solomon (Eds.), *Prevention in health psychology.* Hanover, NH: University Press of New England.

Suchman, E. A. (1965). Stages of illness and medical care. *Journal of Health and Social Behavior, 6,* 114–128.

Sugarman, D. B. (1986). Active versus passive euthanasia: An attributional analysis. *Journal of Applied Social Psychology, 16,* 60–76.

Suls, J., & Fletcher, B. (1985). The relative efficacy of avoidant and nonavoidant coping strategies: A meta-analysis. *Health Psychology, 4,* 249–288.

Suls, J., & Miller, R. L. (1977). *Social comparison processes: Theoretical and empirical perspectives.* Washington, DC: Hemisphere.

Sunshine, A., & Olson, N. Z. (1989). Non-narcotic analgesics. In P. D. Wall & R. Melzack (Eds.), *Textbook of pain* (2d ed.). Edinburgh: Churchill Livingstone.

Surwit, R. S., Feinglos, M. N., & Scovern, A. W. (1983). Diabetes and behavior: A paradigm for health psychology. *American Psychologist, 38,* 255–262.

Swavely, S. M., Silverman, W. H., & Falek, A. (1987). Psychological impact of the development of a presymptomatic test for Huntington's disease. *Health Psychology, 6,* 149–157.

Talbot, J. D., Marrett, S., Evans, A. C., Meyer, E., Bushnell, M. C., & Duncan, G. H. (1991). Multiple representations of pain the human cerebral cortex. *Science, 251,* 1355–1358.

Tanabe, G. (1982). The potential for public health psychology. *American Psychologist, 37,* 942–944.

Tapp, J. T. (1985). Multisystems interventions in disease. In N. Schneiderman & J. T. Tapp (Eds.), *Behavioral medicine: The biopsychosocial approach.* Hillsdale, NJ: Erlbaum.

Tash, R. H., O'Shea, R. M., & Cohen, L. K. (1969). Testing a preventive-symptomatic theory of dental health behavior. *American Journal of Public Health, 59,* 514–526.

Tasker, R. R., & Dostrovsky, J. O. (1989). Deafferentation and central pain. In P. D. Wall & R. Melzack (Eds.),

Textbook of pain (2d ed.). Edinburgh: Churchill Livingstone.

Taylor, S. E. (1979). Hospital patient behavior: Reactance, helplessness, or control? *Journal of Social Issues, 35,* 156–184.

Taylor, S. E. (1983). Adjustment to threatening events: A theory of cognitive adaptation. *American Psychologist, 38,* 1161–1173.

Taylor, S. E. (1984). The developing field of health psychology. In A. Baum, S. E. Taylor, & J. E. Singer (Eds.), *Handbook of health psychology: Vol 4. Social psychological aspects of health.* Hillsdale, NJ: Erlbaum.

Taylor, S. E. (1987). The progress and prospects of health psychology: Tasks of a maturing discipline. *Health Psychology, 6,* 73–87.

Taylor, S. E. (1990). Health psychology: The science and the field. *American Psychologist, 45,* 40–50.

Taylor, S. E., Lichtman, R. R., & Wood, J. V. (1984). Attributions, beliefs about control, and adjustment to breast cancer. *Journal of Personality and Social Psychology, 46,* 489–502.

Taylor, S. E., & Lobel, M. (1989). Social comparison activity under threat: Downward evaluation and upward contacts. *Psychological Review, 96,* 569–575.

Temoshok, L. (1987). Personality, coping style, emotion and cancer: Towards an integrative model. *Cancer Surveys, 6,* 545–567.

Temoshok, L., Heller, B. W., Sagebiel, R. W., Blois, M. S., Sweet, D. M., DiClemente, R. J., & Gold, M. C. (1985). The relationship of prognostic indicators in cutaneous malignant melanoma. *Journal of Psychosomatic Research, 29,* 139–153.

Tempelaar, R., de Haes, J. C. J. M., de Ruiter, J. H., Bakker, D., van den Heuvel, W. J. A., & van Nieuwenhuijzen, M. G. (1989). The social experiences of cancer patients under treatment: A comparative study. *Social Science and Medicine, 29,* 635–642.

Tessler, R., & Mechanic, D. (1978). Psychological stress and perceived health status. *Journal of Health and Social Behavior, 19,* 254–262.

Thomas, L. (1977). On the science and technology of medicine. In J. Knowles (Ed.), *Doing better and feeling worse: Health in the United States.* New York: Norton.

Thompson, J. K., Jarvie, G. J., Lahey, B. B., & Cureton, K. J. (1982). Exercise and obesity: Etiology, physiology, and intervention. *Psychological Bulletin, 91,* 55–79.

Thompson, R. J., & Matarazzo, J. D. (1984). Psychology in United States medical schools: 1983. *American Psychologist, 39,* 988–995.

Thompson, S. C. (1981). Will it hurt less if I can control it? A complex answer to a simple question. *Psychological Bulletin, 90,* 89–101.

Thompson, S. C., Sobowlew-Shubin, A., Graham, M. A., & Janigan, A. S. (1989). Psychosocial adjustment following a stroke. *Social Science and Medicine, 28*, 239–247.

Thorson, J. A., & Powell, F. C. (1990). To laugh in the face of death: The games that lethal people play. *Omega, 21*, 225–239.

Tifft, C. P., & Chobanian, A. V. (1991). Are some antihypertensive therapies more efficacious than others in preventing complications and prolonging life? *Hypertension, 18* (Suppl. I), I146–I152.

Timko, C., & Janoff-Bulman, R. (1985). Attributions, vulnerability, and psychological adjustment: The case of breast cancer. *Health Psychology, 4*, 521–544.

Timko, C., & Moos, R. H. (1989). Choice, control, and adaptation among elderly residents of sheltered care settings. *Journal of Applied Social Psychology, 19*, 636–655.

Tommaso, C. L., Lesch, M., Sonnenblick, E. H. (1984). Alterations in cardiac function in coronary heart disease, myocardial infarction, and coronary bypass surgery. In N. K. Wenger & H. K. Hellerstein (Eds.), *Rehabilitation of the coronary patient* (2d ed.). New York: Wiley.

Tortora, G. J., & Anagnostakos, N. P. (1984). *Principles of anatomy and physiology* (4th ed.). New York: Harper & Row.

Toufexis, A. (1985). Advice on eating right. *Time, 126* (Oct. 7), 61.

Trent, B. (1990). Ottawa lodges add humour to armamentarium in fight against cancer. *Canadian Medical Association Journal, 142*, 163–166.

Triplet, R. G., & Sugarman, D. B. (1987). Reactions to AIDS victims: Ambiguity breeds contempt. *Personality and Social Psychology Bulletin, 13*, 265–274.

Trostle, J. A. (1988). Medical compliance as an ideology. *Social Science and Medicine, 27*, 1299–1308.

Trotter, R. T., III, & Chavira, J. A. (1981). *Curanderismo: Mexican American folk healing.* Athens, GA: University of Georgia Press.

True, W. R., Goldberg, J., & Eisen, S. A. (1988). Stress symptomatology among Vietnam veterans: Analysis of the Veterans Administration Survey of Veterans II. *American Journal of Epidemiology, 128*, 85–92.

Tsalikian, E. (1990). Insulin-dependent (Type I) diabetes mellitus: Medical overview. In C. S. Holmes (Ed.), *Neuropsychological and behavioral aspects of diabetes.* New York: Springer-Verlag.

Tunks, E., & Bellissimo, A. (1991). *Behavioral medicine: Concepts and procedures.* New York: Pergamon.

Turk, D. C., & Fernandez, E. (1990). On the putative uniqueness of cancer pain: Do psychological principles apply? *Behaviour Research and Therapy, 28*, 1–13.

Turk, D. C., & Holtzman, A. D. (1986). Commonalities among psychological approaches in the treatment of chronic pain: Specifying the meta-constructs. In A. D. Holtzman & D. C. Turk (Eds.), *Pain management: A handbook of psychological treatment approaches.* New York: Pergamon.

Turk, D. C., Litt, M. D., Salovey, P., & Walker, J. (1985). Seeking urgent pediatric treatment: Factors contributing to frequency, delay, and appropriateness. *Health Psychology, 4*, 43–59.

Turk, D. C., & Meichenbaum, D. H. (1989). A cognitive-behavioural approach to pain. In P. D. Wall & R. Melzack (Eds.), *Textbook of pain* (2d ed.). Edinburgh: Churchill Livingstone.

Turk, D. C., Meichenbaum, D., & Genest, M. (1983). *Pain and behavioral medicine: A cognitive-behavioral perspective.* New York: Guilford Press.

Turk, D. C., Wack, J. T., & Kerns, R. D. (1985). An empirical examination of the "pain-behavior" construct. *Journal of Behavioral Medicine, 8*, 119–130.

Turnbull, R. (1986). *Terminal care.* Washington, DC: Hemisphere.

Turner, J. A., & Clancy, S. (1988). Comparison of operant behavioral and cognitive-behavioral group treatment for chronic low back pain. *Journal of Consulting and Clinical Psychology, 56*, 261–266.

Turner, J. A., Clancy, S., McQuade, K. J., & Cardenas, D. D. (1990). Effectiveness of behavioral therapy for chronic low back pain: A component analysis. *Journal of Consulting and Clinical Psychology, 58*, 573–579.

Turner, R. D., Polly, S., & Sherman, A. R. (1976). A behavioral approach to individualized exercise programming. In J. D. Krumboltz & C. E. Thoresen (Eds.), *Counseling methods.* New York: Holt, Rinehart, & Winston.

Turner, R. J., & Noh, S. (1988). Physical disability and depression: A longitudinal analysis. *Journal of Health and Social Behavior, 29*, 23–37.

Twaddle, A. C. (1972). The concepts of the sick role and illness behavior. *Advances in Psychosomatic Medicine, 8*, 162–179.

Twycross, R. G. (1984). Relief of pain. In C. Saunders (Ed.), *The management of terminal malignant disease* (2d ed.). London: Edward Arnold.

Twycross, R. G., & McQuay, H. J. (1989). Opioids. In P. D. Wall & R. Melzack (Eds.), *Textbook of pain* (2d ed.). Edinburgh: Churchill Livingstone.

U.S. Department of Health, Education and Welfare (1979). *Healthy people: A report of the Surgeon General on health promotion and disease prevention* (USPHS Publication No. 79-55071). Washington, DC: U.S. Government Printing Office.

Vaccarino, J. M. (1977). Malpractice: The problem in perspective. *Journal of the American Medical Association, 238*, 861–863.

Van den Borne, H. W., Pruyn, J. F., & Van den Heuvel, W. J. (1987). Effects of contacts between cancer patients on their psychosocial problems. *Patient Education and Counseling, 9,* 33–51.

Vandenbos, G. R., DeLeon, P. H., & Pallak, M. S. (1982). An alternative to traditional medical care for the terminally ill: Humanitarian, policy, and political issues in hospice care. *American Psychologist, 37,* 1245–1248.

VanderPlate, C. (1984). Psychological aspects of multiple sclerosis and its treatment: Toward a biopsychosocial perspective. *Health Psychology, 3,* 253–272.

VanderPlate, C., & Aral, S. O. (1987). Psychosocial aspect of genital herpes virus infection. *Health Psychology, 6,* 57–72.

VanderPlate, C., Aral, S. O., & Magder, L. (1988). The relationship among genital herpes simplex virus, stress, and social support. *Health Psychology, 7,* 159–168.

Van Egern, L. F., Abelson, J. L., & Sniderman, L. D. (1983). Interpersonal and electrocardiographic responses to type As and type Bs in competitive socioeconomic games. *Journal of Psychosomatic Research, 27,* 53–59.

van Komen, R. W., & Redd, W. H. (1985). Personality factors associated with anticipatory nausea/vomiting in patients receiving cancer chemotherapy. *Health Psychology, 4,* 189–202.

Varni, J. W., Wilcox, K. T., & Hanson, V. (1988). Mediating effects of family social support on child psychological adjustment in juvenile rheumatoid arthritis. *Health Psychology, 7,* 421–431.

Vartiainen, E., Korhonen, H. J., Pietinen, P., Tuomilehto, J., Kartovaara, L., Nissinen, A., & Puska, P. (1991). Fifteen-year trends in coronary risk factors in Finland, with special reference to North Karelia. *International Journal of Epidemiology, 20,* 651–662.

Veatch, R. (1989). *Death, dying, and the biological revolution* (Rev. ed.). New Haven: Yale University Press.

Velican, C., & Velican, D. (1989). *Natural history of coronary atherosclerosis.* Boca Raton, FL: CRC Press.

Venitt, S. (1990). The dubious evidence for smokeless tobacco. *British Journal of Addiction, 85,* 1100–1102.

Venters, M. H. (1986). Family life and cardiovascular risk: Implications for the prevention of chronic disease. *Social Science and Medicine, 22,* 1067–1074.

Venters, M. H., Jacobs, D., Pirie, P., Luepker, R., Folsom, A., & Gillum, R. (1986). Marital status and cardiovascular risk: The Minnesota Heart Survey and the Minnesota Heart Health Program. *Preventive Medicine, 15,* 591–605.

Verbrugge, L. M. (1979). Female illness rates and illness behavior: Testing hypotheses about sex differentials in health. *Women and Health, 4,* 61–79.

Verbrugge, L. M. (1980). Sex differences in complaints and diagnoses. *Journal of Behavioral Medicine, 3,* 327–355.

Verbrugge, L. M. (1982). Sex differentials in health. *Public Health Reports, 97,* 417–437.

Verbrugge, L. M. (1985a). Gender and health: An update on hypotheses and evidence. *Journal of Health and Social Behavior, 26,* 156–182.

Verbrugge, L. M. (1985b). Triggers of symptoms and health care. *Social Science and Medicine, 20,* 855–876.

Visintainer, M. A., Volpicelli, J. R., & Seligman, M. E. P. (1982). Tumor rejection in rats after inescapable or escapable electric shock. *Science, 216,* 437–439.

Volberding, P. A. (1989). AIDS overview. In I. B. Corless & M. Pittman-Lindeman (Eds.), *AIDS: Principles, practices, & politics* (Ref. ed.). New York: Hemisphere.

von Baeyer, C. L., Johnson, M. E., & McMillan, M. J. (1984). Consequences of nonverbal expression of pain: Patient distress and observer concern. *Social Science and Medicine, 19,* 1319–1324.

von Bertalanffy, L. (1968). *General systems theory.* New York: Braziller.

Wadden, R. A., & Anderton, C. H. (1982). The clinical use of hypnosis. *Psychological Bulletin, 91,* 215–243.

Wadden, T. A., & Brownell, K. D. (1984). The development and modification of dietary practices in individuals, groups, and large populations. In J. D. Matarazzo, S. M. Weiss, J. A. Herd, N. E. Miller, & S. M. Weiss (Eds.), *Behavioral health: A handbook of health enhancement and disease prevention.* New York: Wiley.

Wall, P. D., & Melzack, R. (1989). *Textbook of pain* (2d ed.). Edinburgh: Churchill Livingstone.

Wall, V. J., & Womack, W. (1989). Hypnotic versus active cognitive strategies for alleviation of procedural distress in pediatric oncology patients. *American Journal of Clinical Hypnosis, 31,* 181–191.

Wallston, B. S., & Wallston, K. A. (1984). Social psychological models of health behavior: An examination and integration. In A. Baum, S. E. Taylor, & J. E. Singer (Eds.), *Handbook of psychology and health,* Vol. 4. Hillsdale, NJ: Erlbaum.

Wallston, B. S., Alagna, S. W., DeVellis, B. M., & DeVellis, R. F. (1983). Social support and physical health. *Health Psychology, 2,* 367–391.

Wallston, B. S., Wallston, K. A., Kaplan, G. D., & Maides, S. A. (1976). Development and validation of the Health Locus of Control (HLC) Scale. *Journal of Consulting and Clinical Psychology, 44,* 580–585.

Wallston, K. A., & Wallston, B. S. (1981). Health locus of control scales. In H. M. Lefcourt (Ed.), *Research with the locus of control construct* (Vol. 1). New York: Academic Press.

Wallston, K. A., Wallston, B. S., & DeVellis, R. (1978). Development of the multidimensional health locus of control scales. *Health Education Monographs, 6,* 161–170.

Walsh, A., & Walsh, P. A. (1989). Love, self-esteem, and multiple sclerosis. *Social Science and Medicine, 29,* 793–798.

Ward, C. (1984). Thaipusam in Malaysia: A psycho-anthropological analysis of ritual trance, ceremonial possession and self-mortification practices. *Ethos, 12,* 307–334.

Ward, M. M., Chesney, M. A., Swan, G. E., Black, G. W., Parker, S. D., & Rosenman, R. H. (1986). Cardiovascular responses in type A and type B men to a series of stressors. *Journal of Behavioral Medicine, 9,* 43–49.

Warner, K. E. (1977). The effects of the anti-smoking campaign on cigarette consumption. *American Journal of Public Health, 67,* 645–650.

Warner, K. E., & Murt, H. A. (1983). Premature deaths avoided by the antismoking campaign. *American Journal of Public Health, 73,* 672–677.

Watkins, L. R., & Mayer, D. (1982). Organization of endogenous opiate and nonopiate pain control systems. *Science, 216,* 1185–1192.

Watson, D., & Pennebaker, J. W. (1989). Health complaints, stress, and distress: Exploring the central role of negative affectivity. *Psychological Review, 96,* 234–254.

Watson, D., & Pennebaker, J. W. (1991). Situational, dispositional, and genetic bases of symptom reporting. In J. A. Skelton & R. T. Croyle (Eds.), *Mental representation in health and illness.* New York: Springer-Verlag.

Weber, J. N., & Weiss, R. A. (1988). HIV infection: The cellular picture. *Scientific American, 259*(4), 81–87.

Wegner, D. M., Vallacher, R. R., & Dizadji, D. (1989). Do alcoholics know what they are doing? Identifications of the act of drinking. *Basic and Applied Social Psychology, 10,* 197–210.

Weidner, G., Archer, S., Healy, B., & Matarazzo, J. D. (1985). Family consumption of low fat foods: Stated preference versus actual consumption. *Journal of Applied Social Psychology, 15,* 773–779.

Weidner, G., & Matthews, K. A. (1978). Reported physical symptoms elicited by unpredictable events and the type A coronary-prone behavior pattern. *Journal of Personality and Social Psychology, 36,* 1213–1220.

Weinberg, J., & Emerman, J. T. (1989). Effects of psychosocial stressors on mouse mammary tumor growth. *Brain, Behavior, and Immunity, 3,* 234–246.

Weinstein, A. M. (1987). *Asthma.* New York: McGraw-Hill.

Weinstein, I. B. (1988). The origins of human cancer: Mechanisms of carcinogenesis and their implications for cancer prevention and treatment. *Cancer Research, 48,* 4135–4143.

Weinstein, M. C., & Stason, W. B. (1976). *Hypertension: A policy perspective.* Cambridge: Harvard University Press.

Weinstein, N. D. (1982). Unrealistic optimism about susceptibility to health problems. *Journal of Behavioral Medicine, 5,* 441–460.

Weinstein, N. D. (1984). Why it won't happen to me: Perceptions of risk factors and susceptibility. *Health Psychology, 3,* 431–457.

Weinstein, N. D. (1988). The precaution adoption process. *Health Psychology, 7,* 355–386.

Weisenberg, M. (1977). Pain and pain control. *Psychological Bulletin, 84,* 1008–1044.

Weiss, H. M., Simon, R., Levi, J., Forster, A., Hubbard, M., & Aledort, L. (1991). Compliance in a comprehensive hemophilia center and its implications for home care. *Family Systems Medicine, 9,* 111–120.

Weiss, J. M. (1984). Behavioral and psychological influences on gastrointestinal pathology: Experimental techniques and findings. In W. D. Gentry (Ed.), *Handbook of behavioral medicine.* New York: Guilford Press.

Weiss, S. M. (1982). Health psychology: The time is now. *Health Psychology, 1,* 81–91.

Weiss, S. M. (1984). Community health promotion programs: Introduction. In J. D. Matarazzo, S. M. Weiss, J. A. Herd, N. E. Miller, & S. M. Weiss (Eds.), *Behavioral health: A handbook of health enhancement and disease prevention.* New York: Wiley.

Weitz, R. (1989). Uncertainty and the lives of persons with AIDS. *Journal of Health and Social Behavior, 30,* 270–281.

Wellisch, D. K. (1981). Intervention with the cancer patient. In C. K. Prokop & L. A. Bradley (Eds.), *Medical psychology: Contributions to behavioral medicine.* New York: Academic Press.

Wenger, N. K. (1983). Physical activity and modification of coronary risk. In K. Pyorala, E. Rapaport, K. Konig, G. Schettler, & C. Diehm (Eds.), *Secondary prevention of coronary heart disease.* New York: Thieme-Straton.

Wenger, N. K., & Hurst, J. W. (1984). Coronary bypass surgery as a rehabilitative procedure. In N. K. Wenger & H. K. Hellerstein (Eds.), *Rehabilitation of the coronary patient* (2d ed.). New York: Wiley.

Werry, J. S. (1979). Psychosomatic disorders, psychogenic symptoms, and hospitalization. In H. C. Quay & J. S. Werry (Eds.), *Psychopathological disorders of childhood.* New York: Wiley.

West, D., Horan, J., & Games, P. (1984). Component analysis of occupational stress inoculation applied to registered nurses in an acute care hospital setting. *Journal of Consulting and Clinical Psychology, 31,* 209–218.

West, R., & Krafona, K. (1990). Oral tobacco: Prevalence, health risks, dependence potential and public policy. *British Journal of Addiction, 85,* 1097–1098.

Wexler, M. (1976). The behavioral sciences in medical education: A view from psychology. *American Psychologist, 31,* 275–283.

White, L., Tursky, B., & Schwartz, G. E. (Eds.) (1985). *Placebo: Theory, research and mechanisms.* New York: Guilford Press.

White, L. C. (1988). *Merchants of death: The American tobacco industry.* New York: Beech Tree Books.

Whitehead, W. E., & Bosmajian, L. S. (1982). Behavioral medicine approaches to gastrointestinal disorders. *Journal of Consulting and Clinical Psychology, 50,* 972–983.

Whitehead, W. E., Busch, C. M., Heller, B. R., & Costa, P. T. (1986). Social learning influences on menstrual symptoms and illness behavior. *Health Psychology, 5,* 13–23.

Wicker, A. W. (1969). Attitudes versus actions: The relationship of verbal and overt behavioral responses to attitude objects. *Journal of Social Issues, 25,* 41–78.

Wiebe, D. J., & McCallum, D. M. (1986). Health practices and hardiness as mediators in the stress-illness relationship. *Health Psychology, 5,* 425–438.

Wiens, A. N., & Menustik, C. E. (1983). Treatment outcome and patient characteristics in an aversion therapy program for alcoholism. *American Psychologist, 38,* 1089–1096.

Williams, D. A., Lewis-Faning, E., Rees, A., Jacobs, J., & Thomas, A. (1958). Assessment of the relative importance of the allergic, infective and psychological factors in asthma. *Acta Allergologica, 12,* 376–395.

Williams, R. (1989). *The trusting heart: Great news about type A behavior.* New York: Times Books.

Williams, R. B., Barefoot, J. C., Califf, R. M., Haney, T. L., Saunders, W. B., Pryor, D. B., Hlaky, M. A., Siegler, L. C., & Mark, D. B. (1992). Prognostic importance of social and economic resources among medically treated patients with angiographically documented coronary artery disease. *Journal of the American Medical Association, 267,* 520–524.

Wilson, C., & Renneker, M. (1988). Tobacco as a cause of cancer and death. In M. Renneker (Ed.), *Understanding cancer.* (3d ed.). Palo Alto: Bull Publishing Co.

Wilson, D., Lavelle, S., Greenspan, R., & Wilson, C. (1991). Psychological predictors of HIV-preventive behavior among Zimbabwean students. *Journal of Social Psychology, 131,* 293–295.

Wilson, G. T. (1984). Weight control treatments. In J. D. Matarazzo, S. M. Weiss, J. A. Herd, N. E. Miller, & S. M. Weiss (Eds.), *Behavioral health: A handbook of health enhancement and disease prevention.* New York: Wiley.

Wilson, L. M. (1988). The American revolution in health care. *AAOHN Journal, 36,* 402–407.

Wilson, R. N. (1965). The social structure of a general hospital. In J. K. Skipper & R. C. Leonard (Eds.), *Social interaction and patient care.* Philadelphia: Lippincott.

Wing, R. R., Epstein, L. H., Nowalk, M. P., & Lamparski, D. M. (1986). Behavioral self-regulation in the treatment of patients with diabetes mellitus. *Psychological Bulletin, 99,* 78–89.

Wing, R. R., Lamparski, D., Zaslow, S., Betscart, H., Siminerio, L., & Becker, D. (1985). Accuracy and compliance to blood sugar monitoring among children with type I diabetes. *Diabetes Care, 8,* 214–218.

Wisely, D. W., Masur, F. T., & Morgan, S. B. (1983). Psychological aspects of severe burn injuries in children. *Health Psychology, 2,* 45–72.

Wolf, S. (1950). Effects of suggestion and conditioning on the action of chemical agents in human subjects: The pharmacology of placebos. *Journal of Clinical Investigation, 29,* 100–109.

Wolf, S., & Wolff, H. G. (1947). *Human gastric function* (2d ed.). New York: Oxford University Press.

Wolf, T. M., Elston, R. C., & Kissling, G. E. (1989). Relationship of hassles, uplifts, and life events to psychological well-being of freshman medical students. *Behavioral Medicine, 15,* 37–45.

Wolff, B. B., & Langley, S. (1977). Cultural factors and the response to pain. In D. Landy (Ed.), *Culture, disease, and healing: Studies in medical anthropology.* New York: Macmillan.

Wolff, C. F. (1989). Segmental afferent fibre-induced analgesia: Transcutaneous electrical nerve stimulation (TENS) and vibration. In P. D. Wall & R. Melzack (Eds.), *Textbook of pain* (2d ed.). Edinburgh: Churchill Livingstone.

Wolman, B. B. (1982). Depression and obesity. In B. B. Wolman (Ed.), *Psychological aspects of obesity: A handbook.* New York: Van Nostrand Reinhold.

Wolman, B. B. (1988). *Psychosomatic disorders.* New York: Plenum.

Wolpe, J. (1958). *Psychotherapy by reciprocal inhibition.* Stanford: Stanford University Press.

Wong, M., & Kaloupek, D. G. (1986). Coping with dental treatment: The potential impact of situational demands. *Journal of Behavioral Medicine, 9,* 579–597.

Wood, J. V., Taylor, S. E., & Lichtman, R. R. (1985). Social comparison in adjustment to breast cancer. *Journal of Personality and Social Psychology, 49,* 1169–1183.

Woods, S. M., Natterson, J., & Silverman, J. (1966). Medical students' disease: Hypochondriasis in medical education. *Journal of Medical Education, 41,* 785–790.

Worden, J. K., Flynn, B. S., Solomon, L. J., Costanza, M. C., Foster, R. S., Dorwaldt, A. L., Driscoll, M. A., & Ashikaga, T. (1987). A community-wide breast self-exam education program. In P. F. Engstrom, L. E. Mortenson, & P. N. Anderson (Eds.), *Advances in cancer control: The war on cancer—15 years of progress.* New York: Alan R. Liss, Inc.

Working Group on Apprenticeship (1983). Report. *Health Psychology, 2*(5, Suppl.), 131–134.

Working Group on Postdoctoral Research Training (1983). Report. *Health Psychology, 2*(5, Suppl.), 135–140.

Working Group on Postdoctoral Training for the Health Psychology Service Provider (1983). Report. *Health Psychology, 2*(5, Suppl.), 141–145.

Working Group on Predoctoral Education/Doctoral Training (1983). Report. *Health Psychology, 2*(5, Suppl.), 123–130.

World Health Organization (1982). Trends of mortality from ischemic heart disease and other cardiovascular diseases in 27 countries from 1968 to 1977. *World Health Statistics Quarterly, 35,* 11–47.

Wortman, C. B., & Dunkel-Schetter, C. (1979). Interpersonal relationships and cancer: A theoretical analysis. *Journal of Social Issues, 35*(1), 120–155.

Wysocki, T., Hall, G., Iwata, B., & Riordan, M. (1979). Behavioral management of exercise: Contracting for aerobic points. *Journal of Applied Behavior Analysis, 12,* 55–64.

Young, D. T. (1987). Rehabilitation following myocardial infarction. In D. S. Sheps (Ed.), *The management of postmyocardial infarction patients.* New York: McGraw-Hill.

Young, J. W. (1979). Symptom disclosure to male and female physicians: Effects of sex, physical attractiveness, and symptom type. *Journal of Behavioral Medicine, 2,* 159–169.

Zarit, S. H., Orr, N. K., & Zarit, J. M. (1985). *The hidden victims of Alzheimer's disease: Families under stress.* New York: New York University Press.

Zarski, J. J. (1984). Hassles and health: A replication. *Health Psychology, 3,* 243–251.

Zastowny, T. R., Kirschenbaum, D. S., & Meng, A. L. (1986). Coping skills training for children: Effects on distress before, during, and after hospitalization for surgery. *Health Psychology, 5,* 231–247.

Zborowski, M. (1952). Cultural components in responses to pain. *Journal of Social Issues, 8,* 16–30.

Zimbardo, P. G. (1969). The human choice: Individuation, reason, and order versus deindividuation, impulse, and chaos. In W. J. Arnold & D. Levine (Eds.), *Nebraska symposium on motivation.* Lincoln: University of Nebraska Press.

Zimmerman, B. R. (1990). Non-insulin dependent (type II) diabetes: Medical overview. In C. S. Holmes (Ed.), *Neuropsychological and behavioral aspects of diabetes.* New York: Springer-Verlag.

Zimmerman, M. (1983). Methodological issues in the assessment of life events: A review of issues and research. *Clinical Psychology Review, 3,* 339–370.

Zimmerman, M., O'Hara, M. W., & Corenthal, C. P. (1984). Symptom contamination of life event scales. *Health Psychology, 3,* 77–81.

Zola, I. K. (1964). Illness behavior of the working class: Implications and recommendations. In A. Shostak & W. Gomberg (Eds.), *Blue-collar world: Study of the American worker.* Englewood Cliffs, NJ: Prentice-Hall.

Zola, I. K. (1966). Culture and symptoms—An analysis of patients' presenting complaints. *American Sociological Review, 31,* 615–630.

Zucker, R. A., & Gomberg, E. S. L. (1986). Etiology of alcoholism reconsidered: The case for a biopsychosocial process. *American Psychologist, 41,* 783–793.

Zvaifler, N. J. (1988). Rheumatoid arthritis: Epidemiology, etiology, rheumatoid factor, pathology, and pathogenesis. In H. R. Schumacher, J. H. Klippel, & D. R. Robinson (Eds.), *Primer on the rheumatic diseases* (9th ed.). Atlanta: Arthritis Foundation.

Author Index

Subject Index

Page references followed by b, f, or t indicate boxes, figures, and tables, respectively.